FOUNDATION COURSE IN SPANISH

D. C. HEATH AND COMPANY
Lexington, Massachusetts   Toronto

Foundation Course in

SPANISH

LAUREL H. TURK
DePauw University

AURELIO M. ESPINOSA, JR.
Stanford University

THIRD EDITION

Drawings by JEANETTE P. SLOAN

International Standard Book Number: 0–669–86413–7

Library of Congress Catalog Card Number: 73–5259

Preface

Foundation Course in Spanish, Third Edition, is intended for beginning students who wish to understand and use Spanish. The
materials presented will make possible a development of the
language skills in their natural order—*listening, speaking, reading,*
and *writing*.   At the same time that the student learns to understand and say in Spanish many of the things he says every day
in English and learns to read and write simple Spanish, he will
become informed of something of the civilization, culture, customs, and way of life of the peoples whose language he is
studying.

Throughout the text, emphasis is placed on a practical
vocabulary and oral use of the language.   The dialogues deal with
everyday situations, such as the classroom, the home, meals,
shopping, travel, amusements, and other phases of daily life
within the experience of the average student.   Each lesson presents not only a number of new words and expressions, along with
an explanation of the new grammatical points, but it also repeats
systematically much of the material from earlier lessons.   Individual words in the dialogues have been chosen for their practical
use rather than for their literary frequency, although most of the
words and phrases introduced are those most commonly used.
The *Lecturas* offer a vocabulary which will be of value in reading
Spanish, whether it be novels, plays, short stories, essays, or
newspaper articles.

This edition of *Foundation Course in Spanish* consists of one
preliminary lesson on pronunciation, followed by twenty-five
lessons, five reviews, fifteen *Lecturas,* five *Conversaciones,* a short
section on letter writing, four appendices, and the end vocabularies.   The maps and illustrations form an important part of
the book, offering great variety in topics which supplement the
story of the cultural background in the Spanish-speaking lands.
The art section is a special feature of the book.   Through the use
of carefully selected slides, films, filmstrips, and other visual
materials, the teacher may give the student an even wider
understanding of Hispanic culture.

The first ten lessons are divided into six parts: (*a*) groups of
short dialogues, at times preceded by a brief description of the
setting; (*b*) *Conversación;* (*c*) *Notas gramaticales;* (*d*) *Ejercicios;* (*e*)

Ejercicios de pronunciación; (*f*) *Vocabulario.* The pronunciation section is not included beyond Lesson 15, but it is assumed that the student will constantly apply the elementary principles acquired up to this point as he uses Spanish. Beginning with Lesson 11 a short *Composición* is also included. The new words and expressions listed in each *Vocabulario* are placed at the end of each lesson as a means of encouraging the student to learn them in context.

Habits of speech are formed in the first few weeks of study, hence the dialogues are designed for concentration on the student's hearing and speaking the language. He should listen carefully to the pronunciation and intonation of the teacher, then imitate each phrase or sentence as closely as possible. As an aid to the teacher and student, tape recordings are available for the dialogues and oral exercises of the lessons. Students may memorize parts or all of the model passages, or they may retell similar situations using words already presented. Parts of these passages, or of the *Lecturas,* may be used for dictation.

The *Conversación* section of each lesson will facilitate oral work and comprehension, and it will serve to test the student's knowledge of words and phrases that he needs and wants to learn. In each *Conversación* there are eight questions in Spanish which are based on the dialogue itself, and eight which represent an application of this material.

The *Notas gramaticales* are grouped and presented in logical sequence as far as possible. Care has been taken to state the explanations simply, but adequately, and in terms easily understood by beginning students. Emphasis has been placed upon general principles which arise naturally from Spanish usage, and exceptions are held to a minimum. The examples, drawn largely from the dialogue, are given before the explanations so that the student may be encouraged to make deductions on his own initiative. Frequent cross references are made to similar or contrasting constructions. A short section called *Práctica* is included for further drill after the discussion of certain troublesome points of grammatical usage. The teacher may want to explain the grammatical items before the student works on the dialogue or other parts of the lesson. In any event, the student should study the *Notas gramaticales* carefully before working on the dialogues.

Recognizing the necessity of a thorough knowledge of verb forms and basic grammatical principles, regardless of the purpose for which Spanish is to be used, special attention has been placed first upon a gradual, logical, and clear presentation of all the material, and then upon adequate and varied drill exercises. Some of these exercises may be used in class without having been assigned for study. The *Repasos*, spaced at five-lesson intervals, provide further drill on the material of the preceding lessons.

The *Composición* section may be used at the discretion of the teacher, depending on the amount of emphasis on written work. In this section the student is asked to write only what he should have learned to understand, say, and read correctly. In the first ten lessons, the last exercise is devoted to a series of short, English sentences, which may be used or eliminated, as the teacher desires.

The *Conversaciones*, which follow each third *Lectura*, provide additional oral practice on topics which should be of interest to students. The new words in these selections are repeated in the lesson vocabularies if they are used again in the regular lessons.

The *Lecturas*, introduced after Lesson 6, are designed so that the student can read with understanding without conscious translation. They are closely correlated with the dialogues and grammatical notes, so that the student is not introduced to troublesome constructions before they have been used or explained in the regular lessons. The short notes and exercises in the *Estudio de palabras* section, which in this edition has been placed ahead of the Spanish text should aid greatly in building a working vocabulary. The series of questions in Spanish will test the student's comprehension of the *Lecturas*. Some five per cent of the individual words used in the *Lecturas* are identical cognates, and nearly sixty per cent are recognizable cognates, leaving only approximately thirty-five per cent which may not be recognized from the context. Many words in the latter group are listed in footnotes, to avoid vocabulary thumbing and to facilitate reading. Idioms and difficult phrases are also included in the footnotes. Words and phrases used first in the *Lecturas* are listed in the active vocabularies if used again in the dialogues. Thus, a teacher may omit the *Lecturas* entirely, he may assign them as outside reading, or he may take them up at any subsequent period of the year.

For those who may wish to carry on social or commercial correspondence in Spanish, some commonly used phrases and formulas are given in the special section on letter writing, called *Cartas españolas*.

Appendix A contains songs, to which guitar chords have been added, and gives a free translation of them; Appendix B contains lists of expressions used in the classroom and the laboratory, grammatical terms, punctuation marks, and the abbreviations and signs used in the text; Appendix C contains a summary of Spanish pronunciation, including intonation and Appendix D contains a complete list of verb forms used in the text, as well as a few additional verbs which may be encountered in later study of Spanish.

The Spanish-English vocabulary is intended to be complete with the exception of a few proper and geographical names which are either identical in Spanish and English or whose meaning is clear, a few past participles used as adjectives when the infinitive is given, titles of certain literary works mentioned in the *Lecturas*, the supplementary list of foods on pages 317–318, and Spanish examples translated in the *Cartas españolas* section. Idioms are listed under the most important word in the phrase, and, in most cases, cross listings are given. The English-Spanish vocabulary contains only the English words used in the English-Spanish exercises of the text.

In this third edition of *Foundation Course in Spanish* the dialogues have been revised and reorganized and the content changed in some of them. In addition, the dialogues have been divided into self-contained sequences to facilitate the introduction and preparation of the material, and also to provide more oral practice, as well as to afford flexibility of assignment. The first group of exchanges may be mastered first, and then combined with one or all the other groups in the section. An effort has been made to clarify some of the more difficult matters taken up in the *Notas gramaticales*. The drill exercises, both oral and written, remain essentially the same as in the second edition. One Preliminary Lesson replaces the former two. It, along with the *Ejercicios de pronunciación*, which have been modified and extended through Lesson 15, constitute an elementary, but adequate, survey of the features of Spanish pronunciation which English-speaking students find most troublesome. As stated previously, a summary of Spanish pronunciation is given in Appendix C.

The Workbook has been completely revised. The exercises have been rewritten, except for some of the pronunciation exercises and some of the questions in the *Aplicación del diálogo* of the individual lessons and the items for the *Lecturas* and the *Conversaciones*. Thus, the Workbook offers additional drills on all the major grammatical structures and contains exercises based on the reading material.

To recapitulate, the teacher who wishes to stress hearing and speaking Spanish will emphasize the dialogues and will select from the exercises those which are entirely in the language.   The *Conversaciones* will also be assigned.   If the teacher does not agree with the conviction of the authors concerning the desirability of the presentation of cultural material in a beginning text, the *Lecturas* may be omitted partially or entirely.

For teachers and students who wish to use *Foundation Course in Spanish, Third Edition,* for individualized instruction, a complete individualized program has been prepared.   In programs where individualization procedures are not used, it is recommended that the Achievement Tests contained in the *Student's Manual* of the *Individualized Instruction Program* be made part of the course of instruction to provide an adequate testing program.

As the student begins the study of a foreign language, he should recall the years that he has spent gradually learning his own language.   After completing this text, he will not be able to talk and read Spanish like a native; however, if he has learned what is included in these pages, he will be able to understand much of what a Spanish-speaking person says, he will be able to say in Spanish many of the ordinary things he wants or needs to say, and he will be able to read and write simple Spanish.

In the preparation of this edition the authors are grateful for the valuable suggestions and constructive criticism offered by many colleagues who have used the earlier editions, and by the staff of the Modern Language Department of D. C. Heath and Company.

L. H. T.
A. M. E., Jr.

Contents

PRELIMINARY LESSON. The Spanish alphabet. Spanish sounds. Division of words into syllables. Word stress. Vowels. Diphthongs. Linking. Punctuation. Capitalization   **3**

LECCIÓN 1. Present indicative of the first conjugation. Use of subject pronouns. Gender and plural of nouns. Use of the definite article. Negative and interrogative sentences   **11**

LECCIÓN 2. Present indicative of **ser** and **tener**. The indefinite article. Forms and agreement of adjectives. Use of **hay**. Uses of **que**. The adverbs **aquí, ahí, allí**   **21**

LECCIÓN 3. Present indicative of the second conjugation. Present indicative of **ir**. Preposition **a**. Possession. Cardinal numerals. Time of day. Use of **¿no es verdad?**   **31**

LECCIÓN 4. Present indicative of the third conjugation. Present indicative of **venir**. Possessive adjectives. Position of adjectives. Phrases with **de** plus a noun. Summary of uses of **ser**   **41**

LECCIÓN 5. Present indicative of **estar, querer**, and **saber**. The present participle. Uses of **estar**. Special uses of the definite article. Feminine of nouns. Use of **¿cuál?**   **51**

REPASO I   **60**

LECCIÓN 6. Present indicative of some irregular verbs. The personal **a**. Direct object pronouns. Position of object pronouns. Verbs which require a direct object without a preposition. The infinitive after a preposition. Meaning of **saber** and **conocer**. Demonstrative adjectives   **63**

LECTURA I: *España*   **71**

LECCIÓN 7. Present indicative of **dar** and **decir**. Indirect object pronouns. Reflexive substitute for the passive. Use of **gustar**. Adjectives used as nouns. Comparison of adjectives   **77**

LECTURA II: *La América del Sur*   **87**

LECCIÓN 8.   Present indicative of **hacer** and **poner**.   Present   **95**
indicative of stem-changing verbs, Class I.   Reflexive pronouns.
Present indicative of the reflexive verb **lavarse**.   Position of
pronouns used as objects of an infinitive.   The definite article
for the possessive.   Omission of the indefinite article

LECTURA III: *México*   **105**

LECCIÓN 9.   Commands.   Position of object pronouns in   **113**
commands.   Expressions with **tener**.   Ways to express "time"

CONVERSACIÓN I: *En un café español*   **125**

LECCIÓN 10.   The preterit indicative of regular verbs.   Pret-   **129**
erit of **dar**, **ir**, and **ser**.   Use of the preterit.   Indefinite and
negative expressions.   The definite article with expressions of
time

LECTURA IV: *Los otros países hispanoamericanos*   **137**

REPASO II   **142**

LECCIÓN 11.   The imperfect indicative tense.   Uses of the   **145**
imperfect tense.   Expressions with **hacer**.   Use of the definite
article with the seasons

LECTURA V: *España en América*   **155**

LECCIÓN 12.   Preterit of **traer**.   Cardinal numerals.   Ordi-   **163**
nal numerals.   Days of the week.   The months.   Dates

LECTURA VI: *La Navidad*   **170**

LECCIÓN 13.   Irregular verbs having **i**-stem preterits.   Uses   **175**
of the present participle.   Position of object pronouns with the
present participle.   **Se** used as an indefinite subject.   Pronouns
used as objects of prepositions.   Use of the definite article in a
general sense

CONVERSACIÓN II: *La casa y la familia de María*   **185**

LECCIÓN 14.   Irregular verbs having **u**-stem preterits.   Verbs   **189**
with changes in spelling in the preterit.   Combinations of two
personal object pronouns.   Demonstrative pronouns.   Uses of
volver and **devolver**, of **preguntar**, of **pagar**, and of the idiom
acabar de

LECTURA VII: *Fiestas*   199

LECCIÓN 15. The past participles. The present perfect and 205
pluperfect indicative tenses. The past participle used as an adjective. Other uses of **haber.** **Hace,** meaning "ago, since"

LECTURA VIII: *Los deportes*   215

REPASO III   221

LECCIÓN 16. The future tense. The conditional tense. 225
Verbs irregular in the future and conditional. Uses of the future
tense. Uses of the conditional tense. The future and conditional
perfects. The future and conditional for probability or conjecture.
Forms of **jugar**

LECTURA IX: *Árboles y plantas*   235

LECCIÓN 17. Stem-changing verbs. Familiar singular com- 241
mands of irregular verbs. Irregular comparison of adjectives
and adverbs. The absolute superlative. Summary of comparison of equality. Possessive adjectives that follow the noun

CONVERSACIÓN III: *En un restaurante español*   250

LECCIÓN 18. The present subjunctive of regular verbs. The 255
present subjunctive of irregular and stem-changing verbs. Theory
of the subjunctive mood. The subjunctive in noun clauses

LECTURA X: *La España antigua*   265

LECCIÓN 19. The present perfect subjunctive tense. The 271
present subjunctive of verbs with changes in spelling. The subjunctive in noun clauses (continued). More commands

LECTURA XI: *Exploradores y misioneros*   281

LECCIÓN 20. Adjective clauses and relative pronouns. The 287
subjunctive in adjective clauses. **Hacer** in time clauses. Forms
of **valer**

LECTURA XII: *La cultura española a través de los siglos*   295

REPASO IV   300

LECCIÓN 21. Verbs with changes in spelling. The sub- 305
junctive in adverbial clauses. Review of compound nouns.
Pero and **sino**

CONVERSACIÓN IV: *En un hotel mexicano*   314

LECCIÓN 22. The imperfect subjunctive. The pluperfect 321
subjunctive. Use of the subjunctive tenses. Use of the infinitive
after certain verbs. The subjunctive in a polite or softened
statement. Exclamations

LECTURA XIII: *Miguel de Cervantes*   331

LECCIÓN 23. Possessive pronouns. The definite article used 337
as a demonstrative. The passive voice. **Cuyo** and **¿de quién?**
The neuter **lo.** Forms of verbs in **-uir**

LECTURA XIV: *La literatura española moderna*   347

LECCIÓN 24. Familiar commands. **Si**-clauses. Special use 353
of plural reflexive pronouns. Forms of **enviar** and **continuar.**
Summary of uses of **para.** Summary of uses of **por**

LECTURA XV: *Las artes españolas*   363

LECCIÓN 25. Verbs ending in **-ducir.** Forms of **reír.** The 371
preterit perfect tense. The absolute use of the past participle.
The subjunctive after **tal vez**, **quizá(s).** Translation of "to
become." Use of the infinitive after **oír** and **ver.** Diminutives

CONVERSACIÓN V: *En la Carretera Panamericana*   381

REPASO V   385

CARTAS ESPAÑOLAS. Address on the envelope. Heading 389
of the letter. Salutations and conclusions for familiar letters.
Salutations for business letters or those addressed to strangers.
Conclusions for informal social and business letters. The body
of business letters. Sample letters

APPENDICES

   A. Songs. Translation of songs   400
   B. Frases para la clase. Palabras y expresiones para el labora- 408
     torio. Términos gramaticales. Signos de puntuación.
     Abreviaturas y signos
   C. Pronunciación   413
   D. Verb paradigms   420

SPANISH-ENGLISH VOCABULARY 435

ENGLISH-SPANISH VOCABULARY 473

INDEX 490

MAPS

España	**75**
La América del Sur	**93**
México	**111**
La América Central y el Caribe	**141**
España en los Estados Unidos	**284**
La Carretera Panamericana	**380**

RECORDINGS FOR TURK AND ESPINOSA:

FOUNDATION COURSE IN SPANISH,

Third Edition

TAPES

NUMBER OF REELS: 18 7″ double track

SPEED: 3¾ ips

RUNNING TIME: 18 hours (approximate)

FOUNDATION COURSE IN SPANISH

PRELIMINARY LESSON

— Buenos días,[1] señor (señora).[2]	*"Good morning, sir (madam)."*
— Buenos días, señorita.	*"Good morning (day), miss."*
— ¿Cómo está usted?	*"How are you?"*
— Muy bien, gracias. ¿Y usted?	*"Very well, thanks. And you?"*
— Así, así, gracias.	*"So-so, thank you."*
— Adiós. Hasta mañana, señorita.	*"Goodbye. Until tomorrow, miss."*
— Hasta mañana.	*"Until tomorrow."*

Repeat the Spanish dialogue after your teacher, listening carefully to the linking of words together and to the intonation patterns.   Read the dialogue, either alone or with a classmate, and then memorize each expression.

THE SPANISH ALPHABET[3]

In addition to the letters used in the English alphabet, **ch, ll, ñ,** and **rr** represent single sounds in Spanish and are considered single letters.   In dictionaries and vocabularies words or syllables which begin with **ch, ll,** and **ñ** follow words or syllables that begin with **c, l,** and **n,** while **rr,** which never begins a word, is alphabetized as in English. **K** and **w** are used only in words of foreign origin.   The names of the letters are feminine: **la be,** *(the) b;* **la jota,** *(the) j.*

The Spanish alphabet is divided into vowels (**a, e, i, o, u**) and consonants.   The letter **y** is a vowel when final in a word, and when used as the conjunction **y,** *and.*

The Spanish vowels are divided into two groups: strong vowels (**a, e, o**) and weak vowels (**i, u**).

SPANISH SOUNDS

Even though Spanish uses practically the same alphabet as English, few sounds are identical in the two languages.   It will, however, be necessary to make comparisons between familiar English sounds and the unfamiliar Spanish sounds in order to show how Spanish is pronounced.   Avoid the use of English sounds in Spanish words and imitate good Spanish pronunciation.

[1] **Buenas tardes,** *Good afternoon,* and **Buenas noches,** *Good evening,* are used as greetings in the afternoon or evening, respectively.   **Buenas noches,** *Good night,* is also used in taking leave of persons in the evening.   [2] **Señor (Sr.)** and **señora (Sra.)** also mean *Mr.* and *Mrs.,* respectively.   The abbreviation for **señorita** is **Srta.**   [3] See Appendix C for the Spanish alphabet and a summary of Spanish pronunciation (including intonation).

In general, Spanish pronunciation is much clearer and more uniform than the English. The vowel sounds are clipped short and are not followed by the diphthongal glide which is commonly heard in English, as in *no* (*no^u*), *came* (*ca^ime*), *why* (*why^e*). Even unstressed vowels are pronounced clearly and distinctly; the slurred sound of English *a* in *fireman*, for example, never occurs in Spanish.

Spanish consonants, likewise, are usually pronounced more precisely and distinctly than English consonants, although a few (especially **b, d,** and **g** between vowels) are pronounced very weakly. Several of them (**t, d, l,** and **n**) are pronounced farther forward in the mouth, with the tongue close to the upper teeth and gums. The consonants **p, t,** and **c** (before letters other than **e** and **i**) are never followed by the *h* sound that is often heard in English: *pen* (*p^hen*), *task* (*t^hask*), *can* (*c^han*).

DIVISION OF WORDS INTO SYLLABLES

Spanish words are hyphenated at the end of a line and are divided into syllables according to the following principles:

a. A single consonant (including **ch, ll, rr**) is placed with the vowel which follows: **pa-pel, mu-cho, ca-lle, pi-za-rra.**

b. Two consonants are usually divided: **tar-de, es-pa-ñol, tam-bién.** Consonants followed by **l** or **r**, however, are generally pronounced together and go with the following vowel: **li-bro, pa-dre, a-pren-do.** The groups **nl, rl, sl, tl, nr,** and **sr**, however, are divided: **Car-los, En-ri-que.**

c. In combinations of three or more consonants only the last consonant or the two consonants of the inseparable groups just mentioned (consonant plus **l** or **r**, with the exceptions listed) begin a syllable: **ins-pi-ra-ción, in-glés, en-tra.**

d. Two adjacent strong vowels (**a, e, o**) are in separate syllables: **le-o, tra-e, cre-e.**

e. Combinations of a strong and weak vowel (**i, u**) or of two weak vowels normally form single syllables: **bue-nos, bien, es-tu-dio, gra-cias, ciu-dad, Luis.** Such combinations are called diphthongs. (See page 4 for further discussion of diphthongs.)

f. In combinations of a strong and weak vowel, a written accent mark on the weak vowel divides the two vowels into separate syllables: **dí-a, pa-ís, tí-o.** An accent on the strong vowel of such combinations does not result in two syllables: **lec-ción, tam-bién.**

WORD STRESS

a. Most words which end in a vowel, and in **n** or **s** (plural endings of verbs and nouns, respectively), are stressed on the next to the last syllable: *cla*-se, *to*-mo, *ca*-sas, *en*-tran, *Car*-men.

b. Most words which end in a consonant, except **n** or **s,** are stressed on the last syllable: **pro-fe-*sor*, ha-*blar*, pa-*pel*, ciu-*dad*, es-pa-*ñol*.**

c. Words not pronounced according to these two rules have a written accent on the stressed syllable: **ca-***fé,* **in-***glés,* **lec-***ción,* **tam-***bién.*

The written accent is also used to distinguish between two words spelled alike but different in meaning (**si,** *if,* **sí,** *yes;* **el,** *the,* **él,** *he,* etc.), and on the stressed syllable of all interrogative words (**¿qué?** *what?*).

VOWELS

a is pronounced between the *a* of English *ask* and the *a* of *father:* ***ca*-sa, *ha*-bla, *A*-na.**

e is pronounced like *e* in *café,* but without the glide sound that follows the *e* in English: ***me*-sa, *cla*-se, us-*ted*.**

i (y) is pronounced like *i* in *machine:* **Fe-***li*-pe, *sí, dí*-as, *y*.**

o is pronounced like *o* in *obey,* but without the glide sound that follows the *o* in English: ***no, so*-lo, cho-co-*la*-te.**

u is pronounced like *oo* in *cool:* **us-*ted*, *u*-no, a-*lum*-no.**

The vowels **e** and **o** also have sounds like *e* in *let* and *o* in *for.* These sounds, as in English, generally occur when the **e** and **o** are followed by a consonant in the same syllable: ***el, ser, con,* es-pa-*ñol*.** In pronouncing the **e** in **el** and **ser,** and the **o** in **con** and **español,** the mouth is opened wider, and the distance between the tongue and the palate is greater, than when pronouncing the **e** in **mesa** and **clase,** and the **o** in **no** and **solo.** These more open sounds of **e** and **o** occur also in contact with the strongly trilled **r (rr),** before the **j** sound (written **g** before **e** or **i,** and **j**), and in the diphthongs **ei (ey)** and **oi (oy).** Pay close attention to the teacher's pronunciation of these sounds.

DIPHTHONGS

As stated on page 4, the weak vowels **i (y)** and **u** may combine with the strong vowels **a, e, o,** or with each other to form single syllables. Such combinations of two vowels are called diphthongs. In diphthongs the strong vowels retain their full syllabic value, while the weak vowels, or the first vowel in the case of two weak vowels, lose part of their syllabic value.

As the first element of a diphthong, unstressed **i** is pronounced like a weak English *y* in *yes,* and unstressed **u** is pronounced like *w* in *wet.* The Spanish diphthongs which begin with unstressed **i** and **u** are: **ia, ie, io, iu; ua, ue, uo, ui,** as in ***gra*-cias, *bien*, a-*diós*, ciu-*dad*; *cual*, *bue*-no, an-*ti*-guo, *Luis*.** (The sounds of the other diphthongs will be discussed later.)

Remember that two adjacent strong vowels within a word form separate syllables: ***le*-e, Do-ro-*te*-a.** Likewise, when a weak vowel adjacent to a strong vowel has a written accent, it retains its syllabic value and forms a separate syllable: ***dí*-a, pa-*ís*.** An accent mark on a strong vowel merely indicates stress: **lec-***ción,* **tam-***bién.*

LINKING

In speaking or reading Spanish, words are linked together, as in English, so that two or more may sound as one long word. These groups of words are called breath-groups. It is necessary to practice pronouncing phrases and even entire sentences without a pause between words. Frequently a short sentence will be pronounced as one breath-group, while a longer one may be divided into two or more groups. The meaning of what is being pronounced will help you to determine where the pauses ending the breath-groups should be made.

The following examples illustrate some of the general principles of linking. The syllabic division in parentheses shows the correct linking; the syllable or syllables italicized bear the main stress.

a. Within a breath-group the final consonant of a word is joined with the initial vowel of the following word and forms a syllable with it: **el alumno** (e-la-*lum*-no).

b. Within a breath-group when two identical vowels of different words come together, they are pronounced as one: **el profesor de español** (el-pro-fe-*sor*-de_es-pa-*ñol*).

c. When unlike vowels between words come together within a breath-group, they are usually pronounced together in a single syllable. Two cases occur: (1) when a strong vowel is followed or preceded by a weak vowel, both are pronounced together in a single syllable and the result is phonetically a diphthong (see page 4): **su amigo** (su_a-*mi*-go), **Juan y Elena** (*Jua*-n y E-*le*-na), **mi padre y mi madre** (mi-*pa*-dre_y-mi-*ma*-dre); (2) if both vowels are strong, each loses a little of its syllabic value and both are pronounced together in one syllable: **vamos a la escuela** (*va*-mo-sa-la_es-*cue*-la); **¿Cómo está usted?** (¿*Có*-mo_es-*tá*_us-*ted*?).

PUNCTUATION

Spanish punctuation is much the same as in English. The most important differences are:

1. Inverted question marks and exclamation points precede questions and exclamations. They are placed at the actual beginning of the question or exclamation, not necessarily at the beginning of the sentence:

¿Hablan Carlos y Juan?	Are Charles and John talking?
¡Qué muchacha más bonita!	What a pretty girl!
Usted es español, ¿verdad?	You are a Spaniard, aren't you?

2. In Spanish a comma is not used between the last two words of a series, while in English it usually is:

Tenemos plumas, libros y lápices.	We have pens, books, and pencils.

3. A dash is generally used instead of quotation marks to denote a change of speaker in dialogue.   It appears at the beginning of each speech, but is omitted at the end.

— **¿Es usted peruano?**   "Are you a Peruvian?"
— **Sí, señor.   Soy de Lima.**   "Yes, sir.   I am from Lima."

If quotation marks are used, they are placed on the line:

Juan dijo: «Buenos días».   John said, "Good morning."

CAPITALIZATION

Only proper names and the first word of a sentence begin with a capital letter in Spanish. The subject pronoun **yo** (*I* in English), names of months and days of the week, adjectives of nationality and nouns formed from them, and titles (unless abbreviated) are not capitalized.   In titles of books or works of art, only the first word is capitalized.

Juan y yo hablamos.   John and I are talking.
Hoy es lunes.   Today is Monday.
Buenos días, señor (Sr.) Pidal.   Good morning, Mr. Pidal.
Son españoles.   They are Spanish (Spaniards).
Las hilanderas.   The Spinning Girls.

EXERCISES

A. Vowel sounds.   Pronounce after your teacher, following the explanations given on page 5:

a Ana, Bárbara, hasta, casa, mañana, marchar, Marta, pasar.
e él, en, francés, inglés, José, leer, leche, qué.
o cómo, poco, señor, no, con, Carlos, español, profesor.
i dice, Felipe, libro, lista, así, señorita, y, día.
u alumno, escuchan, lectura, mucho, plumas, pregunta, uno, usted.

B. Spanish diphthongs.   Pronounce after your teacher, following the explanations given on page 5:

i + vowel   gracias, pronuncia; bien, siempre; lección, adiós; ciudad.
u + vowel   cuaderno, cual, cuando; bueno, puede, puerta; muy, Luis.

C. Rewrite the following words, dividing them into syllables, by means of a hyphen (-), and underlining the syllable that is stressed; then pronounce:

1. Carmen, inglés, español, marchar, preparan, señorita.

2. día, lección, país, principio, pronuncian, siempre.

D. Pronounce the following given names after your teacher. If you cannot figure out the English meaning of each name, you will find it in the end vocabulary:

1. Marta, María, Carolina, Luisa, Inés, Dorotea, Isabel, Margarita, Elena, Bárbara, Juanita, Carmen.

2. Felipe, Juan, Jorge, Tomás, Ricardo, Vicente, Ramón, Miguel, Jaime, Carlos, Eduardo, Roberto.

For further practice your teacher may ask you to divide the above names into syllables and underline the syllable that is stressed.

Parque Guell, designed by Gaudí,
the famous Catalan architect,
Barcelona, Spain.

LECCIÓN 1¹

Present indicative of the first conjugation.   Use of subject pronouns
Gender and plural of nouns.   Use of the definite article
Negative and interrogative sentences

EN LA CLASE DE ESPAÑOL

(*La profesora habla con los alumnos.*)

SRTA.² VALDÉS.   Buenos días, Carmen.
CARMEN.   Buenos días, señorita Valdés.
SRTA. VALDÉS.   Carmen, ¿habla usted español?
CARMEN.   Sí, señorita, hablo español un poco.

• • • • •

SRTA. VALDÉS.   Buenas tardes, Felipe.
FELIPE.   Buenas tardes, señorita Valdés.
SRTA. VALDÉS.   ¿Hablamos español en clase?
FELIPE.   Sí, señorita, hablamos español en clase.
SRTA. VALDÉS.   ¿Hablamos español con el profesor de inglés?
FELIPE.   No, señorita, hablamos inglés con el profesor de inglés.

• • • • •

SRTA. VALDÉS.   Ana, ¿estudian mucho los alumnos?
ANA.   Sí, señorita, estudian todas las tardes y todas las noches.

---

¹ SPECIAL NOTE TO THE TEACHER.   In Appendix B, you will find a list of some common classroom expressions which you may wish to introduce to your classes as they come up naturally.   Also, there follows a list of expressions for use in the language laboratory.   ² See page 1, translation of the dialogue and footnote 2, for the meanings of **señor**, **señora**, and **señorita**, and their respective abbreviations.

Srta. Valdés.   Carlos, ¿qué lenguas estudian los alumnos en España?

Carlos.   En España los alumnos estudian el inglés y el francés.

Srta. Valdés.   Sí, Carlos, y estudian el alemán también.   Ana, ¿prepara usted la lección de español en clase?

Ana.   No, señorita, siempre preparo la lección en casa.

Srta. Valdés.   Felipe, ¿prepara usted la lección de español con Carmen?

Felipe.   No, señorita, yo no estudio con las alumnas de la clase.   Preparo las lecciones todos los días con Carlos.

Srta. Valdés.   Muy bien.   Ustedes hablan y pronuncian muy bien el español.

CONVERSACIÓN (*Conversation*)

Answer in Spanish, beginning your reply with **Sí, señor** (**señora, señorita**) or **No, señor** (**señora, señorita**) whenever possible.   Follow the same practice in all subsequent lessons.

A. Preguntas sobre el diálogo (*Questions on the dialogue*)

1. ¿Habla Carmen español?   2. ¿Qué lengua hablamos con el profesor de inglés? 3. ¿Estudian mucho los alumnos?   4. ¿Estudian los alumnos todas las noches? 5. ¿Estudian el inglés en España?   6. ¿Estudian el alemán y el francés en España? 7. ¿Prepara Ana la lección en clase?   8. ¿Prepara Felipe las lecciones con Carmen?

B. Aplicación del diálogo (*Dialogue adaptation*)

1. ¿Qué lengua hablo yo?   2. ¿Habla usted español o inglés en casa?   3. ¿Hablamos español con la profesora de francés?   4. ¿Estudiamos el inglés o el español?   5. ¿Estudia usted el español todos los días?   6. ¿Estudian ustedes mucho?   7. ¿Preparan ustedes la lección de español en casa o en clase?   8. ¿Qué lenguas habla la profesora (el profesor)?

NOTAS GRAMATICALES (*Grammatical notes*)

A. Present indicative of the first conjugation

The infinitive of a Spanish verb consists of a stem (**habl**) and an ending (**-ar**).   The three conjugations in Spanish end in **-ar, -er, -ir** and are usually referred to as the first, second, and third conjugations, respectively.

To form the present tense of regular verbs of the first conjugation, add the endings **-o, -as, -a, -amos, -áis, -an** to the stem of the verb.

hablar, *to speak*

SINGULAR

(yo) hablo	*I speak, do speak, am speaking*
(tú) hablas (*fam.*)	*you speak, do speak, are speaking*
(él) habla	*he speaks, does speak, is speaking*
(ella) habla	*she speaks, does speak, is speaking*
usted habla (*formal*)	*you speak, do speak, are speaking*

PLURAL

(nosotros) hablamos	*we speak, do speak, are speaking*
(nosotras) hablamos	*we* (f.) *speak, do speak, are speaking*
(vosotros) habláis (*fam.*)[1]	*you speak, do speak, are speaking*
(vosotras) habláis (*fam.*)	*you* (f.) *speak, do speak, are speaking*
(ellos) hablan	*they speak, do speak, are speaking*
(ellas) hablan	*they* (f.) *speak, do speak, are speaking*
ustedes hablan (*fam. and formal*)	*you* (pl.) *speak, do speak, are speaking*

Which ending is used when the subject is I? we? she? you (*formal s.*)? you (*pl.*)? you (*fam. s.*)?

Three other verbs used in the dialogue are **estudiar, preparar,** and **pronunciar.** Practice these verbs with the same subjects.

B. Use of subject pronouns

1. **Hablo español.**   I speak Spanish.
   Ella habla y él estudia.   She talks and he studies.
   Carlos y yo preparamos la lección.   Charles and I prepare the lesson.
   Usted estudia mucho.   You study hard (a great deal).

The subject pronouns (**yo,** *I*; **él,** *he*, etc.) are not always required in Spanish since the verb ending often indicates the subject.   The subject pronouns, however, are used for emphasis (**hablamos,** *we speak*, but **nosotros hablamos,** *we speak*), for clearness (**él habla,** *he speaks*; **ella habla,** *she speaks*), or when a pronoun is combined with a noun or another pronoun to form a compound subject (**Carlos y yo hablamos,** *Charles and I*

[1] In Spanish America the second person plural forms in **-áis** are not used; the pronoun **ustedes** is used for the plural *you*, both familiar and formal.   The second person plural forms may be omitted in the early stages of the study of Spanish; they will not be used in the exercises of the first ten lessons of this book.

speak). For the sake of courtesy the pronouns **usted** and **ustedes** (often abbreviated to **Vd.** and **Vds.**) are usually expressed in Spanish. The subject *it* is rarely expressed.

2. Spanish has two forms for *you*. The familiar form **tú** is used by persons who call each other by their first names. Use the formal **usted** (*pl.* **ustedes**) for *you* unless **tú** is required by the context. (As stated above, for the sake of courtesy the pronoun **usted** is usually expressed in Spanish.) Since **usted** is a contraction of **vuestra merced,** *Your Grace*, it requires the third person of the verb; that is, the same form of the verb as **él, ella, Carlos.** In Spanish America **ustedes** is used for the plural *you*, both familiar and formal. In Spain the plural of familiar **tú** is **vosotros, vosotras,** which take the second person plural forms of the verb.

C. Gender and plural of nouns

el alumno	the pupil	**los alumnos**	the pupils
la clase	the class	**las clases**	the classes
el profesor	the teacher	**los profesores**	the teachers
la lección	the lesson	**las lecciones**	the lessons

Nouns in Spanish are either masculine or feminine in gender. Most nouns which end in **-o** are masculine, and those which end in **-a** are generally feminine. An exception is **el día,** *the day*. Since many nouns have other endings, learn the definite article, *the* in English, with each noun. The masculine forms of the definite article are **el** (singular) and **los** (plural); the feminine forms are **la** and **las.** The definite article agrees in gender and number with the noun.

Nouns which end in a vowel regularly add **-s** to form the plural; nouns ending in a consonant add **-es.**

Nouns which end in **-ción,** like **lección** and **conversación,** are feminine in Spanish. Remember that the accent mark is not required in writing the plural of such nouns: **lecciones, conversaciones.**

The masculine plural of nouns referring to persons may include both sexes: **los alumnos,** *the pupils* (boys and girls).

D. Use of the definite article

El profesor y el alumno hablan. The teacher and (the) pupil talk.
Estudian el inglés y el español. They study English and Spanish.
Vds. preparan bien las lecciones. You prepare the lessons well.

BUT: **Ella habla francés.** She speaks French.
¿Habla Vd. español? Do you speak Spanish?
Hablo con la profesora de español. I talk with the Spanish teacher.

The definite article is used more frequently in Spanish than in English. In general, the article is used whenever *the* is used in English, and it is repeated before each noun in a series.

The article is regularly used in Spanish with the name of a language, except after forms of the verb **hablar** and the prepositions **de** and **en**. (Many Spanish-speaking persons, however, also omit the article with a language after verbs such as **estudiar,** *to study*, and **aprender,** *to learn*.)

Note the position of the adverb **bien** in the third example.

E. Negative and interrogative sentences

1. **Yo no estudio con Felipe.** I do not study (am not studying) with Philip.
   Carlos no habla francés. Charles doesn't speak French.
   Ana no estudia el alemán. Ann does not study German.

To make a sentence negative in Spanish place **no** or some other negative word immediately before the verb. The English word *do* is not expressed in a negative sentence in Spanish.

2. **¿Habla Vd. español?** Do you speak Spanish?
   ¿Habla francés el profesor de español? Does the Spanish teacher speak French?
   ¿Estudian mucho los alumnos? Do the pupils study hard?

In questions in Spanish a subject pronoun is usually placed immediately after the verb. If the subject is as long as, or longer than, the object, it is placed at the end of the question (second example). If an adverb such as **mucho** or **bien** is used, the word order is verb, adverb, subject. The word *do* (*does*) is not expressed in Spanish.

3. **¿Qué lenguas estudian?** What languages do they study?
   Carmen, ¿habla Vd. español? Carmen, do you speak Spanish?
   ¿Qué prepara Vd.? What do you prepare? *or* What are you preparing?

If an interrogative word introduces the question, it precedes the verb and always has a written accent. An inverted question mark is placed immediately before the question (second example).

EJERCICIOS (*Exercises*)

A. Substitution drill. Repeat the model sentence after your teacher. He/She will repeat your response, pause slightly, then give a word or expression which you will substitute in your next response. (The teacher may ask part, or all, of the class to reply.)

MODEL: *Teacher.*[1] ¿Habla usted español? *Student.* ¿Habla usted español?

Teacher. ¿Habla usted español?
¿inglés? *Student.* ¿Habla usted inglés?

1. ¿Habla usted francés?
alemán?
mucho?
con Carlos?

2. Estudiamos el español.
el francés.
el inglés.
todos los días.

B. Substitution drill. Repeat the model sentence. When you hear a new subject, give a new sentence, making the verb agree with the subject:

MODEL: Yo hablo español.
Nosotros

Yo hablo español.
Nosotros hablamos español.

1. Felipe habla español.
Ellos
Tú
Usted
Yo

3. Felipe no estudia mucho.
Los alumnos
Carlos y yo
Tú
Ella y él

2. Ella siempre prepara la lección.
Yo
Tú
Nosotros
Ustedes

4. Él pronuncia bien el español.
Tú
Ellos
La alumna
Felipe y yo

C. Repeat after your teacher; then make each sentence negative:

MODEL: Ella habla con Ana.

Ella habla con Ana.
Ella no habla con Ana.

1. Él habla con el alumno.
2. Carmen prepara la lección.
3. El profesor de español habla bien.

4. Usted pronuncia bien el español.
5. Tú estudias el francés.
6. Yo estudio y ella habla.

---

[1] Hereafter the model sentence given by the teacher will be listed at the left, and the student response(s) at the right.

D. Repeat after your teacher; then put all forms in the plural:

> MODEL: Yo estudio la lección. Yo estudio la lección.
> Nosotros estudiamos las lecciones.

1. Él prepara la lección.
2. Usted estudia con la alumna.
3. Ella habla con el profesor.
4. La profesora habla con la alumna.
5. Yo no hablo con el profesor de inglés.
6. ¿Estudia mucho el alumno?

E. Answer affirmatively, beginning with **Sí, señor (señora, señorita)**:

> MODEL: ¿Estudia ella el español? Sí, señor (señora, señorita), ella estudia
> el español.

1. ¿Hablan español Carlos y Ana?
2. ¿Estudian los alumnos en casa?
3. ¿Estudia usted en clase?
4. ¿Pronuncian ustedes bien?
5. ¿Hablo yo español en clase?
6. ¿Preparo yo las lecciones de español?

F. Put into questions, following the models:

> MODELS: Carlos estudia el español. ¿Estudia Carlos el español?
> La alumna pronuncia bien. ¿Pronuncia bien la alumna?

1. Carmen prepara los ejercicios.
2. Los alumnos estudian mucho.
3. Ustedes estudian en casa.
4. Yo hablo con los alumnos.
5. Usted prepara la lección de inglés.
6. Los profesores pronuncian bien.

G. Give in Spanish:

1. Good morning, Philip. Do you speak Spanish? 2. Yes, ma'am, I speak a little in class. 3. Carmen, are you studying English and Spanish? 4. Yes, ma'am, and I study the Spanish lessons well every night. 5. Do you (*pl.*) speak Spanish in the English class? 6. No, we do not speak Spanish with the English teacher. 7. Ann, do you prepare the lessons in class? 8. No, I always study at home. 9. What languages do the students study in Spain? 10. In Spain they study English, French, and German.

EJERCICIOS DE PRONUNCIACIÓN *(Pronunciation exercises)*

A. Spanish **b** and **v**

1. Pronounced exactly alike, they have two sounds. At the beginning of a breath-group, or after **m** and **n,** the sound is that of a weak English *b*. Pronounce after your teacher:

basta	bien	buenos días	Valdés
verde	vida	Vicente	también

2. In other places, particularly between vowels, the sound is much weaker, the lips touching very lightly, and the breath continues to pass through a narrow opening in the center; avoid the English *v* sound. Pronounce after your teacher:

Roberto	hablamos	hablo	Isabel
libro	muy bien	beber	vivir

B. The sounds of Spanish **d**

Spanish **d** has two basic sounds: (1) at the beginning of a breath-group or when after **n** or **l,** it is pronounced like English *d*, but, as in Spanish **t,** the tip of the tongue touches the inner surface of the upper teeth, rather than the ridge above the teeth. Pronounce after your teacher:

donde	día	el día	un día
leyendo	dos	con dos	saldré

(2) In all other cases, the tongue drops even lower, and the **d** is pronounced like a weak English *th* in *this*. The sound is especially weak in the ending **-ado** and when final in a word before a pause. Pronounce after your teacher:

adiós	estudiar	los días	madre
tarde	todos	usted	verdad

C. Review linking, page 6, and pronounce as one breath-group:

en‿España	Buenas tardes, alumnos.	¿Hablan‿ustedes‿inglés?
con‿el profesor	Los‿alumnos‿estudian.	Hablamos‿inglés.
con las‿alumnas	Estudian‿el‿alemán.	Ustedes‿hablan.

VOCABULARIO[1] (*Vocabulary*)

el alemán German (*the language*)
la alumna pupil, student (*girl*)
el alumno pupil, student (*boy*)
Ana Ann, Anna, Anne
bien *adv.* well
bueno, -a[2] good
Carlos Charles
Carmen Carmen
la casa house, home
la clase class, classroom
con with
de of, from, about
el día (*note gender*) day
en in, on, at
España Spain
el español Spanish (*the language*)
estudiar to study
Felipe Philip
el francés French (*the language*)
hablar to speak, talk

el inglés English (*the language*)
la lección (*pl.* **lecciones**) lesson
la lengua language
mucho *adv.* much, hard, a great deal
muy very
no no, not
la noche night, evening
o or, either
preparar to prepare
el profesor teacher (*man*)
la profesora teacher (*woman*)
pronunciar to pronounce
¿qué? what? which?
sí yes
siempre always
también also, too
la tarde afternoon
todo, -a[2] all, every
y and

buenas tardes good afternoon
buenos días good morning (day)
clase de español (**inglés**) Spanish (English) class
en casa at home
en clase in class
lección (**lecciones**) **de español** Spanish lesson (lessons)
profesor *or* **profesora de inglés** (**español**) English (Spanish) teacher
todos los días every day (*lit.*, all the days)
todas las tardes (**noches**) every afternoon (night, evening)
un poco a little

[1] See **Notas gramaticales A** and **C** for the subject pronouns and definite articles.   [2] Agreement of adjectives will be explained in Lesson 2.

LECCIÓN 2

Present indicative of *ser* **and** *tener*.   **The indefinite article**

Forms and agreement of adjectives.   Use of *hay*

Uses of *que*.   **The adverbs** *aquí, ahí, allí*

EN LA SALA DE CLASE

SR. PIDAL.   Carmen, ¿qué hay en la sala de clase?

CARMEN.   Hay mesas y sillas.

SR. PIDAL.   ¿Hay un mapa en la pared?

CARMEN.   Sí, señor, hay un mapa en la pared.

• • • • •

SR. PIDAL.   Ana, ¿hay una pizarra en la pared?

ANA.   Sí, señor, hay una pizarra en la pared.

SR. PIDAL.   ¿De qué color es la pizarra?

ANA.   La pizarra es verde.

• • • • •

SR. PIDAL.   Hoy vamos a hablar de la sala de clase.   Ana, ¿hay cuadros en la pared?

ANA.   Sí, señor, hay dos cuadros en la pared.

SR. PIDAL.   Carlos, ¿qué tengo yo aquí sobre la mesa?

CARLOS.   Vd. tiene ahí papel, un libro y tres lápices.[1]

• • • • •

SR. PIDAL.   Felipe, ¿son azules los lápices?

FELIPE.   No, señor, dos son rojos y uno es amarillo.   El lápiz que tiene Carlos es azul.

SR. PIDAL.   Carmen, ¿qué tiene Vd. ahí sobre la mesa?

CARMEN.   Tengo el libro de español, un lápiz, una pluma y un cuaderno.

SR. PIDAL.   Ana, ¿de qué color es la pared?   ¿Es negra?

ANA.   No, señor, la pared es blanca; pero la pizarra es verde.

• • • • •

SR. PIDAL.   Carlos, ¿de dónde son María y Felipe?

CARLOS.   Ella es de México; es mexicana.   Felipe es de los Estados Unidos; es norteamericano.

[1] Final **z** changes to **c** before **-es**.

21

Sr. Pidal.   Y la profesora de francés, ¿es ella española?

Carlos.   No, señor, ella no es española; es inglesa.

Sr. Pidal.   Carmen es francesa.   Felipe, ¿es Carmen profesora?

Felipe.   No, señor, ella no es profesora; es alumna.

Sr. Pidal.   Muy bien.   Tenemos que hablar español todos los días.

CONVERSACIÓN

A. Preguntas sobre el diálogo

1. ¿Hay mesas y sillas en la sala de clase?   2. ¿Hay un mapa en la pared?   3. ¿Hay cuadros en la pared?   4. ¿De qué color es la pizarra?   5. ¿De qué color es el lápiz que tiene Carlos?   6. ¿De dónde es María?   7. ¿Es española la profesora de francés? 8. ¿Es Carmen profesora o alumna?

B. Aplicación del diálogo

1. ¿Es Vd. alumno (alumna) o profesor (profesora)?   2. ¿Qué soy yo?   3. ¿Qué hay allí en la pared?   4. ¿Tiene el profesor una mesa?   5. ¿Es verde el libro que tengo aquí?   6. ¿Qué tengo yo aquí sobre la mesa?   7. ¿Qué tiene Vd. ahí sobre la mesa? 8. ¿Tiene Vd. que estudiar mucho?

NOTAS GRAMATICALES

A. Irregular present indicative of **ser** and **tener**

	ser, *to be*		**tener,** *to have* (*possess*)	
		SINGULAR		
(yo)	**soy**	*I am*	**tengo**	*I have*
(tú)	**eres** (*fam.*)	*you are*	**tienes** (*fam.*)	*you have*
(él, ella)	**es**	*he, she, it is*	**tiene**	*he, she, it has*
usted	**es** (*formal*)	*you are*	**tiene** (*formal*)	*you have*
		PLURAL		
(nosotros, -as)	**somos**	*we are*	tenemos	*we have*
(vosotros, -as)	**sois** (*fam.*)	*you are*	tenéis (*fam.*)	*you have*
(ellos, -as)	**son**	*they are*	**tienen**	*they have*
ustedes	**son**	*you are*	**tienen**	*you have*

Forms of the irregular verbs must be memorized since there are few rules for conjugating them.

B. The indefinite article

1. **un libro y una pluma**   a book and (a) pen, one book and one pen
   Él tiene dos libros; yo tengo uno.   He has two books; I have one.

The word for *a* or *an* is **un** before a masculine singular noun and **una** before a feminine singular noun.   These words also mean *one*.   **Uno** (*m.*) and **una** (*f.*) are used when the word stands for a noun.   The indefinite article is normally repeated before each noun in a series.   (For the plural forms **unos (-as)** see footnote 2, page 129).

2. **Carlos es español.**   Charles is a Spaniard (is Spanish).
   Ella es profesora.   She is a teacher.

After **ser** the indefinite article is not used with unmodified nouns which indicate nationality or profession.

C. Forms and agreement of adjectives

	SINGULAR		PLURAL	
1.	Masculine	Feminine	Masculine	Feminine
	blanco	**blanca**	**blancos**	**blancas**
	mexicano	**mexicana**	**mexicanos**	**mexicanas**
	verde	**verde**	**verdes**	**verdes**

Adjectives whose masculine singular ends in **-o** have four forms, and the endings are **-o, -a, -os, -as.**   Most other adjectives have only two forms, a singular and a plural. The plurals of these adjectives are formed like those of nouns, by adding **-s, -es.**

2.	**español**	**española**	**españoles**	**españolas**
	francés	**francesa**	**franceses**	**francesas**
	inglés	**inglesa**	**ingleses**	**inglesas**

Adjectives of nationality which end in a consonant add **-a** to form the feminine; those which end in **-és** in the masculine singular drop the accent mark on the other three forms.

3. **La pared es blanca.**   The wall is white.
   Dos lápices son rojos.   Two pencils are red.
   Todas las casas son blancas.   All the houses are white.
   ¿Son azules los lápices?   Are the pencils blue?

Adjectives agree with the nouns they modify in gender and number, whether they modify the noun directly or are in the predicate.   Numerals, except **uno,** do not change in form.   In questions a predicate adjective (*e.g.*, after **ser**) is regularly placed immediately after the verb, and the subject follows the predicate; however, when the subject is shorter than the predicate, it follows the verb: **¿Es ella profesora?**   *Is she a teacher?*

4. **El español habla inglés.**   The Spaniard speaks English.
   La mexicana es alumna.   The Mexican girl is a student.
   Ellas no son francesas.   They are not French (girls).
   ¿Es ella española?   Is she Spanish (a Spanish girl)?

Adjectives of nationality are often used as nouns. When used thus, they have the gender and number of the noun they are replacing.

D.   Use of **hay**

¿Qué hay en la sala de clase?   What is there in the classroom?
Hay dos cuadros en la pared.   There are two pictures on the wall.
¿Hay mapas en la pared?   Are there (any, some) maps on the wall?

The form **hay** has no subject expressed in Spanish and means *there is, there are.* Do not confuse **hay** with **es,** (*it*) *is,* and with **son,** (*they*) *are.*
   Note in the third example that unemphatic *any* or *some* are not expressed in Spanish.

Práctica (*Practice*).   Read in Spanish, keeping the meaning in mind:

1. Hay mapas en el libro de español.   2. También hay cuadernos aquí.   3. ¿Hay cuadros en la sala de clase?   4. ¿Tienen Vds. papel?   5. ¿Tengo yo lápices o plumas sobre la mesa?   6. ¿Tienen Vds. libros de inglés?

E.   Uses of **que**

1. **El lápiz que tiene Carlos es azul.**   The pencil that Charles has is blue.
   El alumno que habla es español.   The pupil who is talking is Spanish.

The relative pronoun **que** refers to things or persons and may mean *that, which, who, whom.* Note that the subject (**Carlos**) follows the verb in the first example.

2. **Tengo que estudiar.**   I have to (I must) study.
   ¿Tiene Vd. que hablar mucho?   Do you have to talk much?

The idiomatic expression **tener que** plus an infinitive expresses necessity and means *to have to, must.*

F.   The adverbs **aquí, ahí, allí**

Tengo aquí un libro de español.   I have a Spanish book here.
¿Qué tiene Vd. ahí?   What do you have there?
¿Qué lengua hablan allí?   What language do they speak there?

The adverb **ahí,** *there*, refers to something near the person addressed, and **allí,** *there*, *over there*, to something at a distance. Adverbs should be placed as near the verb as possible.

EJERCICIOS

A. Repeat after your teacher, then say again, substituting **un (una)** for **el (la)**:

1. Tengo el lápiz. 2. Tienes el libro. 3. Tenemos el mapa. 4. ¿Tiene Vd. el cuadro? 5. ¿Tiene ella el cuaderno? 6. Es la mesa. 7. Es la sala de clase. 8. Es el libro de español.

B. Repeat after your teacher, then make each sentence plural:

MODEL: La pizarra es verde.   La pizarra es verde.
          Las pizarras son verdes.

1. El libro es verde. 2. El cuaderno es negro. 3. La pared es blanca. 4. La mesa no es azul. 5. La pluma no es amarilla. 6. ¿Es rojo el libro de español? 7. ¿Es verde el lápiz? 8. ¿Es amarilla la casa? 9. El alumno es mexicano. 10. La alumna es norteamericana. 11. La profesora es española. 12. Ella no es inglesa.

C. Answer affirmatively:

MODELS: ¿Es verde la pared?   Sí, señor (señora, señorita),[1] la pared es verde.
          ¿Es Vd. alumno?   Sí, señor (señora, señorita), soy alumno.

1. ¿Es Felipe mexicano?
2. ¿Es María norteamericana?
3. ¿Es blanca la casa?
4. ¿Es blanco el papel?
5. ¿Son ingleses los alumnos?

6. ¿Son alumnas María y Carmen?
7. ¿Son Vds. alumnos?
8. ¿Somos Vd. y yo norteamericanos?
9. ¿Soy yo profesor (profesora)?
10. ¿Tiene Vd. un libro de español?

D. Answer negatively:

MODEL: ¿Es Vd. francés?   No, señor (señora, señorita),[1] no soy francés.

1. ¿Es Vd. español (española)?
2. ¿Son Vds. franceses?
3. ¿Eres profesor (profesora)?
4. ¿Son Vds. profesores?
5. ¿Hay cuadros sobre la mesa?

6. ¿Es blanco el libro de inglés?
7. ¿Son negras las sillas?
8. ¿Hay papel en la pared?
9. ¿Tiene Carlos el libro de español?
10. ¿Tienen Vds. lápices verdes?

[1] Hereafter only **Sí** or **No** will be given in the models, but for politeness be sure to include **señor, señora,** or **señorita,** in your reply.

E. Substitution drill:

1. *Carlos* es de España.
   (*Ella, Vd., María y yo, Tú, Yo*)
2. *Yo* tengo dos lápices.
   (*Nosotros, Carmen, Tú, Vds., Ana y yo*)
3. *El alumno* tiene que estudiar.
   (*Ana, Yo, Vd. y yo, Carlos y María, Tú*)

F. Read in Spanish, using the correct form of the verbs given:

(**ser**) 1. ¿De dónde ———— Vd.? 2. ¿De dónde ———— tú? 3. ¿De dónde ————
yo? 4. Los mexicanos ———— de México. 5. Vd. y yo ———— norteamericanos.
6. Carlos y Ana no ———— mexicanos. 7. Carmen no ———— francesa. 8. ¿De qué
color ———— la casa?

(**tener**) 9. Carlos ———— un cuaderno. 10. ¿———— Vd. papel? 11. ¿Qué ————
tú ahí? 12. ¿Qué ———— yo aquí? 13. ¿Qué ———— los alumnos? 14. Felipe
———— que preparar la lección. 15. Él y yo ———— que hablar mucho. 16. ¿————
Vds. que estudiar en casa?

G. Repeat after your teacher; then use the cue words to make new sentences, making the necessary changes in the verb and predicate:

1. La casa es blanca.
   Las casas
   El papel
   La silla
   Los cuadernos
   Las mesas
   La pared

2. El profesor no es español.
   La profesora
   Felipe y yo
   Carlos y María
   Usted
   Tú
   Yo

H. Give in Spanish:

1. Carmen is not [a][1] pupil; she is [a] teacher. 2. Philip is Spanish; [he] is from Spain.
3. Mary is [an] American; [she] is from the United States. 4. The Spanish book is
green; [it] is not red. 5. Is the house white? No, [it] is yellow. 6. The pencils are
not black; [they] are yellow. 7. Is there a map of Mexico on the wall? 8. There are
maps of Mexico and of Spain. 9. Charles, what do I have here on the desk? 10. You
have there [some] books, paper, and two notebooks. 11. Do you[2] have to study hard?
12. Yes, I have to study every night.

---

[1] Words in brackets are not to be translated.   [2] Use the formal **usted** form for *you* unless the context requires the familiar form.

EJERCICIOS DE PRONUNCIACIÓN

A. Sounds of Spanish **c** (and **z**), **qu**, and **k**

1. Spanish **c** before **e** and **i**, and **z** in all positions, are pronounced like English hissed *s* in *sent* in Spanish America and in southern Spain; in northern and central Spain the sound is like *th* in *thin*. Pronounce after your teacher:

ejercicio	francés	lápices	lección
pronunciar	azul	lápiz	pizarra

2. Spanish **c** before all other letters, **qu** before **e** and **i**, and **k** (used only in words of foreign origin) are like English *c* in *cat*, but without the *h* sound that often follows the *c* in English (*cʰat*). The **u** in **que, qui** is never sounded as in English *quest*, *quick*. Pronounce after your teacher:

blanco	Carlos	casa	color
cuadro	lectura	aquí	que
kilo	kilómetro	parque	pequeño

B. Breath-groups, division of words into syllables, and word stress

Rewrite the first four exchanges of the dialogues of this lesson, dividing them into breath-groups and into syllables, and underlining the stressed syllables. Note that conjunctions (**y** and **pero**), prepositions (**a, de, en**), and the forms of the definite article are not considered stressed words in Spanish.

Las Ramblas, Barcelona, Spain.

VOCABULARIO

a to, at
ahí there (*near person addressed*)
allí there (*distant*)
amarillo, -a yellow
aquí here
azul blue
blanco, -a white
el color color
el cuaderno notebook
el cuadro picture
¿dónde? where?
dos two
español, -ola *adj.* Spanish
francés, -esa *adj.* French
hay there is, there are
hoy today
inglés, -esa *adj.* English
el lápiz (*pl.* **lápices**) pencil
el libro book
el mapa (*note gender*) map
María Mary

la mesa table, desk
mexicano, -a Mexican
México Mexico
negro, -a black
norteamericano, -a (North) American (*of the U.S.*)
el papel paper
la pared wall
pero but
la pizarra (black)board
la pluma pen
que that, which, who, whom
rojo, -a red
ser to be
la silla chair
sobre on, upon, about, concerning
tener to have (*possess*)
tres three
un, una, uno a, an, one
verde green

¿de qué color es? what color is (it)?
libro de español Spanish book
los Estados Unidos the United States
sala de clase classroom
tener que + *inf.* to have to + *inf.*
vamos a (**hablar**) we are going to (talk)

LECCIÓN 3

Present indicative of the second conjugation
Present indicative of *ir*. **Preposition** *a*. **Possession**
Cardinal numerals. Time of day. Use of *¿ no es verdad?*

EN EL CUARTO DE LUIS Y DE JORGE

LUIS.   ¿Qué hora es?
JORGE.   Es la una.
LUIS.   ¿Tienes clase ahora?
JORGE.   No, no tengo clase hasta las dos.
LUIS.   ¿Adónde vas?
JORGE.   Voy a la biblioteca a estudiar.

• • • • •

LUIS.   ¿Qué hora es, Jorge?
JORGE.   (*Mira el reloj que tiene sobre la mesita de noche.*)   Son las siete y cuarto de la mañana.
LUIS.   El reloj que tienes ahí anda bien, ¿no es verdad?
JORGE.   Sí, Luis.   El reloj es de Felipe.   Es viejo, pero anda bien.
LUIS.   ¿Es de plata, como el reloj del profesor?
JORGE.   No, es de oro.   Pero, ¿adónde vas tan temprano?
LUIS.   Primero voy al café a tomar el[1] desayuno con Felipe.   Luego vamos a la biblioteca.
JORGE.   Vds. tienen un examen a la una, ¿verdad?
LUIS.   Sí, Jorge.   Vamos a estudiar desde las ocho hasta las diez.
JORGE.   ¿Cuántas clases tienes por la mañana?
LUIS.   Generalmente tengo tres; pero hoy tengo solamente una.

• • • • •

JORGE.   Luis ¿a qué hora tomas el[1] almuerzo?
LUIS.   A las doce.   Y como a las cinco y media o a las seis menos cuarto.   ¿A qué hora cenan Vds.?
JORGE.   En casa nosotros no cenamos hasta las siete o las siete y media.

---

[1] In contrast to English the definite article is used in certain set expressions, such as **tomar el desayuno (almuerzo),** *to take,* *have,* or *eat breakfast (lunch).*

31

Luis.   Vds. comen casi tan tarde como en España.

Jorge.   No, Luis, allí no comen hasta las nueve o las diez de la noche.

Luis.   Sí, es verdad.   Bueno, tengo que ir al café ahora.   Hasta luego, Jorge.

Jorge.   Hasta luego, Luis.

CONVERSACIÓN

A.   Preguntas sobre el diálogo

1. ¿Anda bien el reloj que tiene Jorge?   2. ¿De qué es el reloj?   3. ¿Adónde va Luis primero?   4. ¿Dónde van a estudiar Luis y Felipe?   5. ¿Tiene Luis clases por la mañana?   6. ¿A qué hora toma Luis el almuerzo?   7. ¿A qué hora come Luis? 8. ¿A qué hora comen en España?

B.   Aplicación del diálogo

1. ¿Qué hora es?   2. ¿A qué hora toma Vd. el desayuno?   3. ¿A qué hora comemos generalmente en los Estados Unidos?   4. ¿Tiene Vd. un reloj?   5. ¿De qué es el reloj que tengo aquí?   6. ¿Cuántas clases tiene Vd. por la mañana?   7. ¿Prepara Vd. la lección de español por la mañana o por la tarde?   8. ¿Cuántas alumnas hay en la clase de español?

NOTAS GRAMATICALES

A.   Present indicative of the second conjugation

comer, *to eat*

SINGULAR		PLURAL	
como	*I eat*	comemos	*we eat*
comes	*you* (fam.) *eat*	coméis	*you* (fam.) *eat*
come	*he, she, it eats*	comen	*they eat*
Vd. come	*you* (formal) *eat*	Vds. comen	*you eat*

The present indicative endings of **-er** verbs (second conjugation) are: **-o, -es, -e, -emos, -éis, -en.** Compare with the endings of **-ar** verbs.   Remember that the present tense is translated: **como,** *I eat, do eat, am eating.*

B. Irregular present indicative of **ir**, *to go*

SINGULAR	PLURAL
voy	**vamos**
vas	**vais**
va	**van**
Vd. **va**	Vds. **van**

C. Preposition **a**

Tengo que ir al café.   I have to go to the café.
¿Adónde vas tan temprano?   Where are you going so early?
Vamos a estudiar la lección de hoy.   We are going to study today's lesson.

Ir and other verbs of motion are followed by the preposition **a** before an infinitive or any other object.   Note that **¿adónde?** *where?* is used with **ir** in a question.

When **a** is followed by the definite article **el,** the two words contract into **al.**   The combinations **a la, a los, a las** do not contract: **Vamos a la biblioteca,** *We are going to the library.*

D. Possession

El reloj es de Felipe.   The watch is Philip's.
¿Es de oro el reloj del profesor?   Is the teacher's watch gold?
Carlos tiene la pluma del alumno.   Charles has the student's pen.

BUT: **las plumas de los alumnos**   the students' pens

Spanish uses the preposition **de** to express possession.   The apostrophe is not used in Spanish.   When **de** is followed by the article **el,** the combination is contracted into **del;** however, **de la, de los, de las** are not contracted.   **Del** and **al** are the only two contractions in Spanish.

E. Cardinal numerals

1 **uno**	6 **seis**	11 **once**	16 **diez y seis**
2 **dos**	7 **siete**	12 **doce**	17 **diez y siete**
3 **tres**	8 **ocho**	13 **trece**	18 **diez y ocho**
4 **cuatro**	9 **nueve**	14 **catorce**	19 **diez y nueve**
5 **cinco**	10 **diez**	15 **quince**	20 **veinte**

From 21 to 29 the numerals are: **veinte y un(o), veinte y dos,** etc.   Cardinal numerals do not change their form, except that **uno** and numerals ending in **uno** drop **o** before a masculine noun; **una** is used before a feminine noun: **un libro,** *a* (*one*) *book*; **veinte y un alumnos,** *twenty-one pupils*; **una pluma,** *a* (*one*) *pen*.

Numerals precede the nouns they modify unless they are used in a descriptive sense: **tres lecciones,** *three lessons,* but **Lección tres,** *Lesson Three.*

[From 16 to 19 the numerals are often written as they are always pronounced: **dieciséis, diecisiete, dieciocho, diecinueve.** From 21 to 29 they may also be written together, as they are pronounced: **veintiuno (veintiún), veintidós, veintitrés, veinticuatro, veinticinco, veintiséis, veintisiete, veintiocho, veintinueve.**]

F. Time of day

¿Qué hora es? What time is it?
¿A qué hora tomas el almuerzo? At what time do you take (eat) lunch?
Es la una. It is one o'clock.
Son las tres y veinte. It is twenty minutes past three.
Son las cuatro y media. It is half past four.
Son las doce menos cuarto. It is a quarter to twelve (11:45).

The word **hora** means *time* in asking the time of day. In stating the time, the word **hora** is understood, and the feminine article **la** or **las** is used with the cardinal numeral corresponding to the hour. **Es** is used only when followed by **la una;** in all other cases **son** is used.

Up to and including the half hour, minutes are added to the hour by using the proper numeral after **y;** between the half hour and the next hour they are subtracted from the next hour by using **menos.** The noun **cuarto** is used for a quarter of an hour and the adjective **media** for a half hour. The word *minutes* is seldom expressed.

Son las siete y media de la mañana. It is half past seven A.M. (in the morning).
Ella va a las tres de la tarde. She is going at three P.M. (in the afternoon).
Estudio por la tarde (noche). I study in the afternoon (evening).

When a specific hour is given, the word *in* is translated by **de;** when no definite hour is given, *in* is translated by **por.**

G. Use of ¿no es verdad?

El reloj anda bien, ¿no es verdad? The watch (clock) runs well, doesn't it?
Tú miras el mapa, ¿verdad? You are looking at the map, aren't you?

The expression **¿no es verdad?** (*literally,* 'is it not true?') is the Spanish equivalent of English *isn't it? doesn't it? aren't you? doesn't he?* etc., depending upon the meaning of the verb in the preceding statement. The expression may be shortened to **¿verdad?** or even to **¿no?**

EJERCICIOS

A. Substitution drill:

1. *Luis* come a las seis.
   (*Luis y Jorge, Yo, Nosotros, Tú, Vd.*)
2. *Ella* toma el almuerzo a las doce.
   (*Yo, Nosotros, Luis y yo, Tú, Usted y él*)
3. *Jorge y yo* vamos al café.
   (*Nosotros, Yo, Él y ella, Felipe, Tú*)
4. ¿Adónde va *Vd.?*
   (*Luis, Jorge y Luis, nosotros, Vds., ella*)

B. Repeat after your teacher. When you hear a new subject, use it in a new sentence, making the verb agree with the subject:

1. Yo tomo el desayuno temprano. (Nosotros)
2. Ella toma el almuerzo tarde. (Ella y María)
3. Jorge come a las seis y cuarto. (Él y yo)
4. ¿A qué hora cenas tú? (ustedes)
5. Yo tengo dos clases por la tarde. (Los alumnos)
6. Nosotros tenemos tres clases por la mañana. (El profesor)
7. ¿Miras tú el reloj de oro? (usted)
8. Tú eres norteamericano, ¿verdad? (Usted)
9. Los alumnos y yo vamos a la biblioteca. (Yo)
10. ¿Tienes tú que cenar temprano? (usted y él)

C. Use **a, de, en**, or **por** to complete these sentences:

1. Tomo el desayuno —— las siete —— la mañana. 2. Tengo tres clases —— la mañana. 3. Tengo la clase de español —— la una —— la tarde. 4. ¿—— qué hora va ella —— la biblioteca? 5. ¿Estudias allí —— la tarde? 6. ¿Estudias —— casa todas las noches? 7. Comemos —— el café —— las cinco y media. 8. El reloj —— Luis es —— oro, ¿verdad? 9. ¿Van Vds. —— la biblioteca —— preparar la lección? 10. Vamos —— estudiar hasta las diez —— la noche.

D. Read in Spanish:

1. 4 exámenes. 2. 5 casas. 3. 10 horas. 4. 15 días. 5. 14 cuadros. 6. 11 clases. 7. 13 lecciones. 8. 21 alumnos. 9. 21 alumnas. 10. 18 profesores. 11. 12 lápices. 12. 20 mesas. 13. 2 bibliotecas. 14. 3 mexicanos. 15. 25 norteamericanos.

E. Answer in Spanish:

1. ¿Cuántos son 4 y 8?   2. ¿Cuántos son 12 menos 2?
   7 y 6?   20 menos 11?
   10 y 10?   15 menos 5?
   15 y 14?   16 menos 1?
   12 y 9?   29 menos 9?

F. Listen to the hour given and then to the question. Answer with a complete sentence:

 MODELS: La una. ¿Qué hora es? Es la una.
     Las dos. ¿Qué hora es? Son las dos.

1. La una y cuarto.   5. Las ocho y diez.
2. Las cuatro y media.   6. Las nueve de la noche.
3. Las once menos cuarto.   7. Las tres de la mañana.
4. La una menos veinte.   8. Las dos de la tarde.

G. Give in Spanish, using the familiar form for *you*:

1. Where are you going so early? 2. What time is it? It is a quarter to seven. 3. First I have to go to the café to take breakfast. 4. Do you have an examination today? 5. Yes, I have one at ten o'clock. 6. Do you have to study in the library until ten o'clock? 7. No, I am going to study there only until nine. 8. How many classes do you have in the afternoon? 9. Generally I have two classes, but today only one. 10. At what time do you take lunch? 11. I always take lunch late, at half past twelve. 12. In Spain they eat (dinner) late, at nine or ten P.M., don't they?

EJERCICIOS DE PRONUNCIACIÓN

A. The diphthongs **ie** and **ei** (**ey**)

1. As the first element of a diphthong, unstressed **i** is pronounced like a weak English *y* in *yes*. Pronounce after your teacher:

diecisiete	diez	siete	también
tiene	viejo	él y ella	alemán y español

2. **Ei** (**ey**) is pronounced like a prolonged English *a* in *fate*. Pronounce after your teacher:

coméis	seis	tenéis	veinte
veintiséis	de‿inglés	doce‿y media	siete‿y cuarto

B. The sounds of Spanish **g**

1. Spanish **g** (written **gu** before **e** or **i**) is pronounced like a weak English *g* in *go* at the beginning of a breath-group or after **n.** Pronounce after your teacher:

gracias	inglés	lengua	gusto
guitarra	tengo	en guerra	un guisado

2. In all other cases, except when before **e** or **i** in the groups **ge, gi,** the sound is much weaker, and the breath continues to pass between the back of the tongue and the palate. Pronounce after your teacher:

agua	luego	negro	agosto
Miguel	la guerra	muchas gracias	una guitarra

3. When before **e** or **i** in the groups **ge, gi,** it is pronounced like Spanish **j,** that is, approximately like a strongly exaggerated *h* in *halt*. Pronounce after your teacher:

generalmente	gente	Jorge	ágil
ejercicio	rojo	viejo	gitano

C. Dictado (*Dictation*)

The teacher will select four exchanges of the dialogues of this lesson as an exercise in dictation.

Casa de las conchas, Salamanca, Spain.

VOCABULARIO

¿adónde? where? (*with verbs of motion*)
al = a + el to the
el almuerzo lunch
andar to run (*said of a watch*)
la biblioteca library
bueno *adv.* well, well now, all right
el café café
casi almost
cenar to eat supper
comer to eat, dine, have dinner
como as, like
¿cuánto, -a? how much (many)?
el cuarto quarter; room
del = de + el of the
el desayuno breakfast
desde from, since
el examen (*pl.* **exámenes**) examination
generalmente generally
hasta until, to

la hora hour, time (*of day*)
ir (**a** + *inf.*) to go (to)
Jorge George
luego later, then, next
Luis Louis
la mañana morning
medio, -a half, a half
menos less
mirar to look at
el oro gold
la plata silver
por during, in, through, along, by
primero *adv.* first
el reloj watch, clock
solamente *adv.* only
tan *adv.* so, as
tarde late
temprano early
tomar to take, eat, drink
la verdad truth
viejo, -a old

de *or* **por la mañana** (**tarde, noche**) in the morning (afternoon, evening)
él mira el reloj he looks at the watch (clock)
es de oro (**de plata**) it is (of) gold (silver)
es verdad it is true
hasta luego until later, see you later
la mesita de noche night table
¿(no es) verdad? isn't it? don't you? etc.
tan + *adj. or adv.* + **como** as ... as
tomar el desayuno (**almuerzo**) to take, have *or* eat breakfast (lunch)

LECCIÓN 4

Present indicative of the third conjugation.   Present indicative of *venir*
Possessive adjectives.   Position of adjectives
Phrases with *de* plus a noun.   Summary of uses of *ser*

LA FAMILIA DE TOMÁS

LUIS.   ¡Hola, Tomás!   ¿Qué lees?
TOMÁS.   Leo una carta de mi hermana Carmen.
LUIS.   ¿Dónde estudia ella ahora?
TOMÁS.   Estudia en la Universidad de México.

• • • • •

LUIS.   ¿Escribe tu hermana en español?
TOMÁS.   Todavía no; pero cada día aprende varias palabras nuevas.
LUIS.   ¿Vive en una residencia de estudiantes?
TOMÁS.   No, vive con una familia mexicana.

• • • • •

LUIS.   ¡Hola, Tomás!   Lees una carta.   ¿De quién es?   ¿Es de tu amiga María?
TOMÁS.   No, Luis.   Es de mi hermana Carmen, que estudia en una escuela mexicana.
Ella escribe cartas muy interesantes acerca de la vida del país.
LUIS.   ¿Escribe tu hermana en español?
TOMÁS.   Todavía no; pero vive con una familia mexicana y cada día aprende varias palabras
nuevas.
LUIS.   Vds. hablan español en casa, ¿no es verdad?
TOMÁS.   Un poco.   Mi padre habla español con los amigos mexicanos que vienen a nuestra
casa.
LUIS.   Tus padres reciben un periódico en español, ¿verdad?
TOMÁS.   Sí, y todas las tardes mi madre escucha un programa de televisión en español.

• • • • •

LUIS.   ¿Todavía viven Vds. en su casa de campo?   Es una casa grande y hermosa.
TOMÁS.   No, Luis, ahora vivimos aquí en la ciudad, cerca del parque.   La casa es pequeña,
pero es muy cómoda.
LUIS.   ¿Quién vive en tu casa de campo?
TOMÁS.   Mi hermano vive allí ahora.

Luis.   Bueno, tengo que ir a la biblioteca.   Nuestra lección de español para mañana tiene
una parte muy difícil.

Tomás.   Tenemos que escribir una carta a un estudiante español, ¿no es verdad?

Luis.   Sí.   Yo voy a preparar la carta con mi amigo Carlos.

Tomás.   No es fácil aprender una lengua extranjera.

Luis.   Es verdad.   Es necesario trabajar mucho.

CONVERSACIÓN

A.   Preguntas sobre el diálogo

1. ¿De quién es la carta que lee Tomás?   2. ¿Dónde estudia Carmen?   3. ¿Con quién vive Carmen?   4. ¿Qué aprende ella cada día?   5. ¿Con quiénes habla español el padre de Tomás?   6. ¿Qué escucha la madre de Tomás?   7. ¿Dónde vive ahora la familia de Tomás?   8. ¿Qué tienen que escribir los estudiantes de la clase?

B.   Aplicación del diálogo

1. ¿Dónde estudia Vd., en casa o en la biblioteca?   2. ¿Viven sus padres en el campo?   3. ¿Habla Vd. español o inglés en casa?   4. ¿Qué programas de televisión escucha Vd.?   5. ¿Cuántos periódicos leen Vds.?   6. ¿Son interesantes las cartas de sus amigos?   7. ¿Qué parte de la lección de español es difícil?   8. ¿Es fácil aprender una lengua extranjera?

NOTAS GRAMATICALES

A.   Present indicative of the third conjugation

vivir, *to live*

	SINGULAR		PLURAL
vivo	*I live*	vivimos	*we live*
vives	*you* (fam.) *live*	vivís	*you* (fam.) *live*
vive	*he, she, it lives*	viven	*they live*
Vd. vive	*you* (formal) *live*	Vds. viven	*you live*

The present indicative endings of **-ir** verbs (third conjugation) are: **-o, -es, -e, -imos, -ís, -en.**   These endings are the same as those for **-er** verbs, except in the first and second persons plural.   Remember that **Vd.** and **Vds.** require the third person of the verb; these forms will not be given separately hereafter.   The present tense is translated: **vivo,** *I live, do live, am living.*

B. Irregular present indicative of **venir**, *to come*

SINGULAR	PLURAL
vengo	venimos
vienes	venís
viene	**vienen**

C. Possessive adjectives

SINGULAR	PLURAL	
mi	**mis**	my
tu	**tus**	your (*fam.*)
su	**sus**	his, her, its, your (formal)
nuestro, -a	**nuestros, -as**	our
vuestro, -a	**vuestros, -as**	your (*fam.*)
su	**sus**	their, your (*pl.*)

mi amiga, mis amigas   my (girl) friend, my friends
nuestra casa, nuestras casas   our house, our houses
su escuela   his, her, your, their school
sus padres   his, her, your, their parents
Él viene con sus amigos.   He is coming with his friends.

Possessive adjectives agree with the nouns they modify in <u>gender</u> and <u>number</u>, like other adjectives.   Thus they agree with the thing possessed and not with the possessor.   The possessive adjective never ends in **-s** unless the noun ends in **-s**.   These forms precede the noun and are generally repeated before each noun modified.   Forms will be given later to clarify **su** and **sus**.

D. Position of adjectives

una familia mexicana   a Mexican family
dos cartas interesantes   two interesting letters
varios periódicos españoles   several Spanish newspapers
una casa grande y hermosa   a large, beautiful house

Adjectives which limit as to quantity (*the, a, an, much, several,* numerals, possessive adjectives, etc.) are placed before the nouns they modify.

Adjectives which describe a noun by telling its quality (color, size, shape, nationality, etc.) normally are placed after the noun.

When two adjectives of equal value modify a noun, they are usually placed after the noun and connected by **y** (last example).

E. Phrases with **de** plus a noun

> **un reloj de oro** (**de plata**)   a gold (silver) watch
> **una casa de campo**   a country house
> **un programa de televisión**   a television program
> **la clase** (**lección**) **de español**   the Spanish class (lesson)

Nouns cannot be used as adjectives in Spanish as they often are in English.   When an English noun used as an adjective is put into Spanish, use **de** plus the noun.

Compare **el periódico español**, *the Spanish newspaper*, with **el profesor de español**, *the Spanish teacher* (teacher of Spanish).   A native Spaniard who teaches Spanish would be **un profesor español**, as well as **un profesor de español**.   Also recall the expressions **la lección** (**la clase, el libro**) **de español**.

F. Summary of uses of **ser**

Ser has been used in this lesson and in the two preceding lessons without an explanation of its various uses.   Note carefully the following summary, so that **ser** will not be confused with another verb meaning *to be* which will be given in Lesson 5.

Ser is used:

1. With a predicate noun or pronoun, or adjective used as a noun, to show that the subject and the noun or pronoun in the predicate refer to the same person or thing:

> **María es alumna.**   Mary is a pupil (student).
> **No somos mexicanos.**   We are not Mexicans.

2. With the preposition **de** to denote *ownership, origin,* or *material;* and with the preposition **para** to indicate *for whom* or *for what* a thing is intended:

> **Es de mi hermano.**   It is my brother's.
> **Son de España.**   They are from Spain.
> **El reloj es de oro.**   The watch is (of) gold.
> **La carta es para Carmen.**   The letter is for Carmen.

3. In impersonal expressions (*it* + verb + adjective):

> **Es necesario estudiar mucho.**   It is necessary to study hard.

4. With an adjective to express an inherent, essential, or characteristic quality of the subject that is relatively permanent.   This includes adjectives of color, size, shape, nationality, and the like:

> **La ciudad es grande.**   The city is large.
> **La casa es amarilla.**   The house is yellow.
> **Los programas son interesantes.**   The programs are interesting.

5. To express time of day:

Son las nueve y cuarto.   It is a quarter after (past) nine.

EJERCICIOS

A. Substitution drill:

1. *Yo* vivo en una casa pequeña.
   (*Tú, Tomás, Vds., Nosotros, Ana y Carmen*)
2. *Ellos* no escriben cartas.
   (*Luis, Yo, Ella y yo, Mi hermano, Tú*)
3. *Jorge* viene a las ocho.
   (*Ana, Ana y yo, Yo, Tú, Mis amigos*)

B. Repeat after your teacher. When you hear a new subject, use it with the corresponding verb form to create a new sentence:

1. Mis hermanos escuchan el programa.   (Mi hermana)
2. Carlos no escucha el programa.   (Él y yo)
3. Yo no miro los cuadros.   (Los alumnos)
4. ¿Miras tú el mapa?   (Vd.)
5. ¿Aprendes tú las palabras nuevas?   (Vds.)
6. Tomás y yo aprendemos el español.   (Jorge y sus amigos)
7. Los alumnos leen la lección de español.   (Luis)
8. Mi padre no lee el periódico ahora.   (Mis padres)
9. María recibe cartas de México.   (Sus amigas)
10. Nuestra madre no recibe un periódico extranjero.   (Yo)
11. Luis y yo tomamos el desayuno.   (El amigo de Luis)
12. Mi familia toma el almuerzo.   (Todos los alumnos)

C. Repeat after your teacher, then say again, making the possessive and noun plural:

    MODEL: Preparan *su lección*.   Preparan su lección.
                                   Preparan sus lecciones.

1. Tengo *mi cuaderno*.
2. Estudio *mi lección*.
3. Hablamos mucho en *nuestra clase*.
4. Hay mapas en *nuestro libro*.
5. María y *su hermana* van al café.
6. Jorge y *su padre* leen mucho.
7. ¿Vienen Tomás y *su amigo*?
8. ¿Estudia Luis con *su hermana*?
9. ¿Recibes cartas de *tu amigo*?
10. ¿Hablas con *tu profesora*?
11. ¿Hablan Vds. con *su profesor*?
12. ¿Tienes *tu cuaderno*?

D. Answer affirmatively:

MODELS: ¿Tiene Vd. su pluma?   Sí, tengo mi pluma.
        ¿Tengo yo mi libro?   Sí, Vd. tiene su libro.

1. ¿Habla Vd. con su madre?   5. ¿Leen Vds. sus cartas?
2. ¿Hablas con tus padres?   6. ¿Vienes con tus amigos?
3. ¿Aprende Vd. su lección?   7. ¿Miro yo mi reloj?
4. ¿Tienen Vds. sus lápices?   8. ¿Tengo yo mis libros?

E. Answer negatively:

MODEL: ¿Tienen Vds. libros nuevos?   No, no tenemos libros nuevos.

1. ¿Viven Vds. en casas viejas?   5. ¿Escuchan Vds. programas de television?
2. ¿Reciben Vds. cartas interesantes?   6. ¿Aprenden Vds. palabras fáciles?
3. ¿Leen Vds. libros extranjeros?   7. ¿Trabajan Vds. con alumnos españoles?
4. ¿Miran Vds. cuadros franceses?   8. ¿Tienen Vds. casas de campo?

F. Answer affirmatively, following the models:

MODELS: ¿Es rojo el lápiz?   Sí, es un lápiz rojo.
        ¿Son fáciles las lecciones? Sí, son lecciones fáciles.

1. ¿Es hermoso el parque?   5. ¿Son difíciles las lecciones?
2. ¿Es grande la universidad?   6. ¿Son cómodas las casas?
3. ¿Es interesante la carta?   7. ¿Son grandes las ciudades?
4. ¿Es mexicana la familia?   8. ¿Son nuevas las escuelas?

G. Read in Spanish, supplying the correct form of **ser**:

1. Mi padre ——— profesor. 2. Carlos ——— un amigo de Luis. 3. Carmen y María ——— españolas. 4. Los cuadros ——— hermosos. 5. El país no ——— muy grande. 6. La casa de Jorge no ——— amarilla. 7. ¿Qué hora ———? 8. ——— las diez y media. 9. ——— difícil aprender todas las palabras. 10. Los estudiantes ——— de México. 11. Los libros ——— para mi madre. 12. ¿De quién ——— la carta? 13. Nuestra casa ——— cómoda. 14. El reloj ——— de oro.

H. Give the Spanish for:

1. my letter, my letters. 2. our class, our classes. 3. his brother, his brothers. 4. his sister, his sisters. 5. her notebook, her notebooks. 6. their teacher, their teachers. 7. your father, your parents. 8. your (*fam. s.*) friend, your friends. 9. Mary and her brother. 10. Louis and his sister. 11. the students and their fathers. 12. the (girl) students and their mothers.

I. Give in Spanish:

1. Tom has a letter which he reads to his friends.   2. He receives letters from his sister, who lives in Mexico now.   3. She studies in a Mexican school and each day she learns several new words.   4. In her letters she writes about the interesting life of the country.   5. Louis, there goes our friend Philip.   6. His parents speak Spanish, don't they?   7. Yes, a little, and his mother listens to television programs in Spanish. 8. Also, they receive a Mexican newspaper, which they read every night.   9. Do they still live in their country house?   10. They live near the park in a small, comfortable house.   11. Well, we have a difficult lesson for tomorrow.   12. Yes, it is necessary to work two or three hours.

EJERCICIOS DE PRONUNCIACIÓN

A. Spanish **x** and **j**

1. Before a consonant, the letter **x** is pronounced like English *s* in *sent*.   Pronounce after your teacher:

extranjero   expresión   excursión   excelente

2. Between vowels, **x** is usually a double sound, consisting of a weak English *g* in *go* followed by a hissed *s*.   Pronounce after your teacher:

examen   éxito   existencia   exhibir

3. In a few words, **x,** even when between vowels, is pronounced like English *s* in *sent*. Pronounce after your teacher:

exacto   exactamente

4. The letter **x** in the words **México** and **mexicano,** spelled **Méjico** and **mejicano** in Spain, is pronounced like Spanish **j** (see Lesson 3, page 37).   Spanish **j** is silent in **reloj,** but pronounced in the plural **relojes.**   Repeat after your teacher:

Jorge es mexicano.   Es de México.
Él tiene dos relojes.   El reloj que tengo es viejo.
Aprendo una lengua extranjera.   Trabajo mucho.

B. Spanish intonation

Study the observations on Spanish intonation in Appendix C; then rewrite lines 5–8 of the dialogues of this lesson, dividing them into breath-groups and into syllables, underline the stressed syllables in each breath-group, and outline the intonation patterns.

Painter on the Ramblas, Barcelona, Spain.

Book Fair, Madrid, Spain.

VOCABULARIO

acerca de about, concerning
ahora now
la amiga friend (*f.*)
el amigo friend (*m.*)
aprender to learn
cada (*invariable*) each
el campo country, field
la carta letter
cerca de *prep.* near
la ciudad city
cómodo, -a comfortable
difícil *adj.* difficult, hard
escribir to write
escuchar to listen (to)
la escuela school
el (la) estudiante student
extranjero, -a foreign
fácil easy
la familia family
grande large, big
la hermana sister
el hermano brother
hermoso, -a beautiful, pretty
¡hola! hello!
interesante interesting
leer to read

la madre mother
mañana tomorrow
necesario, -a necessary
nuevo, -a new
el padre father; *pl.* parents
el país country (*nation*)
la palabra word
para for, in order to, to
el parque park
la parte part
pequeño, -a small, little (*size*)
el periódico newspaper
el programa (*note gender*) program
¿quién? (*pl.* **¿quiénes?**) who? whom?
recibir to receive
la residencia residence hall
la televisión television
todavía still, yet
Tomás Thomas, Tom
trabajar to work
la universidad university
varios, -as several, various
venir (**a** + *inf.*) to come (to)
la vida life
vivir to live

escuchar el programa de televisión to listen to the television program
residencia de estudiantes student residence hall
todavía no not yet

LECCIÓN 5

Present indicative of *estar, querer,* **and** *saber*

The present participle. Uses of *estar*

Special uses of the definite article. Feminine of nouns. Use of *¿ cuál?*

ROBERTO QUIERE TRABAJAR EN LA AMÉRICA DEL SUR

(Dorotea está sentada en el patio de su casa. Llega la señora López.[1])

SRA. LÓPEZ. Buenos días, Dorotea. ¿Cómo estás?

DOROTEA. Perfectamente bien, señora López. ¿No quiere Vd. pasar?

SRA. LÓPEZ. Bueno, por un momento solamente si no estás ocupada.

DOROTEA. Pues estoy un poco cansada y necesito descansar un rato.

● ● ● ● ●

SRA. LÓPEZ. ¿Está en casa tu mamá?

DOROTEA. No, señora, ella y mi papá están en casa de mis tíos. Mi tía está enferma.

SRA. LÓPEZ. ¡Qué lástima! Creo que tu tía tiene que descansar más.

DOROTEA. Nosotros también creemos que ella trabaja demasiado.

● ● ● ● ●

SRA. LÓPEZ. Dorotea, necesito hablar con el señor Díaz. ¿Sabes cuál es su casa?

DOROTEA. Es la casa amarilla que está allí cerca del parque.

SRA. LÓPEZ. Como sabes, él es de Chile. Mi hijo Roberto va a trabajar en la América del Sur, y quiero hablar con el señor Díaz.

---

[1] The subject often follows the verb in Spanish, particularly when the verb does not have an object.

DOROTEA. ¿A qué país quiere ir Roberto?

SRA. LÓPEZ. Quiere ir a Chile o a la Argentina.

DOROTEA. Mi primo Carlos está trabajando en Montevideo, la capital del Uruguay.

SRA. LÓPEZ. ¿De veras? Sé que Roberto va a pasar por Montevideo. Pero ya es tarde y estás ocupada ...

DOROTEA. No, señora. ¿No quiere Vd. tomar algo? ¿Una limonada?

SRA. LÓPEZ. Con mucho gusto. (*La señora López toma la limonada.*) Está muy fría. Muchas gracias.

DOROTEA. No hay de qué.

SRA. LÓPEZ. Bueno, hasta la vista, Dorotea.

DOROTEA. Hasta la vista, señora López.

CONVERSACIÓN

A. Preguntas sobre el diálogo

1. ¿Dónde está sentada Dorotea? 2. ¿Están en casa los padres de Dorotea? 3. ¿Con quién quiere hablar la señora López? 4. ¿Cuál es la casa del señor Díaz? 5. ¿De dónde es el señor Díaz? 6. ¿A qué países quiere ir Roberto? 7. ¿Dónde está trabajando el primo de Dorotea? 8. ¿Qué toma la señora López?

B. Aplicación del diálogo

1. ¿Estamos trabajando o descansando ahora? 2. ¿Está Vd. muy ocupado (ocupada) hoy? 3. ¿Está en casa su papá? 4. ¿Cuál es la capital del Uruguay? 5. ¿Quiere Vd. trabajar en la América del Sur? 6. ¿Lee Vd. libros sobre la América del Sur? 7. ¿Están Vds. cansados (cansadas) hoy? 8. ¿Necesitan Vds. descansar un rato?

NOTAS GRAMATICALES

A. Irregular present indicative of **estar, querer,** and **saber**

estar, *to be*

SINGULAR	PLURAL
estoy	estamos
estás	estáis
está	**están**

querer, *to wish, want*		**saber,** *to know, know how*	
SINGULAR	PLURAL	SINGULAR	PLURAL
quiero	queremos	**sé**	sabemos
quieres	queréis	sabes	sabéis
quiere	**quieren**	sabe	saben

Note the accented forms of **estar.** **Querer** may be followed by an infinitive which is not preceded by a preposition: **Roberto quiere ir a Chile,** *Robert wants to go to Chile.*

Followed by an infinitive, **saber** means *to know how to:* **Ella sabe hablar español,** *She knows how to speak Spanish.* **Necesitar** may also be followed by an infinitive: **Necesito descansar,** *I need to rest.*

B. The present participle

hablar:	hablando	*speaking*
comer:	comiendo	*eating*
vivir:	viviendo	*living*

The present participle, which in English ends in *-ing*, is regularly formed in Spanish by adding **-ando** to the stem of **-ar** verbs, and **-iendo** to the stem of **-er** and **-ir** verbs. The present participle always ends in **-o.** Forms of present participles which are irregular will be given later.

C. Uses of **estar**

Estar is used:

1. To express *location* or *position*, whether temporary or permanent:

> **Están en casa de mi tía.** They are at my aunt's.
> **Montevideo está en el Uruguay.** Montevideo is in Uruguay.

2. With an adjective to indicate a state or condition of the subject, which may be non-inherent, accidental, relatively temporary, or variable:

> **Mi tía está enferma.** My aunt is ill.
> **Todos están cansados.** All are tired.
> **No estoy muy ocupado.** I am not very busy.

3. With a present participle to express the progressive forms of the tenses:

> **¿Qué está Vd. escribiendo?** What are you writing?
> **Mi primo está trabajando allí.** My cousin is working there.

The progressive forms of the tenses in Spanish are less frequent and more emphatic than in English. They stress the fact that an action is or was in progress at a certain moment. The progressive forms of **ir** and **venir** are seldom used.

D. Special uses of the definite article

1. **Buenos días, señora López.**   Good morning, Mrs. López.
   La señora López aprende el inglés.   Mrs. López is learning English.
   Los señores Díaz no están en casa.   Mr. and Mrs. Díaz are not at home.

The definite article is used with titles, except when speaking directly to a person. Note that **los señores Díaz** means *Mr. and Mrs. Díaz.*

2. | la Argentina | el Uruguay | el Perú | El Salvador |
   | --- | --- | --- | --- |
   | el Brasil | el Paraguay | el Ecuador | los Estados Unidos |

The definite article regularly forms a part of a few place names, although today many Spanish-speaking people omit the article except with **El Salvador,** which means *The Savior,* and with **la Habana,** *Havana.*

 Remember what has been stated in regard to the use of the definite article with the name of a language (page 15), and in certain set expressions (footnote 1, page 28).

E. Feminine of nouns

el hijo	son	**la hija**	daughter
el hermano	brother	**la hermana**	sister
el primo	cousin (*m.*)	**la prima**	cousin (*f.*)
el tío	uncle	**la tía**	aunt
el amigo	friend (*m.*)	**la amiga**	friend (*f.*)
el alumno	pupil (*m.*)	**la alumna**	pupil (*f.*)

Certain masculine nouns which end in **-o,** particularly those of relationship, change **-o** to **-a** to form the feminine. Others will be used later. Even though **la hija** and **la prima** are not used in the dialogue of this lesson, remember their meanings, for the words will be used in the exercises.

F. Use of ¿**cuál?** *which (one)? what?*

¿Cuál es la capital del Uruguay?   What is the capital of Uruguay?
¿Cuáles son países grandes?   Which (ones) are large countries?
¿Sabes cuál es su casa?   Do you know which (one) is his house?

BUT: **¿A qué país quiere ir Roberto?**   To what (which) country does Robert want to go?

¿**Cuál?** (*pl.* ¿**Cuáles?**) is used as a pronoun, and it usually indicates a choice of one or more things from among several.

An accent mark must be written on interrogatives which introduce indirect questions, the same as in the case of direct questions (third example).

When English *which?* and *what?* modify nouns, the adjective ¿**qué?** is used in Spanish (fourth example). Also compare ¿**Qué libro tiene Vd.?** *Which (What) book do you have?* with ¿**Cuál de los libros tiene Vd.?** *Which (one) of the books do you have?*

EJERCICIOS

A. Substitution drill:

1. ¿Cómo está *Vd.?*
   (*su mamá, tu papá, sus hermanos, tú, Vds.*)
2. *El señor Pidal* está trabajando.
   (*Los alumnos, Él y yo, Yo, Tú, Roberto*)
3. *Yo* quiero ir a la Argentina.
   (*Mi papá, Luis y Jorge, Tú, Dorotea y yo, Ella*)
4. *Nosotros* sabemos hablar bien.
   (*Yo, Tú, Los alumnos y yo, Mi primo, Vds.*)

B. Review the uses of **ser** in Lesson 4, then complete each sentence with the correct form of the verb:

1. Montevideo ——— la capital del Uruguay. 2. La capital ——— una ciudad grande. 3. La ciudad ——— muy interesante. 4. La casa de Roberto ——— nueva. 5. Sus tíos ——— de la Argentina. 6. Roberto y Vd. ——— mexicanos. 7. ¿Qué ——— Vd., señor Díaz? 8. ¿De dónde ——— tú, Carlos? 9. María y yo ——— del Perú. 10. Quiero ——— profesor. 11. No ——— fácil aprender una lengua extranjera. 12. La carta ——— para mi hija. 13. ——— las tres de la tarde. 14. ¿Qué hora ———? 15. ¿——— verdes las paredes? 16. Mi reloj no ——— de plata. 17. ¿Cuál ——— la capital del Ecuador? 18. Yo ——— alumno.

C. Supply the correct form of **estar,** noting the uses of the verb:

1. Mi prima ——— en la Argentina. 2. Creo que mis tíos ——— en El Salvador. 3. Nuestra hija ——— sentada en el patio. 4. Luis y yo ——— muy cansados. 5. Señora López, ¿——— Vd. cansada también? 6. Yo ——— descansando aquí. 7. La limonada ——— fría. 8. ¿Dónde ——— sentados Roberto y María? 9. Mi primo ——— cerca de la mesa. 10. Queremos ——— en casa a la una. 11. ¿Cómo ——— tú hoy? 12. ¿——— tú estudiando? 13. Carlos y yo ——— trabajando aquí. 14. Tú ——— ocupada, ¿verdad? 15. Mi mamá ——— en casa de mis tíos. 16. ¿Dónde ——— Ana?

D. Say after your teacher, then change the verb to the progressive form:

MODEL: Estudio la lección.   Estudio la lección.
            Estoy estudiando la lección.

1. Los alumnos hablan español.
2. Ana prepara los ejercicios.
3. Escucho el programa.
4. Jorge y Tomás trabajan demasiado.
5. Luis y yo miramos el mapa.
6. ¿Toma María el desayuno?
7. ¿Descansan tus padres?
8. ¿Escribes una carta ahora?

E. Answer affirmatively:

1. ¿Es profesor el señor Valdés?
¿Es profesora la señora López?
¿Es española la señorita Gómez?

2. ¿Es verde el libro?
¿Es de España la carta?
¿Son para Carlos los periódicos?

Answer negatively:

3. ¿Está enferma tu mamá?
¿Está cansado tu papá?
¿Están sentados tus padres?
¿Están ocupadas tus primas?

4. ¿Está Felipe en la Argentina?
¿Está Dorotea en el Perú?
¿Están él y ella en México?
¿Están Vds. en casa?

F. Read in Spanish, filling the blanks with the definite or indefinite article, whenever one is needed:

1. Buenas tardes, ——— señora Gómez. 2. ——— señor López quiere trabajar hoy. 3. ——— señores Pidal no están aquí. 4. Roberto escribe ——— cartas interesantes. 5. Mi tía es ——— profesora. 6. Vamos a ——— Argentina. 7. Mis amigos están en ——— España. 8. María escribe cartas en ——— inglés. 9. ¿Estás en la clase de ——— español? 10. ——— español no es fácil. 11. ¿Vas a tomar ——— desayuno ahora? 12. Nuestros amigos españoles quieren hablar ——— inglés. 13. No saben leer ——— francés. 14. Queremos aprender bien ——— español. 15. Quiero ir a ——— América del Sur.

G. Give in Spanish:

1. Good afternoon, Mrs. López. Won't you come in? 2. Yes, thank you, Dorothy. Is your mother at home today? 3. No, she is at my aunt's; my aunt is ill. 4. What a pity! I know that she works too much. 5. I need to talk with Mr. Díaz. Which is his house? 6. It is the white house which is there near the park. 7. Do you know that my son Robert wants to go to South America? 8. Yes, and I know that his uncle

is working (*use progressive form*) in Montevideo, the capital of Uruguay. 9. Well, it is late now and you are very busy. 10. No, ma'am. I am a little tired and I need to rest a while. 11. Won't you take a lemonade? 12. Yes, gladly. (Mrs. López takes the lemonade, which is very cold.)

EJERCICIOS DE PRONUNCIACIÓN

A. Spanish **h**

The letter **h** is silent in modern Spanish. Pronounce:

hasta	hay	hermoso	¡hola!
hijo	hoy	hermana	hora
dos horas	mi hermano	su hija	¿quién habla?

B. Spanish **t**

In the pronunciation of Spanish **t** the tip of the tongue touches the back of the upper front teeth, and not the ridge above the teeth, as in English; furthermore, the sound is never followed by a puff of air, as occurs in English *task* (*t^hask*), for example. To avoid the puff of air, the breath must be held back during the articulation of the sound:

estar	parte	tengo	Argentina
patio	tío	Tomás	perfectamente

C. Spanish **d**

1. Review the sounds of **d**, page 4, then pronounce:

Dorotea	difícil	donde	tarde
demasiado	limonada	sentado	todavía

2. Pronounce each individual word after your teacher, noting the variations of Spanish **d**; then repeat, but as part of a breath-group introduced by the words indicated at the right:

a. doce   dos   diez   a las

b. descansar   Dorotea   para

c. día   desayuno   su

d. del profesor   de mi padre   difícil   es

Plaza de la reina, with its sparkling fountains and the Miguelete Tower of the Cathedral, Valencia, Spain.

Palacio del Pardo near Madrid, where General Franco, the Chief of State, resides, Spain.

VOCABULARIO

algo something, anything
América America
la Argentina Argentina
cansado, -a tired
la capital capital (*city*)
¿cómo? how?
creer to believe, think
¿cuál? (*pl.* **¿cuáles?**) which one (ones)? what?
demasiado *adv.* too, too much
descansar to rest
Dorotea Dorothy
enfermo, -a ill, sick
estar to be
frío, -a cold
gracias thanks, thank you
el gusto pleasure
la hija daughter
el hijo son; *pl.* children
la lástima pity
la limonada lemonade
llegar (**a**) to arrive (at), reach
la mamá mama, mother
más more

el momento moment
mucho, -a much; *pl.* many
necesitar to need
ocupado, -a busy, occupied
el papá papa, dad, father
pasar to pass (by), come in
el patio patio, courtyard
perfectamente fine, perfect(ly)
la prima cousin (*f.*)
el primo cousin (*m.*)
pues well, well then, then
¡qué + *noun*! what a...!
querer to wish, want
el rato while, short time
Roberto Robert
saber to know, know how
sentado, -a seated
el sur south
la tía aunt
el tío uncle; *pl.* uncle(s) and aunt(s)
el Uruguay Uruguay
la vista sight, view
ya already, now

con mucho gusto gladly, with great pleasure
de veras really, truly
en casa de (**mi tía**) at (my aunt's)
hasta la vista until I see you
la América del Sur South America
no hay de qué you are welcome, don't mention it
¿no quiere Vd. (pasar)? won't you (come in)?
perfectamente bien fine, very well
por un momento for a moment
¡qué lástima! what a pity!

REPASO[1] I

A. Answer affirmatively:

1. ¿Sabes la lección?
2. ¿Tienes el mapa?
3. ¿Vas a la biblioteca?
4. ¿Quieres ir al café?
5. ¿Eres alumno (alumna)?
6. ¿Lees una carta interesante?

7. ¿Son Vds. alumnos?
8. ¿Tienen Vds. papel?
9. ¿Van Vds. a tomar algo?
10. ¿Vienen Vds. a trabajar?
11. ¿Quieren Vds. aprender el español?
12. ¿Viven Vds. en la ciudad?

B. Answer negatively:

1. ¿Viene Vd. temprano a la clase?
2. ¿Llega Vd. a las ocho?
3. ¿Recibe Vd. periódicos de México?
4. ¿Escribe Vd. muchas cartas?
5. ¿Quiere Vd. leer libros en inglés?
6. ¿Necesita Vd. descansar un rato?

7. ¿Están Vds. cansados?
8. ¿Aprenden Vds. lenguas extranjeras?
9. ¿Mira Ana cuadros hermosos?
10. ¿Escucha Carlos la televisión?
11. ¿Tomamos Vd. y yo el desayuno?
12. ¿Leemos ella y yo los exámenes?

C. Repeat the model sentence; then substitute the cue words, making any necessary changes:

1. Voy con *mi amigo Roberto*. (amiga Ana, amigos Luis y María, hermano Tomás)
2. Dorotea come con *su papá*. (mamá, hermanos, amigas)
3. Cenamos con *nuestro primo*. (prima, padres, profesor)
4. El señor Díaz viene con *su hija*. (hijo, hijos, amigos)
5. ¿Siempre tienes *tu lápiz*? (lápices, cuaderno, plumas)

D. Repeat each sentence; then, when you hear another verb, make a new sentence using the corresponding form of that verb:

1. Tú escribes todas las palabras. (leer)
2. Los señores Díaz tienen una casa de campo. (querer)
3. La señora López trabaja en el patio. (descansar)
4. El señor Gómez cena muy tarde. (comer)
5. ¿Siempre llegan los estudiantes a la una? (venir)
6. ¿Estudias los ejercicios por la tarde? (preparar)
7. ¿Leen Vds. los libros de español? (tener)
8. Pronuncian bien el alemán. (escribir)
9. Luis y yo queremos descansar un rato. (necesitar)
10. Nuestro papá no vive en el campo. (trabajar)

---

[1] **Repaso**, *Review*.

E. You will hear two sets of one or more words separated by a pause. Make a sentence using the correct form of **estar** or **ser** to join the two sets of words:

1. María ... sentada en la silla.
2. Luis y yo ... muy cansados.
3. Nosotros ... de los Estados Unidos.
4. La capital del país ... grande.
5. El señor López ... de México.
6. La limonada ... muy fría.
7. Los señores Valdés ... en casa.
8. Creo que ... las dos de la tarde.
9. Las casas ... hermosas.
10. La escuela no ... cerca de aquí.
11. Mi tía no ... muy enferma.
12. María y yo no ... mexicanos.
13. Tomás ... trabajando demasiado.
14. Él y yo ... mirando el mapa.
15. Ella no quiere ... profesora.
16. Vds. necesitan ... aquí temprano.

F. Listen to the question. After you hear an adjective or phrase, make an affirmative sentence repeating the subject:

MODEL: ¿Cómo está María? (muy bien)   María está muy bien.

1. ¿Cómo está tu mamá? (enferma)
2. ¿Cómo están tus padres? (cansados)
3. ¿Dónde está la señora Gómez? (en casa)
4. ¿De dónde es el señor López? (de la Argentina)
5. ¿Qué es la señorita Valdés? (profesora de español)
6. ¿De quién es el reloj? (de mi hermano)
7. ¿Cómo está la limonada? (fría)
8. ¿De qué color es la casa? (blanca)

G. Give in Spanish:

1. Good morning, Luis. How are you? 2. Very well, thanks, Mr. López. 3. Miss Díaz is coming now. 4. There are twenty-one students (*m.*) in the class. 5. My sister is at Mary's. 6. Won't you come in? 7. We listen to the television program. 8. I arrive each morning at eight o'clock. 9. We have to study in the evening. 10. It is 3:15 P.M. 11. How many classes do you have in the afternoon? 12. What color is your new house? 13. We are going to the library to study. 14. We need to talk Spanish every day. 15. Many thanks. See you later. 16. You are welcome.

LECCIÓN 6

Present indicative of some irregular verbs. The personal *a*
Direct object pronouns. Position of object pronouns
Verbs which require a direct object without a preposition
The infinitive after a preposition
Meaning of *saber* and *conocer*. Demonstrative adjectives

ENRIQUE BUSCA A TOMÁS ORTEGA

Son las cuatro de la tarde. Enrique sale de la residencia de estudiantes, donde vive, y va a la casa de su amigo José. Llega y llama a la puerta. José la abre y, al ver a Enrique, le invita a entrar. Los dos jóvenes entran en la sala.

José. ¿Qué hay de nuevo, Enrique?

Enrique. Nada de particular. Busco a Tomás Ortega. ¿No pasa a menudo por aquí?

José. Sí, pasa por aquí casi todas las noches si no me ve durante el día. ¿Por qué le buscas?

Enrique. Traigo una carta muy larga de Carlos Padilla y sé que Tomás le conoce bien.

• • • • •

Enrique. Tomás vive en aquella casa nueva que podemos ver por esta ventana, ¿verdad?

José. Sí, Enrique. Pero sé que viene por aquí esta tarde. ¿Por qué no le esperas un rato?

Enrique. Con mucho gusto, si no estás ocupado.

José. La verdad es que tengo que terminar las frases de la lección para mañana. Pero puedes leer el periódico. Aquí lo tienes.

Enrique. Gracias. Lo leo por la mañana, antes de salir de casa.

José. ¿Quieres mirar esa revista que está sobre la mesita cerca de tu silla? ¿La conoces?

Enrique. Sí, la conozco. María Gómez trae revistas españolas a nuestra clase y todos los estudiantes las leen. Conoces a María, ¿verdad?

José. ¡Cómo no! La veo a menudo. Visita a mi hermana casi todos los días.

ENRIQUE. Pero, ¿cuándo vas a terminar las frases si te molesto más? Puedo pasar por aquí esta noche.

JOSÉ. ¡No, hombre! Tengo mi cuaderno aquí y voy a escribir las frases ahora. Después de terminar las frases podemos charlar más.

CONVERSACIÓN

A. Preguntas sobre el diálogo

1. ¿Quién llega a la casa de José? 2. ¿A quién busca Enrique? 3. ¿Qué trae Enrique? 4. ¿Dónde vive Tomás? 5. ¿Qué tiene que terminar José? 6. ¿Cuándo lee Enrique el periódico? 7. ¿Qué leen todos los estudiantes? 8. ¿A quién visita María?

B. Aplicación del diálogo

1. ¿A qué hora sale Vd. de casa por la mañana? 2. ¿A quiénes visita Vd. a menudo? 3. ¿Qué hay sobre esta mesa? 4. ¿Conoce Vd. bien a todas las estudiantes de la clase de español? 5. ¿Qué traen los estudiantes a la clase de español? 6. ¿Cuántas clases tienen Vds. por la tarde? 7. ¿Qué revistas leen Vds.? 8. ¿Saben Vds. dónde vive el profesor de francés?

NOTAS GRAMATICALES

A. Present indicative of some irregular verbs

conocer, *to know, be acquainted with*	poder, *to be able, can*	salir, *to leave, go out*	traer, *to bring*	ver, *to see*
SINGULAR				
conozco	**puedo**	**salgo**	**traigo**	**veo**
conoces	**puedes**	sales	traes	ves
conoce	**puede**	sale	trae	ve
PLURAL				
conocemos	podemos	salimos	traemos	vemos
conocéis	podéis	salís	traéis	veis
conocen	**pueden**	salen	traen	ven

Poder, like **querer,** may be followed by an infinitive which is not preceded by a preposition: **Podemos ver la casa,** *We can see the house.*

B. The personal **a**

> **Enrique ve a su amigo.**   Henry sees his friend.
> **¿Buscas a José?**   Are you looking for Joe?
> **¿A quién ve Vd.?**   Whom do you see?
>
> BUT: **Tengo un amigo mexicano.**   I have a Mexican friend.

An unusual feature of Spanish is the use of **a** before the direct object of a verb when the noun refers to a definite person.   This word **a** is used with **¿quién?** to mean *whom*?, but it is not used after forms of **tener,** nor with direct object pronouns, which are given in section C.

Práctica.   Repeat after your teacher, noting the use of the personal **a**:

1. Conozco a Felipe.   2. ¿Conoce Vd. a mi hermana?   3. No veo a la señorita Ortega.
4. José busca al señor Padilla.   5. ¿A quién llama Vd.?   6. ¿Buscan a su madre?
7. ¿Espera Carmen a María?   8. No puedo escuchar a Tomás ahora.

C. Direct object pronouns

	SINGULAR		PLURAL
me	me	**nos**	us
te	you (*fam.*)	**os**	you (*fam.*)
le	him; you (*formal m.*)	**los**	them (*m.*), you (*m.*)
la	her; it (*f.*); you (*formal f.*)	**las**	them (*f.*), you (*f.*)
lo	it (*m. and neuter*)	**los**	them (*m.*)

Note carefully the third person direct object pronouns and do not confuse them with the definite articles.   In addition to referring to masculine objects, **lo** may refer to an action, a statement, or an idea: **Lo creo,** *I believe it.*

Many Spanish-speaking people, particularly in Spanish America, prefer to use **lo** instead of **le** for *him, you* (formal), but only the **le** form is used in this text.

D. Position of object pronouns

José abre |la puerta|.	Joseph opens the door.
José |la| **abre.**	Joseph opens it.
Ella ve |las revistas|.	She sees the magazines.
Ella |las| **ve.**	She sees them.
Yo no busco |a Tomás|.	I am not looking for Tom.
Yo no |le| **busco.**	I am not looking for him.

Object pronouns are placed <u>immediately before the verb.</u> (Exceptions will be given later.) If the sentence is negative, object pronouns come between **no** and the verb.

Práctica. Read in Spanish, noting particularly the object pronouns and their position with respect to the verb:

1. Yo tengo el cuaderno; yo lo tengo. 2. Ella tiene los lápices; ella los tiene. 3. Escribo la frase; la escribo. 4. José abre las ventanas; José las abre. 5. No veo a José; no le veo. 6. Ellos buscan a los alumnos; ellos los buscan. 7. No miro a mi hermana; no la miro. 8. ¿No espera Vd. a María? ¿No la espera Vd.?

E. Verbs which require a direct object without a preposition

> **Ella busca el periódico.** She is looking for the newspaper.
> **Ella lo mira.** She is looking at it.
> **Escuchan el programa.** They listen to the program.
> **Esperamos a Roberto.** We are waiting for Robert.
> **Le esperamos.** We are waiting for him.

Note that the prepositions *for, at, to* are included in the English meaning of the verbs **buscar, escuchar, esperar, mirar.** The personal **a** is used when the direct object is a person (fourth example).

However, just as **entrar** requires **en** before an object, **salir** requires **de.** If no object is expressed, **en** and **de** are omitted:

> **Salen de (Entran en) la casa.** They leave (enter) the house.
> **Los dos jóvenes salen (entran).** The two young men leave (enter).

F. The infinitive after a preposition

> **al ver** on (upon) seeing, when (he) sees
> **después de terminar las frases** after finishing the sentences

In Spanish the infinitive, not the present participle, is regularly used after a preposition. **Al** plus an infinitive is the equivalent to English *on* (*upon*) plus the present participle. This construction may also be translated as a clause beginning with *when*.

G. Meaning of **saber** and **conocer**

> **Sé que él viene esta tarde.** I know that he is coming this afternoon.
> **Le conozco bien.** I know him well. (I am well acquainted with him.)
> **¿Conoces esa revista?** Do you know that magazine?

Saber means *to know* facts or *to have knowledge* of something. Remember that with an infinitive **saber** means *to know how to*: **Sé leer el español,** *I know how to (can) read Spanish.* **Conocer** means *to know* in the sense of *to be acquainted with* someone or something.

H. Demonstrative adjectives

SINGULAR			PLURAL		
Masc.	Fem.		Masc.	Fem.	
este	**esta**	this	**estos**	**estas**	these
ese	**esa**	that *(nearby)*	**esos**	**esas**	those *(nearby)*
aquel	**aquella**	that *(distant)*	**aquellos**	**aquellas**	those *(distant)*

A demonstrative adjective points out the noun to which it refers. (Do not confuse the demonstrative with the relative **que**.) It comes before its noun and, like all other adjectives in Spanish, it agrees with the noun in gender and number. It is repeated before each noun in a series. **Ese, esa, -os, -as** indicate persons or objects near to, or associated with, the person addressed; **aquel, aquella, -os, -as** indicate persons or objects distant from the speaker and the person addressed.

EJERCICIOS

A. Substitution drill:

1. *Mis amigos* conocen a José.
   (*Vd. y yo, Yo, Tú, Tomás y Carlos, Ana*)
2. *Yo* puedo llamar a María.
   (*Nosotros, Ella y yo, Vd. y él, Tú, Ella*)
3. *Enrique* sale de casa a las ocho.
   (*Yo, Nosotros, Vd., Tú, Ellos*)
4. *Roberto* ve al señor Díaz.
   (*Tú, Tú y yo, Ella, Nuestros amigos, Yo*)

B. Say after your teacher. When you hear the question again, answer it affirmatively. Watch the possessives in sentences 7-12.

1. ¿Conoce Vd. a Felipe?
2. ¿Ve Vd. a la señorita Gómez?
3. ¿Sales de casa temprano?
4. ¿Puedes buscar a Tomás ahora?
5. ¿Tienen Vds. muchos amigos aquí?
6. ¿Escucha Ana a María?
7. ¿Busca Vd. sus lápices?
8. ¿Buscan Vds. a sus amigos?
9. ¿Quieren Vds. ir a ver a sus tíos?
10. ¿Puede José leer sus frases?
11. ¿Espera Carmen a mi hermana?
12. ¿Esperan Vds. a su profesor?

C. Say after your teacher, then repeat making the demonstrative adjective and the noun plural:

    MODEL: Veo a ese hombre.   Veo a ese hombre.   Veo a esos hombres.

1. Entran en este cuarto.
2. Quiero mirar esta revista.
3. Leen ese periódico.
4. Abren esa ventana.
5. No conozco a aquel hombre.
6. No vamos a aquella ciudad.
7. ¿Puedo traer este cuadro?
8. ¿Salen ellos de aquella casa?

D. Say after your teacher. When you hear a new noun, use it to form a new sentence, making the necessary change(s) in agreement:

1. ¿Quiere Vd. este lápiz?
    carta?
    periódicos?
    revistas?
    mapa?

2. Luis no abre ese cuaderno.
    puerta.
    ventanas.
    libros.
    cartas.

3. No puedo ir a aquel parque.
    ciudad.
    países.
    escuelas.
    capital.

4. Esta casa es hermosa.
    casas
    patios
    ventanas
    mesita

E. Read in Spanish, supplying the personal **a** whenever necessary:

1. Yo veo ———— las mesitas. 2. Vds. no ven ———— mi papá. 3. Buscamos ———— un periódico. 4. Ella y él buscan ———— su hermano. 5. ¿Miras ———— tu revista? 6. ¿Mira José ———— su profesora? 7. ¿Tiene Carlos ———— muchas amigas allí? 8. ¿———— quién busca Vd.? 9. ¿No esperan ellos ———— sus amigos? 10. ¿Conoces bien ———— la ciudad? 11. No conozco ———— la señorita Díaz. 12. ¿Escuchan ———— la profesora?

F. Read each sentence in Spanish, then repeat, substituting the correct direct object pronoun for each noun object and modifiers:

    MODEL: Yo abro la puerta.

                  Yo abro la puerta.   Yo la abro.

1. Vd. abre la ventana. 2. Felipe abre las ventanas. 3. Nosotros vemos el cuadro. 4. Vemos los cuadros. 5. Ella no mira la revista. 6. No mira las revistas. 7. Enrique

conoce al hombre.   8. También conoce a los dos jóvenes.   9. Yo no sé la lección.
10. No conozco a María.   11. Carlos llama a Tomás.   12. Ellas buscan a Dorotea.
13. Ella no ve a sus hijas.   14. Los estudiantes escuchan un programa.   15. Esperamos
a nuestro profesor.   16. ¿Espera Vd. a sus padres?   17. Los hombres miran nuestras
casas.   18. ¿No miran esta silla?   19. Veo a Felipe y a su amigo.   20. Visitan a
María y a su hermana.

G. Give in Spanish:

1. I open the door; I open it.   2. I bring the newspaper; I bring it.   3. I do not see the
picture; I do not see it.   4. They do not listen to the program; they do not listen to it.
5. We are looking for the magazines; we are looking for them.   6. The men are looking
for Charles; they are looking for him.   7. Do you see Mary?   Do you see her?   8. Whom
do you see?   Do you see him?   9. George receives long letters in Spanish; he reads them
to the class.   10. Here is the notebook; here it is.   11. Who believes it?   Who believes
him?   12. Don't you know Mary Gómez?   Don't you know her?   13. Do you (*fam. s.*)
call your friends?   Do you call them?   14. Upon seeing Joe, Henry invites him to enter.
15. After opening his book, Charles reads it.   16. Before entering the house, they look
at it.

EJERCICIOS DE PRONUNCIACIÓN

A. The sounds of **r** and **rr**

1. Single **r,** except when initial in a word and when after **l, n,** or **s,** is pronounced with
a single tap of the tip of the tongue against the gums of the upper teeth; the sound is
much like *dd* in *eddy* pronounced rapidly:

pared	eres	amarillo	hora
Carlos	largo	tres	charlar

2. When initial in a word, and when after **l, n,** or **s,** and doubled, the sound is strongly
trilled, the tip of the tongue striking the gums in a series of very rapid vibrations:

un rato	recibir	el reloj	la revista
Roberto	rojo	pizarra	Enrique

B. Linking

Review linking, page 6, giving special attention to the linking of vowels between words,
and pronounce as one breath-group:

1. Ella va a hablar.   Busca a Tomás.   Le esperamos hoy.

Tengo que estudiar.   Es casi inglés.   ¿Dónde vive el hijo?

2. la América española.   Busco a Tomás.   Vamos a estudiar.

No hablo español.   Escucho el programa.   ¿Qué hay de particular?

C. Dictado

The teacher may select the first four exchanges of the dialogues of this lesson as an exercise in dictation.

VOCABULARIO

abrir   to open
antes de   *prep.* before (*time*)
buscar   to look for, seek
conocer   to know, be acquainted with
cuando   when
¿cuándo?   when?
charlar   to chat
después de   *prep.* after
durante   during
Enrique   Henry
entrar (**en** + *obj.*)   to enter, go in
esperar   to wait, wait for; hope
la frase   sentence
el hombre   man
invitar (**a** + *inf.*)   to invite (to)
José   Joseph, Joe
joven (*pl.* **jóvenes**)   young

largo, -a   long
llamar   to call; knock
la mesita   small (little) table
molestar   to bother, molest
nada   nothing
particular   particular, special
poder   to be able, can
¿por qué?   why?   for what reason?
la puerta   door
la revista   magazine, journal
la sala   living room
salir (**de** + *obj.*)   to leave, go (come) out
si   if, whether
terminar   to end, finish
traer   to bring
la ventana   window
ver   to see
visitar   to visit, call on

a menudo   often, frequently
al + *inf.*   on, upon + *pres. part.*
aquí (**lo**) **tienes**   here (it) is
¡cómo no!   of course!   certainly!
esta noche   tonight
¡hombre!   man (man, alive)!
los dos jóvenes   the two (both) young men (*adj. used as noun*; *see Lesson 7*)
nada de particular   nothing special
pasar por aquí   to pass (come) this way *or* by (along) here
¿qué hay de nuevo?   what's new?   what do you know?
salir de casa   to leave home

LECTURA I

ESPAÑA

Estudio de palabras (*Word study*)

The ability to recognize cognates is of enormous value in learning to read a foreign language. In this section and in the "Estudio de palabras" section of subsequent Lecturas a number of principles for recognizing cognates will be introduced. Make every effort to figure out the meaning of new words by their use in the sentence, but if you are unable to do so, you will find them listed in the end vocabulary. A number of words not easily recognized are translated in footnotes. Many of the new words in the reading selections will appear later in the active vocabularies. All examples listed below appear in the reading selection of Lectura I.

a. Exact cognates. Many Spanish and English words are identical in form and meaning, although the pronunciation is different. Pronounce these words in Spanish: capital, central, cultural, general, industrial, natural, Portugal, romance.

b. Approximate cognates. Three principles for recognizing near cognates are:
1. Many Spanish words have a written accent: latín, península, región.
2. Many Spanish words lack a double consonant: comercial.
3. Many Spanish words have a final **-a, -e,** or **-o** (and sometimes a written accent) which is lacking in English: mapa, música, persona; arte, importante, parte; aspecto, italiano, moderno.

Pronounce the words listed in *b* and give the English cognates.

c. Less approximate cognates. Many words should be recognized easily, especially in context or when pronounced in Spanish. Pronounce the following words and then observe the English meaning: arquitectura, *architecture*; centro, *center*; costa, *coast*; cultura, *culture*; Europa, *Europe*; formar, *to form*; frontera, *frontier*; habitante, *inhabitant*; millón, *million*; montaña, *mountain*; norte, *north*; nortecentral, *north-central*; noroeste, *northwest*; oeste, *west*; suroeste, *southwest*; político, *political*; portugués, *Portuguese*; puerto, *port*.

Medieval walls still surround the city of Ávila, Spain.

Hay un mapa en la pared. Es un mapa de España y Portugal. Los dos países forman la Península Ibérica,[1] que está en el suroeste de Europa. Los habitantes de España hablan español, y los habitantes de Portugal hablan portugués. El español y el portugués son lenguas romances. El italiano y el francés son lenguas romances también. Hablan italiano en Italia y francés en Francia. Todas las lenguas romances vienen del latín.

La capital de España es Madrid. Está en el centro del país, en la región de Castilla la Nueva.[2] Castilla la Vieja está en la parte nortecentral, hacia[3] la frontera francesa. Castilla es la tierra[4] de los castillos.[5] Su lengua es el castellano.[6]

Las ciudades de Barcelona y Valencia están en la costa del Mar Mediterráneo. Como Madrid, son importantes[7] centros industriales y comerciales. En el sur hay otras ciudades importantes, como Sevilla, Cádiz, Córdoba, Granada y Málaga. Cádiz y Málaga son puertos del sur; las otras ciudades no están en la costa. Toledo y Segovia, que son ciudades muy antiguas, están en la meseta[8] central, cerca de Madrid. Al oeste, hacia la frontera portuguesa, están

[1] **Ibérica,** *Iberian.*   [2] **Castilla la Nueva,** *New Castile.*   [3] **hacia,** *toward.*   [4] **tierra,** *land.*   [5] **castillos,** *castles.*
[6] **castellano,** *Castilian.*   [7] See pages 265–266 for notes on word order.   [8] **meseta,** *tableland, plateau.*

View of Salamanca from the *Río Tormes*, Spain.

Badajoz y Salamanca. Burgos, Bilbao, San Sebastián y Santander están en el norte del país. Hoy día casi todas las ciudades españolas tienen barrios[1] nuevos con casas y edificios muy modernos y barrios antiguos con casas viejas y calles estrechas.[2]

Las trece regiones naturales de España son Galicia, Asturias, León, Castilla la Vieja, las Provincias Vascongadas,[3] Navarra, Aragón, Cataluña, Valencia, Murcia, Castilla la Nueva, Andalucía y Extremadura.

España tiene cinco ríos importantes y muchas montañas. Al norte está separada de Francia por los altos Pirineos. Toda la parte central es una meseta grande. En el sur están la Sierra Morena y la Sierra Nevada. También hay muchas montañas en la meseta central y en la parte noroeste.

Aunque España es un país pequeño, su lengua es muy importante hoy día. Millones de personas en España, en los diez y ocho países de la América española y en varias partes de los Estados Unidos hablan español. Las relaciones comerciales, políticas y culturales entre los Estados Unidos y los países de habla española[4] son muy importantes. La influencia de España y de los países hispanoamericanos en la vida diaria,[5] la música, el arte, la arquitectura y en otros aspectos de la cultura en general es grande. Estudiamos el español para conocer y apreciar[6] bien la cultura española y su influencia en la vida moderna.

[1] **barrios,** *districts.*   [2] **calles estrechas,** *narrow streets.*   [3] **Vascongadas,** *Basque.*   [4] **de habla española,** *Spanish-speaking.*   [5] **diaria,** *daily.*   [6] **apreciar,** *appreciate.*

Las Cortes, the Spanish Parliament,
in Madrid, Spain.

PREGUNTAS

1. ¿Qué hay en la pared? 2. ¿Qué forman España y Portugal? 3. ¿Dónde está la Península Ibérica? 4. ¿Qué lengua hablan en España? 5. ¿Qué lengua hablan en Portugal? 6. ¿Qué hablan en Italia? 7. ¿Qué hablan en Francia? 8. ¿De qué lengua vienen las lenguas romances?

9. ¿Cuál es la capital de España? 10. ¿Dónde está Madrid? 11. ¿Dónde está Castilla la Vieja? 12. ¿Qué es Castilla?

13. ¿Dónde están Barcelona y Valencia? 14. ¿Cuáles son unas ciudades del sur de España? 15. ¿Qué puertos hay en el sur? 16. ¿Qué otras ciudades hay en España? 17. ¿Qué ciudades están en el norte?

18. ¿Cuáles son las trece regiones naturales de España? 19. ¿Cuántos ríos importantes hay? 20. ¿Qué montañas están en el norte? 21. ¿Qué es toda la parte central? 22. ¿Qué montañas están en el sur?

23. ¿Es España un país grande? 24. ¿En qué países hablan español? 25. ¿Para qué estudiamos el español?

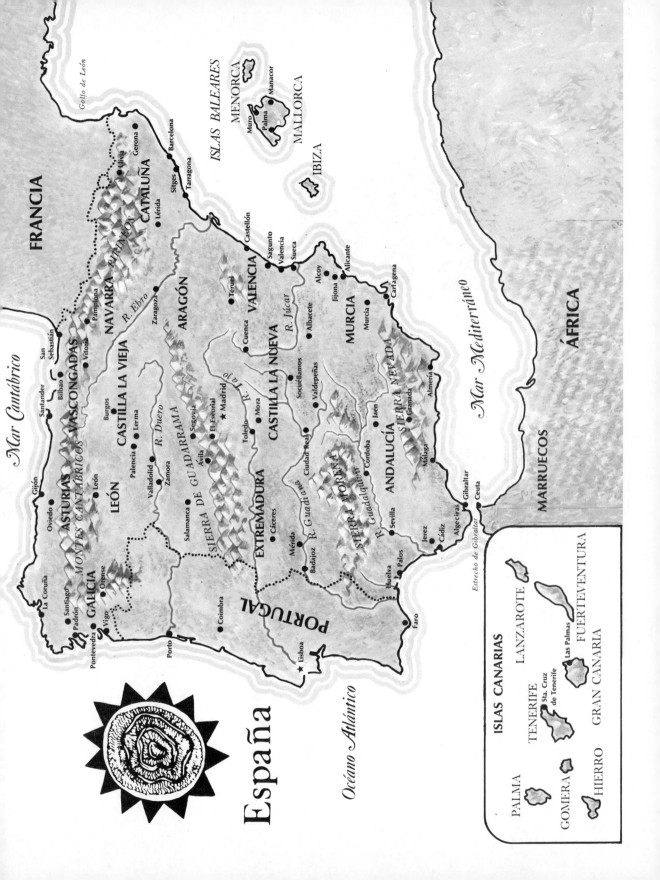

LECCIÓN 7

Present indicative of *dar* **and** *decir*.   **Indirect object pronouns**
Reflexive substitute for the passive.   Use of *gustar*
Adjectives used as nouns.   Comparison of adjectives

LUISA COMPRA UN VESTIDO

(*Luisa está esperando el autobús.   Su amiga Carmen pasa por la calle.*)

CARMEN.   ¡Hola, Luisa!   ¿Adónde vas tan temprano?

LUISA.   Voy al centro.   Como sabes, se abren las tiendas a las nueve.

CARMEN.   ¿Vas a pasar la mañana allí?

LUISA.   Sí, quiero ir a varias tiendas.   Pero, ¿por qué no vienes, Carmen?   Sé que te
gusta ir de compras.

CARMEN.   ¡Ay, hoy no puedo!   No tengo tiempo.

• • • • •

LUISA.   Carmen, si no puedes ir al centro, ¿adónde vas ahora?

CARMEN.   Mi tía llega de California mañana, y tengo que comprar muchas cosas en el
mercado.

LUISA.   ¿Va a estar tu tía mucho tiempo aquí?

CARMEN.   Creo que va a pasar uno o dos meses aquí.

LUISA.   Pues allí viene el autobús.   Hasta luego, Carmen.

CARMEN.   Adiós.   Hasta la vista.

Media hora más tarde llega Luisa al centro. Entra en una tienda y le dice a la empleada que busca un vestido.

EMPLEADA. Tenemos muchos vestidos bonitos, señorita. (*Le enseña a Luisa vestidos de varios estilos.*) Esta semana todos tienen precios especiales.

LUISA. Me gusta este vestido rojo. Es más bonito que el blanco, ¿verdad? Creo que es el más bonito de todos. ¿Qué precio tiene?

EMPLEADA. Hoy lo damos a quince dólares y veinte y nueve centavos.

LUISA. ¡Ay, es demasiado caro! ¿Puedo ver otros, por favor? ¿Qué precio tiene aquel vestido de algodón que se ve en el escaparate?

EMPLEADA. Diez dólares. (*Miran el vestido.*) Se usa mucho este estilo. ¿No le gusta a Vd., señorita?

LUISA. ¿De qué talla es?

EMPLEADA. Talla doce.

LUISA. Muy bien ... Sí, me gusta mucho. Lo tomo.[1] Aquí tiene Vd. el dinero. (*Le da el dinero a la empleada.*)

EMPLEADA. Muchas gracias, señorita. ¿No necesita otra cosa? ¿Un par de guantes, una bolsa ... ?

LUISA. No, gracias, nada más. Adiós.

CONVERSACIÓN

A. Preguntas sobre el diálogo

1. ¿Por qué está esperando Luisa el autobús? 2. ¿A qué hora se abren las tiendas? 3. ¿Le gusta a Carmen ir de compras? 4. ¿Por qué tiene que ir Carmen al mercado? 5. ¿Qué quiere comprar Luisa? 6. ¿Qué le enseña la empleada a Luisa? 7. ¿Qué precio tiene el vestido de algodón? 8. ¿Le gusta a Luisa el vestido de algodón?

B. Aplicación del diálogo

1. ¿Toma Vd. el autobús a menudo? 2. ¿Le gusta a Vd. ir de compras? 3. ¿A qué hora se abren las tiendas en esta ciudad? 4. ¿Le gustan a Vd. los vestidos rojos? 5. ¿Tiene Vd. que ir al centro hoy? 6. ¿Dónde es más cara la vida, en México o en los Estados Unidos? 7. ¿Cuál de sus libros es el más interesante de todos? 8. ¿Quién le da a Vd. dinero para comprar las cosas que necesita?

---

[1] For vividness the present tense is often used in Spanish for the English future: **Lo tomo,** *I'll* (*I shall*) *take it.*

NOTAS GRAMATICALES

A. Irregular present indicative of **dar** and **decir**

dar, *to give*		**decir,** *to say, tell*	
SINGULAR	PLURAL	SINGULAR	PLURAL
doy	damos	**digo**	decimos
das	dais	**dices**	decís
da	dan	**dice**	**dicen**

B. Indirect object pronouns

SINGULAR		PLURAL	
me	(to) me	**nos**	(to) us
te	(to) you (*fam.*)	**os**	(to) you (*fam.*)
le	(to) him, her, it; you (*formal*)	**les**	(to) them, you

Luisa le escribe una carta.   Louise is writing him a letter.
Mi mamá no me da dinero.   My mother doesn't give me money (gives no money to me).
Ella nos (les) enseña el vestido.   She shows us (them) the dress.

An indirect object tells *to* or *for* whom an action is done. In Spanish the indirect object pronoun includes the meaning *to* (sometimes *for:* e.g., **Carmen me abre la puerta,** *Carmen opens the door for me*).   In English the word *to* is omitted if the indirect object precedes a direct object: *He gives me the money,* but *He gives the money to me.*

Be sure to observe that **le** is used for all third person singular indirect object pronouns and **les** for the plural, while **me, te, nos, os** are identical to the direct object pronouns. These forms are placed immediately before the verb.   (Some exceptions will be given later.)   The context of the sentence usually makes the meaning of **le** and **les** clear; however, when these pronouns mean *(to) you* (*formal*), singular and plural, **a usted(es)** is regularly expressed in Spanish also:

¿Le enseñan a Vd. muchos vestidos?   Do they show you many dresses?
Les doy a Vds. los periódicos.   I'm giving you the newspapers.

In Spanish the indirect object pronoun is regularly used in addition to the indirect object noun:

Luisa le da el dinero a la empleada.   Louise gives the money to the clerk.
Yo le digo a Carlos la verdad.   I'm telling Charles the truth.

Práctica.   Repeat in Spanish and indicate whether each pronoun is a direct or an indirect object.

1. Ella no me ve todavía.   2. Yo les enseño mis compras.   3. Yo no le digo el precio.
4. Su madre no le compra un vestido.   5. Nuestros amigos nos escriben muchas cartas.
6. Mi hermano y yo las abrimos y las leemos.   7. Mis padres me esperan en casa.
8. Carmen la invita a ir de compras.   9. La empleada me enseña una bolsa y la compro.
10. Yo le doy dinero a Felipe cuando lo necesita.

C. Reflexive substitute for the passive

Se abren las tiendas a las nueve.   The stores are opened at nine o'clock.
Se ven varios vestidos en el escaparate.   Several dresses are seen in the show window.
Se usa mucho este estilo.   This style is worn a great deal.

In the active voice the subject acts upon an object: *The man opens the doors*, **El hombre abre las puertas.**   In the passive voice the subject is acted upon by the verb: *The doors are opened*, **Se abren las puertas.**

In Spanish the passive is often expressed by using the reflexive object **se** before the third person of the verb, which is singular or plural, depending on the number of the subject.   The subject often follows the verb in this construction.   (See Lesson 8 for the explanation of reflexive verbs.)

D. Use of **gustar,** *to be pleasing, like*

	LITERAL MEANING	USUAL ENGLISH EXPRESSION
Me gusta la bolsa.	The purse is pleasing to me.	I like the purse.
¿No le gusta a Vd.?	Isn't it pleasing to you?	Don't you like it?
Te gusta ir de compras.	To go shopping is pleasing to you.	You like to go shopping.
Me gustan esas cosas.	Those things are pleasing to me.	I like those things.
No le gustan.	They are not pleasing to him.	He doesn't like them.

Spanish has no verb meaning *to like* and uses, instead, the verb **gustar** meaning *to be pleasing*.   An English sentence using the verb *to like* should be changed into one using *to be pleasing (to)* before it can be turned into Spanish.   Instead of *I like the store*, say *The store is pleasing to me* (**Me gusta la tienda**); or instead of *I don't like those stores*, say *Those stores are not pleasing to me* (**No me gustan aquellas tiendas**).

Only two forms of the verb **gustar** are regularly used in the present tense: **gusta** if one thing or an action is pleasing, **gustan** if more than one.   English *it* and *them* are not expressed (second and fifth examples), and the subject usually follows the form of **gustar.**

> **Le gusta a Luisa el vestido.** Louise likes the dress.
> **A Luisa le gustan los vestidos.** Louise likes the dresses.

When a noun is the indirect object of **gustar,** the indirect object pronoun (**le** in the examples) is also used. For greater emphasis the noun indirect object may precede the verb.

Práctica. Read several times in Spanish, noting the meaning:

1. Me gusta este vestido. 2. Me gustan estos vestidos. 3. Le gusta esta silla. 4. Le gustan estas sillas. 5. No nos gusta la revista. 6. No nos gustan las revistas. 7. Les gusta ir al centro. 8. ¿Le gusta a Vd. la bolsa de Luisa? 9. ¿Te gusta mucho? 10. A Luis le gustan estos guantes. 11. Le gusta a María este estilo. 12. Les gusta también a Carlos y a José.

E. Adjectives used as nouns

> **Me gusta este rojo.** I like this red one.
> **El blanco es muy bonito.** The white one is very pretty.
> **No me gustan esos grandes.** I don't like those large ones.
> **La joven** (**La señorita**) **compra un libro.** The young woman buys a book.

Just as adjectives of nationality are used as nouns (page 24), so are many other adjectives, especially when used with the definite article or the demonstrative adjective. In such cases the adjective agrees in gender and number with the noun understood. The word *one(s)* is often included in the English meaning.

F. Comparison of adjectives

1. **bonito** pretty   (**el**) **más bonito** (the) prettier, prettiest
   caro expensive   (**el**) **menos caro** (the) less expensive, least expensive

When we compare adjectives in English we say *pretty, prettier, prettiest; expensive, more (less) expensive, most (least) expensive.* In Spanish we use **más** to mean *more, most,* and **menos** for *less, least.* The definite article is used when *the* is a part of the meaning, and the adjective must agree with the noun in gender and number: **el más bonito, la más bonita, los más bonitos, las más bonitas.** Sometimes the possessive adjective (**mi, tu,** etc.) replaces the definite article. Other examples are:

> **Este vestido es más bonito.** This dress is prettier.
> **El blanco es el más bonito de todos.** The white one is the prettiest of all.

     Es el mercado más grande.   It is the larger (largest) market.
     Es mi bolsa más nueva.   It is my newer (newest) purse.
     Este libro es el menos interesante.   This book is the less (least) interesting.

You can tell from the context when an adjective has comparative or superlative force; that is, whether **más** means *more* or *most* and whether **menos** means *less* or *least*. Note the word order in the last two examples.

     Adverbs are also compared by the use of **más** or **menos: Media hora más tarde llega Luisa,** *Louise arrives a half hour later.*

   2. **Es más bonito que el blanco.**   It is prettier than the white one.
     Ana tiene menos de diez dólares.   Ann has less than ten dollars.

Than is translated by **que** before a noun or pronoun, but before a numeral it is translated by **de.**

   3. **Es la ciudad más grande del país.**   It is the largest city in the country.

After a superlative, *in* is translated by **de.**

EJERCICIOS

A. Substitution drill:

   1. María *me* da el dinero.
     (*le, nos, les, te*)

   2. José no *les* abre la puerta.
     (*me, nos, le, te*)

   3. Nos gusta *este cuarto.*
     (*este estilo, esta calle, este mercado*)

   4. ¿Le gustan a Vd. *estas plumas?*
     (*estos lápices, estas mesas, estos mapas*)

B. Read in Spanish, supplying the correct form of **gustar:**

   1. Me ——— su vestido rojo.   2. No me ——— aquellas tiendas grandes.   3. No nos ——— estas casas.   4. No les ——— comprar mucho.   5. Luis tiene varias cosas que me ——— mucho.   6. A Carlos le ——— mucho este estilo.   7. Le ——— ir de compras.   8. ¿Te ——— leer?   9. ¿Te ——— estos libros?   10. ¿Les ——— a Vds. estos mapas?   11. ¿Le ——— a María los dos vestidos?   12. Le ——— el blanco.

C. Say each sentence as you hear it, then repeat, omitting the noun in your new sentence:

> MODEL: Me gusta el mercado nuevo.　　Me gusta el mercado nuevo.
> Me gusta el nuevo.

1. Me enseña el mercado grande. 2. La casa blanca es de Jorge. 3. ¿Quién vive en la casa amarilla? 4. No nos gustan aquellas casas verdes. 5. No les gustan los autobuses más pequeños. 6. No me gusta el vestido azul. 7. ¿Te gusta la bolsa roja? 8. ¿Es caro el cuadro pequeño? 9. ¿Son más caros los cuadros grandes? 10. Nos gusta la tienda más pequeña. 11. Les gusta la tienda vieja. 12. ¿No te gustan esos guantes nuevos?

D. Say each sentence after your teacher, then make each one plural:

> MODEL: Se abre la puerta.　　Se abre la puerta.
> Se abren las puertas.

1. Allí se ve la casa.
2. Se necesita esta cosa.
3. Se escribe la carta.
4. Se aprende la lección.
5. Aquí se compra el libro.
6. Se recibe el programa.
7. Se usa este lápiz.
8. Se termina la clase.

E. Read each sentence in Spanish, then repeat, changing to the reflexive:

> MODEL: Aquí hablan español.　　Aquí se habla español.

1. Hablan inglés en este país. 2. Aquí compran libros. 3. Abren las puertas a las ocho. 4. Ven muchos autobuses en la calle. 5. Preparan las lecciones en casa. 6. Aprenden bien la lección. 7. Leen muchos periódicos todos los días. 8. No necesitan muchas cosas. 9. Ven otro vestido en el escaparate. 10. Escriben las frases en español.

F. Repeat the question after your teacher; then answer the question affirmatively, following the model:

> MODEL: ¿Es pequeña la casa?　　¿Es pequeña la casa?
> Sí, es más pequeña que la otra.

1. ¿Es caro el vestido?
2. ¿Es interesante el libro?
3. ¿Es grande el mercado?
4. ¿Es bonito el reloj de Luisa?
5. ¿Son caras las bolsas?
6. ¿Son fáciles las lecciones?

G. Repeat the question after your teacher; then answer the question affirmatively, following the model:

> MODEL: ¿Es nuevo el mercado?   ¿Es nuevo el mercado?
>
> Sí, es el más nuevo de todos.

1. ¿Es difícil el ejercicio?   4. ¿Es cómoda la silla?
2. ¿Es larga la frase?   5. ¿Son fáciles los exámenes?
3. ¿Es bonita la alumna?   6. ¿Son hermosas las ciudades?

H. Give in Spanish:

1. Louise leaves home at half past eight in order to go shopping. 2. Her father always gives her money (in order) to buy the things that she needs. 3. A half hour later she arrives downtown. 4. The stores open (are opened) at nine o'clock. 5. Upon entering a store, Louise tells a clerk that she is looking for a dress. 6. The clerk shows Louise [some] dresses of several styles. 7. Louise sees a red dress that she likes a great deal. 8. She says that the red one is prettier than the others. 9. It is too expensive, and she looks at a cotton dress. 10. Louise buys it and she gives the clerk the money.

EJERCICIOS DE PRONUNCIACIÓN

A. The sounds of **ch, y, ll,** and **ñ**

1. **Ch** is pronounced like English *ch* in *church*:

   charlar   Chile   leche   mucho   noche

2. **Y** is pronounced like a strong English *y* in *you*; the conjunction **y**, *and*, when initial in a breath-group before a vowel, or when between vowels within a breath-group, has the sound of Spanish **y**:

   ya   yo   desayuno   ¿y‿usted?   blanco y‿azul

3. **Ll** is pronounced like *y* in *yes* in most of Spanish America and in some parts of Spain; in other parts of Spain and Spanish America it is pronounced somewhat like *lli* in *million*:

   allí   amarillo   llamar   llega   silla

4. **Ñ** is an **n** pronounced with the same tongue position as **ch** and **y**; it sounds somewhat like the English *ny* in *canyon*:

   enseñar   España   mañana   pequeño   señor

B. Spanish intonation

Review the observations on Spanish intonation in Appendix C; then rewrite the first five exchanges of the dialogues of this lesson, dividing them into breath-groups and into syllables, and outline the intonation patterns. Read the exchanges, giving close attention to the intonation patterns.

VOCABULARIO

adiós goodbye
el algodón cotton
el autobús (*pl.* **autobuses**) bus
¡ay! oh! alas! ah!
la bolsa purse
bonito, -a pretty, beautiful
la calle street
caro, -a expensive, dear
el centavo cent (*U.S.*)
el centro center, downtown
la compra purchase
comprar to buy, purchase
la cosa thing
dar to give
decir to say, tell
el dinero money
el dólar dollar (*U.S.*)
la empleada clerk, employee (*woman*)
enseñar (**a** + *inf.*) to show, teach
el escaparate show window

especial special
el estilo style
el favor favor
el guante glove
gustar to be pleasing, like
Luisa Louise
el mercado market
el mes month
otro, -a other, another; *pl.* other(s)
el par pair
pasar to spend (*time*)
el precio price
que than
la semana week
la talla size (*of a dress*)
el tiempo time (*in general sense*)
la tienda store, shop
usar to use, wear
el vestido dress

ir (**llegar**) **al centro** to go (arrive) downtown
ir de compras to go shopping
lo damos a we are offering (selling) it for
lo tomo I'll take it
media hora a half hour
mucho tiempo long, a long time
otra cosa anything (something) else
por favor please (*used at the end of statement*)
¿puedo ver otros? may I see others?
¿qué precio tiene? what is the price of (it)?

Auca indian in Ecuadorian jungle.

LECTURA II

LA AMÉRICA DEL SUR

Estudio de palabras

Additional principles for recognizing approximate cognates will aid you in understanding the reading selections. (Some of the examples listed below are taken from the reading selection of Lectura I.)

a. Certain Spanish nouns ending in **-ia, -io** end in *-y* in English: industria, Italia; contrario.

b. Certain Spanish nouns ending in **-cia, -cio** end in *-ce* in English: edificio (*edifice, building*), Francia, influencia.

c. Certain Spanish nouns ending in **-dad** end in *-ty* in English: realidad.

d. Deceptive cognates. A number of Spanish and English words are similar in form, but quite different in meaning: largo, *long.*

e. Many Spanish words can be recognized by comparing them with related words. *Compare:* alto, *high, and* altura, *height, altitude;* Europe, *Europe, and* europeo, *European;* mesa, *table, and* meseta, *tableland, plateau;* pueblo, *town, village, and* población, *population.*

f. Many Spanish words can be recognized by associating English words from the same source. Careful attention to such related words will aid greatly in improving your vocabulary.

Compare:	antiguo	*old, ancient*	*antique*
	edificio	*building*	*edifice*
	mayor	*larger, greater*	*major*
	mundo	*world*	*mundane*

Hoy vamos a mirar otro mapa que tenemos en la pared. Es el mapa de la América del Sur. Como Vds. saben, es un continente muy grande. Hay nueve repúblicas en que se habla español, y una, el Brasil, donde se habla portugués. El Brasil es un país muy grande; en realidad, es más grande que los Estados Unidos.

Venezuela y Colombia están en el norte del continente. Caracas es la capital de Venezuela, y Bogotá, la[1] de Colombia.

Colombia tiene costas en el Mar Caribe[2] y también en el Océano Pacífico. Además de[3] Colombia, las repúblicas de la costa del Océano Pacífico son el Ecuador, el Perú y Chile. Quito, Lima y Santiago son las capitales de estos tres países. Como Vds. pueden ver, Chile es un país muy largo y estrecho.

La Argentina, en el sur, es un país muy rico. Buenos Aires, su capital, tiene más de nueve millones de habitantes y es una

---

[1] **la,** *that.*   [2] **el Mar Caribe,** *the Caribbean Sea.*   [3] **Además de,** *Besides.*

Fishing boats at Puerto Montt, Chile.

Huatchipato steel plant at night, Chile.

ciudad muy moderna.   En las ciudades de la Argentina hay mucha industria.   En la pampa, una región muy fértil, se produce un poco de todo — trigo,[1] maíz, alfalfa, por ejemplo[2] —, y se cría mucho ganado.[3]

El Uruguay es el país más pequeño de la América del Sur.   Su tierra es fértil también. La tercera parte[4] de sus habitantes viven en la capital, Montevideo.   Hay muchas playas[5] bonitas cerca de la ciudad y en la costa del Río de la Plata.   Bolivia y el Paraguay están en el interior del continente y no tienen costa.   La Paz, Bolivia, es la capital más alta del mundo.   Asunción, una ciudad muy antigua, es la capital del Paraguay.

La América del Sur tiene tres ríos grandes: el Amazonas, que es el río más grande del mundo, el Orinoco, en el norte, y el sistema del Río de la Plata.

---

[1] **trigo,** *wheat.*   [2] **por ejemplo,** *for example.*   [3] **se cría mucho ganado,** *much cattle (livestock) is raised.*   [4] **La tercera parte,** *One (A) third.*   [5] **playas,** *beaches.*

A gaucho with his sheep, Uruguay.

Ocro indians gather to participate in the festival of Q'oyllar'rit'i near the Sinaq'ara glacier, Perú.

El continente tiene montañas, llanuras,[1] desiertos y selvas,[2] y el clima varía según[3] la altura. Una gran[4] parte de los habitantes de Colombia, el Ecuador, el Perú, Bolivia y Chile viven en las altas mesetas y en los valles de la cordillera de los Andes. Es difícil ir de un país a otro, especialmente si uno tiene que cruzar[5] las montañas y los ríos.

La mayor parte de la población[6] de la Argentina y del Uruguay es de origen europeo. En el Ecuador, el Perú y Bolivia, por lo contrario,[7] hay muchos indios, especialmente en los pueblos y ciudades de los Andes. En el Paraguay la población india es muy numerosa. En los otros países la mezcla[8] de razas es la nota más característica de la población.

[1]**llanuras,** *plains.* [2]**selvas,** *forests.* [3]**según,** *according to.* [4]**gran,** *great.* (When **grande** precedes a singular noun it becomes **gran** and means *great.*) [5]**cruzar,** *to cross.* [6]**La mayor parte de la población,** *Most of the population.* [7]**por lo contrario,** *on the contrary.* [8]**mezcla,** *mixture.*

Courtyard, Cuzco, Perú.

New airport facilities in Maracaibo, Venezuela.

PREGUNTAS

1. ¿Qué mapa vamos a mirar hoy? 2. ¿Es grande o pequeño el continente? 3. ¿En cuántas repúblicas se habla español? 4. ¿Qué país es más grande que los Estados Unidos? 5. ¿Qué lengua se habla en el Brasil?

6. ¿Qué países están en el norte? 7. ¿Cuáles son las repúblicas de la costa del Océano Pacífico? 8. ¿Cuál es la capital del Perú? 9. ¿Cuál es la capital de Chile? 10. ¿Cómo es Chile?

11. ¿Cómo es la Argentina? 12. ¿Cuál es su capital? 13. ¿Cuántos habitantes tiene Buenos Aires? 14. ¿Dónde hay mucha industria? 15. ¿Qué se produce en la pampa?

16. ¿Es grande el Uruguay? 17. ¿Cuál es su capital? 18. ¿Tiene muchos habitantes la capital? 19. ¿Qué hay cerca de la ciudad? 20. ¿Qué países están en el interior del continente? 21. ¿Cuál es la capital de Bolivia? 22. ¿Dónde está Asunción?

23. ¿Cuál es el río más grande del mundo? 24. ¿Dónde está el Orinoco? 25. ¿Varía el clima del continente? 26. ¿Dónde viven muchos habitantes de Colombia y Bolivia? 27. ¿Es fácil ir de un país a otro?

28. ¿En qué países es de origen europeo la mayor parte de la población? 29. ¿En qué países hay muchos indios?

Mar Caribe

Océano Atlántico

Canal de Panamá

Santa Marta
Barranquilla
Cartagena
Tolú
Coro
La Guaira
Caracas
TRINIDAD (ENG.)
Port of Spain

L. Maracaibo
R. Orinoco
VENEZUELA
San Cristóbal
Georgetown
Paramaribo
Cayenne
BRITISH GUIANA
SURINAM
FRENCH GUIANA

Buenaventura
Medellín
Cali
Bogotá
Papayán
R. Cauca
R. Guaviare
R. Branco

COLOMBIA

ECUADOR
Quito
R. Putumayo
R. Negro

Guayaquil
PERÚ
Manaus
R. Amazonas
Belem

Callao
Lima
Cuzco
R. Marañón
R. Ucayali
R. Madeira
R. Tapajós
R. Xingú
R. Araguaia
R. Tocantins
R. Parnaiba
Fortaleza
Natal
Recife

SELVAS
BRASIL
Bahia

CORDILLERA DE LOS ANDES
Arequipa
L. Titicaca
La Paz
L. Poopó
Sucre
BOLIVIA
MATO GROSSO
Brasilia
R. São Francisco
MESETA DEL BRASIL

Iquique
Potosí
Belo Horizonte

Antofagasta
PARAGUAY
Cataratas del Iguasú
São Paulo
Río de Janeiro
Santos

Tucumán
Asunción
MISIONES
R. Uruguay
Pôrto Alegre

Aconcagua
Córdoba
R. Salado
R. Paraná

Viña del Mar
Valparaíso
Santiago
Mendoza
Santa Fe
Rosario
Buenos Aires
URUGUAY
Montevideo
R. de la Plata
R. Negro

Océano Pacífico

Concepción
PAMPAS
ARGENTINA
R. Colorado
Bahía Blanca

CHILE
R.

R. Chubut

PATAGONIA

ISLAS FALKLAND
Estrecho de Magallanes

Punta Arenas
Tierra del Fuego

La América del Sur

Present indicative of *hacer* **and** *poner*

Present indicative of stem-changing verbs, Class I

Reflexive pronouns.   Present indicative of the reflexive verb *lavarse*

Position of pronouns used as objects of an infinitive

The definite article for the possessive

Omission of the indefinite article

EL PROFESOR PIENSA HACER UN VIAJE

(*El profesor López encuentra a uno de sus estudiantes en la biblioteca.*)

SR. LÓPEZ.   ¡Hola, Ricardo!   ¿Tiene Vd. un momento?

RICARDO.   ¡Cómo no!   ¿Nos sentamos aquí?

SR. LÓPEZ.   ¿Quiere Vd. acompañarme hasta el garaje que está en la esquina?   Están lavando mi coche allí.

RICARDO.   Con mucho gusto.

• • • • •

SR. LÓPEZ.   Deseo hablarle acerca de un viaje que pienso hacer a México.

RICARDO.   ¿Cuándo piensa Vd. hacer el viaje?

SR. LÓPEZ.   Pronto, durante las vacaciones.   (*Al salir de la biblioteca el Sr. López se pone el sombrero.*)   Veo que Vd., como casi todos los jóvenes, no usa sombrero.

RICARDO.   Es verdad.   Hoy día lo usamos solamente cuando llueve.

• • • • •

SR. LÓPEZ.   Ricardo, tengo que ir a México con la familia y busco un compañero[1] para mi hijo.   Quiero saber si Vd. puede acompañarnos.   ¿Conoce a mi hijo?

---

[1] The personal **a** is not used before **un compañero** since the noun does not refer to a definite person.   Compare the explanation in **Notas gramaticales, B,** page 65.

RICARDO.   Se llama Carlos, ¿verdad? Sí, le conozco muy bien.   Pues, me gusta la idea.

SR. LÓPEZ.   A mi hijo le gusta levantarse temprano y acostarse tarde.   ¿A qué hora se levanta Vd., Ricardo?

RICARDO.   Por lo común me levanto a las siete de la mañana.   Me lavo la cara y las manos y bajo al comedor a desayunarme a las siete y media, más o menos.   Me acuesto a las doce.

SR. LÓPEZ.   Está bien.   Pues, pensamos hacer el viaje en avión.   Como Vd. sabe, hoy día no cuesta mucho viajar en avión.

RICARDO.   Esta noche vuelve mi padre de un viaje.   Creo que puede darme el dinero.

SR. LÓPEZ.   Espero que sí.   Si quiere Vd., yo puedo hablar con su padre esta noche.   Pero ya es hora de volver a casa.   Hasta la vista, Ricardo.

RICARDO.   Hasta luego, señor López.

CONVERSACIÓN

A. Preguntas sobre el diálogo

1. ¿Dónde encuentra el profesor a Ricardo?   2. ¿Se sientan en la biblioteca?   3. ¿Qué se pone el profesor al salir de la biblioteca?   4. ¿Cómo se llama el hijo del profesor? 5. ¿Qué quiere saber el profesor?   6. ¿A qué hora se levanta Ricardo?   7. ¿A qué hora se acuesta Ricardo?   8. ¿Piensan hacer el viaje en coche o en avión?

B. Aplicación del diálogo

1. ¿Cómo se llama Vd.?   2. ¿Le gusta a Vd. viajar?   3. ¿Qué piensa Vd. hacer durante las vacaciones?   4. ¿A qué hora se acuesta Vd.?   5. ¿Se levanta Vd. tarde o temprano?   6. ¿A qué hora se desayuna Vd.?   7. ¿Usa Vd. sombrero al salir de casa?   8. ¿Lava Vd. su coche a menudo?

NOTAS GRAMATICALES

A. Irregular present indicative of **hacer** and **poner**

hacer, *to do, make*		**poner,** *to put, place*	
SINGULAR	PLURAL	SINGULAR	PLURAL
hago	hacemos	**pongo**	ponemos
haces	hacéis	pones	ponéis
hace	hacen	pone	ponen

B. Present indicative of stem-changing verbs, Class I

pensar, *to think*		**volver,** *to return*	
SINGULAR	PLURAL	SINGULAR	PLURAL
pienso	pensamos	**vuelvo**	volvemos
piensas	pensáis	**vuelves**	volvéis
piensa	**piensan**	**vuelve**	**vuelven**

Certain verbs have regular endings, but the stem vowel **e** becomes **ie** and **o** becomes **ue** when stressed; that is, in the three singular forms and in the third person plural. All stem-changing verbs of Class I end in **-ar** and **-er**. Verbs of this type are indicated thus: **pensar (ie), volver (ue).**

C. Reflexive pronouns

SINGULAR		PLURAL	
me	(to) myself	**nos**	(to) ourselves
te	(to) yourself (*fam.*)	**os**	(to) yourselves (*fam.*)
se	(to) himself, herself, yourself (*formal*), itself, oneself	**se**	(to) themselves, yourselves

The reflexive pronouns are used as direct and indirect objects. Notice that in the first and second persons singular and plural they are identical to the direct and indirect object pronouns.

D. Present indicative of the reflexive verb **lavarse,** *to wash (oneself)*

SINGULAR

(yo) me lavo	*I wash (myself)*
(tú) te lavas	*you* (fam.) *wash (yourself)*
(él, ella) se lava	*he, she washes (himself, herself)*
Vd. se lava	*you (formal) wash (yourself)*

PLURAL

(nosotros, -as) nos lavamos	*we wash (ourselves)*
(vosotros, -as) os laváis	*you* (fam.) *wash (yourselves)*
(ellos, -as) se lavan	*they wash (themselves)*
Vds. se lavan	*you wash (yourselves)*

A verb is called reflexive when the subject does something to itself, either directly, **Ricardo se lava,** *Richard washes* (*himself*), or indirectly, **Se compra un coche,** *He buys a car for himself, He buys himself a car.* Reflexive pronouns are in the same person as the subject of the verb.

Many intransitive verbs in English (that is, verbs that cannot have a direct object) are expressed in Spanish by using the reflexive pronoun **se** with a transitive verb. Note that all the reflexive verbs in this lesson, except for **desayunarse,** are used transitively. The third person reflexive **se** attached to an infinitive indicates a reflexive verb: **lavarse.**

For position with respect to the verb, reflexive pronouns follow the same rules as other object pronouns.

The first person singular of reflexive verbs used in this lesson, except for **desayunarse,** is listed here with literal meaning; note, however, the usual meaning:

	LITERAL MEANING	USUAL MEANING
me acuesto	I put myself to bed	I go to bed
me lavo	I wash myself	I wash
me levanto	I raise myself	I get up
me llamo	I call myself	I am called, my name is
me pongo	I put to (on) myself	I put on
me siento	I seat myself	I sit down

Give the meanings of **¿Cómo te llamas? ¿Cómo se llama Vd.? ¿Cómo se llama él?** and **Se llama Carlos.**

E. Position of pronouns used as objects of an infinitive

Ricardo, deseo hablarle. Richard, I want (desire) to talk to you.
Mi padre puede darme el dinero. My father can give me the money.
Vamos a sentarnos. We are going to sit down.
¿Quiere (Vd.) acompañarme? Will you accompany me?
Bajo a desayunarme. I go down to eat breakfast.

Recall that object pronouns are regularly placed immediately before the verb. However, when they are used as objects of an infinitive, they are placed after the verb and are attached to it.

Note that **desear,** like **querer,** is followed by an infinitive (first example). Just as English *to desire* is used less than *to wish* or *to want,* so Spanish **desear** is used less than **querer.**

In the fourth example note that **¿Quiere Vd.?** is used to express *Will you?* meaning *Are you willing to?* Similarly, one says **¿No quiere Vd.?** *Won't you?*

F. The definite article for the possessive

> **Me lavo las manos.** I wash my hands.
> **Se lavan la cara.** They wash their faces.
> **Ella se pone el sombrero.** She puts on her hat.
> **Luis tiene el sombrero en la mano.** Louis has his hat in his hand.
>
> BUT: **Su sombrero está sobre la silla.** His hat is on the chair.

The definite article is often used instead of the possessive adjective with a noun which represents a part of the body or an article of clothing, and sometimes with other articles closely associated with the subject, when this noun is the object of a verb or preposition. Compare the first four examples with the fifth, in which case **su sombrero** is the subject of the verb. Note in the second example that Spanish uses the singular **la cara** to show that each person has one face.

G. Omission of the indefinite article

> **Vd. no usa sombrero.** You don't wear (aren't wearing) a hat.
> **Yo no tengo sombrero.** I don't have a (I have no) hat.
> **¿Usa Vd. sombrero al salir de casa?** Do you wear a hat upon leaving home?

The indefinite article is often omitted before nouns, particularly in negative sentences and when numerical value is not important.

EJERCICIOS

A. Repeat after your teacher. When you hear the cue, make a new sentence:

> MODEL: Enrique se desayuna. Enrique se desayuna.
>   Yo Yo me desayuno.

1. Yo me acuesto temprano. (Tú) 2. Mis padres se acuestan tarde. (Luis y yo)
3. María se sienta a la mesa. (Yo) 4. Ella y yo nos lavamos las manos. (Vd.)
5. Vd. no se llama Jorge. (Tú) 6. Los estudiantes se levantan a las siete. (José)
7. Yo pongo las compras en el coche. (Ella) 8. Tú te pones los guantes. (Nosotros)
9. Vds. no se lavan la cara. (Roberto) 10. Ellos y yo nos desayunamos en el comedor. (Vds.) 11. A menudo yo los encuentro en el parque. (Carlos y yo) 12. Mis tíos no hacen muchos viajes. (Yo)

B. Answer affirmatively, watching the reflexive pronouns:

MODELS: ¿Se pone Vd. el sombrero?   Sí, me pongo el sombrero.
¿Van Vds. a ponerse el sombrero?   Sí, vamos a ponernos el sombrero.

1. ¿Se levanta Vd. temprano?   5. ¿Se levantan Vds. tarde?
2. ¿Se lava Vd. las manos?   6. ¿Se lavan Vds. la cara?
3. ¿Se sienta Vd. a la mesa?   7. ¿Se sientan Vds. en la sala?
4. ¿Se desayuna Vd. en el comedor?   8. ¿Se acuestan Vds. a las diez?

9. ¿Va Vd. a levantarse?   13. ¿Quieren Vds. acostarse?
10. ¿Va Vd. a lavarse?   14. ¿Quieren Vds. lavarse?
11. ¿Va Vd. a sentarse?   15. ¿Pueden Vds. levantarse?
12. ¿Va Vd. a desayunarse?   16. ¿Pueden Vds. sentarse?

C. Read in Spanish, placing the pronoun in its proper position:

1. (me) Yo siento. Voy a sentar. 2. (nos) Carlos y yo lavamos. Queremos lavar. 3. (se) Ana no pone el sombrero. No puede poner el sombrero. 4. (te) ¿Acuestas tú? ¿Piensas acostar? 5. (se) Ricardo levanta. Después de levantar, baja al comedor. 6. (se) Los hijos lavan las manos. Al lavar las manos, se sientan a la mesa. 7. (se) Roberto acuesta tarde. Quiere acostar a las once. 8. (te) ¿Sientas tú allí? ¿No quieres sentar aquí?

D. Read in Spanish, using the correct form of the verb in italics:

1. Me *gustar* este avión. 2. Me *gustar* estos coches. 3. Nos *gustar* la idea. 4. Nos *gustar* aquellas casas. 5. A Ricardo le *gustar* viajar en avión. 6. Les *gustar* a los jóvenes viajar en coche. 7. A Carlos no le *gustar* lavar el coche. 8. No me *gustar* usar sombrero.

9. Yo deseo *lavarse* las manos. 10. Ana y yo vamos a *lavarse* la cara. 11. Yo tengo que *levantarse* temprano. 12. Ella y yo pensamos *sentarse* ahora. 13. Luis y yo *levantarse* tarde. 14. Tú no *desayunarse* a las siete. 15. ¿No *ponerse* tú el sombrero? 16. ¿No espera Vd. *acostarse* pronto?

E. Repeat after your teacher. When you hear a new verb, use the correct form in a new sentence:

1. ¿Quiere Vd. ir a la tienda ahora? (poder)
2. Los hombres no llegan a casa hasta las cinco. (volver)
3. Jorge piensa hacer el viaje. (desear)
4. ¿Quién va a darle a José el dinero? (venir)

5. ¿A qué hora quieres levantarte? (necesitar)
6. Ricardo y yo deseamos hablarle al señor López. (querer)
7. Nuestra familia no cena en el comedor. (desayunarse)
8. Hoy día muchos jóvenes no tienen sombrero. (usar)

F. Repeat after your teacher. When you hear the cue, make a new sentence, following the models:

MODELS: La abro. La abro.
        Voy a   Voy a abrirla.

Nos levantamos. Nos levantamos.
Deseamos   Deseamos levantarnos.

1. Los veo. (Quiero)
2. Se sientan. (Vienen a)
3. Nos lavamos. (Necesitamos)
4. Me pongo el vestido. (Puedo)

5. Les traigo la revista. (¿Puedes?)
6. Te lavas las manos. (¿No quieres?)
7. Nos dicen la verdad. (¿No van a?)
8. ¿La llamas a menudo? (¿Deseas?)

G. Give in Spanish:

1. Richard returns home late and he does not go to bed until twelve o'clock. 2. After getting up, he washes his face and hands. 3. Then he goes down to the dining room in order to eat breakfast. 4. His parents are already seated when he enters. 5. Richard's father tells him that Mr. López intends to take a trip to Mexico during (the) vacation. 6. As Mr. López is going to be very busy, he is looking for a companion for his son Charles. 7. He wants to know whether Richard can accompany them. 8. Richard likes the idea, but he believes that it costs a great deal to travel by plane. 9. His father says that he can give him the money if he works hard after returning from Mexico. 10. That evening the two go to talk with Mr. López about the trip.

A woman of the highland village of Chimú with her flock of sheep on the bank of Lake Titicaca, Perú.

EJERCICIOS DE PRONUNCIACIÓN

A. The sounds of **m** and **n**

    1. Spanish **m** is pronounced like English *m*:

mapa	comer	primo	mes

    2. When initial in a syllable, when final before a pause, or when before any consonant other than those mentioned below, Spanish **n** is pronounced like English *n*:

grande	cansado	pronto	avión

    3. When before **b, v, m,** and **p,** Spanish **n** is pronounced like **m**:

invitar	un par	un poco	un viaje
con papá	están bien	con mamá	un vestido

    4. Before **c, qu, g,** and **j,** Spanish **n** is pronounced like English *n* in *sing*:

encontrar	¿con quién?	en casa	tengo
me pongo	lengua	inglés	con José

B. The sounds of **s**

    1. Spanish **s** is pronounced somewhat like the English hissed *s* in *sent*:

demasiado	desear	desayuno	José
Luisa	televisión	visitar	mis padres

    2. Before **b, d, g, l, ll, m, n, v,** and **y,** however, Spanish **s** is like English *s* in *rose*:

desde	buenas noches	es bueno	las manos
los llama	mis guantes	tres vestidos	varias lenguas

C. The variations of Spanish **s**

Pronounce each individual word after your teacher; then repeat, but as part of a breath-group introduced by the words indicated at the right:

1. grande	bueno	mexicano	viejo		es
2. bolsas	mesas	lecciones	vacaciones		las
3. dólares	libros	meses	viajes		muchos

VOCABULARIO

acompañar to accompany
acostarse (**ue**) to go to bed
el avión (*pl.* **aviones**) (air)plane
bajar (**a** + *inf.*) to go down(stairs)
la cara face
el coche car
el comedor dining room
el compañero companion
costar (**ue**) to cost
desayunarse to take (eat) breakfast
desear to desire, wish, want
encontrar (**ue**) to meet, encounter; find
la esquina corner (*street*)
el garaje garage
hacer to do, make
la idea idea

lavar to wash; *reflex.* wash (oneself)
levantar to raise, lift; *reflex.* get up, rise
llamarse to be called, be named
llover (**ue**) to rain
la mano (*note gender*) hand
pensar (**ie**) to think; + *inf.* intend
poner to put, place; *reflex.* put on (oneself)
pronto soon, quickly
Ricardo Richard
sentarse (**ie**) to sit down
el sombrero hat
las vacaciones vacation (*used in pl.*)
viajar to travel
el viaje trip
volver (**ue**) to return, come back

en avión (**coche**) by plane (car), in a plane (car)
es hora de it is time to
espero que sí I hope so
está bien that's fine, excellent, very well
hacer un viaje to take (make) a trip
hoy día nowadays
más o menos more or less, approximately
¿nos sentamos? shall we sit down?
por lo común generally, commonly
(**volver**) **a casa** (to return) home

University of Guanajuato, México.

LECTURA III

MÉXICO

Estudio de palabras

a. Most Spanish nouns ending in **-ción** are feminine and end in *-tion* in English: civilización, exportación, vegetación.

b. The Spanish ending **-oso** is often equivalent to English *-ous*: famoso, *famous. What are the meanings of* montañoso *and* numeroso?

c. Many English words beginning with *s* followed by a consonant have Spanish cognates beginning with **es** plus the consonant. Give the English for: escuela, España, español, especial, estado, estudiar.

d. As we have seen in the previous Lecturas, the Spanish endings **-cio, -cia** = English *-ce*; **-io, -ia** = *y*; and **-dad** = *-ty*. Give the English cognates of: importancia; colonia, necesario; prosperidad.

e. Compare the meanings of the following pairs of words: centro *and* central; cultura *and* cultural; importancia *and* importante; industria *and* industrial; montaña *and* montañoso.

Hoy vamos a leer algo acerca de México, nuestro buen vecino[1] al sur de los Estados Unidos. El Río Grande, que pasa entre el estado de Texas y cuatro estados mexicanos, forma parte de la frontera con México. En la otra parte de la frontera están nuestros estados de California, Arizona y Nuevo México.

La Carretera[2] Panamericana va desde Nuevo Laredo hasta Guatemala. Pasa por Monterrey, ciudad industrial de mucha importancia, y por la capital, la ciudad de México. Para llegar a la capital, que está en la meseta central, es necesario cruzar muchas montañas muy altas.

La capital está situada en el Distrito Federal y tiene más de seis millones de habitantes. Es el centro comercial y cultural del país. Muchas de las colonias[3] de la capital tienen avenidas anchas[4] y casas nuevas de una arquitectura muy moderna, pero las colonias pobres tienen casas viejas y calles estrechas y antiguas. Por todas partes[5] se ve un gran número de fuentes, árboles y flores, especialmente en los parques que adornan la ciudad. Los magníficos

---

[1] **buen vecino,** *good neighbor.*   [2] **Carretera,** *Highway.*   [3] **colonias,** *districts.*   [4] **avenidas anchas,** *wide avenues.*   [5] **Por todas partes,** *Everywhere.*

View of the University, Mexico City.

Independence Monument, Mexico City.

Central courtyard of the Plaza Satélite Shopping Center, north of Mexico City.

edificios comerciales dan una buena idea del progreso y de la prosperidad de la capital.

Entre las ciudades importantes se encuentran[1] Monterrey, Guadalajara, Saltillo, San Luis Potosí, Puebla y Taxco. Veracruz, un puerto que tiene mucha importancia, está en la costa del Golfo de México. En el este del país también está el puerto de Tampico, importante por la exportación de petróleo. Los puertos de Mazatlán y Acapulco, este último[2] famoso por sus playas bellas y sus hoteles modernos, se encuentran en la costa del Océano Pacífico. Mérida es la ciudad principal de la península de Yucatán.

[1] **se encuentran,** *are found, are.* (**Encontrarse** often means approximately the same as **estar,** although it retains something of its original meaning, *to find itself, be found, be.*)   [2] **este último,** *this last one.*

107

Chapultepec Park directory, Mexico City.

México es el país más montañoso de la América del Norte. Las dos cordilleras principales son la Sierra Madre Occidental, que está en el oeste, y la Sierra Madre Oriental, situada en el este. En las montañas hay oro, plata y otros minerales. México tiene varios volcanes. El Popocatépetl y el Iztaccíhuatl se encuentran cerca del valle central y están cubiertos de nieve[1] casi todo el año. El volcán más nuevo, el Paricutín, está al sudeste de Guadalajara. El Orizaba, el pico más alto del país, se encuentra entre Puebla y Veracruz.

El norte de México es un gran desierto. En el sur, en cambio,[2] en el istmo de Tehuantepec, la vegetación es abundante porque el clima es tropical y llueve mucho. La mayor parte de los mexicanos viven en la meseta central, que tiene un clima muy agradable por[3] la altura en que se encuentra.

Aunque el español es la lengua nacional de México, la civilización del país es una mezcla de la cultura primitiva de los indios y de la cultura de los españoles. Una gran parte de los mexicanos son mestizos, es decir,[4] tienen sangre[5] india y española. Los indios que viven en las ciudades hablan español, pero en ciertas regiones aisladas,[6] hay muchos que todavía hablan sus lenguas indias.

---

[1] **cubiertos de nieve,** *covered with snow.*   [2] **en cambio,** *on the other hand.*   [3] **por,** *because of.*   [4] **es decir,** *that is to say.*   [5] **sangre,** *blood.*   [6] **aisladas,** *isolated.*

View of the Pyramid of the Sun at Teotihuacán during a Sound and Light performance, México.

View of Guadalajara, México.

México

PREGUNTAS

1. ¿Qué vamos a leer hoy? 2. ¿Qué río pasa entre los Estados Unidos y México? 3. ¿Por dónde pasa la Carretera Panamericana? 4. ¿Qué es necesario cruzar para llegar a la capital?

5. ¿Dónde está la capital? 6. ¿Cuántos habitantes tiene la capital? 7. ¿Cómo son muchas colonias? 8. ¿Qué se ve por todas partes? 9. ¿Cómo son los edificios comerciales?

10. ¿Cuáles son algunas ciudades importantes? 11. ¿Qué es Veracruz? 12. ¿Dónde está situada Veracruz? 13. ¿Por qué es importante Tampico? 14. ¿Por qué es famoso Acapulco? 15. ¿Dónde está Mérida?

16. ¿Cómo se llaman las dos cordilleras principales? 17. ¿Qué minerales hay en las montañas? 18. ¿Hay volcanes en México? 19. ¿Dónde se encuentran? 20. ¿Cuál es el pico más alto? 21. ¿Qué parte de México es un gran desierto? 22. ¿Cómo es el clima del istmo de Tehuantepec? 23. ¿Dónde viven la mayor parte de los mexicanos? 24. ¿Cómo es el clima de la meseta central?

25. ¿Cuál es la lengua nacional de México? 26. ¿Qué podemos decir de la civilización del país? 27. ¿Hablan español todos los indios?

LECCIÓN 9

Commands.   Position of object pronouns in commands

Expressions with *tener*.   Ways to express "time"

LA ÚLTIMA CLASE DE LA TARDE

(*La señorita Valdés entra en la sala de clase y saluda a los estudiantes.*)

SRTA. VALDÉS.   Buenas tardes.   Siéntense Vds.   Juan, hágame Vd. el favor de abrir la ventana.

MARTA.   Pero Juan no está escuchando.

SRTA. VALDÉS.   Marta, ¿quiere Vd. decirle a Juan que necesitamos aire fresco?

MARTA.   Juan, abre la ventana, por favor.   Necesitamos aire fresco.   (*Juan abre la ventana.*)

SRTA. VALDÉS.   Muchas gracias, Juan.

● ● ● ● ●

SRTA. VALDÉS.   Ahora, cierren Vds. sus libros y pónganlos en los pupitres.   No los miren y escuchen con atención.   Voy a hacerles algunas[1] preguntas.

MARTA.   Nosotros debemos contestar las preguntas en español, ¿verdad?

SRTA. VALDÉS.   Sí, como siempre.   Vds. deben contestarlas en español.   Inés, ¿tiene Vd. frío?

---

[1] Up to this point unemphatic *some* and *any* (*no* in a negative sentence, *e.g.*, *I have no money*, **No tengo dinero**), so commonly used in English, have not been translated in Spanish.   However, when emphasized, these words are expressed in Spanish.

113

Inés. No, señorita. Siempre tengo mucho calor aquí.

Srta. Valdés. Carlos, ¿tiene Vd. hambre o sed?

Carlos. Tengo mucha hambre. Como me levanto tarde, generalmente no tomo más que café o un vaso de leche antes de venir a la universidad.

• • • • •

Srta. Valdés. Isabel, ¿llega Vd. a tiempo todos los días?

Isabel. No, señorita. Cuando me despierto tarde, no llego a tiempo.

Srta. Valdés. María, ¿tiene Vd. sueño en clase?

María. De vez en cuando tengo sueño. Pero si Vd. ve que no estoy escuchando, me hace alguna pregunta.

Srta. Valdés. A veces lo hago, ¿verdad? Antonio, despierte Vd. a Carlos, por favor. El pobre tiene mucho sueño.

Antonio. (*Despertando a su compañero.*) ¡Despiértate, Carlos! ¡Escucha a la profesora!

Srta. Valdés. Muchas gracias. Carolina, ¿qué hace Vd. los domingos?

Carolina. Por la mañana voy a la iglesia. Por la tarde tengo mucho tiempo para estudiar. A veces doy un paseo con algunos amigos.

Srta. Valdés. Muy bien; ya es la hora. Ahora levántense y tomen sus libros y sus cuadernos. No dejen [1] nada en los pupitres. Salgan despacio, por favor. Hasta mañana.

Alumnos. Hasta mañana, señorita Valdés.

CONVERSACIÓN

A. Preguntas sobre el diálogo

1. ¿Qué les dice la profesora a los estudiantes? 2. ¿Qué le dice Marta a Juan? 3. ¿Qué va a hacer la profesora? 4. ¿En qué lengua deben contestar los estudiantes? 5. ¿Tiene frío Inés? 6. ¿Por qué tiene hambre Carlos? 7. ¿Cuándo llega tarde Isabel? 8. ¿Qué hace la profesora cuando ve que María tiene sueño?

B. Aplicación del diálogo

1. ¿Tiene Vd. sueño en clase a veces? 2. ¿Les hago yo preguntas cuando veo que Vds. tienen sueño? 3. ¿Tiene Vd. hambre ahora? 4. ¿Qué hacemos cuando tenemos hambre? 5. ¿Qué hace Vd. los domingos? 6. ¿Qué les dice la profesora (el profesor) cuando es necesario abrir los libros? 7. ¿Qué les dice la profesora (el profesor) cuando es necesario escuchar? 8. ¿Qué le dice Vd. a su hermano cuando es necesario estudiar?

---

[1] The transitive verb **dejar,** *to leave* (*behind*), requires a direct object. Do not confuse **dejar** with **salir,** *to leave, go out* (of a place).

NOTAS GRAMATICALES

A. Commands

1. Formal commands

INFINITIVE	STEM	SINGULAR	PLURAL	
hablar	habl-	hable Vd.	hablen Vds.	*speak*
comer	com-	coma Vd.	coman Vds.	*eat*
abrir	abr-	abra Vd.	abran Vds.	*open*
decir	**dig-**	**diga** Vd.	**digan** Vds.	*say, tell*
hacer	**hag-**	**haga** Vd.	**hagan** Vds.	*do, make*
poner	**pong-**	**ponga** Vd.	**pongan** Vds.	*put, place*
salir	**salg-**	**salga** Vd.	**salgan** Vds.	*leave, go out*
tener	**teng-**	**tenga** Vd.	**tengan** Vds.	*have*
traer	**traig-**	**traiga** Vd.	**traigan** Vds.	*bring*
venir	**veng-**	**venga** Vd.	**vengan** Vds.	*come*
ver	**ve-**	**vea** Vd.	**vean** Vds.	*see*
pensar	**piens-**	**piense** Vd.	**piensen** Vds.	*think*
volver	**vuelv-**	**vuelva** Vd.	**vuelvan** Vds.	*return*

To the stem of **-ar** verbs add the ending **-e** for the singular formal command and **-en** for the plural. For **-er** and **-ir** verbs the endings are **-a** and **-an**. In Spanish the stem for the formal command form of all but six verbs, four of which are given below, is that of the first person singular present indicative. Stem-changing verbs follow the same rule.

Poder cannot be used as a command, and the forms of **conocer, querer,** and **saber** are not used as commands in this text.

Vd. and **Vds.** are regularly expressed in commands and are placed after the verb; however, in a series of commands it is not necessary to repeat **Vd.** or **Vds.** with each one.

Four verbs whose first person singular present indicative ends in **-oy** do not follow the rule given above.

INFINITIVE	SINGULAR	PLURAL	
dar	**dé** Vd.	den Vds.	*give*
estar	**esté** Vd.	**estén** Vds.	*be*
ir	**vaya** Vd.	**vayan** Vds.	*go*
ser	**sea** Vd.	**sean** Vds.	*be*

Práctica.   Read in Spanish, noting the formal command forms:

ɪ. Deje Vd. el libro aquí; dejen Vds. los cuadernos allí.   2. Lea Vd. la revista; lean Vds. el programa.   3. Escriba Vd. la carta; no escriban Vds. las frases.   4. Cierre Vd. la puerta; no cierren Vds. las ventanas.   5. Traiga Vd. el vaso; traigan Vds. el café. 6. No dé Vd. el paseo ahora; den Vds. un paseo mañana.   7. Salga Vd. del cuarto; no salgan Vds. de la casa.   8. No vaya Vd. a la biblioteca; vayan Vds. al centro.

2. Familiar singular commands

INFINITIVE	AFFIRMATIVE		NEGATIVE	
hablar	habla (tú)	*speak*	no hables (tú)	*don't speak*
comer	come (tú)	*eat*	no comas (tú)	*don't eat*
abrir	abre (tú)	*open*	no abras (tú)	*don't open*
pensar	**piensa** (tú)	*think*	no **pienses** (tú)	*don't think*
volver	**vuelve** (tú)	*return*	no **vuelvas** (tú)	*don't return*

The affirmative familiar singular command, often called the singular imperative, of regular and stem-changing verbs has the same form as the third singular of the present indicative tense.   The pronoun **tú** is omitted, except for emphasis.

To form the negative familiar singular command of these verbs, add **-s** to the formal singular command form: (formal) **No abra Vd. la puerta,** (familiar) **Carlos, no abras la puerta.**   Certain verbs which have irregular affirmative singular command forms will be given later.

Remember that the **Vds.** form is used in this text for all plural commands, affirmative and negative.

In the case of reflexive verbs, the familiar **te** must be used:

levantarse:	levántate (tú)	*get up*	no te levantes	*don't get up*
sentarse:	**siénta**te (tú)	*sit down*	no te **sientes**	*don't sit down*

When object pronouns are attached to command forms in writing, an accent mark must be placed on the stressed syllable of a verb form of more than one syllable.

Práctica.   Read in Spanish, noting the familiar command forms:

ɪ. Compra tú el libro; no compres la pluma.   2. Llama tú a Marta; no llames a Carolina.   3. Mira tú la iglesia; no mires los escaparates.   4. Aprende tú las palabras; no aprendas las frases.   5. Lee tú el periódico; no leas los precios.   6. Lávate tú las manos; no te laves la cara.   7. Acuéstate ahora; no te acuestes todavía.   8. Contesta en español; no contestes en inglés.

B. Position of object pronouns in commands

> **Ábrala Vd.; Ábrela (tú).**   Open it.
> **No la abra Vd.; No la abras (tú).**   Don't open it.
> **Siéntense Vds.; No se sienten Vds.**   Sit down; Don't sit down.
> **Despiértate, Carlos.**   Wake up, Charles.
> **Déjalo (tú) sobre la mesa.**   Leave it on the table.
> **No lo dejes allí todavía.**   Don't leave it there yet.

You have learned that object pronouns are placed immediately before the verb in Spanish except when used as the object of an infinitive, in which case they are attached to it (Lesson 8). Now remember that they are also placed after the verb and are attached to it when used as the object of an affirmative command. In negative commands the object pronouns precede the verb.

Práctica.   Read in Spanish, noting the command forms:

1. Póngalo Vd. allí.   2. No lo ponga Vd. aquí.   3. Tráiganme Vds. sus cuadernos.
4. No me traigan Vds. sus libros.   5. Dénos Vd. café, por favor.   6. No nos dé Vd. café frío.   7. Hágame Vd. el favor de levantarse.   8. Levántese Vd., por favor.   9. Inés, acuéstate.   10. No te acuestes ahora.   11. Ciérrala tú, Carlos.   12. No la cierres todavía.

C. Expressions with **tener**

Juan tiene	{**calor.** **frío.** **hambre.** **sed.** **sueño.**	John is	{warm. cold. hungry. thirsty. sleepy.	

> **Ellos tienen mucho frío.**   They are very cold.
> **Marta y yo tenemos mucha hambre.**   Martha and I are very hungry.
> **El pobre tiene mucho sueño.**   The poor boy is very sleepy.

In describing certain physical and mental conditions of living beings, **tener** is used with nouns in Spanish to express the English equivalent of *to be* with adjectives. Since the words **calor, frío,** etc., are nouns in these expressions, they are modified by the adjective **mucho, -a,** not the adverb **muy.** **Hambre** and **sed** are feminine nouns and require **mucha.**

In the sentence **El café está muy frío,** *The coffee is very cold,* the word **frío** is an adjective and it must be modified by **muy.**

The definite article **el** is used instead of **la** with a few feminine nouns which begin with stressed **a-** or **ha-;** thus, one says **el hambre,** *hunger.* **Yo tengo hambre** means literally *I have hunger.*

Práctica.   Read in Spanish, keeping the meaning in mind:

1. Yo tengo frío; tengo mucho frío.   2. Marta tiene sueño; tiene mucho sueño.   3. Juan y yo tenemos calor; tenemos mucho calor.   4. Inés y Carolina tienen hambre; tienen mucha hambre.   5. ¿Tienes sed?   ¿Tienes mucha sed?   6. La limonada está fría; está muy fría.

D. Ways to express *time*

¿Qué hora es?   What time is it?
Podemos charlar un rato.   We can chat a short time (a while).
¿Siempre llega Vd. a tiempo?   Do you always arrive on time?
Tengo mucho tiempo para estudiar.   I have much time to study.
A veces doy un paseo.   At times I take a walk.
Esta vez no puedo.   This time I cannot.

You have already learned that **hora** is used to express *time of day* and that **un rato** is used for *a short time, a while.*

Tiempo refers to length of time or time in general (third and fourth examples). **Vez** (*pl.* **veces**) is used to express time in a series, such as *this time, the first time (occasion), at times,* etc. (last two examples).

Práctica.   Choose from **hora, rato, tiempo, vez,** or **veces** the correct word to complete each sentence:

1. Marta no va al centro con su mamá esta ———.   2. Mi papá no tiene mucho ——— hoy.   3. ¿Sabe Vd. qué ——— es?   4. Mi mamá va al mercado dos ——— cada semana.   5. Las estudiantes charlan mucho todo el ———.   6. Los jóvenes pasan un ——— aquí todos los días.   7. Yo veo a Juan de ——— en cuando.   8. Hoy no tengo ——— para dar un paseo.   9. ¿Van Vds. a la iglesia a esta ——— de la mañana?   10. ¿Siempre llegan Vds. a ———?

EJERCICIOS

A. Say after your teacher, then change to a singular and a plural formal command:

MODEL: Carlos toma el papel.   Carlos toma el papel.
                                    Tome Vd. el papel.   Tomen Vds. el papel.

1. Juan compra el sombrero.
2. Carmen escribe las frases.
3. Inés contesta en español.
4. Ana lee el periódico.

5. Ricardo sale de casa.
6. Marta trae las cosas.
7. Él no pone los libros aquí.
8. Ella no va con María.

B. Say after your teacher, then change to a familiar singular command, following the model:

>   MODEL: Juan abre la ventana.
>
>   Juan abre la ventana.
>   Juan, abre la ventana, por favor.

1. Carolina mira el cuadro.
2. Inés deja el cuaderno allí.
3. Juan aprende las palabras.

4. Marta abre la puerta.
5. Isabel cierra la ventana.
6. José vuelve a casa pronto.

When you hear the sentences again, make each one a negative familiar command.

>   MODEL: Juan abre la ventana.
>
>   Juan, no abras la ventana.

C. Say after your teacher, then repeat, making each sentence negative:

>   MODEL: Apréndalo Vd.
>
>   Apréndalo Vd.   No lo aprenda Vd.

1. Tráigalos Vd. ahora.
2. Póngalas Vd. aquí.
3. Díganos Vd. la verdad.
4. Levántese Vd. pronto.

5. Enséñenles Vds. los vestidos.
6. Siéntense Vds. allí.
7. Escríbanles Vds. mañana.
8. Ciérrenlas Vds. esta noche.

D. Place the pronoun correctly with each verb:

1. (me) Ellos despiertan. Quieren despertar. Despierte Vd. No despierte Vd.
2. (los) Juan cierra. Va a cerrar. Cierre Vd. No cierre Vd. 3. (lo) Inés hace.
Puede hacer. Haga Vd. No haga Vd. 4. (la) Yo llamo. Tengo que llamar.
Llame Vd. No llame Vd.

E. Listen to each question, then give formal affirmative and negative commands, using object pronouns for the noun objects:

>   MODELS: ¿Tomo el libro?
>   ¿Tomamos los libros?
>
>   Sí, tómelo Vd. *and* No, no lo tome Vd.
>   Sí, tómenlos Vds. *and* No, no los tomen Vds.

1. ¿Abro la puerta?
2. ¿Leo la carta?
3. ¿Cierro las ventanas?

4. ¿Compramos los vestidos?
5. ¿Ponemos las cosas allí?
6. ¿Traemos el dinero?

Answer, giving the familiar affirmative and negative singular commands:

MODELS: ¿Lo abro?   Sí, ábrelo tú *and* No, no lo abras.
       ¿Me lavo ahora?   Sí, lávate tú ahora *and* No, no te laves ahora.

7. ¿La escribo?   9. ¿Me levanto ahora?
8. ¿Los dejo allí?   10. ¿Me siento allí?

F. Read in Spanish, using the correct form of estar, ser, or tener:

1. La limonada no ——— fría. 2. Inés ——— calor. 3. Marta y Carolina ——— hambre. 4. ¿——— Vds. muy cansados? 5. Marta y Juan ——— mucho sueño ahora. 6. ¿——— tú mucha sed? 7. Carlos y yo no ——— mucho frío. 8. Antonio y yo no ——— profesores. 9. ——— necesario ir despacio esta vez. 10. Ya ——— la hora.

G. Give the Spanish for:

1. I bring the coffee. I bring it. Bring it. Do not bring it yet. 2. They sit down. They intend to sit down. Sit down (*pl.*). Don't sit down. 3. We wash our hands. We can wash our hands now. Wash (*pl.*) your hands. Do not wash your hands.

H. Write in Spanish:

1. Please (*pl.*) sit down and put your books on the desks. 2. John, close the door, please, and then open the windows. 3. After opening them, bring me your sentences for today. 4. Put them on the table; do not leave them on your desk. 5. When the teacher asks them questions, they always answer in Spanish. 6. Martha, are you very warm? — No, Miss Valdés, I am cold this morning. 7. Are you sleepy in class at times? — Yes, if I go to bed late. 8. Where do you go on Sundays? — My friends and I go to church. 9. What day is today? — Today is the last day of the week. 10. Very well. Take (*pl.*) your books in your hands; you must (should) not leave them here in the classroom.

EJERCICIOS DE PRONUNCIACIÓN

A. The pronunciation of y, *and*

The following principles govern the pronunciation of the conjunction **y**:

1. When initial in a breath-group before a consonant, or when between consonants, it is pronounced like the Spanish vowel **i**: **Y no la abras** (**Y-no-la-a-bras**), **dos y dos** (**do-s‿y-dos**).

2. When initial in a breath-group before a vowel, or when between vowels, it is pronounced like Spanish **y: ¿y usted? (¿y‿us-ted?), éste y aquél (és-te-y‿a-quél)**.

3. Between **d, s,** or **z** and a vowel within a breath-group, it is also pronounced like Spanish **y: usted y ella (us-ted-y‿e-lla), alumnos y amigos (a-lum-nos-y‿a-mi-gos)**.

4. Between **l, n,** or **r** and a vowel within a breath-group, it is pronounced as the first element of a diphthong, with the preceding consonant, the **y,** and the following vowel in a single syllable: **hablan y escriben (ha-bla-n y es-cri-ben), entrar y esperar (en-tra-r y es-pe-rar)**.

5. Between a vowel and a consonant, it forms a diphthong with the vowel that precedes it: **padre y madre (pa-dre‿y-ma-dre)**.

B. Apply the above principles as you read the following phrases and sentences in single breath-groups:

Hablan y pronuncian muy bien.	Vamos Carlos y yo.
España y América.	Y estudian el alemán, también.
Tengo un lápiz y un libro.	Estudio el inglés y el francés.
Hablar y escribir.	Miren y escuchen.
Tengo hambre y sed.	Tengo sed y hambre.

Sierra Nevada, Granada, Spain.

Indian women, La Paz, Bolivia

VOCABULARIO

el aire   air
  alguno, -a *adj. and pron.*   some, any,
    someone; *pl.* some, a few
  Antonio   Anthony, Tony
la atención   attention
el café   coffee
el calor   heat, warmth
  Carolina   Caroline
  cerrar (ie)   to close
  contestar   to answer, reply
  deber   to owe; must, should, ought to
  dejar   to leave (behind)
  despacio   slowly
  despertar (ie)   to wake up, awaken;
    reflex. wake up (oneself)
el domingo   Sunday, on Sunday
  fresco, -a   cool, fresh
el frío   cold

el hambre (*f.*)   hunger
la iglesia   church
  Inés   Inez, Agnes
  Isabel   Isabel, Betty, Elizabeth
  Juan   John
la leche   milk
  Marta   Martha
el paseo   walk, stroll, ride; boulevard
  pobre   poor
el pupitre   desk (*school*)
  saludar   to greet, speak (say hello) to
la sed   thirst
el sueño   sleep
  último, -a   last (*in a series*)
el vaso   glass
la vez (*pl.* **veces**)   time (*in a series*),
    occasion

a la iglesia   to church
a tiempo   on time
a veces   at times
con atención   attentively, carefully
dar un paseo   to take a walk (ride)
de vez en cuando   from time to time, occasionally
hacer una pregunta (a)   to ask a question (of)
haga (hágame) Vd. *or* **hagan (háganme) Vds. el favor de** + *inf.*   please + *verb*
los domingos   on Sundays
no dejen nada   leave nothing, don't leave anything (*see Lesson 10 for explanation*)
no (tomar) más que   (to take) only, (to take) nothing but
tener tiempo para   to have time to (for)
ya es la hora   the hour is over, it is the end of the hour (period)

Sidewalk café, Plaza Mayor, Salamanca, Spain.

CONVERSACIÓN I[1]

En un café español

(Ana y Carmen son dos jóvenes norteamericanas que están estudiando en Madrid. Salen de su pensión a las cuatro de la tarde para ir a la universidad y pasan por un café al aire libre. Sentado a una mesa, con un compañero, está Carlos, un joven madrileño a quien conocen las muchachas.)

CARLOS. ¡Hola! ¡Qué sorpresa más agradable! ¿Adónde van Vds. a esta hora?

ANA. Pues pensamos dar un paseo antes de ir a la universidad. Tenemos una clase de arte a las seis.

CARLOS. Pues falta mucho tiempo para las seis. ¿Por qué no nos acompañan un rato? Quiero presentar a mi compañero, Felipe Morales.

ANA Y CARMEN. Mucho gusto.

FELIPE. El gusto es mío, señoritas. ¿No quieren Vds. sentarse?

ANA. Parece que en España todo el mundo va al café por la tarde.

CARLOS. Es verdad. Venimos al café para conversar con los amigos. Aquí se habla de todo: de literatura, de música, de la situación política y económica... *(Se sientan las jóvenes y se presenta un camarero.)*

CAMARERO. Buenas tardes. ¿Desean Vds. tomar algo? ¿Café, té, chocolate, un refresco, un helado...?

CARLOS. Ana, ¿qué va a tomar Vd.?

ANA. Café, por favor.

CAMARERO. ¿Café solo o con leche?

ANA. Con leche, por favor.

CARLOS. En los Estados Unidos Vds. toman café con crema, ¿verdad? Mucho café y un poco de crema; en España tomamos mucha leche y poco café.

ANA. Sí, tomamos crema en el café y servimos el café en tazas. ¿Siempre toman Vds. el café en vasos?

FELIPE. No; en casa también usamos tazas, como en los Estados Unidos. Pero en los cafés generalmente sirven el café en vasos.

CARMEN. Y Vds. toman mucha azúcar, ¿verdad?

CARLOS. Sí, creo que tomamos más azúcar que Vds. Y, ¿qué quiere tomar Vd., Carmen?

CARMEN. Voy a tomar té, como siempre.

CAMARERO. ¿Con limón?

CARMEN. Sin limón, por favor, pero con un poco de azúcar.

---

[1] The teacher may assign the **Conversación** for close study, recognition, or comprehension, and students may compose similar dialogues. All new words listed at the end of each **Conversación** will be listed again when introduced in regular lessons.

125

CARLOS.   Y tú, Felipe, ¿qué vas a tomar?

FELIPE.   Por lo común tomo café con leche, pero hoy voy a tomar un helado.

CAMARERO.   ¿De vainilla o de chocolate?

FELIPE.   De vainilla, por favor.

CAMARERO.   ¿Quiere Vd. café con el helado?

FELIPE.   No, gracias.   Un vaso de agua, solamente.

CARLOS.   Pues, yo voy a tomar chocolate.

CAMARERO.   ¿Desean Vds. unos pasteles también?

CARLOS.   Gracias, hoy no deseamos nada más.

CAMARERO.   Muy bien.   Vuelvo en seguida.

PREGUNTAS

Sobre la conversación

1. ¿Son españolas Ana y Carmen?   2. ¿Quiénes están sentados a una mesa en un café al aire libre?   3. ¿Qué piensan hacer las muchachas?   4. ¿A qué hora tienen una clase de arte?   5. ¿Qué dice Ana del café español?   6. ¿De qué hablan los españoles en el café?

7. ¿Qué va a tomar Ana?   8. ¿Cómo toman el café en España?   9. ¿Servimos el café en vasos en los Estados Unidos?   10. ¿Qué toma Carmen?   11. ¿Qué toma Felipe por lo común?   12. ¿Cuál es la última pregunta que les hace el camarero?

Aplicación de la conversación

1. ¿Hay un café al aire libre cerca de esta universidad?   2. ¿Van los estudiantes al café todos los días en los Estados Unidos?   3. ¿Vive Vd. en una pensión?   4. ¿Cuántas clases tiene Vd. por la tarde?   5. ¿Tiene Vd. clase a las seis de la tarde?   6. ¿Le gustan a Vd. las clases de literatura?

7. ¿Generalmente toma Vd. café o té?   8. ¿Tomamos el café con leche en los Estados Unidos?   9. ¿Toma Vd. mucha azúcar en el café?   10. ¿Le gusta a Vd. el té con limón?   11. ¿Tiene Vd. sed ahora?   12. ¿Qué toma Vd. por lo común cuando desea un refresco por la tarde?

PRÁCTICAS ORALES   (*Oral practice*)

Groups of students will be selected to prepare a conversation of six to eight exchanges, using vocabulary already given.

1. In one group two American students meet Spanish friends and speak briefly about their studies.

2. In other groups one student serves as waiter (waitress, **la camarera**) and takes the orders of other students.

VOCABULARIO

el agua (*f.*)[1] water
el(la) azúcar sugar
el camarero waiter
  conversar to converse, talk
la crema cream
el chocolate chocolate
  económico, -a economic
el helado ice cream
el limón (*pl.* **limones**) lemon
la literatura literature
  madrileño, -a native of Madrid
  parecer to appear, seem
el pastel pastry

la pensión (*pl.* **pensiones**)
  boardinghouse
  poco, -a little (*quantity*)
  presentar to present, introduce
  quien who, whom
el refresco cold *or* soft drink
  servimos we serve
  sin *prep.* without
  sirven they serve
la situación (*pl.* **situaciones**) situation
la taza cup
el té tea
la vainilla vanilla

  al aire libre outdoor, open-air
  café solo black coffee
  el gusto es mío the pleasure is mine
  falta mucho tiempo para las seis it is a long time before six
  mucho gusto (I am) pleased *or* glad to know you
  no deseamos nada más we don't want anything else
  ¡qué sorpresa más agradable! what a pleasant surprise!
  se habla one talks, people talk
  se presenta un camarero a waiter appears (presents himself)
  todo el mundo everybody
  vuelvo en seguida I'll be right back, I'll return at once

---

[1] See page 117 for explanation of the use of the definite article **el** with certain feminine nouns.

Bodega Bar in Málaga, Spain.

LECCIÓN 10

The preterit indicative of regular verbs
Preterit of *dar*, *ir*, and *ser*.   Use of the preterit
Indefinite and negative expressions
The definite article with expressions of time

EN EL COMEDOR DE LA RESIDENCIA DE ESTUDIANTES

JOSÉ.   ¡Hola, Juan!   ¿Qué pasó ayer?   Traté de llamarte por teléfono entre las cinco y las seis de la tarde, y nadie me contestó.

JUAN.   Es que llevé[1] a mis padres al aeropuerto.   Salieron para Los Ángeles en el avión de las cinco y media.

JOSÉ.   No cenaste en la residencia, ¿verdad?

JUAN.   No, José.   Cené en el aeropuerto temprano y después fui a casa de María.   Charlamos un rato y miramos unos[2] programas de televisión.

JOSÉ.   ¿No te dio tu padre permiso para usar el coche?

JUAN.   ¡Cómo no!   Después dimos un paseo por el parque y tomamos un refresco en el café.

• • • • •

JUAN.   Y tú, José, ¿no saliste anoche?

JOSÉ.   ¡Hombre, nunca me quedo en casa los sábados por la noche!   Llevé a Isabel al cine. Como salimos tarde del cine, volvimos a casa sin visitar a nadie.

JUAN.   ¿Qué película vieron Vds.?

JOSÉ.   Una magnífica[3] película mexicana.   Hay algunos números de baile muy bonitos, especialmente el *jarabe tapatío*, el baile nacional de México.

JUAN.   Mis padres vieron esa película la semana pasada.   Les gustó mucho.   Hay una orquesta que toca canciones típicas, ¿verdad?

[1] **Llevar** is used when *to take* means *to carry* or *take* (something or someone) to a place.   **Tomar** means *to take* in the sense of *to take up* or *pick up* (*e.g.*, take something in one's hand) or *to take something to eat or drink*.   [2] In Lesson 9 you learned that **algunos, -as,** means *some, a few*.   **Unos, -as,** also means *some, a few, several*.   **Algunos, -as,** has a slightly stronger numerical meaning than **unos, -as.**   [3] Note that the descriptive adjective **magnífica** precedes the noun; also note **hermosos** in line 3, page 130.   There will be no drill on this point in the exercises.   Note similar cases in later lessons and the explanation on pages 265–266.

José.   Sí, y hay dos jóvenes mexicanos — un muchacho y una muchacha — que cantan y bailan bastante bien.

Juan.   A propósito, María y yo vimos unos hermosos bailes españoles en uno de los programas de televisión.   Anunciaron que el grupo que vimos en el programa va a trabajar en Nueva York la semana que viene.

José.   Creo que es el grupo que anuncia un periódico que alguien dejó en mi cuarto.   Espero tener la oportunidad de verlo.

Juan.   Yo también.   Pero ahora tengo que irme.   María me espera en la biblioteca. Hasta la vista, José.

José.   Hasta la vista.

CONVERSACIÓN

A. Preguntas sobre el diálogo

1. ¿Qué le dice José a Juan?   2. ¿Para dónde salieron los padres de Juan?   3. ¿Dónde cenó Juan?   4. ¿Qué miraron Juan y María?   5. ¿Qué película vieron Isabel y José? 6. ¿Cuál es el baile nacional de México? 7. Qué anunciaron acerca del grupo español?   8. ¿Quién espera tener la oportunidad de ver los bailes?

B. Aplicación del diálogo

1. ¿Visitó Vd. a sus amigos ayer?   2. ¿Se queda Vd. en casa los sábados por la noche? 3. ¿Habló Vd. por teléfono con sus padres la semana pasada?   4. ¿Dónde cenó Vd. anoche?   5. ¿A qué cines fueron Vds. el mes pasado?   6. ¿Qué programas de televisión miraron Vds. ayer?   7. ¿Vuelve Vd. a casa temprano cuando estudia con sus amigas?   8. ¿Habla Vd. mucho por teléfono?

NOTAS GRAMATICALES

A. The preterit indicative of regular verbs

hablar		**comer**		**vivir**	
SING.	PLURAL	SING.	PLURAL	SING.	PLURAL
hablé	hablamos	comí	comimos	viví	vivimos
hablaste	hablasteis	comiste	comisteis	viviste	vivisteis
habló	hablaron	comió	comieron	vivió	vivieron

The preterit tense is formed by adding the endings **-é, -aste, -ó, -amos, -asteis, -aron** to the infinitive stem of **-ar** verbs, or the endings **-í, -iste, -ió, -imos, -isteis, -ieron** to the stem of **-er** and **-ir** verbs. Remember that **-er** and **-ir** verbs have identical endings, except in the first and second persons plural of the present indicative tense. The stress is on the ending in the preterit, and the first and third persons singular of regular verbs have a written accent.

The preterit is translated like the English past tense: **hablé,** *I spoke, did speak;* **Vd. comió,** *you ate, did eat;* **vivieron,** *they lived, did live.* In questions and negative statements *did* is used in English, but not in Spanish:

> **¿Escribió Vd. la carta?** Did you write the letter?
> **Juan no se quedó en casa.** John didn't stay at home.

Stem-changing verbs that end in **-ar** and **-er** are regular in the preterit; for example, **pensar: pensé, pensaste, pensó,** etc.; **volver: volví, volviste, volvió,** etc.

B. Irregular preterit of **dar, ir,** and **ser**

dar		**ir, ser**	
SINGULAR	PLURAL	SINGULAR	PLURAL
di	**dimos**	**fui**	**fuimos**
diste	**disteis**	**fuiste**	**fuisteis**
dio	**dieron**	**fue**	**fueron**

Di is translated *I gave, did give;* **fui,** *I went, did go,* or *I was.* **Ir** and **ser** have identical forms, but context makes the meaning clear.

Conocer and **salir** are regular in the preterit. Accents, previously used, are now omitted on **di, dio, fui, fue,** and **vi, vio** (preterit forms of **ver**).

C. Use of the preterit

> **Cené en el aeropuerto temprano.** I ate supper early in (at) the airport.
> **Charlamos un rato.** We chatted a while.
> **¿Qué pasó ayer?** What happened yesterday?
> **Juan no vivió aquí más que dos años.** John lived here only two years.

The preterit, sometimes called the past definite, is the narrative past tense in Spanish. It indicates that an action began, that an action ended, or that a past action or state was completed within a definite period of time, regardless of the length of duration.

D. Indefinite and negative expressions

algo	something, anything	**nada**	nothing, (not) ... anything
alguien	someone, somebody, anybody, anyone	**nadie**	no one, nobody, (not) ... anybody (anyone)
siempre	always	**nunca**	never, (not) ... ever

Los muchachos tienen algo. The boys have something.
No tengo nada *or* **Nada tengo.** I have nothing (I don't have anything).
Nadie me contestó *or* **No me contestó nadie.** No one answered me.
Yo nunca me quedo en casa. I never stay at home.
No hablé con nadie anoche. I did not talk with anyone last night.
Juan estudia más que nunca. John studies more than ever.

The negatives **nada, nadie,** and **nunca** may either precede or follow a verb. When they follow, **no** or some other negative must precede the verb. If these negatives come before the verb or are used without a verb, **no** is not required: **¿Qué está Vd. haciendo?** — **Nada.** *What are you doing?* — *Nothing.* After **que,** *than,* a negative is used.

The pronouns **alguien** and **nadie** refer only to persons, unknown or not mentioned before, and the personal **a** is required when they are used as objects of the verb:

¿Ve Vd. a alguien? Do you see anyone?
No vimos a nadie. We did not see anyone (We saw nobody).
Volvimos sin visitar a nadie. We returned without visiting anyone.

Alguno, used as an adjective or pronoun (see footnote p. 113), refers to persons or things already thought of or mentioned:

Hay algunos números de baile. There are some dance numbers.
Alguno de los hombres llamó. Someone of the men called.
Isabel cantó algunas canciones. Betty sang some (a few) songs.

E. The definite article with expressions of time

Los dos vieron la película la semana pasada. Both saw the film last week.
Ellos fueron a México el año pasado. They went to Mexico last year.
Yo espero verlos el mes que viene. I hope to see them next month.

When an expression of time, such as **semana, mes, año,** a day of the week, is modified by an adjective, the definite article must be used.

Contrast **pasado,** *last, past* (just passed), with **último,** *last* (in a series).

EJERCICIOS

A. Substitution drill:

1. *Yo* hablé con Isabel.
   (*Marta, Nosotros, Ellos, Vd., Tú*)
2. *Los hombres* comieron a las siete.
   (*José, Yo, Luis y yo, Tú, Vds.*)
3. *Ana* no fue con nadie.
   (*Yo, Tú, Ella y yo, María, María y Marta*)
4. *Alguien* volvió a casa.
   (*Nadie, Yo, Ellos, Tú, Juan y yo*)
5. ¿La cerró *Jorge*?
   (*Vds., tú, yo, Carolina, nosotros*)

B. Read each sentence in Spanish, then repeat, changing the verbs from the present tense to the preterit:

1. No me levanto hasta las siete y media. 2. Me lavo las manos y la cara. 3. Después bajo al comedor y me siento a la mesa. 4. Mi hermano se despierta tarde y no se desayuna. 5. Salgo de casa y voy a mi clase de español. 6. Antes de sentarme, abro las ventanas. 7. El profesor entra y saluda a los estudiantes. 8. Nos habla en español y le contestamos. 9. Pero algunos estudiantes no contestan nada. 10. La clase termina a las nueve menos diez, y todos los estudiantes salen despacio. 11. Algunos toman sus libros en las manos y los llevan a casa. 12. Carlos y yo vamos a la biblioteca. 13. No volvemos a la residencia de estudiantes hasta las doce. 14. Nos quedamos allí hasta las dos de la tarde.

C. Answer affirmatively in Spanish:

1. ¿Se despertó Vd. temprano?
2. ¿Se levantó Vd. tarde?
3. ¿Te sentaste en la sala?
4. ¿Te desayunaste en el comedor?
5. ¿Fuiste al cine con Inés?
6. ¿Cantaron Vds. algunas canciones?
7. ¿Se quedaron Vds. en casa?
8. ¿Fueron Vds. a casa de Juan?
9. ¿Dieron Vds. un paseo ayer?
10. ¿Trataron Vds. de ver los bailes?

D. Repeat each negative sentence, then make an affirmative one:

MODELS: Nadie canta ahora. Nadie canta ahora. Alguien canta ahora.
Nunca me dan nada. Nunca me dan nada. Siempre me dan algo.

1. Marta y yo no vimos a nadie.
2. Aquellos hombres no saben nada.
3. Inés no piensa ir con nadie.
4. Juan nunca da nada a nadie.
5. No hay nada en la mesa.
6. Nadie le lleva nada a Juan.

E. Repeat the question after your teacher.   When you hear the question again, use the corresponding negative in your answer:

MODELS: ¿Ve Vd. algo?   ¿Ve Vd. algo?
          ¿Ve Vd. algo?   No, no veo nada.
          ¿Viene alguien?   ¿Viene alguien?
          ¿Viene alguien?   No, nadie viene *or* No, no viene nadie.

  1. ¿Tiene Vd. algo?   5. ¿Canta alguien ahora?
  2. ¿Está Vd. haciendo algo?   6. ¿Siempre llega Vd. a tiempo?
  3. ¿Busca Vd. a alguien?   7. ¿Hay algo en el pupitre?
  4. ¿Vas con alguien?   8. ¿Tienes algo en la mano?

  9. ¿Le llevó Vd. algo a Juan?   11. ¿Fue alguien al cine?
10. ¿Viste a alguien ayer?   12. ¿Le diste algo al profesor?

F. After reviewing the command forms in Lesson 9, read each sentence in Spanish. Then turn each sentence into a command, as indicated:

FAM. SING.:   1. Isabel escribe en español.   3. José no baila con la orquesta.
               2. Juan lleva a Inés al cine.   4. Marta no se queda en casa.

FORMAL SING.: 5. Carlos me hace preguntas.   7. Luis no da un paseo hoy.
               6. Inés se compra una bolsa.   8. José no toma un refresco.

FORMAL PLURAL: 9. Se sientan en el comedor.   11. No me traen nada.
              10. Los llevan al aeropuerto.   12. No les dan permiso para ir.

G. When you hear the question, give the formal affirmative and negative commands, then the familiar:

MODEL: ¿Me acuesto?   Sí, acuéstese Vd. *and* No, no se acueste Vd.
                                               Sí, acuéstate tú *and* No, no te acuestes.

1. ¿Me lavo?   2. ¿Me levanto?   3. ¿Me siento?   4. ¿Me desayuno?

H. Write in Spanish (using familiar forms for *you*):

1. Charles, wait a moment.   Where did you go yesterday?   2. No one answered when I tried to call you by telephone.   3. Well, John, my parents left for New York, and I took them to the airport at four o'clock.   4. Before returning home, Mary and I went to a café where we chatted a while.   5. We ate supper early and then we went to Martha's.   6. Later she and Louis took us to the movies.   7. Did you stay at home or did you go to the movies too?   8. Man!   I never stay at home on Saturday nights.

9. Betty and I saw a film in which there are some Mexican dances.   10. There is an orchestra which plays some songs which are very pretty.   11. After taking cold drinks in another café, we returned home without seeing anyone.   12. Next week we hope to have the opportunity to see a program of Spanish dances.

EJERCICIOS DE PRONUNCIACIÓN

A. The diphthongs **ue** and **eu**

1. As the first element of a diphthong, unstressed **u** is pronounced like *w* in *wet*:

luego	puedo	llueve	escuela
sueño	su hermano	su examen	tu hermana

2. Spanish **eu** has no close equivalent in English.   It consists of a Spanish **e,** followed closely by a glide sound which ends in English *oo*, to sound like *ehoo*:

Europa	¿quiere usted?	¿sabe usted?	busque usted
hable usted	pase usted	pronuncie usted	siéntese usted

B. Spanish intonation

Review the observations on Spanish intonation in Appendix C; then read the first four exchanges of the dialogues of this lesson, paying close attention to the intonation patterns.

C. Dictado

The teacher will select four exchanges of the dialogues of this or of the preceding lesson as an exercise in dictation.

VOCABULARIO

el aeropuerto airport
alguien someone, somebody, any-body, anyone
anoche last night
anunciar to announce, advertise
ayer yesterday
bailar to dance
el baile dance
bastante *adj. and pron.* enough, sufficient; *adv.* quite (a bit), rather

la canción (*pl.* **canciones**) song
cantar to sing
el cine movie(s)
después *adv.* afterwards, later
entre among, between
especialmente especially
el (la) estudiante student
el grupo group
irse to go (away), leave
llevar to take, carry

magnífico, -a magnificent, fine
la muchacha girl
el muchacho boy
nacional national
nadie no one, nobody, (not)... anybody (anyone)
Nueva York New York
el número number
nunca never, (not)... ever
la oportunidad opportunity
la orquesta orchestra
pasado, -a past, last
pasar to happen

la película film
el permiso permission
presentar to present, introduce; give (*a performance*)
quedarse to stay, remain
el refresco refreshment, cold (soft) drink
el sábado Saturday, on Saturday
sin *prep.* without
el teléfono telephone
típico, -a typical
tocar to play (*music*), touch
unos, -as some, a few, several

a propósito by the way
avión de las cinco y media five-thirty (5:30) plane
dar permiso para (usar) to give permission to (use)
en el aeropuerto in (at) the airport
es que the fact is (that)
(ir) a casa de (María) (to go) to (Mary's)
(la semana) que viene next (week)
los sábados por la noche (on) Saturday nights
llamar por teléfono to telephone, call by telephone
número de baile dance number
salir para to leave for
tener la oportunidad de + *inf.* to have the opportunity to + *verb*
tratar de + *inf.* to try to + *verb*

Night view of the Panamá Canal.

LECTURA IV

LOS OTROS PAÍSES HISPANOAMERICANOS

Estudio de palabras

a. Exact cognates. Pronounce the following words in Spanish, taking care to stress the proper syllable: canal, central, general, interior, original, popular, principal, tropical.

b. Adverbs in *-ly*. The Spanish ending **-mente** is often equivalent to English *-ly*: especialmente, *especially*. *What is the meaning of* principalmente?

c. Verb cognates

1. The English verb has no ending: comprender (*to comprehend, understand*), formar, pasar (*to pass*).
2. Spanish verbs in **-ar** often end in *-ate* in English: cultivar, predominar.
3. The English verb ends in *-e*: consumir.

d. Approximate and less approximate cognates. Pronounce the following words aloud and then observe the English meaning: isla, *island*; literatura, *literature*; maíz, *maize, corn*; origen, *origen*; orquesta, *orchestra*; producto, *product*; ritmo, *rhythm*; tabaco, *tobacco*.

Si vamos en avión de México a Panamá, pasamos por cinco de las repúblicas que forman la América Central: Guatemala, El Salvador, Honduras, Nicaragua y Costa Rica. Estos pequeños países cultivan café, bananas y otros productos tropicales que consumimos en los Estados Unidos. Panamá es importante especialmente por el canal del mismo nombre.

En Costa Rica la mayor parte de los habitantes son de origen europeo. En Guatemala predomina la población india. En los otros países de la América Central la mayor parte de los habitantes son mestizos. La población negra se encuentra principalmente en las costas. El clima es tropical en las costas, pero es agradable en las mesetas altas.

Dos pequeñas repúblicas hispanoamericanas se encuentran en el Mar Caribe. Cuba es una isla bastante grande que está muy cerca de los Estados Unidos. En media hora, más o menos, podemos ir en avión desde la Florida hasta la Habana. Muchas canciones y muchos bailes que son muy populares en nuestro país vienen de la[1] Cuba tropical y romántica. Y nuestras orquestas tocan rumbas, congas y otros ritmos latinoamericanos. El tango, otro ritmo popular, no es de Cuba; es de la Argentina. La samba es del Brasil.

La República Dominicana es parte de la isla de Santo Domingo. En esta isla se encuentra Haití, otra república pequeña, en donde se habla francés. Así vemos que se hablan tres lenguas romances en la América

---

[1] The definite article must be used with proper names when they are modified.

Mayan sculpture, Mexico

latina: el español, el portugués y el francés. La isla de Puerto Rico pertenece[1] a los Estados Unidos, pero por su lengua y su cultura forma parte del mundo hispánico.

En todas estas islas la vegetación es tropical y hermosa. Algunos de los productos principales son la caña de azúcar,[2] el café y el tabaco. El tabaco es uno de los productos originales del Nuevo Mundo; también lo[3] es el maíz, que hoy día se encuentra en todas partes de América.

En todas las islas del Mar Caribe se encuentran muchos habitantes de origen africano. Hay una gran influencia negra en la literatura, la música y las costumbres de esta región. Ya sabemos que en todos los países latinoamericanos hay varias razas y no debemos olvidar[4] que cada región tiene sus propias[5] costumbres.

En las lecturas siguientes[6] vamos a continuar nuestro estudio de España y de los países hispanoamericanos. Para comprender los problemas de la América española hay que saber[7] algo acerca de la cultura indígena y de la cultura europea; en realidad, hay que saber algo de la historia, de la vida y del pensamiento[8] de todo el mundo hispánico.

---

[1] **pertenece,** *belongs.*   [2] **la caña de azúcar,** *sugar cane.*   [3] The neuter pronoun **lo** is used to refer to the predicate of the preceding clause, which is understood in this clause.   [4] **olvidar,** *forget.*   [5] **propias,** *own.*   [6] **siguientes,** *following.*   [7] **hay que saber,** *one must (it is necessary to) know.*   [8] **pensamiento,** *thought.*

Students leaving their classes at the University of Costa Rica at San José.

Cristo street, Old San Juan, Puerto Rico.

View of El Morro fortress, built by the Spaniards during colonial times, San Juan, Puerto Rico.

La América Central y el Caribe

PREGUNTAS

1. ¿Cuántos países forman la América Central?   2. ¿Cuáles son?   3. ¿Son grandes?

4. ¿Qué cultivan en la América Central?   5. ¿Por qué es importante Panamá?

6. ¿En qué país son de origen europeo la mayor parte de los habitantes?   7. ¿Dónde hay muchos indios?   8. ¿Hay negros en la América Central?   9. ¿Cómo es el clima?

10. ¿Qué es Cuba?   11. ¿Dónde está situada?   12. ¿Qué tocan nuestras orquestas?
13. ¿De dónde es el tango?   14. ¿De dónde es la samba?

15. ¿Qué repúblicas se encuentran en la isla de Santo Domingo?   16. ¿Qué lengua se habla en Haití?   17. ¿Qué lenguas romances se hablan en la América latina?
18. ¿A qué país pertenece Puerto Rico?

19. ¿Cómo es la vegetación en todas estas islas?   20. ¿Cuáles son algunos de los productos principales?   21. ¿Qué productos son originales de las Américas?

22. ¿En qué encontramos una gran influencia negra?   23. ¿Qué hay en todos los países latinoamericanos?

24. ¿Qué vamos a continuar en las lecturas siguientes?   25. ¿Qué hay que saber para comprender los problemas de la América española?

REPASO II

A. Say after your teacher, then repeat, changing the verbs to the preterit:

1. Yo la veo. 2. Yo no le doy el dinero. 3. Tomás la lleva al baile. 4. Los muchachos van al cine. 5. Luis y Ana ven una película. 6. Después vuelven a casa. 7. Vd. se acuesta tarde, ¿verdad? 8. Vd. se levanta temprano. 9. Marta y yo salimos de casa. 10. Ella y yo damos un paseo. 11. Alguien llama a la puerta. 12. Nadie la abre. 13. ¿Buscas a alguien? 14. ¿Le enseñas a bailar? 15. Dejan los sombreros en la silla. 16. Llueve mucho. 17. Se abren las puertas a las diez. 18. Se cierran a las cinco.

B. Choose from the verbs listed the correct form of the present tense to complete each sentence in the group:

1. (**dar, hacer, llevar, tomar**) a. Juan no ———— más que café. b. A menudo José ———— a Inés a bailar. c. Mis padres no ———— un viaje a España. d. ¿———— Vd. un paseo con María todas las tardes? e. ¿Te ———— tu mamá al parque a veces?

2. (**estar, ser, tener**) a. Mi hermana ———— mucho frío. b. Esta leche no ———— fría. c. Ya ———— la hora. d. ¿———— mucha hambre las muchachas? e. Mi tía no ———— profesora. f. Los estudiantes ———— en el café. g. Ana y yo ———— sueño. h. La orquesta ———— buena. i. Ellas ———— cansadas. j. Hoy ———— el último día de la semana.

3. (**conocer, saber**) a. Creo que Juan ———— la lección. b. ¿———— ella el baile nacional de México? c. Yo ———— bien al señor Valdés. d. ¿———— Vds. si Juan llega en el avión de las dos? e. ¿———— tú aquella película mexicana? f. Yo no ———— dónde están las muchachas.

4. (**dejar, salir**) a. Por lo común yo ———— el sombrero en casa. b. La empleada ———— el vestido en el escaparate. c. ¿A qué hora ———— tú cada mañana? d. A veces el avión ———— tarde del aeropuerto.

C. Repeat after your teacher. When you hear a cue, substitute it and make the necessary changes in the sentence:

1. Me gusta *la bolsa*. (los sombreros)
2. Le gusta a Inés *la película*. (las dos orquestas)
3. No nos gustan *aquellos autobuses*. (aquel avión)
4. ¿Le gustan a Tomás *estas canciones*? (este baile)
5. *Alguien* llamó a la puerta. (Nadie)
6. Escuchamos *unos* programas. (algunos)

D. Listen to each sentence, then change to a singular formal command:

1. Inés compra el vestido.
2. Ricardo vuelve a casa temprano.
3. Isabel se sienta en la sala.
4. Marta se pone el sombrero.
5. Carmen se levanta de la silla.
6. Enrique no da un paseo con Ana.

Change each sentence to an affirmative and negative singular familiar command:

7. Luis abre las ventanas.
8. Roberto deja su libro en la mesa.
9. María cierra la puerta.
10. Carmen se levanta del pupitre.
11. Felipe se lava las manos.
12. Dorotea se queda en casa.

E. Listen to each sentence, then change to an affirmative and a negative singular formal command, substituting object pronouns for the noun objects:

1. Jorge escribe la carta.
2. Dorotea lee las revistas.
3. Carlos mira los cuadros.
4. Tomás trae a su hermano.
5. Inés llama a su hermana.
6. Juan espera a sus amigos.
7. José cierra la ventana.
8. María escucha a su mamá.

F. Listen to each sentence, then repeat, substituting the correct object pronoun for the noun:

1. Juan compró el sombrero. 2. María tomó los guantes. 3. ¿Vio Vd. a las muchachas? 4. ¿Esperó Vd. a Dorotea? 5. ¿Llevó Vd. a Roberto al cine? 6. Deje Vd. el coche aquí. 7. Cante Vd. las canciones ahora. 8. No despiertes al muchacho. 9. No traigas el dinero todavía. 10. Yo debo escuchar el programa. 11. Ella piensa comprar dos vestidos. 12. ¿Puedes dejar la bolsa aquí?

G. Give in Spanish:

1. Are you going to church tomorrow? 2. What's new? 3. What is his name? 4. Betty's sister is at (**en**) the university, isn't she? 5. Why are you taking the trip by car? 6. John is leaving on the four-o'clock plane. 7. Tony went to Martha's. 8. I have only five dollars. 9. Sit down here, please. 10. Please arrive on time. 11. Don't try (*fam. s.*) to call me tonight. 12. Write (*fam. s.*) me from time to time. 13. Mr. Gómez wants to come next week. 14. I don't have time to go shopping. 15. My father gave me permission to use the car. 16. What are you doing? — Nothing special.

H. Answer in a complete Spanish sentence, using words which you have had:

1. ¿Qué lee Vd. todos los días? 2. Por lo común, ¿a qué hora sale Vd. de casa? 3. ¿Le gusta a Vd. levantarse temprano? 4. ¿Se levanta Vd. a las seis? 5. ¿A qué hora se desayunó Vd. esta mañana? 6. ¿Toma Vd. un autobús todas las mañanas? 7. ¿Dónde compramos las cosas que necesitamos? 8. ¿A qué hora se cierran las tiendas aquí? 9. ¿Adónde vamos a menudo los domingos? 10. ¿Fue Vd. al cine la semana pasada? 11. ¿Dio Vd. un paseo el sábado pasado? 12. ¿Llamó Vd. a alguien por teléfono anoche?

LECCIÓN 11

The imperfect indicative tense

Uses of the imperfect tense.   Expressions with *hacer*

Use of the definite article with the seasons

LA COMPOSICIÓN DE PABLO

(*Eduardo entra en el cuarto de su amigo Pablo.*)

PABLO.   ¡Pasa, Eduardo!   Necesito tu ayuda.

EDUARDO.   Pues, ¿qué hacías cuando entré?

PABLO.   Trataba de comenzar una composición en español para mañana.   ¿Quieres darme algunas ideas?

EDUARDO.   Vamos a ver.   ¿Sobre qué pensabas escribir la composición?   Mira, ¿dónde vivían Vds. cuando eras pequeño?

PABLO.   Vivíamos en el campo.

• • • • •

EDUARDO.   ¿Te gustaba vivir en el campo, Pablo?

PABLO.   ¡Cómo no!   Me gustaba mucho.   Mi hermano y yo podíamos montar a caballo todos los días.   A veces mi padre nos llevaba en coche a sitios muy bonitos en las montañas.

145

EDUARDO. Era especialmente agradable dar esos paseos en el verano, ¿verdad?

PABLO. Sí; cuando hacía sol, hacía mucho calor en casa, pero en las montañas siempre hacía fresco. Nos gustaba mucho pasearnos bajo la sombra de los árboles altos y hermosos de los bosques.

• • • • •

EDUARDO. Las otras estaciones eran agradables también, ¿no es verdad?

PABLO. En la primavera siempre hacía buen tiempo. Pero en el invierno hacía mucho frío, y entonces[1] las montañas estaban cubiertas de nieve.

EDUARDO. Recuerdo que un día de otoño fueron Vds. a un sitio que estaba muy lejos y que el paseo no fue muy agradable.

PABLO. Es verdad; salimos de casa muy temprano y comimos bajo los árboles. A las tres de la tarde vimos que había muchas nubes en el cielo. Hacía mucho viento y parecía que iba a llover.

EDUARDO. ¿Por qué no volvieron a casa en seguida?

PABLO. Porque mi hermano y yo insistimos en quedarnos un rato más. Poco después comenzó a llover. El agua[2] corría por todas partes. Sólo eran las cuatro de la tarde, y casi no podíamos ver el camino. El viaje a casa fue muy difícil.

EDUARDO. Pues ya tienes muchas ideas para tu composición.

PABLO. Muchas gracias, Eduardo. Ahora va a ser fácil escribir la composición.

CONVERSACIÓN

A. Preguntas sobre el diálogo

1. ¿Qué hacía Pablo cuando entró Eduardo en su cuarto? 2. ¿Dónde vivía la familia de Pablo? 3. ¿Le gustaba a Pablo vivir en el campo? 4. ¿Qué podían hacer Pablo y su hermano? 5. ¿Qué les gustaba hacer en el verano? 6. ¿En qué estación hacía siempre buen tiempo? 7. ¿Adónde fue la familia un día de otoño? 8. ¿Qué pasó a las tres de la tarde?

B. Aplicación del diálogo

1. ¿Hace buen tiempo hoy? 2. ¿Hace frío hoy? 3. ¿Hace sol ahora? 4. ¿Hay nubes en el cielo? 5. ¿Qué tiempo hace aquí en el verano? 6. ¿En qué estación llueve más aquí? 7. ¿Le gusta a Vd. montar a caballo? 8. ¿Por qué es agradable la primavera?

---

[1] **Entonces** means *then* in the sense of *at that time*. When *then* means *next, later*, **luego** is used. [2] Remember that the article **el** is used instead of **la** with a few feminine nouns which begin with stressed **a-** or **ha-**. See page 117.

NOTAS GRAMATICALES

A. The imperfect indicative tense

1. The regular verbs **hablar, comer, vivir:**

SINGULAR

hablaba	comía	vivía
hablabas	comías	vivías
hablaba	comía	vivía

PLURAL

hablábamos	comíamos	vivíamos
hablabais	comíais	vivíais
hablaban	comían	vivían

The imperfect tense is translated: **hablaba,** *I was talking, used to (would) talk, talked* (habitually).

Note that **-er** and **-ir** verbs have the same endings in the imperfect tense. All forms of these two conjugations bear an accent mark, while only the first person plural of **-ar** verbs is accented. Since the first and third persons singular are identical in all verbs in the imperfect tense, the subject pronouns must be used more often than with other tenses.

2. The irregular verbs **ir, ser,** and **ver:**

ir: **iba, ibas, iba, íbamos, ibais, iban**
ser: **era, eras, era, éramos, erais, eran**
ver: **veía, veías, veía, veíamos, veíais, veían**

Ir, ser, and **ver** are the only verbs in Spanish which have irregular forms in the imperfect tense. The meanings are: **iba,** *I was going, used to go, went;* **era,** *I used to be, was;* **veía,** *I used to see, was seeing, saw.*

B. Uses of the imperfect tense

The imperfect indicative tense, often called the past descriptive, is used to describe past actions, scenes, or conditions which were continuing for an indefinite period of time in the past. The speaker transfers himself mentally to the past and views the action or condition as taking place before him. There is no reference to the beginning or the end of the action or condition. The preterit, as we learned in Lesson 10, indicates that an action was completed or that an existing condition ended. The imperfect tense always translates English *used to* plus the infinitive, and usually *was* (*were*) plus the present participle. Note carefully the following examples in which the imperfect is used:

1. To express description in past time:

El agua corría por todas partes. The water ran (was running) everywhere.
Hacía mucho calor en casa. At home it was very warm.
Había muchas nubes en el cielo. There were many clouds in the sky.
En los bosques siempre hacía fresco. In the forests it was always cool.

2. To indicate repeated or habitual past action, equivalent to English *used to* or *would*:

¿Dónde vivías cuando eras pequeño? Where did you (use to) live when you were small?
Vivíamos en el campo. We lived (used to live) in the country.
A veces mi padre nos llevaba a sitios muy bonitos. At times my father used to (would) take us to very pretty places.

3. To indicate that an action was in progress, or to describe what was going on when something happened (the preterit indicates what happened under the circumstances described):

¿Qué hacías cuando entré? What were you doing when I entered?
Yo estaba cansado cuando volví a casa. I was tired when I returned home.

4. To describe mental activity or state in the past; thus, verbs meaning *believe, know, wish, be able*, etc., are usually translated by the imperfect:

¿Sobre qué pensabas escribir la composición? On (About) what were you intending (did you intend) to write the composition?
Pablo sabía que yo quería quedarme en el parque. Paul knew that I wanted to stay in the park.

5. To express time of day in the past:

Eran las nueve cuando volvió Eduardo. It was nine o'clock when Edward returned.
¿Qué hora era? What time was it?

Práctica. Read in Spanish, substituting the proper imperfect inflected form of each infinitive in italics. Observe carefully how the imperfect tense is used:

1. Cuando yo *ser* pequeño, mi familia *vivir* en el campo. 2. En el verano *hacer* mucho calor. 3. Por lo común *hacer* sol, y a veces *hacer* mucho viento. 4. Los domingos yo *levantarse* tarde. 5. Mis padres siempre me *llevar* a la iglesia. 6. Yo *saber* que *ser*

necesario acompañarlos.   7. Después de comer, mi padre nos *llevar* en coche a las montañas, que no *estar* muy lejos.   8. Me *gustar* pasearme bajo los árboles altos.   9. Allí *hacer* fresco, y yo no *tener* mucho calor.   10. A menudo *ser* muy tarde cuando *volver* nosotros a casa.

C. Expressions with **hacer**

> **¿Qué tiempo hace?**   What kind of weather is it?
> **Hace buen (mal) tiempo.**   It is good (bad) weather.
> **Hace calor (frío, fresco, viento).**   It is warm (cold, cool, windy).
> **No hacía mucho calor (frío).**   It wasn't very warm (cold).
> **Hacía sol.**   It was sunny (The sun was shining).

Hacer is used impersonally with certain Spanish nouns to describe the temperature or weather.   Since **frío, fresco, viento, calor, sol** are nouns when used with **hacer,** they are modified by the adjective **mucho,** not the adverb **muy.**   (Compare the use of **tener** with certain nouns, p. 117.)   One also uses **Hay (Había) sol,** *The sun is (was) shining.*

Recall that **estar** is used with adjectives to express a temporary or changing condition of the subject: **El agua estaba fría,** *The water was cold.*   However, one uses **ser** to express a characteristic quality: **La nieve es fría,** *The snow is cold.*

Bueno and **malo** are shortened to **buen** and **mal** before masculine singular nouns; they retain their regular form otherwise: **un buen camino,** *a good road*; **dos buenos caminos,** *two good roads.*

D. Use of the definite article with the seasons

> **Me gusta la primavera (el invierno).**   I like spring (winter).
> **Es otoño (verano) ahora.**   It is fall (summer) now.

The definite article is regularly used with the seasons; however, it is usually omitted after **ser** or in a **de**-phrase: **un día de otoño,** *a fall day.*   Also in daily speech it is often omitted after **en.**

EJERCICIOS

A. Substitution drill:

   1. *Ana* hablaba español con Pablo.
      (*Yo, Nosotros, Luis y Carmen, Tú, Vd.*)

2. *Mi amigo* vivía en España.
   (*Mis amigos, Juan, Juan y yo, Tú, Vds.*)
3. *Yo* iba al café todos los días.
   (*Vds., Vd. y yo, Mi hermana, Los estudiantes, Tú*)
4. *Nosotros* le veíamos a menudo.
   (*Vd., Yo, Eduardo, Vd. y él, Marta y Pablo*)

B. Say after your teacher, then repeat, changing the verb to the corresponding preterit form, and finally change the verb to the imperfect:

1. Yo necesito tu ayuda.   2. Mis amigos viven en el campo.   3. Eduardo come a las seis.   4. Pablo va al centro.   5. ¿Escribes la composición?   6. ¿Espera Vd. a alguien? 7. Marta y yo no vemos a nadie.   8. Los muchachos cierran la puerta.   9. Carlos lleva a Carolina a bailar.   10. ¿Quién le da a Juan el dinero?   11. José insiste en quedarse.   12. Ana y yo montamos a caballo.

C. Read in Spanish, using the correct preterit or imperfect form of the verb in italics, as required:

1. Cuando yo *vivir* en California, *pasar* mucho tiempo en las montañas.   2. Todos los veranos mi familia *ir* a visitar varios parques nacionales.   3. Uno de los parques, que *ser* muy hermoso, no *estar* lejos, y mi padre nos *llevar* en coche a sitios muy bonitos. 4. *Haber* muchos árboles altos, y nosotros *poder* dar paseos por los bosques.   5. Generalmente *hacer* fresco allí, y nos *gustar* pasearnos bajo la sombra de los árboles.   6. El verano pasado yo *volver* a California.   7. Un amigo y yo *querer* ver un sitio que *visitar* a menudo cuando *ser* jóvenes.   8. *Ser* las ocho de la mañana cuando *salir* de casa. 9. *Hacer* sol y mucho calor en la ciudad, pero *hacer* fresco en el parque.   10. Después de comer allí, nosotros *dar* un paseo largo.   11. A las tres y media *sentarse* a descansar porque *estar* cansados.   12. Poco después *ver* que *haber* muchas nubes en el cielo. 13. Nosotros *volver* al coche, y pronto *comenzar* a llover.   14. No *llover* más que media hora, pero el agua *correr* por todas partes.   15. Mi amigo y yo *salir* del parque a las cinco de la tarde y *llegar* a casa muy tarde.

D. Complete each sentence with the correct present indicative form of **estar, hacer,** or **tener:**

1. ¿Qué tiempo ——— hoy?   2. ——— buen tiempo.   3. ——— sol y no ——— mucho frío.   4. Yo ——— calor y mucha sed.   5. Yo ——— sentado aquí porque ——— muy cansado.   6. ——— fresco bajo la sombra de este árbol.   7. Esta agua ——— fresca.   8. Carolina ——— sentada a la mesa porque ——— hambre.   9. A veces ——— mucho viento en la primavera.   10. También ——— mal tiempo, ¿verdad?   11. A menudo yo ——— frío.   12. Cuando ——— mucho sol, yo no ——— frío.

COMPOSICIÓN

1. When we were young, we used to live in the country.   2. Our house was near the mountains, and our father often took us to some beautiful places.   3. When it was warm at home in summer, it was always cool in the mountains.   4. We liked to stroll through the forest because it was very pleasant there.   5. Generally we ate under the shade of the beautiful trees in (**de**) the parks.   6. We would not go to the mountains in winter if the forest was covered with snow.   7. I recall that one spring day my father took us to a park which was near our house.   8. It was cool, but the sun was shining; really it was a beautiful day.   9. Upon arriving at the park, we ate lunch and rested a while under the tall trees.   10. When my brother and I were taking a walk with some friends, we saw that there were many clouds in the sky.   11. We returned to the car, and shortly afterward it began to rain.   12. It was six o'clock when we arrived home, and we were very tired.

EJERCICIOS DE PRONUNCIACIÓN

A. The sounds of **c, qu,** and **k**

1. As we learned in Lesson 2, the sound of Spanish **c** before all letters except **e** and **i** and of **qu** (also Spanish **k**) is similar to English *k*, but there is no aspiration.   To avoid the aspiration, or puff of air, that follows the English sound (as in $c^h at$), you must hold back your breath during the articulation of the Spanish sound.   Remember, also, that the **u** in **que, qui** is never sounded as in English *quite*:

caballo	camino	cómodo	escuela	cuaderno
bosque	porque	quiero	orquesta	esquina

2. Now watch the sound of Spanish **c** before **e** and **i** (and of **z**) as you pronounce these words:

entonces	estación	composición	precio	canción
cielo	parecer	ciudad	lápiz	almuerzo

B. The sound of **p**

Spanish **p** is similar to English *p*, but the explosion is weaker, and again there is no aspiration (as in $p^h ast$):

Pablo	tiempo	primavera	película	pupitre

Sorting tin, Caracoles, Bolivia.

VOCABULARIO

agradable agreeable, pleasant
el agua (*f.*) water
alto, -a tall, high
el año year
el árbol tree
la ayuda aid, help
bajo *prep.* under, beneath, below
el bosque woods, forest
el caballo horse
el camino road, way
el cielo sky
comenzar (**ie**) (**a** + *inf.*) to begin (to), commence (to)
la composición (*pl.* **composiciones**) composition, theme
correr to run
cubierto, -a (**de**) covered (with)
Eduardo Edward
entonces then, at that time
la estación (*pl.* **estaciones**) season
había there was, there were
insistir (**en** + *obj.*) to insist (on)

el invierno winter
lejos *adv.* far, distant
mal(o), -a bad
la montaña mountain
montar to mount, ride
la nieve snow
la nube cloud
el otoño fall, autumn
Pablo Paul
parecer (*like* **conocer**) to appear, seem
pasearse to walk, stroll
porque because
la primavera spring
recordar (**ue**) to recall, remember
el sitio site, place
el sol sun
sólo only
la sombra shade, shadow
el tiempo weather
el verano summer
el viento wind

día (**de otoño**) (fall) day
en seguida at once, immediately
montar a caballo to ride horseback
¡pasa, Eduardo! come in, Edward!
poco después shortly afterward
por todas partes everywhere
un rato más a while longer
vamos a (**ver**) let's (see)

Convent of San Esteban, Salamanca, Spain.

LECTURA V

ESPAÑA EN AMÉRICA

Estudio de palabras

a. Approximate cognates. Pronounce the following words aloud, give the English cognates, and indicate the variations: civilización, completo, corredor, corresponder, diccionario, especial, introducción, misión, territorio.

b. Deceptive cognates. In Spanish **realizar** means *to realize, carry out*, and not *to realize, understand vividly*. **Recordar** (**ue**) has two meanings: with a personal subject it means *to remember*; with a thing as subject it means *to recall* (*to one*), *remind* (*one*) *of*.

c. Compare the meanings of the following pairs of words: exploración, *exploration, and* explorador, *explorer*; interés, *interest, and* interesante, *interesting*; realidad, *reality, and* realizar, *to realize, carry out*; verdad, *truth*, and verdadero, *true, real*.

d. It will help you in increasing your vocabulary to take note of words of opposite meanings.   How many of the following words do you recognize?

ancho — estrecho	ir — venir	pequeño — grande
bueno — malo	más — menos	recordar — olvidar
este — oeste	mucho — poco	también — tampoco
fácil — difícil	norte — sur	viejo — nuevo

e. **Santo** (not **Santa**) is shortened to **San** before all names of masculine saints, except those beginning with **Do-** or **To-**:

San Francisco St. Francis		**San José** St. Joseph
BUT: **Santo Domingo** St. Dominic		**Santa Inés** St. Agnes
Santo Tomás St. Thomas		**Santa María** St. Mary.

Santa also means *Holy*: **Santa Fe**, *Holy Faith*; **Santa Cruz**, *Holy Cross*.

Try to give the meaning of: San Antonio, San Carlos, San Felipe, San Jorge, San Luis, San Pablo, Santa Ana, Santa Clara, Santa Rosa.

155

La exploración y la colonización de América son principalmente obra[1] de España. Hay que recordar que en realidad la palabra «América» no significa solamente los Estados Unidos, sino los dos continentes, la América del Norte y la América del Sur. A veces usamos la palabra «norteamericano» cuando hablamos de los habitantes de los Estados Unidos, pero este término tampoco es exacto,[2] porque México y la América Central forman parte de la América del Norte también.

Para los norteamericanos las exploraciones que realizaron[3] los españoles en una gran parte de nuestro territorio tienen un interés especial. Exploradores como Ponce de León, Cabeza de Vaca, Hernando de Soto, Coronado y Cabrillo pertenecen también a la historia de los Estados Unidos. Desde San Francisco hasta el sur del continente podemos ver hoy día las ruinas de las antiguas misiones españolas. Hay muchas misiones bien conocidas en California, como las[4] de Santa Bárbara y San Juan Capistrano.

---

[1] **obra,** *work.*   [2] **este término tampoco es exacto,** *this term is not exact either.*   [3] **realizaron,** *carried out, realized.*
[4] **las,** *those.*

"Landing of Hernando de Soto in Florida." Artist unknown.

Balcony in Ronda, southern Spain   Patio of San Miguel Mission, California

En California, Arizona, Nuevo México, Texas, la Florida y otros lugares[1] hay casas y edificios de estilo español. Sus balcones, corredores, portales,[2] tejados,[3] y patios con flores y fuentes recuerdan la arquitectura española. La verdadera casa española tiene ventanas con rejas de hierro[4] y un patio, que está en el centro de la casa y que tiene una fuente, flores y pájaros.[5] En las ciudades y en los pueblos la plaza corresponde al patio de la casa. Muchas veces se encuentran cafés al aire libre en las plazas.

Varios estados de nuestro país tienen nombres de origen español: la Florida, la tierra de las flores; Nevada, la tierra de la nieve; Colorado, la tierra roja; y Montana, la montaña. California tiene el nombre de una isla que se menciona en una antigua novela española. Muchas ciudades tienen nombres españoles, como Fresno, El Paso, San Antonio, Santa Fe, Las Cruces, Las Vegas, San Diego, San José, San Francisco, Sacramento y Los Ángeles, cuyo nombre completo es El pueblo de Nuestra Señora, la Reina[6] de los Ángeles. También muchos ríos, valles y montañas tienen nombres españoles, como el Río Grande, el Sacramento, el Nueces, el Brazos y la Sierra Nevada.

Son innumerables las palabras españolas que se usan todos los días en inglés. Si no saben Vds. lo que significan las palabras

[1] **lugares,** *places.*   [2] **portales,** *doorways.*   [3] **tejados,** *roofs (of tiles).*   [4] **rejas de hierro,** *iron grills, gratings.*
[5] **pájaros,** *birds.*   [6] **Reina,** *Queen.*

Two views of the San Miguel Mission, the oldest church in the United States, Santa Fe, New Mexico.

siguientes, pueden buscarlas en un diccionario inglés: *adiós, adobe, amigo, alpaca, arroyo, banana, bolero, bronco, burro, cargo, cordillera, corral, coyote, chinchilla, chocolate, fiesta, hacienda, hombre, mantilla, mesa, mosquito, parasol, paseo, patio, plaza, pronto, pueblo, rodeo, sierra, sombrero, tapioca.* ¿Conocen Vds. otras?

Entre las muchas palabras que los españoles tomaron de las lenguas indígenas de América, algunas han pasado al inglés, como *alpaca, chinchilla, canoe* (canoa), *coyote, chocolate, hurricane* (huracán), *maize* (maíz) y *tapioca.* Palabras como *banana* (de origen africano) y *adobe* y *tobacco* (tabaco), las dos de origen árabe,[1] también llegaron al inglés por medio de[2] los españoles.

Debemos a los españoles muchas frutas y otros productos y varios animales que tenemos hoy día en las Américas. Las naranjas,[3] los limones, las aceitunas,[4] y las uvas,[5] por ejemplo, son de España; de allí también son el trigo, el arroz,[6] la caña de azúcar y otras plantas, y varios animales domésticos, como el caballo, la vaca,[7] el toro,[8] la oveja[9] y el cerdo.[10] El resto del mundo también debe mucho a España por la introducción en Europa de frutas y legumbres,[11] como el maíz, el chocolate, la patata, el camote,[12] el tabaco, el tomate y la vainilla, que tuvieron[13] su origen en América.

Santa Barbara Mission, California

Mission of San Carlos Borromeo, Carmel, California.

---

[1] **árabe,** *Arabic.*   [2] **por medio de,** *by means of.*   [3] **naranjas,** *oranges.*   [4] **aceitunas,** *olives.*   [5] **uvas,** *grapes.*
[6] **arroz,** *rice.*   [7] **vaca,** *cow.*   [8] **toro,** *bull.*   [9] **oveja,** *sheep.*   [10] **cerdo,** *pig.*   [11] **legumbres,** *vegetables.*
[12] **camote,** *sweet potato.*   [13] **tuvieron** (pret. of **tener**), *had.*

PREGUNTAS

1. ¿A qué país debemos principalmente la exploración y la colonización de América?
2. ¿Qué significa la palabra «América»?   3. ¿Qué palabra usamos cuando hablamos de los habitantes de los Estados Unidos?   4. ¿Por qué no es exacto este término?
5. ¿Qué nombres de exploradores recuerda Vd.?   6. ¿Qué ruinas podemos ver hoy día?   7. ¿Conoce Vd. los nombres de algunas misiones de California?

8. ¿Cómo son las casas y los edificios de estilo español?   9. ¿Cómo es la verdadera casa española?   10. En las ciudades, ¿qué corresponde al patio de la casa?   11. ¿Qué se encuentra muchas veces en las plazas?

12. ¿Cuáles de nuestros estados tienen nombres españoles?   13. ¿Qué significa la palabra «Colorado»?   14. ¿La Florida?   15. ¿Nevada?   16. ¿Qué ciudades tienen nombres españoles?   17. ¿Qué palabras españolas que se usan en inglés recuerda Vd.?   18. ¿Recuerda Vd. algunas palabras españolas de origen indígena?   19. ¿Qué productos debemos a los españoles?   20. ¿Qué animales debemos a España?   21. Mencione Vd. algunos productos que el resto del mundo debe a España.

This statue of Father Junípero Serra stands in front of the San Fernando Mission, California.

VIÑETAS CULTURALES

ESPAÑA

En la página anterior: El Alcázar de Segovia, la residencia
favorita de los reyes durante el siglo XV.
A la izquierda, arriba: Café al aire libre en Puerto de
Santa María (en el sur de España, frente a Cádiz). Abajo:
En Barcelona dos estudiantes comparan notas antes de
entrar en clase. A la derecha: Puesto (*stand*) de libros en el
Rastro, un enorme mercado de cosas viejas en Madrid.

CIUDADES Y PAISAJES

Arriba: Como en la época de Cervantes, los molinos de viento todavía existen en La Mancha, una región árida, sin agua ni árboles, al sur de Madrid. Creyendo que eran gigantes con largos brazos, don Quijote los acometió (*attacked*).

Abajo: Vista de las Ramblas, en Barcelona. Se da este nombre a una serie de hermosas avenidas, con árboles, que atraviesan la ciudad. Barcelona es el puerto más importante de España, con industria y comercio muy activos.

Abajo: Vista de Sevilla. Situada a orillas (*shores*) del río Guadalquivir, en la parte occidental de Andalucía, es una ciudad rica en monumentos históricos. Los conquistadores árabes, que invadieron (*invaded*) la península en 711, se quedaron más de cinco siglos en Córdoba y Sevilla, y casi ochocientos años en Granada. Las tres ciudades reflejan todavía el esplendor de la dominación musulmana (*Moslem*). Hermosas muestras (*samples*) del arte árabe en

Sevilla son el Alcázar—el antiguo palacio real—y la Giralda, construida en el siglo XII como torre de una mezquita (*mosque*) y conservada como torre de la catedral. Después de la conquista de América, Sevilla fue una de las ciudades más populosas y ricas de España. Todo el comercio con el Nuevo Mundo pasaba por su puerto. Hoy día es un activo centro industrial, con más de medio millón de habitantes.

Abajo: Una calle de Sevilla, con la Giralda al fondo.

Arriba, a la izquierda: Dos hombres pescando (*fishing*). En el norte de España la pesca es una de las industrias más importantes. También—como en todas partes—puede ser un deporte o diversión. A la derecha: Desde un mirador (*balcony*) de la Alhambra, el famoso palacio árabe de Granada, se ven hermosos jardines y la torre de un monasterio.

Abajo: Un pueblo andaluz. En Andalucía se acumula la población en grandes pueblos, a veces a muchos kilómetros unos de otros.

Arriba: Una hacienda (*plantation*) en la Costa del Sol. Se da este nombre a una sección de la costa del sur de España, con hermosas playas que atraen (*attract*) a los turistas. Noten que la arquitectura es la misma que los españoles llevaron a América. Abajo: Vista de Madrid al atardecer (*drawing towards evening*). Para terminar nuestro breve paseo por España, volvemos a la vida bulliciosa (*bustling*) de la capital. En Madrid las oficinas y las tiendas quedan abiertas hasta las ocho.

HISPANOAMÉRICA

A la izquierda: Ruinas precolombinas de Tula, al norte de
la ciudad de México. Se cree que Tula fue la capital de los
toltecas, pueblo indio que se estableció en esta región en el
siglo VII. A la derecha, arriba: La Pirámide del Sol,
Teotihuacán. Entre la ciudad de México y Tula se encuentran los restos de un gran centro religioso, construido
tal vez por una raza anterior a los toltecas. La Pirámide
del Sol es la estructura más grande de su tipo en América.

PUEBLOS Y COSTUMBRES

Abajo: Se representan ceremonias indias en este fragmento del grandioso (*magnificent*) mural pintado por Diego Rivera en el Palacio Presidencial de México.

Abajo, a la izquierda: La Iglesia de Santa Prisca y San Sebastián en Taxco, al sur de México. Fue construida hacia 1750 por un minero (*miner*) francés con el producto de sus minas de plata. A la derecha: Una artesana trabaja en una charola de laca (*lacquer tray*) en Uruapan (Michoacán).

A la izquierda, arriba: La biblioteca de la Universidad Nacional de México. La Universidad es una de las más grandes del mundo, con más de cien mil estudiantes. Muchos de los edificios están decorados con mosaicos y pinturas murales. Abajo: Una avenida en el centro de la capital. A la derecha: El mercado de Nochixtlán, en el Estado de Zacatecas.

A la izquierda, arriba: Una plaza típica en la pintoresca (*picturesque*) ciudad de Guanajuato, al norte de la ciudad de México. Fundada en 1548, la ciudad fue un importante centro minero. Abajo: Una parte moderna de Ciudad Guatemala, hoy capital del país en vez de Antigua, abandonada por miedo de los terremotos (*earthquakes*). A la derecha: Una mujer india trabaja en una vasija (*vessel*) de barro en una aldea (*village*) cerca de Chichicastenango.

Arriba, a la izquierda: Ramas del árbol de café, Guatemala. La principal fuente (*source*) de riqueza del país es el cultivo y exportación de café y bananas. A la derecha: Recolectando (*gathering*) bananas en el Ecuador. También en este país las principales industrias son las agrícolas. Abajo: Indios con llamas en el Perú. La llama es el animal de carga (*beast of burden*) de los Andes.

Abajo, a la izquierda: Vista parcial de Machu Picchu, "la ciudad perdida de los incas", descubierta en 1912. Está situada en la cordillera de los Andes, a unos ciento diez kilómetros al noroeste del Cuzco. El imperio de los incas, establecido en el siglo XII, se extendía desde el sur de Colombia hasta el norte de Chile y la Argentina. A la derecha: Vista del altiplano (*high plateau*) peruano. Los indios—que constituyen la mitad de la población del país—viven principalmente en las altas mesetas y valles de los Andes.

Abajo, a la derecha : Calle de Quito, capital del Ecuador. La ciudad conserva hermosos monumentos de la época colonial. A la izquierda , arriba: Vista de Caracas, Venezuela. Abajo: Vista de Bogotá, Colombia. Son grandes ciudades modernas, con industria y comercio muy activos.

Abajo, a la izquierda: Tren, provincia de Corrientes, Argentina. La provincia de Corrientes se encuentra en el extremo (*end*) nordeste del país, entre los ríos Paraná y Uruguay. La agricultura y la ganadería (*livestock*) son las principales fuentes de riqueza. A la derecha: Cataratas del Iguazú, Argentina. Al desembocar (*emptying*) en el río Paraná, el Iguazú, que constituye la frontera entre la Argentina y el Brasil, forma una de las cascadas más notables del mundo.

El final del camino, Tierra del Fuego o Archipiélago de Magallanes (*Magellan*). Es un grupo de islas en el extremo sur del continente, y separado de él por el estrecho (*strait*) de Magallanes. La parte occidental es chilena y la oriental es un territorio argentino. Es una región fría, de fuertes vientos y nieblas (*fog*), y de lluvias (*rains*) y nevadas (*snowfalls*) frecuentes. Magallanes, que murió en las Filipinas, sin poder volver a España, descubrió el estrecho que lleva su nombre en 1520.

VIÑETAS CULTURALES

APLICACIÓN

In addition to presenting a kaleidoscope of information about the Hispanic world, the preceding illustrated section is also intended to serve as a topical basis for oral and written composition. Assignments may be made at several points during the course of instruction. In each instance, the student might include in his presentation the structures and the vocabulary learned so far. It may also be useful and productive to assign the same topic more than once to permit additional development and expansion of a previously completed composition. Some students may wish to use an English-Spanish dictionary in preparing the compositions.

Prácticas orales

Groups of students will be asked to prepare a conversation of 6 to 8 exchanges, using vocabulary already given, on the following topics:

1. La Mancha y los pueblos del sur de España.
2. El pasado y el presente de Sevilla.
3. Restos de la dominación árabe en Andalucía.
4. Aspectos de la vida diaria en Madrid y Barcelona.

Ejercicios escritos

Students will be asked to write a brief essay in Spanish (120–150 words) on one of the following topics:

1. Restos de civilizaciones precolombinas en México y el Perú.
2. El sentido artístico del mexicano.
3. Aspectos de la ciudad de México que atraen al turista.
4. La riqueza agrícola de Hispanoamérica.

LECCIÓN 12

Preterit of *traer*

Cardinal numerals.   Ordinal numerals

Days of the week.   The months.   Dates

HABLAN DE ALGUNAS[1] FIESTAS Y ANIVERSARIOS

SR. PIDAL.   Elena, ¿cuál es la fecha de hoy?

ELENA.   Es el primero de febrero de mil novecientos setenta y cuatro.

SR. PIDAL.   Miguel, ¿qué fechas celebramos en el mes de febrero?

MIGUEL.   El día doce celebramos el nacimiento de Lincoln, y el tercer lunes del mes el nacimiento de Jorge Washington.

SR. PIDAL.   María, ¿en qué fecha celebran su independencia los mexicanos?

MARÍA.   El diez y seis de septiembre, ¿verdad?   Corresponde a la fiesta del cuatro de julio en los Estados Unidos.

• • • • •

SR. PIDAL.   Juanita, ¿celebran alguna fiesta los hispanoamericanos el día doce de octubre?

JUANITA.   ¡Cómo no!   Es el Día de la Hispanidad,[2] el aniversario del día en que Cristóbal Colón descubrió el Nuevo Mundo, en mil cuatrocientos noventa y dos.

SR. PIDAL.   Hoy día algunas de las ciudades más importantes del mundo se hallan[3] en las tierras que descubrió Colón.   Inés, ¿cuáles son algunas de las ciudades más grandes de la América española?

INÉS.   Las dos más grandes son Buenos Aires y México.   Buenos Aires tiene más de nueve millones de habitantes, y México más de seis.

SR. PIDAL.   Es verdad.   Y hay otras ciudades con más de un millón y medio de habitantes.

---

[1] When two or more nouns refer to things and are in the plural, the adjective is plural and may agree with the nearest noun.   [2] The **Día de la Hispanidad,** *Day of Spanish Solidarity* or *Union* (of Spain with the Americas), until recently was called the **Día de la Raza,** *Day of the Race.*   [3] **Hallarse,** like **encontrarse,** often means approximately the same as **estar,** although it retains something of its original meaning.   See page 107, footnote 1.

Sr. Pidal.   A propósito, ¿sabían Vds. que los padres de la profesora Valdés volvieron de un viaje a Santiago la semana pasada?

María.   ¿Fue su primer viaje?   ¿Cuánto tiempo pasaron en Chile?

Sr. Pidal.   Fue su tercer o cuarto viaje.   Partieron de Nueva York el tres de diciembre y volvieron el veinte y cinco de enero.   Trajeron muchas fotografías que sacaron durante el viaje.

Juanita.   ¿Por qué no invita Vd. a la señorita Valdés a enseñarnos las fotografías?

Sr. Pidal.   ¿Les gusta la idea?   Vamos a ver..., hoy es viernes.   Aunque la señorita Valdés está muy ocupada, creo que puedo invitarla a venir a nuestra clase el martes o el miércoles de la semana que viene.

CONVERSACIÓN

A. Preguntas sobre el diálogo

1. ¿En qué fecha celebramos el aniversario del nacimiento de Lincoln?   2. ¿En qué fecha celebran su independencia los mexicanos?   3. ¿Qué fiesta celebramos el cuatro de julio en los Estados Unidos?   4. ¿En qué año descubrió Colón el Nuevo Mundo?   5. ¿Cuáles son algunas de las ciudades más importantes de la América española?   6. ¿Cuándo volvieron de su viaje los padres de la profesora Valdés?   7. ¿Qué ciudad de Chile visitaron?   8. ¿Qué trajeron de su viaje a Chile?

B. Aplicación del diálogo

1. ¿Cuál es la fecha de hoy?   2. ¿Qué día de la semana fue ayer?   3. ¿Cuántas fechas celebramos en el mes de febrero?   4. ¿Cuántos días tiene el mes de enero?   5. ¿Cuántos días hay en un año?   6. ¿Cuántos estudiantes hay en esta escuela?   7. ¿Cuántos habitantes tiene la ciudad de Nueva York?   8. ¿Qué va a hacer Vd. el sábado?

NOTAS GRAMATICALES

A. Irregular preterit of **traer**

SINGULAR	PLURAL
traje	**trajimos**
trajiste	**trajisteis**
trajo	**trajeron**

Note that in the first and third persons singular the stress falls on the stem, instead of the ending; therefore, final **-e** and **-o** are not accented.   Observe the spelling of **trajeron**. **Traje** is translated *I brought, did bring*.

B. Cardinal numerals

30	**treinta**	100	**cien(to)**	700	**setecientos, -as**
31	**treinta y un(o)**	102	**ciento dos**	800	**ochocientos, -as**
40	**cuarenta**	200	**doscientos, -as**	900	**novecientos, -as**
50	**cincuenta**	300	**trescientos, -as**	1000	**mil**
60	**sesenta**	400	**cuatrocientos, -as**	2000	**dos mil**
70	**setenta**	500	**quinientos, -as**	100,000	**cien mil**
80	**ochenta**	600	**seiscientos, -as**	1,000,000	**un millón** (de)
90	**noventa**				

cien (**mil**) **casas**   one hundred (one thousand) houses
cien mil estudiantes   a (one) hundred thousand students
ciento treinta y un días   one hundred thirty-one days
quinientas treinta y una muchachas   five hundred thirty-one girls
un millón de habitantes   a (one) million inhabitants
dos millones de hombres   two million men

Ciento becomes **cien** before nouns and the numerals **mil** and **millones,** but the full form is retained before numerals under a hundred.

Un is omitted before **cien(to)** and **mil,** but is used before **millón.**   If a noun follows **millón** (*pl.* **millones**), **de** is used before the noun.   Recall that **uno** and numerals ending in **uno** drop **-o** before masculine nouns, and that **una** is used before feminine nouns.

Numerals in the hundreds, such as **doscientos,** end in **-as** when used with feminine nouns.

In Spanish **y** is normally used only between the tens and units: **veinte y seis, cincuenta y ocho,** but **doscientos cinco.**

C. Ordinal numerals

1st	**primero, -a**	5th	**quinto, -a**	8th	**octavo, -a**
2nd	**segundo, -a**	6th	**sexto, -a**	9th	**noveno, -a**
3rd	**tercero, -a**	7th	**séptimo, -a**	10th	**décimo, -a**
4th	**cuarto, -a**				

la tercera frase   the third sentence
las primeras canciones   the first songs
el primer (tercer) viaje   the first (third) trip

The ordinal numerals agree in gender and number with the nouns they modify.   **Primero** and **tercero** drop final **-o** before a masculine singular noun (third example); otherwise their regular forms are used.

Ordinal numerals are normally used only through *tenth*; beyond *tenth* the cardinal numerals replace the ordinals and they follow the noun: **Carlos Quinto,** *Charles V* (*Charles the Fifth*); **Alfonso Trece,** *Alfonso XIII* (*the Thirteenth*).

D. Days of the week

el domingo	(on) Sunday	**el jueves**	(on) Thursday
el lunes	(on) Monday	**el viernes**	(on) Friday
el martes	(on) Tuesday	**el sábado**	(on) Saturday
el miércoles	(on) Wednesday		

Hasta el lunes.   Until Monday.
No tenemos clases los sábados.   We have no classes on Saturdays.
Carolina, ¿qué hace Vd. los domingos?   Caroline, what do you do on Sundays?
Hoy es viernes.   Today is Friday.

The definite article is used with the days of the week, except after **ser.**   The article also translates English *on*.   The days of the week are not capitalized in Spanish and they have the same form for the singular and plural, except for **los sábados** and **los domingos.**   (Spanish words of more than one syllable which end in unaccented **-es** and **-is** have the same form for the singular and plural.)

E. The months

enero	January	**mayo**	May	**septiembre**	September
febrero	February	**junio**	June	**octubre**	October
marzo	March	**julio**	July	**noviembre**	November
abril	April	**agosto**	August	**diciembre**	December

The months are not capitalized, except at the beginning of a sentence.   They are masculine and do not require the definite article unless modified.   (See Section E, page 132.)
Memorize this jingle.   You probably know the English version:

> **Treinta días tiene noviembre,**
> **con abril, junio y septiembre;**
> **veintiocho o veintinueve, uno;**
> **y los demás** (*the rest*) **treinta y uno.**

F. Dates

¿Cuál es la fecha (de hoy)?
¿Qué fecha es (hoy)? } What is the date (today)?
(Hoy) es el dos de diciembre.   (Today) is the second of December.

Ayer fue el primero de enero.   Yesterday was the first of January.
Yo salí el treinta y uno de mayo.   I left (on) the thirty-first of May (May 31).
Hoy es viernes, 25 de diciembre de 1970.   Today is Friday, December 25, 1970.

Also commonly used are:

¿A cuántos estamos (hoy)?   What is the date (today)?
Estamos a ocho de noviembre.   (Today) is the eighth of November.

The cardinal numerals are used to express the day of the month, except for **el primero,** *first.*   The definite article **el** translates *the, on the,* with the day of the month.

In counting and in reading dates, use **mil** with numerals of one thousand or more: **el diez de abril de mil novecientos setenta y cinco,** *April 10, 1975.*

EJERCICIOS

A. Substitution drill:

1. *La señora Valdés* trajo muchas fotografías.
   (*Mis padres, Yo, Juan y yo, Tú, Vd.*)
2. *Juanita* partió de allí el martes.
   (*Nosotros, Mis tíos, Yo, Tú, Vds.*)
3. *Yo* no sabía nada del viaje.
   (*Miguel, Tú, Los muchachos, Elena y yo, Vd.*)

B. Say after your teacher, then repeat, changing the verb to the imperfect tense:

1. Yo doy un paseo todos los días.   2. Siempre celebramos la fiesta.   3. A menudo yo les traigo algo.   4. Todos van a la iglesia los domingos.   5. Es un día muy hermoso. 6. Los estudiantes vienen todas las tardes.   7. Me acuesto tarde todas las noches. 8. Me gusta montar a caballo por la tarde.   9. Generalmente yo la veo en el café. 10. Hace fresco bajo los árboles.

C. Review the uses of the preterit and imperfect tenses in Lessons 10 and 11, then use the correct form of the infinitive in italics:

1. Ayer *ser* las tres de la tarde cuando yo *salir* de casa.   2. Aunque *hacer* frío, *ser* un día hermoso.   3. Como yo *querer* comprar un sombrero, *tomar* un autobús que me *llevar* al centro.   4. Cuando yo *entrar* en la tienda, todas las empleadas *estar* ocupadas. 5. Después de un rato una empleada me *enseñar* varios sombreros bonitos.   6. Yo *comprar* uno que no *ser* muy caro.   7. Luego yo *ir* a otra tienda, pero *volver* a casa sin comprar nada más.   8. Al entrar en casa, yo *sentarse* en la sala y *descansar* un rato. 9. Yo no *saber* dónde *estar* mi mamá.   10. Ella y mi papá *llegar* tarde a casa, y nosotros no *cenar* hasta las siete.

D. Read in Spanish:

1. 35 escuelas. 2. 51 autobuses. 3. 41 bibliotecas. 4. 1,000 coches. 5. 500 canciones. 6. 100 libros. 7. 100 sillas. 8. 110 muchachas. 9. 2,000 estudiantes. 10. 750 caballos. 11. 365 días. 12. 1,000,000 de árboles. 13. 5,000,000 de habitantes. 14. 500,000 teléfonos. 15. 41 cuadros. 16. 77 iglesias. 17. 444 palabras. 18. 201 años. 19. 121 semanas. 20. 666 jóvenes. 21. 721 dólares. 22. 114 hombres. 23. 950 muchachos. 24. 21 países. 25. 888 fotografías.

E. Give these dates in Spanish:

MODEL: January 2, 1970   el dos de enero de mil novecientos setenta

1. April 23, 1616   5. July 4, 1776   9. June 29, 1903
2. September 29, 1547   6. August 14, 1909   10. October 12, 1492
3. January 1, 1970   7. May 2, 1808   11. February 20, 1212
4. December 7, 1941   8. November 11, 1918   12. March 31, 1971

F. Answer each question in Spanish, using in your reply the next higher ordinal or cardinal numeral, as required:

MODELS: ¿Mira Vd. el primer cuadro?   No, yo miro el segundo cuadro.
        ¿Volvió Vd. el cinco de diciembre?   No, yo volví el seis de diciembre.

1. ¿Vive Juan en la cuarta casa?   7. ¿Aprendieron Vds. la novena parte?
2. ¿Prepara Vd. la primera lección?   8. ¿Leía Vd. acerca de Felipe Segundo?
3. ¿Hacen ellos el segundo viaje?   9. ¿Estudiaba él la Lección once?
4. ¿Vas a leer la sexta frase?   10. ¿Saliste el primero de noviembre?
5. ¿Tomó Vd. el primer autobús?   11. ¿Partió Ana el diez de mayo?
6. ¿Bailaron Vds. el tercer baile?   12. ¿Tiene enero treinta días?

COMPOSICIÓN

1. Mr. Pidal, from where did Mr. and Mrs. Valdés depart for South America? 2. They left New York by plane on the fifth of July. 3. I believe that it was their third trip to those Spanish American countries. 4. They visited some of the largest cities, and also some of the smaller [ones]. 5. They spent more than six weeks in Chile. 6. Then they went to Buenos Aires, which is the largest city in South America. 7. It is larger than Lima or Santiago, other Spanish American capitals. 8. Nowadays the city has more than 9,000,000 inhabitants. 9. It was good weather there in August even though it was winter. 10. They showed us some beautiful photographs which they took in many places. 11. My uncle and aunt want to take a trip through the lands of the New World next summer. 12. They say that I can accompany them if I do not have to work during vacation (**las vacaciones**).

EJERCICIOS DE PRONUNCIACIÓN

A. The diphthongs **ai** (**ay**) and **oi** (**oy**)

Ai (**ay**) is pronounced like a prolonged English *i* in *mine*; **oi** (**oy**) like a prolonged English *oy* in *boy*.

1. prepráis   habláis   hay
   estudiáis   habla͜ inglés   ella͜ y nosotros

2. hoy   soy   sois
   hablo͜ inglés   español o͜ inglés   negro͜ y blanco

B. The diphthongs **ua** and **au**

As the first element of a diphthong, unstressed **u** is pronounced like *w* in *wet*. Spanish **au** is pronounced like a prolonged English *ou* in *out*.

1. cuaderno   cuadro   ¿cuánto?   cuatro
   Juan   su͜ amiga   su͜ alumno   su͜ almuerzo

2. autobús   la͜ universidad   la͜ usamos   abra͜ usted
   ponga͜ usted   traiga͜ usted   venga͜ usted   vuelva͜ usted

VOCABULARIO

el aniversario   anniversary
aunque   although, even though
celebrar   to celebrate
Colón   Columbus
corresponder   to correspond
Cristóbal   Christopher
descubrir   to discover
Elena   Helen, Ellen
la fecha   date
la fiesta   fiesta, festival, holiday
la fotografía   photograph
el habitante   inhabitant
hallar   to find; *reflex.*   find oneself, be found, be

la Hispanidad   Spanish Solidarity (Union)
hispanoamericano, -a   Spanish American
importante   important
la independencia   independence
Juanita   Juanita, Jane
Miguel   Michael, Mike
el mundo   world
el nacimiento   birth
partir (**de** + *obj.*)   to leave, depart (from)
sacar   to take (out)
la tierra   land

a propósito   by the way
¿cuánto tiempo?   how long?
Nuevo Mundo   New World
sacar fotografías   to take photographs

LECTURA VI

LA NAVIDAD[1]

Estudio de palabras

a. Less approximate cognates. Pronounce the following words aloud, note the English cognates, and indicate the variations: camello, *camel*; círculo, *circle*; conmemorar, *to commemorate*; chimenea, *chimney, fireplace*; entusiasmo, *enthusiasm*; establo, *stable*; extraño, *strange*; indicar, *to indicate*.

b. Deceptive cognates. Note the deceptive meaning of the following: asistir a, *to attend*; colonia, *district* (as well as *colony*); distinto, *different* (a much more frequent meaning than *distinct*); pastor, *shepherd*.

c. Compare the meanings of the following: carta, *letter*, and cartero, *letter carrier, postman*; costumbre, *custom*, and acostumbrar, *to be accustomed to, have the custom of*; noche, *night*, medianoche, *midnight, and* Nochebuena, *Christmas Eve;* puerta, *door,* puerto, *port, and* portero, *doorkeeper, janitor.*

¡Feliz Navidad! ¡Felices Pascuas! En el mundo español se saludan todos[2] así el día 25 de diciembre.

En México las fiestas de Navidad empiezan[3] la noche del 16 de diciembre y no terminan hasta la Nochebuena.[4] Todas las noches se celebran las «posadas», que representan los nueve días que pasaron José y María en su viaje a Belén.[5] En los pueblos y en ciertas colonias de las ciudades los amigos se reúnen[6] y forman una procesión. Van de puerta en puerta[7] llevando las figuritas[8] de José, María, el Niño Jesús, los pastores,[9] las mulas, las vacas y las ovejas. Una persona lleva la estrella[10] de Belén; las otras van detrás cantando. Llaman a cada puerta, pero una voz siempre contesta que la posada[11] está llena. Cuando la procesión llega a la novena puerta, el dueño de la casa les da permiso para pasar la noche en el establo. Todos entran y colocan las figuritas en un altar que representa el nacimiento[12] del Niño Jesús.

En cada «posada», después de preparar el nacimiento, los niños rompen la piñata. Ésta es una olla de barro[13] adornada con papeles de muchos colores y llena de frutas, dulces, nueces[14] y juguetes[15] de toda clase. Se cuelga[16] en el patio o en una sala de la casa, y los niños forman un círculo debajo de ella. Con los ojos vendados,[17] uno de los niños trata tres veces de romper la piñata con un palo.[18] Si no la rompe, otro niño trata de hacerlo. Por fin[19] se rompe

---

[1] **Navidad,** *Christmas.*   [2] **se saludan todos,** *all greet one another.*   [3] **empiezan,** *begin.*   [4] **Nochebuena,** *Christmas Eve.*   [5] **Belén,** *Bethlehem.*   [6] **se reúnen,** *meet, gather.*   [7] **de puerta en puerta,** *from door to door.*   [8] **figuritas,** *small figures.*   [9] **pastores,** *shepherds.*   [10] **estrella,** *star.*   [11] **posada,** *inn.*   [12] **nacimiento,** *manger scene.*   [13] **Ésta...barro,** *This is a clay jar.*   [14] **nueces,** *nuts.*   [15] **juguetes,** *toys.*   [16] **Se cuelga,** *It is hung.*   [17] **Con... vendados,** *Blindfolded.*   [18] **palo,** *stick.*   [19] **Por fin,** *Finally.*

la piñata, y los niños corren a recoger todo lo que cae. Cuando hay varias piñatas, a veces una de ellas está llena de agua o de harina.[1] También hay piñatas en otros países hispanoamericanos, especialmente en la América Central.

En general, no tienen árboles de Navidad en el mundo español. Los niños no cuelgan sus medias[2] en las chimeneas, en primer lugar,[3] porque no las hay,[4] y en segundo lugar, porque la tradición es distinta. Los niños creen que, si han sido[5] buenos, los Reyes Magos[6] les traen regalos, pero no el día de la Navidad, sino el seis de enero, día de la Epifanía.[7] La Epifanía conmemora la visita de los tres reyes de Oriente, Gaspar, Melchor y Baltasar, que siguieron[8] el camino que les indicó la estrella de Belén para ir a **adorar al Niño Jesús y para llevarle ofrendas** de oro, mirra e[9] incienso. Los niños creen que los Reyes Magos van a Belén cada año y que, al pasar por las calles, les dejan sus regalos. La víspera[10] del seis de enero ponen sus zapatos en el balcón y, a veces, un poco de paja[11] para los camellos. La verdad es que hoy día algunas familias han adoptado[12] la costumbre de poner árboles de Navidad, así como la de enviar tarjetas de felicitación.

En España y en los países hispanoamericanos casi todas las familias ponen nacimientos, costumbre que también tienen muchas familias norteamericanas. La víspera de la Navidad, es decir la Nochebuena,

se celebra una misa[13] a la medianoche. Se le llama la misa del gallo.[14] Después de asistir a[15] la misa, todos van a casa a cenar. Durante las fiestas de Navidad acostumbran cantar villancicos[16] y cantos como éstos:

Esta noche no dormimos,
que es santa Nochebuena,
y tenemos que llevarle
a María la enhorabuena.[17]

* * * * * *

¡Oh, Peregrina agraciada![18]
¡Oh, bellísima María!
Yo te ofrezco el alma mía[19]
para que tengas posada.[20]

—Pastores, venid,[21] venid,
veréis lo que no habéis visto,[22]
en el portal de Belén,
el nacimiento de Cristo.

Los pastores y zagalas[23]
caminan hacia el portal,
llevando llenos de frutas
el cesto[24] y el delantal.[25]

El día de Navidad es muy general hacer regalos a todas las personas que durante el año le han prestado[26] a uno algún servicio, como el portero, el sereno[27] y el cartero.

Se celebra la víspera del Año Nuevo en casi todos los países del mundo. En España hay una costumbre muy extraña. Unos

---

[1] **harina,** *flour.* [2] **medias,** *stockings.* [3] **en primer lugar,** *in the first place.* [4] **no las hay,** *there aren't any.* [5] **han sido,** *they have been.* [6] **Reyes Magos,** *Wise Men (Kings).* [7] **Epifanía,** *Epiphany.* [8] **siguieron,** *followed.* [9] Before words beginning with **i-, hi-,** Spanish uses **e,** *and,* for **y.** [10] **víspera,** *eve.* [11] **paja,** *straw.* [12] **han adoptado,** *have adopted.* [13] **misa,** *Mass.* [14] **Se le ... gallo,** *It is called Midnight Mass* (lit., Mass of the cock). [15] **asistir a,** *attending.* [16] **villancicos,** *carols.* [17] **la enhorabuena,** *congratulations.* [18] **¡Oh ... agraciada!** *Oh, graceful Pilgrim!* [19] **el alma mía,** *my heart.* [20] **para ... posada,** *in order that you may have lodging.* [21] **venid,** *come.* [22] **veréis ... visto,** *you will see what (something) you have not (never) seen.* [23] **zagalas,** *shepherdesses.* [24] **cesto,** *basket.* [25] **delantal,** *apron.* [26] **han prestado,** *have performed.* [27] **sereno,** *night watchman.*

minutos antes de la medianoche todos toman doce uvas en la mano. A cada campanada del reloj[1] comen una uva para tener buena suerte[2] durante el año nuevo.

Al sonar la última campanada, todos aplauden mucho y gritan con gran entusiasmo: «¡Feliz Año Nuevo!» o «¡Próspero Año Nuevo!»

PREGUNTAS

1. ¿Cómo se dice *Merry Christmas* en español? 2. ¿Cuándo empiezan las fiestas de Navidad en México? 3. ¿Cuándo terminan? 4. ¿Qué representan las posadas? 5. ¿Qué forma la gente por la noche? 6. ¿Adónde va la procesión? 7. ¿Qué llevan? 8. ¿Qué contesta una voz cuando llaman a las puertas? 9. ¿Qué pasa cuando llegan a la novena puerta? 10. ¿Dónde colocan las figuritas? 11. ¿Qué representa el altar?

12. ¿Qué hacen los niños en cada posada? 13. ¿Qué es la piñata? 14. ¿De qué está llena? 15. ¿Dónde se cuelga la piñata? 16. ¿Qué hacen los niños cuando se rompe la piñata?

17. ¿Dónde cuelgan sus medias los niños norteamericanos? 18. ¿Por qué no cuelgan sus medias los niños españoles? 19. ¿Quiénes les traen regalos a los niños españoles? 20. ¿En qué día los traen? 21. ¿Qué conmemora la Epifanía? 22. ¿Qué hacen los niños españoles la víspera del seis de enero? 23. ¿Qué costumbre han adoptado muchas familias españolas?

24. ¿Cómo se llama la víspera de la Navidad? 25. ¿Qué se celebra esa noche? 26. ¿Qué hacen todos después de asistir a la misa? 27. ¿Qué canciones se cantan durante las fiestas de Navidad?

28. ¿A quiénes se hacen regalos el día de Navidad? 29. ¿Qué costumbre extraña hay en España para celebrar el Año Nuevo? 30. ¿Qué gritan todos al sonar la última campanada?

[1] **cada ... reloj,** *each stroke of the clock.*   [2] **suerte,** *luck.*

Los estudiantes pueden cantar estas dos canciones de Navidad, que son muy populares: «Silent Night» y «Come All Ye Faithful.»

NOCHE DE PAZ, NOCHE DE AMOR

Noche de paz, noche de amor,
Todo duerme en derredor;
Entre los astros que esparcen su luz,
Bella, anunciando al Niño Jesús,
Brilla la estrella de paz,
Brilla la estrella de paz.

Noche de paz, noche de amor,
Oye humilde el fiel pastor
Coros celestes que anuncian salud,
Gracias y glorias en gran plenitud,
Por nuestro buen Redentor,
Por nuestro buen Redentor.

Noche de paz, noche de amor,
Ved que bello resplandor
Luce en el rostro del Niño Jesús
En el pesebre, del mundo la luz,
Astro de eterno fulgor,
Astro de eterno fulgor.

VENID, FIELES TODOS

Venid, fieles todos,
A Belén marchemos,
De gozo triunfantes,
Henchidos de amor;
Al rey de los cielos
Todos adoremos;
Venid, adoremos,
Venid, adoremos,
Venid, adoremos
A nuestro Señor.

Cantad, todos ángeles,
Cantad en regocijo;
Cantad, moradores
Del cielo alto,
Cantad gloria al Dios,
Todos de vosotros;
Venid, adoremos,
Venid, adoremos,
Venid, adoremos
A nuestro Señor.

Irregular verbs having _i_-stem preterits. Uses of the present participle
Position of object pronouns with the present participle
_Se_ **used as an indefinite subject**
Pronouns used as objects of prepositions
Use of the definite article in a general sense

ASPECTOS DE LA CULTURA PERUANA

(*Arturo entra en la oficina del Sr. Blanco.*)

Sr. Blanco. Pase Vd., Arturo. Siéntese, por favor.

Arturo. Muchas gracias. Me alegro mucho de verle a Vd.

Sr. Blanco. Vi a su hermano ayer por la tarde, y me dijo que Vd. quería charlar conmigo.

Arturo. Es que pienso hacer un viaje al Perú el mes que viene y sé que Vd. conoce muy bien el país.

Sr. Blanco. Mi esposa y yo hicimos un viaje por la América del Sur el año pasado, y pasamos varios meses en el Perú.

• • • • •

Arturo. Sr. Blanco, ¿qué parte del país les interesó más?

Sr. Blanco. Nos interesó especialmente el Cuzco, la antigua capital de los incas. Para mí las ruinas de Machu Picchu,[1] no lejos del Cuzco, son las más interesantes de las Américas.

Arturo. ¿Cuánto tiempo se necesita para ir de Lima al Cuzco?

Sr. Blanco. Nosotros hicimos el viaje en dos partes. Primero volamos de Lima a Arequipa

10

[1] **Machu Picchu,** *an old fortress-city of unknown origin, often called the "Lost City of the Incas," discovered in* 1912.

175

— un vuelo de una hora, más o menos.   En Arequipa tomamos el tren.   Salimos a las diez de la noche y llegamos al Cuzco a las seis de la tarde siguiente.

ARTURO.   ¿Puede hacerse el vuelo directamente de Lima al Cuzco?

SR. BLANCO.   También.   Se hace el vuelo en cuarenta y cinco minutos.   Pero mi esposa no quiso hacer el vuelo directamente.

• • • • •

ARTURO.   Sr. Blanco, se dice que la vida en el Perú es más lenta que aquí.   ¿Es cierto?

SR. BLANCO.   Puede decirse que los peruanos saben disfrutar de la vida y que no pasan tanto tiempo pensando en el dinero como en los Estados Unidos.

ARTURO.   Estoy leyendo algunos libros sobre el Perú y estoy de acuerdo con Vd.

SR. BLANCO.   Vd. debe pensar también en las fábricas y en los edificios comerciales que se ven en el país si quiere comprender lo que el Perú está haciendo en el siglo veinte.

ARTURO.   Se ven también muchas casas modernas y escuelas nuevas, ¿verdad?

SR. BLANCO.   En todo el país.   En casa tenemos muchos[1] libros y fotografías que trajimos del Perú.   Creo que Vd. puede aprender mucho mirándolos.   ¿Por qué no nos visita uno de estos días?

ARTURO.   Con mucho gusto, Sr. Blanco.   Tengo muchos deseos de conocer mejor la cultura del país.

CONVERSACIÓN

A. Preguntas sobre el diálogo

1. ¿Adónde piensa ir Arturo? 2. ¿Cuánto tiempo pasaron en el Perú los señores Blanco? 3. ¿Cómo se llaman las ruinas que se hallan no lejos del Cuzco? 4. ¿Cuánto tiempo se necesita para ir en avión de Lima al Cuzco? 5. ¿Qué dice el Sr. Blanco de los peruanos? 6. ¿De qué otros aspectos de la vida moderna del Perú habla el Sr. Blanco? 7. ¿Qué quiere enseñarle a Arturo el Sr. Blanco? 8. ¿Qué quiere conocer mejor Arturo?

B. Aplicación del diálogo

1. ¿Piensa Vd. hacer un viaje este verano? 2. ¿Le gusta a Vd. viajar en avión? 3. ¿Qué ciudades norteamericanas conoce Vd.? 4. ¿Hay algunas ruinas cerca de aquí? 5. ¿Qué libros está leyendo Vd. sobre la cultura norteamericana? 6. ¿Cuánto tiempo necesita uno para volar de San Francisco a Nueva York? 7. ¿Deja Vd. para mañana lo que no es necesario hacer hoy? 8. ¿Pasa Vd. mucho tiempo pensando en el dinero?

---

[1] Note that the masculine plural of the adjective **muchos** is used to modify **libros y fotografías**.   Likewise, **los** is used in the following sentence to refer to these two nouns.

NOTAS GRAMATICALES

A. Irregular verbs having **i**-stem preterits

decir	hacer	querer	venir
		SINGULAR	
dije	hice	quise	vine
dijiste	hiciste	quisiste	viniste
dijo	hizo	quiso	vino
		PLURAL	
dijimos	hicimos	quisimos	vinimos
dijisteis	hicisteis	quisisteis	vinisteis
dijeron	hicieron	quisieron	vinieron

The endings of these four verbs, which have **i**-stem preterits, are the same as for **traer** (Lesson 12). Note the spelling of **dijeron** and **hizo**.

The first person singular preterit is translated as follows: **dije**, *I said, did say, I told, did tell*; **hice**, *I made, did make, I did*; **quise**, *I wanted, did want, I wished, did wish*; **vine**, *I came, did come.*

B. Uses of the present participle

1. In Lesson 5 the forms of the present participles of regular verbs were given and their use in the progressive forms of the tenses was explained: **Estoy (Estaba) leyendo un libro,** *I am (was) reading a book.*

Verbs already used which have irregular present participles are:

decir:	**diciendo**	*saying, telling*		creer:	**creyendo**	*believing*
ir:	**yendo**	*going*		leer:	**leyendo**	*reading*
poder:	**pudiendo**	*being able*		traer:	**trayendo**	*bringing*
venir:	**viniendo**	*coming*				

2. **Ellos no pasan tanto tiempo pensando en el dinero.** They do not spend so much time thinking about money.

Mirando las fotografías, Vd. puede aprender mucho. (By) looking at the photographs, you can learn a great deal.

The present participle may be used alone in Spanish, as in English; it is also used to express *by* plus the present participle.

Remember that the infinitive, not the present participle, is used after a preposition: **Antes de verlos,** *Before seeing them.*

C. Position of object pronouns with the present participle

> **Vd. puede aprender mucho mirándolos.** You can learn much by looking at them.
> **Juan está leyéndolos.** ⎫
> **Juan los está leyendo.** ⎭ John is reading them.

Pronouns used as the object of the present participle are always attached to the participle, except in the progressive forms of the tenses, when the pronouns may be placed before **estar.** An accent mark must be written when a pronoun is attached to the present participle.

Remember that object pronouns are also attached to affirmative commands and to infinitives; otherwise they precede the verb.

Práctica. Read in Spanish, noting the position of the object pronouns and the accented forms:

1. Arturo lo trae. Va a traerlo. Está trayéndolo. Tráigalo Vd. No lo traiga Vd. 2. Ellos las miran. Piensan mirarlas. Están mirándolas. Mírenlas Vds. No las miren Vds. 3. Yo les escribo. Quiero escribirles. Estoy escribiéndoles. Escríbales Vd. No les escriba Vd.

D. **Se** used as an indefinite subject

> **Se dice que es verdad.**   They say ⎫
>   People say ⎬ that it is true.
>   It is said ⎭
> **Se puede decir** *or* **Puede decirse** ...   One can say ... (It can be said ...)
> **Se hace el vuelo** ...   One makes the flight ... (The flight is made ...)
> **¿Cuánto tiempo se necesita (necesita uno)?** How much time does one need (is needed)?

Sometimes an action is expressed without indicating definitely who is doing what the verb implies. In such cases in English we use subjects like *one, people, they, you,* which do not refer to a definite person, while in Spanish we use **se.** When used impersonally (that is, when no subject is expressed), the verb is in the third person singular, since **se** is considered the subject (first two examples).

Compare this use of **se** with that explained in Section C, page 80, in which case the verb may be either third person singular or plural. When used with a singular verb form, **se** may be considered either as an indefinite subject or as a reflexive substitute for the passive (third and fourth examples).

Uno is also used as an indefinite subject (fourth example), particularly with reflexive verbs: **Uno se levanta tarde los domingos,** *One gets up late on Sundays.*

E. Pronouns used as objects of prepositions

1.

	SINGULAR				PLURAL		
	mí	me			**nosotros, -as**	us	
	ti	you (*fam.*)			**vosotros, -as**	you (*fam.*)	
para	**él**	for	him, it (*m.*)	**para**	**ellos**	for	them (*m.*)
	ella	her, it (*f.*)			**ellas**	them (*f.*)	
	usted	you (*formal*)			**ustedes**	you	

With the exception of the first and second persons singular, the forms which are used as objects of prepositions are the same as the subject pronouns. Note, however, the difference in meanings, and remember that direct and indirect object pronouns (**me, te, le,** etc.) are never used after prepositions.

Used with **con,** the first and second persons singular have the special forms **conmigo** and **contigo.**

Occasionally **mí, ti, nosotros, -as, vosotros, -as,** and **sí** (third person singular and plural) are used reflexively: **para mí,** *for myself;* **para nosotros, -as,** *for ourselves;* **para sí,** *for himself, herself, yourself (formal), itself, themselves, yourselves.* When used with **con, sí** becomes **consigo,** *with himself,* etc. This form will be used later in the text.

2. **Yo le doy a ella el dinero.** I give her the money.
   Él me enseñó a mí las fotografías. He showed *me* the photographs.
   ¿Le gustan a Vd.? Do you like them?
   Vi a su hermano y a la amiga de él. I saw your brother and his girl friend.

The prepositional forms are often used with the preposition **a** in addition to the direct and indirect object pronouns for emphasis and, in the third person, also for clearness. In the case of **usted**(**es**) it is more polite to use the prepositional form in addition to the object pronoun. See page 79.

The prepositional forms are also used with **de** (fourth example) to clarify the meaning of **su**(**s**), *his, her, your* (formal singular), *their, your* (plural).

F. Use of the definite article in a general sense

Me gustan los caballos. I like horses (*i.e.,* all horses).
Pensamos en el dinero. We think about money.
Los peruanos saben disfrutar de la vida. Peruvians know how to enjoy life.

If a noun in Spanish denotes a general class, that is, if it applies to all horses, money in general, all Peruvians, etc., the definite article is used with it. Many sentences begin with nouns of this type. Contrast this use, however, with that where unemphatic *some* and *any* are involved: **Él compra libros,** *He buys (some) books*; **¿Tiene Vd. dinero hoy?** *Do you have any money today?*

The definite article is also used in Spanish with abstract nouns, such as life, liberty, etc.

EJERCICIOS

A. Substitution drill:

1. *Arturo* vino a ver la fiesta.
   (*Yo, Luis y yo, Mis hermanos, Tú, Elena*)
2. *Marta* hizo un viaje al Perú.
   (*Mis padres, Yo, Tú, Juan y yo, Vd.*)
3. *Ella y yo* no les dijimos nada.
   (*La profesora, Los muchachos, Yo, Vds., Tú*)
4. *María* no quiso ir al cine.
   (*Yo, Los estudiantes, Tú, Vds., Ellas*)

B. Read each sentence in Spanish, then repeat, changing the inflected verbs to the preterit:

1. Elena viene a darme la fotografía.   2. José hace lo que yo le digo.   3. Ellas dicen que van al baile.   4. Yo no quiero ir con ellos.   5. Se ve que Tomás dice la verdad.   6. Mi papá se sienta a la mesa y se desayuna.   7. Carlos y yo decimos que nos levantamos temprano.   8. Los muchachos vienen cuando los llama su mamá.

C. Read in Spanish, placing the object pronouns in their proper position:

1. (nos) Ella escribe. Quiere escribir. Está escribiendo.   2. (lo) Arturo compra. Compre Vd.   Trató de comprar.   3. (les) Enrique dice la verdad.   Diga Vd. la verdad. Va a decir la verdad.   4. (le) Yo doy un caballo.   No dé Vd. un caballo.   No puedo comprar un caballo.   5. (te) Tú levantas.   Piensas levantar.   Estás levantando.

D. Say after your teacher, then repeat, substituting the correct pronoun for the noun which follows each preposition:

MODEL: Tomás baila con Elena.   Tomás baila con Elena.   Tomás baila con ella.

1. Tráigalo Vd. para Juan.   2. No lo traiga Vd. para Isabel.   3. Arturo quiere ir con los hombres.   4. Elena tiene que quedarse con las muchachas.   5. Ella siempre piensa en Pablo.   6. ¿Vive Vd. cerca de mi tía?   7. ¿Quién vino con sus amigas?   8. ¿Charla Vd. mucho con los profesores?   9. Los jóvenes no pueden partir sin el dinero.   10. Mis padres visitaron muchos de los países.

E. Answer each question twice, following the model:

    MODEL: ¿Lee Vd. los libros?   Sí, estoy leyendo los libros.   Estoy leyéndolos.

  1. ¿Trae Vd. el periódico?   4. ¿Escribe Vd. la carta?
  2. ¿Estudia Vd. las lecciones?   5. ¿Molesta Vd. a Ricardo?
  3. ¿Aprende Vd. las frases?   6. ¿Mira Vd. a los muchachos?

F. Answer negatively, watching the prepositional pronouns in your answer:

    MODEL: ¿Es para mí este papel?   No, no es para Vd.

  1. ¿Son para nosotros estas cosas?   4. ¿Es para ti el cuadro?
  2. ¿Es para ella esta revista?   5. ¿Es para Vd. el reloj?
  3. ¿Son para Vds. los periódicos?   6. ¿Son para mí las frases?

G. Your teacher will ask a question, then give a cue. Answer with a complete sentence:

    MODEL: ¿A qué hora se cena allí? ¿A las seis?   Sí, se cena allí a las seis.

  1. ¿Cómo se viaja en México? ¿En coche?
  2. ¿Qué lengua se habla allí? ¿Español?
  3. ¿Cuándo se levanta uno el domingo? ¿A las nueve?
  4. ¿Dónde se compran estas cosas? ¿En la tienda?
  5. ¿Dónde se leen muchos libros? ¿En la biblioteca?

H. Supply the correct form of the definite article where necessary:

  1. Me gustan ——— películas extranjeras. 2. ——— tiempo es oro. 3. ———
primavera es una estación agradable. 4. Compramos ——— libros de vez en cuando.
5. ——— vida en España es interesante. 6. ——— agua es necesaria. 7. ———
exámenes son difíciles. 8. ¿Tiene Vd. ——— hermanos? 9. Hoy día ——— teléfonos
son de varios colores. 10. ——— españoles trabajan mucho. 11. ——— peruanos
disfrutan de ——— vida. 12. Ayer volaron a ——— América del Sur.

COMPOSICIÓN

1. Arthur told Mr. White that he intended to fly to Peru in April.   2. Mr. White made a long trip through South America last year and he spent several weeks in that country. 3. One of the most interesting places that he visited was Cuzco, the old capital of the Incas.   4. After looking at some photographs of the ruins near Cuzco, Arthur said he wanted to see that part of the country.   5. Mr. White flew from Lima to Arequipa, a flight of approximately one hour, and took the train, which did not reach Cuzco until the following night. 6. Also, one can go directly from Lima to Cuzco by plane in forty-five minutes.   7. It is said that life in Peru is slower than in the United States. 8. Peruvians do not spend so much time thinking about money as North Americans. 9. People say that they know how to enjoy life there.   10. We must also think of the schools, business buildings, and factories which can be seen, especially in Lima. 11. After reading some books about Peru, I can understand well what it is doing in the twentieth century.   12. I am very eager to visit the country.

EJERCICIOS DE PRONUNCIACIÓN

Review of the sounds of Spanish **g** and **j**

1. Remember that Spanish **g** (written **gu** before **e** and **i**) is pronounced like a weak English *g* in *go* at the beginning of a breath-group or after **n**:

gusto	grupo	guitarra	inglés	tengo

2. Also, remember that in all other cases, except when before **e** and **i** (**ge, gi**), the sound is much weaker (see Lesson 3):

siglo	siguiente	regalo	hago	traigan
digo	Miguel	luego	amiga	Santiago

3. When before **e** or **i** in the groups **ge, gi,** it is pronounced like Spanish **j,** that is, somewhat like a strongly exaggerated *h* in *halt* (see Lesson 4):

generalmente	Jorge	viaje	lejos	dejan
mejor	dijimos	julio	garaje	agente

4. In the combinations **gua** and **guo** the **u** is pronounced like English *w* in *wet*:

lengua	agua	antiguo	guapo	guante

VOCABULARIO

el acuerdo agreement
  alegrarse (**de** + *obj.*) to be glad (to)
  antiguo, -a old, ancient
  Arturo Arthur
el aspecto aspect
  cierto, -a certain, true
  comercial commercial, business
  comprender to comprehend, under-
    stand
la cultura culture
el Cuzco Cuzco
el deseo desire, wish
  directamente directly
  disfrutar (**de** + *obj.*) to enjoy
el edificio building
la esposa wife
la fábrica factory
el inca Inca

interesar to interest
lejos de *prep.* far from
lento, -a slow
lo que what, that which
mejor better, best
el minuto minute
moderno, -a modern
la oficina office
el Perú Peru
peruano, -a (*also noun*) Peruvian
las ruinas ruins
el siglo century
siguiente following, next
tanto, -a as (so) much; *pl.* as (so)
    many
el tren train
volar (**ue**) to fly
el vuelo flight

ayer por la tarde yesterday afternoon
estar de acuerdo to agree, be in agreement
me alegro (**mucho**) (**de**) I am (very) glad (to)
pensar (**ie**) **en** (+ *obj.*) to think of (about)
tanto, -a + *noun* + **como** as (so) much ... as; *pl.* as (so) many ... as
tener muchos deseos de to be very eager (wish very much) to

Office building, Barcelona, Spain.

Student's cafeteria, University of Madrid, Spain.

CONVERSACIÓN II

La casa y la familia de María

(*María y Carmen salen juntas del comedor de la residencia de señoritas.*)

CARMEN. ¡Hola, María! ¿Qué hay de nuevo?

MARÍA. Nada de particular… Estudiando, como siempre. Y tú, ¿cómo estás?

CARMEN. Muy bien, gracias. ¿Sales ahora para la universidad? Te acompaño un rato.

MARÍA. Esta mañana no voy a la universidad. No tengo clases y me espera mi madre. Voy a ayudarla a limpiar la casa.

CARMEN. ¿Viven Vds. cerca de aquí?

MARÍA. Sí, vivimos en aquella casa nueva que está cerca de la biblioteca.

CARMEN. Yo no sabía que Vds. vivían allí. Es una casa muy grande y muy bonita. Me interesan mucho las casas y los muebles. ¿Cuántos cuartos tiene?

MARÍA. Tiene una sala, un comedor, una cocina, cuatro alcobas y tres cuartos de baño. Y en el sótano hay una sala de recreo.

CARMEN. La casa tiene muchas ventanas, ¿verdad?

MARÍA. Sí. Hay mucha luz en todos los cuartos, porque cada uno tiene dos o tres ventanas.

CARMEN. ¿Qué muebles hay en la sala?

MARÍA. Hay un sofá, varias sillas, tres sillones, un estante, varias mesitas y un aparato de televisión. Naturalmente hay una alfombra en el suelo, y cuadros en las paredes.

CARMEN. ¿Tienes un aparato de radio también?

MARÍA. Sí, tengo uno de onda corta en mi cuarto. Cuando no quiero mirar los programas de televisión, o cuando mi padre está en casa y quiere leer, escucho la radio en mi cuarto. Me gusta escuchar programas de música española.

CARMEN. ¿Qué muebles hay en tu alcoba?

MARÍA. Tengo una cama, una cómoda, un tocador, una mesita de noche, un estante para libros y varias sillas.

CARMEN. La casa es grande. ¿Tienes hermanos?

MARÍA. Tengo dos hermanos y una hermana. Uno de mis hermanos se llama Felipe, el otro, Luis, y mi hermana, Ana.

CARMEN. ¿Dónde estudian tus hermanos?

MARÍA. Ana y Luis estudian en la escuela superior. Felipe y yo estudiamos en la universidad.

CARMEN. ¿Viven tus abuelos en esta ciudad?

MARÍA. Una de mis abuelas vive aquí. Ella tiene un apartamento cerca de nuestra casa. Es anciana, pero tiene buena salud y es muy simpática. Nos visita a menudo. Pero, ¿dónde vives tú?

CARMEN.   También vivimos cerca de la universidad, en una casa de estilo español.   Tiene
    un patio con una fuente y un jardín, donde tenemos árboles y flores de muchas clases.
MARÍA.   Pues conozco la casa muy bien.   Es muy bonita; en realidad, es una de las más
    bonitas de la ciudad.   Tiene un balcón con flores, ¿no es verdad?
5 CARMEN.   Sí, María.   ¿Por qué no nos visitas uno de estos días?   Voy a estar en casa
    mañana por la tarde.
MARÍA.   Con mucho gusto.   Y también quiero invitarte a mi casa.
CARMEN.   Muchas gracias, María.   Bueno, no trabajes demasiado.   Hasta luego, María.
MARÍA.   Hasta luego, Carmen.

PREGUNTAS

Sobre la conversación

1. ¿Por qué no va María a la universidad hoy?   2. ¿Dónde vive María?   3. ¿Cuántos
cuartos tiene la casa?   4. ¿Qué hay en el sótano?   5. ¿Qué muebles hay en la sala?
6. ¿Tiene María un aparato de radio?

7. ¿Cuándo escucha María programas de radio en su cuarto?   8. ¿Qué muebles hay
en la alcoba de María?   9. ¿Cuántos hermanos tiene María?   10. ¿Dónde estudian
los hermanos de María?   11. ¿Qué dice María de su abuela?   12. ¿Cómo es la casa
de Carmen?

Aplicación de la conversación

1. ¿Dónde vive Vd.?   2. ¿Cuántos cuartos tiene la casa de Vd.?   3. ¿Tiene la casa
una sala de recreo?   4. ¿Qué muebles hay en la sala?   5. ¿Tiene Vd. un aparato de
televisión?   6. ¿Tiene Vd. un aparato de radio de onda corta?

7. ¿Qué programas de radio escucha Vd.?   8. ¿Qué muebles hay en el cuarto de Vd.?
9. ¿Cuántos hermanos tiene Vd.?   10. ¿Cómo se llaman sus hermanos?   11. ¿Dónde
estudian sus hermanos?   12. ¿Cómo son las casas de estilo español?

PRÁCTICAS ORALES

Groups of students will be selected to prepare a conversation of six to eight exchanges,
using vocabulary already given.

1. In several groups two American students meet a Spanish friend and speak briefly
about their homes and families.

2. In other groups two students discuss the pieces of furniture in their dormitory
rooms and whether or not they can study in their rooms.

VOCABULARIO

la abuela grandmother
el abuelo grandfather; *pl.* grandparents
la alcoba bedroom
la alfombra rug, carpet
 anciano, -a old
el apartamento apartment
 ayudar (**a** + *inf.*) to help, aid
el balcón (*pl.* **balcones**) balcony
la cama bed
la clase kind
la cocina kitchen
la cómoda chest of drawers
 corto, -a short
el cuarto de baño bathroom
 donde where, in which
la escuela superior high school
el estante (**para libros**) bookcase
la flor flower

la fuente fountain
el jardín (*pl.* **jardines**) garden
la luz (*pl.* **luces**) light
los muebles furniture
la música music
 naturalmente naturally
la onda wave
el rato while, short time
la radio[1] radio
la sala de recreo recreation room
la salud health
el sillón (*pl.* **sillones**) armchair
 simpático, -a charming, likeable, "nice"
el sofá sofa, davenport
el sótano basement
el suelo floor
el tocador dressing table

aparato de radio (**televisión**) radio (television) set
en realidad in reality, in fact

[1] **La radio** means *radio* as a means of communication; **el radio** is used to mean *the radio set*.

Irregular verbs having *u*-stem preterits
Verbs with changes in spelling in the preterit
Combinations of two personal object pronouns
Demonstrative pronouns.   Uses of *volver* and *devolver*,
of *preguntar*, of *pagar*, and of the idiom *acabar de*

MARTA AYUDA A CAROLINA A HACER UNA COMPRA

(*Al salir de una tienda, Marta se encuentra con Carolina.*)

MARTA.   ¡Hola, Carolina!   ¿Cuándo volviste de tu viaje?   Estuve en tu cuarto ayer por la tarde, y nadie sabía cuándo pensabas volver.

CAROLINA.   Llegué anoche entre las siete y las ocho.   Te busqué, pero no estabas en tu cuarto.

MARTA.   Almorcé con Tomás al mediodía y pasé toda la tarde con él.   Acaba de volver de la Florida.   Y, ¿qué tal el viaje?

CAROLINA.   Pues mucho mejor de lo que[1] esperaba.   Decidí volver cuando supe que mi madre estaba mejor.   Y gracias por las flores que encontré en mi cuarto.

MARTA.   De nada.   María y yo las pusimos allí.

• • • • •

MARTA.   Pero, ¿qué haces aquí en el centro, Carolina?

CAROLINA.   Busco unos regalos para mi hermana Luisa.   Mañana es su cumpleaños.

MARTA.   ¿Cuántos años va a cumplir?

CAROLINA.   Diez y seis años.

[1] Before a verb when an adjective, an adverb, or an idea is compared, **de lo que**, *than* (*what*), is used in Spanish.   See page 82 for the explanation of the use of **que** and **de** for *than*.

Marta. Ya entiendo. Debemos celebrar los grandes[1] momentos de la vida. ¿Qué le compraste?

Carolina. Varias cosas. Empecé con una tarjeta muy bonita. Luego le compré unas medias y, después, una blusa que está muy de moda.

Marta. ¿Cuánto pagaste por la blusa?

Carolina. Pagué nueve dólares por ella. También encontré una bolsa preciosa, pero no pude comprarla porque no tenía bastante dinero.

• • • • •

Marta. Yo tengo un billete de diez dólares que me mandó mi papá esta mañana. Puedo prestártelo si quieres.

Carolina. ¿De veras? ¡Qué amable eres, Marta! Te lo devuelvo[2] esta noche. Ésta es la tienda. Entra conmigo.

Marta. Si no tardas mucho, te acompaño. Tengo una cita con Tomás a las doce. (*Las dos jóvenes entran en la tienda y se detienen frente al mostrador donde se venden las bolsas. Carolina le pregunta a la empleada por la bolsa.*)

Carolina. (*A Marta.*) ¿Te gusta ésta? A mí me gusta más que aquéllas.

Marta. Sí, ésa me gusta. Es preciosa.

Carolina. Pues me la llevo. (*Le da el dinero a la empleada; ésta envuelve la bolsa y se la entrega a Carolina.*) Muchas gracias.

Marta. (*Mirando su reloj.*) Pero ya es tarde; tengo que irme. Hasta luego, Carolina.

Carolina. Hasta la vista, Marta. Gracias por todo. Favor de saludar a Tomás de mi parte.

CONVERSACIÓN

A. Preguntas sobre el diálogo

1. ¿Dónde se encuentra Marta con Carolina? 2. ¿Qué le pregunta Marta a Carolina? 3. ¿Quién puso las flores en el cuarto de Carolina? 4. ¿Qué busca Carolina en el centro? 5. ¿Cuántos años va a cumplir la hermana de Carolina? 6. ¿Qué compró Carolina con el dinero que le prestó Marta? 7. ¿Cuándo va a devolverle el dinero Carolina? 8. ¿Con quién va a almorzar Marta?

B. Aplicación del diálogo

1. ¿Tiene Vd. hermanos? 2. ¿Les compra Vd. regalos a sus hermanos? 3. ¿Cuánto pagó Vd. por el último regalo que le compró a su padre? 4. ¿Les manda Vd. flores a

---

[1] When a form of **grande** precedes a noun it usually means *great*. [2] See footnote 1, page 78. Note two similar constructions in lines 12 and 17.

sus amigas? 5. ¿Les presta Vd. dinero a sus amigos? 6. ¿Qué regalos les gustan a las jóvenes? 7. ¿Acaba Vd. de recibir dinero de sus padres? 8. ¿Qué compras piensa Vd. hacer esta semana?

NOTAS GRAMATICALES

A. Irregular verbs having **u**-stem preterits

estar	**poder**	**poner**	**saber**	**tener**
		SINGULAR		
estuve	pude	puse	supe	tuve
estuviste	pudiste	pusiste	supiste	tuviste
estuvo	pudo	puso	supo	tuvo
		PLURAL		
estuvimos	pudimos	pusimos	supimos	tuvimos
estuvisteis	pudisteis	pusisteis	supisteis	tuvisteis
estuvieron	pudieron	pusieron	supieron	tuvieron

Note that these five verbs have **u**-stem preterits, and that the endings are the same as for the four verbs in Lesson 13 which have **i**-stems in the preterit. They are translated as follows: **estuve,** *I was*; **pude,** *I could, was able to*; **puse,** *I put, did put, I placed, did place*; **tuve,** *I had, did have.* **Tuve** also may mean *I got, received.* The preterit of **saber** is usually translated: **Cuando supe,** *When I learned, found out.*

B. Verbs with changes in spelling in the preterit

buscar: **busqué,** buscaste, buscó, etc.
llegar: **llegué,** llegaste, llegó, etc.
empezar: **empecé,** empezaste, empezó, etc.

Review the sounds of the consonants **c, g,** and **z,** then note that in order to keep the sound of the final consonant of the stem of a Spanish verb, a change in spelling is often necessary. Before the ending **-e** in the first person singular preterit, all verbs ending in **-car** change **c** to **qu;** those ending in **-gar** change **g** to **gu,** and those ending in **-zar** change **z** to **c.**

Note that **empezar** is also a stem-changing verb in the present tense: **empiezo, empiezas, empieza, empezamos, empezáis, empiezan.** **Comenzar** has the same changes.

C. Combinations of two personal object pronouns

Él me lo dio.	He gave it to me.
Ellos nos las escribieron	They wrote them to us.

Ella se lo vende	⎧ **a él.** ⎪ **a ella.** ⎪ **a Vd.** ⎨ **a ellos.** ⎪ **a ellas.** ⎩ **a Vds.**	She sells it	⎧ to him. ⎪ to her. ⎪ to you (*sing.*). ⎨ to them. ⎪ to them (*f.*). ⎩ to you (*pl.*).

Tráigamelos Vd.	Bring them to me.
Yo puedo prestárselo a Vd.	I can lend it to you.
Ella se los puso.	She put them on.
Poniéndoselo, ella salió.	Putting it on, she left.

The indirect object pronoun precedes the direct when two pronouns are used as objects of the same verb. When both pronoun objects are in the third person, **se** replaces the indirect **le** or **les**. Thus **se lo** replaces **le lo, les lo; se la** replaces **le la, les la,** etc. Never use two pronouns together which begin with **l.** Since **se** in this combination may mean *to him, her, you, it,* or *them,* the prepositional forms will often be required in addition to **se** for clearness.

A reflexive pronoun precedes any other object pronoun. When two pronouns are added to an infinitive, an accent mark must be written over the final syllable of the verb. Also note that an accent mark is written on the next to the last syllable of a present participle when either one or two pronouns are added.

Práctica. Say after your teacher:

1. Juan me lo da. Va a dármelo. Está dándomelo. (Me lo está dando.) Démelo Vd. No me lo dé Vd.

2. Yo se lo llevo a él. Quiero llevárselo. Estoy llevándoselo. (Se lo estoy llevando.) Lléveselo Vd. No se lo lleve Vd.

3. Luis no se los prestó a ellos. No pudo prestárselos. Prestándoselos. Présteselos Vd. No se los preste Vd.

4. ¿Se lavaron Vds. las manos? ¿Quieren lavárselas? ¿Están lavándoselas? (¿Se las están lavando?) Lávenselas Vds. No se las laven Vds.

5. ¿Se puso ella los guantes? ¿Se los puso? ¿Pudo ponérselos? ¿Estaba poniéndoselos? (¿Se los estaba poniendo?) Póngaselos Vd.

D. Demonstrative pronouns

éste, ésta, éstos, éstas	this (one), these
ése, ésa, ésos, ésas	that (one), those
aquél, aquélla, aquéllos, aquéllas	that (one), those

> **esto, eso, aquello**   this, that (*neuter*)

> **estos guantes y ésos**   these gloves and those (*near you*)
> **aquella blusa y ésta**   that blouse (*yonder*) and this one
> **¿Qué es esto?**   What is this?
> **Eso es interesante.**   That is interesting.

The demonstrative pronouns are the same in form as the demonstrative adjectives, except for the written accent on the pronouns (see page 67). The use of the pronouns corresponds to that of the adjectives.

The three neuter pronouns are used when the antecedent is a statement, a general idea, or something which has not been identified. Since there are no neuter adjectives, an accent is not required on these three forms.

The demonstrative pronoun **éste** (**-a, -os, -as**) often translates *the latter* in Spanish:

> **Ella le da el dinero a la empleada; ésta envuelve la bolsa.**
> She gives the money to the clerk; the latter wraps up the purse.

E. Uses of **volver, devolver, preguntar, pagar,** and of the idiom **acabar de**

1. **Marta volvió a casa.**   Martha returned home.
   Yo le devolví a ella el dinero.   I returned the money to her.

Volver means *to return, come back*, while **devolver** means *to return, give back, e.g.*, something borrowed.

2. **Pregúntele Vd. si piensa volver.**   Ask him whether he plans to return.
   Le pregunté a ella cuánto costaba.   I asked her how much it cost.
   Carolina le pregunta a la empleada por la bolsa.   Caroline asks the clerk about the purse.

Preguntar means *to ask* a question, which may be direct or indirect (*i.e.*, introduced by an interrogative pronoun or by **si**, *whether, if*) (first and second examples). To ask *about* a thing or person, **por** is used (third example). The verb requires the indirect object of the person.

3. **Yo pagué la bolsa.**   I paid for the purse.
   Le pagué nueve dólares por ella.   I paid her nine dollars for it.

Pagar, *to pay, pay for*, may take as its direct object either the thing paid for or the amount paid; the person paid is the indirect object. The thing paid for is preceded by **por** when the amount is given.

4. **Él acaba de volver de la Florida.**   He has just returned from Florida.
Los muchachos acababan de traerlo.   The boys had just brought it.

The present and imperfect of **acabar de** plus an infinitive translate English *have* (*had*) *just* plus the English past participle.

EJERCICIOS

A. Say after your teacher, then repeat twice, changing the verb to the preterit tense, then to the imperfect tense:

1. Los muchachos están en casa.
2. Ella lo pone sobre la mesa.
3. Yo les entrego las compras.
4. Yo busco a mis amigos.
5. Yo comienzo a leer las frases.
6. Yo llego a tiempo.
7. María se pone el vestido.
8. Las dos se detienen frente a la casa.
9. Yo almuerzo con Tomás.
10. ¿Le pagas a María la bolsa?
11. ¿Los encuentra Vd. en la calle?
12. ¿Te encuentras con María?

B. Say after your teacher, then repeat, substituting the correct object pronoun for each noun (in italics) and placing it in the proper position:

1. Ella me escribió *la carta*.   2. Él me enseñó *los guantes*.   3. Vd. nos trajo *las compras*.
4. Nosotros te dimos *las fotografías*.   5. Ella quería vendernos *la bolsa*.   6. Ellos le dieron a él *los billetes*.   7. Póngase Vd. *el sombrero*.   8. No se ponga Vd. *las medias*.
9. Carolina quiere llevarse *la bolsa*.   10. ¿Quién le vendió a Vd. *ese reloj*?   11. Tú no le llevaste a ella *los regalos*.   12. No te laves *las manos*.   13. ¿Están Vds. lavándose *la cara*?   14. ¿Te prestó ella *el dinero*?   15. Yo me compré *unas blusas*.

C. Answer affirmatively, substituting the correct object pronoun for the noun and making any other necessary changes:

MODELS: ¿Le llevó Vd. a ella la bolsa?   Sí, se la llevé a ella.
          ¿Vas a entregarme el billete?   Sí, voy a entregárselo a Vd.

1. ¿Le dio Vd. a él el regalo?
2. ¿Nos trajeron Vds. el billete?
3. ¿Me traes las compras?
4. ¿Le compras a él el libro?
5. ¿Va Vd. a leerle a ella la carta?
6. ¿Quieres llevarles a ellas esas cosas?
7. ¿Estás trayéndome las flores?
8. ¿Está Vd. llevándoles el dinero?

D. Say after your teacher, then repeat, using the demonstrative pronoun:

> MODEL: Mire Vd. aquella casa.   Mire Vd. aquella casa.   Mire Vd. aquélla.

1. ¿Le gusta a Vd. más este vestido?
2. Yo no quiero comprar esos guantes.
3. Tráigame Vd. aquellas medias.
4. Debes llevarles estas flores.
5. Yo le entregué aquel regalo.
6. Marta abrió esas ventanas.
7. Juan me devolvió estas cosas.
8. ¿Se compró Vd. ese reloj?
9. Entraron en aquella tienda.
10. No salieron de ese cuarto.

E. Answer each question, following the model:

> MODEL: ¿Qué blusa le gusta a Vd.?   ¿Ésta?   No, no me gusta ésa.

1. ¿Qué guantes acabas de comprar?   ¿Éstos?
2. ¿Qué sombrero va Vd. a comprarle a Marta?   ¿Éste?
3. ¿Cuál de los vestidos quiere Vd.?   ¿Ése?
4. ¿Cuál de las tarjetas te gusta más?   ¿Ésa?
5. ¿Qué libros puede Vd. prestarme?   ¿Esos?
6. ¿Qué fotografías te gustan más?   ¿Éstas?

F. Compose original sentences in Spanish using the following:

1. devolver. 2. volver. 3. acabar de. 4. detenerse. 5. ayudar a. 6. llevarse. 7. encontrarse con. 8. favor de. 9. empezar a. 10. gustar más.

G. Give the Spanish for:

1. The money.   Give it to me; don't give it to her.   2. The stockings.   Bring them to her; don't bring them to them (*f. pl.*).   3. The gifts.   Do not take them to him; take them to her.   4. The car.   He wants to sell it to us; he doesn't want to sell it to you.   5. The purse.   Martha is bringing it to her; she has just brought it to her.

COMPOSICIÓN

1. Caroline, who has just returned from Florida, runs across Martha downtown.   2. She returned sooner than she expected because her mother was much better.   3. Caroline said that she was looking for some gifts for her sister Louise's birthday.   4. "What did you buy?,"[1] Martha asked Caroline; the latter answered: "I began with a card and

---

[1] For the use of quotation marks in Spanish, see page 7.

some stockings." 5. "Then I bought her a pretty blouse, which is very stylish." 6. "Also I found a darling purse, but I couldn't buy it because I didn't have enough money." 7. Martha said that she had a ten-dollar bill that she could lend her. 8. The two girls returned to the store and stopped in front of the counter where purses are sold. 9. When Martha says that she likes this purse better than the others, Caroline decides to take it (with her). 10. When Caroline gives the money to the clerk, the latter hands her the purse. 11. It is late now and Martha has to go because her friend Tom is waiting for her. 12. Caroline says to her: "Please say hello to Tom for me."

EJERCICIOS DE PRONUNCIACIÓN

1. Review the sounds of diphthongs (see pages 5, 36, 37, 135, and 169), then pronounce and divide into syllables:

miedo	principio	secretaria	vuelo	encuentra
iglesia	abierto	cuaderno	playa	autobús
baile	reina	veinte	traiga	sois
llevé‿uno	tengo‿una	ruinas	ciudad	muy

2. When a weak vowel adjacent to a strong vowel has a written accent, it retains its syllabic value and forms a separate syllable; divide into syllables:

traía	creí	había	ríos	país

3. An accent on a strong vowel merely indicates stress; divide into syllables:

diálogo	habéis	comió	avión	ayudáis

4. Two adjacent strong vowels form two separate syllables; divide into syllables:

paseo	idea	europeo	leemos	héroe

VOCABULARIO

acabar to end, finish
almorzar (ue) to have (eat) lunch
amable kind
ayudar (a + inf.) to help, aid (to)
el billete bill, bank note
la blusa blouse
la cita date, appointment
el cumpleaños birthday
cumplir to fulfill, keep (one's word);
  reach (one's birthday), be (years old)
decidir to decide
detener (*like* **tener**) to detain, stop;
  reflex. stop (oneself)
devolver (ue) to return, give back
donde where, in which
empezar (ie) (a + inf.) to begin (to)
entender (ie) to understand
entregar to hand (over), give
envolver (ue) to wrap (up)
esperar to expect
la flor flower

la Florida Florida
frente a *prep.* in front of
irse to go (away), leave
llevarse to take away, take with oneself
mandar to send, order
la media stocking; *pl.* stockings, hose
el mediodía noon
la moda style, fashion
el mostrador counter, show case
pagar to pay, pay for
precioso, -a precious, darling, beautiful
preguntar to ask (*a question*)
prestar to lend
el regalo gift
tardar to delay, be long
la tarjeta card (*postal, birthday, etc.*)
todo *pron.* everything
vender to sell

acabar de + inf. to have just + *p.p.*
al mediodía at noon
billete de (diez) dólares (ten)-dollar bill
¿cuántos años (va a cumplir)? how old (is she going to be)?
cumplir (diez y seis) años to reach one's (sixteenth) birthday,
  be (sixteen) years old
de lo que (esperaba) than (I expected)
de mi parte for me, on my part
de nada don't mention it, you are welcome, not at all
en el centro downtown
encontrarse (ue) con to meet, run across
estar (muy) de moda to be (very) stylish, be (very) fashionable
favor de + inf. please + *verb*
gracias por thanks (thank you) for
gustar más (que) to like better (than),
¿qué tal...? how about...? how is (was)...?
toda la tarde all afternoon, the whole (entire) afternoon
tardar mucho to take long (a long time)

Girl wearing regional dress during the Holy Week celebration in Salamanca, Spain.

LECTURA VII

FIESTAS

Estudio de palabras

a. Approximate cognates. Pronounce the following words aloud, give the English cognates, and indicate the principles involved in recognizing them: adornar, aniversario, celebrar, dedicar, independencia, religioso, representar, revolucionario, sociedad.

b. Less approximate cognates. Pronounce the following words aloud, note the English cognates, and indicate the variations: católico, *Catholic*; movimiento, *movement*; héroe, *hero*; máscara, *mask*; grotesco, *grotesque*; solemne, *solemn*; espléndido, *splendid*.

c. Compare the meanings of: baile, *dance, and* bailar, *to dance*; comida, *meal, dinner, and* comer, *to eat, dine*; fiesta, *festival, holiday, and* festivo, *festive*; viaje, *trip,* viajar, *to travel, and* viajero, *traveler.*

d. The opposites of the following words appear in the reading selection: dar, empezar, el fin, entrar. Can you give them?

Los países de habla española celebran muchas fiestas. Algunas son nacionales; otras son religiosas. Nosotros celebramos el aniversario de nuestra independencia el cuatro de julio; los mexicanos celebran el suyo[1] el diez y seis de septiembre. En México esa fecha no conmemora el fin de la guerra de la independencia, sino el principio de una larga lucha contra los españoles. Honra a Miguel de Hidalgo, un sacerdote[2] católico que el día quince de septiembre de 1810 pronunció las palabras que al día siguiente[3] iniciaron el movimiento revolucionario. Todas las repúblicas hispanoamericanas honran a sus héroes nacionales y celebran el aniversario de su independencia. Muchas veces estas fiestas duran dos o tres días.

El mundo católico dedica cada día del año a uno o a varios santos. Cuando bautizan[4] a un niño, éste recibe el nombre de un santo y cada año celebra el día de su santo más bien que[5] el aniversario de su nacimiento. Es un día de mucha alegría en que hay regalos, tertulias y comidas.

En España hay muchas fiestas típicas que combinan elementos religiosos y festivos. Por ejemplo, la verbena, que se celebra la víspera del día del santo patrón, es una feria semejante a los carnavales de nuestro país. La romería, que honra también a algún santo, consiste en una excursión a la capilla[6] del santo, que a veces está lejos del pueblo. Después de las ceremonias religiosas en la capilla, se celebra una fiesta que se parece a[7] un *picnic*. Todos comen y cantan y bailan hasta la hora de volver al pueblo.

El día de San Antón es interesante porque este santo es el patrón de los burros, de las mulas y de los caballos. El diez y siete de enero adornan a los animales y los llevan a recibir la bendición[8] de San Antón.

---

[1] **el suyo,** *theirs.*   [2] **sacerdote,** *priest.*   [3] **al día siguiente,** *on the following day.*   [4] **bautizan,** *they baptize.*
[5] **más bien que,** *rather than.*   [6] **capilla,** *chapel.*   [7] **se parece a,** *resembles.*   [8] **bendición,** *blessing.*

Holy Week celebrations, Salamanca, Spain.

Masked dancers during festival at Urubamba, Perú.

El veinte y ocho de diciembre, Día de los Inocentes,[1] es para los españoles lo que el primero de abril es para nosotros. Todos tratan de dar bromas a[2] sus amigos y se divierten mucho.[3]

Otras fiestas importantes son el Carnaval y la Pascua Florida.[4] El Miércoles de Ceniza[5] marca el fin del Carnaval y el principio de los cuarenta días de la Cuaresma.[6] En las fiestas de Carnaval casi todo el mundo se pone una máscara y un traje grotesco y sale a la calle para tirar confeti y serpentinas. Por la noche hay bailes, y reina[7] la alegría por todas partes.

Durante la Cuaresma se celebran las procesiones religiosas de la Semana Santa, que empieza el Domingo de Ramos[8] y termina el Domingo de Resurrección.[9] En Sevilla, España, se observa esta semana de una manera solemne y espléndida. Muchas sociedades religiosas forman procesiones que pasan por las calles llevando pasos[10] grandes que representan la Pasión de Cristo en forma impresionante y hermosa. Las procesiones terminan el Viernes Santo. Con el Sábado de Gloria[11] vuelve la alegría. Por la noche se tocan las campanas de todas las iglesias. El Domingo de Resurrección se llama la Pascua Florida porque en todas las iglesias adornan de flores los altares. Igual que[12] en nuestro país, la gente se pone la ropa más elegante para ir a la iglesia. Por la tarde generalmente hay corridas de toros.[13]

"Paso" of the Virgin, Holy Week, Seville, Spain

---

[1] **Día de los Inocentes** = *April Fool's Day.* (An **inocente** is a gullible person or one easily duped.)   [2] **dar bromas a,** *to play tricks on.*   [3] **se divierten mucho,** *they have a very good time (amuse themselves very much).*   [4] **Pascua Florida,** *Easter.*   [5] **Miércoles de Ceniza,** *Ash Wednesday.*   [6] **Cuaresma,** *Lent.*   [7] **reina,** *reigns.*   [8] **Domingo de Ramos,** *Palm Sunday.*   [9] **Domingo de Resurrección,** *Easter Sunday.*   [10] **pasos,** *floats.* (**Pasos** are the heavy platforms on which life-sized figures representing Christ, the Virgin, and other persons who figured in the Passion of Christ are carried through the streets of Seville during Holy Week by members of the churches and religious societies.)   [11] **Sábado de Gloria,** *Holy Saturday.*   [12] **Igual que,** *The same as.*   [13] **corridas de toros,** *bullfights.*

Monument to Independence, Dolores Hidalgo, México.

In this church on September 10, 1810, Hidalgo proclaimed the Independence of México.

Charreada, typical Mexican celebration.

PREGUNTAS

1. ¿En qué día celebramos el aniversario de nuestra independencia? 2. ¿Cuándo lo celebran en México? 3. ¿A quién honran los mexicanos? 4. ¿Quién fue Hidalgo?

5. Cuando bautizan a un niño español, ¿qué recibe él? 6. ¿Qué celebran los españoles cada año? 7. ¿Qué hay en ese día? 8. ¿Cuándo se celebra una verbena? 9. ¿A quién honra la romería? 10. ¿Qué hacen todos después de las ceremonias religiosas?

11. ¿De qué es patrón San Antón? 12. ¿Qué día es el veinte y ocho de diciembre? 13. ¿Qué tratan de hacer todos?

14. ¿Qué marca el Miércoles de Ceniza? 15. ¿Qué hace casi todo el mundo en las fiestas de Carnaval? 16. ¿Qué hay por la noche? 17. ¿Cuándo empieza la Semana Santa? 18. ¿Cuándo termina? 19. ¿Qué llevan en las procesiones en Sevilla? 20. ¿Qué hace todo el mundo el Domingo de Resurrección?

Celebration of *Día de Difuntos*, Janitzio, Lake Pátzcuaro, México.

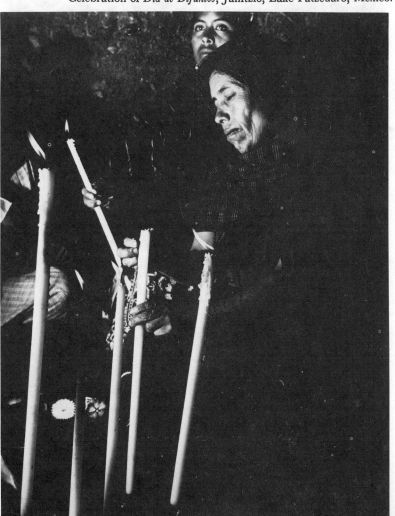

LECCIÓN 15

**The past participles. The present perfect and pluperfect
indicative tenses. The past participle used as an adjective
Other uses of *haber*. *Hace* meaning "ago, since"**

UNA TARDE EN LA PLAYA

(*Ricardo y Vicente, que están de vacaciones, se encuentran en la calle.*)

VICENTE. ¡Hola, Ricardo! ¿Dónde has estado? Pasé por tu casa hace un par de horas y
no había nadie allí.

RICARDO. He estado en la playa, Vicente. Cuando hace calor y tengo tiempo, me gusta ir
a nadar.

5 VICENTE. ¿Había mucha gente?

RICARDO. Sí, mucha. Parecía que todo el mundo había ido a nadar. Nunca he visto
tanta gente en la playa.

• • • • •

VICENTE. Cuando yo era pequeño, me gustaba nadar en un lago que había cerca de nuestra
casa.

RICARDO. Por aquí cerca no hay ni lagos ni ríos. Hay piscinas, pero me gusta más nadar
en el mar.

VICENTE. El martes pasado fui a la playa y no pude nadar porque hacía fresco y el agua
estaba fría.

RICARDO. Recuerdo que llevabas un traje de baño nuevo que habías comprado precisamente para ese día.

VICENTE. Es verdad, pero me senté en la arena un rato a tomar el sol.

• • • • •

RICARDO. Esta tarde llevé a mi hermanito a la playa. Al principio él tenía miedo y no se atrevía a entrar solo.

VICENTE. ¿No sabe nadar?

RICARDO. Estoy enseñándole y ya ha aprendido bastante. Pasamos casi toda la tarde en el agua y cuando salimos del mar, el muchacho se encontraba muy cansado.

VICENTE. ¿Cuántos años tiene tu hermanito?

RICARDO. Creo que tiene nueve años. No, cumplió diez el mes pasado.

VICENTE. Hay que ir a la playa todos los días para aprender rápidamente. No se aprende a[1] nadar tomando el sol en la playa, ¿verdad?

RICARDO. Tienes razón. Pero, ¿qué has hecho tú esta tarde?

VICENTE. He estado trabajando en la oficina de mi padre. Su secretaria ha tenido que ir a Nueva York.

RICARDO. Veo que estás trabajando demasiado, Vicente.

VICENTE. No lo creo. Ahora tengo que bañarme y mudarme de ropa, porque a las siete he de ir al cine con Juan. En realidad, no quiero salir esta noche, pero debo cumplir mi palabra. Hasta luego, Ricardo.

RICARDO. Hasta luego, Vicente.

CONVERSACIÓN

A. Preguntas sobre el diálogo

1. ¿Quiénes hablan en este diálogo? 2. ¿Qué le pregunta Vicente a Ricardo?
3. ¿Dónde ha estado Ricardo? 4. ¿Había mucha gente en la playa? 5. ¿Por qué no pudo nadar Vicente el martes pasado? 6. ¿Sabe nadar el hermanito de Ricardo? 7. ¿Qué ha hecho Vicente esta tarde? 8. ¿Qué ha de hacer Vicente a las siete?

B. Aplicación del diálogo

1. ¿Sabe Vd. nadar bien? 2. ¿En qué meses se puede nadar en esta parte del país?
3. ¿Qué se pone uno para nadar? 4. ¿Le gusta a Vd. nadar cuando hace frío?
5. ¿Dónde se puede nadar por aquí? 6. ¿Hay lagos o ríos cerca de aquí? 7. ¿Le gusta a Vd. tomar el sol en la playa? 8. ¿Qué ha hecho Vd. esta mañana?

---

[1] Note that **aprender** requires **a** before an infinitive object.

NOTAS GRAMATICALES

A. The past participles

hablar: hablado *spoken*   comer: comido *eaten*   vivir: vivido *lived*

Past participles are regularly formed by adding **-ado** to the stem of **-ar** verbs and **-ido** to the stem of **-er** and **-ir** verbs.

If the stem ends in **-a, -e,** or **-o,** the regular ending **-ido** requires an accent:

creer: **creído** *believed*   leer: **leído** *read*   traer: **traído** *brought*

The following verbs which you have learned have irregular past participles:

abrir:	**abierto**	*opened*	poner:	**puesto**	*put, placed*
decir:	**dicho**	*said*	ver:	**visto**	*seen*
escribir:	**escrito**	*written*	volver:	**vuelto**	*returned*
hacer:	**hecho**	*done, made*	devolver:	**devuelto**	*given back*
ir:	**ido**	*gone*	descubrir:	**descubierto**	*discovered*

B. The present perfect and pluperfect indicative tenses

Present Perfect

he		*I have*	
has	hablado	*you* (fam.) *have*	spoken
ha		*he, she has*	
Vd. **ha**		*you* (formal) *have*	

hemos		*we have*	
habéis	hablado	*you* (fam.) *have*	spoken
han		*they have*	
Vds. **han**		*you have*	

Pluperfect

había		*I had*	
habías	comido	*you* (fam.) *had*	eaten
había		*he, she had*	
Vd. había		*you* (formal) *had*	

habíamos		*we had*	
habíais	} comido	*you* (fam.) *had*	} *eaten*
habían		*they had*	
Vds. habían		*you had*	

Nosotros lo hemos escrito.   We have written it.
Ella no se lo ha puesto.   She has not put it on.
¿No lo había hecho Vd.?   Hadn't you (Had you not) done it?

The auxiliary verb **haber** is used with the past participle to form the compound or perfect tenses.   The present tense of **haber** plus the past participle forms the present perfect tense, and the imperfect tense of **haber** plus the past participle forms the pluperfect tense.

Note the following points: (1) Following forms of **haber** the past participle always ends in **-o;** (2) The form of **haber** and the past participle are seldom separated; (3) Negative words precede the form of **haber;** (4) Pronoun objects precede the form of **haber** or come between the negative and the form of **haber.**

Práctica.   Read in Spanish, keeping the meaning in mind:

1. he abierto; había abierto.   2. hemos puesto; habíamos puesto.   3. él ha escrito; había escrito.   4. ellos han hecho; habían hecho.   5. Vd. ha visto; había visto.   6. Vds. han dicho; habían dicho.   7. tú has vuelto; habías vuelto.   8. habéis ido; habíais ido. 9. yo no lo he creído; nosotros no hemos devuelto.   10. nosotros no la hemos leído; yo no me he sentado.

C. The past participle used as an adjective

Las ventanas estaban abiertas.   The windows were open.
La puerta no está cerrada.   The door isn't closed.
José se encontraba cansado.   Joe was (found himself) tired.

Past participles may be used as adjectives, in which case they agree like other adjectives. Remember that certain reflexive verbs like **encontrarse, hallarse, verse** are often substituted for **estar** with past participles, and that in such cases they normally retain something of their literal meanings.   (See footnote 1, page 107, and footnote 3, page 163.)

Do not confuse this use of **estar** with a past participle, used to describe a state or condition which is the result of a previous action, with the reflexive substitute for the passive, page 80, which is used when an action is involved: **Se cerró la puerta a las cinco,** *The door was closed at five o'clock.*

D. Other uses of **haber**

1. **Yo he de ir al cine.**   I am (supposed) to go to the movie.
   Mis padres han de volver hoy.   My parents are to return today.
   Los hombres habían de terminar temprano.   The men were to finish early.

Haber de plus an infinitive expresses commitment or mild obligation and means *to be to, be supposed to.*   The obligation is not so strong as that expressed by **tener que: Yo tengo que salir ahora,** *I have to (must) leave now.*

   For a moral obligation or duty, **deber** is used: **Debo practicar mucho,** *I should (must) practice a great deal.*

   Recall that the third person singular of **haber** is used impersonally; *i.e.,* without a definite personal subject: **hay** (used for **ha**), *there is, there are*; **había,** *there was, there were*; **ha habido,** *there has been, there have been*: **¿Había mucha gente en la playa?** *Were there many people at the beach?*

2. **Hay que estudiar mucho.**   One must study hard.
   Hay que llegar a tiempo.   It is necessary to arrive on time.

Hay que plus an infinitive means *it is necessary to* or the indefinite subject *one, we, you,* etc., *must.*   The imperfect **había que** is less common: **Había que hablar despacio,** *It was necessary to talk slowly.*

Práctica.   Read in Spanish, keeping the meaning in mind:

1. Yo tengo que trabajar esta tarde.   2. Marta tiene que mudarse de ropa.   3. ¿Han de volver ellos mañana?   4. Él y yo hemos de hablar con ella ahora.   5. ¿Habían de pasar por aquí?   6. Hay que hablar con los profesores.   7. Hay que empezar a aprender el diálogo.   8. Había que pronunciar las frases varias veces.   9. Yo debo escribir una tarjeta a mi madre.   10. Debemos esperar a nuestros amigos.

E. **Hace,** meaning *ago, since*

> **Lo compré hace dos semanas** *or* **Hace dos semanas que lo compré.**
>   I bought it two weeks ago *or* It is two weeks since I bought it.
> **Hace un año que los vi** *or* **Los vi hace un año.**
>   It is a year since I saw them *or* I saw them a year ago.

When **hace** is used with an expression of time in a sentence which is in the past tense, it regularly means *ago,* or *since.*   If the **hace**-clause comes first in the sentence, **que** usually (not always) introduces the main clause, but **que** is omitted if **hace** and the time expression follow the verb.

EJERCICIOS

A. Say after your teacher, then repeat using the present perfect tense, and then the pluperfect tense:

1. Yo veo a Vicente.
2. Yo le llevo al lago.
3. Ellos abren la puerta.
4. Marta no dice eso.
5. Tomás me devuelve el dinero.
6. Él y yo vamos a la playa.
7. ¿Qué haces tú?
8. ¿Qué ponen Vds. allí?

B. Say after your teacher, then repeat, using the correct object or prepositional pronouns for the noun objects as required:

1. Luis ha escrito la carta.
2. Tomás se ha puesto el traje.
3. Ellos no han visto a sus amigos.
4. Ana no ha traído el traje de baño.
5. ¿Has estado tomando el sol?
6. Tú no te has mudado de ropa.
7. Elena se ha sentado en la arena.
8. ¿Se han bañado Vds. en aquel lago?

C. Answer in Spanish, following the models in each group:

MODEL: ¿Ha cerrado Vd. la puerta?　　Sí, está cerrada.

1. ¿Ha escrito Vd. las frases?
2. ¿Ha abierto Vd. el cuaderno?
3. ¿Ha cerrado Vd. los libros?
4. ¿Ha terminado Vd. la composición?

MODEL: ¿Habían cerrado ellos las ventanas?　　Sí, ya estaban cerradas.

5. ¿Había hecho María el sombrero?
6. ¿Se había sentado tu mamá?
7. ¿Habían abierto ellos la puerta?
8. ¿Habías puesto las cosas allí?

MODEL: ¿Cuándo llegó él?　¿Hace dos días?　Sí, llegó hace dos días *and* Sí, hace dos días que llegó.

9. ¿Cuándo volvieron?　¿Hace una hora?
10. ¿Cuándo salió Ana?　¿Hace un mes?
11. ¿Cuándo vino José?　¿Hace media hora?
12. ¿Cuándo la compró él?　¿Hace un año?

MODEL: ¿Qué hay que hacer?　¿Sentarse?　Sí, hay que sentarse.

13. ¿Qué hay que hacer?　¿Ir a casa ahora?
14. ¿Qué hay que hacer?　¿Esperar aquí?
15. ¿Qué hay que hacer?　¿Tomar el autobús?
16. ¿Qué hay que hacer?　¿Mudarse de ropa?

MODEL: ¿Vas a ir a la playa?   Sí, he de ir a la playa.

17. ¿Vas a nadar en la piscina?   19. ¿Van Vds. a llevar a Luis al lago?
18. ¿Vas a cantar esa canción?   20. ¿Van Vds. a tomar el sol allí?

MODEL: ¿Has tenido que trabajar?   Sí, he tenido que trabajar.

21. ¿Has tenido que nadar aquí?   23. ¿Has tenido que lavarte las
22. ¿Ha tenido ella que quedarse   manos?
    allí?   24. ¿Han tenido Vds. que bañarse?

D. Say after your teacher, then repeat using the preterit tense, and then the imperfect:

1. Marta toma el sol.   2. Juan se muda de ropa.   3. Carlos va a nadar.   4. El señor Díaz está de vacaciones.   5. Felipe se pone el traje de baño.   6. Mis padres hacen un viaje por México.   7. Yo busco a mi hermano.   8. Elena le trae regalos a su tía.   9. ¿Les vende Vd. los billetes?   10. Los vemos en el parque.

E. Supply the definite article wherever required:

1. Nos gustan ——— flores.   2. No me gusta ——— invierno.   3. Elena cumplió quince años ——— mes pasado.   4. Hoy es ——— jueves.   5. Mis padres quieren partir ——— sábado por ——— mañana.   6. Mis tíos disfrutan de ——— vida en ——— Perú.   7. Casi todos ——— estudiantes van a ——— iglesia ——— domingos.   8. Carolina se puso ——— medias.   9. Tenemos que mudarnos de ——— ropa.   10. Juan acaba de comprar un traje de ——— baño nuevo.   11. Los muchachos se lavaron ——— manos.   12. Pasaron casi todo ——— día en ——— agua.   13. ——— señores Espinosa van a volver ——— semana que viene.   14. Buenas tardes, ——— señorita López.   15. ——— español es una lengua interesante.

View of Segovia, Spain.

COMPOSICIÓN

1. Where has Richard been all afternoon?   2. Vincent passed by his house a couple of hours ago and there was no one there.   3. I believe that he has taken his little brother to a lake which is near their house.   4. Tom doesn't know how to swim yet, but he is learning rapidly.   5. Even though he is not afraid of the water, he doesn't dare to enter alone.   6. Last Sunday my cousin and I went to the beach to spend the day. 7. It was cool when we arrived, and we sat (down) on the sand a while in order to take a sun bath.   8. In the afternoon it was warmer and it seemed that everybody had gone swimming.   9. In fact, I have never seen so many people on the beach.   10. In the park there is a large swimming pool, which was opened last week, and I want to swim there one of these days.   11. Well, I have to take a bath and change clothes now. 12. At seven o'clock I am to take Charles to the airport and I must not arrive late.

EJERCICIOS DE PRONUNCIACIÓN

Review the observations on Spanish intonation (pages 418–419), then read the first four exchanges of the dialogues of this lesson, paying close attention to the intonation patterns.

Department store in Barcelona, Spain.

VOCABULARIO

la arena   sand
atreverse (**a** + *inf.*)   to dare (to)
bañarse   to bathe, take a bath
cerca   *adv.*   near, close, nearby
la gente   people (*requires sing. verb*)
haber   to have (*auxiliary*)
el hermanito   little brother
el lago   lake
el mar   sea
el miedo   fear
mudar   to change
nadar   to swim
ni   neither, nor, (not) ... or
el par   pair, couple

la piscina   swimming pool
la playa   beach
precisamente   precisely, just
el principio   beginning
rápidamente   rapidly
la razón (*pl.* **razones**)   reason
el río   river
la ropa   clothes, clothing
la secretaria   secretary
solo, -a   alone
el traje   suit
el traje de baño   bathing suit
Vicente   Vincent

al principio   at first, at the beginning
¿cuántos años tiene (**él**)**?**   how old is (he)?
en realidad   in reality, in fact
estar de vacaciones   to be on vacation
ir a nadar   to take a swim, go swimming
mudarse de ropa   to change clothes (clothing)
ni ... ni   neither ... nor, (not) ... either ... or
por aquí   around here
tener ... años   to be ... years old
tener miedo (**de** + *obj.*)   to be afraid (of)
tener razón   to be right
todo el mundo   everybody (*requires sing. verb*)
tomar el sol   to take a sun bath

Engraving by Goya depicting an eighteenth-century bullfight. The *matador* is the famous *indiano*, Mariano Ceballos.

Graceful as a ballet dancer, this *novillero* does his *faena* in Salamanca, Spain.

LECTURA VIII

LOS DEPORTES[1]

Estudio de palabras

a. The Spanish ending **-dor** often indicates one who performs or participates in an action: espectador, *spectator*; explorador, *explorer*; jugador, *player*. It may express the means of an action: las boleadoras, *lariat with balls at one end, thrown so as to twist around an animal's legs.*

b. Observe the relation in meaning of the following words: afición, *fondness, and* aficionado, *fan, one who is fond of*; correr, *to run, and* corrida (de toros), *running (of bulls), bullfight*; espectáculo, *spectacle, and* espectador, *spectator*; jugar, *to play,* jugador, *player, and* juego, *game*; varios, *various, several, and* variedad, *variety.*

c. Note the words with deceptive meaning: carrera, *race (as well as career)*; concurso, *contest*; lanzar, *to throw.*

d. The adjectives of nationality **maya,** *Maya, Mayan,* and **azteca,** *Aztec,* have but one ending for both the masculine and the feminine. As we know, adjectives of nationality may be used as nouns: **el (la) maya,** *the Mayan*; **el (la) azteca,** *the Aztec.*

En el mundo hispánico hay una gran variedad de deportes. No sólo los hombres, sino también las mujeres toman parte en los deportes, especialmente en el golf, el tenis y la natación.[2] Muchos deportes son de origen inglés o norteamericano, pero otros, como la pelota o el *jai alai* y la corrida de toros,[3] son de origen español. El fútbol, de estilo *soccer,* es muy popular, y algunos de los estadios tienen una capacidad de 50,000 a 120,000 espectadores. También son populares el béisbol, el básquetbol, las carreras de caballos,[4] el polo, el boxeo, la caza,[5] la pesca,[6] en realidad, todos los deportes que se conocen en los Estados Unidos y en el resto del mundo.

---

[1] **deportes,** *sports.*   [2] **natación,** *swimming.*   [3] **corrida (de toros),** *bullfighting, bullfight.*   [4] **carreras de caballos,** *horse races.*   [5] **caza,** *hunting.*   [6] **pesca,** *fishing.*

Playing "el pato"

Muchas personas creen que hay corridas de toros en todos los países de habla española, pero la verdad es que se encuentran solamente en ciertos países, como en España, México, Colombia, Venezuela y el Perú. En España las corridas de toros constituyen[1] la fiesta nacional y son muy populares también en México y el Perú. En Venezuela y Colombia se celebran con menos entusiasmo y hay países, como el Uruguay y la Argentina, que no permiten este espectáculo.

Hasta fines del[2] siglo diez y ocho las corridas eran una fiesta aristocrática, pero a fines de[3] ese siglo comenzó a perderse el gusto por los toros.[4] Hoy día pueden considerarse[5] como un espectáculo a la vez[6] popular y profesional.

En España el fútbol (o balompié) es un deporte muy popular, sobre todo[7] en el norte. Tiene también miles[8] de aficionados en casi todos los países hispanoamericanos, especialmente en México, la Argentina y el Uruguay. El desarrollo[9] de este deporte ha sido tan notable en el Uruguay que sus equipos[10] han ganado el campeonato mundial[11] en varias ocasiones. (Como se sabe, el Brasil también ha tenido equipos de fama mundial.)

La pelota es el famoso juego vasco,[12] del norte de España. Se juega[13] en un frontón[14] que tiene tres paredes: una alta, que está frente a los jugadores, otra a un lado y la tercera, detrás. Los espectadores se sientan en el lado abierto. Para lanzar la pelota, los jugadores usan una cesta[15] de forma curva. Una pareja de jugadores se opone a otra pareja. Es un juego muy rápido y para jugarlo bien es necesario ser muy ágil.

---

[1] **constituyen,** *constitute.*   [2] **Hasta fines de,** *Up to the end of.*   [3] **a fines de,** *at the end of.*   [4] **comenzó . . . toros,** *the taste for bullfighting began to fade* (lit., *be lost*).   [5] **pueden considerarse,** *it* (= *bullfighting*) *can be considered.*   [6] **a la vez,** *at the same time.*   [7] **sobre todo,** *above all, especially.*   [8] **miles,** *thousands.*   [9] **desarrollo,** *development.*   [10] **equipos,** *teams.*   [11] **el campeonato mundial,** *world championship.*   [12] **vasco,** *Basque.*   [13] **Se juega,** *It is played.*   [14] **frontón,** *court.*   [15] **cesta,** *wickerwork racket.*

Jai alai game, Madrid, Spain.

Es popular no sólo en España, sino también en Cuba, en México y en otros países del Nuevo Mundo. También se juega en algunas ciudades de los Estados Unidos.

El béisbol, el deporte nacional de los Estados Unidos, es también el deporte nacional de Cuba. En Venezuela, en México, en la América Central y en la República Dominicana hay una gran afición por el béisbol. Varios equipos de estos países celebran concursos internacionales. Hoy día muchos jugadores de nuestros equipos profesionales son de la América española.

Las carreras de caballos parecen ser el deporte favorito en Chile y, sobre todo, en la Argentina. Son populares, también, en la República Dominicana y en Puerto Rico.

Hace muchos años los gauchos argentinos tenían un juego llamado «el pato».[1] Era un juego muy peligroso[2] y por eso[3] lo prohibieron las autoridades. Montados a caballo, los jugadores luchaban por la posesión de una pelota bastante grande y pesada[4] que tenía mangos.[5] Los jugadores se arrojaban[6] sobre sus adversarios, les pegaban con el látigo,[7] y con las boleadoras trataban de echar por tierra al caballo.[8] Para ganar la partida había que llevar la pelota unos seis o siete kilómetros. Ahora hay una forma moderna del juego, mucho menos peligrosa, que tiene elementos del polo y del básquetbol.

---

[1] **pato,** *duck.*   [2] **peligroso,** *dangerous.*   [3] **por eso,** *because of that.*   [4] **pesada,** *heavy.*   [5] **mangos,** *handles.*
[6] **se arrojaban,** *threw themselves.*   [7] **les pegaban con el látigo,** *they beat them with their whips.*   [8] **trataban ... caballo,** *they tried to throw the horse to the ground.*

México parece ser el país hispanoamericano donde se practican más los deportes.[1] Es interesante recordar que en la época de los mayas y de los aztecas había un juego de pelota semejante al básquetbol. Sin usar las manos ni la cabeza, los jugadores tenían que pasar una pelota de hule[2] por un anillo[3] que estaba en una pared. La influencia de este juego en el origen del básquetbol moderno es dudosa.[4]   Hoy día el básquetbol es muy popular en todos los países hispanoamericanos.

En Chile y en el Perú se practica algo el alpinismo,[5] pues estos dos países tienen magníficas sierras donde se puede practicar este difícil deporte.

Youngsters playing soccer near the Roman Aqueduct, Segovia, Spain.

---

[1] **se practican más los deportes,** *sports are practiced (people go in for sports) most.*   [2] **hule,** *rubber.*   [3] **anillo,** *ring.*
[4] **dudosa,** *doubtful.*   [5] **alpinismo,** *mountain climbing.*

Vallehermoso stadium during a soccer game, Madrid, Spain.

PREGUNTAS

1. ¿Hay una gran variedad de deportes en el mundo hispánico? 2. ¿En qué deportes toman parte las mujeres? 3. ¿Cuáles son dos deportes de origen español? 4. ¿Qué otros deportes son populares?

5. ¿Hay corridas de toros en todos los países de habla española? 6. ¿Le gusta a todo el mundo la corrida de toros?

7. ¿Es popular el fútbol en España? 8. ¿Tiene muchos aficionados en los países hispanoamericanos? 9. ¿En qué países ha sido muy notable el desarrollo de este deporte?

10. ¿Dónde se juega a la pelota? 11. ¿Cuántas paredes tiene un frontón? 12. ¿Qué usan los jugadores para lanzar la pelota? 13. ¿Es rápido el juego? 14. ¿Dónde es popular?

15. ¿En qué países hay una gran afición por el béisbol? 16. ¿De dónde son muchos jugadores de nuestros equipos profesionales? 17. ¿Cuál parece ser el deporte favorito en Chile?

18. ¿Qué juego tenían los gauchos de la Argentina? 19. ¿Por qué lo prohibieron las autoridades? 20. ¿En qué país hispanoamericano se practican más los deportes? 21. ¿Qué juego había durante la época de los mayas y los aztecas? 22. ¿Qué tenían que hacer los jugadores? 23. ¿Es popular el básquetbol en los países latinoamericanos? 24. ¿Dónde se practica el alpinismo?

Ski resort in the Spanish Pyrenees.

REPASO III

A. Say after your teacher; when you hear a new subject, compose a new sentence using the same tense:

1. Ellos empiezan a leer. (Nosotros)
2. María se pone el sombrero. (Yo)
3. José no encuentra nada. (Tú)
4. Ellos devuelven el dinero. (Vd.)

5. Mi papá llegó a las seis. (Yo)
6. Ellos buscaron a María. (Yo)
7. Tú no hiciste el viaje. (Vd.)
8. Él y yo le trajimos algo. (Ellos)
9. Los jóvenes no pudieron ir. (Él)
10. Yo no les dije nada. (Ellos)

11. Nosotros dábamos un paseo. (Tú)
12. Yo los veía a menudo. (Juan)
13. Ellos iban a la playa. (Ana y yo)
14. El traje era muy caro. (Los trajes)

15. ¿Has visto tú aquel lago? (Vds.)
16. ¿Les ha escrito Ricardo? (tú)
17. Ellos no han dicho eso. (Él y yo)
18. Ella no se lo había puesto. (Yo)
19. Pablo la había abierto. (Ellos)
20. Tú te habías mudado de ropa. (Vd.)

B. Read in Spanish, placing the pronoun objects correctly with each verb (as explained on page 178, in the progressive forms of the tenses there are two possibilities):

1. (me los) Trajeron. Han traído. Van a traer. Están trayendo. Traigan Vds.
2. (nos la) No dé Vd. Ha dado. Está dando. Quería dar. No dio. 3. (se los) Devuelven. Pueden devolver. Están devolviendo. Han devuelto. Devuelvan Vds.
4. (te lo) Enseñan. ¿No han enseñado? Tratan de enseñar. Estaban enseñando. No habían enseñado.

C. Read in Spanish, using the correct form of the verb selected from those in parentheses:

1. (*preterit tense of* dar, tomar, llevar) Ayer Marta ——— el libro en la mano. Yo me lo ———. Luego ellas ——— un paseo. 2. (*present of* haber, tener) Los muchachos no ——— visto la película. ¿La ——— visto Vd.? Yo ——— que irme. Ella ——— de cantar mañana. 3. (*preterit of* volver, devolver) Luis ——— anoche. No me ——— el dinero que le había prestado. 4. (*present of* conocer, saber) ¿——— Vds. a mi amigo Vicente? No le ———, pero ——— donde vive. ¿——— Vds. la ciudad de Nueva York? 5. (*preterit or imperfect of* estar, hacer, ser, tener) El reloj que ——— sobre el mostrador ——— precioso. ——— mucho calor en la tienda, y yo ——— mucha sed. La empleada ——— razón; ——— sol y no ——— un día muy agradable. ——— las cuatro cuando salí de la tienda. Había tanta gente en los autobuses que yo ——— que esperar mucho tiempo. Al llegar a casa, ——— muy cansada.

D. Complete with the necessary preposition:

1. Mi hermanito ha aprendido ——— nadar. 2. Algunos muchachos no se atreven ——— nadar solos. 3. Nuestros padres han ——— volver esta noche. 4. Arturo y yo nos alegramos ——— verlos. 5. José se mudó ——— ropa hace media hora. 6. Yo empecé ——— charlar con él. 7. Él y sus amigos no tienen miedo ——— salir ahora. 8. Luis se encontró ——— María en una tienda. 9. Los dos acaban ——— volver ——— casa. 10. Ricardo tiene muchos deseos ——— ver el mar. 11. Él insiste ——— eso. 12. Los señores López partieron ——— aquí ayer ——— la tarde. 13. En el Perú la gente disfruta mucho ——— la vida. 14. ¿Piensa Vd. ——— Carlos? 15. Favor ——— saludarle de mi parte.

E. Read in Spanish, supplying the preterit or imperfect tense of the verb in parentheses:

1. Esta mañana mi hermano (levantarse) a las ocho. 2. Generalmente (levantarse) más temprano. 3. Nosotros (estar) sentados a la mesa y (desayunarse) cuando él (entrar) en el comedor. 4. Él (tener) que comer rápidamente. 5. (Ser) las ocho y media cuando (salir) de casa. 6. (Hacer) frío, pero él no (ponerse) el sombrero. 7. Él (correr) a la Calle Doce donde (tomar) el autobús. 8. Más tarde yo (decidir) ir de compras, y (llegar) al centro a las diez. 9. (Haber) mucha gente allí, y todas las empleadas (estar) muy ocupadas. 10. Yo (buscar) unos regalos y (poder) hallar varias cosas bonitas. 11. Al mediodía (almorzar) en el centro. 12. Yo (estar) muy cansado cuando (volver) a casa a las tres de la tarde.

F. Answer in Spanish:

1. ¿Le gusta a Vd. el invierno? 2. ¿Cuáles son las otras tres estaciones? 3. ¿Cuál de las estaciones le gusta a Vd. más? 4. ¿Dónde se puede nadar en el verano? 5. ¿Qué hay en las montañas durante el invierno? 6. ¿Hace buen tiempo hoy? 7. ¿Hizo sol ayer? 8. ¿Qué hora era hoy cuando salió Vd. de casa? 9. ¿Cuál es la fecha de hoy? 10. ¿Qué día de la semana es? 11. ¿Tiene Vd. clases los sábados? 12. ¿En qué días de la semana tiene Vd. clases? 13. ¿Cuántos estudiantes hay en esta clase? 14. ¿Cuántos estudiantes hay en esta universidad? 15. ¿En qué siglo vivimos? 16. ¿Cuántos años tiene Vd.? 17. Si Vd. tiene hermanos, ¿cuántos años tienen ellos? 18. ¿Qué hace Vd. cuando está de vacaciones? 19. ¿Ha hecho Vd. un viaje a México? 20. ¿Qué hizo Vd. el sábado pasado?

G. Give the Spanish for:

1. by the way. 2. at first. 3. a good road. 4. the first month. 5. the third week. 6. the ten-o'clock bus. 7. a five-dollar bill. 8. a bathing suit. 9. all afternoon. 10. at once. 11. at noon. 12. everybody.

13. Mary took a sun bath. 14. The blouse is very stylish. 15. You are right. 16. John came an hour ago. 17. I agree. 18. These purses are prettier than those. 19. What kind of weather is it? 20. It is bad weather. 21. Yesterday they went swimming. 22. My father is on vacation. 23. I ran across Tom downtown. 24. He has just returned from Spain. 25. You are welcome.

La Cumbre, a 16,000-foot high peak near La Paz, Bolivia.

LECCIÓN 16

The future tense. The conditional tense
Verbs irregular in the future and conditional
Uses of the future tense. Uses of the conditional tense. The future and
conditional perfects. The future and conditional for
probability or conjecture. Forms of *jugar*

SON AFICIONADOS A LOS DEPORTES

Ha terminado el primer semestre. Para descansar un poco, después de los exámenes, Carlos White, un estudiante norteamericano, ha hecho un viaje a México. Está pasando unos días en la capital del país. Carlos está sentado en el vestíbulo de un hotel de la ciudad de México, leyendo el periódico. Se acerca su amigo Juan Molina, que acaba de salir del comedor del hotel.

• • • • •

JUAN. ¡Hola, Carlos! ¿Qué hay de nuevo?

CARLOS. Nada de particular. Como hoy es sábado, quiero ver si se anuncia algún espectáculo de interés.

JUAN. A propósito, ¿sabe Vd. si habrá un partido de fútbol mañana?

CARLOS. Creo que sí, pero para estar seguro, miraré otra vez lo que se dice en la sección de deportes. Así lo sabremos en seguida … (*Hojea el periódico rápidamente.*) Sí, habrá un partido a las once en punto. ¿Piensa Vd. ir?

JUAN. Sí, con unos amigos norteamericanos que ya habrán llegado a la capital.

CARLOS. Parece que será un partido magnífico — México contra el Uruguay.

Juan.   Me alegro, porque mis amigos tienen muchas ganas de ver un buen partido.   Les escribí hace una semana que compraría billetes para ellos.   Me llamarán por teléfono mañana por la mañana.   ¿Quiere Vd. acompañarnos?

Carlos.   Tendría mucho gusto en hacerlo, pero Pablo Martínez me invitó hace varios días a hacer una excursión a la sierra.   Saldremos al mediodía.

• • • • •

Juan.   A Vd. le interesan mucho los deportes, ¿no es verdad?

Carlos.   Sí, soy muy aficionado a casi todos.   He jugado al fútbol y al béisbol.   No jugué al básquetbol porque resultaba demasiado rápido para mí.   Ahora juego solamente al tenis y al golf.

Juan.   Dicen que el *jai alai*, o la pelota vasca, es muy interesante.   Se juega mucho aquí en la capital, ¿verdad?

Carlos.   ¡Ya lo creo!   Es uno de los juegos más rápidos del mundo, y hay en la ciudad de México algunos jugadores vascos que son excelentes.   ¿Le gustaría a Vd. ir conmigo a ver un partido esta noche?

Juan.   Con mucho gusto.   Sería un gran placer.

Carlos.   Pues, ¿qué hora será? No tengo reloj.

Juan.   (*Mira su reloj.*)   Son las diez menos veinte.

Carlos.   Si Vd. no tiene inconveniente, le buscaré a las seis y media.   Podremos comer en un restaurante vasco que está cerca del frontón.   Le veo a las seis y media, ¿eh?[1]

Juan.   Muy bien.   Estaré listo.

CONVERSACIÓN

A. Preguntas sobre el diálogo

1. ¿Dónde está sentado Carlos?   2. ¿Qué está haciendo Carlos?   3. ¿Qué quiere saber Juan?   4. ¿A qué hora empezará el partido?   5. ¿Quiénes habrán llegado ya a la capital?   6. ¿Qué van a hacer Carlos y su amigo Pablo el domingo?   7. ¿Por qué no jugó Carlos al básquetbol cuando estaba en la universidad?   8. ¿Qué dice Carlos del juego de la pelota vasca?

B. Aplicación del diálogo

1. ¿Es Vd. aficionado a los deportes?   2. ¿Qué deportes le interesan a Vd.?   3. ¿Ha visto Vd. un partido de *jai alai*?   4. ¿Le gustaría a Vd. jugar a la pelota vasca?   5. ¿Ha visto Vd. un partido de fútbol de estilo *soccer*?   6. ¿En qué países juegan al fútbol de estilo norteamericano?   7. ¿Qué deporte le gusta más, el tenis o el golf?   8. ¿Hace Vd. excursiones a la sierra durante el verano?

---

[1] In conversation ¿eh? is often used similarly to ¿(no es) verdad?

NOTAS GRAMATICALES

A. The future tense

FUTURE ENDINGS		**hablar**	
-é	-emos	hablaré	hablaremos
-ás	-éis	hablarás	hablaréis
-á	-án	hablará	hablarán

The future indicative tense is regularly formed by adding the endings of the present indicative of **haber** to the full infinitive form. There is only one set of future endings for all verbs in Spanish.

Observe that three of the endings begin with **e** and three with **a,** and that all the endings except the first person plural have a written accent.

B. The conditional tense

CONDITIONAL ENDINGS		**comer**	
-ía	-íamos	comería	comeríamos
-ías	-íais	comerías	comeríais
-ía	-ían	comería	comerían

The conditional indicative tense is formed by adding the imperfect endings of **haber** to the infinitive. As in the case of the future, there is only one set of conditional endings for all verbs in Spanish. All six forms are accented.

C. Verbs irregular in the future and conditional

Infinitive	*Future*	*Conditional*
1. haber	**habré, -ás, -á,** etc.	**habría, -ías, -ía,** etc.
poder	**podré, -ás, -á,** etc.	**podría, -ías, -ía,** etc.
querer	**querré, -ás, -á,** etc.	**querría, -ías, -ía,** etc.
saber	**sabré, -ás, -á,** etc.	**sabría, -ías, -ía,** etc.
2. poner	**pondré,** etc.	**pondría,** etc.
salir	**saldré,** etc.	**saldría,** etc.
tener	**tendré,** etc.	**tendría,** etc.
venir	**vendré,** etc.	**vendría,** etc.
3. decir	**diré,** etc.	**diría,** etc.
hacer	**haré,** etc.	**haría,** etc.

The future and conditional tenses have the same stem, and the endings are the same as for regular verbs. The irregularity is in the infinitive stem used. In group (1) the final vowel of the infinitive has been dropped; in (2) the final vowel has been dropped and the glide **d** introduced to facilitate the pronunciation of the consonant groups **lr** and **nr**; in (3) the Old Spanish stem **dir, har** (**far**) has been retained. Only two other verbs are irregular in these tenses.

Práctica. Pronounce, then give the corresponding conditional form:

tomaré	saldrás	dirán	podremos
vivirán	tendréis	querrá	dirás
aprenderá	vendrán	habrá	saldrá
podrá	haremos	sabrán	haréis

D. Uses of the future tense

Juan dice que vendrá.   John says that he will come.
Sabemos que él lo hará.   We know that he will do it.
Habrá mucha gente allí.   There will be many people there.

The meaning of the future tense is *shall* or *will* in English, and it is regularly used to express future actions or conditions. The impersonal form **habrá** means *there will be* (last example).

Up to this point substitutions have been used for the future, as is commonly done in English:

Voy a ver a Carlos esta noche.   I'm going to see Charles tonight.
Hemos de ir con ellos.   We are (supposed) to go with them.
Le vemos a Vd. a las nueve.   We'll be seeing you at nine o'clock.
Yo sé que ella viene mañana.   I know that she is coming tomorrow.
¿Nos sentamos?   Shall we sit down?

When *will* means *be willing to*, it is translated by the present tense of **querer**. In the negative it may mean *be unwilling to*:

¿Quiere Vd. ir conmigo?   Will you go with me?
No quieren jugar.   They won't (are unwilling to) play.

E. Uses of the conditional tense

> **Juan dijo que vendría.** John said that he would come.
> **Sabíamos que él lo haría.** We knew that he would do it.
> **Me gustaría ir con Vds.** I should like to go with you.
> **Yo creía que habría más tiempo.** I thought there would be more time.

The conditional tense is translated by *should* or *would*. The impersonal form **habría** means *there would be* (last example).

When *should* means *ought to* (moral obligation), it is expressed by **deber:**

> **Debo escribirles.** I should (ought to, must) write to them.

Remember that *would* is sometimes used to represent a repeated past action in English, in which case it is translated by the imperfect indicative tense in Spanish (Lesson 11):

> **Me levantaba temprano.** I would (used to) get up early.

NOTE: The future and conditional tenses are used after **si** only when it means *whether*, never in a condition when it means *if*: **No sé (sabía) si vendrán (vendrían),** *I do not know (did not know) whether they will (would) come.*

F. The future and conditional perfects

Future Perfect		*Conditional Perfect*	
habré		**habría**	
habrás } hablado		**habrías** } hablado	
habrá		**habría**	
habremos		**habríamos**	
habréis } hablado		**habríais** } hablado	
habrán		**habrían**	

These tenses are regularly used as in English, and translated as *shall* or *will have spoken*, and *should* or *would have spoken*, respectively.

G. The future and conditional for probability or conjecture

> **Marta estará en casa.** Martha is probably (must be) at home.
> **¿Qué hora será?** I wonder what time it is. (What time can it be?)
> **Serían las dos.** It was probably (must have been) two o'clock.
> **Ya habrán llegado.** They have probably (must have) already arrived.

The future tense is used in Spanish to indicate probability, supposition, or conjecture concerning an action or state in the <u>present</u>, while the conditional indicates the same idea with respect to the <u>past</u>. The future perfect, and occasionally the conditional perfect, are also used to indicate probability in the past.

H. Forms of **jugar**, *to play* (a game)

Present Indicative Tense

SINGULAR	PLURAL
juego	jugamos
juegas	jugáis
juega	**juegan**

Jugar is the only verb in Spanish in which **u** changes to **ue** when the stem is stressed. The first person singular preterit is **jugué**.

In everyday conversation **jugar** is often used without **a** and the article: **jugar fútbol**, instead of the more common **jugar al fútbol**.

EJERCICIOS

A. Substitution drill:

1. *Juan* tomará café a las cuatro.
   (*Juan y Ana, Yo, Nosotros, Tú, Vd.*)
2. *Los muchachos* saldrán al mediodía.
   (*Pablo, Vd., Vds., Ella y yo, Tú*)
3. Es cierto que *él* lo pondrá aquí.
   (*yo, nosotros, tú, María y Ana, Vds.*)
4. *Yo* no diría eso.
   (*Mi mamá, Mis hermanos, Nosotros, Ella, Vds.*)
5. *Carlos* tendría mucho gusto en ir.
   (*Yo, Ellos, Vd., Tú, Carlos y yo*)
6. Se sabía que *Juan* podría jugar.
   (*yo, José y Luis, Vds., ella, tú*)
7. Se cree que *Pablo* los habrá visto.
   (*ellas, él y yo, yo, Vd., tú*)
8. *Tomás* juega al golf.
   (*Tomás y yo, Marta, Ella y él, Tú, Vds.*)

B. Answer affirmatively:

1. ¿Comprará Vd. un periódico?
2. ¿Leerá Vd. la sección de deportes?
3. ¿Irás tú a ver el partido?
4. ¿Podrás ir esta noche?
5. ¿Harás tú una excursión mañana?
6. ¿Tendrán Vds. mucho gusto en hacerlo?
7. ¿Saldrán Vds. al mediodía?
8. ¿Vendrá Juan a vernos esta tarde?
9. ¿Dijo Juan que vendría hoy?
10. ¿Dijeron Vds. que podrían jugar?
11. ¿Le gustaría a Vd. jugar al golf?
12. ¿Tendrían Vds. muchas ganas de verla?

C. Read in Spanish, changing the infinitive in parentheses to the tense indicated. Keep the meaning in mind:

(*Future*) 1. Nosotros (ir) al partido de pelota vasca. 2. Yo (comprar) los billetes. 3. Lo (hacer) con mucho gusto. 4. Juan no (poder) acompañarnos. 5. Dice que (tener) que trabajar esta noche. 6. Pablo y yo (salir) de casa temprano. 7. (Tomar) algo en el café antes de ir al frontón. 8. Algunos jugadores (estar) allí. 9. Nosotros (tener) mucho gusto en verlos. 10. (Ser) necesario salir en seguida porque a esa hora (haber) mucha gente en las calles.

(*Conditional*) 1. Carlos dijo que (venir) a mi casa a las tres. 2. Yo sabía que él (hacer) eso. 3. ¿Le (gustar) a Vd. ir con nosotros al partido de fútbol? 4. Sí, gracias, me (gustar) ir con Vds. 5. (Ser) un gran placer. 6. Pues, yo creía que Vd. (tener) muchas ganas de ver el espectáculo.

D. Repeat each sentence twice, following the models:

MODEL: ¿Qué hora es?   ¿Qué hora es?   ¿Qué hora será?

1. ¿Quién es?
2. Juan está en el restaurante.
3. Elena tiene quince años.
4. Son las diez.
5. Los muchachos van al partido.
6. Vicente vuelve esta tarde.

MODEL: ¿Adónde ha ido Juan?   ¿Adónde ha ido Juan?   ¿Adónde habrá ido Juan?

7. Las jóvenes han salido.
8. Carlos ya ha comprado el coche.
9. Ella no ha vuelto todavía.
10. ¿Ha ido Juan al centro?

MODEL: José fue a jugar.   José fue a jugar.   José iría a jugar.

11. Estuvieron en casa anoche.
12. Eran las once.
13. ¿Adónde fueron los jugadores?
14. Llegaron al mediodía.

E. Give in Spanish:

1. What's new? 2. Nothing special. 3. Do you like sports? 4. Of course! 5. I am fond of almost all [of them]. 6. Can you (Do you know how to) play tennis? 7. Yes, but I like golf better (more). 8. Will you accompany me to a football game? 9. Gladly. 10. I shall buy two tickets tomorrow. 11. In Spain (**al**) *jai alai* is played a great deal. 12. About what time is it? 13. It must be half past seven. 14. I'll see you at nine o'clock, right? 15. Yes, I'll be ready.

COMPOSICIÓN

1. Charles is reading a newspaper in the lobby of a Mexico City hotel (hotel of Mexico City) when his friend John approaches.   2. The latter asks whether there will be a football game tomorrow.   3. As Charles is not sure, he looks at the sports section again.   4. He sees that there will be a game at eleven o'clock sharp.   5. Some friends of John have just reached the capital, and they are very anxious to see a game.   6. Charles said that he would be very glad to accompany them, but his friend Paul had already invited him to make an excursion to the mountains.   7. Charles is fond of all sports; when he was in the university he used to play football and golf.   8. He said that he did not play basketball because it was (turned out to be) too fast for him.   9. Then Charles asked John whether he would like to go with him to see a *jai alai* game (match) that night.   10. He answered that it would be a great pleasure to see that game, which is one of the fastest in the world.   11. They decide to eat in a Basque restaurant that is near the (handball) court.   12. John says that he will be ready if Charles comes for him at nine o'clock.

Soccer game at University City's large stadium, which seats more than 100,000 fans, Mexico City.

VOCABULARIO

acercarse (**a** + *obj.*) to approach
aficionado, -a (**a**) fond (of)
algún (*used for* **alguno** *before m. sing.
    nouns*) some, any
así so, thus
el básquetbol basketball
el béisbol baseball
el billete ticket
el deporte sport
¿eh? right? eh? won't I? etc.
el espectáculo spectacle, show
excelente excellent
la excursión (*pl.* **excursiones**) excur-
    sion, trip
el frontón (*pl.* **frontones**) (handball)
    court
el fútbol football
la gana desire
el golf golf
gran (*used for* **grande** *before sing. noun*)
    great
hojear to turn the pages of
el hotel hotel

el inconveniente objection
el interés (*pl.* **intereses**) interest
el juego game
el jugador player
    jugar (**ue**) (**a** + *obj.*) to play (*a
    game*)
    listo, -a ready
el partido match, game
la pelota handball, ball
el placer pleasure
el punto point
    rápido, -a rapid, fast
el restaurante restaurant
    resultar to result, be, turn out
    (to be)
la sección (*pl.* **secciones**) section
    seguro, -a sure, certain, safe
el semestre semester
la sierra mountains, mountain range
el tenis tennis
    vasco, -a Basque
el vestíbulo vestibule, lobby

buscar a uno to come (go) for one
creer que (**sí**) to think *or* believe (so)
en punto sharp (*time*)
estar seguro, -a (**de que**) to be sure (that)
hacer una excursión to take (make) an excursion
la ciudad de México Mexico City
mañana por la mañana (**tarde, noche**) tomorrow morning
    (afternoon, night)
otra vez again
sección de deportes sports section
ser aficionado, -a (**a**) to be fond (of)
si Vd. no tiene inconveniente if you have no objection
tener (**muchas**) **ganas de** to be (very) eager to (desirous of)
tener (**mucho**) **gusto en** to be (very) glad to
¡ya lo creo! of course! certainly!

This region produces both poplar trees, used in the nearby match factories, and corn, Talca, Chile.

LECTURA IX

ÁRBOLES Y PLANTAS

Estudio de palabras

a. Observe the relation in meaning of the following: beber, *to drink, and* bebida, *drink*; conde, *count, and* condesa, *countess*; cultivar, *to cultivate, and* cultivo, *cultivation*; habitar, *to inhabit, and* habitante, *inhabitant*; importante, *important, and* importancia, *importance*; llegar, *to arrive, and* llegada, *arrival*; médico, *doctor, and* medicina, *medicine*; origen, *origin, and* originarse, *to originate*.

b. Since adverbs are often formed by adding **-mente** to the feminine singular of adjectives, give the corresponding adverb for: antiguo, completo, exacto, general, solo.

c. The opposites of the following words appear in the reading selection: buen, después de, frío, mucho, mujer, nuevo, pequeño. Can you give them?

Como ya sabemos, América ha dado al mundo una gran variedad de árboles y de plantas de mucha importancia. Se cree que la planta que hoy día conocemos con el nombre de maíz se originó en el sur de México o en algún lugar de la América Central. En los tiempos de los mayas, los indios que habitaban esa región antiguamente, había una planta silvestre[1] llamada *teocentli*. En la lengua de los mayas *teo* significaba divino y *centli*, maíz. Es evidente que la planta era para ellos una cosa divina, el maíz de los dioses.[2] Poco a poco[3] los mayas y otras tribus indígenas aprendieron a cultivar el *teocentli*, que con el tiempo se convirtió[4] en lo que hoy llamamos el maíz. El cultivo y el desarrollo[5] de esta planta tuvieron una gran influencia en la vida de esas tribus, puesto que[6] muchos hombres tuvieron que quedarse a vivir cerca de los campos de cultivo para cuidar y cosechar[7] el grano. Así se establecieron pueblos permanentes que, al necesitar leyes y crear[8]

una organización social, dieron origen a la civilización indígena. En realidad, puede decirse que el maíz fue la base de esta civilización; todavía hoy, el maíz es uno de los productos más importantes del mundo.

Siglos antes de la llegada de los españoles al Nuevo Mundo, ya se conocía otra planta indígena de las regiones tropicales de América, el cacao. No se sabe exactamente dónde se originó. Las palabras *chocolate* y *cocoa* designan en inglés el producto de las semillas[9] del cacao, cuyo nombre botánico significa alimento[10] de los dioses. La palabra *chocolate* viene de dos palabras: *xococ*, agrio,[11] y *atl*, agua.

Muchos años antes del descubrimiento de América los habitantes de México y de la América Central ya usaban el chocolate. Los aztecas usaban las semillas del cacao para pagar el tributo a su emperador Moctezuma y como moneda en el comercio. Dice una leyenda que el chocolate era la

---

[1] **silvestre,** *wild.*   [2] **dioses,** *gods.*   [3] **Poco a poco,** *Little by little.*   [4] **se convirtió,** *was converted.*   [5] **desarrollo,** *development.*   [6] **puesto que,** *since.*   [7] **cuidar y cosechar,** *to care for and harvest.*   [8] **al necesitar leyes y crear,** *upon needing laws and (needing) to create.*   [9] **semillas,** *seeds.*   [10] **alimento,** *food.*   [11] **agrio,** *sour.*

Some farmers in México prefer to use mules rather than tractors for cotton cultivation. They believe that tractors pack down the soil and cause poor crops.

única bebida[1] que tomaba Moctezuma y que todos los días tomaba por lo menos[2] cincuenta jícaras.[3] El conquistador de México, Hernán Cortés, y sus soldados también tomaban chocolate. Fueron los españoles del Nuevo Mundo quienes[4] llevaron el chocolate a Europa. El chocolate es hoy uno de los alimentos favoritos de todo el mundo.

Otra planta también conocida antes de la llegada de los españoles es la yerba mate. Es parecida al naranjo[5] y se cultiva en la Argentina, el Paraguay y el Brasil. Con ella se hace una bebida que a veces llaman el té paraguayo. Se prepara con agua caliente y se bebe por un pequeño tubo de metal o de madera[6] que se llama bombilla. Se usa la palabra *mate* para referirse a la calabaza[7] en que se sirve; también se emplea como forma abreviada de *yerba mate*. Esta bebida es tan tradicional en esos países como el té en Inglaterra. Todas las clases sociales toman el *mate* además del café.

Ricardo Palma, famoso autor peruano, nos relata una leyenda muy interesante de otra planta. A principios del siglo diez y siete el nuevo virrey[8] don[9] Luis Fernández de Cabrera, conde de Chinchón, llegó al Perú. Su esposa, la condesa, era una mujer muy hermosa. Al poco tiempo[10] la condesa se puso[11] muy enferma de una fiebre alta que hoy día los médicos llaman malaria. Nadie sabía curarla y todos estaban muy tristes. Parecía que la señora iba a morir, y todos decían que solamente un milagro[12] podía salvarla. Un día un indio anciano vino a ver al virrey y le dio un polvo con el que los incas curaban esa misma fiebre desde hacía varios siglos.[13] La condesa pronto quedó completamente bien, y desde entonces el mundo tiene[14] una medicina importante. Por haber curado[15] a la condesa de Chinchón, se dio el nombre de «chinchona» a esta medicina, que se hacía de la cáscara[16] de un árbol peruano. Hoy día se le llama quinina.

En las regiones de los Andes se encuentra otra planta, la coca, que ha tenido mal efecto en la vida de los indios. Para combatir el hambre, el frío y la fatiga, muchos de ellos todavía mascan hojas de coca,[17] que contienen cocaína. Las hojas de coca les sirven de estimulante, pero

---

[1] **bebida,** *drink.* [2] **por lo menos,** *at least.* [3] **jícaras,** *cups.* [4] **Fueron … quienes = Los españoles del Nuevo Mundo fueron quienes** (*the ones who*). [5] **parecida al naranjo,** *similar to the orange tree.* [6] **madera,** *wood.* [7] **calabaza,** *gourd.* [8] **virrey,** *viceroy.* [9] **don,** *a title not translated.* [10] **Al poco tiempo,** *After a short time.* [11] **se puso,** *became.* [12] **milagro,** *miracle.* [13] **un polvo … siglos,** *a powder with which the Incas had been curing that same fever for several centuries.* [14] **tiene,** *has had.* [15] **Por haber curado,** *Because of having cured.* [16] **cáscara,** *bark.* [17] **mascan hojas de coca,** *chew coca leaves.*

Drying sisal hemp, El Salvador

Cacao plant and pods

hacen mucho daño al[1] sistema nervioso. Se dice que si tienen bastantes hojas que mascar, los indios de los Andes pueden trabajar varios días sin comer y sin descansar.

Aquí no podemos mencionar todas las plantas que se originaron en las dos Américas. Algunas de ellas son la vainilla; el chicle, cuya leche se usa para hacer goma de mascar;[2] la yuca, de que se saca la *tapioca*; y un gran número de frutas tropicales que no tienen nombre en inglés. Y no debemos olvidar otros productos como el chile, el tomate, el camote, el tabaco, la calabaza,[3] el algodón y la patata. La patata, que en muchas partes de la América española llaman papa, se originó en los Andes. Los españoles la llevaron a España a principios del siglo diez y seis, y ha llegado a ser[4] uno de los alimentos más importantes del mundo.

[1] **hacen mucho daño al,** *do much harm to the.*   [2] **goma de mascar,** *chewing gum.*   [3] **calabaza,** *pumpkin, squash.*
[4] **ha llegado a ser,** *it has become.*

Studies on beans done at the National
Agricultural Research Center, México.

Banana plantation, Honduras.

PREGUNTAS

1. ¿Dónde se originó el **maíz**?   2. ¿Cómo se llamaba la planta silvestre?   3. ¿Qué indios vivían en esa región?   4. ¿Qué era la planta para ellos?   5. ¿Por qué se quedaron los indios cerca de los campos?   6. En realidad, ¿cuál fue la base de la civilización indígena?

7. ¿Qué otra planta indígena se conocía en las regiones tropicales?   8. ¿Cuáles son algunos productos modernos de las semillas del cacao?   9. ¿Para qué usaban las semillas los aztecas?   10. Según una leyenda, ¿quién tomaba mucho chocolate?   11. ¿Lo tomaban también los españoles?

12. ¿Dónde se cultiva la yerba mate?   13. ¿A qué árbol es parecida?   14. ¿Con qué se prepara el mate?   15. ¿Quiénes toman esta bebida?

16. ¿Quién fue Ricardo Palma?   17. ¿En qué siglo llegó al Perú don Luis Fernández de Cabrera?   18. ¿Quién se puso muy enferma de una fiebre alta?   19. ¿Qué le dio al virrey un indio anciano?   20. ¿Qué nombre se dio a la medicina?

21. ¿Qué hojas mascan hoy día los indios de los Andes?   22. ¿Por qué las mascan?   23. ¿Qué pueden hacer los indios si las mascan?   24. ¿Cuáles son otras plantas de las Américas?   25. ¿Para qué se usa la leche del chicle?   26. ¿Cuáles son otros productos de las Américas?   27. ¿Dónde se originó la patata?   28. ¿Cuándo la llevaron a Europa los españoles?

Workers at sugar mill, Costa Rica.

LECCIÓN 17

**Stem-changing verbs. Familiar singular commands
of irregular verbs. Irregular comparison of adjectives and adverbs
The absolute superlative. Summary of comparison of equality
Possessive adjectives that follow the noun**

JUANITA NO SE SIENTE BIEN

Son las cinco de la tarde. Isabel sale de la oficina y pasa por la casa de su amiga Juanita. Ha notado que su amiga no ha ido a la oficina hoy, y decide detenerse un momento. Aunque siente molestarla, toca el timbre y Juanita abre la puerta.

• • • • •

JUANITA. Buenas tardes, Isabel. Pasa, por favor. ¡Me alegro mucho de verte!

ISABEL. Muy buenas, Juanita. ¿Has estado enferma? No te vi en la oficina hoy.

JUANITA. No me siento bien y pedí permiso para no ir. Tengo un resfriado, y me duele la cabeza, aunque no tanto como ayer.

ISABEL. ¡Lo siento mucho, querida! ¿Por qué no te acuestas?

JUANITA. He pasado la mayor parte del día en la cama. Después de almorzar dormí la siesta y ahora me siento un poco mejor.

ISABEL. ¿Dormiste mucho?

JUANITA. Media hora, más o menos. Pero así es mejor. Si duermo mucho por la tarde, no puedo dormirme por la noche. A propósito, ¿has visto a Bárbara hoy?

ISABEL. Al mediodía la vi en el centro con Elena Martín, una prima suya. Buscaban un regalo para una tía suya. En una joyería vieron una pulsera que les gustó muchísimo y la compraron.

• • • • •

JUANITA. Isabel, ¿qué te ha contado Bárbara del viaje que hizo a Nueva York?

ISABEL. Se divirtió muchísimo y quiere volver lo más pronto posible. Conoció[1] allí a Roberto Molina, el hermano mayor del novio de Carmen, y se enamoró de él.

JUANITA. Conozco a Roberto. Es guapo y muy simpático. No es ni rico ni pobre y tiene un puesto muy bueno.

ISABEL. El viernes por la noche fueron al teatro, y el sábado cenaron y bailaron en uno de los mejores hoteles de la ciudad. Bárbara está contentísima.

JUANITA. ¡Dios mío! ¿Se ha enamorado tan pronto? ¿Crees que podría venir a verme esta noche? Tengo muchas ganas de charlar con ella.

ISABEL. Prometí llamarla por teléfono a eso de las seis y se lo[2] diré.

JUANITA. Pero, ¿ya tienes que irte?

ISABEL. Sí, ya es tarde, y tú debes descansar más. No salgas a la calle esta noche. Esperamos verte en la oficina mañana. ¡Adiós!

JUANITA. Adiós, Isabel. Hasta mañana.

CONVERSACIÓN

A. Preguntas sobre el diálogo

1. ¿Por dónde pasa Isabel al salir de la oficina? 2. ¿Por qué no ha ido Juanita a la oficina hoy? 3. ¿Qué hizo Juanita después de almorzar? 4. ¿Durmió mucho? 5. ¿A quiénes ha visto Isabel en el centro? 6. ¿Qué compraron Bárbara y Elena en una joyería? 7. ¿A quién ha conocido Bárbara en Nueva York? 8. ¿Cómo es Roberto?

B. Aplicación del diálogo

1. ¿Se siente Vd. bien hoy? 2. ¿Tiene Vd. un resfriado? 3. ¿Duerme Vd. la siesta todas las tardes? 4. ¿A qué tienda va Vd. si quiere comprar una pulsera? 5. ¿Se divierte Vd. mucho en los bailes? 6. ¿Qué piensa Vd. hacer el sábado? 7. ¿Qué hizo Vd. el viernes por la noche? 8. ¿Cuántas veces ha ido Vd. al teatro de la universidad?

---

[1] The preterit tense of **conocer** means *met* (someone for the first time); the imperfect means *knew*.   [2] If no direct object is expressed with verbs such as **decir, preguntar, creer,** and **saber,** the neuter pronoun **lo** is normally used: **se lo diré,** *I'll tell her* (*it*).

NOTAS GRAMATICALES

A. Stem-changing verbs

CLASS II		CLASS III
sentir, *to feel*	**dormir,** *to sleep*	**pedir,** *to ask (for)*

Present Indicative

siento	**duermo**	**pido**
sientes	**duermes**	**pides**
siente	**duerme**	**pide**
sentimos	dormimos	pedimos
sentís	dormís	pedís
sienten	**duermen**	**piden**

Preterit

sentí	dormí	pedí
sentiste	dormiste	pediste
sintió	**durmió**	**pidió**
sentimos	dormimos	pedimos
sentisteis	dormisteis	pedisteis
sintieron	**durmieron**	**pidieron**

Present Participles

sintiendo	**durmiendo**	**pidiendo**

When the stem of certain **-ir** verbs is accented, **e** becomes **ie** and **o** becomes **ue,** like Class I verbs, which end in **-ar** and **-er** (Lesson 8). In addition, the verbs of Class II change **e** to **i** and **o** to **u** in the third person singular and plural of the preterit and in the present participle. These verbs are designated in vocabularies: **sentir (ie,i), dormir (ue,u).**

Class III verbs, also of the third conjugation, change the stem vowel in the same forms as Class II verbs; the change, however, is always **e** to **i** (never to **ie**). Such verbs are designated: **pedir (i,i).**

The verb **preguntar** means *to ask* (a question); **pedir** means *to ask for, ask* (request) *someone to do something, ask a favor.*

B. Familiar singular commands of irregular verbs

INF.	AFFIRMATIVE		NEGATIVE	
decir	**di** (tú)	*say, tell*	no **digas** (tú)	*don't say (tell)*
hacer	**haz** (tú)	*do, make*	no **hagas** (tú)	*don't do (make)*
ir	**ve** (tú)	*go*	no **vayas** (tú)	*don't go*
poner	**pon** (tú)	*put, place*	no **pongas** (tú)	*don't put (place)*
salir	**sal** (tú)	*go out, leave*	no **salgas** (tú)	*don't go out (leave)*
ser	**sé** (tú)	*be*	no **seas** (tú)	*don't be*
tener	**ten** (tú)	*have*	no **tengas** (tú)	*don't have*
venir	**ven** (tú)	*come*	no **vengas** (tú)	*don't come*

In Lesson 9 you learned that the familiar singular command is the same in form as the third person singular of the present indicative tense of all but a few verbs. Eight common verbs which have irregular forms are given above.

Review the formal command forms of these verbs in Lesson 9 and the formation of the negative familiar singular commands.

The familiar singular commands for the three model verbs in section A are: **sentir: siente, no sientas; dormir: duerme, no duermas; pedir: pide, no pidas.**

C. Irregular comparison of adjectives and adverbs

1. In Lesson 7 we discussed the regular comparison of adjectives. The comparative of adverbs is also regularly formed by placing **más** or **menos** before the adverb. The definite article is not used in the superlative of adverbs, except that the neuter form **lo** is used when an expression of possibility follows:

Él habla más rápidamente que nunca. He talks more rapidly than ever.
Ella quiere volver lo más pronto posible. She wants to return as soon as possible (the soonest possible).

In the first example note that the negative **nunca** must be used after **que,** *than.*

2. Six adjectives and four adverbs, some of which have already been used, are compared irregularly:

ADJECTIVES

bueno good		(el) **mejor**	(the) better, best
malo bad		(el) **peor**	(the) worse, worst
grande large	{	(el) **más grande**	(the) larger, largest
	{	(el) **mayor**	(the) greater, older, greatest, oldest

pequeño small	{ (el) **más pequeño** { (el) **menor**		(the) smaller, smallest (the) smaller, younger, smallest, youngest	
mucho(s) much (many) **poco(s)** little (few)	**más** **menos**		more, most less, fewer	

Grande and **pequeño,-a** have regular forms which refer to size; the irregular forms **mayor** and **menor** usually refer to persons and mean *older* and *younger,* respectively. **Mejor** and **peor** precede a noun, just as **bueno,-a** and **malo,-a** regularly precede it.

Most (of), the greater part of, is translated **la mayor parte de: la mayor parte del día,** *most of the day.*

Remember that **grande** becomes **gran** before a masculine or feminine singular noun and generally means *great.* The full form is used before plural nouns: **un gran hombre,** *a great man;* **una gran universidad,** *a great university;* **unos grandes jugadores,** *some great players.*

ADVERBS

bien	well	**mejor**	better, best	**mucho**	much	**más**	more, most
mal	badly	**peor**	worse, worst	**poco**	little	**menos**	less, least

D. The absolute superlative

Bárbara está muy contenta (contentísima). Barbara is very happy.
Ella se divirtió muchísimo. She had a very good time.

A high degree of quality, without any element of comparison, is expressed by the use of **muy** before the adjective or adverb, or by adding the ending **-ísimo (-a, -os, -as)** to the adjective. When **-ísimo** is added, a final vowel is dropped. This form is emphatic; it is very common in Spanish. **Muchísimo** (never **muy mucho**) is used for the adjective or adverb *very much (many).*

E. Summary of comparison of equality

Ana tiene tantas cosas como yo. Ann has as many things as I.
Pablo es tan guapo como José. Paul is as handsome as Joseph.
Yo no hablo tan rápidamente como ella. I don't talk so rapidly as she.

Tanto (-a, -os, -as) + a noun + **como** means *as (so) much (many) ... as;* **tan** + an adjective or adverb + **como** means *as (so) ... as.*

Tanto is also used as a pronoun or adverb: **No tengo tantos,** *I don't have so many;* **No me duele la cabeza tanto como ayer,** *My head doesn't ache so much as yesterday.*

Tan is used only as an adverb: **¿Se ha enamorado ella tan pronto?** *Has she fallen in love so quickly?*

F. Possessive adjectives that follow the noun

<table>
<tr><td>SINGULAR</td><td></td><td>PLURAL</td></tr>
<tr><td>**mío, mía**</td><td>my, of mine</td><td>**míos, mías**</td></tr>
<tr><td>**tuyo, tuya**</td><td>your (*fam.*), of yours</td><td>**tuyos, tuyas**</td></tr>
<tr><td>**suyo, suya**</td><td>his, her, your (*formal*), its, of his, of hers, of yours</td><td>**suyos, suyas**</td></tr>
<tr><td>**nuestro, nuestra**</td><td>our, of ours</td><td>**nuestros, nuestras**</td></tr>
<tr><td>**vuestro, vuestra**</td><td>your (*fam. pl.*), of yours</td><td>**vuestros, vuestras**</td></tr>
<tr><td>**suyo, suya**</td><td>their, your (*pl.*), of theirs, of yours, of its</td><td>**suyos, suyas**</td></tr>
</table>

(1) **un amigo mío**   a friend of mine
aquella casa nuestra   that house of ours
Bárbara y una prima suya   Barbara and a cousin of hers
dos hermanos suyos   two brothers of his (hers, yours, theirs)

(2) **querida (amiga) mía**   my dear (friend)

(3) **¡Dios mío!**   heavens!

In Lesson 4 you learned the short forms of possessive adjectives, which always precede the noun.   There is also a set of long forms which follow the noun, agreeing with it in gender and number.   The long forms are most commonly used: (1) to translate *of mine, of his, of yours*, etc.; (2) in direct address; and (3) in certain set phrases.

Since **suyo** (**-a, -os, -as**) has several meanings, the form **de él**, etc., may be substituted to make the meaning clear: **dos hermanos suyos = dos hermanos de él** (**de ella, de ellos, de ellas, de Vd., de Vds.**), *two brothers of his* (*hers, theirs, yours*).   Do not use a prepositional form for any long possessive other than **suyo, -a, -os, -as.**

Práctica.   Read in Spanish, noting the use of the possessives:

1. un compañero mío, dos compañeros míos, un compañero nuestro.   2. un traje de Carlos, este traje suyo, esos trajes suyos.   3. el vestido de Elena, ese vestido suyo, varios vestidos suyos.   4. una amiga nuestra, algunas amigas nuestras, algunas amigas mías. 5. Juanita y un primo suyo, Juanita y una prima suya, Juanita y unos primos suyos. 6. ese regalo tuyo, esos regalos tuyos, esa pulsera tuya.

EJERCICIOS

A. Substitution drill:

1. *Mi mamá* duerme la siesta.
   (*Los muchachos, Yo, Él y yo, Vd., Tú*)

2. *Los jóvenes* siempre se divierten.
    (*Juanita, Nosotros, Yo, Tú, Vds.*)
3. *Ellos* no se sienten muy bien.
    (*Ella, Yo, Ana y yo, Vd., Elena y ella*)
4. *Elena* se durmió tarde.
    (*Los estudiantes, Nosotros, Tú, Isabel, Vds.*)
5. *Jorge* le pidió un favor.
    (*Ellos, Yo, Vd., Bárbara y yo, Tú*)

B. Listen to each sentence, then change to a formal singular command and to a familiar singular command:

> MODELS: Juan le pide algo.   Juan, pídale Vd. algo.   Juan, pídele algo.
> Juan no le pide nada. Juan, no le pida Vd. nada. Juan, no le pidas nada.

1. Isabel vuelve temprano.
2. Ana la llama por teléfono.
3. José duerme la siesta.
4. Carlos viene a verme.
5. Juanita no sale a la calle.
6. Bárbara no le dice eso.

C. Listen to each sentence, then repeat, making it negative:

> MODEL: Hazlo esta tarde.   No lo hagas esta tarde.

1. Dinos el precio de eso.
2. Ponlas sobre la mesa.
3. Ve al centro con ella.
4. Duérmete en el coche.
5. Báñate ahora.
6. Apréndelo hoy.

D. Answer affirmatively, following the models.   Watch the demonstrative pronoun in your answer to questions 1-6:

> MODELS: ¿Es grande la ciudad?   Sí, la ciudad es más grande que ésta.
> ¿Es bueno el camino?   Sí, el camino es mejor que éste.

1. ¿Es pequeña la casa?
2. ¿Son hermosas las flores?
3. ¿Están contentas las muchachas?
4. ¿Son caros los regalos?
5. ¿Es bueno el hotel?
6. ¿Es malo el camino?

> MODEL: ¿Es hermosa María?   Sí, es muy hermosa; es hermosísima.

7. ¿Es guapo su novio?
8. ¿Son altos los árboles?
9. ¿Está contenta su hermana?
10. ¿Son hermosas las pulseras?

MODEL: ¿Es grande la casa?   Sí, es la casa más grande de la ciudad.

11. ¿Es larga la calle?   13. ¿Son bonitos los árboles?
12. ¿Es pequeño el parque?   14. ¿Son nuevas las tiendas?

E. Substitution drill:

1. Mi mamá tiene tantas *flores* como ella.
   (*sombreros, tiempo, pulseras, ropa*)

2. Juan no es tan *alto* como Isabel.
   (*simpático, amable, pequeño, joven*)

3. Bárbara baila *más* que nadie.
   (*menos, mejor, peor, más rápidamente*)

4. Carlos es *mayor* que yo.
   (*menor, menos alto, más pequeño*)

F. Say after your teacher, then repeat, replacing the de-phrase with suyo, -a, -os, -as, as required:

1. Felipe y una hermana *de él*.   2. Felipe y un hermano *de él*.   3. Felipe y dos primos *de él*.   4. Ana y dos primos *de ella*.   5. Isabel y una tía *de ella*.   6. Ana y un tío *de ella*.   7. Los muchachos y algunos amigos *de ellos*.   8. ¿Va Vd. con un amigo *de Vd.*?   9. ¿Va Juanita con un amigo *de ella*?   10. ¿Van los estudiantes con dos profesores *de ellos*?   11. Isabel va a México con dos tías *de ella*.   12. Este reloj es *de él*.   13. Este reloj es *de ella*.   14. Estos trajes no son *de Vd*.   15. Estos regalos no son *de ella*.   16. ¿Es *de Vd.* este coche?

G. Give in Spanish:

1. this watch of mine.   2. these books of mine.   3. this car of ours.   4. those tickets of ours.   5. our father and two sisters of his.   6. Helen and two aunts of hers.   7. my brother and a friend of his.   8. my parents and some friends of theirs.   9. you (*formal sing.*) and a friend of yours.   10. you (*fam. sing.*) and a (girl) friend of yours.   11. an uncle of hers (*two ways*).   12. my dear friends.

COMPOSICIÓN

1. Hello, Jane! How do you feel today? — My head aches and I have a cold.   2. I am very sorry! Why don't you go to sleep now?   3. If I sleep during the day, I cannot go to sleep in the evening.   4. Do you know whether Barbara has returned from her trip to New York?   5. I talked with her an hour ago when I ran across her in the theater.   6. It seems that she fell in love with Mary's younger brother.   7. He intends to visit

her next month because he will be on vacation. 8. Although he isn't handsome, she says that he is very charming. 9. He has a good job in one of the best stores in the city. 10. Barbara is so happy now that she talks about him most of the time. 11. They had a very good time dancing in one of the best hotels Saturday night. 12. Ask her whether she can come (pass) by here tomorrow afternoon. 13. I know that she is very eager to chat with you a while. 14. Are you going already? — Yes, it is late. I'll see you tomorrow.

VOCABULARIO

Bárbara Barbara
la cabeza head
la cama bed
contar (**ue**) to tell, relate
contento, -a happy, pleased, glad
Dios God
divertir (**ie,i**) to divert, amuse; *reflex.* have a good time, amuse oneself
doler (**ue**) to ache, pain
dormir (**ue,u**) to sleep; *reflex.* fall asleep, go to sleep
enamorarse (**de** + *obj.*) to fall in love (with)
guapo, -a handsome, good-looking
la joyería jewelry shop (store)
notar to note, observe

el novio sweetheart, fiancé, boy friend
pedir (**i,i**) to ask, ask for, request
posible possible
prometer to promise
el puesto job, position, place
la pulsera bracelet
querido, -a dear
el resfriado cold (*disease*)
rico, -a rich
sentir (**ie,i**) to feel, regret, be sorry
la siesta nap
simpático, -a charming, likeable, "nice"
tanto *adv.* as (so) much
el teatro theater
el timbre doorbell
tocar to ring

a eso de at about
¿cómo se siente Vd.? how do you feel?
¡Dios mío! heavens!
dormir (**ue,u**) **la siesta** to take a nap
la mayor parte de most (of), the greater part of
lo siento (**mucho**) I am (very) sorry
me duele la cabeza I have a headache, my head aches (*lit.*, the head aches to me)
muy buenas good afternoon (evening) (*used in reply to* **buenas tardes** *or* **buenas noches**)
salir a la calle to go out into the street
sentirse (**ie,i**) **bien** to feel well

CONVERSACIÓN III

En un restaurante español

(Carlos y Felipe, dos jóvenes madrileños, han invitado a dos estudiantes norteamericanas, Ana y Carmen, a almorzar. Son las dos de la tarde, hora en que los españoles acostumbran tomar el almuerzo. Entran en un restaurante cerca de la Plaza Mayor. Se acerca un camarero.)

Typical Spanish restaurant near the Plaza Mayor, Madrid, Spain.

CARLOS. ¿Hay una mesa para cuatro?

CAMARERO. Hay una mesa libre cerca de la ventana. Pasen Vds. por aquí. *(Se sientan los jóvenes. El camarero trae la lista y, mientras los cuatro la examinan, trae vasos de agua, pan, mantequilla y entremeses.)*

CAMARERO. ¿Qué desean tomar, señores?

CARLOS. ¿Encuentran algo de su gusto, señoritas?

CARMEN. No es fácil escoger entre tantos platos. La selección es muy variada.

FELIPE. Es que cada región española tiene su plato típico.

CARMEN. Primero voy a tomar sopa. Y, después, paella valenciana.

CARLOS. ¿No desea un plato de huevos después de la sopa? En España las tortillas son excelentes. Se hacen de patatas, de jamón, de verduras … No son como las mexicanas.

CARMEN. Gracias, hoy no.

ANA. Yo voy a tomar una tortilla española en vez de sopa. Luego no sé si tomar carne o pescado.

CAMARERO. Puede tomar las dos cosas, señorita. Tenemos muchas clases de pescado. La merluza con mayonesa es excelente.

FELIPE. El arroz con pollo es un plato español muy típico y muy sabroso.

ANA. Muy bien. Arroz con pollo, por favor.

FELIPE. Pues yo voy a tomar sopa, pescado y, después, biftec con patatas fritas y una ensalada.

CAMARERO. Muy bien. Y, ¿usted, señor?

CARLOS. Como buen madrileño, tomaré el cocido. Primero sopa y luego los otros elementos que contiene: garbanzos, patatas y albóndigas, con chorizo y tocino. Para terminar, un poco de lomo de cerdo y una ensalada.

CAMARERO. ¿Desean vino, señores?

FELIPE. Naturalmente. Vino tinto. Una botella de vino de la Rioja, por favor. Como verán Vds., los vinos españoles son magníficos.

CAMARERO. ¿Desean algún postre?

CARLOS. ¿Qué postres hay?

CAMARERO. Además de los comunes — arroz con leche, flan, queso, membrillo, pasteles, helados y frutas —, en este restaurante tenemos varias especialidades, como los turrones, los bizcochos borrachos, almíbares de la Rioja …

CARMEN. Para mí, flan y una taza de café con leche y azúcar.

ANA. Pues, yo tomaré frutas y una taza de café solo.

FELIPE. Yo voy a tomar queso, frutas, y café solo.

CARLOS. Y para mí, helado de fresa y una taza de café solo. (*Los jóvenes charlan mientras el camarero trae lo que han pedido. Terminan el almuerzo, pagan la comida y le dan una buena propina al camarero.*)

CARMEN. Se come muy bien aquí, ¿verdad?

CARLOS. ¡Cómo no! Tiene fama de ser uno de los mejores restaurantes de Madrid.

FELIPE. ¿Por qué no cenamos aquí esta noche? Si cenamos a las nueve, podremos ir al teatro después.

CARMEN. ¡Es una idea magnífica!

ANA. ¡Encantada, porque me gustará probar otros platos, como el gazpacho y el lechón y el cordero asados!

CARLOS. Pues, pasaremos a recogerlas a las nueve. Tomaremos un taxi, porque a esa hora habrá mucha gente en los autobuses.

FELIPE. Hasta las nueve, entonces.

ANA Y CARMEN. Muy bien. Estaremos listas. Y, ¡mil gracias por todo!

PREGUNTAS

Sobre la conversación

1. ¿Quiénes son Ana y Carmen?   2. ¿Con quiénes van a almorzar?   3. ¿A qué hora acostumbran almorzar los españoles?   4. Mientras los jóvenes examinan la lista, ¿qué trae el camarero?   5. ¿Qué va a tomar Carmen?   6. ¿De qué se hacen las tortillas en España?

7. ¿Qué dice Felipe del arroz con pollo?   8. ¿Qué elementos contiene el cocido madrileño?   9. ¿Qué dice Felipe acerca de los vinos españoles?   10. ¿Qué postres son comunes a casi toda España?   11. ¿Qué postres recuerda Vd.?   12. ¿Dónde deciden cenar los jóvenes?

Aplicación de la conversación

1. ¿A qué hora acostumbramos almorzar en los Estados Unidos?   2. ¿Qué toma Vd. generalmente para el almuerzo?   3. ¿Cuáles son algunos platos típicos de los Estados Unidos?   4. ¿Conoce Vd. algunos platos típicos de otros países?   5. ¿Qué postres le gustan a Vd.?   6. ¿Cuál será el postre más común de los Estados Unidos?

7. ¿Qué ciudades norteamericanas tienen fama por sus restaurantes?   8. ¿Qué estados son famosos por sus vinos?   9. ¿Qué regiones tienen fama por sus frutas?   10. ¿Le gusta a Vd. la carne de cerdo?   11. ¿Le interesan a Vd. las comidas españolas?   12. ¿Sabe Vd. si se toma fría alguna sopa española?

PRÁCTICAS ORALES

Groups of students will be selected to prepare a conversation of eight to ten exchanges, using vocabulary already given.

1. Groups of students order a Spanish meal, with one acting as waiter (waitress) and others as customers.

2. In other groups two American students meet Spanish friends and discuss the variety of regional dishes in Spain and in the United States.

VOCABULARIO

acostumbrar   to be accustomed to
además de   *prep.*   besides, in addition to
la albóndiga   meat ball
el almíbar   syrup; *pl.* fruit preserves
el arroz   rice
el arroz con leche   rice pudding
asado, -a   roast(ed)

el biftec   steak
el bizcocho borracho   tipsy cake
la botella   bottle
la carne   meat
el cerdo   pork, pig
el cocido   Spanish stew
común (*pl.* **comunes**)   common, ordinary

contener (*like* **tener**) to contain
el cordero lamb
el chorizo smoked pork sausage
el elemento element, ingredient
encantado, -a delighted
la ensalada salad
el entremés (*pl.* **entremeses**) side dish, hors d'oeuvre
escoger to choose, select
la especialidad specialty
examinar to examine
la fama fame, reputation
el flan custard
la fresa strawberry
frito, -a fried
el garbanzo chickpea
el gazpacho cold vegetable soup
el huevo egg
el jamón (*pl.* **jamones**) ham
el lechón (*pl.* **lechones**) suckling pig
la lista menu
el lomo (de cerdo) (pork) loin
la mantequilla butter
el membrillo quince (*fruit and paste*)
la merluza con mayonesa hake with mayonnaise
mientras *conj.* while, as long as
la paella *a rice dish containing meat, vegetables, and shellfish*
el pan bread
la patata potato

el pescado fish
el plato plate, dish, course (*at meals*)
la Plaza Mayor Main Square (*in center of old Madrid*)
el pollo chicken
el postre dessert
probar (**ue**) to try, sample, taste
la propina tip
el queso cheese
recoger to pick up
la región (*pl.* **regiones**) region
la Rioja *part of province of Logroño in northern Old Castile, famous for its wines*
sabroso, -a delicious, tasty
la selección (*pl.* **selecciones**) selection, choice
el señor gentleman
la sopa soup
el taxi taxi
tinto, -a deep red; **tinto** (*m.n.*) red wine
el tocino bacon
la tortilla omelet
el turrón (*pl.* **turrones**) nougat, almond candy
valenciano, -a Valencian, of Valencia
variado, -a varied
las verduras vegetables, greens
el vino wine

de su gusto to his (her, your, their) liking
en vez de instead of, in place of
hora en que the time (hour) when
hoy no not today
mil gracias many (a thousand) thanks
para el almuerzo for lunch
se come muy bien aquí the food is very good here (*lit.*, one eats very well here)
señores ladies and gentlemen
tener fama (de) to have the (a) reputation (of, as)
tener fama por to have a reputation for, be known for

LECCIÓN 18

The present subjunctive of regular verbs
The present subjunctive of irregular and stem-changing verbs
Theory of the subjunctive mood.   The subjunctive in noun clauses

ANA Y ROBERTO CELEBRAN SU ANIVERSARIO CON UN BAILE

Dorotea Gómez acaba de pasar sus vacaciones en Caracas.   En el vuelo a los Estados Unidos conoce a Carlos Molina, un joven argentino que piensa estudiar en la misma universidad que ella.   Una noche Dorotea le lleva a casa de unos amigos suyos, Ana y Roberto White.   Roberto abre la puerta.

• • • • •

ROBERTO.   ¡Cuánto me alegro de verla, Dorotea!   ¡No sabía que estaba Vd. de vuelta! ¿Se divirtió mucho en Venezuela?

DOROTEA.   ¡Muchísimo, Roberto!   En el vuelo conocí a este joven.   Quiero presentarle mi amigo,[1] Carlos Molina.

ROBERTO.   Mucho gusto en conocerle, Carlos.

CARLOS.   El gusto es mío.   Es un gran placer estar en su país.

ROBERTO.   Es Vd. muy amable.   ¿Quieren Vds. pasar?   Ana y yo estamos celebrando nuestro aniversario con un baile, y quiero que Vds. conozcan a nuestros invitados.

---

[1] To avoid confusion with the indirect object **le,** *to you*, the personal **a** is omitted before the direct object **mi amigo.**

255

DOROTEA.   Gracias, Roberto, pero no debemos quedarnos.   Volveremos en otra ocasión. No queremos molestarlos.

ROBERTO.   ¡Dios mío, Dorotea!   ¡No faltaba más!   Les ruego que pasen ahora mismo. Ana también tendrá mucho gusto en verlos.

• • • • •

(*Por fin entran, y Roberto los presenta a todos.   Después de charlar unos minutos, pasan a la sala de recreo.   Ponen varios discos de música popular en el tocadiscos.*)

ANA.   Como Carlos es argentino, sabrá bailar el tango.   ¿Por qué no nos enseña a bailarlo, Carlos?

OTRAS MUCHACHAS.   Sí; queremos que nos enseñe a bailar el tango.   Ninguno de los otros muchachos sabe bailarlo.

CARLOS.   Con mucho gusto.   Y si no conocen la rumba cubana, Dorotea y yo podremos enseñársela.   Quiero que conozcan mejor los bailes hispanoamericanos.

DOROTEA.   Ana, dígale a Roberto que ponga algún disco argentino.   Sé que Vds. tienen una colección magnífica.

CARLOS.   ¿Qué prefieren que les enseñe primero?   El tango, ¿verdad?

ANA.   Sí, y después le pediremos que nos enseñe la rumba.   (*Todos se divierten mucho aprendiendo los diferentes pasos.   A las once y media Ana sirve refrescos.   A la medianoche se despiden todos.*)

LOS INVITADOS.   Muchísimas gracias.   Hemos pasado una noche muy agradable.

ANA Y ROBERTO.   El gusto ha sido nuestro.   Deseamos que todos vuelvan pronto.   Buenas noches.

CONVERSACIÓN

A. Preguntas sobre el diálogo

1. ¿Dónde ha pasado Dorotea sus vacaciones?   2. ¿A quién conoció en el vuelo a los Estados Unidos?   3. ¿Adónde le lleva Dorotea una noche?   4. ¿Qué le dice Roberto a Dorotea al verla?   5. ¿Qué dice Roberto cuando Dorotea le presenta su amigo Carlos?   6. ¿Qué están celebrando Ana y Roberto?   7. ¿Qué bailes les enseña Carlos? 8. ¿A qué hora se despiden todos los invitados?

B. Aplicación del diálogo

1. ¿Dónde va a pasar Vd. sus vacaciones?   2. ¿Le gusta a Vd. la música popular? 3. ¿Tiene Vd. una buena colección de discos?   4. ¿Sabe Vd. bailar el tango?   5. ¿Se baila mucho la rumba cubana en los Estados Unidos?   6. ¿Cuáles son los bailes más populares entre los jóvenes?   7. ¿Qué dice uno al presentar un amigo a otro?   8. ¿Qué dice uno al despedirse, después de una noche agradable?

NOTAS GRAMATICALES

A. The present subjunctive of regular verbs

hablar		**comer**		**vivir**	
SING.	PLURAL	SING.	PLURAL	SING.	PLURAL
hable	hablemos	coma	comamos	viva	vivamos
hables	habléis	comas	comáis	vivas	viváis
hable	hablen	coma	coman	viva	vivan

In the present subjunctive tense the endings of **-ar** verbs begin with **-e,** while those of **-er** and **-ir** verbs begin with **-a.** In earlier lessons we have used the third person singular and plural forms of the present subjunctive in formal commands (Lesson 9), and the second person singular for negative familiar singular commands (Lessons 9 and 17). There is no regular translation for the subjunctive (see section C); however, in drill exercises a conventional translation for the present subjunctive may be: (**que**) **yo hable,** (*that*) *I may speak*; (**que**) **comamos,** (*that*) *we may eat.*

B. The present subjunctive of irregular and stem-changing verbs

Infinitive	*1st Sing.* *Pres. Ind.*	*Present Subjunctive*
conocer	**conozco**	**conozca, conozcas, conozca,** etc.
decir	**digo**	**diga, digas, diga,** etc.
hacer	**hago**	**haga,** etc.
poner	**pongo**	**ponga,** etc.
salir	**salgo**	**salga,** etc.
tener	**tengo**	**tenga,** etc.
traer	**traigo**	**traiga,** etc.
venir	**vengo**	**venga,** etc.
ver	**veo**	**vea,** etc.

As we have found in Lesson 9, in order to form the present subjunctive of all verbs in Spanish, except the six given on page 258, drop the ending **-o** of the first person singular present indicative and add to this stem the subjunctive endings for the corresponding conjugation.

	dar			**estar**			**haber**	
SING.	PLURAL		SING.	PLURAL		SING.	PLURAL	
dé	demos		**esté**	estemos		**haya**	**hayamos**	
des	deis		**estés**	estéis		**hayas**	**hayáis**	
dé	den		**esté**	**estén**		**haya**	**hayan**	

	ir		**saber**			**ser**	
vaya	vayamos	sepa	sepamos		sea	seamos	
vayas	vayáis	sepas	sepáis		seas	seáis	
vaya	vayan	sepa	sepan		sea	sean	

Stem-changing verbs of Class I (ending in **-ar** and **-er**) have the same changes in the present subjunctive as in the present indicative; that is, throughout the singular and in the third person plural. This is also true of **poder** and **querer**.

pensar: **piense, pienses, piense,** pensemos, penséis, **piensen**

volver: **vuelva, vuelvas, vuelva,** volvamos, volváis, **vuelvan**

poder: **pueda, puedas, pueda,** podamos, podáis, **puedan**

querer: **quiera, quieras, quiera,** queramos, queráis, **quieran**

Stem-changing verbs of Class II and Class III (both of which end in **-ir**) have the same four changes in the present subjunctive which they have in the present indicative (throughout the singular and in the third person plural, see Lesson 17). In addition, Class II verbs change **e** to **i** and **o** to **u** in the first and second persons plural, and Class III verbs change **e** to **i** in these two forms also:

	CLASS II					CLASS III	
	sentir		**dormir**			**pedir**	
SING.	PLURAL	SING.	PLURAL		SING.	PLURAL	
sienta	sintamos	duerma	durmamos		pida	pidamos	
sientas	sintáis	duermas	durmáis		pidas	pidáis	
sienta	sientan	duerma	duerman		pida	pidan	

C. Theory of the subjunctive mood

The indicative mood, which has been used up to this point, except in main clauses to express commands, indicates facts.

Spanish uses the subjunctive mood much more than English, particularly in dependent clauses. If the clause is used as a subject or direct object of the verb, it is a noun clause;

e.g., in the sentence *I doubt that he knows it*, the words *that he knows it* make up a noun clause used as the direct object of the verb *I doubt*. The subjunctive mood is generally found in noun clauses that depend on verbs which express *uncertainty* or an *opinion*, an *attitude*, a *wish*, or a *feeling* of the speaker concerning the action of the dependent clause:

> **Yo no creo que él esté aquí.**   I do not believe that he is (will be) here.
> **Ella espera que Juan lo haga.**   She hopes that John may (will) do it.
> **Ellos quieren que Vd. venga.**   They wish that you come, They want you
> to come.

Some of these uses are discussed further in section D; others will be taken up later. Note that the subjunctive has various translations in English: (1) like the English present tense (*that you come*); (2) like the future (*that he will be here*); (3) with the word *may* (*that John may do it*), which carries the idea of something uncertain or not yet accomplished; and (4) by the infinitive (last example).

D. The subjunctive in noun clauses

> **Yo quiero ir.**   I want to go.   (*Subjects the same*)
> **Ellos quieren que yo vaya.**   They want me to go (They wish that
> I go).   (*Subjects different*)
> **José prefiere hacerlo.**   Joe prefers to do it.   (*Subjects the same*)
> **Él prefiere que ella lo haga.**   He prefers that she do it.   (*Subjects different*)

In Spanish the subjunctive is regularly used in a noun clause when the main verb expresses such ideas of the speaker as those of *wish, request, command, order, necessity, permission, approval, advice, cause, suggestion, insistence* and the like, as well as their negatives.

In English an infinitive is most commonly used after such verbs, but in Spanish a clause, usually introduced by **que,** is normally used if the subject of the dependent clause is different from that of the main verb. When there is no change in subject, or no subject is expressed for the English infinitive, the infinitive is also used in Spanish (first and third examples).

The present subjunctive is used for both present and future time in a dependent clause. And since the first and third person singular forms of the present subjunctive tense are the same, the subject pronouns must be used more often than in some other tenses.

With certain verbs, *e.g.*, **decir, pedir, rogar,** and others which require a personal object to be expressed as an indirect object, the subject of the infinitive in English is expressed as the indirect object of the main verb and understood as the subject of the subjunctive verb in the dependent clause. When you have a sentence like *Ask him to leave*, think of it literally as *Ask of (to) him that he leave*:

> **Pídale Vd. a Juan que salga.**   Ask John to leave.   (*Subjects different*)
> **Les ruego a Vds. que pasen.**   I beg you to come in.   (*Subjects different*)
> **Díganles Vds. que me lo den.**   Tell them to give it to me.   (*Subjects different*)
> **Él nos dirá que volvamos.**   He will tell us to return.   (*Subjects different*)

Decir is followed by the subjunctive when it is used to give an order (last two examples). Otherwise the indicative is used, since the verb indicates a fact (unless the verb is used negatively, in which case it becomes a verb which expresses uncertainty; see Lesson 19):

Juan dice que volverá. John says (that) he will return.

EJERCICIOS

A. Say each sentence after your teacher, then express it as a formal command:

1. Pablo habla español. 2. Elena lee la composición. 3. José cierra la ventana. 4. María vuelve temprano. 5. Jorge no lleva a casa el disco. 6. Dorotea sirve el café. 7. Marta va a la tienda. 8. Roberto viene a verme.

B. Say after your teacher, then repeat, changing to the negative:

1. Póngalos Vd. en la mesa. 2. Estúdienlas Vds. para mañana. 3. Levántense Vds. ahora mismo. 4. Enséñeme Vd. su vestido nuevo. 5. Dénoslo Vd. 6. Pónganselo Vds. ahora. 7. Siéntense Vds. 8. Lávenselas Vds.

C. Repeat each familiar command, then change to the negative:

1. Bárbara, sirve el café. 2. Elena, sal ahora mismo. 3. Carolina, ve a la biblioteca. 4. Jorge, ponte el sombrero. 5. Miguel, tráeme el disco. 6. Pablo, llévaselo a ellos.

D. Answer each question with affirmative and negative formal commands, substituting the correct object pronouns for the noun objects:

MODEL: ¿Le doy a Juan el reloj?   Sí, déselo Vd. a él.   No, no se lo dé Vd. a él.

1. ¿Le traigo a Vd. la blusa?
2. ¿Le mando a Luis el billete?
3. ¿Les vendo a Vds. los discos?
4. ¿Les llevo a los muchachos el dinero?
5. ¿Le doy a Marta la pulsera?
6. ¿Les pido a Ana y a María el favor?

E. Substitution drill:

1. Quieren que *yo* hable español.
   (*nosotros, Juan, tú, Vd., los estudiantes*)
2. Prefiere que *él y yo* lo traigamos hoy.
   (*yo, él, Vds., Marta y yo, Bárbara*)
3. *Pídale Vd.* que salga ahora.
   (*Pídales Vd., Ana me pide, José y Miguel le ruegan, Yo le ruego*)
4. *Ellos me dicen* que lo haga.
   (*Dígale Vd., Marta nos dice, Yo les digo, Ella te dice*)

F. Repeat the question after your teacher; when you hear the question again, and then an infinitive, compose an answer using the correct form of the verb, following the model:

> MODEL: ¿Qué quiere ella que él haga?   ¿Qué quiere ella que él haga?
> ¿Qué quiere ella que él haga? ¿Bailar?   Sí, ella quiere que él baile.

1. ¿Qué quiere él que ellos hagan?   ¿Venir?
2. ¿Qué quiere ella que ellos hagan?   ¿Salir?
3. ¿Qué prefieren ellos que José haga?   ¿Ir a casa?
4. ¿Qué prefieres tú que Ana haga?   ¿Cantar?

G. Say the question after your teacher, then answer using a clause, following the model:

> MODEL: ¿Quiere Vd. hacerlo?   ¿Quiere Vd. hacerlo?   No, quiero que Vd. lo haga.

1. ¿Quiere Vd. traerlo?
2. ¿Quiere Vd. servirlos?
3. ¿Quiere Vd. verla?
4. ¿Prefiere Vd. decírselo a él?
5. ¿Prefiere Vd. pedírselo a ellos?
6. ¿Prefiere Vd. ponérselos?

H. Give in Spanish:

1. Louis wants to return.   2. Louis wants John to return (wishes that John return). 3. He and I want to meet her.   4. Helen wants us to meet them (wishes that we meet them).   5. The boys prefer to write the letter.   6. They do not prefer that I write it. 7. Ask them to get up (Ask of them that they get up).   8. Tell him that we are going to eat (*statement of fact*).   9. Tell her not to serve the coffee (Tell to her that she not serve the coffee).   10. I shall ask Ann to teach it to them (I shall ask of Ann that she teach it to them).

COMPOSICIÓN

1. Charles and Dorothy approach the house of some friends of theirs and they ring the doorbell.   2. Upon opening the door, Robert says: "How glad I am to see you, Dorothy! I didn't know that you were back!"   3. And when Dorothy introduces her friend Charles to him, he says: "I am very glad to know you."   4. Charles replies: "The pleasure is mine.   It is a great pleasure to be here."   5. Robert says that he and Ann are celebrating their anniversary with a dance in their recreation room.   6. He wants Dorothy and Charles to meet their guests.   7. He asks them to come in, but they say that they will return another time (on another occasion).   8. He insists that[1] they stay,

---

[1] Use **insistir en que** plus the present subjunctive in the dependent clause.

and they finally decide to do so (it).   9. They play several records of popular music; then Robert puts on some Argentine records.   10. One of the girls wants Charles, who is from Argentina, to teach her the tango.   11. Later another girl asks him to dance the Cuban rumba with her.   12. After dancing two or three hours, Robert tells Ann to serve refreshments.   13. At midnight all the guests take leave, saying: "We have spent a very pleasant evening."   14. Robert and his wife Ann beg them to return soon.

View of the galleries, Museum of Modern Art, Barcelona, Spain.

VOCABULARIO

argentino, -a Argentine
la colección (*pl.* **colecciones**) collection
¡cuánto + *verb*! how!
cubano, -a Cuban
despedirse (**i,i**) (**de** + *obj.*) to say
  goodbye (to), take leave (of)
diferente different
el disco record (*phonograph*)
el fin end
el fonógrafo phonograph, record
  player
el invitado guest
la medianoche midnight
mío, -a *pron. and adj.* mine
mismo, -a same

la música music
ninguno, -a no, none
nuestro, -a *pron. and adj.* ours
la ocasión (*pl.* **ocasiones**) occasion
el paso step
poner to turn on, put on
popular popular
preferir (**ie,i**) to prefer
rogar (**ue**) to ask, beg
la rumba rumba
la sala de recreo recreation room
servir (**i,i**) to serve
el tango tango
la vuelta return; change (*money*)

a la medianoche at midnight
ahora mismo right now, right away
¡cuánto me alegro (**de**)! how glad I am (to)!
el (**la**) **mismo** (**-a**) ... **que** the same ... as
en otra ocasión another (some other) time
estar de vuelta to be back
mucho gusto en conocerle (I am) very pleased (glad) to know you
¡no faltaba más! the very idea! that's the limit!
pasar una noche muy agradable to spend a very pleasant evening
por fin finally, at last

Cathedral of Salamanca, Spain.

LECTURA X

LA ESPAÑA ANTIGUA

Estudio de palabras

a. Less approximate cognates. Pronounce the following words aloud, note the English cognates, and indicate the variations: acueducto, *aqueduct*; avanzado, *advanced*; cantidad, *quantity*; enérgico, *energetic*; espiritual, *spiritual*; establecer, *to establish*; gobierno, *government*; imperio, *empire*; invasor, *invader*; maravilla, *marvel*; matrimonio, *matrimony*, *marriage*; ocupar, *to occupy*; reconquista, *reconquest*; teatro, *theater*; unidad, *unity*.

b. Compare the meanings of: agricultor, *agriculturist, farmer, and* agricultura, *agriculture*; comercio, *commerce, and* comerciante, *merchant*; descubrir, *to discover*; descubridor, *discoverer, and* descubrimiento, *discovery*; explorar, *to explore,* exploración, *exploration, and* explorador, *explorer*; guerra, *war, and* guerrero, -a, *warlike*; nombrar, *to name, appoint, and* nombre, *name*; obra, *work, and* obrero, *workman*; poder, *to be able,* poderío, *power, and* poderoso, -a, *powerful*.

Notas sobre el uso de los adjetivos

In the grammar lessons we have followed the general principle that limiting adjectives (numerals, demonstratives, possessives, a few indefinites, and the like) precede the noun, and that descriptive adjectives which single out or distinguish a noun from another of the same class (adjectives of color, size, shape, nationality, and the like) follow the noun.

Descriptive adjectives may also precede the noun when they express a quality that is generally known or not essential to the recognition of the noun. In such cases there is no desire to single out or to differentiate:

> **los altos Pirineos**   **algunos de los famosos exploradores**
> **las hermosas flores**   **la nueva lengua**

Whenever an adjective is changed from its normal position, the speaker or writer gives a subjective or personal interpretation of the noun. Therefore, position of adjectives may vary according to subject matter, style, and individual feeling or emotion. You have observed that **bueno** and **malo** usually precede the noun, although they may follow to distinguish characteristics of the noun. Other common adjectives like **hermoso, bonito, pequeño,** and the like, may precede or follow the noun. The following sentence from this Lectura offers a good example of adjectives which express qualities which are generally thought of in connection with the nouns in this particular situation:

la famosa Alhambra, con sus magníficos patios, sus bellos jardines y sus alegres fuentes ...

In footnote 3, page 129, we called attention to the fact that a descriptive adjective often precedes the noun: **una magnífica película mexicana; unos hermosos bailes españoles.**

Other examples are: **las antiguas misiones españolas; Ricardo Palma, famoso autor peruano.**

In the Lecturas which follow observe similar cases of adjective position.

La historia de España presenta muchos contrastes. España ha tenido épocas de gloria y períodos de decadencia. En los párrafos siguientes vamos a repasar la historia de España desde sus orígenes hasta el descubrimiento de América, el hecho[1] más notable, sin duda, de su larga historia.

Los primeros pobladores de la península fueron los iberos,[2] pero no se sabe ni su origen ni la época exacta en que entraron en la península. Cerca de Santander, en el norte de España, se conservan, en las cuevas[3] de Altamira, dibujos de animales pintados hace unos veinte o treinta mil años. Los fenicios,[4] considerados como los primeros comerciantes del mundo, llegaron a la península hacia el siglo XI antes de Jesucristo[5] y fundaron la ciudad de Cádiz. Hubo[6] otros invasores: los celtas,[7] en el norte, principalmente en Galicia; los griegos,[8] que se establecieron en la costa del Mar Mediterráneo; y los cartagineses,[9] que

dominaron la península desde el siglo VI hasta el III antes de Jesucristo. Los romanos estuvieron en España unos seis siglos. Durante esa época la península llegó a ser una de las provincias más importantes del imperio romano. En España los romanos dejaron su lengua, sus costumbres, su religión, sus leyes y sus ideas sobre el gobierno; se construyeron[10] teatros, acueductos, caminos, puentes[11] y otras obras públicas.

Buen ejemplo de la obra de los romanos es el acueducto de Segovia, que está en uso todavía. Está construido de piedras grandes, sin argamasa[12] de ninguna clase. Otra obra romana es el teatro de Sagunto, que está al norte de la ciudad de Valencia.

A la caída[13] del imperio romano, ocuparon la península los visigodos[14] y otras tribus germánicas. Los últimos invasores fueron los moros,[15] que entraron en España en 711 y no fueron expulsados hasta 1492. Córdoba fue el centro de la civilización de los

---

[1] **hecho,** *event, deed.* [2] **iberos,** *Iberians.* [3] **cuevas,** *caves.* [4] **fenicios,** *Phoenicians.* [5] **antes de Jesucristo,** *B.C.* [6] **Hubo,** *There were.* [7] **celtas,** *Celts.* [8] **griegos,** *Greeks.* [9] **cartagineses,** *Carthaginians.* [10] **se construyeron,** *were built.* [11] **puentes,** *bridges.* [12] **argamasa,** *mortar.* [13] **caída,** *fall.* [14] **visigodos,** *Visigoths.* [15] **moros,** *Moors.*

Roman theater in Mérida, Spain.

moros, considerada en el siglo X como la más avanzada de Europa. No lejos de Córdoba está Granada, que fue la última capital de los moros. Allí se encuentra la famosa Alhambra, con sus magníficos patios, sus bellos jardines y sus alegres fuentes. Al abandonar a[1] España, los moros dejaron en ella influencias decisivas en la lengua, la literatura, la arquitectura, el arte, la música, el comercio y la agricultura.

Durante la guerra de la reconquista, que duró casi ocho siglos, surgieron los reinos[2] de León, Navarra, Aragón, Galicia y Castilla. Castilla, que se llamó así por la gran cantidad de castillos que se construyeron para la defensa contra los moros, llegó a ser, con el tiempo, el reino principal del país. En el siglo XI el castellano empezó a predominar sobre los demás dialectos romances hablados en la península. Se comenzó a cantar en la nueva lengua la vida guerrera[3] de la época. En ese siglo vivió el Cid, el gran héroe nacional de España, cuya tumba está en la catedral de Burgos, una de las más bellas de Europa.

Para ver la más grande de todas las catedrales góticas de Europa hay que ir a Sevilla. La torre de la catedral, la Giralda, construida por los moros, tiene fama de ser una de las más hermosas del mundo. Hay un refrán[4] español que dice: «Quien[5] no ha visto a Sevilla, no ha visto maravilla». Hay otro que dice: «Quien no ha visto a Granada, no ha visto nada».

Con el matrimonio de Fernando de Aragón con Isabel de Castilla, en 1469, consiguió[6] España la unidad política; poco después los Reyes Católicos terminaron la conquista de Granada para realizar la unidad espiritual. El año de 1492 representa

---

[1] The personal **a** is often used before unmodified place names.   [2] **surgieron los reinos,** (there) appeared the kingdoms.
[3] **guerrera,** warlike.   [4] **refrán,** proverb.   [5] **Quien,** He (The one) who.   [6] **consiguió,** attained.

Tower of the *Mezquita*, Córdoba, Spain.

Conseguida[2] la unidad religiosa y política, los Reyes Católicos comenzaron a interesarse en la expansión del país y por fin decidieron ayudar a un pobre explorador italiano, Cristóbal Colón. Colón salió de España con tres carabelas, la Pinta, la Santa María y la Niña; el doce de octubre de 1492, después de unos setenta días de viaje, llegó a una pequeña isla del Mar Caribe. Tomó posesión de ella en nombre de los Reyes Católicos, y la llamó San Salvador.[3]

Antes de volver a España, Colón exploró otras islas y estableció el primer pueblo español del Nuevo Mundo el 25 de diciembre, por lo cual[4] dio al pueblo el nombre de Navidad. Como Colón creía que había llegado a la India, dio el nombre de «indios» a los habitantes de las islas.

En el segundo viaje de Colón los españoles trajeron semillas, árboles frutales y varios animales domésticos. Los frailes,[5] los obreros[6] y los agricultores que acompañaron a Colón iniciaron la gran obra de la exploración y la colonización del Nuevo Mundo.

La América española ha dado el nombre del gran descubridor a una nación, Colombia, y a dos ciudades de Panamá, Cristóbal y Colón. En los Estados Unidos también hay ciudades que llevan el nombre de *Columbia* o *Columbus*. El mundo debe mucho a Cristóbal Colón. Este hombre enérgico y valiente sentó[7] un buen ejemplo para los hombres que vinieron a América durante las épocas siguientes.

para los españoles el fin de la guerra contra los moros y el principio de una época de gloria y poderío.[1] En el siglo XVI España llegó a ser la nación más poderosa del mundo.

---

[1] **poderío,** *power, dominion.*   [2] **Conseguida,** *After having attained.* **lo cual,** *for which reason.*   [5] **frailes,** *friars.*   [6] **obreros,** *workmen.*   [3] **San Salvador,** *Saint (Holy) Savior.*   [4] **por** [7] **sentó,** *set.*

Replica of the "Santa María" of Columbus, in Barcelona, Spain

PREGUNTAS

1. ¿Quiénes fueron los primeros pobladores de la península? 2. ¿Qué se conserva cerca de Santander? 3. ¿Quiénes fueron los fenicios? 4. ¿Cuándo llegaron a la península? 5. ¿Qué ciudad fundaron ellos? 6. ¿Quiénes fueron otros invasores? 7. ¿Cuántos siglos estuvieron en España los romanos? 8. ¿Qué dejaron allí? 9. ¿Qué construyeron? 10. ¿Cuáles son dos ejemplos de la obra de los romanos?

11. ¿Quiénes ocuparon la península después de los romanos? 12. ¿Quiénes fueron los últimos invasores? 13. ¿En qué año entraron? 14. ¿Hasta cuándo vivieron allí? 15. ¿Por qué fue importante Córdoba? 16. ¿Cuál fue la última capital de los moros? 17. ¿Qué se encuentra allí?

18. ¿Cuántos siglos duró la reconquista? 19. ¿Cuál es el origen del nombre de Castilla? 20. ¿Quién fue el Cid? 21. ¿Dónde está su tumba? 22. ¿Cuál es la catedral gótica más grande de Europa? 23. ¿Qué es la Giralda? 24. ¿Qué refrán hay sobre Sevilla? 25. ¿Sobre Granada?

26. ¿Cómo consiguió España la unidad política? 27. ¿Qué llegó a ser España en el siglo XVI? 28. ¿A quién decidieron ayudar Fernando e Isabel? 29. ¿Cómo se llamaban las tres carabelas de Colón? 30. ¿En qué día llegó a una pequeña isla? 31. ¿Qué nombre dieron a la isla?

32. ¿Cuándo fundó Colón el primer pueblo del Nuevo Mundo? 33. ¿Qué nombre dio a los habitantes de las islas? 34. ¿Quiénes acompañaron a Colón en su segundo viaje? 35. ¿Qué trajeron estos españoles a América? 36. ¿Qué nación lleva el nombre de Colón?

LECCIÓN 19

The present perfect subjunctive tense
The present subjunctive of verbs with changes in spelling
The subjunctive in noun clauses (continued).   More commands

LAS COMPRAS DE JOSÉ

Son las diez de la mañana.   José ha tomado el autobús para ir al centro.   Al bajar del autobús tiene una sorpresa agradable.   Se encuentra con su amigo Jaime, que se ha detenido frente a los escaparates de un gran almacén.

• • • • •

JOSÉ.   ¡Cuánto me alegro de que hayas venido al centro esta mañana!   ¿Puedes acompañarme a hacer algunas compras?

JAIME.   Te acompaño, pero debo advertirte que es urgente que yo llegue a casa antes de las once.   ¿Qué piensas comprar?

JOSÉ.   Papá quiere que yo busque algunas cosas para mi cumpleaños: un par de zapatos, una camisa, una corbata, calcetines …

JAIME.   ¡Qué suerte tienes, José!   Yo quiero un traje nuevo para el verano, pero mi padre me dice que no es preciso que lo compre ahora.

• • • • •

JOSÉ.   Entremos primero en esta zapatería aquí a la derecha.   Voy a pedir que me enseñen zapatos como aquéllos.   (*Señala un par que se exhibe en el escaparate.   Entran en la zapatería.*)

JAIME.   ¡Es extraño que haya tanta gente aquí a esta hora!

JOSÉ.   Temo que tengamos que esperar un rato.   Sentémonos aquí a la izquierda.   (*Pasan cinco o seis minutos.   Por fin se acerca un dependiente.*)

DEPENDIENTE.   ¿En qué puedo servirles, señores?

271

José. Haga Vd. el favor de enseñarme un par de zapatos. Me gusta el estilo que exhiben en el escaparate.

Dependiente. A ver, ¿qué número usa Vd.? (*José se quita el zapato.*) Creo que le sentará bien el número nueve. Pruébese éste, por favor.

José. Es estrecho; no me sienta bien.

Dependiente. ¿Quiere Vd. probarse éstos? Son un poco más grandes.

José. Son bonitos y me sientan bien. ¿Qué precio tienen?

Dependiente. Veinte y cinco dólares. Dudo que encuentre Vd. otros mejores a ese precio.

José. Es lástima que sean tan caros … Pues, me quedo con ellos. Aquí tiene Vd. un billete de veinte dólares y otro de diez. (*El dependiente le da cinco dólares de vuelta, envuelve los zapatos y le entrega el paquete.*)

Jaime. (*Mirando su reloj.*) Ya es tarde. No puedo acompañarte más.

José. Sí, es mejor que te vayas ahora. Siento mucho que hayan tardado tanto.

Jaime. Hasta luego, José. ¡Que te diviertas!

CONVERSACIÓN

A. Preguntas sobre el diálogo

1. ¿Con quién se encuentra José? 2. ¿Qué le pregunta José a Jaime? 3. ¿A qué hora tiene que llegar a casa Jaime? 4. ¿Qué piensa comprar José? 5. Al entrar en la tienda, ¿qué le parece extraño a Jaime? 6. ¿Qué teme José? 7. ¿Cuánto paga José por los zapatos? 8. ¿Qué dice Jaime al mirar su reloj?

B. Aplicación del diálogo

1. ¿Quién le acompaña a Vd. cuando va de compras? 2. ¿Qué regalos recibió Vd. para su último cumpleaños? 3. ¿Necesita Vd. camisas nuevas para el verano? 4. ¿Le gusta a Vd. mirar las cosas que se exhiben en los escaparates? 5. ¿Son caros los zapatos que le gustan a Vd.? 6. ¿Qué le dice su padre cuando Vd. le dice que necesita un traje nuevo? 7. ¿Qué le decimos a un amigo cuando queremos que se divierta mucho? 8. ¿Qué le decimos cuando queremos que tenga mucha suerte?

NOTAS GRAMATICALES

A. The present perfect subjunctive tense

haya		**hayamos**	
hayas	hablado, comido, vivido	**hayáis**	hablado, comido, vivido
haya		**hayan**	

¡Cuánto me alegro de que hayas venido! How glad I am that you have come!

Yo siento mucho que hayan tardado tanto. I am very sorry that it has taken them so long (that they have delayed so much).

The present perfect subjunctive tense is formed by the present subjunctive of **haber** with the past participle. After verbs in the main clause which require the subjunctive in the dependent clause, Spanish uses the present perfect subjunctive to translate *have* or *has* with the past participle. The word *may* is sometimes a part of the English translation: (**que**) **yo haya hablado,** (*that*) *I may have spoken.*

B. The present subjunctive of verbs with changes in spelling

> buscar: **busque, busques, busque, busquemos, busquéis, busquen**
> llegar: **llegue, llegues, llegue, lleguemos, lleguéis, lleguen**
> empezar: **empiece, empieces, empiece, empecemos, empecéis, empiecen**

Just as in the case of the first person singular of the preterit tense, in all six forms of the present subjunctive all verbs which end in **-car** change **c** to **qu,** those in **-gar** change **g** to **gu,** and those in **-zar** change **z** to **c.** This change is made before the vowel **e** to keep the sound of the final consonant of the stem the same as in the infinitive. Note that **empezar** also has the stem change of **e** to **ie.**

Other **-car** verbs already used are: **acercarse, sacar, tocar**; other **-gar** verbs are: **entregar, jugar (ue), pagar, rogar (ue)**; other **-zar** verbs are: **almorzar (ue), comenzar (ie).**

C. The subjunctive in noun clauses (continued)

1. **Me alegro de estar aquí.** I am glad to be here. (*Same subjects*)

   Me alegro (alegraré) de que no te vayas. I am (shall be) glad that you are not going (away).

   Es lástima que sean tan caros. It is too bad that they are so expensive.

   Temo que tengamos que esperar. I fear (that) we shall have to wait.

   Esperamos que no lleguen tarde. We hope they will not arrive late.

The subjunctive is used in noun clauses after verbs which express emotion or feeling, such as *joy, sorrow, fear, hope, pity, surprise,* and the like, as well as their negatives, provided that the subject differs from that of the main verb. Compare the first example, in which there is no change in subject, with those which follow. Remember that **que** regularly introduces a noun clause in Spanish, even though *that* is sometimes omitted in English.

Some common expressions of emotion are:

alegrarse (de que)	to be glad (that)	**sentir (ie, i)**	to regret, be sorry
es lástima	it is a pity, too bad	**temer**	to fear
esperar	to hope	**tener miedo (de que)**	to be afraid (that)

2. **Creo que le sentará bien.** I believe that it will fit you. (*Certainty implied*)

No creo que tengamos que esperar. I don't believe we will have to wait.

Dudo que Vd. encuentre otros mejores. I doubt that you will find other better ones.

No estoy seguro de que vuelvan. I am not sure that they will return.

The subjunctive is regularly used after expressions of *doubt, uncertainty,* or *belief in the negative.* Note that **creer** implies certainty and requires the indicative, while **no creer** implies uncertainty and requires the subjunctive. Likewise, **estar seguro de que** is followed by the indicative (or **estar seguro de** plus an infinitive is used if there is no change in subject), while **no estar seguro de que** requires the subjunctive. **Decir** used negatively also expresses uncertainty: **Yo no digo que Luis sepa eso,** *I do not say that Louis knows (may know) that.*

When **creer** is used in questions, the speaker may imply doubt on the action in the dependent clause, in which case the subjunctive is used. If no implication of doubt is made, the indicative is used. **No creer que** in a question implies certainty:

¿Cree Vd. que salgan hoy? Do you believe (think) they will leave today? (*Doubt in the mind of the speaker*)

¿Cree Vd. que lo comprarán? Do you believe they will buy it? (*The speaker has no opinion*)

¿No creen Vds. que lloverá? Don't you believe it will rain?

The verb **negar (ie),** *to deny,* also requires the subjunctive, but this verb is not used in the dialogues: **Él niega que sea verdad,** *He denies that it is true.*

3. **Es fácil aprender eso.** It is easy to learn that.

Es urgente que yo llegue a casa. It is urgent that I arrive home (for me to arrive home).

Es extraño que haya tanta gente aquí. It is strange that there are so many people here.

Es lástima que sean tan caros. It's too bad that they are so expensive.

No es preciso que él lo compre. It isn't necessary for him to buy it.

Es cierto (verdad) que él lo sabe. It is certain (true) that he knows it.

No es cierto que empiecen. It is not certain that they will begin.

The subjunctive is used after impersonal expressions (which usually begin with *it is*) of *possibility, necessity, probability, uncertainty, strangeness, pity,* and the like, provided that the verb of the dependent clause has a subject expressed. Impersonal expressions of certainty, such as **es cierto** and **es verdad,** require the indicative in the dependent clause; when these expressions are negative, they imply uncertainty and require the subjunctive (last example).

The infinitive may be used after most of these expressions if the subject of the dependent verb (expressed in English as the indirect object of the main verb) is a personal pronoun, not a noun:

> **Me (Les) es preciso ir.** It is necessary for me (them) to go.
> BUT: **Es mejor que Juan se vaya.** It is better for John to go away.

These impersonal expressions really fall under groups 1 and 2 of this section, and section D in Lesson 18, but they are listed separately for convenience and clarity.

Some common impersonal expressions which you have had are:

es difícil	it is difficult	**es mejor**	it is better
es extraño	it is strange	**es necesario**	it is necessary
es fácil	it is easy	**es posible**	it is possible
es importante	it is important	**es preciso**	it is necessary
es lástima	it is a pity, too bad	**es urgente**	it is urgent

D. More commands

1. **Entremos en esta tienda.** Let's (Let us) enter this store.
Abrámosla.
Vamos a abrirla.}Let's open it.
No lo dejemos aquí. Let's not leave it here.

The first person plural of the present subjunctive is used to express commands equal to *let's* or *let us* plus a verb. **Vamos a** plus an infinitive, in addition to meaning *we are going to,* may be used for *let's* or *let us* plus a verb if the intention is to perform the action at once.

Vamos is used for the affirmative *let's (let us) go*: **Vamos a casa ahora,** *Let's go home now.* The subjunctive **vayamos** must be used in the negative for *let's not go*: **No vayamos a casa todavía,** *Let's not go home yet.* **No vamos a casa todavía** can only mean *We are not going home yet.*

For *let's see,* **a ver** is often used without **vamos.**

> **Vámonos.** Let's be going, Let's go.
> **Sentémonos aquí.** (**Vamos a sentarnos aquí.**) Let's sit down here.
> **No nos levantemos.** Let's not get up.

When the reflexive pronoun **nos** is added to this command form, final **-s** is dropped from the verb. Remember that the reflexive pronoun must agree with the subject.

2. **Que lo traiga Juan.**   Have John (May John) bring it.
   Que te diviertas.   May you (I want you to, I hope you) have a good time.

Que, equivalent to English *have, let, may, I wish* or *I hope*, introduces indirect commands in the second and third persons.   In such cases object pronouns precede the verb, and if a subject is expressed, it usually follows the verb.   This construction is really a clause dependent upon a verb of *wishing, hoping, permitting*, and the like, with the main verb understood.

Let, meaning *to allow* or *permit*, will be discussed later (see Lesson 22).

EJERCICIOS

A. Say after your teacher, then repeat making the sentence negative:

1. Démelo Vd.   2. Tráiganoslos Vd.   3. Búsquenlo Vds.   4. Envuélvalo Vd.
5. Entrégueselo Vd. a Juanita.   6. Jueguen Vds. con ellos.   7. Tóquelo Vd. ahora.
8. Sentémonos.   9. Siéntese Vd.   10. Quitémonos el sombrero.   11. Cerrémosla.
12. Diviértanse Vds.   13. Póngaselo Vd.   14. Pongámoslo aquí.   15. Vámonos.

B. Say after your teacher; when you hear the cue, compose a new sentence using the subjunctive in the dependent clause:

> MODEL: Jaime va a casa.   Jaime va a casa.
>   Dudo que   Dudo que Jaime vaya a casa.

1. Juan busca una casa nueva.
   (Quiero que, Me alegro de que, Es necesario que)
2. Yo llego a tiempo.
   (Desean que, Esperan que, No creen que)
3. Ella se sienta a la derecha.
   (Yo dudo que, Es mejor que, Nos alegramos de que)
4. Nosotros no podemos envolverlo.
   (Es lástima que, Ella teme que, Vds. sienten que)
5. Juan ha visto a Jaime.
   (Es posible que, Tengo miedo de que, No creemos que)

C. Say after your teacher, then repeat using the present perfect subjunctive in the dependent clause:

1. Yo espero que los muchachos vengan hoy.   2. Es extraño que ellos lleguen tarde.
3. Me alegro de que ella se ponga el sombrero.   4. Sentimos que Vds. no lo busquen.
5. Es lástima que José no nos traiga el paquete.   6. Tenemos miedo de que ellos no

vuelvan.   7. No estamos seguros de que ella se levante.   8. Es posible que las mucha-chas sirvan refrescos.

D. Repeat the sentence; when you hear the cue, include it in a new sentence:

> MODEL: Yo temo no llegar a tiempo.   Yo temo no llegar a tiempo.
> que Jaime   Yo temo que Jaime no llegue a tiempo.

1. Yo siento no poder comprar los zapatos.   (que José)
2. Es mejor probarse estos zapatos.   (que Vd.)
3. Juan espera tener suerte en el partido.   (que tú)
4. Ella prefiere buscar otro vestido.   (que su hermana)
5. Los muchachos quieren tocar otros discos.   (que nosotros)
6. Nos alegramos de estar aquí.   (de que Vds.)
7. Es mejor no envolverlos todavía.   (que Carolina)
8. No es posible entregarles el paquete.   (que yo)

E. Answer each question twice, using affirmative and negative replies, and (except in questions 6-8) substituting pronouns for the noun objects:

> MODEL: ¿Escribimos la carta?   Sí, escribámosla.   No, no la escribamos.

1. ¿Abrimos la puerta?   2. ¿Cerramos las ventanas?   3. ¿Envolvemos el paquete? 4. ¿Buscamos a Felipe?   5. ¿Nos lavamos las manos?   6. ¿Nos sentamos a la iz-quierda?   7. ¿Nos levantamos ahora mismo?   8. ¿Nos vamos?

F. Listen to each direct command, then give an indirect command with **él,** preceded by the phrase **Yo no puedo:**

> MODEL: Ciérrela Vd.   Yo no puedo, que la cierre él.

1. Llévelo Vd.   2. Tráigalos Vd.   3. Siéntese Vd.   4. Búsquelos Vd.   5. Tóquelo Vd.   6. Pídaselo Vd.   7. Páguelo Vd.   8. Acérquese Vd.

G. Give the Spanish for:

1. Let's open them (*two ways*).   2. Let's get up (*two ways*).   3. Let's not look for shirts today.   4. Let's not give it to him.   5. Let's go to the movie.   6. Let's see.   7. May he return the necktie.   8. Have him ring the doorbell.   9. Have Jane bring me the magazine.   10. Have her bring it (*f.*) to me.

Wood inlay craftsman, Sevilla, Spain.

COMPOSICIÓN

1. John has just stopped in front of a department store when Jim passes along the street.
2. The latter asks his friend to go shopping with him.   3. He says that his father wants him to buy a pair of shoes, a shirt, a necktie, and some socks for his birthday.   4. First they enter a shoe store which is nearby, on the right.   5. There are so many people in the store that Jim fears that they will have to wait a while.   6. "Let's sit down here to the left," says Jim.   7. Finally a clerk approaches and asks: "What can I do for you (*pl.*)?"   8. Jim answers: "Please show me a pair of black shoes.   I like the style which you (*pl.*) are displaying in the show window."   9. Then the clerk asks him: "What size do you wear?   Will you take off your shoe?"   10. The clerk believes that (the) size nine will fit him, but it is [too] tight.   11. Jim tries on other shoes which are a little larger.   12. Even though they are expensive, he says: "I'll take them.   Here is the money."   13. After wrapping up the shoes, the clerk hands the package to Jim.   14. Then John says that it is necessary for him to go to his father's office.   15. Jim is sorry that his friend cannot accompany him longer (more).

VOCABULARIO

advertir (ie,i)   to advise, point out, warn
el almacén (*pl.* **almacenes**)   department store
bajar (**de** + *obj.*)   to get off *or* out of
el calcetín (*pl.* **calcetines**)   sock
la camisa   shirt
la corbata   necktie
el dependiente   clerk
derecho, -a   right
dudar   to doubt
estrecho, -a   narrow, tight
exhibir   to exhibit, display
extraño, -a   strange
izquierdo, -a   left
Jaime   James, Jim

el número   size (*of shoes*)
el paquete   package
preciso, -a   necessary, precise
probarse (ue)   to try on
¡qué + *noun*!   how!
quitar   to remove, take off; *reflex.* take off (oneself)
señalar   to point at (out), indicate
el señor   gentleman
la sorpresa   surprise
la suerte   luck
temer   to fear
urgente   urgent
la zapatería   shoe store
el zapato   shoe

a la derecha (izquierda)   to (on, at) the right (left)
a ver   let's see
¿en qué puedo servirle(s)?   what can I do for you?
me quedo con (ellos)   I'll take (them)
sentar (ie) bien (a uno)   to fit (one) (well)
tardar tanto   to take so long, delay so much (long)
tener (mucha) suerte   to be (very) lucky

Wrought iron gates, forged in the sixteenth century, frame the entrance to the *Capilla Real*, which contains the tombs of the Catholic kings, Granada, Spain.

LECTURA XI

EXPLORADORES Y MISIONEROS

Estudio de palabras

a. Less approximate cognates. Pronounce the following words aloud, note the English cognates, and describe the variations: apóstol, *apostle*; dominico, *Dominican*; estimar, *to esteem*; fabuloso, *fabulous*; fortaleza, *fort, fortress*; jesuita, *Jesuit*; mencionar, *to mention*; navegar, *to navigate, sail*; tempestad, *tempest, storm*.

b. Deceptive cognates. **Conservar** means *to keep, preserve*, as well as *to conserve*. **Desgracia** means *misfortune*, as well as *disgrace*.

c. Compare the meanings of: cristiano, *Christian, and* cristianismo, *Christianity*; esclavo, *slave, and* esclavitud, *slavery*; misión, *mission, and* misionero, *missionary*; relatar, *to relate, and* relato, *tale, story*; rico, *rich, and* riqueza(s), *riches, wealth. Also compare:* la orden, *command, religious order (association),* ordenar, *to order, and* ordenarse (de sacerdote), *to be ordained, take orders (as a priest).* **El orden** means *order* in the sense of *arrangement*.

Durante la primera mitad del siglo XVI los españoles exploraron el territorio de los Estados Unidos que se extiende desde la Florida hasta California. El primer europeo que atravesó[1] el continente fue Cabeza de Vaca. Después de explorar el interior de la Florida con Pánfilo de Narváez en 1528, navegó por las costas del Golfo de México hasta llegar a la región que hoy se conoce como Texas. Una terrible tempestad destruyó su barco, quedando vivos sólo Cabeza de Vaca y tres compañeros. Los cuatro españoles vivieron varios años como esclavos de los indios, pero con el tiempo los indios llegaron a estimar mucho a Cabeza de Vaca como curandero.[2] Poco a poco, caminando de pueblo en pueblo hacia el oeste, atravesó largas distancias y por fin llegó a la costa del Pacífico, en el norte de México, en 1536.

Por desgracia,[3] los españoles creían que todo el Nuevo Mundo era tan rico como la Nueva España,[4] y los indios, sabiendo que nada les interesaba a los españoles tanto como el oro, hablaban de pueblos adornados de oro y de piedras preciosas. La más conocida de estas leyendas es la de las Siete Ciudades de Cíbola, situadas al norte de México, en donde las casas estaban cubiertas de oro puro. Al llegar a México Cabeza de Vaca, renació una vez más el interés en esta leyenda. Fray Marcos de Niza decidió ir en busca de estas ciudades para convertirlas a la fe católica. Después de caminar muchos días por lo que ahora son los estados de Nuevo México y Arizona, un día vio a lo lejos[5] lo que él creyó que eran las Siete Ciudades. Volvió a México a contar su descubrimiento y, naturalmente, cada vez que el relato se repetía, crecía más la riqueza imaginada.

Por fin se organizó una expedición que había de ser una de las más notables de

---

[1] **atravesó,** *crossed.*   [2] **curandero,** *medicine man.*   [3] **Por desgracia,** *Unfortunately.*   [4] **la Nueva España,** *New Spain* = **México.**   [5] **a lo lejos,** *in the distance.*

Father Junípero Serra

Father Bartolomé de las Casas

todas. En 1540 Francisco Vásquez de Coronado salió de México en busca de las Siete Ciudades de Cíbola. Llegó hasta donde ahora están los estados de Texas y Kansas, pero en vez de las fabulosas ciudades de oro y de piedras preciosas, sólo encontró tristes pueblos de adobe. Unos soldados de esta expedición fueron los primeros europeos que vieron el Gran Cañón del Río Colorado. A los dos años [1] Coronado volvió a México, triste y desilusionado.

La ciudad más antigua de los Estados Unidos fue fundada en la Florida el seis de septiembre de 1565 por Menéndez de Avilés. Éste construyó primero una fortaleza cerca del lugar donde ahora está San Agustín, el primer establecimiento permanente construido en nuestro país por los europeos.

El primer pueblo español en el valle del Río Grande fue fundado por Juan de Oñate en 1598, pero al poco tiempo los españoles tuvieron que abandonarlo; once años más tarde establecieron la ciudad de Santa Fe. En seguida, construyeron una iglesia, que es una de las más antiguas del país.

Entre otros muchos [2] exploradores bien conocidos hay que mencionar a Juan Rodríguez Cabrillo, un portugués que estaba al servicio del gobierno español, y que en 1542 descubrió la Alta California. [3]

Los españoles vinieron a América no sólo para buscar riquezas, sino también para

[1] **A los dos años,** *After two years.*   [2] Adjectives of quantity and numerals preferably follow **otros, -as.**
[3] **la Alta California,** *Upper California* (the name used for the present state of California during the colonial period).

convertir a los indios a la fe cristiana. Por eso los misioneros acompañaron a los exploradores por todas partes. Entre los misioneros se destaca[1] el padre Bartolomé de las Casas, el apóstol de los indios. Acompañó a Colón a América y se estableció primero en La Española.[2] Hombre de corazón noble y bondadoso, dedicó toda su vida a defender a los indígenas contra las injusticias de la esclavitud y contra su explotación por los españoles. En 1510 se ordenó de sacerdote y al poco tiempo ingresó en[3] la orden de los dominicos. Predicó[4] por todas partes de la Nueva España, defendiendo a los indios con la pluma y con la palabra.[5]

Los franciscanos también vinieron al Nuevo Mundo con los conquistadores y los exploradores, y durante más de dos siglos habían de acompañarlos por los dos continentes. La orden franciscana convirtió al cristianismo a miles de indios. Los franciscanos aprendieron las lenguas de los indios y les enseñaron artes y oficios[6] útiles y nuevos métodos para el cultivo de plantas y legumbres. Fundaron pueblos, iglesias, misiones, escuelas y universidades.

Las órdenes religiosas fundaron muchas misiones en Texas, Nuevo México, Arizona y California. El que ha visitado San Antonio ha visto sin duda el Álamo, que fue misión en los tiempos coloniales. O si uno ha estado en Tucson, Arizona, ha visto la famosa misión de San Xavier del Bac, fundada por el célebre padre jesuita, Eusebio Kino. El hermoso edificio que vemos allí hoy día se terminó a fines del siglo XVIII.

San Xavier del Bac Mission, Tucson, Arizona

Cuando los jesuitas fueron expulsados de España y de sus colonias en 1769, muchas misiones que ellos habían construido pasaron a manos de los franciscanos. Fray Junípero Serra, que había venido a América desde la isla de Mallorca en la segunda mitad del siglo XVIII, fue nombrado presidente de las misiones de la Baja California y de todas las que habían de establecerse en la Alta California. Durante muchos años dio clases en las escuelas franciscanas de la Nueva España, pero por fin, en 1769, partió de México con don Gaspar de Portolá para establecer misiones en la Alta California. Empezando con la misión de San Diego, fundada en ese mismo año, el padre Junípero Serra estableció una larga serie de misiones. En 1823 había veinte y una misiones entre San Diego y San Francisco. A lo largo del Camino Real[7] todavía se ven los restos de estos monumentos, que conmemoran la gloria de la obra de los misioneros españoles.

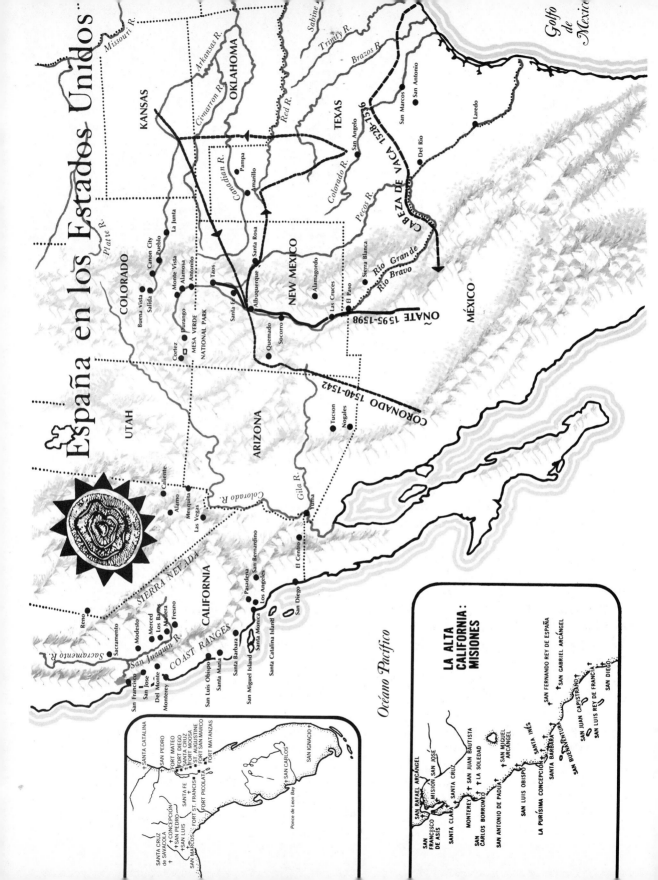

España en los Estados Unidos

Golfo de México

OKLAHOMA

Missouri R.
Platte R.
Arkansas R.
Cimarron R.
Canadian R.
Red R.
Sabine R.
Trinity R.
Brazos R.
Colorado R.
Pecos R.
Sacramento R.
San Juaquin R.
Gila R.
Colorado R.
Rio Grande de Rio Bravo

KANSAS

TEXAS

San Antonio
San Marcos
Laredo
Del Rio
San Angelo

CABEZA DE VACA 1528-1536

COLORADO

Buena Vista
Salida
Canon City
Pueblo
La Junta
Monte Vista
Alamosa
Antonito
Durango
Cortez
MESA VERDE NATIONAL PARK
Taos
Santa Fe
Albuquerque
Las Cruces
El Paso
Sierra Blanca
Alamogordo
Socorro
Quemado

NEW MEXICO

OÑATE 1595-1598

CORONADO 1540-1542

MÉXICO

Pampa
Amarillo
Santa Rosa

UTAH

Caliente
Alamo
Mesquita
Las Vegas

ARIZONA

Tucson
Nogales
Yuma

SIERRA NEVADA

Reno
Sacramento
Modesto
Merced
Los Banos
Madera
Fresno
San Francisco
San Jose
Del Monte
Monterey

CALIFORNIA

COAST RANGES

San Luis Obispo
Santa Maria
Santa Barbara
San Miguel Island
Santa Catalina Island
Santa Monica
Los Angeles
Pasadena
San Bernardino
El Centro
San Diego

Océano Pacífico

LA ALTA CALIFORNIA: MISIONES

SAN RAFAEL ARCÁNGEL
SAN FRANCISCO DE ASÍS
MISIÓN SAN JOSÉ
SANTA CLARA
SANTA CRUZ
SAN JUAN BAUTISTA
MONTEREY
SAN CARLOS BORROMEO
LA SOLEDAD
SAN ANTONIO DE PADUA
SAN MIGUEL ARCÁNGEL
SAN LUIS OBISPO
LA PURÍSIMA CONCEPCIÓN
SANTA INÉS
SANTA BARBARA
SAN BUENAVENTURA
SAN FERNANDO REY DE ESPAÑA
SAN GABRIEL ARCÁNGEL
SAN JUAN CAPISTRANO
SAN LUIS REY DE FRANCIA
SAN DIEGO

SANTA CRUZ de SAVACOLA
SANTA CATALINA
SAN PEDRO
SAN PEDRO
SANTA FE
SAN LUIS
CONCEPCIÓN
SAN MARCOS
FORT MATEO
FORT DIEGO
FORT ST. AUGUSTINE
SANTA CRUZ
ST. AUGUSTINE
FORT SAN FRANCIS
FORT SAN MARCO
FORT PICOLATA
FORT MATANZAS
SAN CARLOS
SAN IGNACIO

Ponce de Leon Bay

PREGUNTAS

1. ¿Qué territorio exploraron los españoles durante el siglo XVI? 2. ¿Quién fue el primer europeo que atravesó el continente? 3. ¿Por dónde navegó? 4. ¿Cuántos españoles quedaron vivos después de la tempestad? 5. ¿Cómo vivieron varios años? 6. ¿Adónde llegó por fin Cabeza de Vaca?

7. ¿Qué creían los españoles acerca del Nuevo Mundo? 8. ¿De qué hablaban los indios? 9. ¿Cuál es la más conocida de estas leyendas? 10. ¿De qué estaban cubiertas las casas? 11. ¿Quién decidió ir en busca de estas ciudades? 12. ¿Por dónde caminó? 13. ¿Halló las Siete Ciudades? 14. ¿Quién salió de México en busca de las Siete Ciudades en 1540? 15. ¿Qué encontró? 16. ¿Cuándo volvió a México?

17. ¿Cuál es la ciudad más antigua de los Estados Unidos? 18. ¿Qué fundó Juan de Oñate? 19. ¿Qué descubrió Cabrillo?

20. ¿Quiénes acompañaron a los españoles a América? 21. ¿Quién fue el apóstol de los indios? 22. ¿A qué dedicó toda su vida? 23. ¿En qué orden religiosa ingresó? 24. ¿Qué otra orden vino al Nuevo Mundo? 25. ¿Qué aprendieron los franciscanos? 26. ¿Qué les enseñaron a los indios? 27. ¿Qué fundaron los franciscanos? 28. ¿Qué fue el Álamo? 29. ¿Qué misión fundó el padre Eusebio Kino?

30. ¿Cuándo vino a América Fray Junípero Serra? 31. ¿De qué fue nombrado presidente? 32. ¿Qué expedición notable partió de México en 1769? 33. ¿Qué misión fundó Fray Junípero Serra en ese mismo año? 34. ¿Cuántas misiones había entre San Diego y San Francisco en 1823?

LECCIÓN 20

Adjective clauses and relative pronouns
The subjunctive in adjective clauses
Hacer in time clauses.   Forms of *valer*

UN PUESTO EN MÉXICO

El señor Carter llama a Carlos a su oficina.   Le dice que acaba de recibir una carta por correo aéreo del gerente de una casa comercial de México.   La carta es del señor que visitó la oficina el verano pasado.   Necesitan un joven que entienda algo de agricultura y de maquinaria agrícola y que pueda trabajar como agente de la casa.   También prefieren un joven que sepa algo de las costumbres del país y que haya tenido algunos años de experiencia en una casa comercial.

• • • • •

SR. CARTER.   Carlos, ¿conoce Vd. a alguien que podamos recomendar para el puesto en México?
CARLOS.   Supongo que buscan una persona que hable español.
SR. CARTER.   ¡Por supuesto!   Es absolutamente necesario que lo hable bien.
CARLOS.   Pues, puedo recomendar a Ricardo Smith.   Hace tres o cuatro años que trabaja en la casa de Blanco y Compañía.   No conozco a nadie que sea tan trabajador como él.

• • • • •

SR. CARTER.   ¿Cuánto tiempo hace que Ricardo habla español?
CARLOS.   Creo que lo habla desde hace ocho o diez años.   Empezó a estudiarlo cuando estaba en la escuela superior, y ha pasado varios veranos en México.

287

Sr. Carter. Su padre trabajó varios años en Colombia, ¿no es verdad?

Carlos. Es cierto. Y sin duda conoce Vd. a los señores Jones, con quienes ha vivido Ricardo, y los que podrán darle informes acerca de él.

Sr. Carter. ¡Cómo no! Los conozco bien. El gerente de la casa mexicana desea que el nuevo empleado empiece a trabajar el primero de mayo, lo cual me sorprende un poco.

Carlos. No sé si Ricardo podrá irse tan pronto. ¿Quiere Vd. que le llame por teléfono para ver si puede venir a su oficina mañana?

Sr. Carter. Valdrá más que venga a verme esta tarde, si es posible. Si le interesa el puesto, le pondré un telegrama al gerente, dándole todos los informes.

Carlos. Muy bien. Voy a telefonearle a Ricardo ahora mismo. Espero que obtenga el puesto.

CONVERSACIÓN

A. Preguntas sobre el diálogo

1. ¿Qué acaba de recibir el Sr. Carter? 2. ¿Qué le dicen en la carta? 3. ¿Buscan una persona que hable español? 4. ¿Qué prefieren también? 5. ¿A quién recomienda Carlos? 6. ¿Cuántos años hace que trabaja Ricardo en la casa de Blanco y Compañía? 7. ¿Cuándo desean que empiece a trabajar el nuevo empleado? 8. ¿Qué hará el Sr. Carter si le interesa a Ricardo el puesto?

B. Aplicación del diálogo

1. ¿Le interesaría a Vd. obtener un puesto en la América del Sur? 2. ¿Entiende Vd. algo de maquinaria agrícola? 3. ¿Conoce Vd. a alguien que haya trabajado en la América española? 4. ¿Cuánto tiempo hace que estudia Vd. el español? 5. ¿Le gustaría a Vd. vivir en la capital de México? 6. Cuando Vd. necesita dinero, ¿a quién se lo pide? 7. Si Vd. busca un puesto, ¿quién podrá dar informes acerca de Vd.? 8. ¿Hay algo que Vd. no entienda en esta lección?

NOTAS GRAMATICALES

A. Adjective clauses and relative pronouns

An adjective clause modifies a noun or pronoun and is introduced by a relative pronoun, usually **que.** In the sentence *I know a man who can do it,* the clause *who can do it* modifies the noun *man.* *Who* is a relative pronoun, and *man* is the antecedent of the clause.

1. **Que,** *that, which, who, whom*:

> (*a*) **el agente que me escribió**   the agent who wrote to me
> (*b*) **el puesto que tiene**   the job (that) he has
> **la joven que conocí**   the young woman (whom) I met
> (*c*) **la casa de que hablaban**   the firm of which they were talking

Que, which is invariable, is the commonest of all the relative pronouns.   Introducing a clause, **que** may be: (*a*) the subject; (*b*) the object of the verb in a clause, and refer to persons or things; or (*c*) used as the object of a preposition, referring to things only. The relative **que** may be omitted in English, but not in Spanish.

2. **Quien** (*pl.* **quienes**), *who, whom*:

> (*a*) **Los hombres, con quienes habla Juan, ...**
> The men, with whom John is talking, ...
> (*b*) **El gerente, quien (que) me ha escrito, desea ...**
> The manager, who has written to me, desires ...
> (*c*) **Son los señores que (a quienes) vi en la oficina.**
> They are the gentlemen (whom) I saw in the office.

Quien (*pl.* **quienes**), which refers only to persons, is used: (*a*) mainly after prepositions; and (*b*) sometimes instead of **que** when *who* is separated from the main clause by a comma. The personal **a** is required (*c*) when **quien(es)** is the direct object of the verb.   **Que** may replace **a quienes** in the last example, and in conversation is more commonly used.

3. **El cual** and **el que,** *that, which, who, whom*:

> (*a*) **La hermana de Ricardo, la cual (la que) trabaja allí, ...**
> Richard's sister, who works there, ...
> **... los señores Jones, con quienes vive Ricardo, y los que podrán ...**
> ... Mr. and Mrs. Jones, with whom Richard lives, and who will be able to ...
> (*b*) **Los edificios cerca de los cuales (los que) dejamos el coche ...**
> The buildings near which we left the car ...

The longer forms of the relative pronouns, **el cual (la cual, los cuales, las cuales)** and **el que (la que, los que, las que)**, are used: (*a*) to make clear which one of two possible antecedents the clause modifies; and (*b*) after prepositions other than **a, con, de, en.**   (Often, however, and particularly in literary style, these long relatives are also used after these short prepositions.   In elegant style the forms of **el cual** are preferred to those of **el que,** as you will see in the Lecturas and other readings.)   Be sure that the long relative agrees with its antecedent.

> **Él tiene que empezar el primero de mayo, lo cual (lo que) me sorprende.**
> He must begin the first of May, which (fact) surprises me.

The neuter form **lo cual** or **lo que,** *which* (*fact*), is used to sum up a preceding idea, statement, or situation.

B. The subjunctive in adjective clauses

Necesitan un joven que entienda algo de agricultura.
They need a young man who understands something of agriculture.   (*Any young man*)

¿Buscan una persona que hable español?
Are they looking for a person who speaks Spanish?   (*Not a definite person*)

¿Conoce Vd. a alguien que podamos recomendar?
Do you know anyone (whom) we can recommend?   (*Indefinite antecedent*)

No conozco a nadie que sea tan trabajador como él.
I do not know anyone who is so industrious as he.   (*Negative antecedent*)

When the antecedent of an adjective clause is indefinite or negative and refers to no particular person or thing, the verb in the dependent clause is in the subjunctive. If the antecedent refers to a certain person or thing, the indicative mood is used: **Busco al muchacho que llamó a la puerta,** *I am looking for the boy who knocked at the door.*

The personal **a** is omitted in the second example since the noun does not refer to a specific person. However, the pronouns **alguien, nadie,** also **alguno** and **ninguno** when referring to a person, and **quien,** require the personal **a** when used as direct objects.

C. **Hacer** in time clauses

Hace tres años que él trabaja aquí *or* **Él trabaja aquí desde hace tres años.**
He has been working here three years (*lit.*, It makes three years that he works here).

¿Cuánto tiempo hace que habla español?
How long has he been speaking (*lit.*, How long does it make that he speaks) Spanish?

Lo habla desde hace ocho años *or* **Hace ocho años que lo habla.**
He has been speaking it (for) eight years.

In Spanish, **hace** followed by a word indicating a period of time (**hora, día, mes, año,** etc.) plus **que** and a present tense verb, or a present tense verb plus **desde hace** plus a period of time, is used to indicate an action begun in the past and still in progress. The present perfect tense is used in English in this construction.

Hacía muchos años que él lo hablaba *or* **Él lo hablaba desde hacía muchos años.**
He had been speaking it (for) many years (*lit.*, It made many years that he spoke it).

Hacía followed by a period of time plus **que** and a verb in the imperfect tense, or the imperfect tense plus **desde hacía** plus a period of time, is used to indicate an action which had been going on for a certain length of time and was still continuing when something else happened.   The pluperfect tense is used in English.

Recall that **hace** plus a verb in a past tense means *ago* or *since* (see Lesson 15): **Hace dos horas que llegué** or **Llegué hace dos horas,** *I arrived two hours ago* or *It is two hours since I arrived.*

D. Irregular forms of **valer,** *to be worth*

PRES. IND.	**valgo,** vales, vale, valemos, valéis, valen
PRES. SUBJ.	**valga, valgas, valga, valgamos, valgáis, valgan**
FUTURE	**valdré, valdrás,** etc. CONDITIONAL **valdría, valdrías,** etc.

The other forms are regular.   The impersonal **vale** (**valdrá,** etc.) **más,** *it is* (*will be,* etc.) *better,* is followed by the subjunctive when the dependent clause has a subject: **Valdrá más que él venga hoy,** *It will be better for him to come* (*that he come*) *today.*

EJERCICIOS

A. Say after your teacher; when you hear the cue, compose a new sentence, following the model:

MODEL: Buscan al joven que habla español.   Buscan al joven que habla español.
Buscan un joven   Buscan un joven que hable español.

1. Tengo una secretaria que escribe bien.   (Necesito una secretaria)
2. Juan tiene un puesto que le gusta.   (Juan quiere un puesto)
3. Tienen una casa que es más grande que ésta.   (Buscan una casa)
4. Quiero ver al señor que es de México.   (Quiero ver una persona)
5. ¿Conoces al hombre que vive aquí?   (¿Conoces a alguien?)
6. Veo a alguien que es tan trabajador como él.   (No veo a nadie)
7. Hay un parque que es más hermoso que éste.   (No hay parque)
8. Hay algo que es muy interesante.   (No hay nada)
9. Busco al joven que ha estudiado en España.   (Busco un joven)
10. Conocen a un joven que ha tenido más experiencia.   (Prefieren un joven)

B. Each group of short sentences is preceded by a phrase which requires the subjunctive in an adjective clause.   Compose complete sentences, changing the verb to the correct subjunctive tense:

MODEL: Buscamos una casa   a. es hermosa.   Buscamos una casa que sea hermosa.

1. Buscamos una secretaria   a. habla español.   b. sabe escribir rápidamente.   c. es joven.   d. ha vivido en México.

2. ¿Conoce Vd. a alguien? a. ha sido gerente de una casa. b. ha trabajado en México. c. quiere vivir en ese país. d. puede irse en seguida.

3. No hay nadie aquí a. es tan trabajador. b. trabaja tanto. c. sabe jugar mejor. d. puede acompañarme.

4. No hay nada allí a. es menos caro. b. me gusta mucho. c. yo puedo usar ahora. d. yo quiero comprar.

C. After you hear two separate sentences, combine them into one sentence using the relative pronoun **que,** following the model:

> MODEL: El libro tiene un mapa de España.   El libro que tiene un mapa de España
> Es nuevo.   es nuevo.

1. El hombre viene ahora. Es mi tío. 2. El telegrama llegó esta mañana. Es de Roberto. 3. La casa tiene un patio. Es de estilo español. 4. El joven está visitándonos. Vive en México.

Combine, using **quien** (**quienes**) and **a quien** (**quienes**), following the model:

> MODEL: Vimos a la joven. Es española.   Vimos a la joven, quien es española *and*
>   La joven a quien vimos es española.

5. Yo saludé al joven. Es mexicano. 6. Vimos a la profesora. Enseña el francés. 7. Ella llamó a la estudiante. Está enferma hoy. 8. Hablamos con aquellos señores. Son profesores de otra universidad.

Combine, using **el** (**la**) **cual, los** (**las**) **cuales** or **el** (**la**) **que, los** (**las**) **que:**

> MODELS: El padre de Ana está enfermo. No puede trabajar hoy.
>   El padre de Ana, el cual (el que) está enfermo, no puede trabajar hoy.
>   Viven cerca de un parque. Es muy hermoso.
>   El parque cerca del cual (del que) viven es muy hermoso.

9. La prima de Carlos salió ayer. Espera volver pronto. 10. El tío de María tiene una casa comercial. Vive en México. 11. Ricardo me escribió acerca de esas costumbres. Son muy interesantes. 12. Dejamos el coche cerca de aquellos edificios. Son muy altos.

D. After you hear the sentence and the cue, combine them into a new sentence:

> MODEL: Él lee el libro. (Hace una hora)   Hace una hora que él lee el libro.

1. Ella mira la televisión. (Hace media hora)
2. Marta escucha unos discos. (Hace quince minutos)

3. Nosotros estudiamos el español.   (Hace siete meses)
4. Miguel juega al golf.   (Hace varios años)
5. Mi tía está enferma.   (Hace dos días)
6. Yo conozco al señor López.   (Hace mucho tiempo)
7. Mis padres viajan por México.   (Hace dos semanas)
8. Mi mamá duerme la siesta.   (Hace veinte minutos)

Give two answers to each question:

MODEL: ¿Cuánto tiempo hace que lee Vd.?   (una hora)   Hace una hora que leo *and*
Leo desde hace una hora.

9. ¿Cuánto tiempo hace que juegan Vds.?   (media hora)
10. ¿Cuánto tiempo hace que conoces a Marta?   (tres años)
11. ¿Cuánto tiempo hacía que estudiaba Vd. el español?   (varios meses)
12. ¿Cuánto tiempo hacía que estaban ellos en el café?   (veinte minutos)

E. After reviewing the subjunctive in noun clauses, read in Spanish, using the correct form of each infinitive in parentheses:

1. No creo que Arturo (estar) en casa.   2. ¿Quiere Vd. que yo le (buscar)?   3. Supongo que Luis no quiere (hacer) eso.   4. Es preciso que Vd. (buscar) un puesto.   5. Yo tengo miedo de que Vds. no le (encontrar) esta tarde.   6. A veces sus amigos le piden a Vd. que (ir) al cine con ellos, ¿verdad?   7. Yo dudo que Bárbara (haber) ido al centro hoy. 8. Si tú la ves, dile a ella que (volver) a casa en seguida.   9. Me alegraré mucho de (ver) a Jaime.   10. Es absolutamente cierto que él no (estar) en la playa.   11. Es posible que él (divertirse) en el parque.   12. Yo espero que tus padres te (dar) permiso para ir a la piscina.

COMPOSICIÓN

1. Richard, do you know an agent who sells farm machinery?   2. No, John, but I hope to sell it some day.   3. I do not know anyone who has worked with (**en**) a foreign firm.   4. My mother's cousin, who lives in the country, recommends that I study agriculture.   5. My father has just received a long letter in which a friend of his wrote of good opportunities in Mexico.   6. Also he has asked my father to look for a secretary who knows Spanish well.   7. He wants a person who has had two or three years of experience.   8. Dad will telephone to Mr. White, who has an office in New York, asking him for information about his daughter.   9. The latter is trying to find a position in South America, but it is possible that she may want to go to Mexico.   10. It is a pity that Joe's sister, who wants to work there, is still studying in the university.

VOCABULARIO

absolutamente absolutely
aéreo, -a air
el agente agent
agrícola (*m. and f.*) agricultural, farm
la agricultura agriculture
la casa firm, house
la compañía company
el correo mail
la costumbre custom
la duda doubt
el empleado employee
la escuela superior high school

la experiencia experience
el gerente manager
los informes information, data
la maquinaria machinery
obtener (*like* **tener**) to obtain, get
la persona person
recomendar (**ie**) to recommend
sorprender to surprise
suponer (*like* **poner**) to suppose
telefonear to telephone
el telegrama (*note gender*) telegram
trabajador, -ora[1] industrious
valer to be worth

poner un telegrama to send a telegram
por correo aéreo by air mail
¡por supuesto! of course! certainly!
sin duda doubtless, without a doubt
valer más to be better

---

[1] Adjectives which end in **-án, -ón, -or** (except such comparative-superlatives as **mejor, peor, mayor, menor, superior,** and a few others) add **-a** to form the feminine: **trabajador, trabajadora.**

Roman aqueduct in Tarragona, Spain.

LECTURA XII
LA CULTURA ESPAÑOLA A TRAVÉS DE LOS SIGLOS

Estudio de palabras

a. Approximate cognates. As we have seen, Spanish nouns in **-ista** = English *-ist*: artista, humanista, novelista. The corresponding adjective presents two forms, as in English: **-ista** = English *-ist*, and **-ístico** = English *-istic*. The choice of ending, however, is not always the same in the two languages, and the correct form can be learned only by observation. The adjectives **idealista**, *idealistic*, and **realista**, *realistic*, are especially troublesome for English speakers, who often tend to give them in Spanish the ending found, for example, in **característico**, *characteristic*.

b. Less approximate cognates. Pronounce the following words aloud, note the English cognates, and describe the variations: arquitecto, *architect*; aventura, *adventure*; científico, *scientific*; enorme, *enormous*; episódico, *episodic*; escultor, *sculptor*; espíritu, *spirit*; filósofo, *philosopher*; fundador, *founder*; igualar, *to equal*; intrínseco, *intrinsic*; lírico, *lyric*; personaje, *personage*, *character* (in literature); reflejar, *to reflect*; Renacimiento, *Renaissance*; sátira, *satire*; teólogo, *theologian*.

c. Compare the meanings of: drama, *drama*, dramático, *dramatic*, and dramaturgo, *dramatist*; hacer, *to do, make*, and hazaña, *deed*; héroe, *hero*, and heroína, *heroine*; historia, *history*, histórico, *historical*, and historiador, *historian*; humanidades, *humanities*, and humanista, *humanist*; origen, *origin*, and originalidad, *originality*; poema, *poem*, poesía, *poetry*, and poeta, *poet*; rico, *rich*, riqueza(s), *riches*, and enriquecer, *to enrich*.

La literatura española, una de las más ricas del mundo, es a la vez[1] una de las manifestaciones más notables de la cultura española. Es importante no sólo por su valor intrínseco y por la creación de nuevos géneros[2] y de personajes universales, sino también por su influencia en otras literaturas modernas, especialmente en las de Inglaterra y de Francia. Desde el siglo XII hasta el siglo XX la literatura ha expresado directamente el alma y el espíritu de los españoles en su larga y gloriosa historia.

El primer monumento literario de España es un poema épico, *El cantar de Mío Cid*,[3] escrito hacia 1140. Este poema trata de las hazañas del Cid, el famoso héroe nacional, en las luchas de Castilla para reconquistar sus tierras de manos de los moros. Del mismo siglo es otro antiguo monumento, el *Auto de los Reyes Magos*,[4] la primera obra del teatro español. Es una breve composición dramática que narra en forma sencilla el viaje de los tres Reyes Magos a adorar al Niño Jesús.

Uno de los géneros más importantes, no sólo de la Edad Media,[5] sino de todos los siglos, ha sido la poesía lírica y narrativa. De interés especial en España ha sido el romance,[6] pequeño poema narrativo y episódico en versos[7] de ocho sílabas. Los

---

[1] **a la vez,** *at the same time.* [2] **género,** *genre, literary type.* [3] **El cantar de Mío Cid,** *The Song (Lay) of the Cid.* [4] **Auto de los Reyes Magos,** *Play of the Magi.* [5] **Edad Media,** *Middle Ages.* [6] **romance,** *ballad.* [7] **verso,** *line* (of poetry).

primeros romances históricos fueron probablemente restos de los antiguos poemas
épicos, y con el tiempo fueron compuestos
otros sobre temas de toda clase. Dando
inspiración a los grandes dramaturgos,
poetas líricos y novelistas de los siglos
siguientes, ninguna poesía ha contribuido
más que el romance a enriquecer la literatura española. Todavía se cantan los romances en España, en la América española y en
el suroeste de los Estados Unidos.

Una de las mayores glorias de los Reyes
Católicos, Fernando e Isabel, fue el impulso
que dieron a las letras y a la cultura en
general a fines del siglo XV. Iniciaron el
estudio de las humanidades y trajeron a

Torre de las damas in the Alhambra, Granada, Spain.

Patio of the Cathedral, Barcelona, Spain.

(*Left*) Ferdinand of Aragon
(*Below*) Isabella of Castile

España muchos humanistas de Italia, donde se originó la época de la cultura que se llama el Renacimiento. Los Reyes Católicos contribuyeron a la introducción de la imprenta[1] en España en 1474 y fundaron bibliotecas, escuelas y universidades, sobre todo la famosa Universidad de Alcalá de Henares en 1508. Durante su reinado aparecieron algunas de las mejores obras de la literatura española, entre ellas *La Celestina*, en 1499, una de las grandes obras de la literatura universal, y el *Amadís de Gaula*, publicado en 1508, que inició la novela de caballerías[2] en España. En 1492 se publicó la *Gramática castellana* de Nebrija, la primera gramática científica de una lengua moderna, y la víspera de Navidad del mismo año se representaron dos piezas dramáticas de Juan del Encina, llamado el padre del teatro español.

La Celestina, célebre novela dramática, relata la triste historia de los amantes Calisto y Melibea, que viven bajo la influencia de una perversa y astuta vieja, llamada Celestina. Esta obra refleja a la vez el espíritu de la Edad Media y el del Renacimiento, y una de sus características más extraordinarias es que se mezclan por primera vez[3] en la prosa el idealismo puro y el realismo crudo. Después de *Don Quijote*, *La Celestina* ocupa el primer lugar en la literatura española.

Un género literario que había de gozar de[4] una gran popularidad durante el siglo XVI fue la novela de caballerías. El *Amadís de Gaula*, según Cervantes, fue «el mejor de todos los libros que de este género

---

[1] **imprenta,** *printing.*   [2] **novela de caballerías,** *novel (romance) of chivalry.*   [3] **por primera vez,** *for the first time.*
[4] **gozar de,** *to enjoy.*

Page of *La Celestina*

se han compuesto, y... único en su arte.»
Esta novela narra las aventuras de Amadís,
el noble, generoso y valiente héroe, que
siempre trata de hacerse digno[1] del amor de
Oriana, la bella y fiel heroína.   Ha influido
poderosamente no sólo en la literatura
española, especialmente en la obra de
Cervantes, sino también, por sus numerosas
traducciones, en la de todo el mundo.

El período comprendido entre mediados
del siglo XVI y fines[2] del siglo XVII es
llamado el Siglo de Oro.[3]   Es la época de la
conquista y la colonización del Nuevo
Mundo; es la época en que España, bajo los
reinados de Carlos V (1516–1556), de
Felipe II (1556–1598) y de Felipe III
(1598–1621), llegó a ser la nación más
poderosa del mundo; es la época de nuevos
géneros literarios, de grandes historiadores,
filósofos y teólogos, de famosos artistas,
escultores y arquitectos; en fin,[4] es la época
en que España llegó a su apogeo[5] en todos
los aspectos de la civilización y la cultura.
Aquí podemos mencionar solamente unos
cuantos[6] nombres de gran importancia en
la literatura del Siglo de Oro.

En el siglo XVI, bajo la influencia del
Amadís de Gaula, se escribieron muchísimas
novelas de caballerías.   Otro tipo de novela
idealista de gran popularidad fue la novela
pastoril,[7] cuya obra maestra[8] fue la *Diana*
(1559) de Jorge de Montemayor.

De carácter realista y enteramente opuesto
al de estos dos tipos idealistas es la novela
picaresca.[9]   En 1554 apareció una de las
obras más bellas y más importantes de la
literatura española, el *Lazarillo de Tormes*,
que dio origen al género.   Esta obra cuenta
la vida de un pícaro astuto, Lazarillo, y a
la vez presenta una sátira poderosa sobre la
sociedad española de la época.   Enorme fue
su influencia en el desarrollo de la novela
del resto del mundo, porque con el tiempo la
novela picaresca se convirtió en la novela de
costumbres.[10]

A Juan del Encina le siguieron en el siglo
XVI varios autores dramáticos de importancia, pero el siglo XVII fue la época
gloriosa del teatro español.   En esta época

---

[1] **hacerse digno,** *to make himself (become) worthy.*   [2] **comprendido... fines,** *comprised between the middle of the ... and the end.*   [3] **Siglo de Oro,** *Golden Age.*   [4] **en fin,** *in short.*   [5] **apogeo,** *height.*   [6] **unos cuantos,** *a few.*   [7] **novela pastoril,** *pastoral romance (novel).*   [8] **obra maestra,** *masterpiece.*   [9] **novela picaresca,** *picaresque novel, romance of roguery.*   [10] **novela de costumbres,** *novel of customs and manners.*

Lope de Vega, llamado el fénix de los ingenios[1] por los españoles, fue el dramaturgo más popular de España y también uno de los más grandes del mundo. Fue el fundador del drama nacional de su país, además de ser un gran poeta lírico. Él mismo dice que compuso unas 1500 comedias; de ellas se conservan hoy día sólo unas 425.

Otros dramaturgos famosos del mismo período son Ruiz de Alarcón, Tirso de Molina y Calderón de la Barca. En *El burlador de Sevilla* Tirso de Molina presenta por primera vez en forma dramática el personaje de don Juan, una de las grandes creaciones de la literatura universal. Según algunos críticos, solamente don Quijote, Hamlet y Fausto[2] le igualan en originalidad y profundidad.

Lope de Vega

PREGUNTAS

1. ¿Es rica la literatura española? 2. ¿Ha tenido influencia en otras literaturas? 3. ¿Qué ha expresado a través de los siglos? 4. ¿Cuál es el primer monumento literario de España? 5. ¿De qué trata el poema? 6. ¿Cuál es la primera obra del teatro español? 7. ¿Qué es un romance? 8. ¿A qué ha contribuido el romance?

9. ¿Cuál fue una de las mayores glorias de los Reyes Católicos? 10. ¿Qué obra inició la novela de caballerías? 11. ¿En qué año se publicó la gramática de Nebrija? 12. ¿Quién fue el padre del teatro español? 13. ¿Qué relata *La Celestina*? 14. ¿Por qué es importante la obra? 15. ¿Qué narra el *Amadís de Gaula*?

16. ¿Qué período comprende el Siglo de Oro? 17. ¿Qué llegó a ser España durante aquella época? 18. ¿Cuál fue la obra maestra de la novela pastoril? 19. ¿Qué género realista apareció en este período? 20. ¿Cuál es la obra maestra del género? 21. ¿Qué cuenta el *Lazarillo de Tormes*? 22. ¿Por qué fue grande su influencia?

23. ¿Quién fue Lope de Vega? 24. ¿Cuántas comedias compuso? 25. ¿Cuáles son los nombres de otros dramaturgos del mismo período? 26. ¿Qué personaje presentó Tirso de Molina por primera vez? 27. ¿Cuáles son otros grandes personajes de la literatura universal?

---

[1] **fénix de los ingenios,** *phoenix (model) of geniuses.* [2] **Fausto,** *Faust* (created by the German writer Goethe, 1749–1832).

REPASO IV

A. Answer each question using a formal affirmative command and the correct object pronoun for the noun object, then compose a new sentence beginning with **Yo quiero que:**

MODEL: ¿Compro el traje?   Sí, cómprelo Vd.
    Yo quiero que Vd. lo compre.

1. ¿Busco un regalo?   4. ¿Toco los discos ahora?
2. ¿Pago las camisas?   5. ¿Me pongo la blusa?
3. ¿Me pruebo los zapatos?   6. ¿Sirvo los refrescos?

B. Say after your teacher; when you hear the cue, compose a new sentence, following the model:

MODEL: Yo prefiero hacerlo.   Yo prefiero hacerlo.
    que Vd.   Yo prefiero que Vd. lo haga.

1. ¿Quiere Vd. jugar al tenis?   (que yo)
2. Nos alegramos de saber eso.   (de que tú)
3. ¿Se alegran Vds. de verlos?   (de que Luis)
4. Sentimos no poder ir al teatro.   (que Marta)
5. ¿Siente Vd. no entenderle?   (que ellos)
6. Es importante estar seguro.   (que Tomás)
7. Me sorprende no encontrarlos.   (que Vds.)
8. Es lástima no conocerla bien.   (que tú)
9. Esperan llegar a tiempo.   (que nosotros)
10. Prefieren quitarse el sombrero.   (que Vd. y yo)
11. Carolina desea comenzar a leer.   (que yo)
12. ¿Quieres ir a nadar esta tarde?   (que nosotros)

C. Say after your teacher; when you hear the cue, compose a new sentence:

MODEL: Han ido al cine.   Han ido al cine.
    Dudo que   Dudo que hayan ido al cine.

1. Ricardo ha vuelto de España.   (Es posible que)
2. Nosotros hemos hecho una excursión.   (Ellos no creen que)
3. Los muchachos no han dicho nada.   (Yo tengo miedo de que)
4. Tú has visto al señor Gómez.   (Nos alegramos de que)

300

5. Isabel no se ha puesto el sombrero.   (Es lástima que)
6. Yo no me he divertido mucho.   (Carlos siente que)
7. Vd. ha dormido la siesta.   (Me sorprende que)
8. Vds. han abierto la puerta.   (No estoy seguro de que)

D. Say after your teacher, then make a new sentence using an indirect command and substituting the pronoun for the noun object:

> MODEL: José quiere buscar un regalo.   José quiere buscar un regalo.
> Que lo busque José.

1. Jorge quiere comprar una camisa.
2. Marta necesita traer unas flores.
3. Jaime va a poner un telegrama.
4. Roberto desea obtener un puesto.
5. Elena prefiere ponerse el vestido.
6. Luis quiere envolver los paquetes.

E. Say after your teacher, then give the alternate form affirmatively and negatively:

> MODEL: Vamos a detenernos.   Vamos a detenernos.
> Detengámonos.   No nos detengamos.

1. Vamos a sentarnos.
2. Vamos a levantarnos.
3. Vamos a lavarnos las manos.
4. Vamos a quitarnos los zapatos.
5. Vamos a ponernos los guantes.
6. Vamos a quedarnos aquí.

F. Repeat each question, then answer it making the first clause negative:

> MODEL: ¿Ve Vd. a alguien que sepa bailar?   ¿Ve Vd. a alguien que sepa bailar?
> No, no veo a nadie que sepa bailar.

1. ¿Conoce Vd. a alguien que juegue bien?
2. ¿Viene alguna joven que pueda cantar?
3. ¿Tiene Vd. algo que yo pueda comprar?
4. ¿Hay algo aquí que le guste a Ana?
5. ¿Conoces a alguien que lo haya creído?
6. ¿Hay alguien que se haya desayunado?

G. Say after your teacher, then make two comparisons, following the model:

> MODEL: Esta casa es grande.   Esta casa es grande.   Es más grande que aquélla.
> Es la más grande de todas.

1. Esta playa es bonita.
2. Este paquete es pequeño.
3. Este jugador es bueno.
4. Esta película es mala.

Falla representing the Statue of Liberty in Valencia, Spain. These elaborate papier maché and wood sculptures are burned during the festival in March.

Street scene, Málaga, Spain.

5. Estos discos son populares.
6. Estas flores son hermosas.

7. Estos lagos son grandes.
8. Estas pulseras son caras.

H. Answer in Spanish:

1. ¿Qué hora será? 2. ¿A qué hora empezó esta clase? 3. ¿Cuánto tiempo hace que estudia Vd. el español? 4. ¿Le gustaría a Vd. pasar un verano en México? 5. ¿Habla Vd. mucho por teléfono? 6. ¿Conoce Vd. a alguien que haya hecho un viaje a México? 7. ¿Juega Vd. al tenis? 8. ¿Es Vd. aficionado al básquetbol? 9. ¿Qué otros deportes tenemos en los Estados Unidos? 10. ¿Ha visto Vd. un partido de pelota vasca? 11. ¿Dónde se juega al *jai alai*? 12. ¿Tenemos corridas de toros en este país? 13. ¿Ha visto Vd. una corrida? 14. ¿Se divierte Vd. mucho en los bailes? 15. ¿Le gusta a Vd. la música popular? 16. ¿De dónde viene el tango? 17. ¿Cómo se siente Vd. hoy? 18. ¿Tiene Vd. un resfriado? 19. ¿Le duele a Vd. la cabeza ahora? 20. ¿Duerme Vd. la siesta todas las tardes? 21. ¿Qué número de zapatos usa Vd.? 22. ¿A qué tienda vamos para comprar una pulsera? 23. Cuando nos acercamos a un dependiente en una tienda, ¿qué pregunta él? 24. Si Vd. decide comprar algo, ¿qué le dice al dependiente? 25. ¿Va Vd. de compras a menudo?

I. Give the Spanish for:

1. Let's go home. 2. Let's be going. 3. Let's not go yet. 4. Let's sit down here. 5. May you (*fam.*) sleep well. 6. May you (*pl.*) have a good time. 7. They will soon be back. 8. I am pleased to meet you. 9. It is a great pleasure to be here. 10. We are very eager to see them. 11. Go to the right, not to the left. 12. The suit fits me. 13. They are very lucky. 14. Send the telegram at once. 15. I arrived at about ten o'clock. 16. How old is your brother? 17. He is sixteen years old. 18. Of course! (*Two ways*) 19. They must have spent most of the day downtown. 20. Two friends of mine have just arrived.

LECCIÓN 21

Verbs with changes in spelling
The subjunctive in adverbial clauses
Review of compound nouns. *Pero* and *sino*

PREPARÁNDOSE PARA EL VIAJE

(*Ricardo se encuentra en la calle con su amigo Tomás.*)

Tomás.   ¡Te felicito, Ricardo!   He oído decir que conseguiste el puesto en México.

Ricardo.   He tenido mucha suerte, Tomás.   Siempre he oído decir que querer es
poder.[1]   Hacía mucho tiempo que trataba de encontrar un puesto como éste.

Tomás.   ¿Cuándo piensas partir?

Ricardo.   El sábado.   Me queda poco tiempo para las mil cosas que tengo que hacer.
En este momento estoy buscando dos maletas nuevas.

• • • • •

Tomás.   Ricardo, como tendrás que hacer viajes de negocios[2] en avión en cuanto llegues a
México, necesitas maletas que sean ligeras.

Ricardo.   Ayer anduve[3] buscándolas, pero no las encontré en ninguna parte.   También
tengo que comprar mi billete.[4]

Tomás.   ¡Hombre!   ¡Hay que hacer eso ahora mismo!   Si quieres, yo reservaré tu asiento
en el avión para que tú puedas escoger las maletas.

Ricardo.   Es que no pensaba comprar el billete hoy sino mañana.

Tomás.   De todos modos, no es seguro que consigas un asiento aunque lo compres ahora
mismo.   Mucha gente va a México en estos días.

Ricardo.   ¿De veras?   Pues, vamos a la agencia de viajes en seguida.   Sigamos por esta
calle a la derecha.

---

[1] This proverb is equivalent to "Where there's a will, there's a way."   [2] For the compound nouns used in this dialogue
see section C.   [3] **Andar,** *to walk*, *go* (often without definite destination,) has a **u**-stem in the preterit: **anduve, andu-
viste, anduvo, anduvimos, anduvisteis, anduvieron.**   [4] In Mexico **el boleto** is regularly used for *ticket*.

(*Ricardo y Tomás llegan a la agencia de viajes.*)

RICARDO. (*Al empleado.*) Quiero salir para Ciudad México el sábado y deseo reservar un asiento.

EMPLEADO. Hay dos vuelos diarios. El vuelo de la mañana hace una parada en Guadalajara.

RICARDO. Prefiero el vuelo de la mañana para llegar a México lo más pronto posible.

EMPLEADO. ¿Puede esperar un momento? Necesito hablar con el aeropuerto para preguntar si quedan asientos. (*Al poco tiempo.*) Por desgracia, no queda ningún asiento en el vuelo de la mañana.

RICARDO. Pues, tendré que ir en el vuelo de la tarde. ¿Cuánto equipaje puedo llevar?

EMPLEADO. Veinte y dos kilos. ¿Billete sencillo o de ida y vuelta?

RICARDO. Billete sencillo, por favor. Aceptan un cheque personal, ¿verdad?

EMPLEADO. ¡Cómo no! Son ciento veinte dólares. Puede Vd. recoger el billete mañana por la mañana.

RICARDO. Muy bien. Hasta mañana.

EMPLEADO. A sus órdenes, señores. Hasta mañana.

CONVERSACIÓN

A. Preguntas sobre el diálogo

1. ¿Qué le dice Tomás a Ricardo? 2. ¿Qué contesta Ricardo? 3. ¿Qué ha oído decir Ricardo? 4. ¿Cuándo piensa partir para México? 5. ¿Qué está buscando Ricardo en este momento? 6. ¿Cómo va a hacer el viaje a la ciudad de México? 7. ¿Qué tiene que comprar Ricardo ahora mismo? 8. ¿Quiere billete sencillo o de ida y vuelta?

B. Aplicación del diálogo

1. ¿Cuántos años le quedan a Vd. para terminar sus estudios en esta universidad? 2. Cuando Vd. viaja, ¿prefiere llevar maletas que sean ligeras? 3. ¿Por qué es necesario reservar los asientos en los aviones? 4. ¿Ha viajado Vd. mucho en avión? 5. Cuando Vd. vuelva a casa este verano, ¿cómo hará el viaje? 6. Si Vd. va en avión, comprará billete sencillo o de ida y vuelta? 7. ¿Dónde se consiguen informes acerca de los viajes en avión? 8. ¿Cuántos aeropuertos hay cerca de esta ciudad?

NOTAS GRAMATICALES

A. Verbs with changes in spelling

1. In verbs ending in **-ger** (**-gir**), **g** changes to **j** before the endings beginning with **-o** or **-a;** that is, in the first person singular present indicative and in all six forms of the present subjunctive: **escoger,** *to choose, select.*

PRES. IND.   **escojo,** escoges, escoge, escogemos, escogéis, escogen
PRES. SUBJ.   **escoja, escojas, escoja, escojamos, escojáis, escojan**

2. In verbs ending in **-guir, u** is dropped after **g** before the endings **-o** and **-a;** that is, in the first person singular present indicative and in all six forms of the present subjunctive.   The model verb for this change, **seguir,** *to follow, continue, go on,* is also a stem-changing verb, Class III, like **pedir.**

PRES. PART.   **siguiendo**
PRES. IND.   **sigo, sigues, sigue,** seguimos, seguís, **siguen**
PRES. SUBJ.   **siga, sigas, siga, sigamos, sigáis, sigan**
PRETERIT   seguí, seguiste, **siguió,** seguimos, seguisteis, **siguieron**
SING. IMPER.   **sigue**

Seguir is followed by the present participle, like the English verb *to continue*: **Ellos siguen charlando,** *They continue chatting*; **Siga Vd. leyendo,** *Continue reading*.

3. In certain verbs whose stem ends in a vowel, unaccented **i** between vowels is written **y** (note the present participle and the third person singular and plural preterit forms below).   Also note the additional forms which have written accent marks.   **Creer** and **leer** are other verbs of this type.   The model verb **oír,** *to hear,* also has an irregular first person singular present indicative, which affects all the present subjunctive forms.

PRES. PART.   **oyendo**   PAST PART.   oído
PRES. IND.   **oigo, oyes, oye,** oímos, oís, **oyen**
PRES. SUBJ.   **oiga, oigas, oiga, oigamos, oigáis, oigan**
PRETERIT   oí, oíste, **oyó,** oímos, oísteis, **oyeron**
SING. IMPER.   **oye**

B. The subjunctive in adverbial clauses

An adverbial clause, which modifies a verb and indicates *time, manner, purpose, condition,* and the like, is introduced by a conjunction, often a compound with **que** as the last element.   The indicative mood is used in adverbial clauses if the act has taken place or is accepted as an accomplished fact; otherwise the subjunctive is normally used.

1. Time clauses:

Cuando yo le veo, charlo con él.   When I see him, I chat with him.
En cuanto le vea yo, charlaré con él.   As soon as I see him, I shall chat with him.
Vámonos antes (de) que vuelvan ellos.   Let's go before they return.
Quédese Vd. hasta que lleguen los muchachos.   Stay until the boys arrive.

The subjunctive is used after time conjunctions when the time referred to in the clause is indefinite and future, from the standpoint of the time of the main clause. When the clause expresses an accomplished fact in the present or past time, the indicative is used (first example). **Antes (de) que** is always followed by the subjunctive. Other common conjunctions (not all of which have been used in earlier lessons, but which will be used in the exercises) which introduce time clauses are:

antes (de) que	before	**después que**	after
cuando	when	**hasta que**	until
en cuanto	as soon as	**mientras (que)**	while, as long as

Así que and **luego que** are less common than **en cuanto** for *as soon as*. They will be found in reading, but they are not used in this text.

2. Concessive and result clauses:

> **Aunque está lloviendo, saldré.** Even though it is raining, I shall leave.
> **Aunque llueva esta noche, saldré.** Although it may rain (rains) tonight, I shall leave.

Aunque, *although*, *even though*, is followed by the indicative mood if an accomplished fact is indicated, and by the subjunctive if the action is yet to happen. Compare the two examples above.

> **Yo hablo despacio de modo que ellos siempre me entienden.**
> I speak slowly so that (as a result of which) they always understand me.
> **Lea Vd. de manera que ellos le entiendan.**
> Read so that they may understand you.

Two other conjunctions, **de modo que** and **de manera que,** both of which mean *so*, *so that*, may express result, in which case they are followed by the indicative mood. They may also express purpose, in which case the subjunctive is used. Compare the two examples, and also compare the use of **para que** in section 3.

3. Purpose, proviso, conditional, negative result clauses:

> **Yo reservaré tu asiento para que tú puedas escoger las maletas.**
> I shall reserve your seat so (in order) that you may select the suitcases.

Certain conjunctions denoting *purpose*, *proviso*, *condition*, *negation*, and the like, always require the subjunctive since they cannot introduce a statement of fact:

a menos que	unless	**para que**	in order (so) that
con tal que	provided that	**sin que**	without

Para que and **con tal que** are used in exercises. The others are given because they will be found in reading. Examples are:

Yo no me iré a menos que él me pague. I shall not go unless he pays me.
Luis entra sin que yo le oiga. Louis enters without my hearing him.
Traiga Vd. el café con tal que esté caliente. Bring the coffee provided that it is hot.

C. Review of compound nouns

> **la agencia de viajes** travel agency
> **el billete de cinco dólares** five-dollar bill
> **el billete sencillo (de ida y vuelta)** one-way (round-trip) ticket
> **la casa de campo** country house
> **el reloj de oro** gold watch
> **la taza para café** coffee cup
> **el viaje de negocios** business trip
> **el vuelo de la mañana (de la tarde)** morning (afternoon) flight

In Spanish a noun is rarely used as an adjective to modify another noun directly. Instead, an adjective phrase introduced by the preposition **de,** or occasionally **para,** is normally used.

D. **Pero** and **sino,** *but*

Juan vino anoche, pero yo no le vi. John came last night, but I did not see him.
Yo no voy en avión, sino en coche. I'm not going by plane, but by car.
Tomás no vio a Juan, sino a Carlos. Tom didn't see John, but Charles.

The English conjunction *but* is usually expressed by **pero** in Spanish. When *but* means *on the contrary, but instead,* **sino** is used in place of **pero** in an affirmative statement which is in direct contrast to a preceding negative statement. Usually no other verb — other than an infinitive — may be used after **sino: Yo no quiero estudiar, sino dormir,** *I don't want to study, but to sleep.*

If clauses containing different verbs are contrasted, **sino que** is used: **Juan no andaba, sino que corría,** *John wasn't walking, but (he was) running.* This construction is not used in the exercises.

EJERCICIOS

A. Substitution drill:

1. *Yo* los oigo todos los días.
   (*Nosotros, Ana, Tú, Vd., Él y ella*)

2. *Ricardo* escoge una maleta.
   (*Mis padres, Yo, Ella y yo, Vd., Tú*)

3. *Las muchachas* siguen charlando.
   (*Él, Vds., Nosotros, Tú, Yo*)

4. *Marta y ella* siguieron andando.
   (*Pablo, Nosotros, Yo, Ella, Vds.*)

B. Repeat the question after your teacher, then follow the same pattern in your replies to the other questions:

> MODEL: ¿Lo hará Vd.?   ¿Lo hará Vd.? Sí, aunque Carlos lo haga también.

1. ¿Lo buscará Vd.?
2. ¿Las escogerá Vd.?
3. ¿Seguirá Vd. trabajando?

4. ¿Saldrá Vd. a la calle?
5. ¿Vendrá Vd. temprano?
6. ¿Empezará Vd. a leer?

C. Repeat the question after your teacher; when you hear the question again and the cue (an infinitive), use the inflected form of the verb in the adverbial clause after **para que,** following the model:

> MODEL: ¿Trae Vd. los libros?   ¿Trae Vd. los libros?
>   ¿Trae Vd. los libros? Ver.   Sí, los traigo para que los vea Vd.

1. Examinar. 2. Leer. 3. Comprar. 4. Vender. 5. Conocer. 6. Llevar a casa.

D. After you repeat the question and answer, your teacher will give other conjunctions to be used in the adverbial clause of the answer:

1. ¿Va Vd. a tocar los discos? Sí, los tocaré en cuanto vuelvan ellos.
   (cuando, antes que, después que, aunque)
2. ¿Vas a seguir trabajando? Sí, seguiré trabajando con tal que me paguen.
   (para que, de manera que, hasta que, mientras)

E. Listen to the two sentences; when you hear the cue (a conjunction), combine the two sentences into one, following the model:

> MODEL: Yo no saldré. Juan paga sus compras. (hasta que)
>   Yo no saldré hasta que Juan pague sus compras.

1. Yo te doy cinco dólares. Puedes comprar un regalo. (para que)
2. Ella hará el viaje. Su padre le dará un cheque. (en cuanto)
3. Los dos pasarán por aquí. Ella saldrá de la biblioteca. (después que)
4. Lean Vds. despacio. Podemos entenderlos. (de manera que)

5. No queremos irnos.   Vienen nuestros amigos.   (antes de que)

6. Tú no podrás llegar a tiempo.   Sales en este momento.   (aunque)

F. Repeat the question, then answer it beginning with **Es posible que,** and substituting the correct pronoun for the noun, following the model:

MODEL: ¿Oye él la música?   ¿Oye él la música?   Sí, es posible que él la oiga.

1. ¿Busca él a su hermana?
2. ¿Consigo yo el puesto?
3. ¿Escojo yo la maleta ahora?
4. ¿Recoge él el billete?
5. ¿Conocen ellos la calle?
6. ¿Trae ella el equipaje?

G. Give in Spanish:

1. at any rate.   2. after a short time.   3. I have five dollars left.   4. He is getting ready for the trip.   5. Let's continue looking for a suitcase.   6. You (*fam.*) can carry the baggage.   7. At your service, gentlemen.   8. I want a round-trip ticket.   9. Let's take the morning flight.   10. It makes a stop in San Antonio.

COMPOSICIÓN

1. "I congratulate you, Richard!   I have heard that you got the position in Mexico." 2. "Yes, Tom, I am very lucky.   I have been looking for a position like this one for several years."   3. "I have to leave Saturday and I have little time left for the many (thousand) things that I have to do."   4. "At this moment I am looking for a suitcase which is light."   5. "This morning I went looking for one, but I couldn't find it anywhere."   6. "Also, I have to buy a ticket and reserve a seat on the plane."   7. Tom says: "Man!   It is necessary to do that right now!   Many people are going to Mexico these days."   8. "Let's go to the travel agency before you continue looking for a suitcase."   9. Upon arriving at the agency, Richard asks for a one-way ticket for Saturday. 10. The employee replies: "Wait a moment so that I can ask what seats remain." 11. After a short time he says: "Unfortunately there isn't any seat left, but I can give you one for Sunday."   12. Richard decides to take it and he pays for the ticket; the employee hands it to him before the boys leave.

Subway Station, Mexico City.

Columbus Circle, Mexico City.

VOCABULARIO

aceptar to accept
la agencia agency
andar to go, walk
el asiento seat
conseguir (i, i) to get, obtain
el cheque check
la desgracia misfortune
diario, -a daily
el equipaje baggage
escoger to choose, select
felicitar to congratulate
la ida departure
el kilo (= **el kilogramo**) kilo(gram)
  (*about 2.2 pounds*)
ligero, -a light

la maleta suitcase
el modo manner, means, way
los negocios business
ningún (*used for* **ninguno** *before m. sing. nouns*) no, (not) ... any
oír to hear, listen
la orden (*pl.* **órdenes**) order, command
la parada stop, stop over
personal personal
recoger to pick up
reservar to reserve
seguir (i, i) to follow, continue, go on
sencillo, -a simple, one-way
sino but

a sus órdenes at your service
agencia de viajes travel agency
al poco tiempo after (in) a short time
Ciudad México Mexico City
de ida y vuelta round-trip
de todos modos at any rate, by all means
en este (ese) momento at this (that) moment
en estos días these days
hacer una parada to stop over, make a stop
(me) queda (poco tiempo) (I) have (little time) left (*used like* **gustar**)
mil cosas many things (*lit.,* a thousand things)
(no) ... en ninguna parte (not) ... anywhere
no queda ningún asiento no seat is left (remains), there isn't any seat left
oír decir que to hear that
por desgracia unfortunately
prepararse para to prepare oneself for, get ready for

Bakery, Mexico City.

CONVERSACIÓN IV

En un hotel mexicano

(Luis y Juan, dos estudiantes norteamericanos, están haciendo un viaje en coche por México. Llegan a la ciudad de Monterrey, donde deciden pasar la noche. Entran en un hotel y hablan con el empleado.)

LUIS.   ¿Tienen Vds. un cuarto para dos personas?

EMPLEADO.   ¿Con baño o sin baño?

LUIS.   ¿Cuánto cuesta un cuarto con baño?

EMPLEADO.   Para dos personas, sin comida, noventa pesos, y, con comida, ciento diez pesos por persona.

LUIS.   El hotel tiene garaje, ¿verdad?

EMPLEADO.   Sí, señor; cobramos tres pesos por el estacionamiento del coche.

JUAN.   ¿Nos permite ver el cuarto?

EMPLEADO.   ¡Cómo no!   Pasen Vds. por aquí.   (*Toman el ascensor al tercer piso y entran en un cuarto.*)   Creo que este cuarto les gustará.   Es grande y tiene dos ventanas que dan a las montañas.   Tengo otro más pequeño; es un poco más barato, pero no tiene cuarto de baño.

JUAN.   ¿Son cómodas las camas?

EMPLEADO.   Son muy cómodas.   Y aquí está el cuarto de baño, con agua caliente y fría a todas horas.   La criada traerá jabón y toallas en seguida.

LUIS.   ¿No te gusta este cuarto, Juan?   Parece muy bueno para el precio, ¿verdad?

JUAN.   Sí, Luis; a mí también me gusta.   Hay una vista magnífica desde la ventana.

EMPLEADO.   Muy bien.   Aquí tienen Vds. la llave.   Pueden firmar el registro cuando bajen.   Estoy seguro de que Vds. van a estar muy cómodos aquí.   El botones subirá las maletas dentro de unos minutos.

JUAN.   ¿A qué hora se abre el comedor?

EMPLEADO.   Aquí se come a las ocho, porque sabemos que a los turistas no les gusta esperar hasta más tarde.   (*Los jóvenes descansan hasta las ocho y bajan al comedor. El mesero se acerca a su mesa y les pregunta qué desean.*)

LUIS.   Deseamos una comida mexicana.   ¿Qué recomienda Vd.?

MESERO.   Primero deben tomar huevos rancheros.   Son huevos fritos, con salsa de chile. Muchas personas los comen con tortillas.

JUAN.   ¿Qué son tortillas?

MESERO.   Son tortas delgadas de maíz.   Después pueden tomar tacos de pollo o mole de guajolote.   Los tacos son tortillas tostadas con pollo o carne y salsa de chile.

JUAN. Y, ¿mole de guajolote?

MESERO. El mole de guajolote es un guisado que se hace de guajolote, chile, cacahuetes, chocolate y otras cosas. Es uno de los platillos más famosos de México.

LUIS. El guacamole es un plato diferente, ¿verdad?

MESERO. ¡Claro! Es una ensalada muy sabrosa. Se hace con aguacate, cebolla, jitomate y chile. Y a muchos mexicanos les gusta tomar frijoles con todas las comidas.

LUIS. Muy bien. Pues, tráiganos huevos rancheros, con tortillas, frijoles, tacos de pollo y guacamole.

MESERO. ¿Desean Vds. una cerveza?

JUAN. No, gracias. Unos vasos de agua purificada, por favor. Después tomaremos café solo, con algún postre.

MESERO. Muy bien. Vuelvo en seguida.

At Cortijo la Morena near Mexico City, one can have lunch while watching tourists play *matador* with baby bulls.

PREGUNTAS

Sobre la conversación

1. ¿A qué ciudad han llegado Luis y Juan en su viaje por México?   2. ¿Qué deciden hacer?   3. ¿Qué le pregunta Luis al empleado del hotel?   4. ¿Cuánto cuesta un cuarto para dos personas, con baño?   5. ¿En qué piso está el cuarto que les enseña el empleado?   6. ¿Qué traerá la criada en seguida?

7. ¿A qué hora se come en el hotel?   8. ¿Qué recomienda el mesero que tomen primero?   9. ¿De qué se hacen las tortillas en México?   10. ¿De qué se preparan los tacos?   11. ¿De qué se hace el mole de guajolote?   12. ¿Qué es el guacamole?

Aplicación de la conversación

1. ¿Qué viajes largos en coche ha hecho Vd.?   2. ¿Le gustaría hacer un viaje en coche por México?   3. ¿Puede Vd. recomendar un buen hotel cerca de la universidad?   4. ¿Cuánto cuesta un cuarto en un buen hotel?   5. ¿Acostumbran los estudiantes celebrar sus fiestas en algún hotel?   6. ¿Qué hay en los hoteles para llegar a los pisos altos?

7. ¿Hay algún restaurante mexicano por aquí?   8. ¿Cuáles son algunos platos típicos de México?   9. ¿Qué plato mexicano le gusta a Vd. más?   10. ¿Cómo se preparan los huevos rancheros?   11. ¿En qué país toman mucha cerveza los estudiantes?   12. ¿Sabe Vd. si se toma mucha cerveza en los partidos de béisbol?

PRÁCTICAS ORALES

Groups of students will be selected to prepare a conversation of eight to ten exchanges, using vocabulary already given.   (For fast learners a supplementary vocabulary is provided below.)

1. Groups of students ask for rooms in a hotel, with one acting as hotel clerk and others as travelers.

2. Groups of students order a Mexican meal, with one acting as waiter (**mesero,** in Mexico) and others as customers.

VOCABULARIO

el aguacate   avocado, alligator pear
el ascensor   elevator
barato, -a   cheap, inexpensive

el botones   bellboy
el cacahuete   peanut
caliente   *adj.*   warm, hot

la cebolla onion
la cerveza beer
  cobrar to charge, collect
la comida dinner, food, meal
la criada maid
el chile chili
  delgado, -a thin
  dentro de *prep.* within
el estacionamiento parking
  firmar to sign
el frijol kidney bean
el guacamole guacamole (*salad*)
el guajolote turkey (*Mex.*)
el guisado stew
el jabón (*pl.* **jabones**) soap
el jitomate tomato (*Mex.*)
la llave key

el maíz maize, corn
el mesero waiter (*Mex.*)
el mole mole (*a stew*)
el peso peso (*Spanish American monetary unit*)
el piso floor, story
el platillo dish (*food*)
  purificado, -a purified
el registro register
la salsa sauce
  subir to bring (take) up
el taco taco
la toalla towel
la torta flat pancake
la tortilla corn pancake (*Mex.*)
  tostado, -a toasted
el (la) turista tourist

¡claro! indeed! of course! certainly!
dar a to face
huevos rancheros eggs ranch style
¿nos permite (ver)? may we (see)? (*lit., do you permit us …?*)
por persona per (for each) person

VOCABULARIO SUPLEMENTARIO (*Supplementary vocabulary*)

(This list of words, not used in the active vocabularies nor in **Conversaciones** III and IV, may be used for further drill. These words are not included in the general vocabulary unless they also appear in the **Lecturas.**)

LEGUMBRES

el apio celery
la batata sweet potato
el betabel beet (*Mex.*)
la calabaza squash, pumpkin
el camote sweet potato (*Am.*)
la col cabbage
la coliflor cauliflower
los chícharos green peas (*Am.*)
los ejotes string beans (*Am.*)
  el elote ear of green corn (*Mex.*)
los espárragos asparagus

los guisantes green peas
las habas lima beans
las judías verdes string beans
  la lechuga lettuce
  el nabo turnip
  la papa potato (*Am.*)
  el puré de patatas mashed potatoes
  el rábano radish
  la remolacha beet
  el tomate tomato
  la zanahoria carrot

CARNES

la **carne de vaca** (**de res**)   beef
el **carnero**   mutton
la **chuleta**   chop, cutlet
los **fiambres**   cold cuts
el **filete**   tenderloin

el **pato**   duck
el **pavo**   turkey (*Spain*)
el **puerco** (**asado**)   (roast) pork
la **salchicha**   sausage
la **ternera**   veal

FRUTAS

el **albaricoque**   apricot
la **banana**   banana
la **cereza**   cherry
la **ciruela**   plum
el **chabacano**   apricot (*Am.*)
el **dátil**   date
el **durazno**   peach
la **frambuesa**   raspberry
el **higo**   fig
la **lima**   lime
la **pera**   pear

la **mandarina**   tangerine
el **mango**   mango
la **manzana**   apple
el **melocotón** (*pl.* **melocotones**)   peach
el **melón** (*pl.* **melones**)   melon
la **naranja**   orange
la **piña**   pineapple
el **plátano**   banana, plantain
la **sandía**   watermelon
la **toronja**   grapefruit
la **uva**   grape

MISCELÁNEA

el **aceite** (**de oliva**)   (olive) oil
la **aceituna**   olive
el **ajo**   garlic
asar   to roast
el **batido de leche**   milk shake
bien cocido, -a   well done
el **bollo**   roll
el **caldo**   broth
el **camarón** (*pl.* **camarones**)   shrimp
la **canela**   cinnamon
el **cangrejo**   crab
la **cocinera**   cook (*f.*)
el **cocinero**   cook (*m.*)
el **consomé**   consommé
la **crema de cacahuete**   peanut butter
el **emparedado**   sandwich

los **encurtidos**   relish, pickles
el **fósforo**   match
la **galleta**   cookie
la **galleta de soda**   soda cracker
la **hamburguesa**   hamburger
la **harina**   flour
el **jugo** (**de naranja**)   (orange) juice
la **mermelada**   marmalade
la **mostaza**   mustard
la **ostra**   oyster
el **pan dulce**   sweet bread, roll
el **panecillo**   hard roll
el **perro caliente**   hot dog
la **pimienta**   pepper
la **sal**   salt
el **vinagre**   vinegar

For use in making up a variety of shopping lists:

la caja box	**media libra** half pound, ½ lb.
la docena dozen	**medio kilo** half kilo
la lata (tin) can	**un cuarto de kilo** ¼ kilogram
la libra pound, lb.	**el litro** liter (*about 1.06 quarts*)

Street market, Bolivia.

LECCIÓN **22**

The imperfect subjunctive.   The pluperfect subjunctive
Use of the subjunctive tenses
Use of the infinitive after certain verbs.   The subjunctive
in a polite or softened statement.   Exclamations

ESPOSAS JÓVENES.   ¿TE ACUERDAS DE MARGARITA?

Clara e[1] Isabel viven en una casa de apartamentos[2] cerca de la Universidad.   Sus esposos estudian en la Facultad de Derecho.   El esposo de Isabel se llama Ramón; tienen una hija, Juanita.   Son las dos de la tarde.   Clara visita a su amiga.

• • • • •

CLARA.   Buenas tardes, Isabel.   ¿Puedes ir de compras conmigo?
ISABEL.   Quisiera decirte que sí, Clara, pero tengo que descansar un rato.   ¡Qué día he tenido!   Primero Ramón me pidió que llevara un traje a la tintorería para hacerlo limpiar, y luego, como él tenía clase, me dijo que llevara a Juanita al dentista.
CLARA.   Juanita acaba de decirme que la llevaste al parque, también.
ISABEL.   Sí; antes de volver a casa, Juanita me pidió que la llevara al parque para ver los animales.
CLARA.   Bueno, ¡se divertirían las dos![1]   ¿Qué pasó después?
ISABEL.   Después le permití jugar un rato, y aunque le aconsejé que tuviera cuidado, se cayó y se hizo daño.   En fin, estoy muy cansada, como puedes suponer.
CLARA.   Pues, siento que no puedas acompañarme.

• • • • •

CLARA.   A propósito, ¿te divertiste mucho anoche en casa de Carolina?
ISABEL.   Muchísimo.   ¡Qué noche tan agradable pasamos!   ¡Es lástima que tuvieras otro compromiso!   ¿Te acuerdas de Margarita Brown, que se casó hace un mes?
CLARA.   Sí, la recuerdo bien y me gustaría volver a verla.

---

[1] See footnote 9, page 171.   [2] In certain regions *apartment* is expressed by **el apartamiento** or **el departamento**.
[3] **¡se divertirían las dos!**   *you two must have had a very good time!*   As we learned in Lesson 16, the conditional tense is used in Spanish to indicate probability or conjecture concerning an action or state in the past.   Also note in this phrase that the subject pronoun **ustedes,** in apposition to **las dos,** need not be expressed.

ISABEL.   Pues acabábamos de sentarnos a jugar a las cartas cuando llegaron Margarita y su esposo Roberto.

CLARA.   ¿De modo que han vuelto de su luna de miel en México?

ISABEL.   Sí, ayer por la tarde.   Cuando supimos que Roberto traía las fotos y transparencias que había sacado en su viaje, le rogamos que nos las enseñara.

CLARA.   ¡Cuánto siento no haber estado allí!   ¡Ojalá que las hubiera visto!   Y, ¿qué te parece Roberto?   Quisiera conocerle.

ISABEL.   ¡Qué guapo es!   Es alto, simpático y muy cortés.

CLARA.   ¿Cuánto tiempo van a pasar aquí?

ISABEL.   Es probable que ya se hayan marchado.   Roberto telefoneó ayer a la oficina de su compañía, e insistieron en que volviera cuanto antes.

CLARA.   ¡Qué interesante!   Pero yo debiera dejarte dormir la siesta.   Que descanses, Isabel.

ISABEL.   Hasta luego, Clara.

CONVERSACIÓN

A. Preguntas sobre el diálogo

1. ¿Qué le pregunta Clara a Isabel?   2. ¿Qué le contesta Isabel?   3. ¿Qué le pidió su esposo primero?   4. ¿Adónde llevó a Juanita después?   5. ¿Adónde fueron Isabel y Juanita antes de volver a casa?   6. ¿Qué pasó en el parque?   7. ¿Se divirtió Isabel en casa de Carolina?   8. ¿Cómo es el esposo de Margarita?

B. Aplicación del diálogo

1. ¿Qué es una tintorería?   2. ¿Qué les aconsejamos a los niños en los parques?   3. ¿Le gusta a Vd. jugar a las cartas?   4. ¿Le gusta a Vd. mirar las fotos que sacan sus amigos en sus viajes?   5. ¿Dónde da Vd. paseos con sus amigas?   6. ¿Es probable que se case Vd. pronto?   7. ¿Dónde piensa Vd. pasar su luna de miel?   8. ¿Quién le aconsejó a Vd. que estudiara el español?

NOTAS GRAMATICALES

A. The imperfect subjunctive

1. Regular verbs:

hablar		**comer, vivir**	
SINGULAR		SINGULAR	
hablara	hablase	comiera	viviese
hablaras	hablases	comieras	vivieses
hablara	hablase	comiera	viviese
PLURAL		PLURAL	
habláramos	hablásemos	comiéramos	viviésemos
hablarais	hablaseis	comierais	vivieseis
hablaran	hablasen	comieran	viviesen

The imperfect subjunctive in Spanish has two forms, often referred to as the **-ra** and the **-se** forms, and the same two sets of endings are used for the three conjugations. To form the imperfect subjunctive of all verbs, regular and irregular, drop **-ron** of the third person plural preterit indicative and add **-ra, -ras, -ra, -́ramos, -rais, -ran** or **-se, -ses, -se, -́semos, -seis, -sen.** Only the first person plural form has a written accent mark.

Except in softened statements (section E) and in conditional sentences (Lesson 24), the imperfect subjunctive tenses are interchangeable in Spanish. Just as the present subjunctive is often translated with *may* as a part of its meaning, so the imperfect subjunctive is translated with *might*: **que hablara,** *that he might talk*; **que comiesen,** *that they might eat.*

2. Stem-changing verbs:

Stem-changing verbs, Class I, are regular in the imperfect subjunctive:

   pensar: pensara, pensaras, etc.   pensase, pensases, etc.
   volver: volviera, volvieras, etc.   volviese, volvieses, etc.

Since stem-changing verbs, Classes II and III, change **e** to **i** and **o** to **u** in the third person singular and plural of the preterit, this change also occurs throughout the imperfect subjunctive:

Inf.	*3rd Pl. Pret.*	*Imperfect Subjunctive*	
sentir	**sintieron**	**sintiera, -ras,** etc.	**sintiese, -ses,** etc.
dormir	**durmieron**	**durmiera, -ras,** etc.	**durmiese, -ses,** etc.
pedir	**pidieron**	**pidiera, -ras,** etc.	**pidiese, -ses,** etc.

3. Irregular verbs:

Inf.	*3rd Pl. Pret.*	*Imp. Subj.*	*Inf.*	*3rd Pl. Pret.*	*Imp. Subj.*
andar	**anduvieron**	**anduviera, -se**	oír	**oyeron**	**oyera, -se**
caer	**cayeron**	**cayera, -se**	poder	**pudieron**	**pudiera, -se**
creer	**creyeron**	**creyera, -se**	poner	**pusieron**	**pusiera, -se**
dar	**dieron**	**diera, -se**	querer	**quisieron**	**quisiera, -se**
decir	**dijeron**	**dijera, -se**	saber	**supieron**	**supiera, -se**
estar	**estuvieron**	**estuviera, -se**	ser	**fueron**	**fuera, -se**
haber	**hubieron**[1]	**hubiera, -se**	tener	**tuvieron**	**tuviera, -se**
hacer	**hicieron**	**hiciera, -se**	traer	**trajeron**	**trajera, -se**
ir	**fueron**	**fuera, -se**	venir	**vinieron**	**viniera, -se**
leer	**leyeron**	**leyera, -se**	ver	vieron	viera, -se

B. The pluperfect subjunctive

hubiera	**hubiese**
hubieras	**hubieses**
hubiera	**hubiese**
hubiéramos	**hubiésemos**
hubierais	**hubieseis**
hubieran	**hubiesen**

⎫ hablado, comido, vivido

Ellos temían que yo no lo hubiera visto.   They feared that I had not seen it.

The pluperfect subjunctive is formed by using either form of the imperfect subjunctive of **haber** with the past participle. Its translation is similar to that of the pluperfect indicative: **que hubiesen vivido,** *that they had lived*; sometimes the word *might* is a part of the translation: *that they might have lived.*

C. Use of the subjunctive tenses

Yo quiero que ella tenga cuidado.   I want her to be careful.
Ella lo ha traído para que Vd. lo vea.   She has brought it so that you may see it.
Ella insistirá en que ellos lo limpien.   She will insist that they clean it.
Es probable que ya se hayan marchado.   It is probable that they have already left.

---

[1] See Lesson 25 for the preterit forms of **haber.**

When the main verb in a sentence requiring the subjunctive in the dependent clause is in the present, future, or present perfect tense, or is a command, the verb in the dependent clause is regularly in the <u>present</u> or <u>present perfect</u> subjunctive tense.

Le rogamos que nos las enseñara. We begged him to show them to us.
No vimos a nadie que le conociese. We saw no one who knew him.
Mamá me dijo que llevara a Juanita al dentista. Mother told me to take Jane to the dentist.
La llevé al parque para que viera los animales. I took her to the park so that she might see the animals.
Yo sentí que ella se hubiera caído. I was sorry that she had fallen down.

When the main verb is in the preterit, imperfect, conditional or pluperfect tense, the verb in the dependent clause is normally in the <u>imperfect</u> subjunctive, unless the English past perfect tense is used in the dependent clause, in which case the pluperfect subjunctive is used in Spanish (last example).

However, the imperfect subjunctive may follow the present, future, or present perfect tense when, as in English, the action of the dependent verb took place in the past:

¡Es lástima que tuvieras otro compromiso! It's a pity that you had another commitment.

D. Use of the infinitive after certain verbs

1. **Déjeme Vd.** *or* **Déjame (tú) mirar la foto.** Let me look at the photo.
   Le permití (a ella) jugar un rato. I permitted (allowed) her to play a while.
   Te dejaré dormir la siesta. I shall let you take a nap.

By exception to the rule which requires a clause in Spanish after certain verbs when there is a change in subject, the infinitive is generally used after **dejar** and **permitir**, particularly when a personal pronoun is the object of the main verb. **Permítame Vd.** or **Permíteme (tú)** may be used in the first example for *Let me.*

For emphasis, or especially when a noun is the object of the main verb and also the subject of the following verb, the subjunctive is used after these verbs:

Permítale Vd. (Permítele tú) a Juan que haga eso. Permit *or* Allow John to (Let John) do that.

2. **Mamá me mandó (hizo) esperar.** Mother ordered me to wait (made me wait).
   Les mandé volver en seguida. I ordered them to return at once.
   Llevé el vestido para mandarlo (hacerlo) limpiar. I took the dress to have it cleaned.

The infinitive is also regularly used after **hacer** and **mandar** when a personal pronoun is the object of the main verb.

Often the infinitive is translated by the passive voice, especially if its subject is a noun referring to a thing (third example).

E. The subjunctive in a polite or softened statement

> **Yo quiero jugar a las cartas.** I want to play cards.
> **Yo quisiera jugar a las cartas.** I should like to play cards.
> **Yo debo descansar un rato.** I must rest a while.
> **Yo debiera dejarte dormir la siesta.** I should (ought to) let you take a nap.

It is considered polite to soften requests by using the **-ra** imperfect subjunctive of forms of **querer.** The **-ra** forms of **deber,** and occasionally **poder,** are also used to form a polite or softened statement. In the case of other verbs, the conditional (as in English) is used: **Me gustaría ir con Vd.,** *I should like to go with you.* (See Lesson 16.)

F. Exclamations

1. **¡Qué!** *What a! How!*

   > **¡Qué noche tan (más) agradable!** What a pleasant evening!
   > **¡Qué guapo es!** How handsome he is!

Before nouns **¡qué!** means *what a!*; before adjectives it means *how!* When an adjective follows the noun, **tan** or **más** is regularly inserted before the adjective.

2. **¡Cuánto!** *How!*

   > **¡Cuánto siento no haber estado allí!** How I regret not having been there!

With verbs the adverb **¡cuánto!** means *how!* The adjective **¡cuánto, -a!** has its literal meaning: **¡Cuántos libros tienes!** *How many books you have!*

3. **¡Ojalá que!** *Would that! I wish that!*

   > **¡Ojalá que ella venga pronto!** Would that she come soon!
   > **¡Ojalá (que) él estuviera aquí!** Would that he were here!
   > **¡Ojalá que yo las hubiera visto!** I wish that I had seen them!

In exclamatory wishes **¡Ojalá!,** with or without **que,** is followed by the subjunctive. The present subjunctive is used in an exclamatory wish which refers to something which may happen in the future (first example). The imperfect subjunctive is used to express a wish concerning something that is contrary to fact (that is, not true) in the present (second example), and the pluperfect subjunctive to express a wish concerning something that was contrary to fact in the past (third example).

EJERCICIOS

A. Answer in Spanish:

> MODELS: ¿Quiere Vd. que yo *limpie* la casa?
>
> Sí, yo quiero que Vd. limpie la casa.
>
> ¿Quería Vd. que yo *limpiara* la casa?
>
> Sí, yo quería que Vd. limpiara la casa.

1. ¿Quiere Vd. que él *hable español?* (*lo aprenda bien, lo escriba*)

2. ¿Quería Vd. que él *hablara español?* (*lo aprendiera bien, lo escribiera*)

3. ¿Le pedirá Vd. que *se marche?* (*tenga cuidado, duerma la siesta*)

4. ¿Le pidió Vd. que *se marchara?* (*tuviera cuidado, durmiera la siesta*)

5. ¿Lo trae Vd. para que yo lo *vea?* (*lea, tenga*)

6. ¿Lo trajo Vd. para que yo lo *viera?* (*leyera, tuviera*)

7. ¿Buscas algo que *cueste menos?* (*sea más barato, te guste más*)

8. ¿Buscabas algo que *costara menos?* (*fuera más barato, te gustara más*)

Students may be asked to use the **-se** form of the imperfect subjunctive in the even-numbered sentences.

B. Say after your teacher; when you hear the cue, compose a new sentence using the **-ra** imperfect subjunctive form in the clause of sentences 1-6 and the **-se** form in sentences 7-12:

> MODEL: Yo temo que Ana no llegue.
>
> Yo temo que Ana no llegue.
>
> Yo temía
>
> Yo temía que Ana no llegara.

1. Juan quiere que yo recoja las cosas pronto.   (Juan quería)
2. Es probable que Clara saque la foto.   (Fue probable)
3. Ellos no creen que ella se sienta bien.   (Ellos no creían)
4. Yo tengo miedo de que Juanita se caiga.   (Yo tenía miedo de)
5. Pídale Vd. a Juan que se siente.   (Yo le pedí a Juan)
6. Yo insisto en que tú te pongas el sombrero.   (Yo insistiría en)
7. Ella dice que lo hará en cuanto volvamos.   (Ella dijo que lo haría)
8. Papá busca una maleta que sea ligera.   (Papá buscaba)
9. Luis lo trae para que Vds. lo lean.   (Luis lo trajo)

10. No hay nadie que sepa la verdad.   (No había nadie)
11. Le aconsejo a Clara que siga andando despacio.   (Le aconsejé)
12. Marta duda que Carlos haya oído decir eso.   (Marta dudaba)

C. Read in Spanish, supplying the correct form of the verb in parentheses; give both the **-ra** and **-se** forms when the imperfect subjunctive is required:

1. Mamá me pide que (tener) cuidado.   2. Mamá me pidió que no (hacerme) daño.
3. Isabel insiste en que Ricardo (volver) cuanto antes.   4. Ella insistió en que él (traer) a su amiga Margarita.   5. Será mejor que ellos no (marcharse) todavía.   6. Sería mejor que Juanita no (jugar) a las cartas ahora.   7. No hay nada que le (gustar) a Felipe.   8. No había nada que yo (poder) hacer.   9. Ana dice que volverá a vernos en cuanto (ser) posible.   10. Ella dijo que volvería en cuanto (tener) tiempo.   11. Me alegro de que Juan no se (haber) hecho daño.   12. Sentíamos que él se (haber) caído.

D. Say after your teacher; when you hear the cue, substitute it in the sentence:

1. *Quiero* ir al parque esta tarde.   (Quisiera)
2. *Yo quisiera* conocer a Roberto.   (Me gustaría)
3. *Debemos* volver a hablar con ella.   (Debiéramos)
4. *Yo debo* descansar un rato.   (Yo debiera)
5. *Mamá me hizo* limpiar el apartamento.   (Mamá me mandó)
6. *Su papá le mandó* lavar el coche.   (Su papá le hizo)
7. *Permítame Vd.* sacar una foto.   (Déjeme Vd.)
8. *Déjame* ayudarte un poco.   (Permíteme)
9. *¡Qué cortés* es!   (¡Qué simpático!)
10. *¡Cuánto me alegro de no* haber estado allí!   (¡Cuánto siento no!)
11. *¡Qué día* tan agradable!   (¡Qué noche!)
12. *¡Ojalá que* ella supiera la canción!   (¡Cuánto me alegré de que!)

E. Give in Spanish:

1. What do you think of Robert?   2. Be careful (*formal and familiar singular*).   3. Let me close the door (*formal and familiar singular*).   4. They were married last month.
5. Do you remember that?   6. He hurt himself yesterday.   7. How tired I am!
8. What a beautiful girl!   9. Mother had me write the letter.   10. I should like to see them again (*two ways*).

COMPOSICIÓN

1. I should like to take a walk, but first I should rest a while.   2. This morning Raymond asked me to take Jane to the dentist.   3. Also he had me take a suit to the cleaning shop in order that they might clean it.   4. Before returning home, I allowed Jane

to play with some friends of hers in the park.   5. Unfortunately, she fell down and hurt herself, and I had to take her home.   6. Do you remember Mary Smith? She and Robert Brown were married two weeks ago.   7. They have just returned from their honeymoon in Mexico.   8. We were playing cards at Caroline's last night when they knocked on the door.   9. How glad we were to see them! Would that you had been there too!   10. We insisted that Robert show us some photos that he had taken on the trip.   11. I am sorry that they have already left.   12. Yesterday Robert telephoned the manager of his company, and the latter asked him to return to the office as soon as possible.

VOCABULARIO

aconsejar (*requires indir. obj. of a person*) to advise, warn

acordarse (**ue**) (**de** + *obj.*) to remember, recall

el **animal** animal

el **apartamento** apartment

caer(**se**) (*like* **oír**) to fall, fall down

la **carta** card (*playing*)

casarse to marry, get married

Clara Clara

el **compromiso** engagement, commitment

cortés (*pl.* **corteses**) courteous

el **cuidado** care

el **daño** harm, damage

dejar to let, permit, allow

el **dentista** dentist

el **derecho** law

e and

el **esposo** husband

la **Facultad** School (*in a university*)

la **foto** (*for* **fotografía**) photo

limpiar to clean

la **luna de miel** honeymoon

marcharse to leave, go away

Margarita Margaret, Marguerite

¡ojalá (**que**)! would that! I wish that!

permitir to permit, allow, let

probable probable

Ramón Raymond

suponer (*like* **poner**) to suppose

la **tintorería** cleaning shop

la **transparencia** transparency, slide

casa de apartamentos apartment house

cuanto antes at once, immediately, as soon as possible

decir que (**sí**) to say (yes)

en fin in short

Facultad de Derecho Law School

hacerse daño to hurt oneself

jugar (**ue**) **a las cartas** to play cards

¿qué te (**le**) **parece** (**Roberto**)? what do you think of *or* how do you like (Robert)?

tener (**mucho**) **cuidado** (**de**) to be (very) careful (to)

volver (**ue**) **a** (**verla**) (to see her) again (*lit.*, to return to see her)

Monument to Cervantes with bronze sculptures representing Don Quixote and Sancho Panza, Madrid, Spain.

LECTURA XIII

MIGUEL DE CERVANTES

Estudio de palabras

a. Compare the meanings of: amor, *love,* amante, *lover,* enamorarse, *to fall in love, and* enamorado, *enamored;* bastante, *enough, and* bastar, *to be enough;* caballo, *horse,* caballero, *one who goes mounted, knight, and* caballerías, *chivalry;* cárcel, *prison, jail, and* encarcelamiento, *imprisonment;* escribir, *to write, and* escritor, *writer;* hablar, *to talk, speak, and* hablador, *talkative;* ideal, *ideal,* idealismo, *idealism, and* idealista, *idealist;* mano, *hand, and* manada, *handful, flock;* noble, *noble, and* nobleza, *nobility;* pensar, *to think, and* pensamiento, *thought;* persona, *person,* personaje, *personage, character* (in literature), *and* personalidad, *personality;* prometer, *to promise, and* promesa, *promise;* real, *real,* realista, *realistic, and* realidad, *reality;* regularidad, *regularity, and* irregularidad, *irregularity;* venta, *inn, and* ventero, *innkeeper.*

b. Deceptive cognates. Some words do not have the apparent meaning: **comedia** may mean *theater, play,* in addition to *comedy;* **éxito,** *success;* **fama** means *name, reputation,* in addition to *fame;* **natural** may mean *native,* as well as *natural;* **suceder,** *to happen.*

Miguel de Cervantes, el escritor más ilustre de España y uno de los más célebres de la literatura universal, nació en Alcalá de Henares en 1547, probablemente el 29 de septiembre, día de San Miguel. De su juventud se sabe muy poco—fuera de que[1] su familia vivía modestamente—, pero es evidente que adquirió un conocimiento notable de la vida española de aquellos días, como se ve claramente en sus obras literarias.

A la edad de veintidós años se hallaba Cervantes en Italia, donde más tarde se alistó como soldado en el ejército español. En 1571, a pesar de estar muy enfermo, tomó parte en la batalla de Lepanto,[2] en la cual se distinguió mucho. Recibió dos heridas en el pecho y otra en la mano izquierda, que se le quedó inútil el resto de su vida.

---

[1] **fuera de que,** *aside from the fact that.* [2] See end vocabulary.

Miguel de Cervantes Saavedra

Cuando volvía a España en 1575, fue hecho prisionero por unos piratas turcos, que le llevaron a Argel,[1] donde permaneció cautivo cinco años. Como llevaba cartas de recomendación de personas de alta posición, los turcos le tomaron por hombre de gran importancia, pero su familia no tenía bastante dinero para rescatarle.[2] Cinco veces trató de escaparse, pero fue en vano. Por fin, en 1580, fue rescatado y logró volver a su patria, donde esperaba encontrar una vida más próspera.

Habiéndose distinguido en las armas, ahora se dedicó a las letras. Compuso poesías, comedias y una novela pastoril, *La Galatea* (1585), pero no consiguió triunfar en ninguno de estos géneros. En 1587 obtuvo el cargo de comisario para proveer la Armada Invencible, pero no le pagaban con regularidad y en 1592, por irregularidades en sus cuentas, le condenaron a la cárcel por unos meses.

Se cree que en otro encarcelamiento empezó a escribir la primera parte del *Quijote*, que publicó en 1605. Aunque logró la novela un éxito tremendo, Cervantes ganó poco de su venta. Diez años después, en 1615, apareció la segunda parte de la célebre novela. En el mismo año Cervantes publicó sus *Ocho comedias y ocho entremeses*.[3] Las comedias son de poca importancia, pero los entremeses figuran entre los mejores que se han escrito en español. Dos años antes, en 1613, publicó sus *Novelas ejemplares*, que bastarían para, establecer la fama del autor. Su última obra, una novela de aventuras, fue *Los trabajos de Persiles y Sigismunda*. Murió Cervantes el día 23 de abril de 1616.

El ingenioso hidalgo don Quijote de la Mancha es una de las obras inmortales de la literatura universal. Un pobre hidalgo, Alonso Quijano el Bueno, se aficionó tanto a[4] la lectura de libros de caballerías que llegó a perder el juicio. Por fin decidió « ... así para el aumento de su honra, como para el servicio de su república,[5] hacerse caballero andante,[6] e irse por todo el mundo con sus armas y caballo a buscar aventuras y a ejercitarse en[7] todo aquello que él había leído que los caballeros se ejercitaban, deshaciendo todo género de agravio,[8] y poniéndose en ocasiones y peligros donde, acabándolos, cobrase eterno nombre y fama.»

Después de limpiar unas armas antiguas y de dar nombre a su caballo, decidió llamarse don Quijote de la Mancha, nombre que, según él, indicaba claramente su linaje y su patria. Luego se dio cuenta de[9] la necesidad de «buscar una dama de quien enamorarse, porque el caballero andante sin amores era árbol sin hojas y sin fruto, y cuerpo sin alma. En un lugar cerca del suyo había una moza labradora de muy buen parecer,[10] de quien él un tiempo anduvo enamorado,[11] aunque, según se entiende, ella jamás lo supo. Se llamaba Aldonza Lorenzo, y a ésta le pareció ser bien darle título[12] de señora de sus pensamientos, y... vino a llamarla Dulcinea del Toboso, porque era natural del Toboso...»

Hechas todas estas prevenciones,[13] salió

---

[1] **Argel,** *Algiers* (in North Africa).   [2] **rescatar,** *to ransom.*   [3] **entremés,** *a short farce.*   [4] **se aficionó tanto a,** *became so fond of.*   [5] **república,** *country.*   [6] **caballero andante,** *knight errant.*   [7] **ejercitarse en,** *to practice.*   [8] **deshaciendo...agravio,** *righting every type of wrong.*   [9] **se dio cuenta de,** *he realized.*   [10] **moza... parecer,** *very good-looking, young farm girl.*   [11] **de quien...enamorado,** *with whom he was in love once upon a time.*   [12] **a ésta...título,** *he thought it proper to confer upon her the title.*   [13] **Hechas... prevenciones,** *Having made all these preparations.*

Battle of Lepanto.

don Quijote una mañana, sin que nadie le viese, en busca de aventuras. Al anochecer llegó a una venta[1] que tomó por castillo, y aquella misma noche el ventero le armó caballero.[2] Volvió a su pueblo, donde «solicitó a un labrador vecino suyo… Tanto le dijo, tanto le persuadió y prometió, que el pobre villano[3] determinó salirse con él y servirle de escudero. Le decía entre otras cosas don Quijote que se dispusiese a ir con él de buena gana,[4] porque tal vez le podía suceder[5] aventura en que ganase alguna ínsula[6] y le dejase a él gobernador de ella. Con estas promesas y otras tales, Sancho Panza, que así se llamaba el labrador, dejó su mujer e hijos y asentó por[7] escudero de su vecino.»

En la larga serie de aventuras de la novela Cervantes representa el eterno conflicto entre el espíritu ideal e imaginativo del amo y el sentido realista y práctico del escudero. Aunque la locura de don Quijote mueve a risa en muchas ocasiones, no le supera nadie en cortesía, dignidad, humildad, nobleza y generosidad. En cambio, su fiel compañero Sancho Panza es un aldeano[8] crédulo, tímido, hablador, socarrón,[9] algo glotón,[10] y, además, una figura muy graciosa.[11] ·En vano Sancho trata de hacerle a su amo volver a la realidad; en vano trata de convencerle que no son gigantes los molinos de viento,[12] que no son ejércitos las manadas de carneros,[13] etcétera. A medida que[14] progresa la acción de la novela, especialmente en la segunda parte, las personalidades de caballero y de escudero se desarrollan hasta tal punto que el pobre escudero acaba por creer en la existencia real de los caballeros andantes. Cuando muere su amo, ya en su cabal juicio,[15] a Sancho ya no le parece locura la vida de los caballeros andantes con todos sus nobles ideales.

En esta obra maestra pasa ante nuestros ojos todo el rico panorama del siglo XVII en España. Ninguna obra literaria es más nacional y a la vez más universal, porque su fondo es la humanidad de todos los tiempos y de todos los países del mundo. *El Quijote*, síntesis de todos los géneros de ficción del Siglo de Oro, se ha llamado, y con razón, la novela más célebre del mundo.

---

[1] **venta,** *inn.* [2] **el ventero le armó caballero,** *the innkeeper dubbed him knight.* [3] **villano,** *peasant, villager.* [4] **se dispusiese…gana,** *he should make up his mind to go with him willingly.* [5] **suceder,** *to happen.* [6] **ínsula,** *island.* [7] **asentó por,** *took service as.* [8] **aldeano,** *villager.* [9] **socarrón,** *crafty.* [10] **algo glotón,** *something of a glutton.* [11] **graciosa,** *witty, amusing.* [12] **que no … viento,** *that the windmills are not giants.* [13] **manadas de carneros,** *flocks of sheep.* [14] **A medida que,** *As.* [15] **cabal juicio,** *right mind.*

Roman bridge, Córdoba, Spain.

Puerta de Bisagra, Toledo, Spain.

Torre de la Calahorra, Córdoba, Spain.

PREGUNTAS

1. ¿En qué año nació Cervantes? 2. ¿Se sabe mucho de su juventud? 3. ¿Dónde se hallaba a la edad de veintidós años? 4. ¿En qué batalla tomó parte? 5. ¿Cuántas heridas recibió?

6. ¿Qué le pasó cuando volvía a España? 7. ¿Adónde le llevaron los piratas? 8. ¿Cuántos años quedó cautivo? 9. ¿Cuántas veces trató de escaparse? 10. ¿Cuándo volvió a España?

11. ¿Qué clase de obras compuso Cervantes primero? 12. ¿Triunfó en estos géneros? 13. ¿Qué cargo obtuvo en 1587?

14. ¿Cuándo publicó la primera parte del *Quijote*? 15. ¿Ganó mucho en la venta de la novela? 16. ¿Cuándo apareció la segunda parte? 17. ¿Qué interés tienen sus entremeses? 18. ¿Qué otras obras publicó? 19. ¿Cuándo murió Cervantes?

20. ¿Cómo llegó a perder el juicio don Quijote? 21. ¿Qué decidió hacer? 22. ¿Por qué decidió buscar una dama de quien enamorarse? 23. ¿Qué hizo don Quijote una mañana? 24. ¿Quién le armó caballero? 25. ¿Qué le prometió don Quijote a Sancho Panza?

26. ¿Qué representa Cervantes en la larga serie de aventuras de don Quijote? 27. ¿Cuáles son algunos de los ideales que representa don Quijote? 28. ¿Qué clase de persona es Sancho Panza? 29. ¿En qué acciones de Sancho podemos ver su sentido realista y práctico? 30. ¿En qué llega a creer Sancho a medida que progresa la acción de la novela?

31. ¿Qué interés social tiene la novela? 32. ¿Por qué puede decirse que ninguna obra literaria es más universal que esta novela? 33. ¿Qué más se ha dicho de esta novela?

Ancient University of Alcalá de Henares, near Madrid.

Possessive pronouns. The definite article used as a demonstrative
The passive voice. *Cuyo* **and** *¿de quién?*
The neuter *lo.* **Forms of verbs in** *-uir*

BUSCANDO UN APARTAMENTO

Dos estudiantes, Carlos Guzmán y Juan Martínez, están buscando un apartamento que sea más cómodo que el que ocupan ahora. Se encuentran frente a una casa de apartamentos que ha sido recomendada por un profesor suyo.

● ● ● ● ●

CARLOS. Ésta parece ser la casa de apartamentos que recomienda el profesor Gómez. La calle es ancha y bonita y no hay mucho tránsito.

JUAN. ¿Sabes de quién es?

CARLOS. Pronto lo sabremos. (*Tocan el timbre y abre la puerta un señor.*)

JUAN. Buenos días. Nos ha dicho un amigo nuestro, el profesor Gómez, que Vd. alquila apartamentos. Vd. es el dueño, ¿verdad?

SR. BROWN. Sí, señor, lo soy. Pasen Vds. Me llamo José Brown, a sus órdenes.

JUAN. Mucho gusto en conocerle, Sr. Brown. Yo me llamo Juan Martínez. Quiero presentarle mi compañero, Carlos Guzmán. ¿Tiene Vd. algún apartamento vacante?

SR. BROWN. Sí, señor. Acaban de marcharse dos estudiantes que lo ocupaban.

CARLOS. ¿Cuántas habitaciones tiene?

SR. BROWN. Tiene cuatro, sin contar el cuarto de baño: la sala, con espacio para poner una mesa de comer, la cocina y dos alcobas. Está en el piso bajo. Permítanme Vds. enseñárselo. (*Examinan con cuidado el apartamento de los Sres. Brown.*)

Juan. El apartamento parece nuevo, Sr. Brown. ¿Cuándo se construyó el edificio?

Sr. Brown. Hace cinco años. Fue construido por un buen amigo mío. El que está allí enfrente, cuyo tejado es de tejas, es mío también, pero todos los apartamentos están ocupados.

Juan. Veo que hay familias con niños en el edificio.

Sr. Brown. Solamente la mía. De las tres niñas que están jugando en el jardín, dos son hijas nuestras. Son las que tienen el pelo castaño; la del pelo rubio es una amiguita suya.

Carlos. A mí me gusta el apartamento. Los muebles son mejores que en el nuestro — es decir, el que estamos alquilando.

Juan. Y éste tiene un jardín bonito y una piscina, donde podremos bañarnos.

Carlos. Lo malo es que probablemente será muy caro.

Sr. Brown. Como vienen recomendados por el Sr. Gómez, puedo alquilárselo por ciento treinta dólares al mes.

Carlos. Agradecemos mucho su amabilidad. Supongo que nos permitirá Vd. esperar hasta mañana para llegar a una decisión.

Sr. Brown. ¡Por supuesto! Pero si deciden Vds. tomar el apartamento no dejen de avisarme lo más pronto posible.

CONVERSACIÓN

A. Preguntas sobre el diálogo

1. ¿Qué están buscando los dos estudiantes? 2. ¿Quién ha recomendado la casa de apartamentos que están visitando? 3. ¿Cómo se llama el dueño del edificio? 4. ¿Cuántas habitaciones tiene el apartamento? 5. ¿Cuándo se construyó el edificio? 6. ¿Cuántas hijas tienen los Sres. Brown? 7. ¿Por qué le interesa a Juan el apartamento? 8. ¿Por cuánto puede alquilarles el apartamento el Sr. Brown?

B. Aplicación del diálogo

1. ¿Cuáles son las habitaciones de una casa? 2. ¿Se ven muchos tejados de tejas en esta parte del país? 3. ¿Viven los padres de Vd. en una casa o en un apartamento? 4. ¿Cuántas alcobas tiene la casa en que Vd. vive? 5. ¿Cuáles tienen más espacio, las casas modernas o las antiguas? 6. ¿Les gustan a los estudiantes los apartamentos con mucho espacio? 7. ¿Tiene Vd. el pelo rubio, castaño o negro? 8. ¿Conoce Vd. a alguien que tenga el pelo rubio?

NOTAS GRAMATICALES

A. Possessive pronouns

el mío	la mía	los míos	las mías	mine
el tuyo	la tuya	los tuyos	las tuyas	yours (*fam.*)
el nuestro	la nuestra	los nuestros	las nuestras	ours
el vuestro	la vuestra	los vuestros	las vuestras	yours (*fam.*)
el suyo	la suya	los suyos	las suyas	his, hers, its, yours (*formal*), theirs

1. **mi coche, nuestro coche; el mío, el nuestro**   my car, our car; mine, ours
   nuestra casa, mi casa; la nuestra, la mía   our house, my house; ours, mine
   sus flores; las suyas   his (her, your, their) flowers; his (hers, yours, theirs)

   ¿Tiene Vd. el suyo?   Do you have yours?
   Alquilaron la suya.   They rented theirs.
   Este jardín es nuestro.   This garden is ours.
   El coche es de Juan (suyo).   The car is John's (his).

The possessive pronouns are formed by using the definite article **el** (**la, los, las**) with the long forms of the possessive adjectives (Lesson 17). After **ser** the article is usually omitted (last two examples).

2. **mi madre y la de ella**   my mother and hers
   nuestros padres y los de él   our parents and his
   el coche de ellos y el de Vd.   their car and yours

Since **el suyo** (**la suya, los suyos, las suyas**) may mean *his, hers, its, yours* (formal), *theirs*, these pronouns may be clarified by substituting **el de él, el de ella, el de Vd(s).,** **el de ellos (ellas)**.   The article agrees with the thing possessed.

B. The definite article used as a demonstrative

1. **mi habitación y la de Juan**   my room and that of John (John's)
   este apartamento y el del Sr. Gómez   this apartment and that of Mr. Gómez
   la del sombrero rojo   the one in (with) the red hat
   las del pelo rubio   the ones with the blond hair

Before a phrase beginning with **de**, Spanish uses the definite article (which originated from the Latin demonstrative), instead of the demonstrative pronoun. **El** (**la, los, las**) **de** is translated *that (those) of, the one(s) of (with, in)*, and occasionally by an English possessive (first example).

2. **La que está allí es mía también.**   The one which is there is mine also.
   Son las que tienen el pelo castaño.   They are the ones who have dark hair.
   El que salió es un amigo suyo.   The one who left is a friend of his.

Spanish also regularly uses the definite article before a relative clause introduced by **que,** instead of the demonstrative pronoun.   **El (la, los, las) que** is translated *he who, the one(s) who (that, which), those who (which).*   These forms, which may refer to persons or things, are often called compound relatives because the article serves as the antecedent of the **que-**clause.   (Do not use **el cual** in this construction.)

   Quien (*pl.* **quienes**), which refers to persons only, sometimes means *he (those) who, the one(s) who,* particularly in proverbs:

        Quien busca, halla.   He (The one) who seeks, finds.
        Son quienes lo hicieron.   They are the ones who did it.

Lo que is the neuter form of **el que** and means *what, that which*:

   Lo que dicen es verdad.   What they say is true.
   Agradezco mucho lo que ha hecho Vd.   I am very grateful for what you
      have done.

C. The passive voice

   La casa fue construida por un amigo mío.   The house was built by a friend
      of mine.
   Las puertas fueron cerradas por Juan.   The doors were closed by John.
   La casa ha sido recomendada por una amiga suya.   The house has been
      recommended by a friend of theirs.
   Las niñas fueron vistas en la calle.   The (little) girls were seen in the street.

When an action is performed by an agent, Spanish uses **ser** and the past participle. The past participle agrees with the subject in gender and number, and the agent is usually expressed by **por.**   (In the third example note that **sido** completes the compound tense with **haber** and is invariable, whereas **recomendada** agrees with the subject.)

Remember that when the agent is not expressed, and the subject is a thing, the reflexive substitute for the passive is regularly used (Lesson 7): **Aquí se habla español,** *Spanish is spoken here.*

If the subject is a person (fourth example), **ser** and the past participle are normally used even though no agent is expressed.   **Las niñas se vieron** would mean *The girls saw themselves.*   In actual practice this use of the passive is often avoided by changing the sentence to active voice: **Vieron a las niñas,** *They saw the girls.*

Do not confuse the true passive, which expresses action, with the use of **estar** plus a past participle to express the state which results from the action of a verb (see Lesson 15):

La casa está bien construida.   The house is well built.
Esta carta está escrita en español.   This letter is written in Spanish.

D. **Cuyo** and **¿de quién?**

La casa, cuyo tejado es de tejas, es mía.   The house, whose roof (the roof of which) is of tiles, is mine.
¿De quién(es) es la casa?   Whose house is it?
¿Sabes de quién es?   Do you know whose it is?

The relative adjective **cuyo, -a, -os, -as,** *whose, of whom, of which,* agrees in gender and number with the object possessed and refers to persons as well as things.
   ¿De quién(es)? expresses *whose?* in a question.   Note that the second example means literally *Of whom is the house?*

E. The neuter **lo**

1. **Él prefiere lo bueno a lo malo.**   He prefers the good (what is good) to the bad.
    Lo malo es que probablemente será muy cara.   What is bad (The bad thing) is that it will probably be too expensive.

The neuter article **lo** is used with masculine singular adjectives to form an expression almost equivalent to an abstract noun.   The word *thing* or *part* is often a part of the translation.
   Recall that the neuter article **lo** is also used with an adverb when an expression of possibility is used (Lesson 17): **No dejen de avisarme lo más pronto posible,** *Don't fail to inform me the soonest (as soon as) possible.*

2. **¿Es Vd. el dueño?** — **Lo soy.**   Are you the owner? — I am.

The neuter pronoun **lo** is used with **ser** and a few other verbs to represent a previously expressed idea.   In the example, **lo** stands for **el dueño.**

F. Forms of verbs in **-uir: construir,** *to construct*

PRES. PART.	**construyendo**
PRES. IND.	**construyo, construyes, construye,** construimos, construís, **construyen**
PRES. SUBJ.	**construya, construyas, construya, construyamos, construyáis, construyan**
PRETERIT	construí, construiste, **construyó,** construimos, construisteis, **construyeron**
IMP. SUBJ.	**construyera,** etc. **construyese,** etc.
SING. IMPER.	**construye**

Verbs ending in **-uir** insert **y** except before the endings beginning with **i,** and change unaccented **i** between vowels to **y.**

EJERCICIOS

A. Substitution drill:

1. *Mi padre* no construye casas.
   (*Yo, Tú, Vds., Nosotros, El Sr. López*)
2. *Carlos* sigue buscando apartamento.
   (*Yo, Ella y yo, Tú, Mi tío, Los Sres. Gómez*)
3. *Ella* agradece lo que ha hecho Luis.
   (*Yo, Nosotros, Los jóvenes, Tú, Vds.*)
4. *Marta* tiene el pelo rubio.
   (*Las niñas, Tú, Yo, Ella y yo, Vds.*)

B. Say the sentence or question after your teacher, then repeat it, using a possessive pronoun:

MODELS: Yo tengo el libro de Ana.   Yo tengo el libro de Ana.   Yo tengo el suyo.
       ¿Tiene Vd. su libro?   ¿Tiene Vd. su libro?   ¿Tiene Vd. el suyo?

1. Juan tiene su equipaje.
2. José lleva sus maletas.
3. ¿Tiene María su billete?
4. ¿Tienen ellos sus billetes?
5. Vamos a nuestra casa.
6. ¿Vas tú a tu escuela?
7. Traigo los vestidos de Ana.
8. No dejes allí tus zapatos.
9. Nuestros amigos están de vuelta.
10. Nuestras flores son hermosísimas.
11. Quítese Vd. el sombrero.
12. ¿Quiere ella mis discos?

C. Listen to the question, then answer affirmatively, using the correct possessive pronoun:

MODELS: ¿Es suyo este reloj?   Sí, es mío.
       ¿Es de Juan este reloj?   Sí, es suyo.

1. ¿Es suya esta camisa?
2. ¿Son suyos estos calcetines?
3. ¿Son de María estas medias?
4. ¿Es de ella esta blusa?
5. ¿Son de ella estos zapatos?
6. ¿Es tuya esta corbata?
7. ¿Son tuyos estos discos?
8. ¿Es mío ese paquete?
9. ¿Son míos esos billetes?
10. ¿Es nuestro ese equipaje?

D. Listen to the sentence, then repeat, following the models:

> MODELS: Quiero ese libro y el libro de Ana.   Quiero ese libro y el de Ana.
> Esa foto y las fotos que tengo son   Esa foto y las que tengo son
> bonitas.   bonitas.

1. Me gustan este jardín y el jardín de su mamá.
2. Esta alcoba y la alcoba de Marta son grandes.
3. Aquella niña y la niña del pelo rubio son primas mías.
4. Este joven y el joven que se acerca son estudiantes.
5. Este disco y los discos que compraste ayer son buenos.
6. ¿Te gustan estas flores y las flores que ella tiene?
7. Aquel coche y el coche que pasa por la calle son nuevos.
8. Esta casa y la casa del Sr. López son muy cómodas.

E. Say after your teacher, then repeat, using the reflexive substitute for the passive (see Lesson 7):

> MODELS: Allí hablan español.   Allí hablan español.   Allí se habla español.
> Aquí venden zapatos.   Aquí venden zapatos.   Aquí se venden zapatos.

1. Cierran la puerta a las cinco.
2. Abren las tiendas a las diez.
3. ¿Cómo dicen eso en español?
4. No venden libros en la biblioteca.
5. Exhiben muchas cosas en el escaparate.
6. En México oímos mucha música popular.
7. Aquí construyen muchas casas nuevas.
8. ¿Dónde limpian los trajes?

F. Say after your teacher, then repeat, using the passive voice. Watch the agreement of the verb and the past participle:

> MODEL: Él cerró la puerta.   Él cerró la puerta.   La puerta fue cerrada por él.

1. Ricardo abrió las ventanas.
2. María escribió la tarjeta
3. La madre de Marta hizo el vestido.
4. Mi hermano trajo los discos.
5. Tomás sacó todas las fotos.
6. Ella puso las flores sobre la mesa.
7. Elena no vio a las niñas.
8. Mi padre no construyó esta casa.

G. Repeat the sentence; when you hear the cue, compose a new sentence using the **-ra** imperfect subjunctive form in the clause:

> MODEL: Él quiere una casa que tenga patio.   Él quiere una casa que tenga patio.
> Él quería una casa   Él quería una casa que tuviera patio.

1. Ellos buscan una casa que sea más grande. (Ellos buscaban una casa)
2. Quieren mucho espacio para que jueguen las niñas. (Querían mucho espacio)

3. Prefieren una casa que tenga dos pisos.   (Preferían una casa)

4. Yo les recomiendo que alquilen la del Sr. López.   (Yo les recomendé)

5. Yo temo que no encuentren otra más cómoda.   (Yo temía)

6. Les pediré que vayan a verla lo más pronto posible   (Yo les pedí)

7. Me prometen irse en cuanto vuelva el Sr. López.   (Me prometieron irse)

8. Será mejor que la examinen con cuidado.   (Sería mejor)

H. Give in Spanish:

1. He closed the door.   2. The door was closed at five o'clock.   3. The door was closed by the teacher.   4. The door is closed at this moment.   5. Whose flowers are these?   6. Are they hers?   7. They are prettier than mine.   8. This (little) girl and the one with the blond hair are sisters of his.   9. Jane has dark hair, doesn't she?   10. Is Mr. Gómez a dentist?   — Yes, he is.   11. The best thing is to be careful.   12. Don't fail (*fam. sing.*) to call me.

I. Learn the following proverbs:

1. Poco a poco se va lejos.

2. Quien mal (*evil*) dice, peor oye.

3. Lo que mucho vale, mucho cuesta.

4. Lo que no se empieza, no se termina.

5. Más vale tarde que nunca.

6. Más vale algo que nada.

7. Quien mucho duerme, poco aprende.

8. Mañana será otro día.

9. Nunca lo bueno fue mucho.

10. La mejor salsa (*sauce*) es el hambre.

COMPOSICIÓN

1. Charles and John want to find an apartment that is larger than the one (that) they are occupying.   2. They go to see an apartment house which was recommended by Professor Gómez, a friend of theirs.   3. They approach the building, and, after they ring the doorbell, a gentleman opens the door.   4. When John asks him whether he is the owner, the latter replies that he is and that his name is Joseph Brown.   5. The apartment has four rooms without counting the bathroom: a (**la**) living room with space (in order) to eat, a (**la**) kitchen, and two bedrooms.   6. The building has four floors, but the apartment is on the first floor.   7. Mr. Brown said that the apartment house was built three years ago.   8. It was built by a good friend of his, who has been building houses for many years.   9. Mr. Brown says that the one that is opposite is his also, but all the apartments are occupied.   10. The two young men like the apartment house very much because it has a garden and a swimming pool where they can take a swim.   11. Also, it seems to them that there is little traffic on the street even though it is very wide.   12. When the owner says that he can rent it to them for one hundred thirty dollars a month, they decide to take it.

VOCABULARIO

agradecer (*like* **conocer**) to be grateful (thank) for
la alcoba bedroom
alquilar to rent
la amabilidad kindness
la amiguita little (girl) friend
ancho, -a broad, wide
avisar to advise, inform
bajo, -a low, lower
bañarse to take a swim (dip)
castaño, -a dark, brown, brunet(te)
la cocina kitchen
construir to construct, build
contar (**ue**) to count
el cuarto de baño bathroom
cuyo, -a whose
la decisión (*pl.* **decisiones**) decision
el dueño owner
enfrente *adv.* in front, opposite

el espacio space, room
examinar to examine
la habitación (*pl.* **habitaciones**) room
la mesa de comer dining table
los muebles furniture
el jardín (*pl.* **jardines**) garden
la niña little girl
el niño little boy, child; *pl.* children
ocupar to occupy
el pelo hair
el piso floor, story
probablemente probably
rubio, -a fair, blond(e)
Sres. = señores Mr. and Mrs.
la teja tile
el tejado roof (*of tiles*)
el tránsito traffic
vacante vacant, empty

con cuidado carefully
es decir that is (to say)
llegar a una decisión to reach (make) a decision
no dejar de + *inf.* not to fail to + *verb*
piso bajo first floor
por ... al mes for ... a month
tener el pelo (**castaño**) to have (dark) hair

Performance of Don Juan Tenorio by Zorrilla. Stage design and costumes by Salvador Dalí, Madrid, Spain.

Performance of *Man from la Mancha*.

LECTURA XIV
LA LITERATURA ESPAÑOLA MODERNA

Estudio de palabras

a. Less approximate cognates. Pronounce the following words aloud, note the English cognates, and describe the variations: andaluz, *Andalusian*; consecuencia, *consequence*; contemporáneo, *contemporary*; desilusión, *disillusion*; espontáneo, *spontaneous*; extenso, *extensive*; filólogo, *philologist*; genio, *genius*; interrumpir, *to interrupt*; maestría, *mastery, skill*; melancolía, *melancholy*; modificado, *modified*; reaccionar, *to react*; ruta, *route, direction*; sutil, *subtle*; técnico, *technical*.

b. Compare the meanings of: carácter, *character*, característica, *characteristic, trait*, and caracterizar, *to characterize*; conocer, *to know*, and conocimiento, *knowledge*; día, *day*, and diario, *daily*; dominio, *domination*, dominar, *to dominate*, and predominar, *to predominate*; ensayo, *essay*, and ensayista, *essayist*; libre, *free*, libertad, *liberty, freedom*, and liberal, *liberal*; país, *country*, and paisaje, *countryside, landscape*; pensar, *to think*, and pensador, *thinker*; perder, *to lose*, and pérdida, *loss*; presentar, *to present*, and presentación, *presentation, introduction*; producir, *to produce*, and producción, *production*; sentir, *to feel*, and sentimiento, *sentiment, feeling*; tipo, *type*, and típico, *typical*; vivir, *to live*, and vivo, *live, living*.

c. Deceptive cognates. **Actual** means *present, present-day*. **Diverso**, as in the case of English *diverse*, means both *different* and *varied*.

Durante el siglo XVII España comenzó a perder su poderío político y militar. A la decadencia política la siguió la cultural, y en el siglo siguiente se produjeron[1] pocas obras de valor literario. Solamente en el último tercio del siglo XVIII, con escritores como Gaspar Melchor de Jovellanos y Juan Meléndez Valdés, empezaron a renacer las actividades literarias, si bien[2] fueron interrumpidas otra vez por las guerras contra Napoleón y las represiones de Fernando VII.

Con el fin del reinado de Fernando VII en 1833 y la vuelta a España de los liberales que habían sido desterrados[3] o que se habían refugiado en tierras extranjeras, brotó[4] el romanticismo, especialmente en la poesía y en el drama. Por lo general, este movimiento en España se caracteriza por su índole[5] nacional; los escritores empezaron de nuevo a buscar inspiración en la historia nacional, en el paisaje, en el cristianismo y en la completa libertad artística. Para ellos el arte era individualista y les proporcionaba[6] oportunidad para la libre expresión de sus sentimientos y de su emoción personal.

Entre los escritores del período romántico en España se destacan José de Espronceda, poeta lírico, el Duque de Rivas y José Zorrilla, poetas también y autores de leyendas y dramas históricos basados en la historia nacional. El último de los grandes poetas románticos fue Gustavo Adolfo Béc-

---

[1] **se produjeron,** *were produced.* [2] **si bien,** *although.* [3] **desterrados,** *exiled.* [4] **brotó,** *burst forth.* [5] **índole,** *character, nature.* [6] **proporcionaba,** *it offered.*

Jacinto Benavente

Miguel de Unamuno

quer, autor también de cuentos y leyendas en prosa. Sus famosas *Rimas* expresan su desilusión, su melancolía y su pesimismo, características de la obra romántica en general. Ejemplos de sus *Rimas* son:

Los suspiros son aire y van al aire.
Las lágrimas son agua y van al mar.
Dime, mujer: cuando el amor se olvida,
      ¿Sabes tú adónde va?

* * * * *

Hoy la tierra y los cielos me sonríen;[1]
Hoy llega al fondo de mi alma el sol;
Hoy la he visto...la he visto y me ha
   mirado...
      ¡Hoy creo en Dios!

¿Qué es poesía? dices mientras clavas [2]
En mi pupila tu pupila azul;
¿Qué es poesía? ¿Y tú me lo preguntas?
      Poesía...eres tú.

En el mismo período había escritores que comenzaron a cultivar el artículo de costumbres,[3] en que presentaban cuadros y tipos realistas de la vida diaria, y en que a la vez señalaban los defectos de los españoles de la época. Los costumbristas prepararon el terreno para la novela realista, que surgió en el último tercio del siglo XIX. Entre los muchos novelistas ocupa el primer lugar Benito Pérez Galdós (1843–1920), el

---

[1] **me sonríen,** *smile at (upon) me.*   [2] **clavas,** *you fix.*   [3] **artículo de costumbres,** *article of customs and manners.*

José Ortega y Gasset

Juan Ramón Jiménez

maestro de la novela española moderna. No fue un novelista regional, como Alarcón, Pereda, Palacio Valdés, Blasco Ibáñez y otros escritores de la época, sino el novelista de toda España. Presenta en su extensa obra todas las regiones y todos los tipos—en fin, toda la historia española del siglo XIX. Ningún otro novelista español, con la excepción de Cervantes, le supera en el genio creador y en el conocimiento de la vida y del carácter humano. Es el novelista más nacional y al mismo tiempo el más universal de la España moderna. En algunas de sus mejores novelas, como *Doña Perfecta* y *Gloria*, se presenta el conflicto entre lo antiguo y lo moderno, entre el

fanatismo y la tolerancia, y casi siempre el protagonista trata de elevarse sobre el medio social en que vive. Pérez Galdós luchó siempre por la verdad, la justicia, la libertad y el progreso.

El año de 1898 tuvo grandes consecuencias en España, primero en la historia política y después en la vida intelectual. Con la pérdida de Cuba, de Puerto Rico y de las Islas Filipinas en la guerra con los Estados Unidos, un grupo de escritores jóvenes, que se ha llamado «la generación del 98», comenzó a protestar contra el tradicionalismo, los defectos del gobierno español y la falta de ideas progresivas en el país. En su clamor por un nuevo espíritu nacional, ensayistas,[1] novelistas, dramaturgos y poetas produjeron un notable renacimiento de las letras españolas que llegó a su apogeo en los primeros años del siglo veinte.

Algunas de las personalidades más importantes de este grupo fueron el gran pensador Miguel de Unamuno, que ha dejado una larga serie de ensayos, de novelas y de poesías, Azorín, ensayista y fino crítico literario, y Ortega y Gasset, filósofo y ensayista.

Otro movimiento literario que influyó mucho en la España de los primeros años del siglo actual[2] fue el modernismo, contribución del Nuevo Mundo a la madre patria. El nicaragüense Rubén Darío fue el maestro reconocido de este movimiento, que realizó muchas innovaciones de metro, de forma, de lenguaje y de ideas. Enorme ha sido la influencia de Darío y de otros poetas hispanoamericanos sobre la poesía española del siglo XX. Con el tiempo los poetas españoles, como Juan Ramón Jiménez, que en 1956 recibió el premio Nobel de literatura, y Antonio Machado, reaccionaron contra el modernismo para buscar rutas más personales en su producción artística.

El dramaturgo más eminente del teatro contemporáneo es Jacinto Benavente, otro escritor español que recibió el premio Nobel de literatura (1923). Aunque su teatro es muy diverso, sus mejores comedias se caracterizan por la ironía sutil, por la fina sátira, por la maestría en la estructura técnica y por la presentación exacta y artística de la sociedad contemporánea, con todos sus defectos e injusticias.

Las obras dramáticas más espontáneas del siglo actual son los sainetes[3] y las comedias de los hermanos Álvarez Quintero, que han dejado en sus producciones cuadros vivos de la vida andaluza, llenos de gracia, de emoción y de optimismo. Otro dramaturgo del siglo XX es Gregorio Martínez Sierra, autor de una larga serie de comedias en que interpreta de una manera optimista e idealista el carácter español, especialmente el alma femenina.

No se ha cultivado la novela tanto como el ensayo, la poesía y el teatro en el siglo XX. En la primera parte del siglo el vasco Pío Baroja fue uno de los novelistas más populares. Continúa en él el realismo de los novelistas anteriores, pero modificado por el fondo lírico y personal de su sensibilidad. Subjetivo, apasionado e impresionista, es un escritor típico de «la generación del 98.»

Entre los novelistas que comenzaron a escribir después de la guerra civil española de 1936–1939 se ha distinguido especialmente don Camilo José Cela. La producción novelística de Cela muestra muchos rasgos de la novela europea contemporánea. Uno de sus rasgos principales es la nota personal; otros son la presencia de preocupaciones morales y sociales y su dominio del lenguaje.

Otras grandes figuras de la literatura española del siglo XX son el poeta y dramaturgo Federico García Lorca, autor del *Romancero gitano*,[4] y de tres tragedias rurales bien conocidas en nuestro país, *Bodas de sangre*,[5] *Yerma* y *La casa de Bernarda Alba*, y los dramaturgos Alejandro Casona y Antonio Buero Vallejo.

---

[1] **ensayistas,** *essayists.*   [2] **actual,** *present.*   [3] **sainete,** *one-act farce.*   [4] **Romancero gitano,** *Gypsy Ballad Book.*
[5] **Bodas de sangre,** *Blood Wedding.*

El filólogo más eminente de la España contemporánea ha sido don Ramón Menéndez Pidal, autor, entre otros muchos estudios, de *Orígenes del español*, y *La España del Cid*.

En estos últimos años, especialmente desde la guerra civil española, un gran número de escritores y eruditos se han trasladado a las Américas. Algunos, como los poetas Jorge Guillén y Pedro Salinas y los eruditos Américo Castro y Tomás Navarro Tomás, han trabajado como profesores en este país. Otros, como el dramaturgo Alejandro Casona y el poeta Juan Ramón Jiménez, se dedicaron a sus labores en varios países hispanoamericanos, pero todos han continuado cultivando las letras para la mayor gloria de la cultura hispana.

PREGUNTAS

1. ¿Cuándo empezó España a perder su poderío político y militar? 2. ¿Qué puede decirse de la literatura en el siglo XVIII? 3. ¿Cuándo brotó el romanticismo? 4. ¿En qué géneros se vio especialmente? 5. ¿Dónde empezaron a buscar inspiración los escritores? 6. ¿Cuáles son los nombres de tres escritores románticos? 7. ¿Qué escribió Bécquer? 8. ¿Qué expresan sus *Rimas*?

9. ¿Qué comenzaron a cultivar otros escritores del mismo período? 10. ¿Qué presentaban en los artículos de costumbres? 11. ¿Quién fue el maestro de la novela moderna? 12. ¿Cuáles son los nombres de algunos novelistas regionales? 13. ¿Qué presentó Pérez Galdós en su obra? 14. ¿Qué conflictos se presentan en algunas de sus novelas? 15. ¿Qué ideales defendió siempre?

16. ¿Qué perdió España en 1898? 17. ¿Qué nombre se ha dado al grupo de escritores jóvenes de este período? 18. ¿Contra qué comenzaron a protestar? 19. ¿Quiénes son algunos escritores de este grupo? 20. ¿Quién fue el maestro del modernismo?

21. ¿Quién es el autor más eminente del teatro contemporáneo español? 22. ¿Qué escribieron los hermanos Álvarez Quintero? 23. ¿Quién es otro dramaturgo contemporáneo? 24. ¿Quién es Pío Baroja? 25. ¿Qué rasgos muestra Camilo José Cela en su producción novelística? 26. ¿Quiénes son otras grandes figuras de la literatura española del siglo XX? 27. ¿Cuáles son algunas de las obras de García Lorca? 28. ¿Cuáles son algunas obras de Menéndez Pidal? 29. ¿Dónde han vivido muchos escritores y eruditos en los últimos años? 30. ¿Qué han continuado cultivando?

Rubén Darío

LECCIÓN 24

Familiar commands. *Si*-**clauses.** **Special use of plural reflexive pronouns.** **Forms of** *enviar* **and** *continuar* **Summary of uses of** *para.* **Summary of uses of** *por*

«*LOS QUE TIENEN BUENOS AMIGOS SON RICOS.*»

Ricardo Smith vive en un apartamento con dos compañeros, Miguel Cruz y Luis Hernández. Suena el despertador en el cuarto que ocupan Miguel y Ricardo. Como éstos no dan señales de vida, Luis llama a la puerta. Esta semana le toca a Luis preparar el desayuno para los tres. Luis es español y emplea formas peninsulares.

• • • • •

LUIS. ¡Despertaos, muchachos! ¡Ya son casi las ocho! No os olvidéis de que Ricardo ha de estar en la oficina del Sr. Ortiz a las nueve. ¡Daos prisa!

RICARDO. (*Desperezándose.*) ¿De veras son las ocho? Dime la verdad, Miguel.

MIGUEL. (*Bostezando.*) Luis está llamando, y está sonando el despertador.

RICARDO. ¡Ay, si pudiera dormir un poco más, sería el hombre más feliz del mundo!

LUIS. ¡Levantaos y vestíos, dormilones! El desayuno estará listo dentro de diez minutos. (*Los dos jóvenes se levantan, se afeitan y se visten rápidamente. Pasan al comedor, donde se desayunan despacio, charlando como si no tuviesen nada que hacer.*)

LUIS. Oíd, si continuáis charlando, vais a perder el autobús. (*Ricardo y Miguel se miran sorprendidos.*) No me digáis que no os desperté a tiempo. Poneos el abrigo, porque hace fresco. ¡Hala, idos ahora mismo!

(Media hora más tarde Ricardo entra en la oficina del Sr. Ortiz.)

SR. ORTIZ.   Pase Vd., Ricardo.   He oído decir que Vd. ha conseguido el puesto en México.
Le felicito muy cordialmente.

RICARDO.   Muchas gracias, Sr. Ortiz.   Sé por el Sr. Carter que sin la ayuda de Vd. me
habría sido difícil conseguirlo.   Le agradezco mucho cuanto[1] ha hecho por mí.

SR. ORTIZ.   He enviado por Vd. porque quisiera darle algunas cartas de presentación para
varios amigos míos que viven en México.   Si lo hubiera sabido antes, les habría
escrito directamente.

RICARDO.   ¡Es Vd. muy amable!   ¿Viven los señores en la ciudad de México?

SR. ORTIZ.   Sí; son abogados, ingenieros, comerciantes … Si yo estuviera en su lugar, iría a
hablar con esos señores en cuanto llegara.   Todos se pondrán a su disposición y
harán todo lo que puedan para hacer más agradable su estancia en México.

RICARDO.   Esto me recuerda el viejo refrán que dice: «Los que tienen buenos amigos son
ricos.»

SR. ORTIZ.   Pues, ¿para qué sirven los amigos?   Me gustaría charlar más con Vd., pero sé
que tendrá mucho que hacer antes de salir para México.   Para norteamericano, Vd.
habla muy bien el[2] español.

RICARDO.   Hace muchos años que lo estudio.

SR. ORTIZ.   Podría uno tomarle por mexicano.   Los que saben el español como Vd. pueden
hacer mucho para mejorar las relaciones entre nuestros dos países.

RICARDO.   Quisiera poder colaborar en la labor de estrechar las relaciones entre los dos
pueblos.   Mil gracias por todo, Sr. Ortiz.

SR. ORTIZ.   No hay de qué, Ricardo.   ¡Que tenga mucha suerte!   Envíeme una tarjeta
de vez en cuando.

CONVERSACIÓN

A. Preguntas sobre el diálogo

1. ¿Se despiertan Ricardo y Miguel al sonar el despertador?   2. ¿Qué les dice Luis?
3. ¿Dónde ha de estar Ricardo a las nueve de la mañana?   4. ¿Cuándo estará listo
el desayuno?   5. ¿Dónde se encuentra Ricardo media hora más tarde?   6. ¿Por
qué ha enviado por él el Sr. Ortiz?   7. ¿Qué haría el Sr. Ortiz si estuviera en el lugar
de Ricardo?   8. ¿De qué refrán se acuerda Ricardo?

---

[1] **Cuanto,** *all that,* is often used instead of **todo lo que.**   [2] When an adverb comes between the verb **hablar** and
the name of a language, the definite article must be used.

B. Aplicación del diálogo

1. ¿Se levanta Vd. en seguida cuando suena el despertador? 2. ¿Le gusta a Vd. desayunarse rápidamente? 3. ¿Lee Vd. el periódico durante el desayuno? 4. ¿Le despierta alguien cuando Vd. tiene que salir de casa temprano? 5. ¿Qué lenguas debe uno saber si desea trabajar en la América del Sur? 6. ¿A quiénes envía Vd. tarjetas cuando viaja? 7. ¿Le tomarían a Vd. por español en España? 8. ¿Continúa Vd. charlando cuando sus compañeros desean estudiar?

NOTAS GRAMATICALES

A. Familiar commands

Recall that the form of the affirmative familiar singular command is the same as the third person singular of the present indicative tense of all but a few irregular verbs (see Lessons 9 and 17). Recall that this form is often called the singular imperative.

Also, remember that the negative familiar singular command form is the same as the second person singular of the present subjunctive. Examples: **hablar, habla (tú), no hables; hacer, haz (tú), no hagas.**

1. Familiar plural commands:

hablar:	hablad	no habléis	dormir:	dormid	no **durmáis**
comer:	comed	no comáis	pedir:	pedid	no **pidáis**
escribir:	escribid	no escribáis	venir:	venid	no **vengáis**

To form the affirmative familiar plural commands (the plural imperative) of <u>all</u> verbs, drop **-r** of the infinitive and add **-d.** For the negative familiar plural commands, use the second person plural of the present subjunctive.

In this text we have followed the practice, which is common in Spanish America, of using **Vds.** with the third person plural present subjunctive in familiar plural commands: **Hablen Vds.; Vengan Vds.** The familiar plural forms used in this lesson will be needed for recognition in reading.

2. Familiar commands of reflexive verbs:

	SINGULAR			PLURAL	
levantarse:	levántate	no te levantes		levantaos	no os levantéis
despertarse:	**despiérta**te	no te **despiertes**		despertaos	no os despertéis
ponerse:	**pon**te	no te **pongas**		poneos	no os **pongáis**
vestirse:	**víste**te	no te **vistas**		vestíos	no os **vistáis**
irse:	**ve**te	no te **vayas**		**id**os	no os **vayáis**

Remember: (*a*) that the second person reflexive object pronouns are **te** and **os,** and (*b*) that all object pronouns are attached to affirmative commands, while they precede in negative commands. An accent mark must be written when **te** is added to a singular command form of more than one syllable; also when **os** is added to an **-ir** reflexive verb, except for **idos,** an accent mark must be written: **vestíos.**

In forming the affirmative plural familiar commands of reflexive verbs, final **-d** is dropped before **os** in all forms except **idos.**

B. **Si**-clauses

In earlier lessons we have had simple conditions in which the present indicative tense is used in the English *if*-clause and the same tense in the Spanish **si**-clause:

Si él tiene el dinero, me lo dará.
　If he has the money, he will give it to me.

Si continuáis charlando, vais a perder el autobús.
　If you continue chatting, you are going to miss the bus.

Now contrast these sentences with the following:

Si él tuviera (tuviese) el dinero, me lo daría.
　If he had the money (*but he doesn't*), he would give it to me.

Si yo estuviera (estuviese) en su lugar, iría a hablar con esos señores.
　If I were in your place (*but I'm not*), I would go to talk with those gentlemen.

Si yo lo hubiera (hubiese) sabido antes, les habría escrito.
　If I had known it before (*but I didn't*), I would have written to them.

Si ellos vinieran (viniesen) mañana, lo harían.
　If they should (were to) come tomorrow, they would do it.

Continúan charlando como si no tuviesen (tuvieran) nada que hacer.
　They continue chatting as if they had nothing to do.

To express something that is contrary to fact (*i.e.*, not true) at the present time (first two examples), or something that was contrary to fact in the past (third example), Spanish uses either form of the imperfect (or pluperfect) subjunctive. The result or main clause is usually expressed by the conditional (or conditional perfect), as in English. (In reading you will also find the **-ra** form of the imperfect subjunctive in the result clause, but not in this text.) **Como si** also expresses a contrary-to-fact condition (last example).

Likewise, either form of the imperfect subjunctive is used in the **si**-clause to express something that is not expected to happen, but which might happen in the future (fourth example). Whenever the English sentence has *should, were to,* in the *if*-clause, the imperfect subjunctive is used in Spanish.

The future indicative, the conditional, and the present subjunctive tenses are not used after **si** meaning *if* in conditional sentences. Also see page 229, section E, Note.

C. Special use of plural reflexive pronouns

> **Se miraron sorprendidos.** They looked at each other surprised.
> **Nos vemos mañana.** We'll be seeing one another (each other) tomorrow.

The plural forms of the reflexive pronouns (**nos, os, se**) may be used with verbs to translate *each other, one another*.

D. Forms of **enviar,** *to send*; **continuar,** *to continue*

PRES. IND.	**envío, envías, envía,** enviamos, enviáis, **envían**
PRES. SUBJ.	**envíe, envíes, envíe,** enviemos, enviéis, **envíen**
SING. IMPER.	**envía**
PRES. IND.	**continúo, continúas, continúa,** continuamos, continuáis, **continúan**
PRES. SUBJ.	**continúe, continúes, continúe,** continuemos, continuéis, **continúen**
SING. IMPER.	**continúa**

A few verbs ending in **-iar** and **-uar** require an accent mark on the final stem vowels **i** and **u** in the singular and third person plural of the present indicative tense, in the same forms of the present subjunctive, and in the singular familiar command. All other forms are regular.

E. Summary of uses of **para**

Para and **por** are not interchangeable, even though both often mean *for*.

Para is used:

1. To express the purpose, the use, the person, or the destination for which something is intended:

> **Él lo trajo para ellos.** He brought it for them.
> **La carta es para mí.** The letter is for me.
> **Ellos partieron para México.** They left for Mexico.

2. To express a point or farthest limit of time in the future, often meaning *by*:

> **La lección es para mañana.** The lesson is for tomorrow.
> **Estén Vds. aquí para las seis.** Be here by six o'clock.

3. With an infinitive to express purpose, meaning *to, in order to*:

> **Pueden hacer mucho para mejorar las relaciones entre nuestros dos países.** They can do much (in order) to improve relations between our two countries.

4. To express *for* in comparisons which are understood:

> **Para norteamericano, Vd. habla muy bien el español.**
> For a North American, you speak Spanish very well.

F. Summary of uses of **por**

Por is used:

1. To express *for* in the sense of *because of, on account of, for the sake of, in behalf of, in exchange for, as*:

> **Por eso te llamé.** Because of that (For that reason) I called you.
> **Ella lo ha hecho por mí.** She has done it for me (for my sake).
> **Podría uno tomarle por mexicano.** One could take him for (as) a Mexican.
> **Él lo vendió por cinco dólares.** He sold it for five dollars.
> **¡Por Dios!** For heaven's sake!
> **por ejemplo** for example

2. To express the space of time during which an action continues, *for, during*:

> **Bárbara estudia por la noche.** Barbara studies in (during) the evening.
> **Miguel estuvo allí por tres días.** Michael was there for three days.

3. To express the place *through, along*, or *around* which motion takes place:

> **Pensamos viajar por México.** We intend to travel through Mexico.
> **por aquí** this way, around here

4. To express the agent by which something is done, *by*:

> **La carta fue escrita por mi hermana.** The letter was written by my sister.
> **Luis me llamó por teléfono.** Louis called me by telephone.
> **Yo la envié por correo aéreo.** I sent it (by) air mail.

5. To express *for* (the object of an errand or search) after verbs such as **ir, mandar, enviar, venir, preguntar**:

> **He enviado (venido) por Vd.** I have sent (come) for you.
> **Ellos preguntaban por él.** They were asking for (about) him.

6. To form certain idiomatic expressions:

por desgracia unfortunately	**por fin** finally, at last
por eso therefore, because of that	**por lo menos** at least
por favor please	**¡por supuesto!** of course! certainly!

EJERCICIOS

A. Say after your teacher, then make negative formal and negative familiar singular commands:

> MODEL: Juan se cae. Juan se cae.
> Juan, no se caiga Vd.   Juan, no te caigas.

1. Tomás se olvida del libro.
2. Ricardo se levanta ahora.
3. Marta se pone el sombrero.
4. Elena se da prisa.
5. Enrique se sienta a la derecha.
6. Isabel se hace daño.
7. Pablo se va temprano.
8. Carlos se viste despacio.

B. Say after your teacher, then make each familiar plural command negative:

> MODEL: Buscad a vuestra tía.   Buscad a vuestra tía.   No busquéis a vuestra tía.

1. Id por vuestra hermana.
2. Enviad por vuestro hermanito.
3. Hacedlo esta noche.
4. Sentaos aquí cerca de mí.
5. Poneos los guantes ahora.
6. Daos prisa, por favor.
7. Vestíos en este momento.
8. Dormíos antes que vuelva ella.

C. Say these sentences after your teacher, and explain briefly the differences in meaning in each series:

1. Si yo veo a Tomás en la calle, hablo con él.
   Si yo viera a Tomás en la calle, hablaría con él.
   Si yo hubiera visto a Tomás en la calle, habría hablado con él.
2. Si ellos tienen tiempo, vendrán a vernos.
   Si ellos tuviesen tiempo, vendrían a vernos.
   Si ellos hubiesen tenido tiempo, habrían venido a vernos.
3. Si Luis va a México, verá muchas cosas interesantes.
   Si Luis fuera a México, vería muchas cosas interesantes.
   Si Luis hubiera ido a México, habría visto muchas cosas interesantes.

Your teacher may repeat the first sentence in each series, then follow with the two **si**-clauses and ask you to complete the sentences.

D. Say after your teacher, then repeat, substituting the imperfect subjunctive for the present indicative tense in the **si**-clause and the *conditional* for the future tense in the main clause:

1. Si Carlos está en su cuarto, escribirá la carta.
2. Si ellos se dan prisa, no perderán el autobús.
3. Si Marta no puede salir, me lo dirá.
4. Bárbara vendrá a verte si la llamas por teléfono.
5. Felipe no tendrá frío si se pone el abrigo.
6. Si él va a México, me enviará varias tarjetas.
7. Si suena el despertador, Juan se despertará.

Substitute the pluperfect subjunctive for the present perfect tense in the **si**-clause, and the *conditional perfect* for the future perfect in the main clause:

8. Si él ha escrito la composición, habrá ido al cine.
9. Si Luis ha traído el dinero, se lo habrá dado a Miguel.
10. Juan les habrá enviado el regalo si lo ha comprado.

E. Give in Spanish:

1. If Richard is in Mexico, he will send me a card. 2. If Richard were in Mexico, he would send me a card. 3. If Richard had been in Mexico, he would have sent me a card. 4. If the boys come tonight, they will bring us the tickets. 5. If the boys should come tonight, they would bring us the tickets. 6. If the boys had come last night, they would have brought us the tickets. 7. If Richard should spend the night with us, we would talk about the trip. 8. That young man talks as if he were from Spain.

F. Read in Spanish, supplying **para** or **por,** as required:

1. Se dice que comemos ——— vivir. 2. Mis amigos saldrán ——— México el lunes. 3. Yo quisiera darle a Vd. una carta de presentación ——— un amigo mío. 4. Ricardo compró un billete ——— el sábado. 5. ¿Cuánto tuvo que pagar ——— el billete? 6. Mi madre estuvo en el centro ——— tres horas. 7. Escoja Vd. algunas flores ——— su amiga. 8. Juan vendrá ——— mí al mediodía. 9. Cuando conocí a Carlos Molina, le tomé ——— argentino. 10. Ellos tomaron un autobús ——— ir a casa de Vicente. 11. Carlos no se despertó; ——— eso perdió el autobús. 12. Tenemos que estar en casa ——— las seis. 13. Clara hizo este vestido ——— ti (*i.e. for your use*). 14. Carolina es muy alta ——— una muchacha de quince años. 15. ¿No sabe Vd. ——— qué sirven los amigos? 16. Nuestra casa fue construida ——— un amigo nuestro. 17. Será mejor enviar esta carta ——— correo aéreo. 18. Mis padres piensan viajar ——— la América del Sur. 19. Mil gracias ——— cuanto has hecho. 20. ——— norteamericanos, ellos conocen muchas costumbres mexicanas.

G. Say after your teacher, then compose a new sentence, using **nos** or **se,** following the models:

MODELS: Ricardo vio a Tomás anoche.

          Yo veo a Tomás a menudo.

Ricardo vio a Tomás anoche.
Ricardo y Tomás se vieron anoche.
Yo veo a Tomás a menudo.
Tomás y yo nos vemos a menudo.

1. Vd. entiende bien al señor Díaz.
2. Elena mira a Carlos a menudo.
3. ¿Veían Vds. a Pablo todos los días?
4. Yo le escribo a Luis de vez en cuando.
5. Ana encontró a María en el centro.
6. ¿Envía él muchas cartas a Juanita?

COMPOSICIÓN (Use familiar forms for the verbs in sentences 2, 3, 7.)

1. Richard and Michael do not show [any] signs of life when the alarm clock sounds. 2. Louis awakens them, saying: "Get up, sleepyheads! Shave and get dressed at once!" 3. "Don't forget that Richard is to be at Mr. Ortiz's office at nine o'clock." 4. Richard says that he would be the happiest man in the world if he could sleep until noon. 5. Finally the two young men go downstairs to the dining room and they begin to eat breakfast slowly, chatting as if they had nothing to do. 6. When Louis tells them that they will miss the bus if they don't hurry, they look at each other surprised. 7. Then he continued: "Get going, boys! Don't delay [any] longer! Put on your topcoats, because it is very cool this morning." 8. Mr. Ortiz had sent for Richard in order to give him some letters of introduction. 9. The letters were for some friends of his — engineers, lawyers, and merchants —, who lived in Mexico City. 10. He said that if he were in Richard's place, he would present them to those gentlemen as soon as he arrived. 11. Richard is very grateful to Mr. Ortiz for all that he has done for him, and he says to him: "Many thanks for everything." 12. The latter answers: "You are welcome. Good luck to you (May you have much luck)! Don't fail to send me a card from time to time."

VOCABULARIO

el abogado lawyer
el abrigo topcoat, overcoat
afeitarse to shave (oneself)
antes *adv.* before, formerly
bostezar to yawn
colaborar to collaborate
el comerciante merchant, tradesman, businessman
como si as if
continuar to continue
cordialmente cordially
cuanto all that
dentro de *prep.* within
desperezarse to stretch (one's arms and legs)
el despertador alarm clock
la disposición (*pl.* **disposiciones**) disposition, service
el dormilón (*pl.* **dormilones**) sleepy-head
emplear to employ, use
enviar to send
la estancia stay

estrechar to tighten, bring closer together
feliz (*pl.* **felices**) happy
la forma form
¡hala! come on! get going!
el ingeniero engineer
la labor work, labor
el lugar place
el médico doctor, physician
mejorar to better, improve
olvidarse (**de** + *obj.*) to forget
peninsular peninsular (*of Spain*)
perder (**ie**) to lose, miss
la presentación (*pl.* **presentaciones**) introduction
la prisa haste
el pueblo people, nation
el refrán (*pl.* **refranes**) proverb
la relación (*pl.* **relaciones**) relation
la señal sign
sonar (**ue**) to sound, ring
vestir (**i,i**) to dress; *reflex.* dress (oneself), get dressed

a su disposición at your service
dar señales de to show signs of
darse prisa to hurry
(**no**) **tener** (**nada**) **que** (**hacer**) to have (nothing) to (do), (not) to have (anything) to (do)
¿para qué? for what purpose? why?
¿para qué sirven los amigos? what are friends (good) for?
¡que tenga mucha suerte! good luck (may you have much luck)!
tocar a (**uno**) (*used like* **gustar**) to be (one's) turn

LECTURA XV

LAS ARTES ESPAÑOLAS

Estudio de palabras

a. Less approximate cognates. Pronounce the following words aloud, note the English cognates, and describe the variations: adecuadamente, *adequately*; anónimo, *anonymous*; detalle, *detail*; discípulo, *disciple, pupil*; escena, *scene*; espontaneidad, *spontaneity*; maravilloso, *marvelous*; melodía, *melody*; método, *method*; místico, *mystic*; perfeccionar, *to perfect*; simplificar, *to simplify*.

b. Compare the meanings of: color, *color,* colorido, *coloring, and* colorista, *colorist*; componer, *to compose,* compositor, *composer, and* composición, *composition*; dibujar, *to draw, paint,* dibujo, *drawing, and* dibujante, *draftsman*; flor, *flower, and* florecer, *to flourish*; fuerte, *strong,* fuertemente, *strongly, and* fuerza, *strength*; intérprete, *interpreter, and* interpretación, *interpretation*; música, *music,* músico, *musician, and* musical, *musical*; pintor, *painter,* pintar, *to paint, and* pintura, *painting*; rey, *king,* reina, *queen,* reinar, *to reign, and* reinado, *reign*; varios, *various, several,* variado, *varied, and* variedad, *variety*.

c. Deceptive cognates. Note the following: **la infanta,** *princess* (daughter of royalty); **el representante,** *representative (noun)*; **el sentido,** *sense, feeling,* and, also, *meaning*.

No solamente la literatura sino todas las artes han florecido en España: la pintura, la música, la arquitectura, la escultura y las artes manuales. Se necesitarían muchas páginas para tratar adecuadamente de todas ellas. Aquí sólo podremos hacer algunas observaciones sobre la pintura a partir de fines[1] del siglo XV. A continuación se dedicarán algunos párrafos a la música en la época moderna.

Como la política española dominaba en los Países Bajos[2] y en Italia desde fines del siglo XV, los artistas españoles iban a aquellos países a estudiar, y los flamencos[3] y los italianos venían a España a trabajar. Gracias a este intercambio llegaban a España las ideas y métodos de afuera. Sin embargo,[4] el espíritu nacional era tan fuerte que en general el arte de los españoles nunca se sometió mucho a las influencias extranjeras.

El pintor más importante de la última parte del siglo XV fue Bartolomé Bermejo. Hacia 1474–1477 pintó el magnífico cuadro, «Santo Domingo de Silos,»[5] en el cual a la técnica flamenca agregó[6] elementos hispánicos, como el vigoroso realismo y la gran riqueza de detalles. Se observan rasgos

[1] **a partir de fines,** *since the end.*   [2] **Países Bajos,** *Low Countries* (the Netherlands or Holland).   [3] **flamencos,** Flemish.   [4] **Sin embargo,** *Nevertheless.*   [5] For this painting and others mentioned in this **Lectura,** see art section between pages 368–369.   [6] **agregó,** *he added.*

semejantes en una hermosa obra anónima de la misma época, «La Virgen de los Reyes Católicos» (hacia 1491).

En el primer tercio del siglo XVI el arte de Hernando Yáñez de la Almedina representa el triunfo del Renacimiento italiano. A pesar de la fuerte influencia italiana, el alto sentido religioso de la pintura española prevalece en el arte de Luis de Morales, *el Divino* (¿1517?–1586).

En la segunda mitad del siglo Alonso Sánchez Coello (1531–1588), discípulo del holandés Antonio Moro, crea el tipo del nuevo retrato cortesano,[1] como en el retrato de una de las hijas de Felipe II, la Infanta[2] Isabel Clara Eugenia. Con la escuela de los continuadores de este pintor se relaciona el bello retrato anónimo de la Reina Isabel de Borbón, primera mujer · de Felipe IV (murió en 1644).

El primer gran pintor del Siglo de Oro fue El Greco (¿1548?–1614). Desde la isla de Creta, donde nació, fue a Venecia, como tantos otros artistas, para estudiar con los maestros italianos. Hacia el año 1577 llegó a Toledo, no lejos de Madrid, donde desarrolló y perfeccionó su arte, llegando a ser uno de los pintores más originales e individualistas del mundo. Gran parte de su obra artística comprende una larga serie de retratos e innumerables cuadros religiosos, en que demuestra su sentido místico y su maestría en el uso del colorido. Su obra maestra, «El entierro[3] del Conde de Orgaz,» que encierra muchos aspectos del alma española, fue pintada para la pequeña

iglesia de Santo Tomé de Toledo, donde podemos admirarla hoy día.

Diego Velázquez (1599–1660), de Sevilla, tiene el honor de ser el genio más ilustre de la pintura de su época. Gran realista, este pintor de la corte del rey Felipe IV (1621–1665), presentó en sus lienzos[4] todos los aspectos de la vida y la sociedad de su tiempo, todo ello con una claridad y una precisión no conocidas antes. Para ver las obras maestras de Velázquez hay que visitar el Museo del Prado en Madrid, uno de los museos más importantes de Europa. Algunas de sus mejores obras son «Las meninas,»[5] «Las hilanderas,»[6] «Los borrachos»[7] y «La rendición de Breda,»[8] llamado a menudo «Las lanzas».

En el cuadro «Las meninas,» considerado por muchos como la obra maestra de Velázquez, vemos a la infanta Margarita, rodeada de su corte de meninas y enanos.[9] Detrás de ellos aparecen una dueña[10] y un cortesano,[11] y al lado de ellos se halla el pintor mismo, ocupado en dibujar al rey y a la reina, quienes se supone están parados donde se halla el espectador y se reflejan en un espejo que está en la pared del fondo.

Realista también fue José de Ribera (1591–1652), que muy joven pasó a Italia para perfeccionar su arte. El dominio de los efectos de luz, forma y color, el naturalismo y la nota dramática y apasionada caracterizan la obra de este gran pintor, que halló su inspiración en los motivos[12] religiosos. La fusión del realismo con el idealismo espiritual se realiza en Francisco

---

[1] **cortesano,** *courtly.*   [2] **Infanta,** *Princess.*   [3] **entierro,** *Burial.*   [4] **lienzos,** *canvases.*   [5] **meninas,** *Little Ladies in Waiting.*   [6] **hilanderas,** *Spinning Girls.*   [7] **borrachos,** *Drinkers.*   [8] **La rendición de Breda,** *The Surrender of Breda* (a town in Holland taken from the Flemish in 1625 by the Italian General Spínola, who was serving in the Spanish army).   [9] **enanos,** *dwarfs.*   [10] **dueña,** *chaperone.*   [11] **cortesano,** *courtier.*   [12] **motivos,** *motifs, themes.*

de Zurbarán (1598–1664) y en Bartolomé Esteban Murillo (1618–1682). Continuaron con éxito las excelencias del arte naturalista de Ribera, pero se distinguen de éste por su manera de serenar y simplificar la realidad. Zurbarán es considerado como el más fiel intérprete de la vida religiosa. Los dos saben producir también maravillosas figuras femeninas, en que realzan[1] la belleza y elegancia de la mujer andaluza.

Tanto en la pintura como[2] en la literatura, el siglo XVIII ofrece poco de interés. Sin embargo, a fines del siglo aparecieron las primeras obras de Francisco Goya (1746–1828), uno de los pintores más originales del mundo moderno. Aunque de familia humilde, Goya llegó a ser el pintor de la corte de Carlos IV y de Fernando VII y dejó una gran cantidad de retratos de las dos familias reales, pintados con un realismo y una franqueza que asombran.[3] En su extensa y variada obra vemos, en realidad, toda la historia de su época. Al lado de los cuadros que representan claramente la brutalidad de la guerra de la independencia, después de la invasión de Napoleón en 1808, hay una larga serie de cartones[4] o modelos para tapices,[5] en que

---

[1] **realzan,** *they enhance.*   [2] **Tanto...como,** *Both...and.*   [3] **asombran,** *are amazing.*   [4] **cartón,** a painting or drawing on strong paper.   [5] **tapices,** *tapestries.*

Etching from "The Disasters of War" by Goya

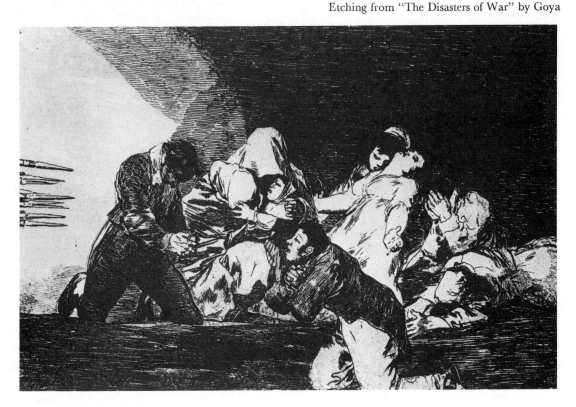

"Young Girl on a Swing," pen and ink drawing by Goya

Etching from "The Caprices" by Goya

pinta escenas y tipos del pueblo, fiestas, bailes populares y otros aspectos de la vida diaria de la época. Por su realismo, su maestría en la técnica, su espontaneidad, su espíritu crítico, su individualismo y su conocimiento de la época en que vivía, Goya es considerado como uno de los genios de la pintura moderna.

Durante el período romántico la pintura española se vuelve convencional, y los artistas buscan inspiración en obras extranjeras. Sin embargo, hacia fines del siglo XIX, cuando reina el realismo en la literatura y las artes, la pintura tiene su mejor representante en el valenciano Joaquín Sorolla (1863–1923), que se ha distinguido por la luz y el colorido de sus hermosos cuadros de la vida y de las costumbres de su región. Algunos de sus mejores lienzos se encuentran en el museo de la Sociedad Hispánica de Nueva York y en el Museo Metropolitano de la misma ciudad. La obra vigorosa y dramática de Ignacio Zuloaga (1870–1945), gran pintor de la España vieja y tradicional, contrasta fuertemente con la de Sorolla.

La influencia de pintores españoles en el arte de nuestro tiempo es incalculable. Pablo Picasso (1881–1973), que pasó muchos años en Francia, ha sido, sin duda, el artista que ha ejercido mayor influencia en la pintura contemporánea. Su arte ha atravesado distintas etapas, desde su período azul («El guitarrista») y período rosa,[1] a través del cubismo («Tres músicos»,) hasta volver, hacia 1920, a las formas naturalistas, aunque no olvida su atracción por las composiciones abstractas y cubistas.

Juan Gris (1887–1927), compañero y discípulo de Picasso, superó a su maestro en el estilo cubista. Juan Miró (1893–) es uno de los más grandes pintores de la escuela surrealista. Las obras cubistas y surrealistas del gran dibujante y colorista Salvador Dalí (1904–) representan el triunfo de la interpretación libre de la realidad, típica del arte actual.

Puede decirse que la música siempre ha sido muy popular en España entre todas las clases sociales. Gracias a las composiciones de los grandes artistas Albéniz y Granados, la música española moderna ya es conocida en todo el mundo. Albéniz (1860–1909),

[1] **rosa,** *pink.*

"Peasant from Segovia" by Zuloaga

"Beach of Valencia by Morning Light" by Sorolla

notable pianista y compositor, ha dado a conocer[1] una gran variedad de ritmos, especialmente melodías andaluzas. Las escenas del pintor Goya han servido de inspiración para *Goyescas*, seis famosas piezas para piano, compuestas por Granados (1867–1916).

Según muchos músicos, Manuel de Falla (1876–1946) es el mejor compositor español moderno. Natural de Andalucía, como Albéniz, compuso las encantadoras melodías llamadas *Noches en los jardines de España*. Se oye mucho en los Estados Unidos su *Danza del fuego*,[2] del famoso ballet *El amor brujo*.[3] Para conocer la pasión, la fuerza y la gran variedad de la música española, uno debe escuchar la música de Manuel de Falla.

Gracias a *la Argentina*, célebre intérprete del baile español en la primera parte del siglo actual, conocemos mejor no sólo el antiguo arte del baile español, sino también la música de Albéniz, Granados, Falla y otros compositores.

Otras grandes figuras españolas del mundo musical que conocemos hoy día en los Estados Unidos son Pablo Casals, violoncelista incomparable, Andrés Segovia, guitarrista sin igual, y José Iturbi, eminente pianista, compositor y director de orquesta.

PREGUNTAS

1. ¿Qué artes han florecido en España? 2. ¿Puede decirse que el arte de los españoles se sometió mucho a las influencias extranjeras? 3. ¿Qué gran pintor español vivió en la última parte del siglo XV? 4. ¿Qué rasgos pueden observarse en la obra de Bermejo? 5. ¿Qué representa Yáñez de la Almedina en la historia del arte español? 6. ¿Qué sentido característico da Morales al arte aprendido en Italia? 7. ¿Qué tipo de arte crea Sánchez Coello? 8. ¿Quién fue El Greco? 9. ¿Dónde estudió? 10. ¿A qué ciudad de España llegó? 11. ¿Qué clase de obras pintó? 12. ¿Cuál es su obra maestra?

13. ¿Quién fue el gran pintor realista del Siglo de Oro? 14. ¿Qué presentó en sus lienzos? 15. ¿Dónde están sus obras maestras? 16. ¿Cuáles son algunas de sus obras? 17. ¿Qué personas hay en «Las meninas»? 18. ¿Qué rasgos caracterizan la pintura de Ribera? 19. ¿Qué representan Zurbarán y Murillo en el arte español? 20. ¿Qué puede decirse de sus figuras femeninas?

21. ¿De qué siglo es Francisco Goya? 22. ¿Qué llegó a ser? 23. ¿Qué clase de obras pintó? 24. ¿Cuándo reinó el realismo en las artes? 25. ¿Quién es su mejor representante en la pintura? 26. ¿Dónde se encuentran algunos de sus mejores lienzos? 27. ¿Quiénes son otros pintores contemporáneos?

28. ¿Qué etapas pueden señalarse en la evolución del arte de Picasso? 29. ¿Supera Picasso a Juan Gris en el estilo cubista? 30. ¿Con qué escuela se relaciona Juan Miró? ¿Salvador Dalí?

31. ¿Quién fue Albéniz? 32. ¿Quién fue otro pianista famoso? 33. ¿Qué compuso Falla? 34. ¿Quién ha sido la intérprete más célebre del baile español? 35. ¿Quién es Pablo Casals? 36. ¿Quién es Andrés Segovia? 37. ¿José Iturbi?

---

[1] **ha dado a conocer,** *has made known.* [2] **Danza del fuego,** *Fire Dance.* [3] **El amor brujo,** *Wedded by Witchcraft.*

LA PINTURA ESPAÑOLA

A la derecha:
Anónimo LA VIRGEN DE LOS REYES CATÓLICOS
Cortesia, Museo del Prado, Madrid

Debajo, a la derecha:
Luis de Morales LA VIRGEN Y EL NIÑO
Cortesia, Museo del Prado, Madrid

Debajo, a la izquierda:
Bartolomé Bermejo SANTO DOMINGO DE SILOS
Cortesia, Museo del Prado, Madrid

A la izquierda:
Alonso Sánchez Coello LA INFANTA ISABEL CLARA EUGENIA
Cortesía, Museo del Prado, Madrid

Debajo, a la izquierda:
Anónimo LA REINA ISABEL DE BORBÓN
Cortesía, Museo del Prado, Madrid

Debajo, a la derecha:
Hernando Yáñez de la Almedina SANTA CATALINA
Cortesía, Museo del Prado, Madrid

EL ENTIERRO DEL CONDE DE ORGAZ
Cortesía, Iglesia de Santo Tomé, Toledo. Fotografía de MAS

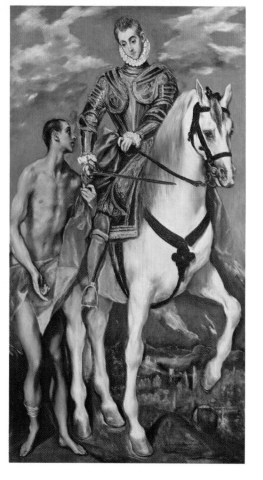

Arriba, a la izquierda:

SAN MARTÍN Y EL MENDIGO

Cortesía, National Gallery of Art, Washington, D.C.,
Widener Collection

Arriba, a la derecha:

LA CORONACIÓN DE LA VIRGEN

Cortesía, Museo del Prado, Madrid

A la derecha:

LA SAGRADA FAMILIA

Cortesía, National Gallery of Art, Washington, D.C.,
Samuel H. Kress Collection

EL GRECO

EL GRECO

LA TRINIDAD
Cortesía, Museo del Prado, Madrid

SAN ANDRÉS Y SAN FRANCISCO
Cortesía, Museo del Prado, Madrid

LAS MENINAS

Cortesía, Museo del Prado, Madrid

EL PRÍNCIPE BALTASAR CARLOS (detalle)
Cortesía, Museo del Prado, Madrid

LOS BORRACHOS
Cortesía, Museo del Prado, Madrid

VELÁZQUEZ

LA RENDICIÓN DE BREDA
Cortesía, Museo del Prado, Madrid

VELÁZQUEZ

LA CORONACIÓN DE LA VIRGEN
Cortesía, Museo del Prado, Madrid

LAS HILANDERAS
Cortesía, Museo del Prado, Madrid

RIBERA

EL SUEÑO DE JACOB
Cortesía, Museo del Prado, Madrid

LA TRINIDAD
Cortesía, Museo del Prado, Madrid

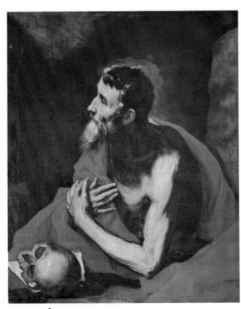

SAN JERÓNIMO
Cortesía, Museo del Prado, Madrid

ZURBARÁN

A la derecha:
LA VISIÓN DE SAN PEDRO NOLASCO
Cortesía, Museo del Prado, Madrid

Debajo, a la derecha:
SANTA CASILDA
Cortesía, Museo del Prado, Madrid

Debajo, a la izquierda:
SANTA LUCÍA
*Cortesía, National Gallery of Art, Washington, D.C.,
Gift of Chester Dale*

MURILLO

LOS NIÑOS DE LA CONCHA
Cortesía, Museo del Prado, Madrid

EL DIVINO PASTOR
Cortesía, Museo del Prado, Madrid

LA ADORACIÓN DE LOS PASTORES
Cortesía, Museo del Prado, Madrid

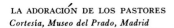

MURILLO

LA PURÍSIMA CONCEPCIÓN
Cortesía, Museo del Prado, Madrid

EL REGRESO DEL HIJO PRÓDIGO
Cortesía, National Gallery of Art, Washington, D.C.,
Gift of the Avalon Foundation

GOYA

EL GENERAL RICARDOS
Cortesía, Museo del Prado, Madrid

EL DOS DE MAYO
Cortesía, Museo del Prado, Madrid

EL TRES DE MAYO
Cortesía, Museo del Prado, Madrid

GOYA

LA VENDIMIA
Cortesía, Museo del Prado, Madrid

EL PARASOL
Cortesía, Museo del Prado, Madrid

AQUELARRE DE BRUJAS
Cortesía, Museo del Prado, Madrid

PICASSO

TRES MÚSICOS
Collection, The Museum of Modern Art, New York.
Mrs. Simon Guggenheim Fund

EL VIEJO GUITARRISTA
Cortesía, "The Art Institute of Chicago"

GRIS

NATURALEZA MUERTA CON UN PLATO
DE FRUTAS Y UNA BOTELLA DE AGUA
Cortesía, Rijksmuseum Kröller-Müller Stichting, Otterlo, Holanda

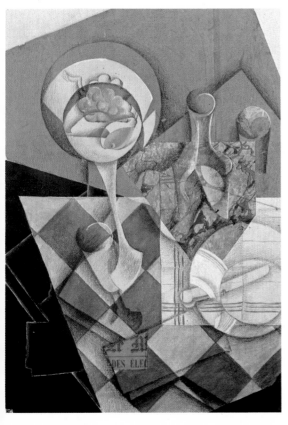

MIRÓ

MURAL DE CERÁMICA (detalle), UNESCO, PARÍS
Cortesía, UNESCO*, París. Fotografía de* MAS

DALÍ

EL DESCUBRIMIENTO DE AMÉRICA POR CRISTÓBAL COLÓN

*Cortesía, Salvador Dalí y The Gallery of Modern Art including the Huntington
Hartford Collection*

El Prado Museum, Madrid, Spain.

Museum of Modern Art, Barcelona, Spain.

LECCIÓN 25

Verbs ending in -*ducir*. Forms of *reír*. The preterit perfect tense
The absolute use of the past participle
The subjunctive after *tal vez, quizá(s)*
Translation of "to become". Use of the infinitive after *oír* and *ver*
Diminutives

¡QUE LO PASES BIEN! ¡BUEN VIAJE!

(Ramón y Luis pasan por la casa de Tomás. Vuelven del aeropuerto, donde se han despedido de su amigo Ricardo.)

RAMÓN. ¿Qué pasó, Tomás? No te vimos en el aeropuerto.

LUIS. ¿No pensabas ir a la casa de Ricardo esta mañana?

TOMÁS. No se[1] pueden imaginar lo que pasó en casa esta mañana. Quizás no vayan a creer lo que les voy a contar; pero no se rían de mí.

RAMÓN. No nos reiremos. Cuéntanos lo que pasó.

LUIS. ¿Te pusiste enfermo? ¿Tuviste que cuidar a Juanito y a tus hermanitas?

TOMÁS. Algo peor que eso. Se cortó la electricidad durante la noche sin saberlo yo.[2] Casi me volví loco cuando comprendí que no me había levantado a las siete sino a las ocho y media.

---

[1] Up to this point, following usual practice in Spanish, object pronouns have been attached to an infinitive. However, object pronouns may be placed before inflected forms of verbs such as **ir, poder, querer,** when these verbs precede an infinitive: **No se pueden imaginar,** instead of **No pueden imaginarse; lo que les voy a contar,** instead of **lo que voy a contarles.** [2] **sin saberlo yo,** *without my knowing it.* The infinitive, which is a verbal noun in Spanish, may have a subject. The latter, when expressed, must follow the infinitive.

Luis. ¡Qué mala suerte! Y, ¿por eso decidiste no salir?

Tomás. ¡Claro! Sabida la hora, me di cuenta de que no llegaría a tiempo.

● ● ● ● ●

Tomás. Pero olvidémonos de todo eso. ¿Qué pasó en el aeropuerto?

Luis. Primero tengo que contarte lo que ocurrió en casa de Ricardo. Al llegar a su casa, oímos que el Sr. Smith gritaba desde el garaje que el coche tenía una llanta desinflada.

Ramón. En vista de que no podían usar el coche, tuve que ir por el mío y conduje a todos al aeropuerto.

Tomás. Estarían[1] todos muy nerviosos.

Ramón. Me gritaban todos: «¡Date prisa! ¡Tal vez pierda Ricardo el avión!» Pero por fin se calmaron cuando vieron que llegábamos a tiempo.

Tomás. ¿Hubo tiempo para facturar las maletas?

Luis. Sí; nos dijo el empleado que se había retrasado la hora de la salida.

Ramón. En cuanto Ricardo hubo entrado en el aeropuerto, se dio cuenta de que varios amigos suyos le aguardaban allí. Uno de ellos llevaba su cámara y le sacó algunas fotos.

Tomás. Quedaría poco tiempo antes de la salida del avión, ¿verdad?

Ramón. Exactamente. Pasamos a la sala de espera inmediatamente. Y apenas hubimos llegado, oímos anunciar a alguien que el avión estaba para salir.

Luis. Ricardo abrazó a su padre y les dio un beso a su madre y a su novia.

Ramón. Cuando Ricardo subió al avión, empezamos a gritar: «¡Que lo pases bien! ¡No dejes de escribirnos a menudo! ¡Que te hagas rico pronto! ¡Buen viaje!»

Tomás. ¡Cuánto siento no haber estado![2] Pero sería triste verle partir.

Ramón. Sí; cerradas las puertas del avión, quedamos algo[3] tristes.

Luis. Pero también quedamos muy contentos por saber que le esperaba en México una carrera útil e interesante.

CONVERSACIÓN

A. Preguntas sobre el diálogo

1. ¿Dónde han estado Ramón y Luis? 2. ¿Qué le preguntan a Tomás? 3. ¿Qué había pasado durante la noche? 4. Sabida la hora, ¿de qué se dio cuenta Tomás? 5. ¿Qué gritaba el Sr. Smith desde el garaje? 6. ¿Qué gritaban todos mientras los conducía Ramón al aeropuerto? 7. ¿Qué anunciaba alguien cuando entraron en la sala de espera? 8. ¿Quedaron tristes todos al ver partir a Ricardo?

---

[1] See Lesson 16, page 229. Also, see lines 16 and 22 below for similar uses.   [2] When location is clear from the context, it is not necessary to use **aquí, allí**, etc., with **estar**.   [3] **Algo** may be used as an adverb meaning *somewhat*, *rather*. Note that the adjective agrees with the subject, which is understood in this sentence.

B. Aplicación del diálogo

1. ¿Qué hacemos generalmente cuando se pone enferma una persona? 2. Cuando Vd. está enfermo, ¿prefiere estudiar o mirar la televisión? 3. ¿Se pone Vd. nervioso cuando cree que no va a llegar a clase a tiempo? 4. ¿Le parecen a Vd. simpáticas las personas que se ríen de Vd.? 5. ¿Qué frases les decimos a los amigos al despedirnos de ellos? 6. ¿Por qué no debemos ponernos tristes al ver partir a los amigos? 7. ¿Qué carrera le interesa a Vd. más, la de médico o la de ingeniero? 8. Terminado este año, ¿piensa Vd. continuar sus estudios en esta universidad?

NOTAS GRAMATICALES

A. Verbs ending in **-ducir: conducir,** *to conduct, drive*

PRES. IND.	**conduzco,** conduces, conduce, conducimos, conducís, conducen
PRES. SUBJ.	**conduzca, conduzcas, conduzca, conduzcamos, conduzcáis, conduzcan**
PRETERIT	**conduje, condujiste, condujo, condujimos, condujisteis, condujeron**
IMP. SUBJ.	**condujera, condujeras,** etc. **condujese, condujeses,** etc.

B. Forms of **reír,** *to laugh*

PRES. PART.	**riendo**	PAST PART.	reído
PRES. IND.	**río, ríes, ríe,** reímos, reís, **ríen**		
PRES. SUBJ.	**ría, rías, ría, riamos, riáis, rían**		
PRETERIT	reí, reíste, **rió,** reímos, reísteis, **rieron**		
IMP. SUBJ.	**riera, rieras,** etc. **riese, rieses,** etc.		
SING. IMPER.	**ríe**	PL. IMPER.	reíd

Reír is a stem-changing verb, Class III. Also note that the accent mark is used on several forms since the stem ends in a vowel. The other tenses are regular.

C. The preterit perfect tense

hube hablado	**hubimos** hablado
hubiste hablado	**hubisteis** hablado
hubo hablado	**hubieron** hablado

En cuanto (Cuando) él hubo entrado, vio a varios amigos suyos.
As soon as (When) he had entered, he saw several friends of his.
Apenas hubimos llegado, oímos anunciar a alguien ...
Scarcely had we arrived, when we heard someone announce (announcing) ...

The preterit perfect tense is formed with the preterit of **haber** and the past participle. It is translated like the English past perfect tense, but is used only after conjunctions such as **cuando, en cuanto, después que, apenas.** In the case of **apenas,** the word *when* is carried over to the following clause in English. In spoken Spanish the simple preterit often replaces the preterit perfect. The Spanish pluperfect tense is used to translate the English past perfect in other cases: **Habían vuelto,** *They had returned.*

The third person singular preterit form **hubo** is used impersonally, meaning *there was (were).* The form has been used in the Lecturas.

D. The absolute use of the past participle

Sabida la hora, me di cuenta de que ...
Having found out (After I had found out) the time, I realized that ...
Cerradas las puertas, quedamos algo tristes.
The doors closed (After the doors had been closed), we were (remained) somewhat sad.

The past participle is often used absolutely with a noun or pronoun to express *time, manner, means,* and the like. Used thus, the participle precedes the noun or pronoun it modifies and with which it agrees in gender and number. The translation depends on the context.

E. The subjunctive after **tal vez, quizá(s),** *perhaps*

Tal vez lo han terminado. Perhaps they have finished it.
Tal vez (Quizás) perdamos el avión. Perhaps we'll (we may) miss the plane.
Quizás Vds. no vayan a creerlo. Perhaps you aren't going to believe it.

The indicative mood is used after **tal vez, quizá(s),** *perhaps,* when certainty is expressed or implied. The subjunctive, however, is used when doubt or uncertainty is implied.

F. Translation of *to become*

¡Que te hagas rico pronto! May you become (get) rich soon!
¿Te pusiste enfermo? Did you become ill?
Casi me volví loco. I almost became (went) crazy.

Hacerse plus a noun or a few adjectives like **rico** and **feliz** means *to become,* denoting conscious effort. **Llegar a ser** means approximately the same, indicating final result: **Él llegó a ser (se hizo) médico,** *He became a doctor.*

Ponerse followed by an adjective or past participle, which agrees with the subject of the verb, expresses a physical, mental, or emotional change. A violent change is expressed by **volverse.**

Se is used with many transitive verbs to express the idea of *become.* Contrast **Los calmé,** *I calmed them,* with **Se calmaron,** *They became calm (calmed themselves).*

G. Use of the infinitive after **oír** and **ver**

> **Oímos gritar a alguien.** We heard someone shout (shouting).
> **Sería triste verle partir.** It was probably (must have been) sad to see him leave (leaving).

After **oír** and **ver** the infinitive is regularly used in Spanish, while the present participle is often used in English. Note the word order in the first example. A subject of the infinitive is considered the direct object of **oír** and **ver**.

H. Diminutives

amiga	(girl) friend	**amiguita**	little (girl) friend
hermana	sister	**hermanita**	little sister
hermano	brother	**hermanito**	little brother
mesa	table, desk	**mesita**	small (little) table
señora	lady, woman	**señorita**	young lady (woman)

In Spanish diminutive endings are often used to express not only small size, but pity, affection, scorn, ridicule, and the like. The most common endings are: **-ito, -a; -illo, -a; -(e)cito, -a.** Frequently, the use of these suffixes with nouns precludes the need for adjectives. For the choice of ending you must rely upon observation.

A final vowel is often dropped before adding the ending. Sometimes a change in spelling is necessary to preserve the sound of a consonant when a final vowel is dropped: **amiga, amiguita; poco,** *little* (quantity), **poquito,** *very little.*

Applied to baptismal names these endings indicate affection (whether or not connected with smallness): **Juanita,** *Jane*; **Juanito,** *Johnny*; **Anita,**[1] *Annie*; **Carlitos,** *Charlie*; **Tomasito,** *Tommy.*

Give the base word to which each diminutive has been added:

casita	nice (little) house, cottage	**momentito**	(short) moment
chiquilla	(cute) little girl	**mujercita**	pleasant little woman
florecita	small (tiny) flower	**pequeñito, -a**	very small, tiny
hijito	(dear) son	**pobrecito**	poor boy (man, thing)
jovencito	nice young man (fellow)	**pueblecito**	small town, village
madrecita	dear mother, mom	**regalito**	small gift

---

[1] The diminutives given in the rest of this section are not listed in the end vocabulary since they are not used elsewhere in this text. Watch for similar and other uses of diminutives in reading.

EJERCICIOS

A. Substitution drill. Watch the agreement of the adjective in sentences 5 and 6.

   1. *Ramón* condujo ese coche.
      (*Yo, Él y yo, Los muchachos, Tú, Vd.*)
   2. Tal vez *José* pierda el autobús.
      (*yo, nosotros, Vds., tú, mis padres*)
   3. *Yo* no me río de él.
      (*Juanito, Ellos, Ella y yo, Tú, Vds.*)
   4. *Vd.* se dio cuenta de eso.
      (*Yo, Tú, Vds., Él y yo, Carlos y Luis*)
   5. *Roberto* no se ha hecho rico.
      (*Juanita, Yó, Vd., Tú, Nosotras, Las muchachas*)
   6. *Luis* se puso nervioso.
      (*Él y yo, Ana, Ana y Luisa, Tú, Vds.*)

B. Say after your teacher, then give the negative familiar singular command:

   1. Corta tú la electricidad.
   2. Sube tú al avión.
   3. Conduce tú a todos al aeropuerto.
   4. Cuéntanos lo que pasó.
   5. Ríete de aquel muchacho.
   6. Date prisa.

C. Say after your teacher; when you hear the cue, substitute it in the sentence:

   1. *Tal vez* no le guste a él la televisión. (Quizás)
   2. *Quizás* perdamos el avión. (Tal vez)
   3. *Juanito debe* darse prisa. (Juanito debiera)
   4. *Yo quiero* ir al aeropuerto con Vds. (Yo quisiera)
   5. ¡*Que* te hagas rico pronto! (¡Ojalá que!)
   6. *Después de hacer todo eso*, me senté un rato. (Hecho todo eso)
   7. *Después que salió el avión*, volvimos a casa. (Salido el avión)
   8. *Al terminar la composición*, se la di al profesor. (Terminada la composición)
   9. *Mi primo se hizo* médico. (Mi primo llegó a ser)
  10. *Los oímos* salir de la casa. (Los vimos)
  11. *Oí tocar* a María algunas canciones. (Oí cantar)
  12. *Cuando* él hubo entrado, vio a algunos amigos. (En cuanto)
  13. *Después que* hubimos llegado, oímos gritar a alguien. (Apenas)
  14. *Ella no mandó* facturar sus maletas. (Ella no hizo)
  15. *Ricardo vio* que ellos le aguardaban. (Ricardo se dio cuenta de)

D. Read in Spanish, changing the infinitive in parentheses to the correct form of the preterit tense whenever a change is required:

   1. Mi hermano (hacerse) ingeniero. 2. Un amigo mío (llegar a ser) abogado. 3. Mi mamá (ponerse) muy nerviosa. 4. La novia de Ricardo (quedar) algo triste.

5. Cuando Ramón perdió su puesto, su madre casi (volverse) loca. 6. Mi hermanito (caerse) y (hacerse) daño. 7. No oímos (gritar) al niño. 8. Yo le mandé (quedarse) en casa el resto del día. 9. Todos (calmarse) cuando vieron que llegábamos a tiempo. 10. Ricardo (darse) cuenta de que varios amigos suyos le aguardaban. 11. Ellos (despedirse) de Ricardo en el aeropuerto. 12. Ricardo y su padre (abrazarse).

E. Say after your teacher, then repeat, changing the verbs in the present tense to the future and those in the imperfect tense to the conditional, thereby suggesting probability:

1. ¿Qué ocurre en casa de Ricardo?
2. Su hermanito está enfermo hoy.
3. El coche tiene una llanta desinflada.
4. Él quiere facturar las maletas.
5. Todos estaban muy nerviosos.
6. Quedaba poco tiempo.
7. Era triste verle partir.
8. Había mucha gente en el aeropuerto.

F. Give in Spanish:

1. The boys got into the car. 2. Richard had his suitcases checked. 3. We did not realize that he was back. 4. I imagine that they are about to leave. 5. John's cousin became a lawyer. 6. Johnny fell down and cut himself. 7. His mother became somewhat nervous. 8. Don't laugh at him. 9. Let him (*fam. sing.*) drive the car. 10. It was probably sad to see them leave. 11. Raymond isn't here; perhaps he may arrive later. 12. Did you hear Mary sing last night?

G. Learn the following proverbs:

1. No dejes para mañana lo que puedas hacer hoy.
2. Haz bien y no mires a quién.
3. Antes que te cases, mira lo que haces.
4. Dime con quién andas y te diré quién eres.
5. Hablando se entiende la gente.
6. Comida hecha, compañía deshecha.[1]

[1] The English equivalent is "Once the favor has been done, the favored one disappears."   [2] Use **consigo**.

COMPOSICIÓN

1. Raymond and Louis have just returned from the airport, where they took leave of Richard.   2. Tom said to his two friends: "You cannot imagine what happened at home this morning."   3. "The electricity was cut off during the night and my alarm clock did not sound; therefore, I did not get up until half past eight."   4. At this moment Louis said: "Let me (*fam. sing.*) tell you what occurred at Richard's."   5. Upon arriving at his house, Raymond and Louis found out that Mr. Smith's car had a flat tire. 6. Raymond had to go home for his car and he drove all to the airport.   7. They feared that he wouldn't arrive on time, and they were shouting: "Hurry!   Perhaps Richard will (may) miss the plane!"   8. There was time to check the suitcases because the time of departure had been set back.   9. Upon entering the airport, we realized that many friends of his were waiting for him.   10. As soon as we had reached the waiting room, we heard someone announce that the plane was about to leave.   11. When Richard got on the plane, we began to shout: "Have a good trip!   Don't forget to write often! Goodbye!"   12. After the doors of the plane had been closed (The doors of the plane closed), we were (remained) somewhat sad, but we knew that an interesting career awaited him in Mexico.

Suburban Madrid apartment complexes viewed from the road to Talavera, Spain.

VOCABULARIO

abrazar to embrace
aguardar to wait, wait for, await
algo *adv.* somewhat, rather
apenas scarcely, hardly
el beso kiss
calmar to calm; *reflex.* calm oneself, become calm
la cámara camera
la carrera career
conducir to conduct, drive (*a car*)
cortar to cut, cut off
la cuenta account, bill
cuidar to care for, take care of, look after
desinflado, -a flat (*tire*)
la electricidad electricity
exactamente exactly
facturar to check (*baggage*)
gritar to shout

la hermanita little sister
hubo (*pret. of* **haber**) there was (were)
imaginarse to imagine
inmediatamente immediately
Juanito Johnny
loco, -a crazy, wild
la llanta tire
nervioso, -a nervous
la novia fiancée, sweetheart, girl friend
ocurrir to occur, happen
quizá(s) perhaps
reír (i, i) to laugh
retrasar to delay, set back
la salida departure
subir (**a** + *obj.*) to go up, get into, climb up (into)
triste sad
útil useful

¡buen viaje! (have) a good trip!
¡claro! of course! certainly! indeed!
darse cuenta de (**que**) to realize (that)
en vista de que in view of the fact that
estar para to be about to
hacerse + *noun* to become
ponerse + *adj.* to become
¡que lo pase(s) bien! goodbye (*lit.*, may you fare well)!
reírse (i, i) (de) to laugh (at)
sala de espera waiting room
tal vez perhaps
volverse (ue) (loco, -a) to become *or* go (crazy *or* wild)

LA CARRETERA PANAMERICANA

Cosmopolitan cities of over one million inhabitants

Important pre-Columbian archaeological sites

Urban centers of historical and artistic interest; important colonial buildings

Scenic areas, lakes, mountains and volcanic regions

Areas rich in folk arts and festivals

Great waterfalls

Winter sports centers

Beaches and water sports centers

1. Guadalajara **(Mexico)**
2. Mexico City; Toluca, Cuernavaca, Puebla, Taxco, Teotihuacán, San Miguel Allende, Morelia, Guanajuato, Pátzcuaro, Querétaro **(Mexico)**
3. Veracruz, Jalapa **(Mexico)**
4. Acapulco **(Mexico)**
5. Oaxaca; ruins of Monte Albán and Mitla **(Mexico)**
6. Mérida; ruins of Uxmal and Chichén-Itzá **(Mexico)**
7. Guatemala City; Antigua, Lake Atitlán, Chichicastenango, ruins of Tikal* **(Guatemala)**
8. San Salvador and surroundings; ruins of Tazumal, Izalco Volcano National Park **(El Salvador)**
9. Tegucigalpa; ruins of Copán* **(Honduras)**
10. Managua; León, Lake Nicaragua **(Nicaragua)**
11. San José; Irazú and Poás Volcanoes, Cartago **(Costa Rica)**
12. Canal Zone; Panama City, Portobelo, San Blas Islands* **(Panama)**
13. Cartagena and surroundings **(Colombia)**
14. Caracas and surroundings; Maracay, Angel Falls*, Margarita Island* **(Venezuela)**
15. Mérida, Trujillo, Lake Maracaibo **(Venezuela)**
16. Bogotá; Tequendama Falls, Tunja **(Colombia)**
17. Cali and Popayán in the Cauca Valley **(Colombia)**
18. Route of the Incas; Otavalo, Quito, Ambato, Cuenca, ruins of Incapirca, Mt. Cotopaxi and Mt. Chimborazo **(Ecuador)**
19. Guayaquil; Galápagos Islands* **(Ecuador)**
20. Trujillo; ruins of Chavín, Callejón de Huaylas, Cajamarca **(Peru)**
21. Lima; Callao **(Peru)**
22. Cuzco area; Chincheros, Ayacucho, Machu Picchu* **(Peru)**
23. Lake Titicaca Region: Arequipa and Puno **(Peru)**; La Paz, Copacabana, and ruins of Tiahuanaco **(Bolivia)**
24. Sucre and Potosí **(Bolivia)**
25. Asunción and surroundings **(Paraguay)**
26. Iguazú Falls and surroundings; Jesuit mission ruins **(Argentina, Paraguay, Brazil)**
27. São Paulo **(Brazil)**
28. Rio de Janeiro and surroundings **(Brazil)**
29. Belo Horizonte; Ouro Prêto **(Brazil)**
30. Brasilia **(Brazil)**
31. Brasilia-Belém Highway; Araguia National Park, Belém **(Brazil)**
32. Salvador (Pelourinho) **(Brazil)**
33. Recife (Pernambuco) **(Brazil)**
34. Fortaleza **(Brazil)**
35. River Plate Region: Greater Buenos Aires **(Argentina)**; Montevideo **(Uruguay)**
36. Córdoba, Rosario, Santa Fe **(Argentina)**
37. Bariloche **(Argentina)**
38. Santiago de Chile; Valparaíso, Viña del Mar, Portillo, Farellones, Juan Fernández Archipelago* **(Chile)**
39. Tierra del Fuego: Punta Arenas **(Chile)**; Ushuaia **(Argentina)**

*Reached by train, boat, or plane.

Drawn by OAS Graphic Services Unit, 1973

CONVERSACIÓN V

En la Carretera Panamericana

(*Luis y Juan se desayunan temprano en el hotel y, después de pagar su cuenta, van al garaje donde han guardado su coche. El botones baja el equipaje y lo mete en la cajuela del coche.*)

JUAN. Luis, ayer manejé yo casi todo el día, de manera que te toca a ti manejar un rato esta mañana.

LUIS. Está bien. (*Entra en el coche y pone en marcha el motor.*) Parece que necesitamos gasolina, ¿no?

JUAN. No falta mucha, pero es mejor estar seguros. Vamos a pararnos en una de las estaciones que vimos anoche al llegar a la ciudad. (*Quince minutos más tarde se paran en una gasolinera que encuentran en la Carretera Panamericana.*)

EMPLEADO. Buenos días, señores. ¿En qué puedo servirles? ¿Gasolina? ¿Aceite?

LUIS. Necesitamos gasolina.

EMPLEADO. ¿Desean llenar el tanque?

LUIS. Sí, llénelo, por favor. Siempre es bueno llevar suficiente gasolina. Habrá muchas estaciones de gasolina por la carretera, ¿verdad?

EMPLEADO. Pues, sí, señor, si van por esta carretera. Hasta en los pueblos pequeños las[1] hay ... Puse (Eché) treinta y un litros de gasolina. ¿Qué tal el aceite? ¿Quieren que lo mire?

LUIS. Lo cambiamos ayer en San Antonio, pero es posible que necesitemos un poco. El coche ya no es nuevo y gasta bastante.

EMPLEADO. Pues, vale más mirarlo ... Sí, necesita un litro. ¿Qué marca?

LUIS. Es igual. Uno que sea bueno. Y, ¿quiere ver si el radiador tiene bastante agua?

EMPLEADO. Está lleno. Y la batería tiene agua también. ¿Ponemos (Echamos) aire en las llantas?

LUIS. Sí, veinte y ocho libras; y en la llanta de repuesto también, por favor. Aquí tiene la llave de la cajuela.

EMPLEADO. Ya está hecho. No necesitan aire. El parabrisas está muy sucio. Lo limpio en un momento ... Bueno, todo está listo.

LUIS. ¿Cuánto es?

EMPLEADO. Treinta y siete, sesenta.[2]

LUIS. Aquí tiene Vd. un billete de cincuenta pesos.

---

[1] Used with impersonal forms of **haber** the direct object pronouns **lo, la, los, las** usually mean *one, some,* expressed or understood: **Hasta en los pueblos pequeños las hay,** *Even in the small towns there are (some).* Also see page 340, line 14: **Los hay muy buenos,** *There are some very good ones.* In negative sentences, these object pronouns may mean *any (one)*: **¿Hay estación allí? — No, no la hay.** *Is there a station there? — No, there isn't any.* [2] That is, **Treinta y siete pesos, sesenta centavos.**

EMPLEADO.　Y aquí tiene Vd. el cambio, señor.

JUAN.　¿Está la carretera en buenas condiciones?

EMPLEADO.　Hay algunos puentes angostos y algunos tramos en reparación, pero, en general, está en muy buenas condiciones.　Pero les advierto una cosa, señores; no excedan la velocidad máxima o los detiene la policía.

JUAN.　Muchas gracias por la advertencia.　Tendremos mucho cuidado, si bien no tenemos mucha prisa.　Pensamos pararnos de vez en cuando para sacar fotografías y para mirar el paisaje.　¿Qué distancia hay de aquí a la capital?

EMPLEADO.　Unos mil ciento cincuenta kilómetros.　No tratarán de hacer el viaje en un día, ¿verdad?　Les aconsejo que pasen la noche en Valles o en Tamazunchale.

LUIS.　Eso pensamos hacer.　Así no tendremos que viajar de noche y podremos cruzar las montañas mañana por la mañana.

JUAN.　Hay buenos hoteles en esos lugares, ¿verdad?

EMPLEADO.　¡Ya lo creo!　Los hay muy buenos.　También hay campos de turismo (moteles), como en su país.

JUAN.　Muchísimas gracias.

EMPLEADO.　De nada.　¡Que les vaya bien!　¡Buen viaje!

PREGUNTAS

Sobre la conversación

1. ¿Qué hacen Luis y Juan después de desayunarse?　2. ¿Qué hace el botones?
3. ¿Quién va a manejar un rato?　4. ¿Qué van a hacer antes de salir de la ciudad?
5. ¿Por qué prefieren llenar el tanque?　6. ¿Qué le pregunta Luis al empleado?
7. ¿Por qué dice Luis que es posible que el coche necesite aceite?　8. ¿Qué tiene que limpiar el empleado?　9. ¿Cuántos litros de gasolina puso en el tanque?　10. ¿Qué dice el empleado de la carretera?　11. ¿Qué distancia hay de Monterrey a la capital?
12. ¿Dónde van a pasar la noche?

Aplicación de la conversación

1. ¿Qué le damos al botones cuando nos ayuda con nuestro equipaje?　2. ¿Le gusta a Vd. manejar de noche?　3. ¿Cuántos años tenía Vd. cuando aprendió a manejar?
4. ¿Dónde guarda Vd. su coche?　5. ¿Qué es una gasolinera?　6. ¿Hay muchas gasolineras cerca de la universidad?
7. ¿Cuántas libras de aire pone Vd. en las llantas de su coche?　8. ¿Por qué es importante que esté en buenas condiciones la llanta de repuesto?　9. ¿Qué pasa algunas veces cuando excedemos la velocidad máxima?　10. ¿Qué distancia hay desde esta ciudad hasta la capital del estado?　11. ¿Sabe Vd. si hay buenos moteles por aquí?　12. ¿Hay que tener mucho cuidado al manejar en las carreteras de este país?

Bridge on the new Atlantic Highway, Guatemala

PRÁCTICAS ORALES

Groups of students will be selected to prepare a conversation of eight to ten exchanges, using vocabulary already given, on:

1. Servicing a car at a filling station.
2. Paying a hotel bill, loading luggage into the car, and departing.
3. Asking for directions and about road conditions.

VOCABULARIO

el **aceite** oil
la **advertencia** warning
  angosto, -a narrow
  bajar to bring down
la **batería** battery
la **cajuela** auto trunk
  cambiar to change
el **cambio** change
el **campo de turismo** tourist camp,
   motel
la **carretera** highway
la **condición** (*pl.* **condiciones**)
   condition
  cruzar to cross, pass (go) across
la **distancia** distance
  echar to throw, put (in)
la **estación** (*pl.* **estaciones**) station
  exceder to exceed
  faltar to lack, be lacking (*used like*
   gustar)
la **gasolina** gasoline
la **gasolinera** filling (gas) station
  gastar to waste, use (up)
  guardar to keep, guard
  hasta *adv.* even
  igual equal

la **libra** pound
el **litro** liter (*about 1.06 quarts*)
la **llanta de repuesto** spare tire
  llenar to fill
  lleno, -a full
  manejar to drive (*Mex.*)
la **marca** brand, kind, make
  máximo, -a maximum
  meter to put (in)
el **motel** motel
el **motor** motor
el **paisaje** landscape, countryside
  panamericano, -a Pan American
  pararse to stop
el **parabrisas** windshield
la **policía** police
el **pueblo** village, town
el **puente** bridge
el **radiador** radiator
la **reparación** (*pl.* **reparaciones**)
   repairing, repairs
  sucio, -a dirty
  suficiente sufficient, enough
el **tanque** tank
el **tramo** stretch, section
  unos, -as about (*quantity*)
la **velocidad** speed

de nada don't mention it, you're welcome, not at all
de noche at night
en buenas condiciones in good condition
es igual it's all the same, it doesn't matter
estación de gasolina gasoline station
poner en marcha to start
¡que les vaya bien! good luck (*lit.*, may it go well with you)!
¿qué distancia hay? how far is it?
si bien though, while
te toca a ti it's your turn
tener mucha prisa to be in a big hurry
tramo en reparación section under repairs
ya no no longer

REPASO V

A. Answer in Spanish, following the models:

MODEL: ¿Quiere Vd. ese sombrero? No, quiero el que Vd. tiene.

1. ¿Quiere Vd. esos guantes?
2. ¿Le gusta a Vd. esa blusa?
3. ¿Vas a comprar esas camisas?
4. ¿Te gusta ese abrigo?

MODEL: ¿Llegó ese joven ayer? Sí, es el que llegó ayer.

5. ¿Vino esa joven anoche?
6. ¿Vinieron esas muchachas ayer?
7. ¿Llamó ese señor por teléfono?
8. ¿Enviaron esos jóvenes las flores?

B. Say after your teacher, then repeat, using a possessive pronoun for the noun or prepositional phrase:

MODELS: Tengo la maleta de Juan. Tengo la maleta de Juan. Tengo la suya.
Nuestro coche es viejo. Nuestro coche es viejo. El nuestro es viejo.

1. No conduzca Vd. el coche de él.
2. Yo traigo el equipaje de Marta.
3. Póngase Vd. el abrigo.
4. Deja tú aquí nuestras flores.
5. Fui por mi billete.
6. Mis amigos me aguardaban.
7. Dame tú tus paquetes.
8. El jardín de mi mamá es bonito.

C. Listen to the question, then reply affirmatively, using the correct possessive pronoun:

MODEL: ¿Es de Vd. este disco? Sí, es mío.

1. ¿Es de Vd. este abrigo?
2. ¿Es de ellos este coche?
3. ¿Es tuya esa blusa?
4. ¿Es mía esta pulsera?
5. ¿Son de Ramón estas corbatas?
6. ¿Son de ella estas maletas?
7. ¿Son nuestros esos billetes?
8. ¿Son de Vds. esas cartas?

D. Answer affirmatively, using the passive voice in your reply:

MODEL: ¿Escribió Juan la tarjeta? Sí, la tarjeta fue escrita por Juan.

1. ¿Escribió Elena las frases?
2. ¿Envió Juanita las flores?
3. ¿Hizo María los dos vestidos?
4. ¿Vio Ana a los muchachos?
5. ¿Abrió la puerta la Sra. Valdés?
6. ¿Construyó la casa el tío de Pablo?

E. Repeat the sentence; when you hear the cue, compose a new sentence:

> MODEL: Yo hablé con él cuando le vi.   Yo hablé con él cuando le vi.
> Yo hablaré con él   Yo hablaré con él cuando le vea.

1. Ellos volvieron a casa en cuanto yo los llamé. (Ellos volverán a casa)
2. Nosotros tuvimos que salir aunque llovía. (Nosotros tendremos que salir)
3. Yo hablaba despacio de modo que ellos me entendían. (Yo hablaré despacio)
4. Nos quedamos en casa hasta que llegaron ellos. (Nos quedaremos en casa)
5. Yo le pagué a él cuando me trajo el paquete. (Yo le pagaré a él)
6. Juan no pudo irse aunque consiguió el puesto. (Juan no podrá irse)
7. Ella y yo fuimos a verlos en cuanto fue posible. (Ella y yo iremos a verlos)
8. Yo charlaba con ella cuando estaba aquí. (Yo charlaré con ella)

F. Listen carefully to the sentence, then compose a conditional sentence. Use the **-ra** imperfect subjunctive in the first three sentences, and the **-se** form in the last three:

> MODEL: Juan escribiría la carta,   Si Juan estuviera aquí, escri-
> pero no está aquí.   biría la carta.

1. Ellos irían al parque hoy, pero no tienen tiempo.
2. Carolina les daría el paquete, pero no los ve.
3. Nosotros saldríamos con Vds., pero no estamos listos.
4. Yo compraría la maleta, pero no voy a hacer el viaje.
5. Ana podría llegar a tiempo, pero no se da prisa.
6. Me gustaría ir al cine, pero la película no es buena.

G. Read in Spanish, supplying the correct form of the infinitive in parentheses:

1. Mi hermanito corría como si (tener) miedo.
2. ¡Ojalá que ellos (haber) llegado a tiempo anoche!
3. Los padres de él buscan una casa que (ser) más grande.
4. Yo no conozco a nadie que (construir) casas tan bien como el Sr. Smith.
5. No había nadie que (conducir) el coche mejor que Pablo.
6. Déjame el coche, por favor, para que yo lo (conducir) esta tarde.
7. Juan dijo que se iría mañana aunque (hacer) mucho frío.
8. Yo insistí en que los dos (seguir) andando por el parque.
9. Mi hermana no pudo hallar ninguna bolsa que le (gustar).
10. Ellos me llamaron en cuanto (volver) a casa.
11. Aunque (llover) mucho anoche, fuimos al cine.

12. Aunque ellas (vestirse) pronto, van a perder el autobús.
13. Les aconsejé a ellos que (tener) cuidado.
14. Diles a las niñas que (ponerse) los zapatos.
15. No creo que Eduardo (reírse) de Carlos ahora.
16. ¿Duda Vd. que Elena (haber) oído decir eso?
17. Yo sentía mucho que las muchachas no (haber) limpiado su habitación.
18. ¿Fue preciso que ellas (volver) a la universidad?
19. Será mejor que Carlos (escoger) un regalo para su novia esta tarde.
20. ¿Se alegra Vd. de que ésta (ser) la última lección del libro?

H. Listen carefully to each sentence, then answer the question based on it:

1. Roberto partió ayer y fue a México.
   ¿Para dónde partió Roberto?
2. El señor Gómez escribió una carta de presentación.
   ¿Por quién fue escrita la carta de presentación?
3. Vicente le vendió un libro a Luis y éste le pagó cinco dólares por él.
   ¿Cuánto le pagó Luis a Vicente por el libro?
4. Ricardo estuvo aquí por tres días antes de salir para California.
   ¿Por cuántos días estuvo aquí Ricardo?
5. Los jóvenes tomaron un autobús para ir a casa de Margarita.
   ¿Qué tomaron los jóvenes para ir a casa de Margarita?
6. Yo tengo un regalo y se lo voy a dar a Eduardo.
   ¿Para quién es el regalo?
7. Ramón y Luis pasaron por la casa de Tomás para hablar con él.
   ¿Para qué pasaron los dos por la casa de Tomás?
8. Aunque llegaron tarde al aeropuerto, hubo tiempo para hacer facturar sus maletas.
   ¿Para qué hubo tiempo?

I. Give in Spanish:

1. At your service. 2. Drive carefully (*formal and fam. sing.*). 3. Don't fail (*fam. sing.*) to write to me. 4. We have to hurry. 5. Jane has blond hair. 6. What do you think of Paul? 7. What are friends good for? 8. Send her a card today. 9. Get dressed at once (*formal and fam. sing.*). 10. Let's sit down near the window. 11. Let's not eat breakfast yet. 12. Henry forgot to reserve a seat. 13. He bought a round-trip ticket. 14. I did not see Mary anywhere. 15. Jane's little brother hurt himself. 16. Johnny's mother became ill.

J.   Answer in Spanish:

1. Cuando Vd. tiene que hacer un viaje largo, ¿prefiere hacerlo en coche o en avión? 2. Si Vd. tuviera dinero, ¿qué país hispanoamericano le gustaría visitar? 3. ¿Qué les enviamos a nuestros amigos cuando viajamos? 4. ¿Qué les decimos a los amigos cuando nos despedimos de ellos? 5. ¿Dónde conseguimos informes acerca de los viajes en avión? 6. ¿Qué les pedimos a los amigos cuando buscamos un puesto?

7. ¿Hay mucho tránsito en la calle en que vive Vd.? 8. ¿Cuándo fue construida la casa en que viven sus padres? 9. ¿Es su casa más grande o más pequeña que las otras de la misma calle? 10. ¿Cuántas habitaciones tiene su casa en el piso bajo?

11. ¿Qué hacemos cuando creemos que no vamos a llegar a tiempo a algún sitio? 12. ¿A quién llamamos cuando una persona está muy enferma? 13. ¿Adónde llevamos los trajes y los vestidos para hacerlos limpiar? 14. ¿Se levanta Vd. temprano los domingos? 15. ¿Qué hizo Vd. ayer después de almorzar?

16. ¿Juega Vd. a menudo a las cartas? 17. ¿Con quiénes juega Vd. a las cartas? 18. ¿Cómo termina el refrán que comienza, «Antes que te cases»? 19. ¿Qué otros refranes españoles sabe Vd.? 20. ¿Cuánto tiempo hace que estudia Vd. el español?

Parque Guell, designed by Gaudí, the famous Catalan architect, Barcelona, Spain.

CARTAS
ESPAÑOLAS

In the following pages will be given some of the essential principles for personal and business letters in Spanish. Even though many formulas used in Spanish letters are less formal and flowery than formerly, in general they are still less brief and direct than in English letters, and at times they may seem rather stilted. There is no attempt to give a complete treatment of Spanish correspondence, but careful study of the material included should serve for ordinary purposes.

The new words and expressions whose English equivalents are given throughout this section are not included in the Spanish-English vocabulary, unless used elsewhere in the text.

A. Address on the envelope

The title of the addressee begins with **señor** (**Sr.**), **señora** (**Sra.**), or **señorita** (**Srta.**). **Sr. don** (**Sr. D.**) may be used for a man, **Sra. doña** (**Sra. Dª.**) for a married woman, and **Srta.** for an unmarried woman:

Señor don Carlos Morelos	**Sr. D. Pedro Ortega y Moreno**
Srta. Carmen Alcalá	**Sra. Dª. María López de Martín**

In the third example note that Spanish surnames often include the name of the father (**Ortega**), followed by that of the mother (**Moreno**). Often the mother's name is dropped (first two examples). A woman's married name is her maiden name followed by **de** and the surname of her husband (fourth example).

The definite article is not used with the titles **don** and **doña,** which have no English equivalents.

Two complete addresses follow:

Sr. D. Luis Montoya	**Srta. Elena Pérez**
Calle de San Martín, 25	**Avenida Bolívar,** 245
Santiago, Chile	**Caracas, Venezuela**

Business letters are addressed to a firm:

Suárez Hermanos (Hnos.)	**Señores (Sres.) López Díaz y Cía., S. A.**
Apartado (Postal) 867	**Paseo de la Reforma,** 12
Buenos Aires, Argentina	**México, D. F., México**

In an address in Spanish one writes first **Calle** (**Avenida,** *avenue*; **Paseo,** *boulevard*; **Camino,** *road*; **Plaza,** *square*), then the house number. **Apartado (Postal),** *post office box*, may be abbreviated to **Apdo. (Postal).** The abbreviation **Cía.** = **Compañía; S. A.** = **Sociedad Anónima,** equivalent to English *Inc. (Incorporated)*; and **D. F.** = **Distrito Federal,** *Federal District.*

Air mail letters are marked **Vía aérea, Correo aéreo,** or **Por avión.** Special delivery letters are marked **Urgente,** and registered letters, **Certificada.**

B. Heading of the letter

The usual form of the date line is:

México, D. F., 27 de enero de 1974

The month is usually not capitalized unless it is given first in the date. For the first day of the month 1° (**primero**) is commonly used; the other days are written 2, 3, 4, etc. Other less common forms for the date line are:

Lima, Junio 15 de 1968
Bogotá, 1° agosto 1970

The address which precedes the salutation of the business and formal social letter is the same as that on the envelope. In familiar letters only the salutation need be used.

C. Salutations and conclusions for familiar letters

Forms used in addressing relatives or close friends are:

Querido hermano (Luis):	**(Mi) querida hija:**
Querida amiga mía:	**Queridísima**[1] **mamá:**

---

[1] **Queridísima,** *Dearest.*

In conclusions of familiar letters a great variety of formulas may be used.   Some commonly used endings for letters in the family are:

> (**Un abrazo de**) **tu hijo,** (*one boy signs*)
> **Tu hijo** (**hija**), **que te quiere,**[1] (*one boy or girl signs*)
> **Con todo el cariño**[2] **de tu hermano** (**hermana**), (*one boy or girl signs*)

For friends (also for the family) the following, with many possible variations, are suitable:

> **Un abrazo de tu** (**su**) **amiga, que te** (**le**) **quiere,**
> **Tuyo** (**Suyo**) **afectísimo** (**afmo.**),[3] *or* **Tuya** (**Suya**)
>   **afectísima** (**afma.**),
> **Cariñosos saludos**[4] **de tu amigo** (**amiga**),
> (**Con el cariño de**) **tu buen amigo** (**buena amiga**),
> **Sinceramente,** *or* **Afectuosamente,**[5]

In the first few letters to a Spanish friend one normally uses the polite forms of address; as the correspondence continues, more familiar forms may be used.

D. Salutations for business letters or those addressed to strangers

Appropriate salutations, equivalent to "My dear Sir," "Dear Sir," "Dear Madam," "Gentlemen," etc., are:

> **Muy señor** (**Sr.**) **mío:** (*from one person to one gentleman*)
> **Muy señor nuestro:** (*from a firm to one gentleman*)
> **Muy señores** (**Sres.**) **míos:** (*from one person to a firm*)
> **Muy señores nuestros:** (*from one firm to another firm*)
> **Muy señora** (**Sra.**) **mía:** (*from one person to a woman*)
> **Muy señorita nuestra:** (*from a firm to a young woman*)

Formulas which may be used in less formal letters are:

> **Muy estimado Sr. Salas:** Dear Mr. Salas:
> **Estimada amiga** (**Isabel**)**:** Dear friend (Betty):
> **Mi distinguido amigo** (**colega**)**:** Dear Friend (Colleague):

---

[1] When **querer** has a personal object, it means *to love*.   [2] **cariño,** *affection*.   [3] **Tuyo** (**Suyo**) **afectísimo,** *Affectionately yours*.   [4] **Cariñosos saludos,** *Affectionate greetings*.   [5] **Afectuosamente,** *Affectionately, Sincerely*.

E. Conclusions for informal social and business letters

Common forms equivalent to "Sincerely yours," "Cordially yours," "Affectionately yours," are:

> **Suyo afectísimo (afmo.),** *or* **Suyos afectísimos (afmos.),**
> **Queda**[1] **(Quedo) suyo afmo. (suya afma.),**
> **Le saluda cariñosamente (muy atentamente),**
> **Se despide afectuosamente tu amigo,**

F. The body of business letters

The Spanish business letter usually begins with a brief sentence which indicates the purpose of the letter. A few examples, with English translations, follow. Note that the sentences cannot always be translated word for word:

Acabo (Acabamos) de recibir su carta del 10 de septiembre.
I (We) have just received your letter of September 10.

Le doy a usted las gracias por el pedido que se sirvió hacerme ...
Thank you for the order which you kindly placed with me ...

He recibido con mucho agrado su amable carta ...
I was very glad to receive your (good) letter ...

Le acusamos recibo de su atenta[2] **del 2 del corriente ...**
We acknowledge receipt of your letter of the 2nd (of this month) ...

Mucho agradeceré a usted[3] **el mandarme ...**
I shall thank you if you will send me ...

Le envío giro postal por $3.00 ...
I am sending you a postal money order for $3.00 ...

Con fecha 8 del actual me permití escribir a Vd., informándole ...
On the 8th (of this month) I took the liberty of writing to you, informing you ...

Some proper conclusions which might accompany such salutations are:

Muy agradecidos por la buena atención que se dignará Vd. prestar a la presente, saludamos a Vd. con nuestro mayor aprecio y consideración,
Thanking you for your kind attention to this letter, we remain, Very truly yours,

---

[1] **Queda** is in the third person if the signee is the subject. Also note the next example. [2] **Carta** is often replaced with **favor, grata, atenta.** [3] Since **usted** is technically a noun (coming from **vuestra merced**), the object pronoun **le** may be omitted before the verb. This practice is noted particularly in letter writing.

En espera de su envío y con gracias anticipadas, quedo de Vd. atto. S.S.,[1]
Awaiting the shipment and thanking you in advance, I remain, Sincerely yours,

Aprovechamos esta ocasión para ofrecernos sus attos. y ss. ss.,
We take advantage of this opportunity to remain, Yours truly,

Quedamos de ustedes afmos. attos. y Ss. Ss.,
We remain, Very truly yours,

Me repito[2] **su afmo. s. s.,** *or* **Nos repetimos sus afmos. ss. ss.,**
I (We) remain, Sincerely,

As noted above, the Spanish conclusion usually requires more than a mere "Very truly yours," or "Sincerely yours." However, there is a tendency nowadays to shorten conclusions of business letters, particularly as correspondence continues with an individual or firm.

Great care must be taken to be consistent in the agreement of salutations and conclusions of letters, keeping in mind whether the letters are addressed to a man or a woman, or to a firm, and whether the letters are signed by one person or by an individual for a firm.

---

[1] **Seguro servidor** (*sing.*) may be abbreviated to **S.S.** or **s. s.**; **seguros servidores** (*pl.*) to **SS. SS., Ss. Ss.,** or **ss. ss. Atto. = atento; attos. = atentos.**   [2] After the first letter (where the verb **aprovechar** may have been used) **Me repito** is a good follow-up.

Mailman, Tarragona, Spain.

G. Sample letters

The following letters translated freely from Spanish to English will show how natural, idiomatic phrases in one language convey the same idea in another.   Read the following letters aloud for practice, and be able to write any of them from dictation.   The teacher may want to test comprehension by asking questions in Spanish on the content of the letters.   At the end of this section are listed some words and phrases, not all of which are used in the sample letters, which should be useful in composing original letters.

1

12 de marzo de 1974

Librería de Porrúa Hnos. y Cía.
Apartado 7990
México, D. F., México

Muy señores míos:

Tengo el gusto de avisarles a ustedes que acabo de recibir su atenta del 8 del actual y el ejemplar de su catálogo con la lista de precios que se sirvieron remitirme por separado.

Sírvanse enviarme a la mayor brevedad posible la lista de libros que envío anexa. También hallarán adjunto un cheque por pesos 196,40[1] en pago de la factura del 20 del pasado.

Quedo de ustedes su atto. y S. S.,

March 12, 1974

Porrúa Brothers and Co., Bookstore
Post Office Box 7990
Mexico City, Mexico

Gentlemen:

I am glad to inform you that I have just received your letter of March 8 and the copy of your catalogue with the list of prices which you kindly sent me under separate cover.

Please send me as soon as possible the list of books which I am including (in this letter).   Also you will find enclosed a check for $196.40 (196.40 pesos) in payment of your bill of February 20 (of the 20th of last month).

Sincerely yours,

---

[1] Read **ciento noventa y seis pesos, cuarenta centavos**.   While the comma between the **pesos** and **centavos** has largely been replaced in Spanish by a period, it is still used.   The English comma is often written as a period in Spanish: **pesos** 1.250,35.

2

16 de marzo de 1974

Muy señor nuestro:

Acusamos recibo de su favor del 12 del presente, en que hallamos adjunto su cheque por pesos 196,40, que abonamos en su cuenta, y por el cual le damos a usted las gracias.

Hoy le enviamos a vuelta de correo el pedido de libros que se sirvió hacernos, cuyo importe cargamos en su cuenta.

En espera de sus nuevos gratos pedidos, nos place ofrecernos sus afmos. attos. y ss. ss.,

March 16, 1974

Dear Sir:

We acknowledge receipt of your letter of March 12, in which we found enclosed your check for 196.40 pesos, which we are crediting to your account, and for which we thank you.

Today we are sending by return mail the order for books which you kindly sent us (made of us), the amount of which we are charging to your account.

Awaiting other kind orders from you, we remain, Sincerely yours,

EJERCICIO

1. Write to a foreign student, describing some of your daily activities. Try to use words which you have had in this text.
2. Write to a member of your family, describing some shopping you have done.
3. Assume that you are the Spanish secretary for an American exporting firm. Write a reply to a Spanish American firm which has asked for a recent catalogue and prices.

Post office, Barcelona, Spain.

VOCABULARIO ÚTIL

abonar   to credit
adjunto, -a   enclosed, attached
anexo, -a   enclosed, attached
el buzón   mailbox
cargar   to charge
la casa de correos   Post office
el catálogo   catalogue
certificar   to register
comunicar   to inform, tell
dirigir   to address, direct
el ejemplar   copy
el envío   shipment, remittance
la estampilla   (postage) stamp (Am.)
la factura   bill, invoice
la firma   signature
el folleto   folder, pamphlet
el franqueo   postage
el giro   draft

grato, -a   kind, pleased
el importe   cost, amount
la muestra   sample
las noticias   news, information
ofrecer(se)   to offer, be, offer
   one's services
el pago   payment
el pasado   last month
el pedido   order
permitirse   to take the liberty (to)
el recibo   receipt
remitir   to remit, send
el saldo   balance
el sello   (postage) stamp (Spain)
servirse (i,i)   to be so kind as to
el sobre   envelope
la solicitud   request
suplicar   to beg, ask
el timbre   (postage) stamp (Am)

acusar recibo de   to acknowledge receipt of
a la mayor brevedad posible   as soon as possible
anticipar las gracias   to thank in advance
a vuelta de correo   by return mail
dar las gracias (a)   to thank
de acuerdo con   in compliance with
del corriente (actual)   of the present month
echar al correo   to mail
en contestación a   in reply to
en espera de   awaiting
en pago de   in payment of
en su cuenta   to one's account
estar encargado, -a de   to be in charge of
giro postal   money order
hacer un pedido   to place (give) an order
lista de precios   price list
(nos) es grato   (we) are pleased
nos place   we are pleased
paquete postal   parcel post
por separado   under separate cover
sírva(n)se + *inf.*   to please, be pleased to
tener el agrado (gusto) de   to be pleased to
tener la bondad de   to have the kindness to, please

APPENDICES

VOCABULARIES

INDEX

Appendix A

ME GUSTAN TODAS

Me gus - tan to - das, me gus - tan to - das, me gus - tan
to - das en ge - ne - ral. Pe - ro e - sa ru - bia, pe - ro e - sa
ru - bia, pe - ro e - sa ru - bia me gus - ta más.

VILLANCICO DE NAVIDAD

La Vir - gen la - va __ pa - ña - les __ y los
tien - de en el ro - me - ro __ y los pa - ja - ri - tos

Note: The guitar chords for these songs were prepared by Mr. Robert P. Sullivan of the New England Conservatory of Music.

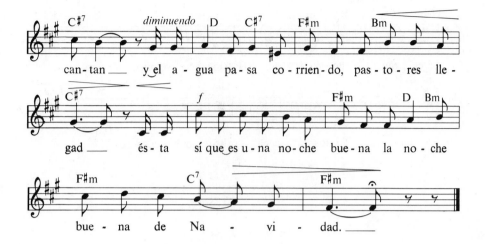

can - tan ___ y el a - gua pa - sa co - rrien - do, pas - to - res lle -

gad ___ és - ta sí que es u - na no - che bue - na la no - che

bue - na de Na - vi - dad. ___

ALLÁ EN EL RANCHO GRANDE[1]

A - llá en el ran - cho gran - de A - llá don - de vi - ví - a, ___

___ Ha - bía u - na ran - che - ri - ta Que a - le - gre me de -

cí - a, Que a - le - gre me de - cí - a, ___

Te voy a ha - cer tus cal - zo - nes, ___ Co - mo los u -

sa el ran - che - ro; _____ Te los co - mien - zo de

la na, _____ Te los a - ca - bo de cue - ro.

D.S.

LAS MAÑANITAS

És - tas son las ma - ña - ni - tas que can -
Si el se - re - no de la es - qui - na me qui -

ta - ba el Rey Da - vid, pe - ro no e - ran tan bo -
sie - ra ha - cer fa - vor, de a - pa - gar su lin - ter -

ni - tas, co - mo las can - tan a - quí.
ni - ta, mien - tras que pa - sa mi a - mor.

Des - pier - ta, mi bien, des - pier - ta, mi -

ra que ya a - ma - ne - ció, ya los pa - ja - ri - llos

can - tan, ya la lu - na se o - cul - tó.

CANTO DE ROMERÍA

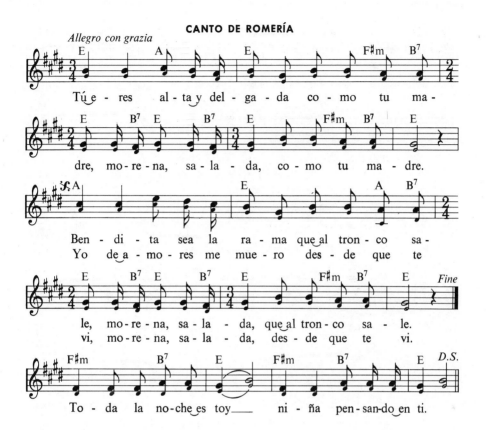

Tú e - res al - ta y del - ga - da co - mo tu ma -

dre, mo - re - na, sa - la - da, co - mo tu ma - dre.

Ben - di - ta sea la ra - ma que al tron - co sa -
Yo de a - mo - res me mue - ro des - de que te

le, mo - re - na, sa - la - da, que al tron - co sa - le.
vi, mo - re - na, sa - la - da, des - de que te vi.

To - da la no - che es toy___ ni - ña pen - san - do en ti.

LA GOLONDRINA

¿A - dón - de i - rá, ve - loz y fa - ti - ga - da,

la go - lon - dri - na que de a - quí se va?___ Oh, si en el

ai - re ge - mi - rá ex - tra - via - da, bus - can - do a -
bri - go y no lo en - con - tra - rá. Jun - to a mi
le_____ cho le pon - dré____ su ni____ do,
en - don - de pue - da_____ la es - ta - ción_____ pa -
sar; tam - bién yo es - toy_____ en la re - gión per -
di - do, ¡oh cie - lo san - to! sin po - der vo - lar.____

ADELITA

A - de - li - ta se lla - ma la jo - ven a quien yo

quie - ro y no pue - do_ol - vi - dar; en el mun - do yo

ten - go_u - na ro - sa, que con el tiem - po la

Estribillo

voy a cor - tar. Si A - de - li - ta qui -

sie - ra ser mi_es - po - sa, si_A - de - li - ta fue -

ra mi mu - jer, le com - pra - ría un

ves - ti - do de se - da pa - ra lle - var - la_a bai -

lar al cuar - tel. Si_A - de -

ÁBREME LA PUERTA

Á - bre - me la puer - ta, do - ra - do cla - vel, á - bre - me la

TRANSLATION OF SONGS[1]

Me gustan todas (*I Like All the Girls*)

I like all the girls, I like all the girls, in general, I like them all.   But that blonde, that blonde, but that blonde (is the one) I like best.

Villancico de Navidad (*Christmas Carol*)

The Virgin is washing baby clothes and laying them to dry on the rosemary bush; the little birds are singing as the water rushes by.   Shepherds, come, this is indeed a holy night, the holy night of Christmas.

[1] No attempt has been made at a literal or poetic translation of these songs.

Allá en el rancho grande (*There on the Big Ranch*)

There on the big ranch, where once I used to live, there was a little farm girl who happily used to tell me (*repeat*): I am going to make your breeches like those the rancher wears; I'll start them with wool, I'll trim them with hide.

Las Mañanitas (*Early Morning Song*)

This is the early morning song which King David used to sing, but it was not quite so pretty as (the one) they sing here.

If the night watchman on the·corner would only do me the favor of putting out his lantern while my love passes by.

Awake, my love, awake. See, the dawn has come, the little birds are singing, and the moon has gone to rest.

Canto de romería (*Picnic Song*)

You are tall and slender like your mother, charming brunette, just like your mother. Blessed be the branch which resembles the trunk, charming brunette, which resembles the trunk. I have been dying of love ever since I saw you, charming brunette, ever since I saw you. All night long, dear, I think of you.

La golondrina (*The Swallow*)

Whither can the swallow be bound which is leaving here, swiftly, though weary? Oh, if it wails, when lost in the air, looking for shelter, unable to find it!

Near my bed I shall put its nest, where it can spend the whole season. I, too, am lost in this region, oh, merciful heaven, unable to fly!

Adelita (*Adelita*)

Adelita is the name of the girl whom I love and cannot forget; in the world I have a rose, which in time I am going to pick.

If Adelita would like to be my bride, if Adelita were my wife, I would buy her a silk dress to take her to a dance at the barracks.

Ábreme la puerta (*Open the Door for Me*)

(*He*) Open the door for me, radiant carnation, open the door for me because I am coming to see you. (*She*) If you come all alone, I shall burn only one light. (*He*) Just to see my sweetheart I shall go all around the world. (*Both*) To see my sweetheart, to see my love, to see the darling of my heart.

Appendix B

FRASES PARA LA CLASE (*Classroom expressions*)

A number of expressions and grammatical terms which may be used in the classroom and laboratory are listed below. They are not included in the end vocabularies unless used in the preceding lessons. Other common expressions are used in the text.

Voy a pasar lista.	I am going to call the roll.
Presente.	Present.
¿Qué lección tenemos hoy?	What lesson do we have today?
Tenemos la Lección primera (dos).	We have Lesson One (Two).
¿En qué página empieza?	On what page does it begin?
¿Qué línea (renglón)?	What line?
(La lectura) empieza en la página ...	(The reading) begins on page ...
Al principio de la página.	At the beginning of the page.
En el medio (Al pie) de la página.	In the middle (At the bottom) of the page.
Abra(n) Vd(s). su(s) libro(s).	Open your book(s).
Cierre(n) Vd(s). su(s) libro(s).	Close your book(s).
Lea Vd. en español.	Read in Spanish.
Empiece Vd. a leer.	Begin to read.
Siga Vd. leyendo.	Continue (Go on) reading.
Traduzca Vd. al español (inglés).	Translate into Spanish (English).
Repítalo Vd.	Repeat it.
Pronuncie Vd.	Pronounce.
Basta.	That is enough, That will do.
Vayan (Pasen) Vds. a la pizarra.	Go (Pass) to the blackboard.
Escriban Vds. (al dictado).	Write (at dictation).
Corrijan Vds. las oraciones (frases).	Correct the sentences.
Vuelva (n) Vd(s). a su(s) asiento(s).	Return to your seat(s).
Siénte(n)se Vd(s).	Sit down.
Haga(n) Vd(s). el favor de (+*inf.*) ...	Please (+*inf.*) ...
Está bien.	All right, That's fine.
¿Qué significa la palabra ... ?	What does the word ... mean?
¿Cómo se dice ... ?	How does one say ... ?
¿Quién quiere hacer una pregunta?	Who wants to ask a question?
Escuchen Vds. bien.	Listen carefully.
Preparen Vds. para mañana ...	Prepare for tomorrow ...
Ha sonado el timbre.	The bell has rung.
La clase ha terminado.	The class has ended.
Vds. pueden marcharse.	You may leave (You are excused).

PALABRAS Y EXPRESIONES PARA EL LABORATORIO

(Words and expressions for the laboratory)

el alto parlante loud speaker
los auriculares (audífonos) ear(head)phones
la cabina booth
el carrete reel
la cinta (magnetofónica) (magnetic) tape
la cinta maestra (matriz) master tape
la corriente (eléctrica) power; (electric) current
el disco (fonográfico) disc, (phonograph) record
empalmar to splice
el enchufe plug
la entrada input
externo, -a external
la grabadora (de cinta) (tape) recorder
grabar to record
el interruptor switch
el micrófono microphone
la perilla knob
reparar to repair
la salida output
el sonido sound
el volumen volume
Acérquese más al micrófono. Get closer to the microphone.
Aleje más el micrófono. Move the microphone away from you.
Apriete el botón. Push the button.
Aumente el volumen. Turn it louder (Increase the volume).
Escuche la grabación. Listen to the recording.
Hable en voz más alta (más baja, natural). Speak in a louder (lower, natural) voice.
Hable más rápido (despacio). Speak faster (slower).
Imite lo que oiga. Imitate what you hear.
Mi máquina no funciona. My machine does not work.
Pare (Apague) su máquina. Stop (Turn off) your machine.
Ponga en marcha (Encienda) . . . Start, turn on . . .
Póngase (Quítese) los audífonos. Put on (Take off) your headphones.
Repita la respuesta. Repeat the answer.
Se oirá (Vd. oirá) cada frase una vez (dos veces), seguida de una pausa.
    You will hear each sentence once (twice), followed by a pause.
Se oirá (Vd. oirá) luego la respuesta (correcta).
    You will hear the (correct) answer later.
¿Se oye claramente la señal? Is the signal clear?
Vuelva a enrollar la cinta. Rewind the tape.

TÉRMINOS GRAMATICALES *(Grammatical terms)*

el adjetivo	adjective
demostrativo	demonstrative
posesivo	possessive
el adverbio	adverb
el artículo	article
definido	definite
indefinido	indefinite
el cambio ortográfico	change in spelling
la capitalización	capitalization
la cláusula	clause
la comparación	comparison
el comparativo	comparative
el complemento	object
directo	direct
indirecto	indirect
la composición	composition
la concordancia	agreement
la conjugación	conjugation
la conjunción	conjunction
la consonante	consonant
el diptongo	diphthong
el género	gender
masculino	masculine
femenino	feminine
el gerundio	gerund, present participle
el infinitivo	infinitive
la interjección	interjection
la interrogación	interrogation, question (mark)
la letra	letter (of the alphabet)
mayúscula	capital
minúscula	small
el modo indicativo (**subjuntivo**)	indicative (subjunctive) mood
el nombre (**substantivo**)	noun, substantive
el nombre propio	proper noun
el número	number, numeral
cardinal (**ordinal**)	cardinal (ordinal)
el objeto	object
la palabra (**negativa**)	(negative) word
las partes de la oración	parts of speech
el participio pasado (**presente**)	past (present) participle
la persona	person
primera	first

segunda	second
tercera	third
el plural	plural
la posición	position
el predicado	predicate
la preposición	preposition
el pronombre	pronoun
interrogativo	interrogative
personal	personal
relativo	relative
la puntuación	punctuation
el radical (**la raíz**)	stem
el significado	meaning
la sílaba	syllable
última	last
penúltima	next to the last
el singular	singular
el subjuntivo	subjunctive
el sujeto	subject
el superlativo (**absoluto**)	(absolute) superlative
la terminación	ending
el tiempo	tense
el tiempo simple (**compuesto**)	simple (compound) tense
presente	present
imperfecto	imperfect
pretérito	preterit
futuro	future
condicional	conditional
perfecto	perfect (present perfect)
pluscuamperfecto	pluperfect
futuro perfecto	future perfect
condicional perfecto	conditional perfect
el triptongo	triphthong
el verbo	verb
auxiliar	auxiliary
impersonal	impersonal
irregular	irregular
reflexivo	reflexive
regular	regular
(in)transitivo	(in)transitive
la vocal	vowel
la voz	voice
activa	active
pasiva	passive

SIGNOS DE PUNTUACIÓN *(Punctuation marks)*

,	coma	( )	(el) paréntesis
;	punto y coma	« »	comillas
:	dos puntos	′	acento escrito
.	punto final	¨	(la) diéresis
...	puntos suspensivos	~	(la) tilde
¿ ?	signo(s) de interrogación	-	(el) guión
¡ !	signo(s) de admiración	—	raya

ABREVIATURAS Y SIGNOS *(Abbreviations and signs)*

adj.	adjective	*lit.*	literally
adv.	adverb	*Mex.*	Mexican
Am.	American	*m.*	masculine
cond.	conditional	*masc.*	masculine
conj.	conjunction	*n.*	noun
dir.	direct	*obj.*	object
e.g.	for example	*p.*	page
etc.	and so forth	*p.p.*	past participle
f.	feminine	*part.*	participle
fem.	feminine	*pl.*	plural
fam.	familiar	*prep.*	preposition
i.e.	that is	*pres.*	present
imp.	imperfect	*pret.*	preterit
imper.	imperative	*pron.*	pronoun
ind.	indicative	*reflex.*	reflexive
indef.	indefinite	*sing./s.*	singular
indir.	indirect	*subj.*	subjunctive
inf.	infinitive	*trans.*	transitive
		U.S.	United States

( ) Words in parentheses are explanatory or they are to be translated in the exercises.

[ ] Words in brackets in the exercises are not to be translated.

— In the general vocabularies a dash indicates a word repeated, while in the exercises it usually is to be supplied by some grammatical form.

+ = followed by.

Appendix C

PRONUNCIATION

THE SPANISH ALPHABET

LETTER	NAME	LETTER	NAME	LETTER	NAME
a	a	j	jota	r	ere
b	be	k	ka	rr	erre
c	ce	l	ele	s	ese
ch	che	ll	elle	t	te
d	de	m	eme	u	u
e	e	n	ene	v	ve, uve
f	efe	ñ	eñe	w	doble ve
g	ge	o	o	x	equis
h	hache	p	pe	y	i griega
i	i	q	cu	z	zeta

In addition to the letters used in the English alphabet, **ch, ll, ñ,** and **rr** represent single sounds in Spanish and are considered single letters. In dictionaries and vocabularies words or syllables which begin with **ch, ll,** and **ñ** follow words or syllables that begin with **c, l,** and **n,** while **rr,** which never begins a word, is alphabetized as in English. **K** and **w** are used only in words of foreign origin. The names of the letters are feminine: **la be,** (*the*) *b*; **la jota,** (*the*) *j*.

The Spanish alphabet is divided into vowels (**a, e, i, o, u**) and consonants. The letter **y** is a vowel when final in a word, and when used as the conjunction **y,** *and*.

The Spanish vowels are divided into two groups: strong vowels (**a, e, o**) and weak vowels (**i, u**).

SPANISH SOUNDS

Even though Spanish uses practically the same alphabet as English, few sounds are identical in the two languages. It will, however, be necessary to make comparisons between the familiar English sounds and the unfamiliar Spanish sounds in order to show how Spanish is pronounced. Avoid the use of English sounds in Spanish words and imitate good Spanish pronunciation.

In general, Spanish pronunciation is much clearer and more uniform than the English. The vowel sounds are clipped short and are not followed by the diphthongal glide which is commonly heard in English, as in *no* (*no*^u), *came* (*ca*^i*me*), *why* (*why*^e). Even unstressed vowels are pronounced clearly and distinctly; the slurred sound of English *a* in *fireman*, for example, never occurs in Spanish.

Spanish consonants, likewise, are usually pronounced more precisely and distinctly than English consonants, although a few (especially **b, d,** and **g** between vowels) are pronounced very weakly. Several of them (**t, d, l,** and **n**) are pronounced farther forward in the mouth, with the tongue close to the upper teeth and gums. The consonants **p, t,** and **c** (before letters other than **e** and **i**) are never followed by the *h* sound that is often heard in English: *pen* (*p*^h*en*), *task* (*t*^h*ask*), *can* (*c*^h*an*).

DIVISION OF WORDS INTO SYLLABLES

Spanish words are hyphenated at the end of a line and are divided into syllables according to the following principles.

a. A single consonant (including **ch, ll, rr**) is placed with the vowel which follows: **pa-pel, mu-cho, ca-lle, pi-za-rra.**

b. Two consonants are usually divided: **tar-de, es-pa-ñol, tam-bién.** Consonants followed by **l** or **r,** however, are generally pronounced together and go with the following vowel: **li-bro, pa-dre, a-pren-do.** The groups **nl, rl, sl, tl, nr,** and **sr,** however, are divided: **Car-los, En-ri-que.**

c. In combinations of three or more consonants only the last consonant or the two consonants of the inseparable groups just mentioned (consonant plus **l** or **r,** with the exceptions listed) begin a syllable: **ins-pi-ra-ción, in-glés, en-tra.**

d. Two adjacent strong vowels (**a, e, o**) are in separate syllables: **le-o, tra-e, cre-e.**

e. Combinations of a strong and weak vowel (**i, u**) or of two weak vowels normally form single syllables: **bue-nos, bien, es-tu-dio, gra-cias, ciu-dad, Luis.** Such combinations of two vowels are called *diphthongs.* (See page 417 for further discussion of diphthongs.)

f. In combinations of a strong and weak vowel, a written accent mark on the weak vowel divides the two vowels into separate syllables: **dí-a, pa-ís, tí-o.** An accent on the strong vowel of such combinations does not result in two syllables: **lec-ción, tam-bién.**

WORD STRESS

a. Most words which end in a vowel, and in **n** or **s** (plural endings of verbs and nouns, respectively), are stressed on the next to the last syllable: *cla-***se,** *to-***mo,** *ca-***sas,** *en-***tran,** *Car-***men.**

b. Most words which end in a consonant, except **n** or **s**, are stressed on the last syllable: **pro-fe-***sor***, ha-***blar***, pa-***pel***, ciu-***dad***, es-pa-***ñol***.

c. Words not pronounced according to these two rules have a written accent on the stressed syllable: **ca-***fé***, in-***glés***, lec-***ción***, tam-***bién***.

The written accent is also used to distinguish between two words spelled alike but different in meaning (**si**, *if*, **sí**, *yes;* **el**, *the*, **él**, *he*, etc.), and on the stressed syllable of all interrogative words (**¿qué?** *what?*).

VOWELS

a is pronounced between the *a* of English *ask* and the *a* of *father*: **ca-***sa***, ha-***bla***, *A***-na.**

e is pronounced like *e* in *café*, but without the glide sound that follows the *e* in English: *me***-sa,** *cla***-se,** us-***ted***.

i (**y**) is pronounced like *i* in *machine*: **Fe-***li***-pe, sí,** *dí***-as, y.**

o is pronounced like *o* in *obey*, but without the glide sound that follows the *o* in English: *no***,** *so***-lo, cho-co-***la***-te.**

u is pronounced like *oo* in *cool*: **us-***ted***, u-no, a-***lum***-no.**

The vowels **e** and **o** also have sounds like *e* in *let* and *o* in *for*. These sounds, as in English, generally occur when the **e** and **o** are followed by a consonant in the same syllable: *el***, ser,** *con***, es-pa-***ñol***. In pronouncing the **e** in **el** and **ser**, and the **o** in **con** and **español**, the mouth is opened wider, and the distance between the tongue and the palate is greater, than when pronouncing the **e** in **mesa** and **clase**, and the **o** in **no** and **solo**. These more open sounds of **e** and **o** occur also in contact with the strongly trilled **r** (**rr**), before the **j** sound (written **g** before **e** or **i**, and **j**), and in the diphthongs **ei** (**ey**) and **oi** (**oy**). Pay close attention to the teacher's pronunciation of these sounds.

CONSONANTS

b and **v** are pronounced exactly alike. At the beginning of a breath-group (see page 6), or after **m** and **n**, the sound is that of a weakly pronounced English *b*: *bien***, bue-nas,** *ver***-de, *vi*-da.** In other places, particularly between vowels, the sound is much weaker than the English *b*. The lips touch very lightly, leaving a narrow opening in the center, and the breath continues to pass between them. Avoid the English *v* sound. Examples: *li***-bro, es-***cri***-bo, la-vo, *Cu*-ba.** Note the two different sounds in **vi-***vir***, be-***ber***.

c before **e** and **i**, and **z** in all positions, are pronounced like the English hissed *s* in *sent* in Spanish America and in southern Spain. In northern and central Spain this sound is like *th* in *thin*. Examples: **cen-***ta***-vo, *ci*-ne, gra-cias, *lá*-piz.**

c before all other letters, **k**, and **qu** are like English *c* in *cat*, but without the *h* sound that often follows the *c* in English: **ca-***sa***, *cla*-se, ki-***ló***-me-tro, *que*, par-que.** Note both sounds of **c** in *cin***-co, lec-***ción***.

ch is pronounced like English *ch* in *church*: *mu*-cho, *le*-che, cho-co-*la*-te.

d has two sounds.   At the beginning of a breath-group or following **l** or **n,** it is pronounced like a weak English *d*, but with the tongue touching the back of the upper front teeth rather than the ridge above the teeth, as in English: *dos, don*-de, sal-*dré*.   In other places, particularly between vowels and at the end of a word, the sound is like a weakly articulated English *th* in *this*: *ca*-da, *to*-do, us-*ted*, Ma-*drid*.

f is pronounced like English *f*: ca-*fé*, Fe-*li*-pe.

g before **e** and **i,** and **j** in all positions, have no English equivalent.   They are pronounced approximately like a strongly exaggerated *h* in *halt* (rather like the rasping German **ch** in **Buch**): *gen*-te, *hi*-jo, *Jor*-ge, re-*gión*.   (The letter **x** in the words **México** and **mexicano**, spelled **Méjico** and **mejicano** in Spain, is pronounced like Spanish **j.**)

g in other positions and **gu** before **e** or **i** are pronounced like a weak English *g* in *go* at the beginning of a breath-group or after **n.**   In other cases, especially between vowels, the sound is much weaker, and the breath continues to pass between the back of the tongue and the palate.   Examples: *gra*-cias, gui-*ta*-rra, *ten*-go; but *ha*-go, *lue*-go, por-tu-*gués*.   (In the combinations **gua** and **guo** the **u** is pronounced like English *w* in *wet*: *len*-gua, *a*-gua, an-*ti*-guo; when the diaeresis is used over **u** in the combinations **güe** and **güi,** the **u** has the same sound: ni-ca-ra-*güen*-se.)

h is always silent: ha-*blar*, *has*-ta, *hoy*.

l is pronounced like *l* in *leap*, with the tip and front part of the tongue well forward in the mouth: *la*-do, pa-*pel*.

ll is pronounced like *y* in *yes* in most of Spanish America and in some sections of Spain; in other parts of Spain it is somewhat like *lli* in *million*: *e*-lla, *ca*-lle, lla-*mar*.

m is pronounced like English *m*: *to*-ma, *me*-sa.

n is pronounced like English *n*: *no*, *Car*-men.   Before **b, v, m,** and **p,** however, it is pronounced like *m*: *un*-po-co, con-*Bár*-ba-ra.   Before **c, qu, g,** and **j** it is pronounced like English *n* in *sing*: *blan*-co, *ten*-go, *án*-gel.

ñ is somewhat like the English *ny* in *canyon*: se-*ñor*, ma-*ña*-na, es-pa-*ñol*.

p is pronounced like English *p*, but without the *h* sound that often follows the *p* in English: *pe*-lo, pa-*pel*.

q (always written with **u**): see page 4 1 5, under **c, k,** and **qu.**

r and **rr** represent two different sounds.   Single **r,** except at the beginning of a word, or after **l, n,** or **s,** is pronounced with a single tap produced by the tip of the tongue against the gums of the upper teeth.   The sound is much like *dd* in *eddy* pronounced rapidly: *ca*-ra, *to*-ro, ha-*blar*.   Initial **r, r** after **l, n,** or **s,** and **rr** are strongly trilled: *ri*-co, *ro*-jo, Ro-*ber*-to, pi-*za*-rra, *co*-rre, En-*ri*-que.

s is pronounced somewhat like the English hissed *s* in *sent*: *ca*-sa, *es*-tos.   Before **b, d, g, l, ll, m, n, v,** and **y** the sound is like the English *s* in *rose*: *mis*-mo, *des*-de, *es* ver-*dad*, los *li*-bros.

t is pronounced with the tip of the tongue touching the back of the upper front teeth (rather than the ridge above the teeth, as in English); it is never followed by the *h* sound that is often heard in English: *to*-do, *tar*-des, *tiem*-po.

v: see page 4 1 5, under **b.**

x is pronounced as follows: (1) Before a consonant it is pronounced like English hissed *s* in *sent*: **ex-plo-*rar*, ex-tran-*je*-ro**; (2) between vowels it is usually a double sound, consisting of a weak English *g* in *go* followed by a hissed *s*: **e-*xa*-men, *é*-xi-to.**

y is pronounced like a strong English *y* in *you*: ***ya, yo, ma*-yo.** The conjunction **y,** *and,* when combined with the initial vowel of a following word is similarly pronounced: *Car*-los *y⁀A*-na.

DIPHTHONGS

As stated on page 415, the weak vowels **i** (**y**) and **u** may combine with the strong vowels **a, e, o,** or with each other to form single syllables. Such combinations of two vowels are called diphthongs. In diphthongs the strong vowels retain their full syllabic value, while the weak vowels, or the first vowel in the case of two weak vowels, lose part of their syllabic value.

As the first element of a diphthong, unstressed **i** is pronounced like a weak English *y* in *yes*, and unstressed **u** is pronounced like *w* in *wet*. The Spanish diphthongs which begin with unstressed **i** and **u** are: **ia, ie, io, iu; ua, ue, ui, uo,** as in *gra*-cias, *bien*, a-*diós*, ciu-*dad*; *cual, bue*-no, *Luis*, an-*ti*-guo.

The diphthongs in which unstressed **i** and **u** occur as the second element of the diphthong are nine orthographically, but phonetically only six, since **i** and **y** have the same sound here. They are: **ai, ay; au; ei, ey; eu; oi, oy; ou.** They are pronounced as follows:

    ai, ay like a prolonged English *i* in *mine*: ***bai*-le, *hay***

    au like a prolonged English *ou* in *out*: **au-*tor*, au-to-*bús***

    ei, ey like a prolonged English *a* in *fate*: ***seis, ley***

    eu has no close equivalent in English. It consists of a clipped *e* as in English *eh*, followed closely by a glide sound which ends in *oo*, to sound like *ehoo*: **Eu-*ro*-pa**

    oi, oy like a prolonged English *oy* in *boy*: ***sois, soy***

    ou like a prolonged English *o* in *note*: **lo⁀u-*sa*-mos**

Remember that two adjacent strong vowels within a word do not combine in a single syllable, but form two separate syllables: ***le*-e, Do-ro-*te*-a.** Likewise, when a weak vowel adjacent to a strong vowel has a written accent, it retains its syllabic value and forms a separate syllable: ***di*-a, pa-*ís*.** An accent mark on a strong vowel merely indicates stress: **lec-*ción*, tam-*bién*.**

TRIPHTHONGS

A triphthong is a combination in a single syllable of a stressed strong vowel between two weak vowels. There are four combinations: **iai, iei, uai (uay), uei (uey),** as in **es-tu-*diáis*, Pa-ra-*guay*.**

LINKING

In reading or speaking Spanish, words are linked together, as in English, so that two or more may sound as one long word. These groups of words are called breath-groups. The pronunciation of certain Spanish consonants depends upon their position at the beginning of, or within, a breath-group. Similarly, the pronunciation of many individual sounds will be modified depending on the sounds with which they are linked within the breath-group. Since the words that make up the breath-group are pronounced as if they formed one long word, the principles which govern the structure of the syllable must be observed throughout the entire breath-group.

In speech, words normally are uttered in breath-groups. Thus it is necessary to practice pronouncing phrases and even entire sentences without a pause between words. Frequently a short sentence will be pronounced as one breath-group, while a longer one may be divided into two or more groups. The meaning of what is being pronounced will help you to determine where the pauses ending the breath-groups should be made.

The following examples illustrate some of the general principles of linking. The syllabic division in parentheses shows the correct linking; the syllable or syllables italicized bear the main stress.

a. Within a breath-group the final consonant of a word is joined with the initial vowel of the following word and forms a syllable with it: **el alumno** (e-la-*lum*-no).

b. Within a breath-group when two identical vowels of different words come together, they are pronounced as one: **el profesor de español** (el-pro-fe-*sor*-de‿es-pa-*ñol*).

c. When unlike vowels between words come together within a breath-group, they are usually pronounced together in a single syllable. Two cases occur: (1) when a strong vowel is followed or preceded by a weak vowel, both are pronounced together in a single syllable and the result is phonetically a diphthong (See above, page 417): **su amigo** (su‿a-*mi*-go), **Juan y Elena** (*Jua*-n‿y‿E-*le*-na), **mi padre y mi madre** (mi-*pa*-dre‿y-mi-*ma*-dre); (2) if both vowels are strong, each loses a little of its syllabic value and both are pronounced together in one syllable: **vamos a la escuela** (*va*-mo-sa-la‿es-*cue*-la); **¿ Cómo está usted?** (¿ *Có*-mo‿es-*tá*‿us-ted?).

INTONATION

The term intonation refers to the variations in pitch which occur in speech. Every language has its characteristic patterns of intonation. The intonation of Spanish is quite different from that of English.

The alternate rise and fall of the pitch depends upon the particular meaning of the sentence, the position of stressed syllables, and whether the sentence expresses command, affirmation, interrogation, exclamation, request, or other factors. In general, three meaningful levels of pitch can be distinguished in Spanish: one below the speaker's normal pitch (level 1); the speaker's normal tone (level 2), and a tone higher than the normal one (level 3). Study carefully the examples on page 419.

EXAMPLES

Declarative statement	LEVEL 3 LEVEL 2 LEVEL 1	

Estudiamos el español.   Es-tu-dia-mo-se-les-pa-ñol.

Interrogative sentences   3 2 1

¿Estudiamos el español?   ¿Es-tu-dia-mo-se-les-pa-ñol?

3 2 1

¿Cómo está usted?   ¿Có-mo‿es-tá‿us-ted?

Or, more politely   3 2 1

¿Có-mo‿es-tá‿us-ted?

Exclamatory sentence   3 2 1

¡Qué muchacha más bonita!   ¡Qué-mu-cha-cha-más-bo-ni-ta!

Or, with special interest   3 2 1

¡Qué-mu-cha-cha-más-bo-ni-ta!

With respect to the use of these levels, the following basic principles should be observed:

a. At the beginning of a breath-group the voice begins and continues in a relatively low pitch (level 1) as long as the first accented syllable is not reached.

b. When the first accented syllable of a breath-group is reached, the voice rises to the speaker's normal tone (level 2) and continues in the same pitch as long as the last accented syllable is not reached.

c. When the last accented syllable of the breath-group is reached, the voice falls or rises, depending on the following circumstances:

(1) At the end of a declarative statement, the voice falls to a pitch even lower than that of the initial unaccented syllable or syllables.

(2) At the end of an interrogative sentence, or of an incomplete sentence interrupted by a pause, the voice rises to a pitch above the normal tone (level 3).

Appendix D

REGULAR VERBS

hablar, *to speak*   **comer,** *to eat*   **vivir,** *to live*

PRESENT PARTICIPLE

hablando, *speaking*   **comiendo,** *eating*   **viviendo,** *living*

PAST PARTICIPLE

hablado, *spoken*   **comido,** *eaten*   **vivido,** *lived*

THE SIMPLE TENSES

INDICATIVE MOOD

PRESENT

I speak, do speak, am speaking, etc.	*I eat, do eat, am eating, etc.*	*I live, do live, am living, etc.*
hablo	como	vivo
hablas	comes	vives
habla	come	vive
hablamos	comemos	vivimos
habláis	coméis	vivís
hablan	comen	viven

IMPERFECT

I was speaking, used to speak, spoke, etc.	*I was eating, used to eat, ate, etc.*	*I was living, used to live, lived, etc.*
hablaba	comía	vivía
hablabas	comías	vivías
hablaba	comía	vivía

hablábamos	comíamos	vivíamos
hablabais	comíais	vivíais
hablaban	comían	vivían

PRETERIT

I spoke, did speak, etc.	*I ate, did eat, etc.*	*I lived, did live, etc.*
hablé	comí	viví
hablaste	comiste	viviste
habló	comió	vivió
hablamos	comimos	vivimos
hablasteis	comisteis	vivisteis
hablaron	comieron	vivieron

FUTURE

I shall (will) speak, etc.	*I shall (will) eat, etc.*	*I shall (will) live, etc.*
hablaré	comeré	viviré
hablarás	comerás	vivirás
hablará	comerá	vivirá
hablaremos	comeremos	viviremos
hablaréis	comeréis	viviréis
hablarán	comerán	vivirán

CONDITIONAL

I should (would) speak, etc.	*I should (would) eat, etc.*	*I should (would) live, etc.*
hablaría	comería	viviría
hablarías	comerías	vivirías
hablaría	comería	viviría
hablaríamos	comeríamos	viviríamos
hablaríais	comeríais	viviríais
hablarían	comerían	vivirían

SUBJUNCTIVE MOOD

PRESENT

(that) I may speak, etc.	*(that) I may eat, etc.*	*(that) I may live, etc.*
hable	coma	viva
hables	comas	vivas
hable	coma	viva

hablemos	comamos	vivamos
habléis	comáis	viváis
hablen	coman	vivan

-ra IMPERFECT

(that) I might speak, etc.	(that) I might eat, etc.	(that) I might live, etc.
hablara	comiera	viviera
hablaras	comieras	vivieras
hablara	comiera	viviera
habláramos	comiéramos	viviéramos
hablarais	comierais	vivierais
hablaran	comieran	vivieran

-se IMPERFECT

(that) I might speak, etc.	(that) I might eat, etc.	(that) I might live, etc.
hablase	comiese	viviese
hablases	comieses	vivieses
hablase	comiese	viviese
hablásemos	comiésemos	viviésemos
hablaseis	comieseis	vivieseis
hablasen	comiesen	viviesen

IMPERATIVE

speak	*eat*	*live*
habla (tú)	come (tú)	vive (tú)
hablad (vosotros)	comed (vosotros)	vivid (vosotros)

THE COMPOUND TENSES

PERFECT INFINITIVE

haber hablado (comido, vivido), *to have spoken (eaten, lived)*

PERFECT PARTICIPLE

habiendo hablado (comido, vivido), *having spoken (eaten, lived)*

INDICATIVE MOOD

PRESENT PERFECT	PLUPERFECT	PRETERIT PERFECT
I have spoken, eaten, lived, etc.	*I had spoken, eaten, lived, etc.*	*I had spoken, eaten, lived, etc.*

he has ha hemos habéis han } hablado comido vivido	había habías había habíamos habíais habían } hablado comido vivido	hube hubiste hubo hubimos hubisteis hubieron } hablado comido vivido

FUTURE PERFECT

I shall (will) have spoken, etc.

habré
habrás
habrá
habremos
habréis
habrán } hablado comido vivido

CONDITIONAL PERFECT

I should (would) have spoken, etc.

habría
habrías
habría
habríamos
habríais
habrían } hablado comido vivido

SUBJUNCTIVE MOOD

PRESENT PERFECT

(that) I may have spoken, etc.

haya
hayas
haya
hayamos
hayáis
hayan } hablado comido vivido

-ra AND -se PLUPERFECT

(that) I might have spoken, etc.

hubiera *or* hubiese
hubieras *or* hubieses
hubiera *or* hubiese
hubiéramos *or* hubiésemos
hubierais *or* hubieseis
hubieran *or* hubiesen } hablado comido vivido

IRREGULAR PAST PARTICIPLES OF REGULAR AND STEM-CHANGING VERBS

abrir:	**abierto**	escribir:	**escrito**
cubrir:	**cubierto**	morir:	**muerto**
descubrir:	**descubierto**	romper:	**roto**
devolver:	**devuelto**	volver:	**vuelto**
envolver:	**envuelto**		

COMMENTS CONCERNING FORMS OF VERBS

INFINITIVE decir	PRES. PART. **diciendo**	PAST PART. **dicho**	PRES. IND. **digo**	PRETERIT **dijeron**
IMP. IND. decía FUTURE **diré** CONDITIONAL **diría**	PROGRESSIVE TENSES **estoy,** etc. **diciendo**	COMPOUND TENSES **he,** etc. **dicho**	PRES. SUBJ. **diga** IMPERATIVE **di** decid	IMP. SUBJ. **dijera** **dijese**

a. From five forms (infinitive, present participle, past participle, first person singular present indicative, and third person plural preterit) all other forms may be derived.

b. The first and second persons plural of the present indicative of all verbs are regular, except in the cases of **haber, ir, ser.**

c. The third person plural is formed by adding **-n** to the third person singular in all tenses, except the preterit and in the present indicative of **ser.**

d. All familiar forms (second person singular and plural) end in **-s,** except the second person singular preterit and the imperative.

e. The imperfect indicative is regular in all verbs, except **ir (iba), ser (era), ver (veía).**

f. If the first person singular preterit ends in unaccented **-e,** the third person singular ends in unaccented **-o;** the other endings are regular, except that after **j** the ending for the third person plural is **-eron.** Eight verbs of this group, in addition to those which end in **-ducir,** have a **u**-stem preterit (**andar, caber, estar, haber, poder, poner, saber, tener**); four have an **i**-stem (**decir, hacer, querer, venir**); **traer** has a regular stem with the above endings. (The third person plural preterit forms of **decir** and **traer** are **dijeron** and **trajeron,** respectively. The third person singular form of **hacer** is **hizo.**) **Ir** and **ser** have the same preterit, while **dar** has second-conjugation endings in this tense.

g. The conditional always has the same stem as the future. Only twelve verbs have irregular stems in these tenses. Five drop **e** of the infinitive ending (**caber, haber, poder, querer, saber**); five drop **e** or **i** and insert **d** (**poner, salir, tener, valer, venir**); and two (**decir, hacer**) retain the Old Spanish stems **dir-, har- (far-).**

h. The stem of the present subjunctive of all verbs is the same as that of the first person singular present indicative, except for **dar, estar, haber, ir, saber, ser.**

i. The imperfect subjunctive of all verbs is formed by dropping **-ron** of the third person plural preterit and adding the **-ra** or **-se** endings.

j. The singular imperative is the same in form as the third person singular present indicative, except in the case of ten verbs (**decir, di; haber, he; hacer, haz; ir, ve; poner, pon; salir, sal; ser, sé; tener, ten; valer, val** or **vale; venir, ven**). The plural imperative is always formed by dropping final **-r** of the infinitive and adding **-d.** (Remember that the imperative is used only for familiar affirmative commands.)

k. The compound tenses of all verbs are formed by using the various tenses of the auxiliary verb **haber** with the past participle.

IRREGULAR VERBS

(Participles are given with the infinitive; tenses not listed are regular.)

1. **andar,** andando, andado, *to go, walk.*

PRETERIT	**anduve**	**anduviste**	**anduvo**	**anduvimos**	**anduvisteis**	**anduvieron**
IMP. SUBJ.	**anduviera,** etc.		**anduviese,** etc.			

2. **caber,** cabiendo, cabido, *to fit, be contained in*

PRES. IND.	**quepo**	cabes	cabe	cabemos	cabéis	caben
PRES. SUBJ.	**quepa**	**quepas**	**quepa**	**quepamos**	**quepáis**	**quepan**
FUTURE	**cabré**	**cabrás,** etc.		COND.	**cabría**	**cabrías,** etc.
PRETERIT	**cupe**	**cupiste**	**cupo**	**cupimos**	**cupisteis**	**cupieron**
IMP. SUBJ.	**cupiera,** etc.		**cupiese,** etc.			

3. **caer, cayendo, caído,** *to fall*

PRES. IND.	**caigo**	caes	cae	caemos	caéis	caen
PRES. SUBJ.	**caiga**	**caigas**	**caiga**	**caigamos**	**caigáis**	**caigan**
PRETERIT	caí	**caíste**	**cayó**	**caímos**	**caísteis**	**cayeron**
IMP. SUBJ.	**cayera,** etc.		**cayese,** etc.			

4. **dar,** dando, dado, *to give*

PRES. IND.	**doy**	das	da	damos	dais	dan
PRES. SUBJ.	**dé**	des	**dé**	demos	deis	den
PRETERIT	**di**	**diste**	**dio**	**dimos**	**disteis**	**dieron**
IMP. SUBJ.	**diera,** etc.		**diese,** etc.			

5. **decir, diciendo, dicho,** *to say, tell*

PRES. IND.	**digo**	**dices**	**dice**	decimos	decís	**dicen**
PRES. SUBJ.	**diga**	**digas**	**diga**	**digamos**	**digáis**	**digan**
IMPERATIVE	**di**				decid	
FUTURE	**diré**	**dirás,** etc.		COND.	**diría**	**dirías,** etc.
PRETERIT	**dije**	**dijiste**	**dijo**	**dijimos**	**dijisteis**	**dijeron**
IMP. SUBJ.	**dijera,** etc.		**dijese,** etc.			

6. **estar,** estando, estado, *to be*

PRES. IND.	estoy	estás	está	estamos	estáis	están
PRES. SUBJ.	esté	estés	esté	estemos	estéis	estén
PRETERIT	estuve	estuviste	estuvo	estuvimos	estuvisteis	estuvieron
IMP. SUBJ.	estuviera, etc.		estuviese, etc.			

7. **haber,** habiendo, habido, *to have* (auxiliary)

PRES. IND.	he	has	ha	hemos	habéis	han
PRES. SUBJ.	haya	hayas	haya	hayamos	hayáis	hayan
IMPERATIVE	he				habed	
FUTURE	habré	habrás, etc.		COND.	habría	habrías, etc.
PRETERIT	hube	hubiste	hubo	hubimos	hubisteis	hubieron
IMP. SUBJ.	hubiera, etc.		hubiese, etc.			

8. **hacer,** haciendo, **hecho,** *to do, make*

PRES. IND.	hago	haces	hace	hacemos	hacéis	hacen
PRES. SUBJ.	haga	hagas	haga	hagamos	hagáis	hagan
IMPERATIVE	haz				haced	
FUTURE	haré	harás, etc.		COND	haría	harías, etc.
PRETERIT	hice	hiciste	hizo	hicimos	hicisteis	hicieron
IMP. SUBJ.	hiciera, etc.		hiciese, etc.			

9. **ir,** yendo, ido, *to go*

PRES. IND.	voy	vas	va	vamos	vais	van
PRES. SUBJ.	vaya	vayas	vaya	vayamos	vayáis	vayan
IMPERATIVE	ve				id	
IMP. IND.	iba	ibas	iba	íbamos	ibais	iban
PRETERIT	fui	fuiste	fue	fuimos	fuisteis	fueron
IMP. SUBJ.	fuera, etc.		fuese, etc.			

10. **oír,** oyendo, oído, *to hear*

PRES. IND.	oigo	oyes	oye	oímos	oís	oyen
PRES. SUBJ.	oiga	oigas	oiga	oigamos	oigáis	oigan
IMPERATIVE	oye				oíd	
PRETERIT	oí	oíste	oyó	oímos	oísteis	oyeron
IMP. SUBJ.	oyera, etc.		oyese, etc.			

11. **poder, pudiendo,** podido, *to be able*

PRES. IND.	puedo	puedes	puede	podemos	podéis	pueden
PRES. SUBJ.	pueda	puedas	pueda	podamos	podáis	puedan
FUTURE	podré	podrás, etc.		COND.	podría	podrías, etc.
PRETERIT	pude	pudiste	pudo	pudimos	pudisteis	pudieron
IMP. SUBJ.	pudiera, etc.		pudiese, etc.			

12. **poner,** poniendo, **puesto,** *to put, place*

PRES. IND.	**pongo**	pones	pone	ponemos	ponéis	ponen
PRES. SUBJ.	**ponga**	**pongas**	**ponga**	**pongamos**	**pongáis**	**pongan**
IMPERATIVE	**pon**				poned	
FUTURE	**pondré**	**pondrás,** etc.		COND.	**pondría**	**pondrías,** etc.
PRETERIT	**puse**	**pusiste**	**puso**	**pusimos**	**pusisteis**	**pusieron**
IMP. SUBJ.	**pusiera,** etc.		**pusiese,** etc.			

Like **poner:** componer, *to compose*; suponer, *to suppose.*

13. **querer,** queriendo, querido, *to wish, want*

PRES. IND.	**quiero**	**quieres**	**quiere**	queremos	queréis	**quieren**
PRES. SUBJ.	**quiera**	**quieras**	**quiera**	queramos	queráis	**quieran**
FUTURE	**querré**	**querrás,** etc.		COND.	**querría**	**querrías,** etc.
PRETERIT	**quise**	**quisiste**	**quiso**	**quisimos**	**quisisteis**	**quisieron**
IMP. SUBJ.	**quisiera,** etc.		**quisiese,** etc.			

14. **saber,** sabiendo, sabido, *to know*

PRES. IND.	**sé**	sabes	sabe	sabemos	sabéis	saben
PRES. SUBJ.	**sepa**	**sepas**	**sepa**	**sepamos**	**sepáis**	**sepan**
FUTURE	**sabré**	**sabrás,** etc.		COND.	**sabría**	**sabrías,** etc.
PRETERIT	**supe**	**supiste**	**supo**	**supimos**	**supisteis**	**supieron**
IMP. SUBJ.	**supiera,** etc.		**supiese,** etc.			

15. **salir,** saliendo, salido, *to go out, leave*

PRES. IND.	**salgo**	sales	sale	salimos	salís	salen
PRES. SUBJ.	**salga**	**salgas**	**salga**	**salgamos**	**salgáis**	**salgan**
IMPERATIVE	**sal**				salid	
FUTURE	**saldré**	**saldrás,** etc.		COND.	**saldría**	**saldrías,** etc.

16. **ser,** siendo, sido, *to be*

PRES. IND.	**soy**	**eres**	**es**	**somos**	**sois**	**son**
PRES. SUBJ.	**sea**	**seas**	**sea**	**seamos**	**seáis**	**sean**
IMPERATIVE	**sé**				sed	
IMP. IND.	**era**	**eras**	**era**	**éramos**	**erais**	**eran**
PRETERIT	**fui**	**fuiste**	**fue**	**fuimos**	**fuisteis**	**fueron**
IMP. SUBJ.	**fuera,** etc.		**fuese,** etc.			

17. **tener,** teniendo, tenido, *to have*

PRES. IND.	**tengo**	**tienes**	**tiene**	tenemos	tenéis	**tienen**
PRES. SUBJ.	**tenga**	**tengas**	**tenga**	**tengamos**	**tengáis**	**tengan**
IMPERATIVE	**ten**				tened	
FUTURE	**tendré**	**tendrás,** etc.		COND.	**tendría**	**tendrías,** etc.
PRETERIT	**tuve**	**tuviste**	**tuvo**	**tuvimos**	**tuvisteis**	**tuvieron**
IMP. SUBJ.	**tuviera,** etc.		**tuviese,** etc.			

Like **tener:** contener, *to contain*; detener, *to stop*; obtener, *to obtain.*

18. **traer, trayendo, traído**, *to bring*

PRES. IND.	**traigo**	traes	trae	traemos	traéis	traen
PRES. SUBJ.	**traiga**	**traigas**	**traiga**	**traigamos**	**traigáis**	**traigan**
PRETERIT	**traje**	**trajiste**	**trajo**	**trajimos**	**trajisteis**	**trajeron**
IMP. SUBJ.	**trajera**, etc.		**trajese**, etc.			

19. **valer,** valiendo, valido, *to be worth*

PRES. IND.	**valgo**	vales	vale	valemos	valéis	valen
PRES. SUBJ.	**valga**	**valgas**	**valga**	**valgamos**	**valgáis**	**valgan**
IMPERATIVE	**val**(vale)				valed	
FUTURE	**valdré**	**valdrás**, etc.			COND. **valdría**	**valdrías**, etc.

20. **venir, viniendo,** venido, *to come*

PRES. IND.	**vengo**	**vienes**	**viene**	venimos	venís	**vienen**
PRES. SUBJ.	**venga**	**vengas**	**venga**	**vengamos**	**vengáis**	**vengan**
IMPERATIVE	**ven**				venid	
FUTURE	**vendré**	**vendrás**, etc.			COND. **vendría**	**vendrías**, etc.
PRETERIT	**vine**	**viniste**	**vino**	**vinimos**	**vinisteis**	**vinieron**
IMP. SUBJ.	**viniera**, etc.		**viniese**, etc.			

21. **ver,** viendo, **visto,** *to see*

PRES. IND.	**veo**	ves	ve	vemos	veis	ven
PRES. SUBJ.	**vea**	**veas**	**vea**	**veamos**	**veáis**	**vean**
PRETERIT	**vi**	viste	**vio**	vimos	visteis	vieron
IMP. IND.	**veía**	**veías**	**veía**	**veíamos**	**veíais**	**veían**

VERBS WITH CHANGES IN SPELLING

Changes in spelling are required in certain verbs in order to preserve the sound of the final consonant of the stem. The changes occur in only seven forms: in the first four types below the change is in the first person singular preterit, and in the remaining types in the first person singular present indicative, while all types change throughout the present subjunctive.

	a	o	u	e	i
Sound of *k*	ca	co	cu	que	qui
Sound of *g*	ga	go	gu	gue	gui
Sound of *th* (*s*)	za	zo	zu	ce	ci
Sound of *h*	ja	jo	ju	ge, je	gi, ji
Sound of *gw*	gua	guo		güe·	güi

1. Verbs ending in **-car** change **c** to **qu** before **e**: **buscar,** *to look for.*

PRETERIT	**busqué**	buscaste	buscó, etc.			
PRES. SUBJ.	**busque**	**busques**	**busque**	**busquemos**	**busquéis**	**busquen**

Like **buscar:** acercarse, *to approach*; colocar, *to place*; dedicar, *to dedicate*; indicar, *to indicate*; marcar, *to mark*; practicar, *to practice*; predicar, *to preach*; publicar, *to publish*; sacar, *to take out*; significar, *to mean*; simplificar, *to simplify*; tocar, *to play* (music).

2. Verbs ending in **-gar** change **g** to **gu** before **e**: **llegar,** *to arrive.*

PRETERIT	**llegué**	llegaste	llegó, etc.			
PRES. SUBJ.	**llegue**	**llegues**	**llegue**	**lleguemos**	**lleguéis**	**lleguen**

Like **llegar:** *agregar,* to add; colgar (ue),[1] *to hang*; entregar, *to hand (over)*; jugar (ue), *to play* (a game); navegar, *to sail*; negar (ie), *to deny*; pagar, *to pay*; pegar, *to beat*; rogar (ue), *to beg, ask.*

3. Verbs ending in **-zar** change **z** to **c** before **e**: **gozar,** *to enjoy.*

PRETERIT	**gocé**	gozaste	gozó, etc.			
PRES. SUBJ.	**goce**	**goces**	**goce**	**gocemos**	**gocéis**	**gocen**

Like **gozar:** abrazar, *to embrace*; almorzar (ue), *to take lunch*; bautizar, *to baptize*; bostezar, *to yawn*; caracterizar, *to characterize*; comenzar (ie), *to commence, begin*; cruzar, *to cross*; desperezarse, *to stretch*; empezar (ie), *to begin*; lanzar, *to hurl*; organizar, *to organize*; realizar, *to realize, carry out.*

4. Verbs ending in **-guar** change **gu** to **gü** before **e**: **averiguar,** *to find out.*

PRETERIT	**averigüé**	averiguaste	averiguó, etc.			
PRES. SUBJ.	**averigüe**	**averigües**	**averigüe**	**averigüemos**	**averigüéis**	**averigüen**

5. Verbs ending in **-ger** or **-gir** change **g** to **j** before **a** and **o**: **escoger,** *to choose.*

PRES. IND.	**escojo**	escoges	escoge, etc.			
PRES. SUBJ.	**escoja**	**escojas**	**escoja**	**escojamos**	**escojáis**	**escojan**

Like **escoger:** dirigir, *to direct*; recoger, *to pick up*; surgir, *to surge, appear.*

6. Verbs in **-guir** change **gu** to **g** before **a** and **o**: **distinguir,** *to distinguish.*

PRES. IND.	**distingo**	distingues	distingue, etc.			
PRES. SUBJ.	**distinga**	**distingas**	**distinga**	**distingamos**	**distingáis**	**distingan**

Like **distinguir:** conseguir (i,i), *to get;* seguir (i,i), *to follow.*

7. Verbs ending in **-cer** or **-cir** preceded by a consonant change **c** to **z** before **a** and **o**: **vencer,** *to overcome.*

PRES. IND.	**venzo**	vences	vence, etc.			
PRES. SUBJ.	**venza**	**venzas**	**venza**	**venzamos**	**venzáis**	**venzan**

Like **vencer:** convencer, *to convince*; ejercer, *to exert.*

[1] See pages 431–433 for stem changes.

8. Verbs ending in **-quir** change **qu** to **c** before **a** and **o**: **delinquir,** *to be guilty.*

PRES. IND. **delinco** delinques delinque, etc.
PRES. SUBJ. **delinca** **delincas** **delinca** **delincamos** **delincáis** **delincan**

VERBS WITH SPECIAL ENDINGS

1. Verbs ending in **-cer** or **-cir** following a vowel insert **z** before **c** in the first person singular present indicative and throughout the present subjunctive: **conocer,** *to know, be acquainted with.*

PRES. IND. **conozco** conoces conoce, etc.
PRES. SUBJ. **conozca** **conozcas** **conozca** **conozcamos** **conozcáis** **conozcan**

Like **conocer**: agradecer, *to be thankful for*; aparecer, *to appear*; crecer, *to grow*; establecer, *to establish*; florecer, *to flourish*; nacer, *to be born*; ofrecer, *to offer*; parecer, *to seem*; pertenecer, *to belong*; prevalecer, *to prevail*; reconocer, *to recognize.*

2. Verbs ending in **-ducir** have the same changes as **conocer,** with additional changes in the preterit and imperfect subjunctive: **conducir,** *to conduct, drive.*

PRES. IND. **conduzco** conduces conduce, etc.
PRES. SUBJ. **conduzca** **conduzcas** **conduzca** **conduzcamos** **conduzcáis**
    conduzcan
PRETERIT **conduje** **condujiste** **condujo** **condujimos** **condujisteis**
    condujeron
IMP. SUBJ. **condujera,** etc. **condujese,** etc.

Like **conducir**: producir, *to produce.*

3. Verbs ending in **-uir** (except **-guir**) insert **y** except before **i,** and change unaccented **i** between vowels to **y**: **construir,** *to construct.*

PARTICIPLES **construyendo** construido
PRES. IND. **construyo** **construyes** **construye** construimos construís
    construyen
PRES. SUBJ. **construya** **construyas** **construya** **construyamos** **construyáis**
    construyan
IMPERATIVE **construye** construid
PRETERIT construí construiste **construyó** construimos construisteis
    construyeron
IMP. SUBJ. **construyera,** etc. **construyese,** etc.

Like **construir**: constituir, *to constitute*; contribuir, *to contribute*; destruir, *to destroy*

4. Certain verbs ending in **-er** preceded by a vowel replace unaccented **i** of the ending by **y**: **creer,** *to believe.*

PARTICIPLES	**creyendo**		**creído**			
PRETERIT	creí	**creíste**	**creyó**	**creímos**	**creísteis**	**creyeron**
IMP. SUBJ.	**creyera**, etc.		**creyese**, etc.			

Like **creer**: leer, *to read.*

5. Some verbs ending in **-iar** require a written accent on the **i** in the singular and third person plural in the present indicative and present subjunctive and in the singular imperative: **enviar,** *to send.*

PRES. IND.	**envío**	**envías**	**envía**	enviamos	enviáis	**envían**
PRES. SUBJ.	**envíe**	**envíes**	**envíe**	enviemos	enviéis	**envíen**
IMPERATIVE	**envía**				enviad	

Like **enviar**: criar, *to grow*; variar, *to vary.*

However, such common verbs as **anunciar,** *to announce*; **apreciar,** *to appreciate*; **cambiar,** *to change*; **estudiar,** *to study*; **iniciar,** *to initiate*; **limpiar,** *to clean*; **pronunciar,** *to pronounce*, do not have the accented **i.**

6. Verbs ending in **-uar** have a written accent on the **u** in the same forms as verbs in section 5:[1] **continuar,** *to continue.*

PRES. IND.	**continúo**	**continúas**	**continúa**	continuamos	continuáis	**continúan**
PRES. SUBJ.	**continúe**	**continúes**	**continúe**	continuemos	continuéis	**continúen**
IMPERATIVE	**continúa**				continuad	

STEM-CHANGING VERBS

CLASS I (**-ar, -er**)

Many verbs of the first and second conjugations change the stem vowel **e** to **ie** and **o** to **ue** when the vowels **e** and **o** are stressed, *i.e.*, in the singular and third person plural of the present indicative and present subjunctive and in the singular imperative.   Class I verbs are designated: **cerrar (ie), volver (ue).**

cerrar, *to close*

PRES. IND.	cierro	cierras	cierra	cerramos	cerráis	cierran
PRES. SUBJ.	cierre	cierres	cierre	cerremos	cerréis	cierren
IMPERATIVE	cierra					

Like **cerrar**: atravesar, *to cross*; comenzar, *to commence*; despertar, *to awaken*; empezar, *to begin*; encerrar, *to enclose*; negar, *to deny*; pensar, *to think*; recomendar, *to recommend*; sentarse, *to sit down.*

---

[1] **Reunir(se),** *to gather*, has a written accent on the **u** in the same forms as **continuar**:

PRES. IND.	**reúno, reúnes, reúne . . . reúnen**
PRES. SUBJ.	**reúna, reúnas, reúna . . . reúnan**

perder, *to lose*

PRES. IND.	**pierdo**	**pierdes**	**pierde**	perdemos	perdéis	**pierden**
PRES. SUBJ.	**pierda**	**pierdas**	**pierda**	perdamos	perdáis	**pierdan**
IMPERATIVE	**pierde**					

Like **perder**: defender, *to defend*; entender, *to understand*.

contar, *to count*

PRES. IND.	**cuento**	**cuentas**	**cuenta**	contamos	contáis	**cuentan**
PRES. SUBJ.	**cuente**	**cuentes**	**cuente**	contemos	contéis	**cuenten**
IMPERATIVE	**cuenta**					

Like **contar**: acordarse, *to remember*; acostarse, *to go to bed*; almorzar, *to take lunch*; colgar, *to hang*; costar, *to cost*; demostrar, *to demonstrate*; encontrar, *to find*; mostrar, *to show*; probarse, *to try on*; recordar, *to remember*; rogar, *to beg, ask*; sonar, *to sound, ring*; volar, *to fly*.

volver,[1] *to return*

PRES. IND.	**vuelvo**	**vuelves**	**vuelve**	volvemos	volvéis	**vuelven**
PRES. SUBJ.	**vuelva**	**vuelvas**	**vuelva**	volvamos	volváis	**vuelvan**
IMPERATIVE	**vuelve**					

Like **volver**: devolver, *to give back*; doler, *to ache*; envolver, *to wrap up*; llover, *to rain*; mover, *to move*.

jugar, *to play* (a game)

PRES. IND.	**juego**	**juegas**	**juega**	jugamos	jugáis	**juegan**
PRES. SUBJ.	**juegue**	**juegues**	**juegue**	juguemos	juguéis	**jueguen**
IMPERATIVE	**juega**					

CLASS II (-ir)

Certain verbs of the third conjugation have the changes in the stem indicated below. Class II verbs are designated: **sentir (ie,i), dormir (ue,u)**.

PRES. IND.	1, 2, 3, 6	
PRES. SUBJ.	1, 2, 3, 6	e > ie
IMPERATIVE	Sing.	o > ue

PRES. PART.		
PRETERIT	3, 6	e > i
PRES. SUBJ.	4, 5	
IMP. SUBJ.	1, 2, 3, 4, 5, 6	o > u

sentir, *to feel*

PRES. PART.	**sintiendo**					
PRES. IND.	**siento**	**sientes**	**siente**	sentimos	sentís	**sienten**
PRES. SUBJ.	**sienta**	**sientas**	**sienta**	**sintamos**	**sintáis**	**sientan**

[1] The past participles of **volver, devolver, envolver**, are: **vuelto, devuelto, envuelto**.

IMPERATIVE	**siente**					
PRETERIT	sentí	sentiste	**sintió**	sentimos	sentisteis	**sintieron**
IMP. SUBJ.	**sintiera,** etc.		**sintiese,** etc.			

Like **sentir:** adquirir,[1] *to acquire*; advertir, *to advise*; convertir, *to convert*; divertirse, *to amuse oneself*; preferir, *to prefer*; referir, *to refer*.

dormir, *to sleep*

PRES. PART.	**durmiendo**					
PRES. IND.	**duermo**	**duermes**	**duerme**	dormimos	dormís	**duermen**
PRES. SUBJ.	**duerma**	**duermas**	**duerma**	**durmamos**	**durmáis**	**duerman**
IMPERATIVE	**duerme**					
PRETERIT	dormí	dormiste	**durmió**	dormimos	dormisteis	**durmieron**
IMP. SUBJ.	**durmiera,** etc.		**durmiese,** etc.			

Like **dormir:** morir,[2] *to die*.

CLASS III (-ir)

Certain verbs in the third conjugation change **e** to **i** in all forms in which changes occur in Class II verbs. These verbs are designated: **pedir (i,i)**.

pedir, *to ask*

PRES. PART.	**pidiendo**					
PRES. IND.	**pido**	**pides**	**pide**	pedimos	pedís	**piden**
PRES. SUBJ.	**pida**	**pidas**	**pida**	**pidamos**	**pidáis**	**pidan**
IMPERATIVE	**pide**					
PRETERIT	pedí	pediste	**pidió**	pedimos	pedisteis	**pidieron**
IMP. SUBJ.	**pidiera,** etc.		**pidiese,** etc.			

Like **pedir:** conseguir, *to get*; despedirse, *to take leave*; repetir, *to repeat*; seguir, *to follow*; servir, *to serve*; vestir, *to dress*.

reír, *to laugh*

PARTICIPLES	**riendo**		reído			
PRES. IND.	**río**	**ríes**	**ríe**	reímos	reís	**ríen**
PRES. SUBJ.	**ría**	**rías**	**ría**	**riamos**	**riáis**	**rían**
IMPERATIVE	**ríe**				reíd	
PRETERIT	reí	reíste	**rió**	reímos	reísteis	**rieron**
IMP. SUBJ.	**riera,** etc.		**riese,** etc.			

Like **reír:** sonreír, *to smile*.

---

[1] Forms of **adquirir:** PRES. IND. **adquiero, adquieres, adquiere,** adquirimos, adquirís, **adquieren**
PRES. SUBJ. **adquiera, adquieras, adquiera,** adquiramos, adquiráis, **adquieran**

[2] Past participle: **muerto.**

Vocabulary

A

a to, at, in, from, by, *etc.*
abandonar to abandon
abierto, -a *p.p. of* **abrir** *and adj.* open, opened
el **abogado** lawyer
abrazar to embrace
abreviado, -a abbreviated, shortened
el **abrigo** topcoat, overcoat
abril April
absolutamente absolutely
abrir to open
abstracto, -a abstract
la **abuela** grandmother
el **abuelo** grandfather; *pl.* grandparents
abundante abundant
acabar to end, finish, complete
  acabar de + *inf.* to have just + *p.p.*
  acabar por + *inf.* to end up by + *pres. part.*
la **acción** (*pl.* **acciones**) action
el **aceite** oil
la **aceituna** olive
aceptar to accept
acerca de about, concerning
acercarse (**a** + *obj.*) to approach
acompañar to accompany
aconsejar to advise, warn
acordarse (**ue**) (**de** + *obj.*) to remember, recall
acostarse (**ue**) to go to bed
acostumbrar to be accustomed to, be in the habit of

la **actividad** activity
actual *adj.* present, present-day
el **acueducto** aqueduct
el **acuerdo** agreement
  estar de acuerdo to agree, be in agreement
adecuadamente adequately
además *adv.* besides, furthermore
  además de *prep.* besides, in addition to
adiós goodbye
el **adjetivo** adjective
admirar to admire
el **adobe** *brick made of clay and straw*
¿adónde? where? (*with verbs of motion*)
adoptar to adopt
la **adoración** adoration
adorar to adore, worship
adornado, -a (**de, con**) adorned (with), decorated (with)
adornar (**de, con**) to adorn (with), decorate (with)
adquirir (**ie**) to acquire
el **adversario** adversary, opponent
la **advertencia** warning
advertir (**ie,i**) to advise, point out, warn
aéreo, -a air
  por correo aéreo by air mail
el **aeropuerto** airport
afeitarse to shave (oneself)
la **afición** fondness
aficionado, -a (**a**) fond (of)
  ser aficionado, -a (**a**) to be fond (of)

el aficionado fan
aficionarse (tanto) a to become (so) fond of
africano, -a African
afuera *adv.* outside, abroad
la agencia agency
  agencia de viajes travel agency
el agente agent
ágil agile
agosto August
agraciado, -a graceful, charming
agradable agreeable, pleasant
agradecer to be grateful for, thank for
el agravio wrong
agregar to add
agrícola (*m. and f.*) agricultural, farm
el agricultor agriculturist
la agricultura agriculture
agrio, -a sour
el agua (*f.*) water
el aguacate avocado, alligator pear
aguardar to wait (for), await
Agustín Augustine
ahí there (*near person addressed*)
ahora now
  ahora mismo right now, right away
el aire air
  al aire libre outdoor, (in the) open air
aislado, -a isolated
al = a + el to the
  al + *inf.* on (upon) + *pres. part.*
la albóndiga meat ball
la alcoba bedroom
el aldeano villager
alegrarse (de + *inf.*) to be glad (to)
alegrarse (de + *obj.*) to be glad (of)
  ¡cuánto me alegro (de)! how glad I am (to)!
  me alegro (mucho) de I am (very) glad to
alegre cheerful, joyful, lively
la alegría joy
el alemán German (*language*)
la alfalfa alfalfa
la alfombra rug, carpet
algo *pron.* something, anything; *adv.* somewhat, rather

el algodón cotton
alguien someone, somebody, anybody, anyone
algún *used for* **alguno** *before m. sing. nouns*
alguno, -a *adj. and pron.* some, any, someone; *pl.* some, a few
el alimento food
alistarse to enlist
el alma (*f.*) soul, heart, spirit
  el alma mía my heart
el almacén (*pl.* **almacenes**) department store
el almíbar syrup; *pl.* fruit preserves
almorzar (**ue**) to have (eat) lunch
el almuerzo lunch
  para el almuerzo for lunch
  tomar el almuerzo to take (have, eat) lunch
Alonso Alphonsus
el alpinismo mountain climbing
alquilar to rent
el altar altar
alto, -a tall, high, upper; lofty
la altura altitude, height
la alumna pupil, student (*girl*)
el alumno pupil, student (*boy*)
allí there (*distant*)
la amabilidad kindness
amable kind
el amante lover
amarillo, -a yellow
el Amazonas Amazon (River)
América America
  la América del Norte (Sur) North (South) America
  la América española Spanish America
la amiga friend (*f.*)
el amigo friend
la amiguita little (girl) friend
el amo master
el amor love; *pl.* love affairs
Ana Ann, Anna, Anne
anciano, -a old
ancho, -a wide, broad
Andalucía Andalusia (*territory of southern Spain*)

andaluz, -uza Andalusian
andante: caballero —, knight errant
andar to go, walk; run (*said of a watch*)
  anduvo enamorado (he) was in love
los Andes Andes
el ángel angel
angosto, -a narrow
el anillo ring
el animal animal
el aniversario anniversary
anoche last night
anochecer: al —, at nightfall
anónimo, -a anonymous
ante *prep.* before, in the presence of
anterior earlier, preceding
antes *adv.* before, formerly
  antes de *prep.* before (*time*)
  antes (de) que *conj.* before
antiguamente formerly, in ancient times
antiguo, -a ancient, old
  lo antiguo the (what is) old
Antón, Antonio Anthony, Tony
anunciar to announce, advertise
el año year
  a los dos años after two years
  ¿cuántos años tiene (él)? how old is (he)?
  cumplir (diez y seis) años to reach one's (sixteenth) birthday, be (sixteen) years old
  tener ... años to be ... years old
el aparato de radio (televisión) radio (television) set
aparecer to appear
el apartamento (apartamiento) apartment
  casa de apartamentos apartment house
apasionado, -a tender, passionate
apenas scarcely, hardly
aplaudir to applaud
la aplicación application, adaptation
el apogeo height
el apóstol apostle
apreciar to appreciate
aprender (a + *inf.*) to learn (to)
aquel, aquella (-os, -as) *adj.* that, those (*distant*)

aquél, aquélla (-os, -as) *pron.* that (one), those
el aquelarre witches' Sabbath
aquello *neuter pron.* that
aquí here
  por aquí by (around) here, this way
árabe Arabic
Aragón Aragon (*region and former kingdom in northeastern Spain*)
el árbol tree
la arena sand
la argamasa mortar
Argel Algiers (*in North Africa*)
la Argentina Argentina
argentino, -a Argentine
aristocrático, -a aristocratic
la armada armada, fleet
  Armada Invencible Invincible Armada
armar to arm
  armar caballero to dub (as a) knight
las armas arms, weapons
el arquitecto architect
la arquitectura architecture
arrojarse to throw oneself
el arroz rice
  arroz con leche rice pudding
el arte art; skill, artifice, craft
  las artes arts
el artículo article
  artículo de costumbres article of customs and manners
el (la) artista artist
artístico, -a artistic
Arturo Arthur
asado, -a roast(ed)
el ascensor elevator
asentar (ie) por to take service as
así so, thus
  así, así so-so
  así ... como both (as much) ... and (as)
  así como as well as, just as
el asiento seat
asistir a to attend
asombrar to amaze, be amazing
el aspecto aspect
el astro star, planet
astuto, -a astute, clever

la **atención**   attention
   con **atención**   attentively, carefully
la **atracción**   attraction
  atravesar (**ie**)   to cross; pass through
  atreverse (**a** + *inf.*)   to dare (to)
el **aumento**   increase
  aunque   although, even though
el **autobús** (*pl.* **autobuses**)   bus
el **autor**   author
la **autoridad**   authority
  avanzado, -a   advanced
la **avenida**   avenue
la **aventura**   adventure
el **avión** (*pl.* **aviones**)   (air)plane
  avión de las cinco   five-o'clock plane
  en avión   by plane
  avisar   to advise, inform
  ¡ay!   oh! alas! ah!
  ayer   yesterday
  ayer por la tarde   yesterday afternoon
la **ayuda**   aid, help
  ayudar (**a** + *inf.*)   to aid (to), help (to)
el **azteca**   Aztec
el (**la**) **azúcar**   sugar
  azul   blue

B

  bailar   to dance
el **baile**   dance
  número de baile   dance number
  bajar   to go down(stairs), bring down
  bajar (**a** + *inf.*)   to go down(stairs) (to)
  bajar (**de** + *obj.*)   to get off (out of)
  bajo *prep.*   under, beneath, below
  bajo, -a   low, lower
  piso bajo   first floor
el **balcón** (*pl.* **balcones**)   balcony
el **balompié**   football
  Baltasar   Balthasar (*one of the Three Wise Men*)
el **ballet**   ballet
la **banana**   banana
  bañarse   to bathe, take a bath; take a swim (dip)
el **baño**   bath

  cuarto de baño   bathroom
  traje de baño   bathing suit
  barato, -a   cheap, inexpensive
  Bárbara   Barbara
el **barco**   boat
el **barrio**   district
el **barro**   clay
  Bartolomé   Bartholomew
  basado, -a   based
la **base**   base, basis
el **básquetbol**   basketball
  bastante *adj. and pron.* enough, sufficient; *adv.* quite, quite a bit, rather
  bastar   to be enough, be sufficient
la **batalla**   battle
la **batería**   battery
  bautizar   to baptize
  beber   to drink
la **bebida**   drink
el **béisbol**   baseball
  Belén   Bethlehem
la **belleza**   beauty
  bellísimo, -a   very (most) beautiful
  bello, -a   beautiful, pretty
la **bendición**   blessing
el **beso**   kiss
la **biblioteca**   library
  bien   well
    está bien   that's fine, excellent, very well
    más bien (**que**)   rather (than)
    parecer ser bien a uno   to think it proper for one, seem proper to one
    si bien   although, though, while
el **biftec**   steak
el **billete**   bill, bank note; ticket
    billete de (**diez**) **dólares**   (ten)-dollar bill
    billete de ida y vuelta   round-trip ticket
    billete sencillo   one-way ticket
el **bizcocho borracho**   tipsy cake
  blanco, -a   white
la **blusa**   blouse
la **boda**   wedding
las **boleadoras**   *lariat with balls at one end, thrown so as to twist around an animal's legs*

el **boleto**   ticket (*Mex.*)
la **bolsa**   purse

la **bombilla**   small tube
bondadoso, -a   kind
bonito, -a   pretty, beautiful
el **borracho**   drinker
el **bosque**   woods, forest
bostezar   to yawn
botánico, -a   botanical
la **botella**   bottle
el **botones**   bellboy
el **boxeo**   boxing
el **Brasil**   Brazil
el **brazo**   arm
breve   brief, short
brillar   to shine
la **broma**   trick, joke
dar bromas a   to play tricks on
brotar   to burst forth
la **bruja**   witch
la **brutalidad**   brutality
buen   *used for* **bueno** *before m. sing. nouns*
bueno   *adv.*   well, well now, all right
bueno, -a   good
lo bueno   the (what is) good
muy buenas   good afternoon (evening)
el **burlador**   deceiver
el **burro**   burro, donkey
la **busca**   search
buscar   to look for, search, seek
buscar a uno   to come (go) for one

C

cabal   complete, right
caballerías: novela (libro) de —, novel (book) of chivalry
el **caballero**   knight
armar caballero   to dub (as a) knight
caballero andante   knight errant
el **caballo**   horse
a caballo   on horseback
montar a caballo   to ride horseback
la **cabeza**   head
me duele la cabeza   I have a headache, my head aches

Cabeza de Vaca: (Álvar Núñez)   *Spanish explorer of the southwestern U.S. in the early sixteenth century*
Cabrillo: (Juan Rodríguez)   *Portuguese-born navigator and explorer, discoverer of California, 1542*
el **cacahuete**   peanut
el **cacao**   cacao (*plant*)
cada (*invariable*)   each, every
caer(se)   to fall (down)
el **café**   café; coffee
café solo   black coffee
taza para el café   coffee cup
la **caída**   fall
la **cajuela**   auto trunk (*Am.*)
la **calabaza**   pumpkin, squash, gourd
el **calcetín** (*pl.* **calcetines**)   sock
caliente   *adj.*   warm, hot
calmar   to calm; *reflex.* calm oneself, become calm
el **calor**   heat, warmth
hacer (mucho) calor   to be (very) warm *or* hot (*weather*)
tener (mucho) calor   to be (very) warm (*living beings*)
la **calle**   street
la **cama**   bed, berth
la **cámara**   camera
la **camarera**   waitress
el **camarero**   waiter
cambiar   to change
el **cambio**   change
en cambio   on the other hand
el **camello**   camel
caminar   to walk, go, travel
el **camino**   road, way
Camino Real   King's (Royal) Highway
la **camisa**   shirt
el **camote**   sweet potato
la **campana**   bell
la **campanada**   stroke (*of clock or bell*)
el **campeonato**   championship
el **campo**   country, field
campo de turismo   tourist camp, motel
casa de campo   country house (home)
el **canal**   canal

la **canción** (*pl.* **canciones**) song
 cansado, -a tired
 cantar to sing
la **cantidad** quantity
el **canto** song
la **caña de azúcar** sugar cane
el **cañón** canyon
la **capacidad** capacity
la **capilla** chapel
la **capital** capital (*city*)
la **cara** face
la **carabela** caravel, boat
el **carácter** (*pl.* **caracteres**) character
la **característica** characteristic
 característico, -a characteristic
 caracterizar to characterize
la **cárcel** prison, jail
el **cargo** post, position, job
 caribe *adj.* Caribbean
 Carlos Charles
 Carmen Carmen
el **carnaval** carnival
la **carne** meat
el **carnero** sheep
 caro, -a expensive, dear
 Carolina Caroline
la **carrera** career; race
 carrera de caballos horse race
la **carretera** highway
la **carta** letter; card (*playing*)
 jugar (ue) a las cartas to play cards
el **cartaginés** (*pl.* **cartagineses**) Carthaginian
el **cartero** postman, letter carrier
el **cartón** (*pl.* **cartones**) *painting or drawing on strong paper*
la **casa** house, home; firm
 a (la) casa de (María) to (Mary's)
 en casa at home
 en casa de (mi tía) at (my aunt's)
 (ir) a casa (to go) home
 salir de casa to leave home
 casarse to marry, be (get) married
la **cáscara** bark
 casi almost
 castaño, -a dark, brown, brunet(te)
 castellano, -a Castilian

el **castellano** Castilian (*language*)
 Castilla Castile
 Castilla la Nueva New Castile
 Castilla la Vieja Old Castile
el **castillo** castle
 Catalina Katherine
la **catedral** cathedral
 católico, -a Catholic
 catorce fourteen
el **cautivo** captive
la **caza** hunting
la **cebolla** onion
 celebrar to celebrate
 célebre celebrated, famous
 celeste celestial
el **celta** Celt
 cenar to eat supper
 Ceniza: Miércoles de —, Ash Wednesday
el **centavo** cent (*U.S.*); centavo (*Spanish American monetary unit*)
 central central
el **centro** center; downtown
 (estar) en el centro (to be) downtown
 (ir) al centro (to go) downtown
la **cerámica** ceramics, pottery
 cerca *adv.* near, close, nearby
 cerca de *prep.* near
el **cerdo** pig, pork
 (lomo) de cerdo pork (loin)
la **ceremonia** ceremony
 cerrar (ie) to close
la **cerveza** beer
la **cesta** basket; wickerwork racket
el **cesto** basket

 Cíbola: Siete Ciudades de —, *supposed cities in southwestern U.S. for which the Spaniards searched in vain in the sixteenth century*

el **cielo** sky, heaven
 científico, -a scientific
 ciento (cien) one (a) hundred
 ciento (dos) one hundred (two)
 cierto, -a (a) certain, true
 cinco five

cincuenta fifty
el cine movie(s)
el círculo circle
la cita date, appointment
la ciudad city
    la ciudad de México Mexico City
    Ciudad México Mexico City
    civil civil
la civilización civilization
    civilizador, -ora civilizing
el clamor clamor, outcry
    Clara Clara, Clare, Claire
    claramente clearly
la claridad clarity, clearness
    ¡claro! indeed! of course! certainly!
la clase class, classroom; kind
    clase (de español) (Spanish) class
    dar clases to teach
    de toda clase of all kinds
    en clase in (the) class
    (no) ... de ninguna clase (not) ... of any kind
    sala de clase classroom
    clavar to fix
el clima climate
    cobrar to charge, collect; gain
la coca *a plant whose leaves are chewed as a stimulant*
la cocaína cocaine
el cocido Spanish stew
la cocina kitchen
el coche car
    en coche by car
    colaborar to collaborate
la colección (*pl.* **colecciones**) collection
    colgar (**ue**) to hang
    colocar to put, place
    Colón Columbus
la colonia colony, district
    colonial colonial
la colonización colonization
el color color
    ¿de qué color es? what color is (it)?
    colorado, -a red
el colorido coloring, color
el (la) colorista colorist
    combatir to combat

    combinar to combine
la comedia play, comedy
el comedor dining room
    comenzar (**ie**) (**a** + *inf.*) to begin (to), commence (to)
    comer to eat, dine, have dinner
    se come muy bien aquí the food is very good here
    comercial commercial, business
el comerciante merchant, trader, tradesman, business man
el comercio commerce, trade
la comida meal, dinner, food
el comisario commissary
    como as, like, since
        así ... como both (as much) ... and (as)
        como si as if
        tan + *adj. or adv.* + **como** as ... as
        tanto ... como both ... and
    ¿cómo? how?
        ¿cómo es (Chile)? what is (Chile) like? how is (Chile)?
        ¿cómo se llama (Vd.)? what is (your) name?
    ¡cómo no! of course! certainly!
la cómoda chest of drawers
    cómodo, -a comfortable
el compañero companion
la compañía company
    completamente completely
    completo, -a complete
    componer to compose
la composición (*pl.* **composiciones**) composition, theme
el compositor composer
la compra purchase
    ir de compras to go shopping
    comprar to buy, purchase
    comprender to comprehend, understand; comprise, include
el compromiso engagement, commitment
    compuesto, -a *p.p. of* **componer** *and adj.* composed
    compuso *pret. of* **componer**
    común (*pl.* **comunes**) common, usual, ordinary
    por lo común commonly, generally

con   with; to
la concepción   conception
el concurso   contest, competition
la concha   shell
el conde   count
condenar   to condemn
la condesa   countess
la condición (*pl.* **condiciones**)   condition
  en buenas condiciones   in good condition
conducir   to conduct, drive (*a car*)
el confeti   confetti
el conflicto   conflict
la conga   conga
conmemorar   to commemorate
conmigo   with me
conocer   to know, be acquainted with, meet
  dar a conocer   to make known
conocido, -a   known, recognized
  la más conocida   the best known
el conocimiento   knowledge
la conquista   conquest
el conquistador   conqueror
la consecuencia   consequence
conseguir (**i,i**)   to get, obtain, attain, succeed in
conservar   to conserve, keep, preserve
considerar   to consider
consigo   with himself (herself, etc.)
consiguió   *pret. of* **conseguir**
consistir (**en**)   to consist (of)
constituir   to constitute
constituyen   *pres. ind. of* **constituir**
construido, -a de   constructed (built) of (with)
  construido, -a por   built by
construir   to construct, build
construyeron, construyó   *pret. of* **construir**
consumir   to consume, eat
contar (**ue**)   to count; tell, relate
contemporáneo, -a   contemporary
contener   to contain
contento, -a   happy, pleased, glad
contestar   to answer, reply
contigo   with you (*fam.*)

el continente   continent
continuación: a —,   immediately, afterwards
el continuador   follower
continuar   to continue
contra   against
contrario: por lo —,   on the contrary
contrastar   to contrast
el contraste   contrast
la contribución   contribution
contribuir   to contribute
convencer   to convince
convencional   conventional
la conversación (*pl.* **conversaciones**)   conversation
conversar   to converse, talk
convertir (**ie,i**)   to convert; *reflex.* be converted
convirtió   *pret. of* **convertir**
el corazón   heart
la corbata   necktie
el cordero   lamb
cordialmente   cordially
la cordillera   cordillera, mountain range
el coro   chorus
la coronación   coronation
Coronado: (Francisco Vásquez de) *Spanish explorer of the southwestern U.S., 1540-42*
el corredor   corridor
el correo   mail
  por correo aéreo   by air mail
correr   to run
corresponder   to correspond
corrida (de toros)   bullfight; *pl.* bullfighting
cortar   to cut, cut off
la corte   court
cortés (*pl.* **corteses**)   courteous
cortesano, -a   courtly
el cortesano   courtier
la cortesía   courtesy
corto, -a   short
la cosa   thing
  otra cosa   anything (something) else
cosechar   to harvest
la costa   coast

costar (ue) to cost
la costumbre custom
    novela (artículo) de costumbres novel (article) of customs and manners
el costumbrista writer of articles of customs and manners
la creación (*pl.* **creaciones**) creation
creador, -ora creative
crear to create
crecer to grow, increase
crédulo, -a credulous
creer to believe, think
    creer que (sí) to think *or* believe (so)
    ¡ya lo creo! of course! certainly!
la crema cream
Creta Crete (*an island near Greece*)
la criada maid
criar to grow; *reflex.* be raised
el cristianismo Christianity
cristiano, -a Christian
Cristo Christ
Cristóbal Christopher
crítico, -a critical
el crítico critic
crudo, -a crude, stark
la cruz (*pl.* **cruces**) cross
cruzar to cross, pass (go) across
el cuaderno notebook
el cuadro picture, scene, vivid description
cual: el —, la — (**los, las cuales**) that, which, who, whom
    lo cual which (fact)
¿cuál? which (one)? what?
cuando when
    de vez en cuando from time to time
¿cuándo? when
cuanto *neuter pron.* all that
cuanto: en —, *conj.* as soon as
    cuanto antes at once, immediately, as soon as possible
cuanto, -a all that (who)
    unos(-as) cuantos (-as) some, a few
¿cuánto, -a (-os, -as)? how much (many)?
    ¿a cuántos estamos? what is the date?
    ¿cuánto tiempo? how long?
¡cuánto + *verb*! how!

cuarenta forty
la Cuaresma Lent
cuarto, -a fourth
el cuarto quarter; room
    cuarto de baño bathroom
cuatro four
cuatrocientos, -as four hundred
cubano, -a Cuban
cubierto, -a (de) covered (with)
el cubismo cubism
cubista (*m. and f.*) cubist, of the cubist school
la cuenta account, bill
    darse cuenta de (que) to realize (that)
el cuento short story, tale
el cuerpo body
la cueva cave
el cuidado care
    con cuidado carefully
    tener (mucho) cuidado (de) to be (very) careful (to)
cuidar to care for, look after, take care of
cultivar to cultivate, raise
el cultivo cultivation
    campo de cultivo cultivated field
la cultura culture
cultural cultural
el cumpleaños birthday
cumplir to fulfill, keep (one's word); reach (one's birthday), be (years old)
    ¿cuántos años va a cumplir? how old is he going to be?
    cumplir (diez y seis) años to reach one's (sixteenth) birthday, be (sixteen) years old
el curandero medicine man
curar to cure
curvo, -a curved
cuyo, -a whose, of whom (which)
el Cuzco Cuzco

Ch

charlar to chat
el cheque check
la chica (little) girl
el chicle chicle (*used for making chewing gum*)

el **chile** chili
la **chimenea** chimney, fireplace
el **chocolate** chocolate
el **chorizo** smoked pork sausage

D

la **dama** lady
la **danza** dance
el **daño** harm, damage
 hacer daño a to do harm to, harm, hurt
 hacerse daño to hurt oneself
dar to give
 dar a to face
 dar a conocer to make known
 dar a uno to confer upon one
 dar clases to teach
 dar permiso para to give permission to
 dar señales de to show signs of
 dar un paseo to take a walk (ride)
 darse cuenta de (que) to realize (that)
 darse prisa to hurry
 lo damos a we are offering (selling) it for
de of, from, about, by, to, with, as; in (*after a superlative*); than (*before numerals*)
debajo de below, under, beneath
deber to owe; must, should, ought to
debiera (I) ought to, should
la **decadencia** decadence
decidir to decide
décimo, -a tenth
decir to say, tell
 decir que (sí) to say (yes)
 es decir that is (to say)
 oír decir que to hear that
la **decisión** (*pl.* **decisiones**) decision
decisivo, -a decisive
dedicar to dedicate
 dedicarse a to dedicate (devote) oneself to, be dedicated to
el **defecto** defect
defender (ie) to defend
la **defensa** defense

dejar *trans.* to leave (behind), abandon; let, allow, permit
 no dejar de + *inf.* not to fail to + verb
del = de + el of the
el **delantal** apron
delgado, -a thin
demás *adj. and pron.* (the) rest, other(s)
demasiado *adv.* too, too much
demasiado, -a *adj. and pron.* too much (many)
demostrar (ue) to demonstrate, show
el **dentista** dentist
dentro de *prep.* within
el **departamento** apartment
el **dependiente** clerk
el **deporte** sport
 sección de deportes sports section (pages)
el **derecho** law
 Facultad de Derecho Law School (*in a university*)
derecho, -a right
 a la derecha to (on, at) the right
derredor: en —, around
desarrollar to develop
el **desarrollo** development
desayunarse to take (eat) breakfast
el **desayuno** breakfast
 tomar el desayuno to take (have, eat) breakfast
descansar to rest
el **descubridor** discoverer
el **descubrimiento** discovery
descubrir to discover
desde from, since; for (*time*)
desear to desire, wish, want
el **deseo** desire, wish
 tener muchos deseos de to be very eager (wish very much) to
el **desfile** parade
la **desgracia** misfortune
 por desgracia unfortunately
deshacer to right, undo
el **desierto** desert
designar to designate
la **desilusión** disillusion

desilusionado, -a disillusioned

desinflado, -a flat (*tire*)

despacio slowly

despedirse (i,i) (de + *obj.*) to say good-bye (to), take leave (of)

desperezarse to stretch (one's arms and legs)

el despertador alarm clock

despertar (ie) to awaken, wake up; *reflex.* wake up (oneself)

después *adv.* afterwards, later

después de *prep.* after

después que *conj.* after

poco después shortly afterward

destacarse to stand out

desterrado, -a exiled, banished

destruir to destroy

destruyó *pret. of* **destruir**

el detalle detail

detener to detain, stop; *reflex.* to stop (oneself)

determinar to determine, decide

detrás *adv.* behind

detrás de *prep.* behind

devolver (ue) to return, give back

el día day

al día siguiente on the following day

buenos días good morning (day)

en estos días these days

hoy día nowadays

todos los días every day

el dialecto dialect

el diálogo dialogue

diario, -a daily

el (la) dibujante draftsman; illustrator, master in the art of drawing

dibujar to draw, paint

el dibujo drawing

el diccionario dictionary

diciembre December

el dictado dictation

Diego James

diez ten

diez (y seis) (six)teen

diferente different

difícil difficult, hard

la dignidad dignity

digno, -a worthy

dime = di + me, tell me

el dinero money

Dios God

¡Dios mío! heavens!

el dios god

directamente directly

el director director

el discípulo pupil, disciple

el disco record (*phonograph*)

disfrutar (de + *obj.*) to enjoy

disponerse a to make up one's mind to

la disposición (*pl.* **disposiciones**) disposition, service

a su disposición at your service

dispusiese *imp. subj. of* **disponer**

la distancia distance

¿qué distancia hay? how far is it?

distinguirse to distinguish oneself, become distinguished

distinguirse de to differ from

distinto, -a different, distinct

el distrito district

diverso, -a diverse, varied

divertir (ie,i) to divert, amuse; *reflex.* have a good time, amuse oneself

divino, -a divine

doce twelve

el dólar dollar (*U.S.*)

doler (ue) to ache, pain

me duele la cabeza my head aches

doméstico, -a domestic

dominar to dominate, control, subdue

Domingo Dominic

el domingo Sunday

Domingo de Ramos Palm Sunday

Domingo de Resurrección Easter Sunday

los domingos on Sundays

los domingos por la tarde (on) Sunday afternoons

dominicano, -a Dominican

la República Dominicana Dominican Republic

el dominico Dominican (*of religious order*)

el dominio domination, control

don Don (*title used before first names of men*)

donde   where, in which
  en donde   where, in which
¿dónde?   where?
el dormilón (*pl.* **dormilones**)   sleepyhead
dormir (**ue,u**)   to sleep; *reflex.* fall asleep, go to sleep
Dorotea   Dorothy
dos   two
  los (**las**) **dos**   the two, both
doscientos, -as   two hundred
el drama   drama
dramático, -a   dramatic
el dramaturgo   dramatist
la duda   doubt
  sin duda   doubtless, without a doubt
dudar   to doubt
dudoso, -a   doubtful
la dueña   chaperone
el dueño   owner
los dulces   sweets, candy
durante   during
durar   to last

E

e   and (*used for* **y** *before* **i-, hi-,** *but not* **hie-**)
económico, -a   economic
el Ecuador   Ecuador
echar   to throw; put (in)
  echar por tierra (**a**)   to throw to the ground
la edad   age
  Edad Media   Middle Ages
el edificio   building
Eduardo   Edward
el efecto   effect
¿eh?   right? eh? won't I? etc.
ejemplar *adj.* exemplary
el ejemplo   example
  por ejemplo   for example
ejercer   to exert
el ejercicio   exercise
ejercitarse (**en**)   to practice
el ejército   army
el (*pl.* **los**)   the (*m.*)
  el (**los**) **de**   that (those) of, the one(s) of (with, in)

el (**los**) **que**   that, who, which, he (those) who (whom), the one(s) who (that, which)
él   he, him (*after prep.*)
la electricidad   electricity
la elegancia   elegance, grace, distinguished manner
elegante   elegant
el elemento   element, ingredient
Elena   Helen, Ellen
elevarse   to rise, elevate oneself
ella   she, her (*after prep.*)
ello   *neuter pron.* it
  todo ello   all of it
ellos, -as   they, them (*after prep.*)
embargo: sin —,   nevertheless, however
eminente   eminent, prominent
la emoción   emotion
el emperador   emperor
empezar (**ie**) (**a** + *inf.*)   to begin (to)
la empleada   clerk, employee (*woman*)
el empleado   employee
emplear   to employ, use
en   in, on, at, into, of
  en casa   at home
  en (**el aeropuerto**)   at *or* in (the airport)
enamorado, -a   enamored
  anduvo enamorado   (he) was in love
enamorarse (**de** + *obj.*)   to fall in love (with)
el enano   dwarf
encantado, -a   delighted
encantador, -ora   enchanting, delightful
el encarcelamiento   imprisonment
encerrar (**ie**)   to enclose, include
encontrar (**ue**)   to meet, encounter; find; *reflex.* find oneself, be found, be
  encontrarse con   to meet, run across
enérgico, -a   energetic
enero   January
enfermo, -a   ill, sick
enfrente *adv.* in front, opposite
la enhorabuena   congratulations
enorme   enormous, great
Enrique   Henry
enriquecer   to enrich
la ensalada   salad

el ensayista essayist
el ensayo essay
  enseñar to teach, show
    enseñar (a + *inf*.) to show *or* teach (how to)
  entender (ie) to understand
  enteramente entirely
  entero, -a entire
el entierro burial
  entonces then, at that time
  entrar (en + *obj*.) to enter, go (get) in
  entre among, between
  entregar to hand (over), give
el entremés (*pl*. **entremeses**) side dish, hors d'oeuvre; interlude (*a short farce*)
el entusiasmo enthusiasm
  con entusiasmo enthusiastically
  enviar to send
  envolver (ue) to wrap up
  épico, -a epic
la Epifanía Epiphany (*January 6*)
  episódico, -a episodic
la época epoch, period, time
el equipaje baggage, luggage
el equipo team
el erudito scholar, learned man
el escaparate show window
  escaparse to escape
la escena scene
la esclavitud slavery
el esclavo slave
  escoger to choose, select
  escribir to write
  escrito, -a *p.p. of* **escribir** *and adj*. written
el escritor writer
  escuchar to listen (to)
el escudero squire
la escuela school
  escuela superior high school
el escultor sculptor
la escultura sculpture
  ese, esa (-os, -as) *adj*. that, those (*nearby*)
  ése, ésa (-os, -as) *pron*. that (one), those
  eso *neuter pron*. that
  a eso de at about

  por eso because of that, therefore
el espacio space, room
España Spain
  español, -ola (*also noun*) Spanish
el español Spanish (*language*)
    (clase) de español Spanish (class)
    (libro) de español Spanish (book)
la Española Hispaniola
  esparcir to spread, scatter
  especial special
la especialidad specialty
  especialmente especially
el espectáculo spectacle, show
el espectador spectator
el espejo mirror
  espera: sala de —, waiting room
  esperar to wait, wait for, await; hope, expect
  esperar to wait, wait for, await; hope, expect
    esperar que (sí) to hope (so)
el espíritu spirit
  espiritual spiritual
  espléndido, -a splendid
la espontaneidad spontaneity
  espontáneo, -a spontaneous
la esposa wife
el esposo husband
la esquina corner (*street*)
  establecer to establish, settle; *reflex*. settle, establish oneself
el establecimiento establishment, settlement
el establo stable
la estación (*pl*. **estaciones**) season; station
el estacionamiento parking
el estadio stadium
el estado state
  los Estados Unidos United States
la estancia stay
el estante (para libros) bookcase
  estar to be
    ¿a cuántos estamos? what is the date?
    está bien that's fine, excellent, very well
    estamos a (ocho de noviembre) it is (November 8)
    estar para to be about to

este, esta (**-os, -as**) *adj.* this, these
éste, ésta (**-os, -as**) *pron.* this (one), these; the latter
el este east
Esteban Stephen
el estilo style
estimar to esteem
el estimulante stimulant
esto *neuter pron.* this
estrechar to tighten, bring closer together, narrow (down)
estrecho, -a narrow, tight
la estrella star
la estructura structure
el (la) estudiante student
   residencia de estudiantes student residence hall
estudiar to study
el estudio study
   estudio de palabras word study
la etapa period, stage
etcétera and so forth, etcetera
eterno, -a eternal
Eugenia Eugenie
Europa Europe
europeo, -a (*also noun*) European
evidente evident
la evolución evolution
exactamente exactly
exacto, -a exact
el examen (*pl.* **exámenes**) examination
examinar to examine
exceder to exceed
la excelencia excellence, superiority, refinement
excelente excellent
la excepción exception
la excursión (*pl.* **excursiones**) excursion, trip
   hacer una excursión to make (take) an excursion
exhibir to exhibit, display
la existencia existence
el éxito success
la expansión expansion
la expedición expedition
la experiencia experience

la exploración (*pl.* **exploraciones**) exploration, search
el explorador explorer
explorar to explore
la explotación exploitation
la exportación exportation
expresar to express
la expresión (*pl.* **expresiones**) expression
expulsar to expel, drive out
extenderse (**ie**) to extend
extenso, -a extensive, vast
extranjero, -a foreign
el extranjero foreigner
extraño, -a strange, foreign, unusual
extraordinario, -a extraordinary

F

la fábrica factory
fabuloso, -a fabulous
fácil easy
facturar to check (*baggage*)
la Facultad School (*in a university*)
   Facultad de Derecho Law School
la falta lack
faltar to lack, be lacking
   falta mucho tiempo para it is a long time before
   ¡no faltaba más! the very idea! that's the limit!
la fama fame, reputation, name
   tener fama (**de**) to have the (a) reputation (of, as)
   tener fama por to have a reputation for, be known for
la familia family
famoso, -a famous
el fanatismo fanaticism
la fatiga fatigue
el favor favor
   favor de + *inf.* please + *verb*
   haga(n)me Vd(s). el favor de + *inf.* please + *verb*
   por favor please (*used at end of request*)
favorito, -a favorite
la fe faith

febrero February
la fecha date
Federal Federal
la felicitación congratulation(s)
felicitar to congratulate
Felipe Philip
feliz (*pl.* **felices**) happy
 ¡**Felices Pascuas**! Merry Christmas!
 ¡**Feliz Navidad**! Merry Christmas!
femenino, -a feminine
el fenicio Phoenician
el fénix phoenix, model
la feria fair
Fernando Ferdinand
el ferrocarril railroad
 estación de ferrocarril railroad station
fértil fertile
festivo, -a festive
la ficción fiction
la fiebre fever
fiel faithful
la fiesta fiesta, festival, holiday
la figura figure, person
figurar to figure, appear
la figurita small figure
filipino, -a Philippine
el filólogo philologist
el filósofo philosopher
el fin end
 a (**hacia, hasta**) **fines de** at (towards, until) the end of
 a partir de fines since the end
 en fin in short
 por fin finally, at last
 y fines de and the end of
fino, -a fine, keen
firmar to sign
flamenco, -a Flemish, from Flanders
el flamenco Flemish
el flan custard
la flor flower
florecer to flourish
la Florida Florida
florido, -a flowery
 Pascua Florida Easter
el fondo background, substance, bottom, depth

 del fondo at the back, in the background
el fonógrafo phonograph, record player
la forma form, shape
formar to form, make up
la fortaleza fort, fortress
la foto (*for* **fotografía**) photo
la fotografía photograph, snapshot
 sacar fotografías to take photographs
el fraile friar
francés, -esa French
el francés French (*language*)
Francia France
franciscano, -a (*also noun*) Franciscan
Francisco Francis
la franqueza frankness
la frase sentence
Fray Friar (*title*)
frente a *prep.* in front of
la fresa strawberry
fresco, -a cool, fresh
el fresco coolness, fresh air
 hacer fresco to be cool (*weather*)
el frijol kidney bean
frío, -a cold
el frío cold
 hacer (**mucho**) **frío** to be (very) cold (*weather*)
 tener (**mucho**) **frío** to be (very) cold (*living beings*)
frito, -a fried
la frontera frontier
el frontón (handball) court
frutal *adj.* fruit
las frutas fruit(s)
el fruto fruit, product
el fuego fire
la fuente fountain
 fuera de *prep.* outside (of)
  fuera de que aside from the fact that
fuerte strong
fuertemente strongly
la fuerza force, strength
el fulgor radiance, brilliance
el fundador founder
fundar to found, settle
la fusión fusion
el fútbol football

G

el gallo   cock

    misa del gallo   midnight Mass

la gana   desire

    de buena gana   willingly

    tener (muchas) ganas de   to be (very) eager to (desirous of) eager (wish very much)

el ganado   cattle, livestock

    ganar   to gain, earn, win

el garaje   garage

el garbanzo   chickpea

la gasolina   gasoline

    de gasolina   gasoline

la gasolinera   filling (gas) station

    Gaspar   Jasper (*one of the Three Wise Men*)

    gastar   to waste, use (up)

el gaucho   gaucho, South American cowboy

el gazpacho   cold vegetable soup

la generación   generation

    general   general

        en (por lo) general   in general, generally

el general   general

    generalmente   generally

el género   genre, literary type; sort, kind

la generosidad   generosity

    generoso, -a   generous, highborn

el genio   genius

la gente   people

el gerente   manager

    germánico, -a   Germanic

el gigante   giant

    gitano, -a   gypsy

la gloria   glory

    Sábado de Gloria   Holy Saturday

    glorioso, -a   glorious

el glotón   glutton

    algo glotón   something of a glutton

el gobernador   governor

el gobierno   government

el golf   golf

el golfo   gulf

la goma de mascar   chewing gum

    gótico, -a   Gothic

    gozar (de + *obj.*)   to enjoy

el gozo   joy

la gracia   grace, charm

gracias   thanks, thank you

    gracioso, -a   witty, amusing

la gramática   grammar

    gramatical   grammatical

    gran *adj.*   great, large (*used for* **grande** *before a sing. noun*)

grande   large, big, great

el grano   grain

el griego   Greek

    gritar   to shout

    grotesco, -a   grotesque

el grupo   group

el guacamole   guacamole (*salad*)

el guajolote   turkey (*Mex.*)

el guante   glove

    guapo, -a   handsome, good-looking

    guardar   to keep, guard

la guerra   war

    guerrero, -a   warlike

el guisado   stew

la guitarra   guitar

el guitarrista   guitarist, guitar player

    gustar   to be pleasing (to), like

        gustar más (que)   to like better (than), prefer (to)

        ¿le gustaría a Vd.?   would you like?

        me gustaría   I should like

el gusto   pleasure; taste

    con mucho gusto   gladly, with great pleasure

    de su gusto   to your liking

    el gusto es mío   the pleasure is mine

    mucho gusto   (I am) pleased *or* glad to know you

    mucho gusto en conocer(le)   (I am) very pleased (glad) to know (you)

    tener (mucho) gusto en   to be (very) glad to

H

la Habana   Havana

    haber   to have (*auxiliary*); be (*impersonal*)

    haber de + *inf.*   to be to, be supposed to

había there was (were)

habrá there will be

habría there would be

hay there is (are)

hay (había) que + *inf.* it is (was) necessary to, one must (should)

hubo there was (were)

los (las) hay there are (some)

no hay de qué you're welcome, don't mention it

¿qué hay de nuevo? what's new? what do you know?

la habitación (*pl.* **habitaciones**) room

el habitante inhabitant

habitar to inhabit, live in

habla: de — española Spanish-speaking

hablador, -ora talkative

hablar to talk, speak

oír hablar de to hear of

se habla one talks, people talk

hacer to do, make; be (*weather*)

desde hacía varios siglos for several centuries

hace (muchos años) (many years) ago

hacer (calor) to be (warm) (*weather*)

hacer daño a to do harm to, harm, hurt

hacer regalos to give gifts

hacer un viaje to take (make) a trip

hacer una excursión to take (make) an excursion

hacer una parada to stop over, make a stop

hacer (una) pregunta (a) to ask (a) question (of)

hacerse daño to hurt oneself

hacerse (digno) to make oneself *or* become (worthy)

hacerse + *noun* to become

hága(n)me Vd(s). el favor de + *inf.* please + *verb*

¿qué tiempo hace? what kind of weather is it?

hacia toward(s); about (*time*)

a (hacia, hasta) fines de at (towards, until) the end of

Haití Haiti

¡hala! come on! get going!

hallar to find; *reflex.* find oneself, be found, be

el hambre (*f.*) hunger

tener (mucha) hambre to be (very) hungry

la harina flour

hasta *prep.* until, to, up to, as far as; *adv.* even

hasta luego until later, see you later

hasta que *conj.* until

hay there is (are)

hay que + *inf.* it is necessary to, one must

los (las) hay there are (some)

no hay de qué you're welcome, don't mention it

¿qué hay de nuevo? what's new? what do you know?

la hazaña deed

hecho, -a *p.p. of* **hacer** *and adj.* done, made

el hecho deed, event, act

el helado ice cream

henchido, -a filled up

la herida wound

la hermana sister

la hermanita little sister

el hermanito little brother

el hermano brother

hermosísimo, -a very pretty (beautiful)

hermoso, -a beautiful, pretty

Hernán, Hernando Ferdinand

Hernando de Soto *Spanish explorer in the Americas, and discoverer of the Mississippi River, 1541*

el héroe hero

la heroína heroine

el hidalgo nobleman

el hierro iron

la hija daughter

el hijo son; *pl.* children

la hilandera spinning girl

hispánico, -a Hispanic

la Hispanidad Spanish Solidarity (Union)

hispano, -a Hispanic

hispanoamericano, -a Spanish American

la **historia**   history
el **historiador**   historian
histórico, -a   historical
la **hoja**   leaf
hojear   to turn the pages of
¡hola!   hello!
el **holandés**   Dutchman
el **hombre**   man
¡hombre!   man (man alive)!
el **honor**   honor
la **honra**   honor
honrar   to honor
la **hora**   hour, time (*of day*)
¿a qué hora?   at what time?
es hora de   it is time to
hora en que   the time (hour) when
¿qué hora es?   what time is it?
ya es la hora   the hour is over
el **hotel**   hotel
hoy   today
hoy día   nowadays
hoy no   not today
hubo   *pret. of* **haber**   there was (were)
el **huevo**   egg
huevos rancheros   eggs ranch style
el **hule**   rubber
la **humanidad**   humanity; *pl.* humanities
el **humanista**   humanist
humano, -a   human
la **humildad**   humility
humilde   humble

I

ibérico, -a   Iberian
la **Península Ibérica**   Iberian Peninsula
el **ibero**   Iberian
la **ida**   departure
billete de ida y vuelta   round-trip ticket
la **idea**   idea
ideal *adj.*   ideal
el **ideal**   ideal
el **idealismo**   idealism
idealista (*m. and f.*)   idealistic
la **iglesia**   church

a la iglesia   to church
igual   equal
es igual   it's all the same, it doesn't matter
igual que   the same as
sin igual   matchless, without equal
igualar   to equal
ilustre   illustrious, famous
la **imagen** (*pl.* **imágenes**)   image
imaginado, -a   imagined
imaginarse   to imagine
imaginativo, -a   imaginative
el **imperio**   empire
la **importancia**   importance
importante   important
la **imprenta**   printing
impresionante   impressive
impresionista (*m. and f.*)   impressionistic
el **impulso**   impulse, impetus
el **inca**   Inca
incalculable   incalculable, inestimable
el **incienso**   incense
incomparable   incomparable
el **inconveniente**   objection
si Vd. no tiene inconveniente   if you have no objection
la **independencia**   independence
la **India**   India
indicar   to indicate
indígena (*m. and f.*)   native
el (**la**) **indígena**   native, Indian
indio, -a (*also noun*)   Indian
el **individualismo**   individualism
individualista (*m. and f.*)   individualistic
la **índole**   character, nature
la **industria**   industry
industrial   industrial
Inés   Inez, Agnes
la **infanta**   *daughter of royalty*, princess
la **influencia**   influence
influir (**en**)   to influence, have influence (on)
los **informes**   information, data
el **ingeniero**   engineer
el **ingenio**   genius
ingenioso, -a   ingenious
Inglaterra   England

inglés, -esa English
el inglés English (*language*)
   (**profesor**) **de inglés** English (teacher)
ingresar (**en** + *obj.*) to enter, become a member of
iniciar to initiate, begin
la injusticia injustice
inmaculado, -a immaculate, without stain
inmediatamente immediately
inmortal immortal
la innovación (*pl.* **innovaciones**) innovation, novelty
innumerable innumerable, numberless
el inocente person easily duped
   Día de los Inocentes *December 28, equivalent to April Fool's Day*
insistir (**en** + *obj.*) to insist (on)
   insistir en que to insist that
la inspiración inspiration
la ínsula island
intelectual intellectual
el intercambio interchange, exchange
el interés (*pl.* **intereses**) interest
interesante interesting
interesar to interest
   interesarse en to be interested in, be concerned with
el interior interior
internacional international
la interpretación interpretation
interpretar to interpret
el (**la**) **intérprete** interpreter
interrumpir to interrupt
intrínseco, -a intrinsic
la introducción introduction
inútil useless
la invasión invasion
el invasor invader
invencible invincible
el invierno winter
el invitado guest
invitar (**a** + *inf.*) to invite (to)
ir (**a** + *inf.*) to go (to); *reflex.* go (away), leave
   ir al centro to go downtown
   ir de compras to go shopping

irse por to go (set out) through
   ¡que les vaya bien! good luck (may it go well with you)!
   vámonos let's be going
   vamos a (**ver**) let's (see)
la ironía irony
la irregularidad irregularity
   Isabel Isabel, Betty, Elizabeth
la isla island
el istmo isthmus
   Italia Italy
   italiano, -a (*also noun*) Italian
el italiano Italian (*language*)
   izquierdo, -a left
      a la izquierda to (on, at) the left

J

el jabón (*pl.* **jabones**) soap
   Jaime James, Jim
   jamás ever, never
el jamón (*pl.* **jamones**) ham
el jardín (*pl.* **jardines**) garden
el jefe chief, leader
   Jerónimo Jerome
   Jesucristo: antes de —, B.C.
   jesuita (*m. and f.*) Jesuit
   Jesús Jesus
la jícara cup
el jitomate tomato (*Mex.*)
   Jorge George
   José Joseph, Joe
   joven (*pl.* **jóvenes**) young
      la joven young woman
      los dos jóvenes the two young men
      los jóvenes (the) young people
la joyería jewelry shop (store)
   Juan John
   Juanita Juanita, Jane
   Juanito Johnny
el juego game
el jueves (on) Thursday
el jugador player
   jugar (**ue**) (**a** + *obj.*) to play (*a game*)
el juguete toy, plaything
el juicio judgment, mind

julio July
junio June
la justicia justice
la juventud youth

K

el kilo(gramo) kilo(gram) (*about 2.2 pounds*)
el kilómetro kilometer (*5/8 mile*)

L

la (*pl.* **las**) the (*f.*)
  la(s) de that (those) of, the one(s) of (with, in)
  la(s) que who, that, which, she who, the one(s) who (that, whom, which), those who (which, whom)
la *obj. pron.* her, it (*f.*), you (*formal f.*)
la labor (*also pl.*) work, labor
el labrador farmer, peasant
  labrador vecino peasant (who was a) neighbor
la labradora farm girl
el lado side
  al lado de beside, at the side of, along with
el lago lake
la lágrima tear
la lanza lance
  lanzar to throw, hurl
el lápiz (*pl.* **lápices**) pencil
  largo, -a long
  a lo largo de along
  las *obj. pron.* them (*f.*), you (*formal f.*) (*also see* **la**)
  las hay there are (some)
la lástima pity
  es lástima it is a pity (too bad)
  ¡qué lástima! what a pity!
el látigo whip
el latín Latin (*language*)
  latino, -a Latin
  latinoamericano, -a Latin American
  lavar to wash; *reflex.* wash (oneself)
  le *obj. pron.* him, you (*formal m.*); to him, her, it, you

la lección (*pl.* **lecciones**) lesson
  lección (de español) (Spanish) lesson
la lectura reading
la leche milk
  arroz con leche rice pudding
el lechón (*pl.* **lechones**) suckling pig
  leer to read
la legumbre vegetable
  lejos *adv.* far, distant
  a lo lejos in the distance
  lejos de *prep.* far from
la lengua language, tongue
el lenguaje language, style
  lento, -a slow
  Lepanto *a seaport in Greece, near which the Spanish and Italian fleets defeated the Turks, October 7, 1571*
las letras letters, learning
  levantar to raise, lift; *reflex.* get up, rise
la ley law
la leyenda legend
el liberal liberal (person)
la libertad liberty, freedom
la libra pound
  libre free
  al aire libre outdoor, (in the) open-air
el libro book
  libro de español Spanish book
el lienzo canvas
  ligero, -a light
el limón (*pl.* **limones**) lemon
la limonada lemonade
  limpiar to clean
el linaje lineage
  lírico, -a lyric
la lista menu
  listo, -a ready
  literario, -a literary
la literatura literature
el litro liter (*about 1.06 quarts*)
  lo *neuter article* the; that, what is
  de lo que (esperaba) than (I expected)
  lo (bueno) what is (good), the (good) part
  lo que what, that which
  todo lo que all that (which)
  lo *obj. pron.* him, it (*m. and neuter*), you (*formal m.*)

(**lo**) **es**   he (it) is
loco, -a   crazy, wild
la locura   madness
lograr   to attain, succeed in, obtain
el lomo (de cerdo)   (pork) loin
los   the (*m.*)
Los Angeles   Los Angeles
los de   those of, the ones of (with, in)
los que   who, that, which, the ones *or*
   those who (that, which, whom)
los *obj. pron.*   them, you (*formal*)
   los hay   there are (some)
Lucía   Lucy
lucir   to shine
la lucha   struggle
luchar   to struggle, fight
luego   later, then, next
   hasta luego   until (see you) later
el lugar   place
   en (primer) lugar   in the (first) place
Luis   Louis
Luisa   Louise
la luna de miel   honeymoon
el lunes   (on) Monday
la luz (*pl.* **luces**)   light

Ll

llamado, -a   called
llamar   to call; knock; *reflex.*   be called,
   be named, call (name) oneself
   ¿cómo se llama (Vd.)?   what is
      (your) name?
   llamar por teléfono   to telephone,
      call by telephone
   se le llama   it is called
   se llama (Carlos)   his name is *or* he
      is called (Charles)
la llanta   tire
   llanta de repuesto   spare tire
la llanura   plain
la llave   key
la llegada   arrival
   llegar (a)   to arrive (at), reach, come to
      llegar a ser   to come to be, become
   llegar a una decisión   to reach (make)
      a decision

llenar   to fill
lleno, -a (de)   full (of), filled (with)
llevar   to take, carry; *reflex.*   take away,
   take with oneself
llorar   to cry, weep
llover (ue)   to rain

M

la madera   wood
la madre   mother
   madre patria   motherland
madrileño, -a   native of Madrid
maestra: obra —,   masterpiece
la maestría   mastery, skill
el maestro   master, teacher
magnífico, -a   magnificent, fine
Magos: Reyes —,   Wise Men (Kings),
   Magi
el maíz   maize, corn
mal *adv.*   badly
mal   *used for* **malo** *before m. sing. nouns*
el mal   evil, harm
la malaria   malaria
la maleta   suitcase
malo, -a   bad
   lo malo   the (what is) bad
Mallorca   Majorca (*largest of the Balearic
   Islands, in the Mediterranean Sea*)
la mamá   mama, mother
la manada   flock
la Mancha   *region in southern New Castile*
mandar   to send, order
   mandarlo limpiar   to have it cleaned
manejar   to drive (*Mex.*)
la manera   manner, way
   de manera que *conj.*   so, so that
   de una manera (solemne)   in a
      (solemn) way
el mango   handle
la manifestación (*pl.* **manifestaciones**)
   manifestation
la mano   hand
   a manos de   into the hands of
   de manos de   from the hands of
la mantequilla   butter
manual   manual

mañana *adv.* tomorrow
la mañana morning
    (mañana) por la mañana (tomorrow) morning
    por (de) la mañana in the morning
    vuelo de la mañana morning flight
el mapa map
la maquinaria machinery
el mar sea
la maravilla marvel, wonder
maravilloso, -a marvelous, wonderful
la marca brand, kind, make
marcar to mark, indicate
marcha: poner en —, to start
marchar to go; march; *reflex.* to leave, go away
Margarita Margaret, Marguerite
María Mary
Marta Martha
el martes (on) Tuesday
marzo March
más more, most, *(time)* longer
    la más conocida the best known
    más bien (que) rather (than)
    más o menos more or less, approximately
    (no) ... nada más (not) ... anything else
    no (tomar) más que (to take) only, (to take) nothing but
    (un rato) más (a while) longer
mascar to chew
    goma de mascar chewing gum
la máscara mask
matar to kill
el mate maté *(a green South American tea)*; gourd
el matrimonio marriage
máximo, -a maximum
el maya Maya, Mayan
mayo May
la mayonesa mayonnaise
mayor greater, greatest; older, oldest
    la mayor parte de most of
me *obj. pron.* me, to me, (to) myself
la media stocking; *pl.* stockings, hose

mediados: entre — de between the middle of
la medianoche midnight
    a la medianoche at midnight
la medicina medicine
el médico doctor, physician
medida: a — que as
medio, -a half, a half
    (a las siete) y media (at) half past (seven)
    dos horas y media two hours and a half
    Edad Media Middle Ages
    media hora a half hour
el medio medium, environment; means
    por medio de by means of
el mediodía noon
    al mediodía at noon
mediterráneo, -a Mediterranean
mejor better, best
mejorar to better, improve
la melancolía melancholy, sadness
Melchor Melchior *(one of the Three Wise Men)*
la melodía melody
el membrillo quince *(fruit and paste)*
mencionar to mention
el mendigo beggar
la menina Little Lady in Waiting
menor smaller, younger, lesser, smallest, youngest, least
menos less, least, fewer
    a menos que *conj.* unless
    más o menos more or less, approximately
    por lo menos at least
menudo: a —, often, frequently
el mercado market
la merluza hake
el mes month
    al mes a (per) month
la mesa table, desk
    mesa de comer dining table
el mesero waiter *(Mex.)*
la meseta tableland, plateau
la mesita small (little) table

mesita de noche   night table
el mestizo   mestizo (*person of white and Indian blood*)
el metal   metal
meter   to put (in)
el método   method
el metro   meter (*verse*)
metropolitano, -a   metropolitan
mexicano, -a   Mexican
México   Mexico
la ciudad de México, Ciudad México   Mexico City
Nuevo México   New Mexico
la mezcla   mixture
mezclar   to mix, mingle
mi   my
mí   me, myself (*after prep.*)
el miedo   fear
tener miedo (de + *obj.*)   to be afraid (of)
tener miedo de que   to be afraid that
mientras (que) *conj.*   while, as long as
el miércoles   (on) Wednesday
Miércoles de Ceniza   Ash Wednesday
Miguel   Michael, Mike
mil   a (one) thousand; *pl.* thousands, many
mil cosas   many things
mil (gracias)   many *or* a thousand (thanks)
el milagro   miracle
militar   military
el millón (*pl.* **millones**)   million
el mineral   mineral
el minuto   minute
mío, -a *adj.*   my, (of) mine
(el) mío, (la) mía, (los) míos, (las) mías *pron.*   mine
mirar   to look at
se miraron   they looked at each other
la mirra   myrrh
la misa   Mass
misa del gallo   midnight Mass
la miscelánea   miscellany
la misión (*pl.* **misiones**)   mission
el misionero   missionary
mismo, -a   same, very

ahora mismo   right now, right away
el (la) mismo (-a) ... que   the same ... as
él mismo   he himself
místico, -a   mystic(al)
la mitad   half
Moctezuma   Montezuma
la moda   style, fashion
estar (muy) de moda   to be (very) stylish
el modelo   model
el modernismo   modernism
moderno, -a   modern
lo moderno   the (what is) modern
modestamente   modestly
modificado, -a   modified
el modo   manner, means, way
de modo que *conj.*   so, so that
de todos modos   at any rate, by all means
el mole   mole (*a sauce*)
molestar   to bother, molest
el molino de viento   windmill
el momento   moment
en este (ese) momento   at this (that) moment
por el (un) momento   for the (a) moment
la moneda   money, coin, currency
la montaña   mountain
montañoso, -a   mountainous
montar   to mount, ride
montar a caballo   to ride horseback
el monumento   monument
el morador   dweller, inhabitant
moral   moral
moreno, -a   brown, dark
morir (ue,u)   to die
el moro   Moor
el mosaico   tile
el mostrador   counter, show case
mostrar (ue)   to show
el motel   motel
el motivo   motive; motif, theme
el motor   motor
mover (ue)   to move
mueve a risa   (it) moves one to laughter

el **movimiento** movement
mozo, -a young
la **muchacha** girl
el **muchacho** boy
muchísimo *adv.* very much
muchísimo, -a (-os, -as) very much (many)
mucho *adv.* much, hard, a great deal
mucho, -a (-os, -as) much, (many); very
mudar to change
   mudarse de ropa to change clothes (clothing)
los **muebles** furniture
la **mujer** woman; wife
la **mula** mule
el **mundo** world
mundial *adj.* world
   Nuevo Mundo New World
   todo el mundo everybody
el **museo** museum
la **música** music
musical musical
el **músico** musician
muy very

N

nacer to be born
el **nacimiento** birth; manger scene
la **nación** nation
nacional national
nada nothing, (not) ... anything
   de nada don't mention it, you are welcome, not at all
   nada de particular nothing special
   (no) ... nada más (not) ... anything else
nadar to swim
   ir a nadar to take a swim, go swimming
nadie no one, nobody, (not) ... anyone (anybody)
Napoleón Napoleon
la **naranja** orange
el **naranjo** orange tree
narrar to narrate, tell

narrativo, -a narrative
la **natación** swimming
natural natural
el **(la) natural** native
el **naturalismo** naturalism
naturalista (*m. and f.*) naturalistic
naturalmente naturally
Navarra Navarre (*province, and former kingdom, in northern Spain*)
navegar to sail, navigate
la **Navidad** Christmas
   (día) de Navidad Christmas (day)
   ¡Feliz Navidad! Merry Christmas!
necesario, -a necessary
la **necesidad** need, necessity
necesitar to need
negar (ie) to deny
los **negocios** business
   viaje de negocios business trip
negro, -a black; Negro
el **negro** Negro
nervioso, -a nervous
nevado, -a snow-covered
ni neither, nor, (not) ... or
   ni ... ni neither ... nor, (not) ... either ... or
el **nicaragüense** native of Nicaragua
la **nieve** snow
ningún *used for* **ninguno** *before m. sing. nouns*
ninguno, -a no, none, (not) ... any
   de ninguna clase of any kind (*after negative*)
   (no) ... en ninguna parte (not) ... anywhere
la **niña** little girl
el **niño** little boy, child; *pl.* children
   Niño Jesús Child Jesus
no no, not
noble noble
la **nobleza** nobility
la **noche** night, evening
   buenas noches good evening (night)
   de la noche in the evening, at night, p.m.
   de noche at night
   (el sábado) por la noche (Saturday) night

esta noche   tonight
pasar una noche   to spend an evening
por (de) la noche   in the evening
todas las noches   every night (evening)
la **Nochebuena**   Christmas Eve
nombrar   to name, appoint
el **nombre**   name; fame, reputation
dar nombre a   to name
en nombre de   in the name of
noroeste *adj.*   northwest
el **norte**   north
al norte   to (in) the north
la **América del Norte**   North America

norteamericano, -a   (North) American (*of the U.S.*)
nortecentral *adj.*   northcentral
nos *obj. pron.*   us, to us, (to) ourselves
nosotros, -as   we, us (*after prep.*)
la **nota**   note; touch
notable   notable, noteworthy
notar   to note, observe
novecientos, -as   nine hundred
la **novela**   novel, romance, tale
novela de caballerías   novel of chivalry
novela de costumbres   novel of customs and manners
Novelas ejemplares   Exemplary Tales (Stories)
el **novelista**   novelist
novelístico, -a   novelistic
noveno, -a   ninth
noventa   ninety
la **novia**   fiancée, sweetheart, girl friend
noviembre   November
el **novio**   fiancé, sweetheart, boy friend
la **nube**   cloud
nuestro, -a *adj.*   our, (of) ours
(el) nuestro, (la) nuestra, (los) nuestros, (las) nuestras *pron.*   ours
Nueva York   New York
nueve   nine
nuevo, -a   new
de nuevo   again, anew
¿qué hay de nuevo?   what's new? what do you know?
Nuevo México   New Mexico

la **nuez** (*pl.* **nueces**)   nut
el **número**   number, size (*of shoes*)
número de baile   dance number
numeroso, -a   numerous, many, large
nunca   never, (not) ... ever

O

o   or, either
la **obra**   work
obra maestra   masterpiece
el **obrero**   workman
la **observación** (*pl.* **observaciones**)   observation
observar   to observe
obtener   to obtain, get
la **ocasión** (*pl.* **ocasiones**)   occasion, opportunity
en otra ocasión   another (some other) time
occidental   occidental, western
el **océano**   ocean
Océano Pacífico   Pacific Ocean
octavo, -a   eighth
octubre   October
ocupado, -a   busy, occupied
ocupar   to occupy
ocurrir   to occur, happen
ochenta   eighty
ocho   eight
ochocientos, -as   eight hundred
el **oeste**   west
la **oficina**   office
el **oficio**   craft, trade
ofrecer   to offer
la **ofrenda**   offering
ofrezco *pres. ind. of* **ofrecer**
¡oh!   oh!
oír   to hear, listen
oír decir que   to hear that
¡ojalá (que)!   would that! I wish that!
el **ojo**   eye
olvidar   to forget
olvidarse (de + *obj.*)   to forget
la **olla**   jar
once   eleven
la **onda**   wave
oponerse a   to oppose, face

la **oportunidad**   opportunity
    tener la oportunidad de   to have the
    opportunity to
el **optimismo**   optimism
    optimista (*m. and f.*)   optimistic
    opuesto, -a   opposite
    oral   oral
el **orden**   order, arrangement
la **orden** (*pl.* **órdenes**)   order, command;
    religious order
    a sus órdenes   at your service
    ordenar   to order; ordain
    ordenarse de   to be ordained as, take
    orders as
la **organización**   organization
    organizar   to organize
    oriental   oriental, eastern
el **Oriente**   Orient, East
el **origen** (*pl.* **orígenes**)   origin
    dar origen a   to begin, start
    original   original
la **originalidad**   originality
    originar(se)   to originate
el **oro**   gold
    (es) de oro   (it is) gold
    reloj de oro   gold watch
    Siglo de Oro   Golden Age
la **orquesta**   orchestra
    director de orquesta   orchestra di-
    rector
    os *obj. pron.*   you (*fam. pl.*), to you, (to)
    yourselves
el **otoño**   fall, autumn
    día de otoño   fall day
    otro, -a   other, another; *pl.* other(s)
    otra cosa   anything (something) else
    otros, -as (**muchos, -as**)   (many)
    other(s)
la **oveja**   sheep

P

Pablo   Paul
pacífico, -a   pacific, peaceful
el **Pacífico**   Pacific (Ocean)
el **padre**   father; priest; *pl.* parents
la **paella**   *a rice dish containing meat, vegetables,
    and shellfish*

pagar   to pay, pay for
la **página**   page
el **país**   country (*nation*)
el **paisaje**   landscape, countryside
la **paja**   straw
el **pájaro**   bird
la **palabra**   word
    con la pluma y con la palabra   writ-
    ing and talking
el **palo**   stick
la **pampa**   pampa, plain (*of Argentina*)
el **pan**   bread
    Panamá   Panama
    panamericano, -a   Pan American
el **panorama**   panorama
la **papa**   potato (*Am.*)
el **papá**   papa, dad, father
el **papel**   paper
el **paquete**   package
el **par**   pair; couple
    para *prep.*   for, in order to, to, by
    estar para   to be about to
    para que *conj.*   so that, in order that
    ¿para qué?   why? for what purpose?
el **parabrisas**   windshield
la **parada**   stop, stop over
    hacer una parada   to stop over, make
    a stop
    parado, -a   standing
el **Paraguay**   Paraguay
    paraguayo, -a   Paraguayan
    pararse   to stop
    parecer   to appear, seem
    parecer ser bien a uno   to think it
    proper for one, seem proper to one
    parecerse a   to resemble
    ¿qué le (te) parece...?   what do you
    think of...? how do you like...?
el **parecer**   appearance
    de muy buen parecer   very good-
    looking
    parecido, -a   similar
la **pared**   wall
la **pareja**   pair, couple
el **parque**   park
el **párrafo**   paragraph
la **parte**   part
    de mi parte   for me, on my part

la mayor parte de most of, the greater part of

la tercera parte one (a) third

(no) ... en ninguna parte (not) ... anywhere

por todas partes through (in) all parts, everywhere

particular particular, special

nada de particular nothing special

la partida match, game

el partido match, game

partir (de + *obj.*) to leave, depart

a partir de starting with, from ... on

a partir de fines since the end

pasado, -a past, last

pasar to pass (by), come in, run (along), go; happen; spend (*time*)

¡pasa! (**¡pase Vd.!**) come in!

pasar por aquí to pass (come) this way *or* by here

¡que lo pase(s) bien! good-bye! (*lit.*, may you fare well!)

la Pascua Florida Easter

¡Felices Pascuas! Merry Christmas!

pasearse to walk, stroll

el paseo walk, stroll, ride; boulevard

dar un paseo to take a walk (ride)

la pasión passion

el paso step; float

el pastel pastry, pie

el pastor shepherd

pastoril pastoral

la patata potato

el patio patio, courtyard

el pato duck

la patria fatherland, native country

madre patria motherland

el patrón patron, patron saint, protector

santo patrón patron saint

la paz peace

el pecho chest, breast

pedir (i,i) to ask, ask for, request

Pedro Peter

pegar to beat, lash

la película film

el peligro danger

peligroso, -a dangerous

el pelo hair

tener el pelo (castaño) to have (dark) hair

la pelota handball, ball

la península peninsula

peninsular peninsular (*of Spain*)

el pensador thinker

el pensamiento thought

pensar (ie) to think; + *inf.* intend

pensar en (+ *obj.*) to think of (about)

la pensión (*pl.* **pensiones**) boardinghouse

peor worse, worst

pequeño, -a small, little (*size*)

perder (ie) to lose, miss

la pérdida loss

la peregrina pilgrim (*f.*), wanderer (*f.*)

perfeccionar to perfect

perfectamente fine, perfect(ly)

perfectamente bien fine, very well

el periódico newspaper

el período period

permanecer to remain

permanente permanent

el permiso permission

dar (pedir) permiso para (usar) to give (ask) permission to (use)

permitir to permit, allow, let

¿nos permite (ver)? may we (see)?

pero but

la persona person

por persona per (for each) person

el personaje personage, character (*theater*)

personal personal

la personalidad personality

persuadir to persuade

pertenecer a to belong to

el Perú Peru

peruano, -a (*also noun*) Peruvian

perverso, -a perverse, evil

pesado, -a heavy

pesar: a — de in spite of

la pesca fishing

el pescado fish

el pesebre manger

el pesimismo pessimism

el peso peso (*Spanish American monetary unit*)

el petróleo petroleum, oil

el pianista pianist
el piano piano
picaresco, -a picaresque
el pícaro rogue
el pico peak
la piedra stone
la pieza piece (*of music*), play, drama
pintar to paint
el pintor painter
la pintura painting
la piñata *jar filled with sweets and toys*
el pirata pirate
los Pirineos Pyrenees
la piscina swimming pool
el piso floor, story
    piso bajo first (lower) floor
la pizarra (black)board
el placer pleasure
la planta plant
la plata silver
    (es) de plata (it is) silver
el platillo dish (*food*)
el plato plate, dish, course (*at meals*)
la playa beach
la plaza plaza, square
    plaza de toros bullring
    Plaza Mayor Main Square (*in center of Old Madrid*)
la plenitud fullness, abundance
la pluma pen
    con la pluma y con la palabra writing and talking
la población population
el poblador populator, settler
pobre poor; humble, modest
    el pobre the poor boy (fellow)
poco, -a *adj., pron., and adv.* little (*quantity*); *pl.* (a) few
    al poco tiempo after (in) a short time
    poco a poco little by little
    poco después shortly afterward
    un poco (de) a little (of)
poder to be able, can
    ¿puedo (ver otros)? may I (see others)?
el poderío power, dominion

poderosamente powerfully
poderoso, -a powerful
el poema poem
la poesía (*also pl.*) poetry
el poeta poet
la policía police (force)
la política politics
político, -a political
el polo polo (*game*)
el polvo powder
el pollo chicken
Ponce de León: (Juan) *Spanish explorer, early sixteenth century, discoverer of Florida*
poner to put, put on, place, set (put) up, turn on; *reflex.* put on (oneself)
    poner en marcha to start
    poner un telegrama to send a telegram
    ponerse + adj. to become
popular popular
la popularidad popularity
poquito *adv.* very little
por for, during, in, through, along, by, around, in behalf of, for the sake of, on account of, because of, per, as (a), in exchange for
    por aquí by here, this way, around here
    por eso therefore, because of that
    ¿por qué? why? for what reason?
porque because
el portal doorway, city gate; (*Am.*) Christmas crèche
el portero doorkeeper, janitor
Portugal Portugal
portugués, -esa Portuguese
el portugués Portuguese (*language*)
la posada inn, lodging; *religious celebration* (*Mex.*)
la posesión possession
posible possible
la posición position
el postre dessert
la práctica practice
practicar to practice
    practicar deportes to practice (go in for) sports

práctico, -a practical

el precio price

    ¿qué precio tiene? what is the price of (it)?

precioso, -a precious, darling, beautiful

precisamente precisely, just

la precisión precision

preciso, -a necessary, precise

predicar to preach

predilecto, -a favorite

predominar to predominate, stand out

preferir (ie,i) to prefer

la pregunta question

    hacer una pregunta (a) to ask a question (of)

preguntar to ask (*a question*)

el premio prize

la preocupación (*pl.* **preocupaciones**) preoccupation

preparar to prepare, make

    prepararse para to prepare oneself for, get ready for

la presencia presence

la presentación (*pl.* **presentaciones**) presentation, introduction

    presentar to present, introduce; give (*a performance*); *reflex.* present oneself, appear

el presidente president

prestar to lend; perform (*a service*)

prevalecer to prevail

la prevención (*pl.* **prevenciones**) preparation

la prima cousin (*f.*)

la primavera spring

primer *used for* **primero** *before m. sing. nouns*

primero *adv.* first

primero, -a first

primitivo, -a primitive

el primo cousin (*m.*)

principal principal, main

principalmente principally, mainly

el príncipe prince

el principio beginning

    a principios (de) at the beginning (of)

    al principio at first, at the beginning

la prisa haste

    darse prisa to hurry

    tener (mucha) prisa to be in a (big) hurry

el prisionero prisoner

probable probable

probablemente probably

probar (ue) to try, sample, taste; *reflex.* try on

el problema problem

la procesión (*pl.* **procesiones**) procession

pródigo, -a prodigal

la producción (*pl.* **producciones**) production

producir to produce, yield; *reflex.* be produced

el producto product

produjeron *pret. of* **producir**

profesional professional

el profesor teacher, professor (*man*)

    profesor (de inglés) (English) teacher, professor

la profesora teacher, professor (*woman*)

la profundidad depth, profundity

el programa program

progresar to progress, move forward

progresivo, -a progressive

el progreso progress

prohibir to prohibit, forbid

la promesa promise

prometer to promise

pronto soon, quickly, suddenly

    lo más pronto posible as soon as possible

la pronunciación pronunciation

pronunciar to pronounce

la propina tip

propio, -a (one's) own

proporcionar to offer

propósito: a —, by the way

la prosa prose

la prosperidad prosperity

próspero, -a prosperous

el protagonista protagonist, central figure

protestar to protest

proveer to supply (*with provisions*)

la provincia province

publicar to publish
público, -a public
el pueblo town, village; people, nation
  de pueblo en pueblo from village to village
el puente bridge
la puerta door
  de puerta en puerta from door to door
el puerto port
pues well, well then, then
puesto que *conj.* since
el puesto position, place, job
la pulsera bracelet
el punto point
  en punto sharp (*time*)
la pupila pupil (*of eye*)
el pupitre desk (*school*)
purificado, -a purified
purísimo, -a immaculate, very pure
puro, -a pure

Q

que that, which, who, whom; than; *indirect command* have, let, may, I wish (hope)
  el (la, los, las) que that, which, who, whom, he (she, those) who (*etc.*), the one(s) who (*etc.*)
  el (la) mismo (-a) ... que the same ... as
  de lo que (esperaba) than (I expected)
  hora en que the hour (time) when
  igual que the same as
  lo que what, that which, which (fact)
  todo lo que all that (which)
¿qué? what? which?
  no hay de qué you're welcome, don't mention it
  ¿para qué? why? for what purpose?
  ¿por qué? why? for what reason?
  ¿qué tal ...? how about ...? how is (was) ...?
¡qué! what a! how!
quedar(se) to stay, remain; be
  (me) queda (poco tiempo) (I) have (little time) left

me quedo con (ellos) I'll take (them)
no queda ningún asiento no seat is left (remains), there isn't any seat left
querer to wish, want
  ¿no quiere Vd. (pasar)? won't you (come in)?
  no quieren ir they won't (are unwilling to) go
  ¿quiere Vd. (decirle)? will you (tell him)?
querido, -a dear
el queso cheese
quien (*pl.* **quienes**) who, whom, he (those) who, the one(s) who
¿quién(es)? who? whom?
  ¿a quién? whom?
  ¿de quién es? whose is (it)?
quince fifteen
quinientos, -as five hundred
la quinina quinine
quinto, -a fifth
quisiera (I) should like
quitar to remove, take off; *reflex.* take off (oneself)
el quitasol parasol
quizá(s) perhaps

R

el radiador radiator
el radio radio (*set*)
la radio radio (*communication*)
Ramón Raymond
Ramos: Domingo de —, Palm Sunday
rancheros: huevos —, eggs ranch style
rápidamente rapidly
rápido, -a rapid, fast
el rasgo trait, characteristic; *pl.* features
el rato while, short time
  un rato más a while longer
la raza race
la razón (*pl.* **razones**) reason
  con razón rightly
  tener razón to be right
reaccionar to react
real real, actual; royal

Real: Camino —, King's (Royal) Highway
la **realidad** reality
en **realidad** in reality, in fact
el **realismo** realism
realista (*m. and f.*) realistic
el **realista** realist
realizar to realize, carry out; *reflex.* to
become fulfilled, be carried out
realzar to enhance, emphasize
recibir to receive
recoger to pick up
la **recomendación** recommendation
recomendar (**ie**) to recommend
reconocer to recognize
la **reconquista** reconquest
reconquistar to reconquer
recordar (**ue**) to recall, remember
recreo: sala de —, recreation room
el **Redentor** The Redeemer
referirse (**ie,i**) (**a**) to refer (to)
reflejar to reflect
el **refrán** (*pl.* **refranes**) proverb
el **refresco** refreshment, cold (soft) drink
refugiarse to take refuge
el **regalo** gift
la **región** (*pl.* **regiones**) region
regional regional
el **registro** register
el **regocijo** joy
el **regreso** return
la **regularidad** regularity
con **regularidad** regularly
la **reina** queen
el **reinado** reign
reinar to reign, rule
el **reino** kingdom
reír (**i,i**) to laugh
reírse (**de**) to laugh (at)
la **reja** grating, grille
la **relación** (*pl.* **relaciones**) relation
relacionar to relate, connect; *reflex.* to
be connected, related
relatar to relate, tell
el **relato** story, tale
la **religión** religion
religioso, -a religious

el **reloj** watch, clock
renacer to be born again, spring up
again, be revived
el **renacimiento** rebirth, revival, renaissance
el **Renacimiento** Renaissance
la **rendición** surrender
la **reparación** (*pl.* **reparaciones**) repairing, repairs
tramo en reparación section under
repair
repasar to review, retrace
el **repaso** review
repetir (**i,i**) to repeat
el **representante** representative
representar to represent; show, express,
perform
la **represión** (*pl.* **represiones**) repression
la **república** republic; country
la **República Dominicana** Dominican Republic
repuesto: llanta de —, spare tire
rescatar to ransom
reservar to reserve
el **resfriado** cold (*disease*)
la **residencia** residence hall
residencia de estudiantes student
residence hall
residencia de señoritas women's
dormitory (residence hall)
el **resplandor** brilliance
el **restaurante** restaurant
el **resto** rest; *pl.* remains
resultar to result, be, turn out (to be)
Resurrección: Domingo de —, Easter
Sunday
retrasar to delay, set back
el **retrato** portrait, picture
reunirse to meet, gather
la **revista** magazine, journal
revolucionario, -a revolutionary
el **rey** king
Reyes Católicos Catholic King and
Queen
Reyes Magos Wise Men (Kings),
Magi
Ricardo Richard

rico, -a   rich
el río   river
la Rioja   *province in northern Old Castile, famous for its wines*
la riqueza (*also pl.*)   riches, wealth
la risa   laughter
el ritmo   rhythm
Roberto   Robert
rodeado, -a (**de**)   surrounded (by)
rogar (**ue**)   to ask, beg
rojo, -a   red
romance *adj.*   Romance, Romanic
el romance   ballad
el romancero   ballad book, collection of ballads
romano, -a (*also noun*)   Roman

el romanticismo   romanticism
romántico, -a   romantic
la romería   pilgrimage, excursion
romper   to break
la ropa   clothing, clothes
mudarse de ropa   to change clothes
rosa (*m. and f.*)   pink, rose (color)
el rostro   face
rubio, -a   fair, blonde
las ruinas   ruins
la rumba   rumba
rural   rural
la ruta   route, direction

S

el sábado   (on) Saturday; Sabbath
los sábados por la noche   Saturday nights
Sábado de Gloria   Holy Saturday
saber   to know, know how; *in pret.* learn, find out
sabroso, -a   delicious, tasty
sacar   to take, take out
el sacerdote   priest
sagrado, -a   sacred, holy
la Sagrada Familia   The Holy Family
el sainete   *one-act farce*
la sala   living room
sala de espera   waiting room

sala de clase   classroom
sala de recreo   recreation room
la salida   departure
salir (**de** + *obj.*)   to leave, go (come) out
salir a la calle   to go out into the street
salir de casa   to leave home
salir para   to leave for
salirse con   to set out with
la salsa   sauce
la salud   health
saludar   to greet, speak to, say hello to
el Salvador   Savior
El Salvador   El Salvador
salvar   to save
la samba   samba
san   *used for* **santo** *before m. name of saint not beginning with* **To-, Do-**
la sangre   blood
santo, -a   saint, holy
el santo   saint
día de su santo   his saint's day
santo patrón   patron saint
la sátira   satire
se   *pron. used for* **le, les**   to him, her, it, them; you (*formal*); *reflex.* (to) himself, herself, *etc.*; *reciprocal pron.*   each other, one another; *indef. subject* one, people, you, *etc.*
la sección (*pl.* **secciones**)   section
la secretaria   secretary
la sed   thirst
tener (**mucha**) **sed**   to be (very) thirsty
seguida: en —, at once, immediately
seguir (**i,i**)   to follow, continue, go on
según   according to
segundo, -a   second
seguro, -a   sure, certain, safe
estar seguro, -a (**de que**)   to be sure (that)
seis   six
seiscientos, -as   six hundred
la selección (*pl.* **selecciones**)   selection, choice
la selva   forest
la semana   week

Semana Santa Holy Week
semejante similar
el semestre semester
la semilla seed
sencillo, -a simple
  billete sencillo one-way ticket
la sensibilidad sensibility, sensitivity
sentado, -a seated
sentar (ie) to seat, set; *reflex.* sit down
  ¿nos sentamos? shall we sit down?
  sentar bien (a uno) to fit (one)
el sentido sense, feeling, reason, judgment, meaning
el sentimiento sentiment, feeling
sentir (ie,i) to feel, regret, be sorry
  ¿cómo se siente Vd.? how do you feel?
  lo siento (mucho) I am (very) sorry
  sentirse bien to feel well
la señal sign
  dar señales de to show signs of
señalar to point at (out), indicate
señor sir, Mr.
  los señores (López) Mr. and Mrs. (López)
  ¡señores viajeros! travelers!
el señor gentleman; *pl.* gentlemen, ladies and gentlemen
  El Señor The Lord
señora madam, Mrs.
la señora woman, lady, mistress
  Nuestra Señora Our Lady
señorita Miss
la señorita Miss, young lady (woman)
  Residencia de Señoritas Women's Dormitory (Residence Hall)
separado, -a separated
septiembre September
séptimo, -a seventh
ser to be
  es decir that is (to say)
  es que the fact is (that)
serenar to calm down, to make serene
el sereno night watchman
la serie series
la serpentina streamer; serpentine
el servicio service

estar al servicio de to be in the service of
servir (i,i) to serve
  ¿en qué puedo servirle(s)? what can I do for you?
  ¿para qué sirven los amigos? what are friends (good) for?
  servir de to serve as
setecientos, -as seven hundred
setenta seventy
Sevilla Seville
sexto, -a sixth
si if, whether
  si bien although, though, while
sí yes
  (esperar) que sí (to hope) so
sí *reflex. pron.* himself, herself, yourself (*formal*), themselves, yourselves
siempre always
la sierra mountains, mountain range
la siesta nap
  dormir (ue, u) la siesta to take a nap
siete seven
el siglo century
  Siglo de Oro Golden Age
significar to signify, mean
siguiente following, next
siguieron, siguió *pret. of* **seguir**
la sílaba syllable
silvestre wild
la silla chair
el sillón (*pl.* **sillones**) armchair
simpático, -a charming, likeable, nice
simplificar to simplify
sin *prep.* without
  sin embargo nevertheless, however
  sin que *conj.* without
sino but
  no sólo (solamente) … sino (también) not only … but (also)
  sino que *conj.* but
la síntesis synthesis
sirve, sirven *pres. ind. of* **servir**
el sistema system
el sitio site, place
la situación (*pl.* **situaciones**) situation

situado, -a   situated, located

sobre   on, upon, about, concerning

  sobre todo   especially, above all

socarrón, -ona   crafty

social   social

la sociedad   society

el sofá   sofa, davenport

el sol   sun

  hace (hacía) sol *or* **hay (había) sol**   it is (was) sunny, the sun is (was) shining

  tomar el sol   to take a sun bath

solamente   only

el soldado   soldier

solemne   solemn

solicitar   to solicit, ask (for)

solo, -a   alone

  café solo   black coffee

sólo   only

  no sólo ... sino (también)   not only ... but (also)

la sombra   shade, shadow

el sombrero   hat

someterse   to submit, be subjected

sonar (ue)   to sound, ring

sonreír (i,i)   to smile (at)

la sopa   soup

sorprender   to surprise

la sorpresa   surprise

el sótano   basement

Soto: Hernando de —,   *Spanish explorer in the Americas, and discoverer of the Mississippi River, 1541*

Sr. = señor

Sra. = señora

Sres. = señores

Srta. = señorita

su   his; her; your (*formal*); its, their

subir   to bring (take, carry) up

  subir a   to go up, get into, climb up (into)

subjetivo, -a   subjective

suceder   to happen

sucio, -a   dirty

el sudeste   southeast

el suelo   floor

el sueño   sleep; dream

tener (mucho) sueño   to be (very) sleepy

la suerte   luck

  ¡que tenga mucha suerte!   good luck!

  tener (mucha) suerte   to be (very) lucky

suficiente   sufficient, enough

superar   to surpass, excel

superior: escuela —,   high school

suplementario, -a   supplementary

suponer   to suppose

¡supuesto: por —!   of course! certainly!

el sur   south

  la América del Sur   South America

surgir   to appear, surge, arise

el suroeste   southwest

surrealista (*m. and f.*)   surrealist, surrealistic

el suspiro   sigh

sutil   subtle

suyo, -a *adj.*   his; her; your (*formal*); their, of his (hers, yours, theirs)

  (el) suyo, (la) suya, (los) suyos, (las) suyas *pron.*   his, hers, theirs, yours (*formal*)

T

el tabaco   tobacco

el taco   taco

tal   such, such a; similar

  con tal que *conj.*   provided that

  ¿qué tal ...?   how about ...?   how is (was) ...?

  tal vez   perhaps

la talla   size (*of a dress*)

también   also, too

tampoco   neither, (not) ... either

tan *adv.*   as, so

  tan + *adj. or adv.* + como   as ... as

el tango   tango

el tanque   tank

tanto, -a (-os, -as) *adj. and pron.*   as (so) much (many); *adv.*   as (so) much

  tanto ... como   both ... and

  tanto, -a (-os,-as) ... como   as (so) much (many) ... as

la tapioca tapioca

el tapiz (*pl.* **tapices**) tapestry

tardar to delay, be long

> **tardar mucho** to take long (a long time)
>
> **tardar tanto** to take so long, delay so much (long)

tarde late

la tarde afternoon

> **(ayer) por la tarde** (yesterday) afternoon
>
> **buenas tardes** good afternoon
>
> **de (por) la tarde** in the afternoon
>
> **toda la tarde** all afternoon, the whole (entire) afternoon
>
> **todas las tardes** every afternoon

la tarjeta card (*postal, birthday, etc.*)

el taxi taxi

la taza cup

> **taza para café** coffee cup

te *pron.* you (*fam.*), to you, (to) yourself

el té tea

el teatro theater

la técnica technique

> **técnico, -a** technical

la teja tile

el tejado roof (*of tiles*)

telefonear to telephone

el teléfono telephone

> **llamar por teléfono** to telephone, call by telephone

el telegrama telegram

> **poner un telegrama** to send a telegram

la televisión television

> **programa de televisión** television program

el tema theme, subject

temer to fear

la tempestad storm, tempest

temprano early

tener to have (*possess*)

> **aquí (lo) tienes (tiene Vd.)** here (it) is
>
> **¿cuántos años tiene (él)?** how old is (he)?
>
> **¿qué precio tiene?** what is the price of (it)?

tener ... años to be ... years old

tener (calor) to be (warm) (*living beings*)

tener (mucha) prisa to be in a (big) hurry

tener (muchas) ganas de to be (very) eager to (desirous of)

tener muchos deseos de to be very eager (wish very much)

tener que + *inf.* to have to (must) + *inf.*

tener ... que + *inf.* to have ... to + *inf.*

tener razón to be right

el tenis tennis

el teólogo theologian

> **tercer** *used for* **tercero** *before m. sing. nouns*
>
> **tercero, -a** third

el tercio third

terminar to end, finish

el término term

el terreno ground, land, terrain

terrible terrible

el territorio territory

la tertulia party, social gathering

> **ti** *pron.* you (*fam.*), yourself (*after prep.*)

la tía aunt

el tiempo time (*in general sense*); weather

> **a tiempo** on time
>
> **al poco tiempo** after (in) a short time
>
> **con el tiempo** in (in the course of) time
>
> **¿cuánto tiempo?** how long?
>
> **falta mucho tiempo para** it is a long time before
>
> **hacer buen (mal) tiempo** to be good (bad) weather
>
> **hacer calor (frío, fresco, viento)** to be warm (cold, cool, windy)
>
> **mucho tiempo** long, a long time
>
> **¿qué tiempo hace?** what kind of weather is it?
>
> **tener tiempo para** to have time to (for)

la tienda store, shop

la tierra land

> **echar por tierra (a)** to throw to the ground

el timbre   doorbell
tímido, -a   timid
tinto, -a   deep red; **el tinto** red wine
la tintorería   cleaning shop
el tío   uncle; *pl.* uncle(s) and aunt(s)
típico, -a   typical
el tipo   type, kind
tirar   to throw
el título   title
la toalla   towel
el Toboso   *a Spanish village in New Castile*
el tocador   dressing table
el (los) tocadiscos   record player
tocar   to play (*music*), touch; ring
tocar a (uno)   to be (one's) turn
el tocino   bacon
todavía   still, yet
todavía no   not yet
todo, -a   all, whole, entire, every; *pron.*
everything
por todas partes   everywhere
sobre todo   especially, above all
toda la (tarde)   all (afternoon), the
whole (entire) afternoon
todas ellas   all of them
todas las tardes (noches)   every
afternoon (evening, night)
todo ello   all of it
todo el mundo   everybody
todos los días   every day
la tolerancia   tolerance
tomar   to take, eat, drink
lo tomo   I'll take it
tomar el desayuno   to take (have,
eat) breakfast
tomar el sol   to take a sun bath
Tomás   Thomas, Tom
el tomate   tomato
el toro   bull
corrida de toros   bullfight
plaza de toros   bullring
la torre   tower
la torta   flat pancake
la tortilla   omelet (*Spain*); corn pancake
(*Mex.*)
tostado, -a   toasted
trabajador, -ora   industrious
trabajar   to work, perform

el trabajo   work; *pl.* hardships, tribulations
la tradición   tradition
tradicional   traditional
el tradicionalismo   traditionalism
la traducción (*pl.* **traducciones**)   translation
traer   to bring
la tragedia   tragedy
el traje   suit, costume
traje de baño   bathing suit
el tramo   stretch, section
tramo en reparación   section under
repair
el tránsito   traffic
trasladarse (a)   to move (to)
tratar (de + *obj.*)   to treat, deal (with)
tratar de + *inf.*   to try to + *verb*
través: a — de   across, through
trece   thirteen
treinta   thirty
treinta y un(o)   thirty-one
tremendo, -a   tremendous
el tren   train
tres   three
trescientos, -as   three hundred
la tribu   tribe
el tributo   tribute
el trigo   wheat
la Trinidad   The Trinity
triste   sad
triunfante   triumphant
triunfar   to triumph
el triunfo   triumph
tropical   tropical
tu   your (*fam.*)
tú   you (*fam.*)
el tubo   tube
la tumba   tomb
turco, -a   Turkish
el turco   Turk
turismo: campo de —,   tourist camp,
motel
el (la) turista   tourist
el turrón (*pl.* **turrones**)   nougat, almond
candy
tuyo, -a *adj.*   your (*fam.*), of yours
**(el) tuyo, (la) tuya, (los) tuyos, (las)
tuyas** *pron.*   yours

U

último, -a last (*in a series*)
un, una, uno a, an, one
único, -a only, unique
la unidad unity
unido, -a united
   los Estados Unidos the United States
universal universal
la universidad university
unos, -as some, a few, several; about
   (*quantity*)
urgente urgent
el Uruguay Uruguay
usar to use, wear
el uso use
usted you (*formal*)
útil useful
la uva grape

V

la vaca cow
las vacaciones vacation
   estar de vacaciones to be on vacation
   vacante vacant, empty
la vainilla vanilla
valenciano, -a Valencian, of Valencia
valer to be worth
   valer más to be better
valiente valiant, brave
el valor value
el valle valley
vamos we are going
   vamos a + *inf.* we are going to, let's
   + *verb*
vano, -a vain
variado, -a varied
variar to vary
   varía it varies
la variedad variety
varios, -as various, several
vasco, -a Basque
vascongado, -a Basque
el vaso glass
Vd(s). = usted(es)
vecino, -a neighboring
   labrador vecino peasant (who was a)
   neighbor

el vecino neighbor
la vegetación vegetation
veinte twenty
   veinte (y uno) twenty(-one)
   veintidós twenty-two
   veintinueve twenty-nine
   veintiocho twenty-eight
   veintiuno (veintiún) twenty-one
la velocidad speed
   vendado, -a bandaged
   vendados los ojos blindfolded
vender to sell
la vendimia vintage
Venecia Venice
venir (a + *inf.*) to come (to)
   (la semana) que viene next (week)
la venta sale; inn
la ventana window
la ventanilla small window; ticket window
el ventero innkeeper
ver to see; *reflex.* be, be seen
   nos vemos we'll be seeing each other
   (vamos) a ver let's see
el verano summer
veras: de —, really, truly
la verbena *night festival on the eve of a*
   saint's day
la verdad truth
   es verdad it is true
   ¿no es verdad? isn't it (true)? don't
   you? *etc.*
verdadero, -a true, real
verde green
las verduras vegetables, greens
el verso line (*of poetry*)
el vestíbulo vestibule, lobby
el vestido dress
   vestir (i,i) to dress; *reflex.* dress (oneself), get dressed
la vez (*pl.* **veces**) time (*in a series*), occasion
   a la vez at the same time
   a veces at times
   alguna vez some time, ever (*in a*
   question)
   de vez en cuando from time to time
   en vez de instead of, in place of
   muchas veces many times, often
   otra vez again

por primera vez for the first time
tal vez perhaps
una vez once
viajar to travel
el viaje trip, voyage, journey
¡buen viaje! (have) a good trip!
hacer un viaje to take (make) a trip
el viajero traveler
¡señores viajeros! travelers!
Vicente Vincent
la vida life
viejo, -a old
la vieja old woman
el viento wind
hacer (mucho) viento to be (very) windy
molino de viento windmill
el viernes (on) Friday
Viernes Santo Good Friday
vigoroso, -a vigorous
el villancico carol
el villano peasant, villager
el vino wine
el violoncelista violoncellist, cellist
la Virgen Blessed Virgin (Mary)
el virrey viceroy
el visigodo Visigoth
la visión vision
la visita visit, call
visitar to visit, call on
la víspera eve
víspera de la Navidad Christmas Eve
víspera del Año Nuevo New Year's Eve
la vista sight, view
en vista de que in view of the fact that
hasta la vista until I see you
vivir to live
vivo, -a live, alive, living
el vocabulario vocabulary

volar (ue) to fly
el volcán (*pl.* **volcanes**) volcano
volver (ue) to return, come back
volver a (verla) (to see her) again
volverse (+ *adj.*) to become
vuelvo en seguida I'll be right back, I'll return at once
vosotros, -as you (*fam. pl.*), yourselves
la voz (*pl.* **voces**) voice
el vuelo flight
vuelo de la mañana (tarde) morning (afternoon) flight
vuelo de la tarde afternoon flight
la vuelta return; change (*money*)
billete de ida y vuelta round-trip ticket
estar de vuelta to be back
vuestro, -a *adj.* your (*fam. pl.*), of yours
(el) vuestro, (la) vuestra, (los) vuestros, (las) vuestras *pron.* yours

Y

y and
(a la una) y (diez) (at ten minutes) after (one)
ya already, now
¡ya lo creo! of course! certainly!
ya no no longer
la yerba mate *tree whose leaves are used to make maté*
yo I
la yuca yucca

Z

la zagala shepherdess
la zapatería shoe store
el zapato shoe

Vocabulary

A

a, an un, una; *often untranslated*
able: be —, poder
about *prep.* de, acerca de, en, sobre; (*probability*) *use future tense*
  at about a eso de
  be about to estar para
accept aceptar
accompany acompañar
ache doler (ue)
  my (her) head aches me (le) duele la cabeza
across: run —, encontrarse (ue) con
advise aconsejar (*requires indir. obj. of a person*)
afraid: be — (of, that) tener miedo (de, de que)
after *prep.* después de; *conj.* después que; (*in giving time*) y
  after a short time al poco tiempo
afternoon la tarde
  afternoon flight el vuelo de la tarde
  all afternoon toda la tarde
  every afternoon todas las tardes
  good afternoon buenas tardes
  in the afternoon por la tarde; (*when the hour is given*) de la tarde
  (tomorrow) afternoon (mañana) por la tarde
afterward(s) *adv.* después
  shortly afterward poco después
again otra vez; volver a + *inf.*
agency la agencia
  travel agency agencia de viajes
agent el agente
ago: (an hour) —, hace (una hora)
agree estar de acuerdo
agriculture la agricultura
air: by — mail por correo aéreo
airport el aeropuerto
  at the airport en el aeropuerto
alarm clock el despertador
all todo, -a; *pl.* todos, -as
  all that todo lo que, cuanto
allow dejar, permitir

almost casi
alone solo, -a
along por
already ya
also también
always siempre
America América
  South America la América del Sur
American *adj. and noun* norteamericano, -a
  Spanish American hispanoamericano, -a
ancient antiguo, -a
and y
Ann Ana
anniversary el aniversario
announce anunciar
another otro, -a
  another one otro, -a
answer contestar
any *adj. and pron.* alguno, -a, (*before m. sing. nouns*) algún, (*after negative*) ninguno, -a (ningún); *often not translated*
  at any rate de todos modos
anyone alguien, (*after negative or comparative*) nadie
anything algo, (*after negative*) nada
  anything else algo más
anywhere (*after negative*) en ninguna parte
apartment el apartamento
  apartment house casa de apartamentos
approach acercarse (a + *obj. or inf.*)
approximately más o menos
April abril
Argentina la Argentina
Argentine argentino, -a
arm el brazo
arrive llegar (a + *obj.*)
  arrive downtown llegar al centro
Arthur Arturo
as como
  as + *adj. or adv.* + as tan ... como
  as if como si
ask (*question*) preguntar; (*request*) pedir (i, i)
  ask a question (of) hacer una pregunta (a)

473

ask for (*inquire about*)   preguntar por
ask for (*request*)   pedir (i, i)
at   a, en, de
   at first   al principio
   at (**my aunt's**)   en casa de (mi tía)
   at noon   al mediodía
August   agosto
aunt   la tía
   at my aunt's   en casa de mi tía
avenue   la avenida
await   aguardar, esperar
awaken (*trans.*)   despertar (ie)

B

back: be —,   estar de vuelta
   be set back   retrasarse
bad   malo, -a, (*before m. sing. nouns*) mal
baggage   el equipaje
Barbara   Bárbara
baseball   el béisbol
basketball   el básquetbol
Basque   vasco, -a
bath   el baño
   take a bath   bañarse
   take a sun bath   tomar el sol
bathing suit   el traje de baño
bathroom   el cuarto de baño
be   estar, ser; encontrarse (ue), hallarse, (*remain*) quedar(se)
   aren't they, isn't it, *etc.*   ¿(no es) verdad?
   be ... years old   tener (cumplir) ... años
   be able   poder
   be about to   estar para
   be afraid (**of, that**)   tener miedo (de, de que)
   be back   estar de vuelta
   be on vacation   estar de vacaciones
   be right   tener razón
   be set back   retrasarse
   be to, be supposed to   haber de + *inf.*
   be very eager to   tener muchos deseos (muchas ganas) de (+ *inf.*)
   be (**very**) **glad to**   tener (mucho) gusto en
   here (**it**) **is**   aquí (lo) tienes (tiene Vd.)
   there is (**are**)   hay
   there was (**were**)   *imp.* había; *pret.* hubo
   there will be   habrá

   what are friends good for?   ¿para qué sirven los amigos?
   you are welcome   no hay de qué
beach   la playa
beautiful   bonito, -a, hermoso, -a
because   porque
become + *adj.*   ponerse; +*noun* hacerse, llegar a ser
   become calm   calmarse
bed   la cama
   go to bed   acostarse (ue)
bedroom   la alcoba
before *prep.*   antes de; *conj.* antes (de) que
beg   rogar (ue)
begin (**to**)   comenzar (ie) (a + *inf.*), empezar (ie) (a + *inf.*)
believe   creer
   believe so   creer que sí
best, better   mejor
   like better   gustar más
   the best thing   lo mejor
Betty   Isabel
bill   el billete
   (**ten-dollar**) **bill**   billete (de diez dólares)
birthday   el cumpleaños
black   negro, -a
blond(e)   rubio, -a
blouse   la blusa
blue   azul
book   el libro
box (*post office*)   el apartado postal
boy   el muchacho
   poor (**little**) **boy**   el pobrecito
bracelet   la pulsera
breakfast   el desayuno
   eat (**take**) **breakfast**   desayunarse, tomar el desayuno
bring   traer
brother   el hermano
   little brother   el hermanito
build   construir
building   el edificio
bus   el autobús
   (**ten-o'clock**) **bus**   el autobús (de las diez)
business   los negocios; *adj.* comercial
   (**take**) **a business trip**   (hacer) un viaje de negocios
busy   ocupado, -a
but   pero, (*after negative*) sino

buy comprar
by por
  by car (plane) en coche (avión)
  by the way a propósito

C

café el café
call llamar
calm calmar
  become calm calmarse
can poder, (*know how*) saber; *for conjecture use future tense*
capital la capital
car el coche
  by car en coche
card (*playing*) la carta; (*postal, birthday, etc.*) la tarjeta
  play cards jugar (ue) a las cartas
career la carrera
careful: be —, tener cuidado
carefully con cuidado
Carmen Carmen
Caroline Carolina
carry llevar
  carry with oneself llevar consigo
celebrate celebrar
cent el centavo
century el siglo
certain cierto, -a
change clothes mudarse de ropa
Charles Carlos
charming simpático, -a
chat charlar
check el cheque; (*baggage*) facturar
  have checked hacer (mandar) facturar
children los niños
church la iglesia
  to church a la iglesia
city la ciudad
class la clase
  (come) to class (venir) a clase
  in class en (la) clase
classroom la sala de clase
clean limpiar
cleaning shop la tintorería
clerk el dependiente, la empleada
clock: alarm —, el despertador

close cerrar (ie)
clothes la ropa
  change clothes mudarse de ropa
cloud la nube
coffee el café
cold *adj.* frío, -a
  cold drink el refresco
cold el frío, (*disease*) el resfriado
  be (very) cold (*living beings*) tener (mucho) frío
color el color
  what color is (it)? ¿de qué color es?
come venir
  come by pasar por
  come for (one) buscar (a uno)
  come in pasar, entrar (en)
comfortable cómodo, -a
companion el compañero
company la compañía
congratulate felicitar
continue seguir (i, i), continuar
cool fresco, -a; (*noun with* hacer)
  be (very) cool (*weather*) hacer (mucho) fresco
corner (*street*) la esquina
cost costar (ue)
cotton el algodón
  cotton dress vestido de algodón
could *pret. or imp. of* poder
count contar (ue)
counter el mostrador
country el campo, (*nation*) el país
  country house casa de campo
couple el par
course: of —! ¡ya lo creo! ¡cómo no! ¡por supuesto! ¡claro!
court (*handball*) el frontón
cousin el primo, la prima
covered (with) cubierto, -a (de)
cry llorar
Cuban cubano, -a
custom la costumbre
cut (off) cortar
  cut oneself cortarse
Cuzco el Cuzco

D

dad (el) papá
daily diario, -a
dance el baile; bailar
  dance number número de baile
dare (to) atreverse (a + *inf.*)
dark (*color*) castaño, -a
darling precioso, -a
date la fecha
daughter la hija
day el día
  all day todo el día
  every day todos los días
  these days en estos días
deal: a great —, mucho
dear querido, -a
December diciembre
decide decidir
decision la decisión
delay tardar; (*set back*) retrasar
dentist el dentista
depart (from) partir (de + *obj.*)
  depart for partir para
department store el almacén
departure la salida
desk la mesa, (*student*) el pupitre
different diferente
difficult difícil
dining room el comedor
dining table mesa de comer
directly directamente
discover descubrir
display exhibir
do hacer; *not translated as an auxiliary*
  don't *or* **didn't (they), doesn't (she)**
    ¿(no es) verdad?
  what can I do for you? ¿en qué puedo
    servirle(s)?
doctor el médico
dollar (*U.S.*) el dólar
  (ten)-dollar bill billete de (diez) dólares
door la puerta
doorbell el timbre
Dorothy Dorotea
down: go — (to) bajar (a)
  fall down caerse
  sit down sentarse (ie)
downstairs: go —, bajar

downtown el centro
  (be) downtown (estar) en el centro
  (go) downtown (ir) al centro
dress el vestido
dress (*oneself*), **get dressed** vestirse (i, i)
drink: cold —, el refresco
drive conducir
during durante

E

each cada (*invariable*)
  (look at) each other (mirar)se
eager: be very — to tener muchos deseos
  (muchas ganas) de (+*inf.*)
early temprano
easy fácil
eat comer
  eat breakfast desayunarse, tomar el
    desayuno
  eat lunch tomar el almuerzo, almorzar (ue)
  eat supper cenar
eight ocho
  eight hundred ochocientos, -as
eighty ochenta
  eighty (-eight) ochenta (y ocho)
electricity la electricidad
eleven once
else: anything —, algo más
embrace abrazar
employee el empleado
engineer el ingeniero
English *adj.* inglés, inglesa; (*language*) el
  inglés
  English (class) (clase) de inglés
enjoy disfrutar (de + *obj.*)
enough bastante
enter entrar (en + *obj.*)
especially especialmente
even though aunque
evening la noche
  in the evening por la noche
every todo, -a
  every afternoon (night) todas las tardes
    (noches)
  every day todos los días
everybody todo el mundo, todos
everything *pron.* todo

everywhere   por todas partes
examination   el examen (*pl.* exámenes)
examine   examinar
excellent   excelente
excursion   la excursión
   make an excursion   hacer una excursión
exercise   el ejercicio
expect   esperar
expensive   caro, -a
experience   la experiencia

F

face   la cara
fact: in —,   en realidad
factory   la fábrica
fail: not to — to   no dejar de (+*inf.*)
fall   el otoño
   fall day   día de otoño
   fall down   caerse
   fall in love (with)   enamorarse (de)
family   la familia
far **(away)** *adv.*   lejos
farm *adj.*   agrícola (*m. and f.*)
fast   rápido, -a
father   el padre, el papá
fear   temer
February   febrero
feel   sentir(se) (ie, i)
   feel well (better)   sentirse (ie, i) bien
      (mejor)
   how do (you) feel?   ¿cómo se siente (Vd.)?
few: **(a)** —,   unos (-as) pocos (-as), algunos,
      -as, unos, -as
fifteen   quince
fifty   cincuenta
   fifty-one   cincuenta y un(o)
film   la película
finally   por fin
find   encontrar (ue), hallar
   find out (*in pret.*)   saber
fine: that's —,   está bien
finger   el dedo
finish   terminar
firm   la casa
first *adj.*   primero, -a, (*before m. sing. nouns*)
      primer; *adv.* primero
   at first   al principio

first floor   piso bajo
fit **(one)**   sentar (ie) bien a (uno)
five   cinco
   before five o'clock   antes de las cinco
flat (*tire*)   desinflado, -a
flight   el vuelo
   afternoon (morning) flight   el vuelo de la
      tarde (mañana)
floor (*story*)   el piso
   first floor   piso bajo
   upper floor   piso alto
Florida   la Florida
flower   la flor
fly   volar (ue)
following   siguiente
fond **(of)**   aficionado, -a (a)
   be fond (of)   ser aficionado, -a (a)
football   el fútbol, el balompié
   football game   partido de fútbol
for   para, por
   for (many years)   desde hace (muchos
      años) *or* hace (muchos años) que (+*verb*)
   for me (on my part)   de mi parte
foreign   extranjero, -a
forest   el bosque
forget **(to)**   olvidarse (de + *obj.*)
   forget that   olvidarse de que
forty   cuarenta
   forty-one   cuarenta y un(o)
   forty-five   cuarenta y cinco
four   cuatro
fourteen   catorce
French (*language*)   el francés
friend   el amigo, la amiga
   girl friend   la novia, la amiga
from   de, desde
front: in — of   frente a
furniture   los muebles

G

game   el juego, (*match*) el partido
garage   el garaje
   garage door   puerta del garaje
garden   el jardín
generally   generalmente, por lo común
gentleman   el señor
   gentlemen   señores

George Jorge
German (*language*) el alemán
get conseguir (i, i), obtener
  get dressed vestirse (i, i)
  get going! ¡hala!
  get into (**the car**) subir al *or* entrar en (el coche)
  get off bajar (de + *obj.*)
  get on the plane subir al avión
  get ready for prepararse para
  get up levantarse
  let's get up vamos a levantarnos, levantémonos
gift el regalo
girl la muchacha
  girl friend la amiga, la novia
  little girl la niña
give dar
glad: be (**very**) **— to** alegrarse (mucho) de, tener (mucho) gusto en
  how glad I am to (**that**) **...!** ¡cuánto me alegro de (de que) ...!
gladly con mucho gusto
glass el vaso
glove el guante
go ir (a + *obj.*), andar
  go (**away**) irse
  go down(**stairs**) (**to**) bajar (a)
  go looking for andar (ir) buscando
  go out into the street salir a la calle
  go shopping ir de compras
  go swimming ir a nadar
  go to bed acostarse (ue)
  go to sleep dormirse (ue, u)
  get going! ¡hala!
  let's be going vámonos
  let's go vamos (a + *obj.*)
  let's not go no vayamos
  we are going (**to**) vamos (a)
gold el oro
  (**it**) **is** (**of**) **gold** es de oro
golf el golf
good bueno, -a, (*before m. sing. nouns*) buen
  good afternoon buenas tardes
  good morning buenos días
  what are friends good for? ¿para qué sirven los amigos?
goodbye adiós, que lo pase(s) bien
  say goodbye to despedirse (i, i) de

grateful: be (**very**) **— to** agradecer (mucho) a
great (*before sing. nouns*) gran; *pl.* grandes
  a great deal mucho
green verde
  the green one (*m.*) el verde
guest el invitado

H

hair el pelo
  have (**dark**) **hair** tener el pelo (castaño)
  the one (*f.*) **with the blond hair** la del pelo rubio
half medio, -a
  a half hour media hora
  half past (**twelve**) (las doce) y media
hall; residence-, la residencia
hand la mano
hand (**over**) entregar
handball la pelota
handsome guapo, -a
happen pasar, ocurrir
happy contento, -a, feliz (*pl.* felices)
hard *adv.* mucho
hat el sombrero
have tener; (*auxiliary*) haber
  have (*causative*) hacer *or* mandar + *inf.*
  have (*indir. command*) que + *pres. subj.*
  have a good trip! ¡buen viaje!
  have a (**very**) **good time** divertirse (ie, i) (mucho)
  have just acabar de (+*inf.*)
  have left quedar a (uno)
  have to tener que (+*inf.*)
  have ... to tener ... que (+*inf.*)
he él, (*the latter*) éste
head la cabeza
  my head aches me duele la cabeza
headache: she has a —, le duele (a ella) la cabeza
hear oír
  hear that oír decir que
heavens! ¡Dios mío!
Helen Elena
hello hola
  say hello saludar
help ayudar (a + *inf.*)
Henry Enrique

her *adj.* su(s); su(s) *or* el (la, los, las) ... de ella
her *dir. obj.* la; *indir. obj.* le; *after prep.* ella
here aquí
  here (it) is aquí (lo) tienes (tiene Vd.)
hers *pron.* (el) suyo, (la) suya, *etc.*, (el, la, los, las) de ella
  of hers *adj.* suyo, -a, de ella
high school la escuela superior
him *dir. and indir. obj.* le; *after prep.* él
  with him(self) consigo
his *adj.* su(s); su(s) *or* el (la, los, las) ... de él; *pron.* (el) suyo, (la) suya, *etc.*, (el, la, los, las) de él
  of his *adj.* suyo, -a, de él
home la casa
  at home en casa
  leave home salir de casa
  (return) home (volver) a casa
honeymoon la luna de miel
hope esperar
  hope so esperar que sí
horseback: ride —, montar a caballo
hose las medias
hotel el hotel
hour la hora
  a half hour media hora
house la casa
how? ¿cómo?
  how long? ¿cuánto tiempo?
  how much (many)? ¿cuánto, -a (-os, -as)?
  how old is (he)? ¿cuántos años tiene (él)?
how! + *adj. or adv.* ¡qué!
  how! + *verb* ¡cuánto!
hundred: a (one) —, ciento, (*before nouns and* mil) cien
  five hundred quinientos, -as
  one hundred (two) ciento (dos)
  (two) hundred (dos)cientos, -as
hungry: be (very) —, tener (mucha) hambre
hurry darse prisa
hurt oneself hacerse daño
husband el esposo

I

I yo
idea la idea
  the very idea! ¡no faltaba más!

if si
ill enfermo, -a
imagine imaginarse
immediately inmediatamente
important importante
in en, por, de, a; (*after a superlative*) de
Inca el inca
independence la independencia
industrious trabajador, -ora
information los informes
inhabitant el habitante
insist (on) insistir (en)
  insist that insistir en que
intend pensar (ie) (+*inf.*)
interest interesar
interesting interesante
introduce presentar
introduction la presentación
  letters of introduction cartas de presentación
invite invitar (a + *inf.*)
it *dir. obj.* lo (*m. and neuter*), la (*f.*); *indir. obj.* le; (*usually omitted as subject*) él (*m.*), ella (*f.*); *after prep.* él (*m.*), ella (*f.*)

J

James Jaime
Jane Juanita
January enero
jewelry shop la joyería
Jim Jaime
job el puesto
Joe José
John Juan
Johnny Juanito
Joseph José
July julio
June junio
just: have —, acabar de (+*inf.*)

K

keep one's word cumplir la palabra
kind: what — of weather is it? ¿qué tiempo hace?
kiss el beso

give a kiss to dar un beso a
kitchen la cocina
knock (on) llamar (a)
know (*facts*) saber, (*be acquainted with*) conocer
  know how to saber (+*inf.*)

L

lake el lago
land la tierra
language la lengua
large grande
  the larger one (*f.*) la más grande
last pasado, -a, (*in a series*) último, -a
  last night anoche
late tarde
later más tarde, después
  see you later hasta la vista
latter: the —, éste, ésta (-os, -as)
laugh at reírse (i, i) de
lawyer el abogado
learn aprender (a + *inf.*)
least menos
  at least por lo menos
leave salir (de + *obj.*), partir (de + *obj.*),
    irse, marcharse; (*trans.*) dejar
  leave for salir (partir) para
  leave home salir de casa
  take leave (of) despedirse (i, i) (de)
left izquierdo, -a
  on (to) the left a la izquierda
left: have —, quedar (a)
  I have (five dollars) left me quedan
    (cinco dólares)
  there isn't any seat left no queda
    ningún asiento
lemonade la limonada
lend prestar
less menos
lesson la lección (*pl.* lecciones)
  (**Spanish**) **lesson** lección (de español)
let dejar, permitir
  let me + *verb* déjeme Vd. (permítame Vd.)
    or déjame (permíteme) + *inf.*
  let's (let us) + *verb* vamos a + *inf. or first
    pl. pres. subj.*
  let's go vamos
letter la carta

library la biblioteca
life la vida
light ligero, -a
like como; gustar
  (**he**) **would like** (le) gustaría
  how do you like (**him**)? ¿qué te (le)
    parece (él)?
  I should like (yo) quisiera, me gustaría
  like better gustar más
listen (to) escuchar
  listen! (*fam. sing. command*) ¡oye (tú)!
    ¡escucha!; (*fam. pl.*) ¡oíd! ¡escuchad!
little *adj.* (*quantity*) poco, -a; *adv.* poco
  a little un poco
  little brother el hermanito
  little girl la niña
  little time poco tiempo
live vivir
living room la sala
lobby el vestíbulo
long largo, -a
  a long time mucho tiempo
  how long? ¿cuánto tiempo?
  longer más (tiempo)
  take so long tardar tanto
look at mirar
  look at each other mirarse
look for buscar
Los Angeles Los Ángeles
Louis Luis
Louise Luisa
love: fall in — (with) enamorarse (de)
lower bajo, -a
luck: may you (*pl.*) **have good —,** que
    tengan (Vds.) mucha suerte
lucky: be (very)—, tener (mucha) suerte
lunch el almuerzo
  eat (have) lunch tomar el almuerzo,
    almorzar (ue)

M

ma'am señora, señorita
machinery la maquinaria
madam señora, señorita
Madrid Madrid
magazine la revista
mail: by air —, por correo aéreo

make hacer
  make a stop hacer una parada
  make a trip hacer un viaje (una excursión)
man el hombre
  man (alive)! ¡hombre!
  young man el joven
  young men los jóvenes
manager el gerente
many muchos, -as; mil
  as (so) many tantos, -as
  how many? ¿cuántos, -as?
  many (a thousand) things mil cosas
  many people mucha gente
  so many people tanta gente
map el mapa
March marzo
Margaret Margarita
market el mercado
married: be —, casarse
Martha Marta
  to Martha's a casa de Marta
Mary María
  at Mary's en casa de María
match el partido
may (*wish, indir. command*) que + *subj.*; *sign of pres. subj.*
  may I (see)? ¿puedo (ver)?
May mayo
me *dir. and indir. obj.* me; *after prep.* mí
  for me (on my part) de mi parte
  with me conmigo
meet (*a person for the first time*) conocer
merchant el comerciante
Mexican mexicano, -a
Mexico México
  Mexico City México, D.F.; la ciudad de México; Ciudad México
Michael Miguel
midnight la medianoche
  at midnight a la medianoche

might *sign. of imp. subj.*
Mike Miguel
milk la leche
million el millón (*pl.* millones)
  a (one) million un millón de
  (three) million(s) (tres) millones de
mine *pron.* (el) mío, (la) mía, *etc.*
  of mine *adj.* mío, -a

minute el minuto
miss perder (ie)
Miss (la) señorita, Srta.
moment el momento
  at this (that) moment en este (ese) momento
  for a moment por un momento
money el dinero
month el mes
  a (per) month por (al) mes
more más
morning la mañana
  good morning buenos días
  in the morning por la mañana; (*when the hour is given*) de la mañana
  morning flight el vuelo de la mañana
  (tomorrow) morning (mañana) por la mañana
most más
  most of la mayor parte de
mother la madre, (la) mamá
mountain la montaña; *pl.* las montañas, la sierra
movie(s) el cine
Mr. (el) señor, Sr.
  Mr. and Mrs. (Valdés) los señores (Valdés)
Mrs. (la) señora, Sra.
much *adj.* mucho, -a; *adv.* mucho
  as (so) much or many (... as) tanto, -a, -os, -as (... como)
  too much *adv.* demasiado
  very much *adv.* mucho, muchísimo
music la música
must deber, tener que (+*inf.*); *for probability use future tense*
my *adj.* mi(s), mío, -a (-os, -as)

N

name: one's — is, be named llamarse
  his name is (él) se llama
  what is (his) name? ¿cómo se llama (él)?
nap la siesta
  take a nap dormir (ue, u) la siesta
national nacional
near *prep.* cerca de
nearby *adv.* cerca

nearly casi
necessary necesario, -a, preciso, -a
necktie la corbata
need necesitar
neither ... nor (no) ... ni ... ni
nervous nervioso, -a
never nunca
new nuevo, -a
  New World Nuevo Mundo
  New York Nueva York
  what's new? ¿qué hay de nuevo?
newspaper el periódico
next (week) (la semana) que viene
night la noche
  every night todas las noches
  last night anoche
  (on) Saturday night(s) el (los) sábado(s)
    por la noche
nine nueve
  nine hundred novecientos, -as
  the nine o'clock plane el avión de las
    nueve
nineteen diez y nueve
no *adv.* no; *adj.* ninguno, -a, (*before m. sing.*
  nouns) ningún
  no one nadie
noon el mediodía
  at noon al mediodía
  until noon hasta el mediodía
nor: neither ... —, (no) ... ni ... ni
North American el norteamericano
not no
  not yet todavía no
note notar
notebook el cuaderno
nothing nada
  nothing special nada de particular
November noviembre
now ahora, ya
  right now ahora mismo
nowadays hoy día
number el número
  dance number número de baile

O

obtain obtener, conseguir (i, i)
occasion la ocasión (*pl.* ocasiones)

occupied ocupado, -a
occupy ocupar
occur ocurrir
o'clock: at one —, a la una
  at (ten) o'clock a las (diez)
  ten-o'clock bus el autobús de las diez
October octubre
of de, a
off: get —, bajar (de + *obj.*)
  take off (*oneself*) quitarse
office la oficina
  at Mr. Ortiz's office en la oficina del Sr.
    Ortiz
often a menudo
old antiguo, -a, viejo, -a
  be...years old tener (cumplir) ... años
  how old is (he)? ¿cuántos años tiene (él)?
  how old is (he) going to be? ¿cuántos
    años va a tener (cumplir)?
older mayor
on en, sobre
  on the fifth of July el cinco de julio
once: at —, en seguida, cuanto antes
one un, una, uno; *indef. subj.* se, uno
  at one o'clock a la una
  no one nadie
  one-way sencillo, -a
  the one in (of, with) el (la) de
  the one(s) that (who, which) el (la) que,
    pl. los (las) que, quien(es) (*persons only*)
  the (red) one el (rojo), la (roja)
only solamente, sólo, no ... más que
open abrir
opportunity la oportunidad
  have the opportunity to tener la opor-
    tunidad de
opposite *adv.* enfrente
or o
orchestra la orquesta
order mandar
order: in — that *conj.* para que, de manera
  (modo) que
  in order to *prep.* para
other otro, -a
  (look at) each other (mirar)se
  the other one (*f.*) la otra; (*m.*) el otro
  the others los otros
ought to deber
our nuestro, -a

ours *pron.* (el) nuestro, (la) nuestra, *etc.*
  of ours. *adj.* nuestro, -a
out: go — into salir a
owner el dueño

P

package el paquete
pair el par
paper el papel
parents los padres
park el parque
part la parte
pass pasar
  pass by pasar por
past: half — (twelve) (las doce) y media
patio el patio
Paul Pablo
pay (for) pagar
pencil el lápiz (*pl.* lápices)
people la gente (*requires sing. verb*); *indef.*
  subject se
perhaps tal vez, quizá(s)
permission el permiso
  give permission to dar permiso para
  permit permitir
person la persona

personal personal
Peru el Perú
Peruvian el peruano
Philip Felipe
photo la foto
photograph la fotografía
  take photographs sacar fotografías (fotos)
pick up recoger
picture el cuadro
pity la lástima
  it is a pity es lástima
  what a pity! ¡qué lástima!
place el sitio, el lugar
plane el avión
  by plane en avión
  (on) the (four o'clock) plane (en) el
  avión (de las cuatro)
play (*game*) jugar (ue) (a + *obj.*), (*music*)
  tocar
player el jugador
pleasant agradable, simpático, -a

please + *verb* hága(n)me Vd(s). el favor de +
  inf.; favor de + *inf.*; (*after request*) por favor
pleased contento, -a
  I am pleased to meet you mucho gusto
  en conocerle (-la) a Vd.
pleasure el placer, el gusto
p.m. de la tarde (noche)
pool: swimming —, la piscina
poor pobre
  poor (little) boy el pobrecito
popular popular
position el puesto
possible posible
  as soon as possible cuanto antes, tan
  pronto como posible, lo más pronto posible
prefer preferir (ie, i)
prepare preparar
present presentar
pretty bonito, -a, hermoso, -a
probably *use future or cond. tense*
program el programa
pronounce pronunciar
pupil el alumno, la alumna
purse la bolsa
put poner
  put on (*oneself*) ponerse
  put on (*record*) poner

Q

quarter el cuarto
  at a quarter after nine a las nueve y
  cuarto
  until a quarter to (ten) hasta las (diez)
  menos cuarto
question la pregunta
  ask a question (of) hacer una pregunta (a)

R

radio (*set*) el radio, (*communication*) la radio
rain llover (ue)
raise cultivar
rapidly rápidamente
rate: at any —, de todos modos
Raymond Ramón
reach llegar (a + *obj.*)

reach a decision   llegar a una decisión
read   leer
ready   listo, -a
  be ready to   estar listo, -a para
  get ready for   prepararse para
realize (that)   darse cuenta de (que)
really   de veras
recall   recordar (ue)
receive   recibir
recommend   recomendar (ie)
record (*phonograph*)   el disco
recreation room   la sala de recreo
red   rojo, -a
  the red one   el rojo, la roja
refreshment   el refresco
remain   quedar(se)
remember   recordar (ue), acordarse (ue)
  (de + *obj.*)
rent   alquilar
reply   contestar
reserve   reservar

rest   el resto; descansar
restaurant   el restaurante

return   volver (ue), (*give back*) devolver (ue)
Richard   Ricardo
ride horseback   montar a caballo

right   derecho, -a
  be right   tener razón

  on (to) the right   a la derecha
  right?   ¿eh?
  right now   ahora mismo

ring   tocar
road   el camino
Robert   Roberto
roof   el tejado

room   el cuarto, la habitación (*pl.* habitaciones)

  dining room   el comedor
  living room   la sala

  recreation room   la sala de recreo
  waiting room   la sala de espera
round-trip   de ida y vuelta

ruins   las ruinas
rumba   la rumba
run   correr
  run across   encontrarse (ue) con

S

sad   triste
sand   la arena
Saturday   el sábado
  (on) Saturday   el sábado
  (on) Saturday night(s)   el (los) sábado(s)
    por la noche
say   decir
  say hello   saludar
  say yes   decir que sí
scarcely   apenas
school   la escuela
  high school   la escuela superior
seat   el asiento
seated   sentado, -a
secretary   la secretaria
section   la sección
see   ver
  I'll see you   le (te) veo
  let's see   (vamos) a ver
  see each other   verse
  see you later   hasta la vista
seem   parecer
sell   vender
send   enviar, mandar
  send for   enviar (mandar) por
  send a (the) telegram   enviar· (poner) un
    (el) telegrama
sentence   la frase
September   septiembre
serve   servir (i, i)
service: at your —,   a sus órdenes, a su
    disposición
set: be — back   retrasarse
seven   siete
  seven hundred   setecientos, -as
seventy   setenta
seventy(-seven)   setenta (y siete)
several   varios, -as
shade   la sombra
shall *sign of future tense; occasionally translated by*
    pres. tense
  shall we sit down?   ¿nos sentamos?
sharp (*time*)   en punto
shave (*oneself*)   afeitarse
she   ella
shining: the sun was —,   hacía (había) sol
shirt   la camisa

shoe el zapato
shoe store la zapatería
shop: cleaning —, la tintorería
  jewelry shop la joyería
shopping: go —, ir de compras
short: after a — time al poco tiempo
shortly afterward poco después
should *sign of cond. and imp. subj.*; deber,
  (*softened statement*) debiera
shout gritar
show enseñar (a + *inf.*)
  show signs of dar señales de
show window el escaparate
since como
sign la señal
  show signs of dar señales de
sing cantar
sir señor
sister la hermana
  little sister la hermanita
sit down sentarse (ie)
  let's sit down sentémonos, vamos a
  sentarnos
  shall we sit down? ¿nos sentamos?
six seis
sixteen diez y seis
sixty sesenta
  sixty(-five) sesenta (y cinco)
size (*shoes*) el número
sky el cielo
sleep dormir (ue, u)
  go to sleep dormirse (ue, u)
sleepy: be (very) —, tener (mucho) sueño
sleepyhead el dormilón (*pl.* dormilones)
slide la transparencia
slow lento, -a
slowly despacio
small pequeño, -a
  the smaller ones los más pequeños, las
  más pequeñas
snow la nieve
so (*with adj. or adv.*) tan
  hope (believe) so esperar (creer) que sí
  so many tantos, -as
  so many people tanta gente
  so much (+*noun*) **... as** tanto, -a ... como
  so-so así, así
  so that *conj.* para que, de modo (manera)
  que

sock el calcetín (*pl.* calcetines)
some *adj. and pron.* alguno, -a, (*before m. sing.*
  nouns) algún; *pl.* algunos, -as; unos, -as;
  often not translated
someone alguien
somewhat *adv.* algo
son el hijo
song la canción (*pl.* canciones)
soon pronto
  as soon as en cuanto
  as soon as possible cuanto antes, tan
  pronto como posible, lo más pronto posible
sorry: be —, sentir (ie, i)
  I am very sorry lo siento mucho
sound sonar (ue)
south el sur
  South America la América del Sur
space el espacio
Spain España
Spanish *adj.* español, -ola; (*language*) el
  español
  Spanish American hispanoamericano, -a
  Spanish (book) (libro) de español
  Spanish (lesson) (lección) de español
speak hablar
special: nothing —, nada de particular
spend (*time*) pasar
sport el deporte
  sports section la sección de deportes
spring la primavera
  spring day día de primavera
square la plaza
States: United —, los Estados Unidos
stay quedarse
step el paso
still todavía
stocking la media
stop la parada; detenerse
  make a stop hacer una parada
store la tienda
  department store el almacén
  shoe store la zapatería
strange extraño, -a
street la calle
  go out into the street salir a la calle
stroll pasearse
student el alumno, la alumna, el (la)
  estudiante
study estudiar

study hard   estudiar mucho
style   el estilo
stylish   de moda
suit   el traje
  bathing suit   el traje de baño
suitcase   la maleta
summer   el verano
sun   el sol
  take a sun bath   tomar el sol
  the sun was shining   hacía (había) sol
Sunday   el domingo
  on Sundays   los domingos
supper: eat —,   cenar
suppose   suponer
sure   seguro, -a
surprise   sorprender
surprised   sorprendido, -a
swim   nadar
  take a swim   bañarse
swimming: go —,   ir a nadar
swimming pool   la piscina

T

table   la mesa
  dining table   la mesa de comer
take   tomar, (*carry*) llevar, (*photos*) sacar
  I'll take it (*f.*)   la tomo, me quedo con ella
  take a bath   bañarse
  take a business trip   hacer un viaje de negocios
  take a nap   dormir (ue, u) la siesta
  take a sun bath   tomar el sol
  take a swim   bañarse
  take a trip   hacer un viaje (una excursión)
  take a walk   dar un paseo
  take breakfast   desayunarse, tomar el desayuno
  take leave (of)   despedirse (i, i) (de)
  take lunch   tomar el almuerzo, almorzar (ue)
  take off (*oneself*)   quitarse
  take so long   tardar tanto
  take with oneself   llevarse, llevar consigo
talk   hablar
tall   alto, -a
tango   el tango
teach   enseñar (a + *inf.*)

teacher   el profesor, la profesora
  (**English**) **teacher**   profesor *or* profesora (de inglés)
telegram   el telegrama
  send a (**the**) **telegram**   poner un (el) telegrama
telephone   el teléfono; telefonear, llamar por teléfono
  by telephone   por teléfono
television   la televisión
  television program   programa de televisión
tell   decir, contar (ue)
ten   diez
tennis   el tenis
than   que, (*before numerals*) de
  than (**she**) **expected**   de lo que (ella) esperaba
thank you, thanks   gracias
  many thanks   muchas (mil) gracias
that *adj.* (*near person addressed*) ese, esa (-os, -as), (*distant*) aquel, aquella (-os, -as); *pron.* ése, ésa (-os, -as), aquél, aquélla (-os, -as), (*neuter*) eso, aquello; *relative pron.* que
  all that   todo lo que, cuanto
  that's fine   está bien
  that which   lo que
  the one(s) that   el (la, los, las) que
the   el, la, los, las
theater   el teatro
their *adj.*   su(s), de ellos (-as)
theirs *pron.*   (el) suyo, (la) suya, *etc.*, (el, la, los, las) de ellos (-as)
  of theirs *adj.*   suyo, -a, de ellos (-as)
them *dir. obj.* los, las; *indir. obj.* les, se; *after prep.* ellos (-as)
then   luego
there (*near person addressed*) ahí, (*distant*) allí
  there is (are)   hay
  there was (were) *imp.* había; *pret.* hubo
therefore   por eso
these *adj.* estos, estas; *pron.* éstos, éstas
they   ellos, ellas
thing   la cosa
  the best thing   lo mejor
think   pensar (ie)
  think of (about)   pensar en + *obj.*
  what do you think of ...?   ¿qué le (te) parece ...?

third tercero, -a *(before m. sing. nouns)* tercer

thirsty: be —, tener sed

thirty treinta

  thirty(-five) treinta (y cinco)

this *adj.* este, esta; *pron.* **this (one)** éste, ésta; *neuter* esto

those *adj.* *(near person addressed)* esos (-as), *(distant)* aquellos (-as); *pron.* ésos (-as), aquéllos (-as)

though: even —, aunque

thousand: a (one) —, mil

three tres

through por

Thursday el jueves

  on Thursday el jueves

ticket el billete

  one-way ticket billete sencillo

  round-trip ticket billete de ida y vuelta

tight estrecho, -a

tile la teja

time *(in general sense)* el tiempo; *(of day)* la hora; *(series)* la vez *(pl.* veces*)*

  a long time mucho tiempo

  after a short time al poco tiempo

  another time (occasion) en otra ocasión

  at times a veces

  at what time? ¿a qué hora?

  be time to ser hora de

  from time to time de vez en cuando

  have a (very) good time divertirse (ie, i) (mucho)

  have little time left quedar poco tiempo a (uno)

  have time to tener tiempo para

  on time a tiempo

  there was time to había tiempo para

  what time is it? ¿qué hora es?

tire la llanta

tired cansado, -a

to a, de, para, que, *(in time)* menos

  to (Martha's) a casa de (Marta)

today hoy

Tom Tomás

tomorrow mañana

  tomorrow (afternoon) mañana (por la tarde)

tonight esta noche

Tony Antonio

too también, demasiado

too much *adv.* demasiado

topcoat el abrigo

traffic el tránsito

train el tren

travel viajar

  travel agency la agencia de viajes

tree el árbol

trip el viaje, la excursión

  have a good trip! ¡buen viaje!

  take a business trip hacer un viaje de negocios

  take (make) a trip hacer un viaje (una excursión)

true: be —, ser verdad (cierto)

truth la verdad

try tratar; *(test)* probar (ue)

  try on (the hat) probarse (ue) (el sombrero)

  try to (find) tratar de (hallar)

turn out (to be) resultar

twelve doce

  at twelve o'clock a las doce

twenty veinte

twenty-one veinte y un(o)

two dos

  the two los (las) dos

U

uncle el tío

  my uncle and aunt mis tíos

under *prep.* bajo

understand comprender

unfortunately por desgracia

United States los Estados Unidos

university la universidad

until *prep.* hasta; *conj.* hasta que

up: get —, levantarse

up to *prep.* hasta

upon + *pres. part.* al + *inf.*

upper alto, -a

Uruguay el Uruguay

us *dir. and indir. obj.* nos; *after prep.* nosotros, -as

use usar

used to *sign of the imperfect tense*

V

vacant   vacante
vacation   las vacaciones
  be on vacation   estar de vacaciones
very *adv.*   muy, mucho; *adj.*   mucho, -a
very much *adv.*   mucho, muchísimo
  very well   muy bien, está bien
Vincent   Vicente
visit   visitar

W

wait (for)   esperar, aguardar
waiter   el camarero, la camarera
waiting room   la sala de espera
wake up *(someone)* despertar (ie), *(oneself)*
    despertarse (ie)
walk   el paseo; andar, pasearse
  take a walk   dar un paseo
wall   la pared
want   querer, desear
warm *(noun with* hacer*)*   el calor
  be (very) warm *(living beings)* tener
    (mucho) calor
  be warm *(weather)*   hacer calor
wash   lavar, *(oneself)* lavarse
watch   el reloj
water   el agua *(f.)*
way: by the —,   a propósito
we   nosotros, -as
wear   usar
weather   el tiempo
  be good (bad) weather   hacer buen (mal)
    tiempo
  what kind of weather is it?   ¿qué tiempo
    hace?
week   la semana
welcome: you are —,   no hay de qué, de
    nada
well *adv.*   bien; bueno, pues
  very well   muy bien, está bien
what *pron.*   lo que
what?   ¿qué? ¿cuál? ¿cómo? *(indirect question)*
  what color is (it)?   ¿de qué color es?
  what's new?   ¿qué hay de nuevo? qué
what a ...!   ¡qué ...!

when   cuando
when?   ¿cuándo?
where   donde
where?   ¿dónde?, *(with verbs of motion)*
    ¿adónde?
  where is (George) from?   ¿de dónde es
    (Jorge)?
whether   si
which   que, el (la, los, las) que, el (la) cual,
    los (las) cuales
  that which   lo que
  which (fact)   lo que, lo cual
  which (one)?   ¿cuál?
  which (ones)?   ¿cuáles?
while   el rato
white   blanco, -a
who   que, quien(es), el (la) cual, los (las)
    cuales, el (la, los, las) que
  the one who   el que, quien
who?   ¿quién(es)?
whom   que, a quien(es)
whom?   ¿a quién(es)?
  from whom?   ¿de quién(es)?
whose *relative adj.*   cuyo, -a
whose?   ¿de quién(es)?
why?   ¿por qué? ¿para qué?
wide   ancho, -a
wife   la esposa
will *sign of future tense*
  will you + *verb?*   ¿quiere Vd. (quieres) +
    inf.?
window   la ventana
  show window   el escaparate
winter   el invierno
wish   querer, desear
  I wish that!   ¡ojalá (que) + *subj.!*
with   con, de, en
within *prep.*   dentro de
without *prep.*   sin
won't you?   ¿no quiere Vd. (quieres)?
word   la palabra
  keep one's word   cumplir la palabra
work   trabajar
  work hard   trabajar mucho
world   el mundo
  New World   Nuevo Mundo
would *sign of imperfect or cond. tense*
  would that!   ¡ojalá (que) + *subj.!*
wrap up   envolver (ue)

write escribir

Y

year el año
  be ... years old tener (cumplir) ... años
  for (several years) desde hace (varios
    años)
yellow amarillo, -a
yes sí
  say yes decir que sí
yesterday ayer
yet todavía
  not yet todavía no
you (*fam. sing.*) tú, (*pl.*) vosotros, -as; *dir. and
  indir. obj.* te, os; *after prep.* ti, vosotros, -as

you (*formal*) *subject pron. and after prep.* usted
  (Vd.), ustedes (Vds.); *dir. obj.* le, la, los,
  las; *indir. obj.* le, les, se
young joven (*pl.* jóvenes)
  young man el joven
  young men los jóvenes
  younger más joven, menor
your (*fam.*) *adj.* tu(s), vuestro(s), -a(s);
  (*formal*) su(s), de Vd. (Vds.)
yours (*fam.*) *pron.* (el) tuyo, (la) tuya, (los)
  tuyos, (las) tuyas, (el) vuestro, (la) vuestra,
  (los) vuestros, (las) vuestras; (*formal*) (el)
  suyo, (la) suya, (los) suyos, (las) suyas, (el,
  la, los, las) de Vd. (Vds.)
  of yours *adj.* tuyo(s), -a(s), vuestro(s),
    -a(s); suyo, -a, de Vd. (Vds.)

Index

(References are to page numbers)

a: + **el,** 33; omission of personal **a,** 65, 95 note, 255 note, 290; personal, 65, 66, 132, 267 note, 289, 290; preposition, 33, 179, 206 note; verbs which take **a** before an infinitive, 33, 179, 206 note

abbreviations and signs, 3, 14, 389, 390, 393 note, 412

absolute: superlative, 245; use of the past participle, 374

acabar de, 194

address: forms of, 13 note, 14, 116, 355

adjective clauses, 288–290; subjunctive in, 290

adjectives: agreement of, 23–24, 34, 43, 67, 81, 163 note, 165, 176 note, 208, 245, 341, 372 note, 374; comparison of, 81–82, 244–245; demonstrative, 67, 193; feminine of, 23, 294 note; forms of, 23; of nationality, 23–24, 215; past participle used as, 208, 340; plural of, 23; position of, 34, 43, 67, 90 note, 129 note, 165, 166, 245, 265–266, 282 note; possessive (short forms), 43, 81, (long forms), 246; shortened forms of, 33–34, 90 note, 149, 165, 245; used as nouns, 24, 81, 215; with **estar,** 53, 117, 149; with neuter article **lo,** 341; with **ser,** 44, 340

adverbial clauses: subjunctive in, 307–309

adverbs: comparison of, 82, 244; formation of, 137; position of, 14–15, 24–25, 354 note; with neuter article **lo,** 244, 341

agreement: of adjectives, 23–24, 34, 43, 67, 81, 163 note, 165, 176 note, 208, 245, 341, 372 note, 374; of cardinal numerals, 23, 33–34, 165; of ordinal numerals, 165–166

al: + infinitive, 66

alphabet: Spanish, 3, 413

andar, 305 note

'any,' 24, 113 note, 180, 381 note

article, definite: contraction with **el,** 33; **el** with feminine nouns, 117, 146 note; for the possessive, 99; forms, 14; general use of, 14–15; in a general sense and with abstract nouns, 179–180; in comparison of adjectives, 81–82; in dates, 166–167; in expressing time of day, 34; **lo,** *see* neuter **lo;** omission with **hablar, de, en,** 14–15; to form possessive pronouns, 339; used as a demonstrative, 339–340; with a meal, 31 note; with days of the week, 166; with expressions of time, 132; with place and proper names, 54, 137 note; with seasons, 149; with the months, 166; with the name of a language, 14–15, 354 note; with titles, 54, 389

article, indefinite: forms of, 23; omission with **ciento** and **mil,** 149; omission with other nouns and after a negative, 99; omission with predicate noun, 23

'become,' 374

breath-group, 6

'by,' translated by **para,** 357; translated by **por,** 340–341, 358; with passive, 340–341; with present participle, 177

capitalization, 7, 166

-car verbs, 191, 273, 429

cardinal numerals, 23, 33–34, 165, 166, 167; in dates, 167; to express time of day, 34

-cer and **-cir** verbs, 430, 431

cien(to), 165

classroom expressions, 408

commands: equal to *let's,* 275; familiar plural, 355–356; familiar singular, 116, 244, 355; formal direct, 115; indirect, 276; negative familiar singular forms, 116, 244; object pronouns with, 116, 117, 356; plural, 116, 355–356

comparison: of adjectives, 81–82, 244–245; of adverbs, 82, 244; of equality, 245 compound nouns, 44, 149, 309

compound tenses, 207–208, 229, 272–273, 324, 373-374, 422–423

con: conmigo, contigo, consigo, 179

conditional: for probability, 229–230, 322 note; irregular forms of, 227-228; perfect, 229; sentences, 356–357; tense, 227–228; uses of, 229, 326, 357

conducir, 373, 430

conocer: use of, 66-67, 242

construir, 341–342, 430

continuar, 357, 431

contractions: **a + el,** 33; **de + el,** 33

contrary-to-fact sentences, 356

¿cuál(es)? 54–55

cuanto, 354 note

¡cuánto! 326

cuyo, 341

dates, 166–167

days of the week, 166

de: after a superlative; before a numeral, 82; for *than,* 82; in expressing time, 34; phrases with, 44, 149, 309, 339; plus **el,** 33; possession, 33

¿de quién(es)? 341

deber, 209, 229, 326

definite article, *see* article, definite

dejar, 114 note, 325

demonstrative: adjectives, 67, 193; article, 339–340; pronouns, 192-193

desear, 98

devolver, 193

diminutives, 375

diphthongs, 4, 5, 36–37, 135, 169, 414, 417

direct object, *see* pronouns

division of words into syllables, 4, 414

-ducir verbs, 373, 430

e, 'and,' 171 note

¿eh? 226 note

encontrarse: for **estar,** 107 note, 163 note, 208

entrar: use of, 66

enviar: forms, 357, 431

estar: uses of, 53-54, 117, 149, 177, 208, 340-341; verbs used for, 107 note, 163 note, 208

éste, 'the latter,' 193

exclamations, 6, 326–327

expressions: for the classroom, 408; for the laboratory, 409

feminine: article **el,** 117, 146 note; of adjectives, 23, 294 note; of nouns, 14, 54

future: for probability, 229–230; irregular forms of, 227–228; perfect, 229; present tense for, 78 note, 228; tense, 227–228; uses of, 228, 229, 357

-gar verbs, 191, 273, 429

gender of nouns, 14

-ger and **-gir** verbs, 306–307, 429

grammatical terms, 410–411

gran(de), 90 note, 190 note, 245

-guar verbs, 429

-guir verbs, 307, 429

gustar, 80-81, 326

haber: impersonal use of, 24, 149, 209, 228, 374, 381 note; to form perfect tenses, 207–208, 229, 272–273, 324, 373–374; use of **haber de,** 209; use of **haber que,** 209

hacer: for *ago* or *since,* 209, 291; in time clauses, 290–291; plus infinitive, 325-326; to express weather, 149

hallarse: for **estar,** 163 note, 208

hay, 24, 209

-iar verbs, 357, 431

imperative, 116, 355, 422

imperfect: contrasted with preterit, 148; indicative forms, 147; of **hacer** in time clauses, 290–291; subjunctive forms, 323–324; uses of imperfect indicative, 147-148, 229; uses of imperfect subjunctive, *see* subjunctive

impersonal expressions, 44, 274–275, 291; subjunctive after, 274–275, 291 indefinite article, *see* article, indefinite

indefinite expressions, 132

indefinite subject, 178–179, 209

indirect object, *see* pronouns

indirect questions, 55

infinitive: after **al**, 66; after **dejar, permitir, hacer, mandar** 325-326; after impersonal expressions, 275; after **oír** and **ver**, 375; after prepositions, 33, 66, 178, 358, 371 note; after **tener que**, 24, 209; after verbs without a preposition, 53, 64, 67, 98; position of object pronouns with, 98, 178, 371 note; translated as passive, 325–326

interrogative sentences, 6, 15, 23, 54–55

intonation, 418–419

ir: a + infinitive, 33

-ísimo, 245

jugar, 230

laboratory expressions, 409

'leave,' **66,** 114 note

'let,' 275–276, 325

letter writing, 389–395

'like,' 80–81

linking, 6, 418

lo, see neuter **lo**

llevar, 129 note

mandar, 325–326, 358

months, 166

'most of,' 245

'must,' 24, 209

negation: double negatives, 132; simple, 15

neuter **lo**: article with adjectives, 341; article with adverbs, 244, 341; object pronoun, 65; pronoun to complete sentence, 139 note, 242 note, 341; to express *than*, 189 note; with **que,** 340

¿**(no ès) verdad?** 34, 226 note

noun clauses: subjunctive in, 259–260, 273–275, 291, 325

nouns: adjectives used as, 24, 81, 215; feminine of, 14, 54; gender of, 14; phrases with **de** plus a noun, 44, 149, 309, 339; plural of, 14, 21 note, 166; plural referring to persons, 14; predicate, 23–24, 44

numerals: cardinal, 23, 33–34, 165, 166, 167; ordinal, 165–166

oír: followed by infinitive, 375; forms of, 307

¡**ojalá (que)!** 326–327

ordinal numerals, 165-166

pagar, 193

para: uses of, 44, 309, 357–358

passive: infinitive translated by, 325–326; reflexive substitute for, 80, 178, 208, 340; voice, 340–341

past participle: absolute use of, 374; forms of, 207; in perfect tenses, 207–208, 229, 257–258, 272–273, 324, 373–374, 422–423; irregular forms of, 207, 423, 432 note, 433 note; to express passive voice, 340–341; used as adjective, 208, 340

pedir: use of, 243, 259

pero, sino, sino que, 309

personal **a,** 65, 66, 132, 267 note, 289, 290; omission of, 65, 95 note, 255 note, 290

phrases with **de** + a noun, 44, 149, 309, 339

pluperfect: indicative, 207–208, 374; subjunctive, 324

plural: of adjectives, 23; of nouns, 14, 21 note, 166; of nouns referring to persons, 14

poder, 64, 115

por: uses of, 34, 193, 340, 357–359

position: of adjectives, 34, 43, 67, 90 note, 129 note, 165, 166, 245, 265–266, 282 note; of adverbs, 14–15, 24–25, 354 note; of object pronouns, 65–66, 79, 98, 116, 117, 178, 192, 208, 355, 356, 371 note

possession, 33; with parts of the body, 99

possessive adjectives: agreement of, 43; definite article used for, 99; forms (short), 43, 81, (long), 246; position of, 34, 43, 67, 246 possessive pronouns, 339; clarification of **el suyo, la suya,** etc., 339

predicate noun, 23–24, 44

preguntar: uses of, 193, 242 note, 243, 358

preposition **a,** 33, 179, 206 note

present participle: after **seguir,** 307; forms, 53; other use of, 177; position of object pronouns with, 178; to express progressive forms of tense, 53–54, 177

present tense: for future, 78 note, 228; indicative of regular verbs, 12–13, 32, 42; indicative of stem-changing verbs, 97, 191, 230, 243; of **hacer** in time clauses, 290–291; perfect indicative, 207–208; perfect subjunctive, 272–273; subjunctive, 257–258

preterit: contrasted with imperfect, 148; regular forms of, 130–131; uses of, 131, 374; verbs with special meanings in, 191, 242

preterit perfect tense, 373–374

probability: future and conditional of, 229–230, 322 note

progressive forms of the tenses, 53–54, 177

pronouns: demonstrative, 192–193; direct object, 65, 116, 381 note; indirect object, 79; neuter **lo** to complete sentence, 139 note, 242 note; position of object, 65–66, 79, 98, 116, 117, 178, 192, 208, 355, 356, 371 note; possessive, 339; redundant use of indirect object pronoun, 79, 81; reflexive, 97–98, 116, 192, 275, 355–356, 357; relative, 24, 288–290, 340, 354 note; special use of indirect object, 259; subject, 13–14, 42, 116, 322 note; two object, 192; use of **lo** for **le** in Spanish America, 65; used as objects of prepositions, 79, 179, 291

pronunciation, 3–6, 18, 27, 36–37, 47, 57, 69–70, 84, 102, 120–121, 135, 151, 169, 182, 196, 413–419

punctuation, 6–7, 15, 55, 394 note, 412

que: meaning *let, have, may,* 276; meaning *than,* 82, 132, 244; relative pronoun, 24, 288–289

¿qué? 54–55

¡qué! 326

querer: quisiera, 326; uses of, 53, 64, 98, 228, 391 note

questions, 6, 15, 23, 54–55

quien: use of, 289, 340

-quir verbs, 430

quotation marks, 7

reflexive pronouns, 97–98, 116, 192, 275, 355–356, 357

reflexive substitute for the passive, 80, 178, 208, 340

reflexive verbs: forms of, 97–98, 116, 275; familiar plural commands of, 116, 335–336; familiar singular commands of, 116, 355; **uno** for indefinite subject with, 179

reír, 373

relative pronouns, 24, 288–290, 340, 354 note

saber: uses of, 53, 66–67, 191, 242 note

salir: use of, 66, 114 note

san(to), 155

se: as indefinite subject, 178; as substitute for the passive, 80, 178, 208, 340; for **le** and **les,** 192; reflexive pronoun, 97–98; used to express *become,* 374

seasons, 149

seguir, 307

ser: uses of, 23, 24, 34, 44–45, 149, 340

shortened forms of adjectives, 33–34, 90 note, 149, 165, 245

'should,' 229, 356

si-clauses, 356–357

sino, sino que, 309

'some,' 24, 113 note, 129 note, 180, 381 note

songs, 173, 400–406; translation of, 406–407

stem-changing verbs, 97, 115, 131, 191, 230, 243, 244, 258, 307, 323, 373; summary of, 431–433

su(s): clarification of, 179

subject pronouns: use of, 13 note, 13–14, 42, 116, 322 note

subjunctive: after impersonal expressions, 274, 275, 291; ¡ojalá (que)! 326–327; after **tal vez, quizá(s),** 374; imperfect, 323–324; in adjective clauses, 290; in adverbial clauses, 307–309; in conditional sentences, 356–357; in familiar commands, 116, 355; in indirect commands, 275–276; in noun clauses, 259–260, 273–275, 291, 325; in formal commands, 115; in **si-**clauses, 356–357; in softened statement, 326; pluperfect, 324; present, 257–258; present perfect, 272–273; theory of, 258–259; use of subjunctive tenses, 324–325, 356–357

superlative: absolute, 245; comparative, 81–82, 244–245

suyo, -a: clarification of, 246; clarification of **el suyo, la suya,** etc., 339

'take,' 129 note

tener: idioms with, 117; special meaning in preterit of, 191; **tener que** + infinitive, 24, 209

tenses, *see* present, etc.

'than,' 82, 132, 189 note, 244

'then,' 146 note

time: of day, 34, 45, 118, 148; ways to express, 34, 118

tomar, 129 note

triphthongs, 417

-uar verbs, 357, 431

-uir verbs, 341–342, 430

uno: used as indefinite subject, 179

usted(es): use of, 13 note, 14, 42, 79, 115, 116, 179, 322 note, 355

valer, 291

ver: followed by infinitive, 375

verbs: *see* each separately and tables in Appendix C; followed by an infinitive without a preposition, 53, 64, 67, 98; requiring a direct object without a preposition, 66; requiring the indirect object of a person, 193, 259; stem-changing, 97, 115, 131, 191, 230, 243, 244, 258, 307, 323, 373, 431–433; with changes in spelling, 191, 273, 306–307, 428–430; with special endings, 430–431; with special meanings in the preterit, 191, 242

verse: used for **estar,** 208

volver, 193

weather: expression of, 149

'will,' 98, 228

word order, 15, 23, 24, 51 note, 80, 81, 371 note, 374, 375

word stress, 4–5, 414–415

words and expressions for the classroom, 408; for the laboratory, 409

'would,' 148, 199, 229

-zar verbs, 191, 273, 429

PHOTOGRAPH CREDITS

9   Parque Guell, Barcelona, Spain   P. Menzel
17   Ocarina   Courtesy, United Fruit Co.
27   Pre-columbian stone relief   Courtesy, Mexican National Tourist Office
28   Las Ramblas, Barcelona, Spain   P. Menzel
37   Ceramic dish   Courtesy, Spanish Tourist Office
38   House of the Shells, Salamanca, Spain   P. Menzel
48   Painter on the Ramblas, Barcelona, Spain   P. Menzel
48   Book Fair, Madrid, Spain   P. Menzel
58   Plaza de la reina, Valencia, Spain   G. Engelhard
58   View of El Pardo Palace near Madrid, Spain   B. Bailey
61   Aqueduct, Mexico   E. Anderson
72   City walls, Avila, Spain   P. Menzel
73   View of Salamanca, Spain   P. Menzel
74   View of Las Cortes, Madrid, Spain   P. Menzel
86   Indian in jungle, Ecuador   C. Capa
88   Fishing boats, Puerto Montt, Chile   Courtesy, Chilean Consulate
88   Steel plant, Chile   Courtesy, United Nations
89   Gaucho with sheep, Uruguay   P. Conklin
90   Indian festival, Peru   Sergio Larrain
91   Courtyard, Cuzco, Peru   K. Muldoon
92   Airport, Maracaibo, Venezuela   Courtesy, Venezuelan Government Tourist Bureau
101   Indian woman near Lake Titicaca, Peru   Courtesy, United Nations
104   University of Guanajuato, Mexico   P. Menzel
106   Mexico City   Courtesy, Mexican National Tourist Office
106   Independence Monument, Mexico City   Courtesy, Mexican National Tourist Office
107   Shopping Center, Mexico City   Monkmeyer, M. Pease
108   Lottery Stand, Mexico City   Rapelye
108   Chapultepec Park Directory, Mexico City   Rapelye
109   Pyramid of the Sun, Teotihuacan, Mexico   Courtesy, Mexican National Tourist Office
110   View of Guadalajara, Mexico   P. Menzel
121   Sierra Nevada, Spain   C. Morris
122   Indian women, Bolivia   Sergio Larrain
124   Sidewalk cafe, Salamanca, Spain   P. Menzel
127   Bar, Malaga, Spain   P. Menzel
136   Night view of Panama Canal   Courtesy, Pan Am
138   Mayan sculpture, Mexico   I. Groth
139   University of Costa Rica   F. Vikar
140   Cristo Street, Puerto Rico   Courtesy, Puerto Rico News Agency
140   View of El Morro, San Juan, Puerto Rico   Courtesy, Puerto Rico News Agency
152   Sorting tin, Caracoles, Bolivia   C. Capa
153   Indian women, Bolivia   Courtesy, Braniff
154   Convent, Salamanca, Spain   P. Menzel
156   Landing of Hernando de Soto in Florida   Culver Pictures Inc.

157   Balcony in Ronda, Spain   Courtesy, Spanish Tourist Office
157   San Miguel Mission, California   W. Linton
158   Two views of San Miguel Mission, New Mexico   Courtesy, V. Dermer
159   Santa Barbara Mission, California   W. Linton
159   San Carlos Borromeo Mission, California   Courtesy, V. Dermer
160   San Fernando Mission, California   Monkmeyer
161   View of the Alcazar, Segovia   Photo by H. Krieger for Burlington House
172   Nativity scene   Courtesy, Spanish Tourist Office
185   Office building, Barcelona, Spain   P. Menzel
185   Cafeteria, University of Madrid, Spain   P. Menzel
187   Spanish style house, California   Monkmeyer
196   Southern Chile   K. Muldoon
198   Holy Week, Salamanca, Spain   P. Menzel
200   Holy Week, Salamanca, Spain   P. Menzel
200   Masked dancers, Urubamba, Peru   P. Conklin
201   Holy Week, Seville, Spain   Burye for Monkmeyer
202   Monument, Dolores Hidalgo, Mexico   Rapelye
202   Church, Mexico   Courtesy, Mexican National Tourist Office
202   Charreada, Mexico   Courtesy, Mexican National Tourist Office
203   Religious Celebration, Janitzio, Lake Patzcuaro, Mexico   Courtesy Mexican National Tourist Office
211   View of Segovia, Spain   P. Menzel
212   Department store, Barcelona, Spain   P. Menzel
214   Engraving by Goya   Courtesy, Museum of Fine Arts, Boston
214   Bullfight, Salamanca, Spain   P. Menzel
216   Playing "el pato"   E. M. Crawford
217   Jai alai game, Madrid   Photo by Roger Coster. Reprinted by special permission from Holiday. Copyright 1952, the Curtis Publishing Co.
218   The Roman Aqueduct, Segovia, Spain   P. Menzel
219   Soccer game, Madrid, Spain   P. Menzel
220   Ski resort in the Spanish Pyrenees   P. Menzel
223   Mountain range, Bolivia   P. Conklin
232   Soccer game, Mexico City   Courtesy, Mexican Railroad Co.
234   Poplar trees, Chile   Courtesy, United Nations
236   Cotton fields, Mexico   Courtesy United Nations
237   Cacao plant and pods   Courtesy, American Airlines
237   Drying sisal hemp, El Salvador   Photo by Sawders for Cushing
238   Research on beans, National Agricultural Research Center, Mexico   Courtesy, Mexican National Tourist Office
238   Banana plantation, Honduras   Courtesy, United Fruit Co.
239   Sugar mill, Costa Rica   Courtesy, United Nations
250   Spanish restaurant, Madrid, Spain   P. Menzel

262 Museum of Modern Art, Barcelona, Spain P. Menzel
264 Cathedral of Salamanca, Spain P. Menzel
267 Roman theatre, Merida, Spain Courtesy, Spanish Tourist Office
268 Tower of the Mezquita, Cordoba, Spain Courtesy, Spanish Tourist Office
269 Reproduction of the "Santa María" of Columbus, Barcelona, Spain M. Hurlimann
279 Craftsman, Seville, Spain P. Menzel
280 Entrance to the Royal Chapel, Granada, Spain Courtesy, Spanish Tourist Office
282 Father Junipero Sierra, Father Bartolome de las Casas Historical Pictures Service
283 San Xavier del Bac Mission, Tucson, Arizona Courtesy, Sunchine Climate Club, Visitors and Convention Bureau, Tucson, Arizona
294 Roman Aqueduct, Tarragona, Spain P. Menzel
296 View of the Alhambra, Granada, Spain Courtesy, Spanish Tourist Office
296 Patio of the Cathedral, Barcelona, Spain P. Menzel
297 Ferdinand of Aragon, Isabella of Castile Historical Pictures Service
298 Page of La Celestina Courtesy, Hispanic Society of America
299 Lope de Vega Historical Pictures Service
302 Fallas, Valencia, Spain P. Menzel
302 Street in Malaga, Spain P. Menzel
311 Fence with inscription, Peru F. Vikar
312 Subway station, Mexico City P. Menzel
312 Columbus Circle, Mexico City Courtesy, Mexican National Tourist Office
313 Bakery shop, Mexico City Rapelye
315 Cortijo La Morena near Mexico City Courtesy, Mexican National Tourist Office
319 Street market, Bolivia Magnun
322 Don Quijote and Sancho, drawing by Daumier Courtesy, Metropolitan Museum of Art, New York
330 Monument to Cervantes, Madrid, Spain P. Menzel
331 Portrait of Cervantes Photo by MAS
334 Roman bridge, Cordoba, Spain Courtesy, Iberia Airlines

334 Puerta de Bisagra, Toledo, Spain Courtesy Spanish Tourist Office
334 Tower of Calahorra, Cordoba, Spain P. Menzel
335 University of Alcala de Henares, Spain Hurlimann
346 Performance of Don Juan Tenorio, Madrid, Spain Courtesy, Spanish Tourist Office
346 Performance of Man from la Mancha
348 Portraits of Jacinto Benavente and Miguel de Unamuno Courtesy, Spanish Society of America, New York
349 Portraits of José Ortega y Gasset and Juan Ramón Jiménez Courtesy, Hispanic Society of America
351 Rubén Darío PAU
361 Still Life, oil on canvas Courtesy, El Prado Museum, Madrid
362 Still life with dried fruit, oil on canvas Courtesy, El Prado Museum, Madrid
365 Etching by Goya Courtesy, El Prado Museum, Madrid
366 Drawing by Goya Courtesy, Metropolitan Museum of Art, New York
366 Etching by Goya Courtesy, El Prado Museum, Madrid
367 Peasant from Segovia, oil on canvas by Zuluaga Courtesy, Museum of Modern Art, Madrid
367 Beach of Valencia by Morning Light, oil on canvas by Sorolla Courtesy Spanish Society of America, New York
369 El Prado Museum in Madrid, and a view of the galleries in the Museum of Modern Art, Barcelona, Spain P. Menzel
377 Hand painted Spanish fan from the XVIII century Courtesy, El Prado Museum, Madrid
378 Apartment complexes near Madrid, Spain P. Menzel
383 Bridge, Guatemala Courtesy, United Nations
388 View of Parque Guell, Barcelona, Spain P. Menzel
389 Mailbox, Granada, Spain P. Menzel
393 Mailman, Tarragona, Spain P. Menzel
395 Post Office, Barcelona, Spain P. Menzel
396 Post Office, Barcelona, Spain P. Menzel